A CHURCH OBSERVED

A Church Observed

Being Anglican as Times Change

ANDREW NORMAN

GILEAD
B O O K S
PUBLISHING

Gilead Books Publishing
Corner Farm
West Knapton
Malton
North Yorkshire
YO17 8JB UK
www.GileadBooksPublishing.com

First published in Great Britain in 2018
2 4 6 8 10 9 7 5 3 1

British Library Cataloguing-in-Publication Data:
A catalogue record for this book is available from the British Library.

ISBN-13: 978-0-9932090-7-9

Typesetting, index and cover design by Dona McCullagh.

Front cover images: mementos from the Great War including a *Gospel of John,* from the author's personal
archives, photo © Dona McCullagh (left); St Andrew's Weeley, photo © Andrew Norman (top right);
bishops' spouses at the 2008 Lambeth Conference, photo © Anglican Communion Office (lower right);
order of service for the laying up of the colours of the Cinque Ports Battalion at Holy Trinity Hastings
in 1915, reproduced by kind permission of West Sussex Record Office RSR/MSS/11/23 (background).
Back cover image (background): inauguration of the ministry of the 105th Archbishop of Canterbury,
Justin Welby, photo © Andrew Dunsmore / Picture Partnership / Lambeth Palace.

To the next generation of Anglicans

Contents

Acknowledgements

THIS BOOK started out as a sabbatical project during my fifth year as Principal of Ridley Hall theological college. I am grateful to Ridley Hall for its tradition of regular staff sabbaticals and for the inspiration of colleagues who prioritise writing and publishing in the midst of the many competing demands on theological educators in the Church of England. Making headway was helped by taking over the much-loved *Château de Tourville* in Normandy for several weeks, spreading piles of books and papers around the downstairs rooms. *'Merci!'* to Fabienne and Wilfrid Petrie for providing this haven of tranquillity for uninterrupted study.

A Church Observed is a mosaic of personal stories which together reveal something of the bigger saga of the Anglican family. I am indebted to all those whose stories are told and to those who helped me to tell them. Particular thanks should go to my mother, Anna Norman, whose recollections inform much of the earlier chapters. Several archivists should also be thanked for unearthing unfamiliar details of my grandparents' lives, notably Catherine Wakeling (USPG archivist), Bernice Pilling (archivist for the Diocese of Calgary) and Melanie Delva (archivist for Vancouver School of Theology).

I am grateful to Revd Dr John Corrie and Dr Martin Davie for reading over the manuscript and offering comments, though of course responsibility for the final version is entirely mine. And I would like to thank my colleague Dona McCullagh for her thoroughness in preparing the manuscript for publication.

Finally, I would like to thank my wife, Amanda, for all her love and support and for bearing with what escalated into, in the words of Paris city planners, *un grand projet.*

An archetypal Anglican
scene: Dry Drayton parish
church, viewed from
my study at home

Photo © Andrew Norman

Introduction

THE SNOW WAS FALLING. I was looking out of the window towards Dry Drayton parish church, as I began writing this book. It was the kind of scene found on Christmas cards, year after year: timeless, it might seem. Yet inside the church, things had changed. For the first time in eight hundred years, a toilet had been installed. Wooden pews had been removed and the floor levelled, creating a more flexible space. Unusually, there had been little resistance from parishioners with fond memories of the church's traditional ambience. In a neighbouring parish, similar proposals had sparked forceful objections and the convening of a consistory court, a legal provision dating back to the eleventh century and King William I.

I was not the vicar of Dry Drayton, contrary to what you might have expected, if you had seen me leaving the house wearing a clerical collar. Nor was I living in a house owned by the Church of England. The former vicarage was a decaying shell, held together by scaffolding. The vicar now lived in a neighbouring village. She was not the first female vicar with responsibility for Dry Drayton. But she was the first vicar to combine cure of souls for Dry Drayton with the villages of Coton and Hardwick. It was not just buildings that had changed in this parish.

By precedent, I should have been living six miles away, in central Cambridge. All the previous principals of Ridley Hall theological college had lived within the college grounds, in the three-storey Principal's Lodge. But things had changed there too. Since it first opened in 1881, Ridley Hall's activities had expanded. Originally designed for forty students preparing for ordination, it was now catering for seventy ordinands and fifty students training for youth ministry. Its teaching facilities were used by other colleges in the Cambridge Theological Federation too. So the Principal's Lodge had been

1

requisitioned for classrooms and offices. As a consequence, I was living in rented accommodation, which just happened to be opposite a village church.

Things change for the Church of England, even if outwardly things may look the same, whether in a local parish church or a theological college. This is a book about what it means to be Anglican as things change. Its point of departure is the British Isles. But the Church of England is no longer the beginning and end of what it means to be Anglican. The total number of Anglicans has risen to 85 million. They gather for worship in over 165 countries.[1] In Nigeria, there are 260 times more Anglicans than there are in Wales.[2] A form of Christianity that was minted in sixteenth-century England has now been exported to a vast range of cultural settings. Up until recently, it flourished as a unique family of churches, with a strong shared identity. But these churches have found it increasingly difficult to respond in unison to the forces of change. Their members have struggled to keep in step. Its senior bishops have been contemplating walking apart for more than a decade.

In British society, things have not exactly stood still either. Over ten years, the number of people with no religion doubled to fourteen percent, according to the 2011 census. The number calling themselves Christian declined by thirteen percent. In a much-publicised case, a British Airways employee found herself forbidden to wear a cross around her neck.[3] With Christianity increasingly pushed to the margins of public life in England, preoccupation with the wider Anglican Communion might seem like an exotic distraction. As candidates were considered for Archbishop of Canterbury in 2012, there were plenty of advocates for an Archbishop who focussed exclusively on England, washing his hands of contentious Anglican Communion affairs.

Yet, whether the focus is on church life in England or the coherence of the Anglican Communion, a similar question emerges. What does it mean to be authentically yet creatively Anglican, as times change? This question faces the English vicar spread ever more thinly, the pioneer minister in a housing estate and the active lay person perplexed by the Church's public image. At the same time, it is a question faced by the bishops of the Anglican Communion, as they eye one another warily in the debates over sexuality or mutual accountability in a globalised world.

Looking to the future, Anglicans seem not to have a satellite navigation system they can simply programme and switch on. So what is the night-sky constellation by which Anglicans can navigate?

This is not just a matter for idle curiosity. There is a sense of urgency, especially for those who believe that the Church is more than a human institutional construct. If Jesus truly prayed that his followers might be one, we cannot cheerily opt for fragmentation. Nor can we confine our attention to our own back yard, blithely turning our backs on our Christian sisters and brothers around the world. Neither can we simply adhere blindly to inherited patterns of church life, if active church involvement is declining year by year.

Paradoxically, this forward-looking question about Anglican identity cannot be answered without looking back. We must seek to discern distinctive Anglican characteristics. Some would say 'comprehensiveness' is one of these characteristics, but this cannot mean the same as 'anything goes'. For a start, if that had been so up until now, Anglicans would have made far less progress in ecumenical agreements. When talking to us, other churches like to know what we stand for.

This book will therefore attempt to identify fixed points for Anglicanism as we look to the future. But in doing so, it will acknowledge that appearances can be deceptive. Some fixed points may be partially concealed. Not everything is as non-negotiable as it might look. For Anglicans, things have already changed a great deal since King Henry VIII chose to marry Anne Boleyn and nationalised the Church of England. There is a further complication. No-one ever masterminded a new global brand of Christianity called the Anglican Communion. That means that things have often changed in an unplanned and haphazard way. As Archbishop Michael Ramsey famously put it, there is an untidiness to Anglicanism. In his view at least, that untidiness contributes to its distinctive vocation and charm.[4] With this untidiness, there is a sense in which Anglican identity is caught as much as taught. The Latin phrase 'lex orandi, lex credendi' is often applied to Anglican identity. 'How you pray reveals what you believe' is how it is loosely translated, signalling the need to observe, if you want to appreciate what 'being Anglican' means.[5]

To understand what it means to be Anglican, therefore, it is necessary to spend time with Anglicans. This not only means going back in time. It means getting out and about. To do so opens up the possibility of capturing something of the lived reality of Anglican experience as things have changed, both in church life and in the wider world. In the midst of this, guiding principles can be sought and conclusions offered about ways in which things have changed.

But where can we begin? Did 'being Anglican' begin with the break from Rome? Or with the arrival of the papal envoy on the shores of Kent in 597AD? Or with the Celtic Christians who had been active as missionaries before St Augustine arrived in 597AD? Or with the martyrdom of St Alban in Roman times? Come to that, should we go back even further, and let our imaginations be enlivened by the hymn beloved of English public schools? 'And did those feet in ancient times, walk upon England's mountains green? And was the holy Lamb of God on England's pleasant pastures seen?'

Unsurprisingly, this book will not begin with the fanciful conceit of William Blake's poem and Hubert Parry's rousing music, much as we all liked to sing it at school. Jesus, we can safely say, never made it to England, with or without Joseph of Arimathea. This book does however draw on my own experience, of which singing the patriotic hymn 'Jerusalem' in school chapel was a fleeting part. It begins, though, not with my own experience but with that of my immediate forebears. It does so, not because that is the optimum starting point, but because it is what I have to hand. This means picking up the Anglican story when it is already in full swing: a century ago, to be precise, when most of my grandparents were young adults. Others could embark on similar exercises, drawing on their own unique raw data, to assess what it means to be Anglican.

In my own case, however, I am emboldened to offer this personal account because of the range of situations in which 'being Anglican' can be sampled. They constitute a suitably potent cocktail from which to acquire a taste of what it means to be Anglican. My mother, for example, still has a lively recollection of her father's ministry as an Anglican priest in Canada, Scotland and England. Growing up on a farm, I had first-hand experience of a country parish, the setting so often associated with classic Anglicanism. Secondary school introduced me to Anglo-Catholic churchmanship, while university was a whirlwind of evangelical activism. The decade leading to ordination exposed me to Anglican life in Africa and in various provincial towns and cities around England, including inner city Liverpool. Ordination then took me to mainland Europe and to Bristol, before bringing me to London and the historic residence of the Archbishop of Canterbury. In supporting the Archbishop of Canterbury, I witnessed Anglican life and ecumenical engagement in dozens of countries, including England. During a particularly troubled time for Anglicans, I had a ringside seat at many of the seminal Anglican gatherings. I found myself serving on strategic working groups, such as the international consultations of TEAC (Theological Education in the Anglican Communion), with its brief for articulating 'the Anglican Way' to inform theological education in the Anglican Communion.[6] As an Anglican theological college Principal, I had to make it my business to observe and imagine the church in which future clergy of the Church of England would serve. As a teacher of Anglicanism, I cannot get away with reducing this to a pragmatic exercise.

The title, *A Church Observed,* is deliberately reminiscent of a book by a writer in the Anglican hall of fame, C. S. Lewis, who died the year I was born. His short book, *A Grief Observed,* is far less well known than his bestselling Narnia children's stories. But it forms the backdrop to the movie *Shadowlands,* in which Hollywood star Anthony Hopkins plays C. S. Lewis. *Shadowlands* tells the extraordinary story of Lewis' love affair with the American poet, Joy Gresham. An Oxford University academic, a Christian apologist and a confirmed bachelor, Lewis marries Gresham so she can live in England. It is only after this marriage of convenience that friendship blossoms into love. When Gresham is diagnosed with cancer and dies, Lewis is devastated. *A Grief Observed* is C. S. Lewis observing his own aching grief. 'I am not afraid, but the sensation is like being afraid', he writes. 'The same fluttering in the stomach, the same restlessness, the yawning. I keep on swallowing.'[7] In observing his own grief, he is anything but a passive bystander.

Likewise, in observing the Church, I make no pretence at being a passive bystander. No Anglican priest would be. Being Anglican has been an uninterrupted part of my life for five decades. The same could be said for my grandparents for the fifty years that preceded my own first watery encounter with Anglican ritual in the baptismal font. Like Lewis writing *A Grief Observed,* I write as one who is not a detached observer. Yet that is where the similarity to Lewis' work ends. This is not an elegy for a Church seemingly in terminal decline, whose time-honoured ways are no longer cherished. There are such books.[8] This instead is a book which looks back not to mourn but to extrapolate into the future. Inevitably, given my own personal engagement, it cannot claim to be entirely neutral. No-one's take on Anglican identity can be. Much of what it means to be authentically Anglican has been contested at one time or another, often fiercely. I will attempt, nonetheless, to guard against offering too idiosyncratic an account of what it might mean to be Anglican. I will do my best to situate personal experience within the wider context of Anglican history, theological reflection and tradition. I will inevitably be selective, noting those things which catch my eye. But in doing so I will seek to be alert to ways in which their significance is more widely viewed. So for example, having worked for two Archbishops of Canterbury, I will be reflecting periodically on ways in which successive Archbishops have shaped what it means to be Anglican. Yet I do so, not arbitrarily, or even to give in to the cult of celebrity. Rather, I do so in recognition that the Archbishop of Canterbury has been a lynchpin within Anglican ecclesiology, serving as a focus of unity for the Church. Archbishops of Canterbury therefore merit our attention.

I must come clean and admit from the outset that there is a strong 'missional' motivation in this exercise. Even the term 'missional' bears witness to the ways things change, when it comes to being Anglican. The truth is that Anglicans have not always been great enthusiasts for mission. The very idea of 'mission' can sound a bit pushy in parishes where clergy and laity have been quietly and unostentatiously serving their local communities for generations. Yet in recent years, talk of 'mission' has become increasingly prominent in Anglican circles. In the Church of England, there is even talk of 'a quiet revolution', as the pastoral emphasis in parish life is increasingly combined with efforts to make the Church more 'mission-shaped'.[9]

At the same time, and sometimes in tension with this, there has been a move away from conceiving mission in narrowly denominational terms. The notion of *missio Dei* ('mission of God') has gained currency across denominations.[10] The idea of *missio Dei* is that mission is ultimately *God's* mission. Churches engaging in mission are joining God's missionary endeavour. They are not simply engaging in institutional self-preservation. From this trans-denominational perspective, Anglicans should guard against an exaggerated sense of their own importance for the future of God's mission. Nonetheless, commitment to God's mission can energise consideration of what it means to be Anglican. Mission-minded Anglicans must assess how they can faithfully play their part in God's mission. This cannot mean rigid adherence to forms of Christian expression designed for bygone eras. Anglicans must assess what to preserve from their much-cherished past, along with discerning which 'new ways of being church' may be appropriate for tomorrow. Anglican bishops meeting in 1948 spoke of having been entrusted, by God, 'a special service to render to the whole church'.[11] As we look to the future, we need to consider whether Anglicans still have a special service to render in the universal church, in their participation in God's mission.

This missional motivation means taking seriously the interface between Anglican life and the society in which it is set. Observing the Church therefore means much more than time-lapse photography in the church sanctuary. It means recognising how the country in which Anglicanism was incubated has changed. It also means observing the wider world into which Anglicanism has migrated and considering how it too has changed. It includes noting the changing demography of non-Anglican churches. The Church of England may have started as a monopoly. Now it is but one form of Christianity. Compared with 1.2 billion Roman Catholics and 250 million Pentecostals, 85 million Anglicans are quite a small presence. Yet, after the Roman Catholic Church,

Anglicans are geographically the most widespread; who their Christian neighbours are and how they relate to them matters.

Achieving all this in a short book is an ambitious task, especially when it is linked to the particularities of one family's experiences. Yet by charting ways in which 'being Anglican' has both changed and stood firm over time, and by situating them in their wider context, this book seeks to offer a vantage point for further enquiry. By cutting a vertical cross-section though Anglican experience, it seeks to expose raw material for constructing a shared frame of reference for Anglicans looking to the future.

This book does not presuppose in-depth knowledge of Anglican life and theology. For those unfamiliar with the unfolding Anglican story, it should provide an induction into distinctive features of Anglicanism. Anglican characteristics, as times change, will be viewed through the lens of particular experiences and set in their wider context. The book does not follow a textbook approach, with themes being classified chapter by chapter. Rather, themes are explored as they emerge in the narrative. It is only towards the end of the book that more structured analysis is offered, with conclusions drawn about implications for the future. However, those who feel they are already familiar with Anglican life and theology should resist the temptation to race ahead to the conclusions and skip the narrative section of the book. It may be that they are familiar with Anglican expression within their own tradition or country, but less so with that in other traditions or Anglican provinces. In addition, the narrative sections are intended not simply to inform but to act as a stimulus for re-imagining Anglican life and witness. In the Church of England, General Synod agreed in 2011 that 're-imagining the church's ministry' should be one of the three major objectives during its five-year term. To re-imagine means seeing things differently. A deeper appreciation both of the past and how things have changed can also help us to see things differently. I hope this book may help all its readers to discern more clearly what being Anglican means as times change.

Three years before 'marching
as to war': my grandfather,
William Norman

Author's personal archives

1

Conflict, Colonies and Home Truths

BOTH MY GRANDFATHERS survived World War One; against the odds. William Norman left the family farm for the infantry six weeks after war was declared. Harry Nobbs joined the Canadian Medical Corps sixteen months later, abandoning his life in Canada as a lay church worker. They would both experience the full horrors of the 'war to end all wars', a conflict which issued a wake-up call to the Church of England. As we accompany them to the war zone, we will see how much of a rude awakening this really was.

On the way to church: the Cinque Ports Battalion in Hastings

Reproduced by kind permission of West Sussex Record Office RSR/PH/5/80

On 19 February 1915, William Norman disembarked at the French port of Le Havre, with his 'Cinque Ports' Battalion. He was 22 years old. That same Friday, his battalion was being prayed for in the parish church of Hastings, one of the 'Cinque Ports' towns on the south coast of England. A detachment from his battalion had marched through the town to attend a service at Holy Trinity church. During the service, the old battalion colours were laid up in the church. The congregation sang 'Onward Christian soldiers, marching as to war'. As the Cinque Ports Battalion of the Royal Sussex Regiment made its way by ship and train to Northern France, it enjoyed the blessing of the church at home.[1]

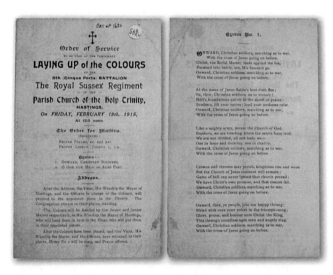

'Onward Christian Soldiers' was sung at Holy Trinity Hastings the day my grandfather left for the front line with his Cinque Ports Battalion

Reproduced by kind permission of West Sussex Record Office RSR/MSS/11/23

By that time, the German Army had occupied Northern France and built its four hundred mile barbed-wire barricade from Belgium to Switzerland. Initial hopes of a swift victory had evaporated. British and French forces now lined muddy trenches along the German front. By the time the Cinque Ports Battalion assembled on a football field to celebrate Easter Sunday, the French were planning a major offensive to break through German lines, north of Arras.[2] In support, British forces would aim to capture Aubers Ridge, a vantage point used by the Germans to survey enemy troops. My grandfather's Royal Sussex Cinque Ports Battalion would join the assault. The scene was set for William Norman's baptism into the trauma that was starting to shake the Church that had sanctioned it.

The attack was scheduled for the beginning of May. The plan was for the French to attack first, preceded by heavy artillery bombardment over several days. The British knew they could only manage a brief bombardment, as they were short of artillery shells, but they thought this would be sufficient to flatten the barbed wire. In the event, bad weather delayed the French attack. On 9 May 1915, the French and British simultaneously launched their attacks. At 5am, the British bombarded the German lines for half an hour. Waves of soldiers, including my grandfather, then scrambled out of the trenches into the one hundred metre stretch of no-man's land. The tacticians had fatally misjudged. The Germans had strengthened their defences, including their barbed wire, and set up machine guns behind thick steel plates. Soldiers were cut down as they advanced or struggled with the barbed wire. At 6am, as German artillery shelled survivors in no man's land, the order was given to stop the attack, just thirty minutes after it had started.[3]

Somehow my grandfather survived. Of the men attacking from his battalion, three quarters were killed, wounded or missing presumed dead: two hundred officers and men.[4] 'My mates fell like skittles', reported one of the survivors of my grandfather's B Company to the Eastbourne Gazette. 'The last words I heard our captain say were "Now lads, another two minutes and England expects. You know the rest." Then he said "Come on B!". He was the first to go down.'[5] In all, 11,000 British soldiers were killed or wounded that day. And that was just the beginning. William Norman would serve on the front line for another three and a half years, including the Battle of the Somme, which claimed half of the 1.2 million Allied troops as casualties, during its five bitter months. By then Cinque Ports Battalion had been designated a Pioneer Battalion, specialising in digging and clearing trenches and gun emplacements. Even that was a hazardous business, thanks to the incessant shelling. As the battalion gathered for a church parade on 30 July 1916, its war diarist recorded 118 casualties during that first month of the Battle of the Somme. William Norman himself was wounded that summer.[6]

Back to the farm
from the trenches

Author's personal archives

My other grandfather, Harry Nobbs, chose not to fight. Yet serving in the Medical Corps was no soft option. Of the 21,453 in the Canadian Medical Corps, 1,325 became casualties.[7] Harry Nobbs was 29 years old when he reported to the enlisting officer for 8th Field Ambulance in Calgary, Western Canada. He had little formal education, having left school at thirteen. As a lay church worker, he had pastoral experience, but was not a trained medic. His first few weeks in 8th Field Ambulance began to remedy this with some rudimentary training in stretcher bearing and first aid, along with the inevitable military drill. On 1 April 1916, he set sail on the SS *Adriatic* for England, along with the other 182 members of 8th Field Ambulance. He was returning to his country of birth, as were ninety-five of his new comrades. They arrived in Liverpool on 9 April 1916 and were boarding a ship in Southampton a month later, bound for Normandy. Arriving at the port at Le Havre, as William Norman had done, they travelled north by train to Belgium. Their destination was the bustling rest area of Poperinghe, just West of Ypres and close to the Salient front line.[8]

Though a small Belgium town with 11,000 inhabitants, the number of troops at Poperinghe would swell to as many as a quarter of a million during the course of the war.[9] When my grandfather arrived, his unit was marched to a farm outside the town, where they would take over a rest station for wounded men from the 3rd Canadian Division.[10] In the town itself was a facility for troops which would come to symbolise the Church of England's need to rethink its ministry during World War One, in order to make it more accessible. Talbot House, also known as 'Toc H', had been founded six months earlier by two chaplains. They quickly turned it into a place that was 'full of friendship, homeyness, fun, music, games, laughter, books, pictures and discussion.'[11] In the attic was a chapel, which became known as the Upper Room. I visited it earlier this year. The month my grandfather's unit arrived, the Archbishop of Canterbury, Randall Davidson, confirmed thirty-seven men there. A few weeks earlier, on Easter Day, there had been ten celebrations of the Eucharist.[12]

In the Upper Room, the green and gold altar frontal had been provided by Anglican sisters from Haywards Heath, a few miles from the farm my other grandfather, William Norman, had left behind.[13] Such connections with home would doubtless have been welcomed by him and his fellow members of his Royal Sussex Regiment, when they saw active service around Ypres. But Talbot House was intended to be a 'home from home' not just for English troops. When Archbishop Davidson arrived, it was a Canadian sergeant major, serving as vicar's warden, who had welcomed him.[14] On the wall were maps of Canada and Australia, as well as of England.[15] All this must have felt custom-made for my grandfather, freshly arrived from Canada. He would gratefully recall the work of 'Toc H' throughout his life.

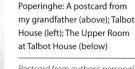

Poperinghe: A postcard from my grandfather (above); Talbot House (left); The Upper Room at Talbot House (below)

Postcard from author's personal archives
Photos © Andrew Norman

But my grandfather's unit was not stationed at Poperinghe to rest and socialise at Talbot House. As soon as they arrived, they started to receive fifty sick or wounded men each day. A Field Ambulance Unit was responsible for evacuating the wounded and providing initial treatment to alleviate pain. The first major duties for 8th Field Ambulance came two weeks after arrival, when the Germans launched an attack on the Canadian forces. On the evening of 2 June 1916, ninety-nine stretcher bearers from the unit were mobilised. Some were assigned to a hastily prepared dressing station in Brandhoek. Others were dispatched to the established 'Asylum' Dressing Station in Ypres. Motor and horse ambulances evacuated the wounded from the battlefield to these two dressing stations, under heavy shelling. The men working at Brandhoek would receive 153 casualties over the next twenty-four hours.[16]

This set the pattern for the months ahead, when my grandfather's unit would support Canadian troops in the Somme and the capture of Vimy Ridge and Hill 70. In September 1917, they were preparing dressing stations near Lens in Northern France. Before they could use them, they were instructed to move on and await orders. By 15 October, it was clear they were returning to Belgium. The weather was miserable and rainy.[17] They were joining the Battle of Passchendaele. The heaviest rains for thirty years had saturated the battlefield. 'I died in hell. They called it Passchendaele' went Siegfried Sassoon's poem.[18]

For their main dressing station, 8th Field Ambulance took over a mill from a New Zealand Ambulance Corps. All available stretcher bearers would join 10th Field Ambulance for clearance of the battle front. Two former German pill-boxes would serve as Regimental Aid Posts on the battlefield itself. A relay post (the Somme Redoubt) would serve as the Assembly Point for loading the wounded onto trucks to take to the Advanced Dressing Station, located in a disused mine shaft. From there, they would be taken by ambulance to the Main Dressing Station at the Mill.[19]

This would be the Battle of Passchendaele Ridge. Canadian troops attacked twice between 26 October and 1 November 1917. The Commanding Officer of my grandfather's unit did his best to record the unit's valiant work during the first attack.

> It is not possible to describe the conditions which existed during this operation, as no imagination would be sufficient to realise exactly how the difficult work of the stretcher bearers was accomplished. With no cover or shelter of trenches, the work was proceeded with in the open, the area along which the cases was brought [sic] was greatly exposed to enemy shell fire, and throughout the whole of the work this hostile shelling continued with increasing activity. The distance of the carry would be approximately 2½ miles, the state of the ground can best be described as a 'quagmire' as the result of heavy rains and continuous shelling. Trench mats had been placed along the route, but these, being so narrow, to avoid the dangerous possibility of the bearers slipping from the side of these into the sinking ground beneath, it was impossible to adopt the usual system of a 4-man carry shoulder high, and necessary to resort to a two man system.... The accommodation at most of the Stations was limited to the 'Pill-Boxes', but these [were] required for wounded as they came in, [so] the stretcher bearers had usually to be content to rest where they could in the open.[20]

Three stretcher bearers were killed that day and sixteen wounded. All 'worked cheerfully throughout under dangerous conditions'. Four medals were awarded. 'The evacuation during the whole operation was a complete success', he concluded, despite the cost. 'The men behind the line had to be possessed of as much courage and endurance as the men who went over the top' the Commander of 3rd Canadian Division told 8th Field Ambulance.[21]

Army chaplains played their part too. 'Patients were quickly received, transmitted through the waiting room into the dressing room, attended to carefully and passed out for evacuation', recorded the Commanding Officer of 8th Field Ambulance. 'When needed, the friendly padres who were on duty stepped into any breach, would hand the wounded man a drink, or take their end of the stretcher, as the case may be.'[22]

Added to the shells and mud, another deadly feature of World War One was included in the day's report: chemical weapons. Mustard gas shells were used on Passchendaele Ridge. 8th Field Ambulance had experienced their blinding effect three months earlier at the Battle of Hill 70. On Passchendaele Ridge the stretcher bearers were now equipped with box respirators, but were still vulnerable in the pandemonium.[23] My grandfather would speak later of being gassed himself during these battles, though never went into detail.

The Canadians succeeded in breaking through enemy lines at Passchendaele Ridge. Things eventually quietened down for 8th Field Ambulance after Christmas and remained less intense throughout the winter. They were even planting vegetables in the spring.[24] As the year progressed, a virulent influenza epidemic competed with their other duties.[25] But they would see further intensive action before the Armistice was finally declared at the end of the year.

Meanwhile, around the time Harry Nobbs was struggling in the mud of Passchendaele, William Norman found himself moving to very different terrain: the shell-splintered rocks of the Alpine foothills. His regiment was transferred to Italy, just North of Venice. From there, it reinforced Italian resistance to the Austrians, including the Battle on the Piave in June 1918. The Piave River was where Ernest Hemingway was wounded while serving in the Medical Corps. It was this experience on the Italian front that inspired his first novel, *A Farewell to Arms*.

Italy was where William Norman finished World War One. His mementos of that great ordeal are in my mother's loft. They include his helmet and bayonet; a map of the countryside around Ypres; a collection of trench art, containing a cross, two rings, and an anchor, all made from shrapnel. They also include three pocket books: a *Gospel of John* (well thumbed), a *Book of Psalms* (not so well thumbed) and *Book of Prayer and Praise in Times of Peace and War* (scarcely used).

John's Gospel with instructions to 'Carry this in your pocket', among my grandfather's
Great War mementos   *Author's personal archives; photo © Dona McCullagh*

Also amongst his mementos is a letter from the Senior Chaplain of the 48th Division in Italy, dated January 1919. Sent to 'every member of the Church in the Division', it confronts the problem of 'lack of support and response to the efforts of the chaplains'. With restrained understatement, A. S. Crawley points out that 'the life of the Church is not quite as strong and vigorous as it ought to be'. At Sunday services, despite hundreds of invitations, 'sometimes no officers and a mere handful of men were present'.

In an effort to reverse the trend, the Senior Chaplain appeals rather lamely to patriotism and pride in the Church of England. 'In these things the honour of our Church in the eyes of other religious bodies and of the Italian people is at stake'. With surer footing, he looks ahead to peacetime and presents religion as playing a crucial role in 'making the world and our Country after the war, better and happier than it was before, more worthy of the price paid to preserve it'. But the tone is not high-handed. 'I hope that I have not struck too much the note of complaint', he writes. The shortcomings of the chaplains are candidly acknowledged. 'The Clergy in general, myself in particular, I know are often wanting in ability and the power of leadership.'

This self-deprecation is significant. When war broke out, Stafford Crawley had been chaplain to Cosmo Lang, Archbishop of York. He had first come across Cosmo Lang as an undergraduate at Oxford University. He and his family would go on to be lifelong friends of the future Archbishop of Canterbury, naming one of their sons Cosmo. As a Canon at St George's Windsor, he would prepare the future Queen Elizabeth II for confirmation.[26] He was at home in the highest echelons of British society. As soon as he had persuaded Cosmo Lang to let him serve as a military chaplain in 1915, he was assigned to a field ambulance unit, similar to the one in which my grandfather served.

It was linked to the Guards Division commanded by his brother-in-law, the Earl of Cavan. He was provided with a horse and a servant called Raddenby.[27] He was most definitely officer class.

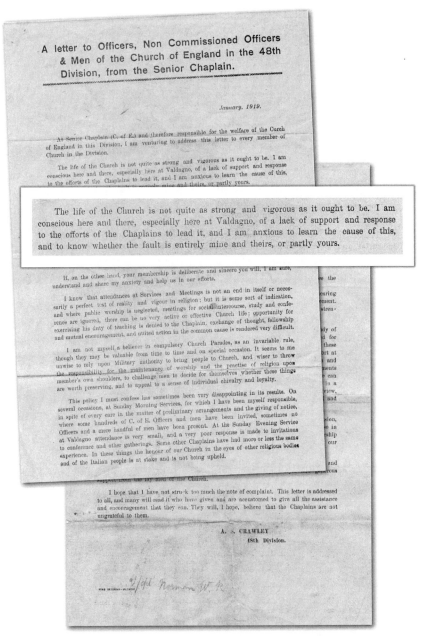

A letter to Officers, Non Commissioned Officers & Men of the Church of England in the 48th Division, from the Senior Chaplain.

January, 1919.

As Senior Chaplain (C. of E.) and therefore responsible for the welfare of the Curch of England in this Division, I am venturing to address this letter to every member of Church in the Division.

The life of the Church is not quite as strong and vigorous as it ought to be. I am conscious here and there, especially here at Valdagno, of a lack of support and response to the efforts of the Chaplains to lead it, and I am anxious to learn the cause of this, and to know whether the fault is entirely mine and theirs, or partly yours.

If, on the other hand, your membership is deliberate and sincere you will, I am sure, understand and share my anxiety and help us in our efforts.

I know that attendances at Services and Meetings is not an end in itself or necessarily a perfect test of reality and vigour in religion; but it is some sort of indication, and where public worship is neglected, meetings for social intercourse, study and conference are ignored, there can be no very active or effective Church life; opportunity for exercising his duty of teaching is denied to the Chaplain, exchange of thought, fellowship and mutual encouragement, and united action in the common cause is rendered very difficult.

I am not myself a believer in compulsory Church Parades, as an invariable rule, though they may be valuable from time to time and on special occasion. It seems to me unwise to rely upon Military authority to bring people to Church, and wiser to throw the responsibility for the maintenance of worship and the practise of religion upon member's own shoulders, to challenge men to decide for themselves whether these things are worth preserving, and to appeal to a sense of individual chivalry and loyalty.

This policy I must confess has sometimes been very disappointing in its results. On several occasions, at Sunday Morning Services, for which I have been myself responsible, in spite of every care in the matter of preliminary arrangements and the giving of notice, where some hundreds of C. of E. Officers and men have been invited, sometimes no Officers and a mere handful of men have been present. At the Sunday Evening Service at Valdagno attendance is very small, and a very poor response is made to invitations to conference and other gatherings. Some other Chaplains have had more or less the same experience. In these things the honour of our Church in the eyes of other religious bodies and of the Italian people is at stake and is not being upheld.

I hope that I have not struck too much the note of complaint. This letter is addressed to all, and many will read it who have given and are accustomed to give all the assistance and encouragement that they can. They will, I hope, believe that the Chaplains are not ungrateful to them.

A. S. CRAWLEY
48th Division.

The aftermath of war: the Senior Chaplain troubled by low turnout for worship, as my grandfather awaits demobilisation *Author's personal archives*

Yet by the end of World War One, he was suffering from the nervous disorder alopecia and had lost all his hair.[28] Writing home from the front line to his wife in 1916, he had expressed serious doubts about the effectiveness of the Church of England's ministry. He had regularly conducted church services for several hundred servicemen. On one occasion they knelt upright on the grass for much of the service.[29] But appearances could be deceptive, especially where church parades were compulsory. 'Our Church in order to be true and comprehensive has failed to present its faith in a clear and definite way that simple people can understand', he lamented.[30] Despite being decorated for bravery, he had returned to civilian life before accepting the posting to Italy. During this time away from the trenches, he had suffered serious doubts about his vocation. He had even considered resigning his orders.[31] 'Your printed letter, though quite excellent, made me feel sad for you', his wife Nancy wrote to him in Italy.[32]

Stafford Crawley's deeply unsettling experiences and his appeal to the troops in Italy both corresponded to the wider soul-searching in the Church of England as World War One progressed. On the front line, the life of the Church had not been 'quite as strong and vigorous as it ought to be' from the start. As the war dragged on, the Church had to contend with its precipitous endorsement of it, the harrowing impact of war on combatants and the realities revealed about the spirituality of the millions who were supposedly members of the Church of England.

The Church of England's actions at the start of the First World War had done little to build up its long-term credibility. Unaware of what lay in store, Church leaders dutifully encouraged civilians to sign up to fight. 'No household or home will be acting worthily' wrote the Archbishop of Canterbury, 'if, in timidity or self-love, it holds back any of those who can loyally bear a man's part in the great enterprise.... The well-being, nay the very life of our Empire may depend on the response which is given.'[33] A few months later, the Archbishop refused to urge clergy to use their pulpits to appeal for recruits, but by then the damage had been done. As disillusion set in, the Church was irrevocably associated with blessing the war.

To make matters worse, in the early stages of the war, Church of England chaplains were not allowed to go to the front, as the author Robert Graves damningly observed in his *Goodbye to All That*. It was felt they would be in the way.[34] At a safe distance from the action, 'No work for you today, padre' meant little more than no corpses for burial.[35] The chaplains themselves pressed for change. 'Had a really v. fine service at the Heavy Batteries... in a large dugout with a gun', Stafford Crawley wrote to his wife in October

1915. 'It was a weird sight 50 men in the dugout lit by lanterns, a little talk arranged for me back to the gun.'[36] By 1916 chaplains were administering Holy Communion in the trenches and ministering to the wounded and dying. But they were hardly doing so from a position of strength.

The chaplains discovered they were ill-equipped to minister outside the familiar framework of parish life. They were 'peddling unmarketable C. of E. goods', according to Neville Talbot.[37] The Prayer Book was not enough, he argued. It assumes so much as 'going without being said'. In June 1916, Stafford Crawley wrote to Nancy about a talk given by Neville Talbot the previous day, where he had spoken of the soldier's 'strange and utter ignorance of Christianity as an organised religion—or of what we clergy stand for. He said that tho' they like us personally they don't seem to want us as clergy or understand what we are after.... It's very largely what I have been feeling so much.'[38] Roman Catholic chaplains at least had rites for ministering to the dying, Talbot observed. Most of the time, Anglican chaplains had to content themselves with being friendly, burying the dead and trying to be helpful.[39]

The Revd Geoffrey Studdert Kennedy epitomised that approach. Woodbine Willie, as he is remembered, said that of 'purely spiritual work', there was 'very little; it is all muddled and mixed'. His advice: 'Take a box of fags in your haversack and a great deal of love in your heart.... You can pray with them sometimes; but pray for them always.' Crawley was quick to follow suit. 'Here I am sweetheart v. hard at it in a ruined village behind the firing line', he wrote to Nancy in September 1915. 'Send me 1000 Woodbines in smallish packets to give to the men.'[40]

It was Neville Talbot who found there was a niche for the Church when soldiers were on rest breaks. In 1915, he and a fellow chaplain, Tubby Clayton, rented the house in Poperinghe that would carry his family name, Talbot House. Its mission was summed up in a poem written by one appreciative serviceman:

> *Refreshment, rest and cheer for all those men*
> *Who hapless roam,*
> *And over all—a touch of sanctity—*
> *A breath of home.*[41]

With restrictions on them lifted, chaplains were typically found amongst the wounded, instead of just at rest centres like Poperinghe. At the Battle of Passchendaele Ridge, as we have observed, my grandfather's Commanding Officer was able to commend the role of padres at the main dressing station for 8th Field Ambulance. 'I am generally to be found with the Advanced Dressing stations where I think we can be most useful', wrote Stafford Crawley. 'We can help with the wounded men as they come in and when there is a lull we can go and visit the Battalions when they are resting or in reserve trenches.'[42]

In 1914, there had been just eighty-nine Anglican chaplains. Almost exactly that number of chaplains had been killed by the end of the war, of the final total of 1,985 who had served. Eight of these casualties had trained at Ridley Hall, where I would serve as Principal. I have visited some of their graves. A number of chaplains had been decorated for bravery, including Stafford Crawley, Woodbine Willie and my father's future headmaster, Ernest Crosse, all of whom were awarded the Military Cross. The reputation of chaplains had been salvaged, but there was no cause for triumphalism, as the letter my grandfather received in Italy from Stafford Crawley had made plain.

The war revealed 'a very heart-searching shock', as a chaplain who went on to be Bishop of Southwark put it. For many of the soldiers, 'religion apparently meant nothing to them'.[43] 'Nice fine day', Stafford Crawley wrote to his wife one Sunday in Italy, 'but it was a vv poor congregation. No Sussex came at all, officers or men.'[44] The scale of the challenge had led the Archbishop of Canterbury to set up five Committees of Enquiry in 1916. Their mandate was to look beyond the war itself to longer term reforms within the Church of England. They covered teaching, worship, evangelism, administrative reform and 'industrial problems'. Military chaplains were invited to contribute, with Toc H's Neville Talbot serving on one of the Committees.

The challenge before the Church of England was laid bare: it was 'the grave fact that the instinct for worship has diminished in the people as a whole'. The war had brought 'a startling and vivid revelation of need and opportunity'. Though seventy percent of those in the army were known as 'Church of England', only a very small proportion knew the faith and received the sacraments.[45] The Church lacked a sense of fellowship. Clergy were out of touch with 'ordinary people'. The laity were failing to spread the faith, in part because clergy were neglecting to teach them and give them responsibility. Most had little training in everyday prayer and devotion. The Church was held back from responding because of its reliance on Parliament for changing its regulations. It had neglected to engage prophetically with industrial life.

This critique set an agenda for the Church of England following the end of World War One. Recommendations included improved training for clergy, with greater emphasis on their roles as teachers and more attention given to the principles of evangelistic work. The laity needed to be taught how to develop their prayer life. They should be more involved in teaching and the conduct of worship. They were not simply there for 'approval or disapproval of the proposals of the incumbent'. Holy Communion should be given a more prominent role in Sunday worship, rather than being treated as a bolt-on to Morning Prayer (matins). We shall see in later chapters that most of the issues took much longer to address than expected, especially when legislation by Parliament was needed. This was true of Prayer Book revision, which in the eyes of the military chaplains called for 'bold and wide experiment' and 'changes as regards uniformity of services'.[46] They warned that 'we shall be unable to go back merely to the pre-war grooves' and 'we cannot go on with such a narrow range of method'.[47] But it would be another sixty years before a revised Prayer Book was successfully introduced.

One issue that did not require sanction from Parliament was the Church's engagement with 'industrial problems'. This last point had been taken to heart by William Norman's senior chaplain in Italy, Stafford Crawley. There were strikes back home and Russia's Bolshevik Revolution made it impossible to ignore the protests of workers. Crawley's letter to servicemen spoke of conferences he was running in the Music Room of Division HQ, on the subject of industrial problems and 'creating greater harmony between capital management and labour'. These well-intentioned seminars were hardly likely to appeal to my grandfather, whose father had just written to support his demobilisation, stressing it was 'very important that this man should be released for agricultural work'. But they reflect an awakened social conscience among the chaplains, expressed later, for example, by Woodbine Willie in his work in the Industrial Christian Fellowship.

Shielded from the prospect of unemployment and industrial disputes, Lance Corporal William Norman finally returned to the farm in March 1919. During his fifty-four months of service, he had not been awarded any medals for bravery. But his papers commended him as 'steady and very reliable—a good worker'. He re-joined a rural community where the Church of England was still symbolically at its heart. The parish church in Uckfield would soon have its roll of remembrance. William would join the annual Remembrance Day parade, instituted by King George V 'to perpetuate the memory of that Great Deliverance and of those who laid down their lives to achieve it'. He would exchange trench warfare for the routine of milking the cows twice a day, where qualities of steadiness and reliability were just as applicable.

My other grandfather, Harry Nobbs, would encounter military chaplains in a different guise towards the end of the war. They would help improve his education. The Khaki University was set up by the Canadian Army in Britain in 1917, at the instigation of the chaplains and the YMCA. It began with study groups in Canadian Army Camps in England. By July 1917, 300,000 were attending classes and lectures at camps in England and France.[48] Classes were available for 8th Field Ambulance in marquees in the Vimy Sector, in the quiet months after Passchendaele.[49] Having left school at thirteen, by the time he was demobilised my grandfather had passed exams in English, History and Chemistry with the Khaki University.

Scarred by his wartime experiences, but with horizons broadened, Harry Nobbs boarded the SS *Olympic* on 17 March 1919. His faith had survived the war, even if he would always jump when doors were slammed. On his return to Canada, he settled back into church work and was soon being considered as a candidate for ordination. His credentials hardly matched his counterparts in England, most of whom were 'officer class' like Stafford Crawley and studied at Oxford and Cambridge. But he could at least draw on considerable experience of church work before the war.

He had been born on the Isle of Wight in 1886, the only child of his father's second wife. As a teenager, he worked in a furniture shop on the island before moving with his parents to Romford Green in Essex, just a few miles from where his mother grew up in the East End of London. Earning a wage as a draper's assistant, he became actively engaged in church work and worked side-by-side with the young vicar of Hackney, Murray Tapply. He was put in charge of a mission in Beacontree Heath, near where he lived. He also took on responsibility for missions elsewhere in East and North London.[50] But in 1911, the draper's shop burned down and he was out of work. He made up his mind to travel to Canada, as a lay missionary with the Anglican mission agency, the Society for the Propagation of the Gospel (SPG).

This might seem a bold step for a 25-year-old of such limited education. However, his father's life experience helped him look beyond South East England. John Nobbs, by then aged 70, had been an engineer with an exotic job. The crowning achievement of his working life was serving as chief engineer on the yacht of a world-famous businessman, Sir Thomas Lipton. 'Tommy' Lipton had made his fortune with his grocery stores in England and his tea plantations in Ceylon. Lipton's tea is still a world-famous brand. He also had a passion for sailing and competed five times in the America's Cup in his state-of-the-art yachts. He had a steam yacht, *Erin*, which he used for lavish hospitality and for towing his racing yachts across the Atlantic. John Nobbs was its chief engineer. Harry Nobbs' father was not a man of limited horizons. It remains something of a puzzle that he allowed his son to leave school so young, though my grandfather believed his father was acquiescing to his mother's wishes. Whatever the reason, the chief engineer's global outlook would undoubtedly make it easier for Harry Nobbs to look further afield to make something of his life.

Harry Nobbs was to spend four years as a lay church worker in Canada before joining the Canadian Medical Corps, describing his trade as 'Licensed Lay Reader, Church of England'. After the war, en route to ordination, he moved to the coastal city of Vancouver to start training at its Anglican theological college. He entered wholeheartedly into student life, serving on the committee of the Literary and Athletic Association.[51] His vacations in 1922 and 1923 were spent on mission teams in his sending diocese, including a placement in the prairie town of Coronation. During term-time, he was on placement at St Martin's, North Vancouver.[52] To the dismay of fellow students, the Bishop of Calgary decided his five ordinands should move colleges for their third and final year.[53] So they travelled more than a thousand miles east, just south of Lake Winnipeg. Their destination, St John's Winnipeg, had been founded in 1866 by Robert Machray, a Scotsman who went on to become Canada's first Anglican Archbishop. In 1877, under Machray's direction, it joined with two other church colleges to form the University of Manitoba. In 1923, when my grandfather enrolled, St John's was a thriving liberal arts college within the University, co-educational, well-endowed financially and with a distinctive Anglican identity.

He was fortunate to arrive when he did. The founder's nephew had been appointed as bursar, as well as secretary general of the local Anglican diocese and financial director of the University. He declined to be audited, on the grounds that it would impugn his good name. Free from scrutiny, he speculated recklessly with all their funds. He lost everything, was convicted, died in prison and left St John's in a precarious state for the next two decades. Its survival is owed to the fact that in Winnipeg 'a disproportionate number of the Protestant elite' was Anglican. Wealthy businessmen eventually stepped in, in support of the dynamic leadership of a Principal appointed in the 1950s.[54]

Completing his studies in 1924, when St John's was still buoyant, Harry Nobbs was ordained deacon. It was the year his father died. He would start out as curate in Cardston, Coutts and Warner, in the Diocese of Calgary. The congregations were a far cry from the church of the Anglican elite in Winnipeg. Cardston was then, and still remains, a mainly Mormon area. It was on the edge of the Blood Reserve Indian settlement with its Indian residential school and its own clergy. Coutts was the border crossing to the US state of Montana, so clergy from both sides of the border used to take services. As deacon, Harry Nobbs was not yet in a position to take communion services himself. Over the next eighteen months, he concentrated on Cardston, often conducting two services each Sunday, usually with around eight worshippers in the pews. Using the Church of England Prayer Book, he sometimes took the morning service (matins) or the evening service (evensong) at St Peter's Coutts, again with a typical attendance of eight people. He buried a 1-month-old baby and baptised a couple and their child.[55]

Once ordained priest, he was given a new assignment and moved eighty miles north to be curate-in-charge of Blairmore with Coleman. It was a coal-mining area in Crow's Nest Pass, a route through the Rocky Mountains. St Luke's, Blairmore had been founded in 1904, three years after a massive rock-slide, which crushed seventy people. St Alban's Coleman served a neighbouring town, founded by International Coal and Coke at about the same time.

In his eighteen months as curate-in-charge, his duties included three marriages and seven baptisms.[56] Still associated with the mission agency SPG, he sent regular reports back for the benefit of its supporters. He describes his work as a series of 'ups and downs'. To his disappointment, the settlers seemed more attracted to the non-Anglican 'Union Church of Canada'. There were nonetheless encouragements. A Lancastrian had recently arrived. 'On arriving at the place where he has been living for the past four years, he found a church that had not been used for eight years owing to the lack of priests in the West. He was from Lancashire, in the Old Land, and desired that his children should continue in the old Faith. As there was no minister he started a Sunday school, and succeeded in getting together about thirty children, Sunday by Sunday.' Now living four miles from Blairmore, the Lancastrian planned to start a Sunday school there too. Despite such 'ups', my grandfather was frustrated by his own limited resources. 'I found on a twelve mile walk a family that have not seen a minister of the church for eight years.... I plan to... visit there again and give him and his two confirmed descendants Communion. Our urgent need is priests and support for them. Many lonely settlers are without means of grace and in danger of falling from all observances of religion altogether.'[57]

He nonetheless did what he could. Back in town, he arranged children's services and prepared six candidates for confirmation. The Bishop of Calgary conducted the confirmation service in April 1926.[58] He clearly felt Harry Nobbs was ready for a bigger challenge. On 1 August 1926, he inducted him as priest-in-charge of Drumheller, a fast-growing mining community, two hundred miles north-east of Coleman.[59] Bordering the Rockies in one direction and the prairies in the other, these were the badlands, thus named by trappers because they were 'bad lands to cross'. The dry terrain with its ravines and gullies has made the Drumheller badlands a popular location for filming. In 1992, it was a perfect setting for Clint Eastwood's Oscar-winning western, *Unforgiven*.

The Bishop of Calgary preparing to confirm six candidates at Blairmore in 1926

Author's personal archives

Drumheller had been established as a village thirteen years before my grandfather was inducted, following the opening of the Calgary–Drumheller Railway. Its location was close to the spot where a dinosaur head had been found by coal-mining prospector, Joseph Tyroll. After World War One, it quickly became known as the 'Wonder town of the west—the fastest growing town in Canada', with 3,000 inhabitants by 1931.[60] The year my grandfather moved to Drumheller, there had been 233 attending worship at St Magloire's on Easter Day. It was in a different league from his duties so far.[61]

The Church of England in Canada had started out as the established Church in 'Upper Canada', where Calgary was located. In the early days this had brought funding, through strips of land set aside for the Church ('clergy reserves'). But all this was long gone. Clergy reserves were discontinued in 1854. The Church was now disestablished and self-financing. With so much opportunity, and limited finances, Harry Nobbs was clear he would need to draw further on his links with SPG. As he explained to SPG's faithful supporters, frequent pastoral visits to Drumheller's hospital had revealed that 'a good many Church members are living in various small places scattered over the adjoining country.... Our urgent need', he wrote, 'is a priest with a motor lorry, fitted up similarly to the Sunday School Mission vans that operate in various dioceses in Western Canada.... The scattered people badly need visiting, and if a car were available we could reach them occasionally, baptise their children, give communion, and get the names of their children for our Sunday school by post. It would also be possible to combine something of the nature of the Church Army evangelistic work.'[62]

It was not SPG's usual policy to provide cars, but the appeal was heeded by one of SPG's supporters. Thus my grandfather found himself in possession of an expenses-paid Rolls Royce, large enough for him to sleep in when doing his parish visiting.[63] On Easter Day in 1927, there were an impressive 390 worshippers at St Magloire's, a seventy percent increase on the previous year. There were a further 105 worshippers in 'other places', testifying to the usefulness of his SPG-funded Rolls Royce.[64]

The Revd Harry Nobbs, my grandfather (above), parish visiting in the Canadian badlands, in his SPG-supplied Rolls Royce, complete with bedding (left)

Author's personal archives

Harry Nobbs seemed to be thriving on this ministry. There was active lay involvement at Drumheller, including a choir, an altar guild and the Women's Auxiliary. He opened services in seven other locations.[65] He took on civic duties, serving as justice of the peace, judge of the juvenile court and member of the Provincial Council of the Canadian Red Cross. Being mobile, and in any case only a short train journey from Calgary, he could take on wider diocesan roles, serving on the Diocesan Social Services Council and as chaplain of the Canadian Legion, drawing on his military experience. One might have expected his newly appointed bishop, Ralph Sherman, to be pleased with the appointment made by his predecessor.

Unfortunately, things were not going as smoothly as the reports to SPG suggested. Harry Nobbs might have been impressively enterprising; handling conflict, however, was not his strong suit. Yet as soon as he started at Drumheller, conflict is precisely what he encountered. The issue, bizarre as it might seem today, was candles.[66]

We shall be looking more closely at churchmanship and differing traditions in later chapters. For now, it is enough to recall that the nineteenth century had seen a revival of practices that had been suppressed when the Church of England broke with Rome in the sixteenth century. In Canada, as in England, this sparked bitter controversy. In England, the so-called Oxford Movement emphasised the 'catholic' nature of the Church. This was not just a matter of re-instating practices characteristic of the Roman Catholic Church. The 'catholic' Church needed to retain its integrity and resist being compromised by its association with the state. In Canada, this ecclesiology struck a chord at a time when the Church was being disestablished. It made a virtue out of necessity. Two parties had thus emerged in Canada: the 'church party', with its Anglo-Catholic convictions and the 'evangelical party', retaining a more Protestant and 'low church' conception of Anglican identity.

Harry Nobbs' predecessor at Drumheller, the Revd J. L. Smith, had received a petition requesting him to put candles on the communion table. When he tabled this for discussion, it provoked a vigorous response from those church members who identified with the 'evangelical party'. In face of this opposition, he chose not to press the matter and instead developed an overall approach that the evangelical party regarded as a 'happy medium'. As soon as Harry Nobbs arrived, he re-opened the matter. Things quickly came to a head. On 10 October 1926, ten weeks after he was inducted, a congregational meeting was held to consider his terms for remaining in post. For this new priest-in-charge, candles on the communion table were non-negotiable. There would nonetheless be 'strict observance of the canons with regard to the conduct of church services as laid down by the Prayer Book'. This prompted 'considerable discussion, during which the accuracy of Mr Nobbs' statement with regard to the reading of certain sections of the Prayer Book was called into question'. The sections were read out and 'found to vindicate Mr Nobbs'. Candles were not prohibited in the prayer book rubric.

His terms were therefore accepted, twenty-seven for, five against and he was invited to remain as priest-in-charge with 'full confidence and support'.

But the matter did not end there. The 'evangelical party' set up a rival weekly gathering elsewhere in town. They started advertising Sunday school classes under the name of 'Bishop Ridley Memorial Church of England', taking the name of one of the iconic bishops from the time of the Reformation. Ironically, the theological college where I would serve as Principal was also named after him. The rival activities of the Bishop Ridley Memorial Church were on the agenda at the next Vestry meeting. Harry Nobbs' mind had been made up: this was a schism. It was brought to the attention of the new bishop, who quickly decided a pastoral visit should be one of his first assignments in post. He met with Harry Nobbs and the churchwardens and urged them to make every effort both to heal the schism and to remain fully within the protocols of the Church of England in Canada. Harry Nobbs explained that regrettably he had reached a dead end in efforts at reconciliation, but that weekly attendance numbers at St Magloire's had increased by a third in the meantime. The bishop agreed the diocese would contest the use of 'Church of England' by the so-called 'Ridleyite' schism.

A month later, the title 'Church of England' was still being used in adverts in the local press. Harry Nobbs decided to resort to a more drastic measure. He wrote to all present and former communicants, excommunicating those associated with the 'Bishop Ridley Memorial Schism', so long as they failed to repent of the schism. This he based on the Prayer Book requirement that 'it is required of persons who come to the Lord's Supper, to examine themselves, whether they repent them truly of their former sins'.

The leader of the breakaway group wrote to the bishop in protest, enclosing a copy of a petition that had been sent to Harry Nobbs requesting more 'low church' services. Nothing was resolved and the dispute simmered on. A year later, despite his newly-acquired Rolls Royce, Harry Nobbs began to feel he needed a break. He came up with the idea of returning to England for a year. It was 1928, the year my other grandfather finally married, aged 36. It was also ten years after the end of World War One. Harry Nobbs was 41.

✠

Through the exploits of these two men, Harry Nobbs and William Norman, we have been able to observe the Church of England from a number of angles. We have seen its working assumptions under severe stress in the turmoil and devastation of World War One. The Church of England's association with privilege presented obstacles for effective ministry. Its identification with the state proved a delicate balancing act. Its patterns of worship and its clergy seemed ill-suited for nurturing a resilient and attractive faith in demanding times.

We have also observed the Church within the Empire the British fought to preserve. In one of the oldest colonies, we have seen a Church acclimatising to less privilege. We have seen it operating at a distance from the state, while still playing a civic role. Within its patterns of worship, we have seen conflict over the kind of worship that is fitting; we have witnessed resistance to change.

We have also seen active lay involvement, in local church life, in funding Church enterprises and in the work of the mission agency, SPG. We have noted the challenge of finance. And we have seen the Church's commitment to education, whether in the Khaki University or the University of Manitoba.

Time and again, when faced with new challenges, we have seen enterprise and a pioneering mentality. We have seen this in Talbot House, in the development of St John's Winnipeg and in the parish work of Harry Nobbs with his Rolls Royce.

All these themes we will pick up again in later chapters, as we explore further what 'being Anglican' means as times change.

Poised to move on: Amy
Gander, shortly before
marrying my grandfather

Author's personal archives

2

Vision, Enterprise and Anglican Communities

FOR BOTH MY GRANDFATHERS, 1928 was time to move. For the Church of England, it looked like time to move too, but in practice things mostly stayed put. Randall Davidson finally retired aged 80, having been Archbishop of Canterbury for twenty-five years. His successor, Cosmo Lang, showed little inclination to bring fresh energy to the challenges identified during World War One. The Church of England now had more control over its own affairs, with the establishment of the Church Assembly in 1919. Cosmo Lang's successor as Archbishop of York, William Temple, embodied a more easygoing, evangelistic and reform-minded approach to the national life of the Church. But at grass roots level, not much seemed to be changing, apart from the number of clergy (declining) and acceptance (increasing) of the kind of 'Catholic' practices that had alarmed the 'Ridleyite' lobby in my grandfather's parish in Canada. A revised Prayer Book was rejected by Parliament for making too many concessions in the 'Catholic' direction. There was little sign of a concerted effort to engage more effectively with the people of England or to equip churchgoers more fully to live out their faith.

William Norman's move in 1928 was to Heasewood Farm, the home of his new in-laws. He left his kid brother, Jim, to take over running Streele Farm, as their father was now 66 years old. My grandfather was marrying into one of the oldest farming families in mid-Sussex. Amy Gander, his 37-year-old fiancée, was the eldest of three children. Her father, Warden Gander, had moved to Heasewood Farm as co-tenant with his brothers thirty-eight years earlier, from Rookery Farm, just down the road in Haywards Heath. He had set up a dairy in the town centre of Haywards Heath, with his brothers. They then left him to run the farm. In 1928, he was 71 years old and was pleased to pass the tenancy on to his new son-in-law and take a back seat, his own two sons having left home. Thus William and Amy Norman began their married life. A year later, their only child was born: my father, John Warden Norman.

Harry Nobbs' move was less straightforward than William Norman's. His plan was to move back to England for a year, then return to his parish in Drumheller, no doubt hoping that the conflict over candles had subsided by then. He wanted to be active while in England, so he needed permission to officiate, as Canadian clergy were not automatically entitled to minister in England. For that, approval from the Archbishop of Canterbury was required. So he wrote to the elderly Archbishop Davidson at Lambeth Palace, proposing he might minister with his former mentor in the East End of London, the Revd Murray Tapply.

The Archbishop's Assistant Secretary wrote back to enquire whether Harry Nobbs' bishop was willing to receive him back after a year in England. 'I have told him', Bishop Ralph Sherman responded, 'that if he leaves I will not be able to keep the important town of Drumheller open for him, but will fill it.' He added 'I have told him that I cannot definitely promise to take him back on the staff of the Diocese one year hence'.[1] Four weeks later, and a few months before his retirement, Archbishop Davidson wrote a two-page letter to Harry Nobbs. He knew first-hand about the Church in my grandfather's adopted country, as the first Archbishop of Canterbury to have visited Canada.[2] His verdict: 'My strong advice would be that you should remain in Canada and I can accept no responsibility for your coming to England'.

Archbishop Davidson recognised that my grandfather had 'obviously undergone great strain and difficulty' but felt bound by his responsibility for 'securing that those who minister in England have shown evidence of due qualification'. The problem was twofold. 'Your examination for ordination was very far inferior to the kind of examination you would have had to pass for ordination in this country', he pointed out. 'You were excused both Latin and Greek, and there is no evidence before me of your having other educational attainments to compensate for this great deficiency'. Added to this was his age at ordination: 38 years old. 'You were ordained at an age much beyond that at which we ordinarily accept men for Ordination in this country, and this clearly may increase your difficulties.'[3]

By modern standards this seems hard-line, when Greek or Latin are no longer considered essential and more than sixty percent of candidates are over 40 years old when they start training.[4] Even by the standards of the time it seems a little harsh. In 1916, Archbishop Davidson and Cosmo Lang (then Archbishop of York) had written to all soldiers commending the possibility of ordination after the war. 'The Church of the future will need recruits for its ministry from men of all kinds of upbringing, circumstances and education.' They conceded there may 'be instances in which even the elementary knowledge of Greek' might be dispensed with.[5] They were heeding the recommendations of a Committee tasked with considering possible vocations among those who lacked 'early education'.[6] As war ended, there were imaginative efforts to provide training pathways for those who had served in the forces and lacked the usual qualifications.[7] However, by 1928, Latin was obligatory and Archbishop Davidson had no intention of bending the rules. Harry Nobbs had to resort to contingency plans.

He tried moving dioceses in Canada. But his bishop blocked the move. 'He could not be classed as one of our successful men' he explained in an informal reference, despite the growth in numbers at Drumheller. 'He is excitable and has no grounding either of education, culture or churchmanship.' In the bishop's view, the Archbishop of Canterbury was right to refuse permission for him to work in England.[8]

So Harry Nobbs finally identified a viable destination: Scotland. In the early part of the twentieth century, there were three categories of church in what we now call the Anglican Communion, from the Church of England's point of view. There were 'sister churches' such as the Scottish Episcopal Church and the Church of the United States of America; 'colonial churches', such as the Church of England in Canada, referred to also as 'daughter churches'; and 'missionary churches', in Asia and Africa.[9] Both sister churches and colonial churches had their own procedures for authorising clergy, independent from the Church of England. Harry Nobbs duly left Canada for Glasgow. He was appointed curate at St Bride's.

The Scottish Episcopal Church was not the established church in Scotland. Back in 1688 the Scottish bishops had refused to back the new king of England, William III. From that point on, the established Church of Scotland did without bishops altogether. Meanwhile, for another hundred years, those still identifying with Scottish bishops were treated suspiciously. For almost half that time, following the Jacobite rising in 1745, Scottish Episcopalian clergy were banned from taking services altogether. In the nineteenth century, the Oxford Movement had understandably struck a chord with this non-established church, just as it had in Canada; the independent authority of the church made good sense for a church used to being shunned by the British Crown. The ceremonial emphases emanating from the Oxford

Movement therefore followed suit, though not without controversy. Just before Harry Nobbs joined St Bride's, there had been a major row about incense. Complaints had been made to the bishop.[10] With Harry Nobbs' experience of candlestick controversy, the incumbent at St Bride's, Philip Lempriere, must have felt that Harry Nobbs would understand his world.

Harry Nobbs stuck to his original plan of a one-year interlude. As Randall Davidson had now been replaced by Cosmo Lang at Canterbury, he decided to try for a post in England again. Perhaps because Cosmo Lang's own church-manship was more Catholic than Davidson, this time he was successful. He was appointed curate at All Saints, Twickenham, alongside his ebullient mentor, Revd Murray Tapply. Not mincing his words, Revd Tapply rejoiced in the appointment in the local press. 'We have at last got a priest who is a staunch Catholic without the "spike virus", which has done so much harm by its copying a foreign cult and spoiling the Liturgy by acts of "personal revision". Now our troubles are at an end. Father Nobbs is not here to share my work, but to add his quota in what must now be a time of advance.'[11]

As things turned out, the alliance did not last long enough to put this to the test. Later in 1929, Murray Tapply moved to be Vicar of All Saints Hornsey and Harry Nobbs returned to Scotland, to serve as Diocesan Missioner in Argyll and the Isles. His efforts as Missioner were appreciated and in Oban he earned respect for his services for the sick and his association with the men's club.[12] After two years, he decided it was time to try for another spell in England and he moved to Bristol. But after just a few months as curate at Bedminster, he was lured once again by a more senior appointment in Scotland. In 1931, he was inducted as Rector of Campbeltown, a fishing town on the west coast.

With far fewer members than the Presbyterian Church of Scotland, the Scottish Episcopal Church had the reputation of being elitist. Presbyterians viewed it as 'supported mainly by people who hope the laird will ask them to dinner' mused one Scottish historian around this time, herself an Epis-copalian.[13] In Campbeltown, however, St Kiaran's Episcopal Church was by no means a church exclusively for the privileged and upwardly mobile. 'Hardly thirty episcopal families now live in the district, which is probably the most depressed area of unemployment in the Highlands', my grandfather wrote. At one point it had described itself as the whisky capital of the world, with thirty-four distilleries and its Campbeltown Single Malt. But in 1931 it had been hit hard by the slump in the whisky trade which followed prohibition in the United States and the Great Depression.

Harry Nobbs was quick off the mark as usual. A few weeks after his arrival, he was making a national appeal for help in running the institute for mission work among the poor of Campbeltown. The work would be spearheaded by his housekeeper's husband, J. D. Mayo. An ex-naval officer, he had experience of similar work at St Dunstan's, Bedminster, from where Harry Nobbs had just relocated, bringing the Mayos with him. Readers of the *Scottish Guardian* were urged to support a social centre that would be 'a haven for fishermen and youths'. As well as money and God's blessing, they needed 'woollies, notepaper, games, a piano, books and magazines etc'.[14] 'Local church people will do their best but are few in numbers', he added.

The following summer, with local church people 'few in numbers', Harry Nobbs was enthusiastic about plans for evangelism in the town and local area. A Church Army Motor Mission Van would be stationed near the War Memorial for four days of outreach. It would also visit local villages. Sunday services would be held on the seafront by the 'Mission to Seamen'. In addition, a Church Army sister would join them for the month of August, to work amongst the 'fisher girls' engaged in the herring trade.

Scottish 'fisher girls' enjoying Church Army tea and cakes
Author's personal archives

The Church Army had been founded in 1882 by an enterprising clergyman, Revd Wilson Carlile. Its initial focus was the slums of Westminster. Ahead of his time, Carlile recognised the gulf that existed between the educated 'gentlemanly' clergy and the urban poor, long before this had been exposed by World War One. He therefore drew together an 'army' of soldiers, working men and women, who were trained to act as Church of England evangelists. A Church Army training institution was set up in London, near Marble Arch, and its workers were soon active outside London and in other countries. By the turn of the century, four hundred Church Army captains and two hundred Church Army nurses were ministering in settings ranging from lodging houses and bars to dockyards.[15] During World War One, eight hundred Church Army centres were in operation in Europe. At peak times, 200,000 men used the centres every day. There were also wartime Church

Army centres in Egypt (200), British East Africa and India (30), Mesopotamia (30) and Malta (20).[16]

Church Army Mission Vans had inspired Harry Nobbs in his vision for the Rolls Royce SPG supplied him in Drumheller. The evangelical ethos of the Church Army was entirely compatible with his more Catholic churchmanship. 'I am as evangelical as anyone—I am also a Catholic' he explained to his bishop in the midst of the candles controversy at Drumheller.[17]

Preparatory work for Campbeltown's mission included house-to-house visiting and distribution of Church Army pamphlets to the local poorhouse, the fisher folk and hospitals. To complement the work of the Church Army Mission Van, Sister Margaret Reynolds arrived as planned in August. She had trained as a State Registered Nurse in London. She also had a certificate in theology, pastoral and evangelistic work from the Board of Women's Work in the Diocese of London. Her task was to offer first aid and friendship to the fisher girls who often suffered nasty cuts while gutting the herrings. Her training at the Church Army College in London had included open air preaching across the street from the college, at Hyde Park Corner. She had already worked amongst fisher girls in Suffolk and the Shetlands. She was well equipped to play her part in this evangelistic enterprise.

Church Army sister Margaret Reynolds (left of centre) on a 'lugger' fishing boat

Author's personal archives

It was a busy summer. The supply of books and magazines ran out and Harry Nobbs made another national appeal. He conducted off-shore services on board ships moored in the loch. Some were on the naval vessel HMS *Lucia*, for the crews of the submarine flotilla in the harbour. Fortuitously, in all the activity, the Rector was not too busy to appreciate his co-workers. Sister Reynolds caught his eye. By May the following year, they would be married.

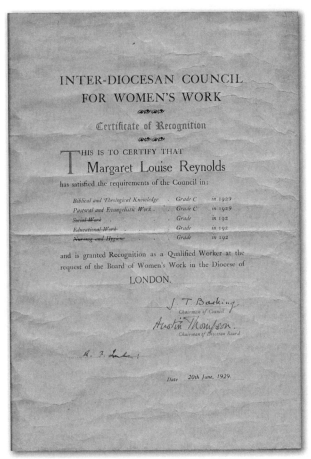

INTER-DIOCESAN COUNCIL
FOR WOMEN'S WORK

Certificate of Recognition

THIS IS TO CERTIFY THAT
Margaret Louise Reynolds
has satisfied the requirements of the Council in:

Biblical and Theological Knowledge	Grade C	in 1929
Pastoral and Evangelistic Work	Grade C	in 1929
Social Work	Grade	in 192
Educational Work	Grade	in 192
Nursing and Hygiene	Grade	in 192

and is granted Recognition as a Qualified Worker at the request of the Board of Women's Work in the Diocese of

LONDON.

J. T. Backing.
Chairman of Council

Austin Thompson.
Chairman of Diocesan Board

Date   20th June, 1929.

Recognised by the Bishop of London: Margaret Reynolds' qualification in
biblical and theological knowledge, pastoral and evangelistic work
Author's personal archives

As my grandparents' wedding plans were being put in place, Harry Nobbs once again was responding to seamen afflicted by wintry weather. 'The woollies that you so kindly sent came in very useful during the weekend' he reported to readers of the *Scottish Guardian*. 'Two large trawlers sought shelter from the gale—one of them was badly battered about in the Atlantic, with two men injured. I have almost exhausted the woollies as the crew lost nearly everything, except what they stood up in, overboard.' A grateful captain 'sent a basket of fish up to the Rectory on New Year's Day' which was passed on to the secretary of the unemployed workers. 'So the helped helped others. The best kind of Christian Socialism, you will agree', my grandfather observed, alluding to the approach being popularised south of the border by William Temple, Archbishop of York.

Margaret Reynolds and Harry Nobbs chose a more accessible wedding venue than St Kiaran's, Campbeltown. They opted for St Bride's, Glasgow, where Harry Nobbs had served as curate four years earlier. Margaret Reynolds had spent her childhood in Shropshire, Kent and Surrey, but her family were used to Glasgow weddings. By coincidence, her brother Charles had been married in Glasgow Cathedral two years earlier. At both these Glasgow weddings, they would be joined by their mother and younger sister, Elizabeth ('Birdie'). Their father, a building contractor, had died of war wounds in 1918, aged 50, and their two other siblings had died as babies.

Margaret and Harry decided they needed a fresh start, despite their shared endeavours in Campbeltown. They took the bold decision of moving to Glasgow, but not to the prosperous suburbs served by St Bride's. They went for a 'slum parish', St Mark's Kinning Park. Anglo-Catholics had developed a reputation for ministry amongst the urban poor. At the time evangelicals were ministering amongst the urban poor through the Church Army, Anglo-Catholics were active in deprived parishes with their own distinctive emphases. Harry Nobbs had first-hand experience of this before World War One, through his association with Murray Tapply in Bethnal Green. 'Altogether in the east of London,' an observer wrote seventy years before then, 'in Bethnal Green, Stepney, Shoreditch, and that neighbourhood, the church is doing wonders; and here the *Morning Chronicle* says Puseyism is all but universal.'[18] 'Slum priests' tended to be unmarried, even if Edward Pusey and other donnish founders of the Oxford Movement, such as John Keble, chose not to be. An Anglo-Catholic priest serving in a slum parish with a trained Church Army worker was a novelty and potentially a winning combination.

Kinning Park was described then as being 'in a backwater of the main stream of life' but it was a far cry from the coastal remoteness of Campbeltown. To the south were the LMS railway yards, used for shunting freight wagons; to the north was the busy Paisley Road West. Many of Glasgow's dockyard workers lived in the parish. Work was erratic and in the mid-1930s there was chronic unemployment. 'St Marks has broken one or two of the clergy who have served it in the past' a report noted ominously at the time. 'The ceaseless work, the strain of financial anxiety, the floating and ever-changing population, and the dank atmosphere of depression that enwraps the surroundings, make demands almost too severe on the faith and physical energy of most men'.[19]

Undaunted, Harry Nobbs launched energetically into the work. Margaret began to carve out her distinctive role as rector's wife, playing an active part in parish organisations such as the Mothers' Union. Before long, they were preparing to be parents. Margaret's sister-in-law, whose wedding had been celebrated in Glasgow three years earlier, had died giving birth. Margaret would thankfully not suffer the same fate. On 24 August 1934, the only child of Margaret and Harry Nobbs was born: Anna Louise, my mother. My grandmother was 35, my grandfather 46, the same age his own father had been when he was born.

In October, my mother was baptised at St Mark's, with her mother's brother and sister, Charlie and Birdie, serving as godparents. The baptism certificate left no doubt about the obligations which accompanied infant baptism. Her parents and sponsors should ensure she is:

1. Taught about religion as soon as possible.
2. Brought to Holy Communion to hear sermons.
3. Taught the church catechism.
4. Trained in Christian habits.
5. Brought to be confirmed as soon as the Catechism is known and understood.

The expectation was that she would automatically wish to continue in the faith in which she was baptised, as soon as she was old enough to understand it sufficiently well.

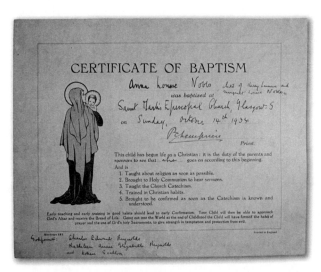

My mother's baptism certificate, making it clear she was expected to 'go on after this beginning'

Author's personal archives

After the baptism, parish activity continued unabated. The church was dedicated that same October, with no fewer than five services on the Sunday, as well as Sunday school. The following afternoon there was a Home Mission rally, with a fundraising 'bring and buy' sale in the evening. Harry Nobbs also found time for engagements outside the parish in the months that followed. On Wednesday evenings in Lent, he delivered a series at Holy Trinity, Paisley on the theme 'The Kingdom that must be built'.

However, as they entered their fourth year at St Mark's, the strain of this demanding parish was beginning to show. With their daughter approaching school age, they felt it was time to move on. For the fourth time, Harry Nobbs tried for an appointment in England. This time he would go for the north of England. It was the Archbishop of York who would need to give his consent. William Temple duly obliged and the family of three moved to the Diocese of Durham, along with my grandfather's widowed mother.

Harry Nobbs was put in charge of a mission church, eight miles upriver from Durham. Binchester was best known for its Roman Fort, Vinovium, in the valley of the river Wear. Built around 79AD, the fort was a staging post en route to Hadrian's Wall. Alongside garrisons of Spanish cavalry and Dutch infantry, a thriving community of farmers, traders and craftsmen developed. Archaeological excavations began in 1878, with the local vicar, Robert Hoopell, a prime mover. By then, the site was owned by the Diocese of Durham. Ownership passed to the Church Commissioners, who in 2007 bought the nearby Binchester Hall to open as a visitor centre. In 2008, the site attracted the *Time Team* from Channel 4 television.[20]

Ministry in England, eventually authorised by Archbishop Cosmo Lang, and later by Archbishop William Temple, for the Province of York (on top) *Author's personal archives*

Auckland Castle, historic residence of the Bishop of Durham, as viewed from the entrance to Binchester Fort

Photo © Andrew Norman

Serving a coal-mining community — the graveyard of St Barnabas Binchester

Photo © Andrew Norman

From the entrance to the fort, you can look across the golf course to Auckland Castle, residence of the Bishop of Durham from the twelfth century until 2012. The Roman site and Auckland Castle are now both tourist attractions, with Auckland Castle hosting some of the most valuable paintings in the north of England. Back in 1937, however, the neighbourhood of Binchester was far from being a highbrow National Trust destination. The village itself was the other side of the hill to the Roman remains. Its graveyard included a tombstone commemorating 'James, accidentally killed at Westerton Colliery, aged 23, son of James and Sarah Merritt'. It was a mining community, surrounded by countryside. Masonry from the Roman fort was used as props inside the pits.

Harry and Margaret Nobbs, 3-year-old Anna and 'Granny' moved into the clergy house next to the church. St Barnabas had a corrugated iron roof and was gas-lit. It had been built in 1876 for £500, the Victorian equivalent of a portakabin. A permanent stone or brick building would have cost ten times as much.[21] Of the two mission churches in the parish, the one at Binchester was more Anglo-Catholic. Although the population of Binchester was less than three hundred, there were also two Methodist churches in the village: a Primitive Methodist Church, built in 1886 and a Wesleyan Methodist Church, built in 1903. The Bishop of Durham, Hensley Henson, noted drily that the established religion in his diocese was not Anglicanism, but Methodism.[22]

'Three main movements of thought and experience are lodged within our household', Cosmo Lang had observed at his enthronement in Canterbury Cathedral ten years earlier, 'Catholic, Evangelical and Liberal. Is any one of these an intruder?'[23] Hensley Henson had already been Bishop of Durham for eight years by then and had established his reputation as one of the more prominent liberals on the bench of bishops, albeit something of a maverick. He was outspoken and convinced—in the words of his biographer—that 'the old language must be restated in the light of new knowledge'.[24] His nomination as Bishop of Hereford in 1917 had provoked what he regarded as a heresy hunt. He was accused of denying the resurrection and the virgin birth. The preacher at his installation at Durham Cathedral had been Dean Inge, the leader of the so-called Modernist movement. Objections to Henson and Inge were cited by the writer G. K. Chesterton when he justified becoming a Roman Catholic.[25] Henson ended up falling out with Dean Inge when he distanced himself from the Modernist movement. But he remained more liberal than Catholic or evangelical. He described himself as 'like a circus rider with a foot on both horses'.[26]

Henson's predecessor at Durham was mine too: the evangelical former Principal of Ridley Hall, Handley Moule. Henson thought him 'a very good man and a bad bishop'. In particular, he felt he had been too willing to take on 'ill-educated' clergy.[27] When he arrived in Durham, Henson hoped to replace clergy from humble origins with those educated at Oxbridge and Durham University.[28] Henson was no fan of Catholic traditions either. This might sound unpromising for my grandfather, as a non-Oxbridge Anglo-Catholic. But Henson was prepared to find Catholic-minded clergy for Catholic-minded parishes, even if he preferred to recruit his Anglo-Catholic curates straight from Cuddesdon theological college in Oxfordshire.[29]

When my grandfather began as curate, just across the fields from the Bishop's palatial but chilly residence, Henson had just published his views on the role of parish clergy. In *Ad Clerum,* marking fifty years since his own ordination, he offered twelve charges to ordinands on the eve of their ordination. A parson should be marked out from the people without being ostentatious, wearing a clerical collar; he should stay in the parish and visit house-to-house, seldom 'rushing away in a motor car'; he should read, prioritising Scripture over the newspaper; he should be interested in people yet discreet; by service to the people he should hold before them the Lordship of Christ.[30]

Harry Nobbs ticked most of the boxes in his bishop's book. But as an Anglo-Catholic, he would want to give celebration of communion a higher profile than his bishop. In doing so, he was in step with both Archbishops and a growing movement to see communion established as the main Sunday service in all Church of England parishes. The influential collection of essays *The Parish Communion* was published that year and proved itself an inspiration for what became the 'Parish and People Movement'.[31] St Barnabas Binchester may have been Anglo-Catholic in churchmanship, but that did not mean its worshippers already accepted the logic of this emerging movement. When my grandfather began his ministry there, the most popular service at Binchester was not a morning service at all. It was evensong. Average evensong attendance was forty in 1938. At the 9am Eucharist, average weekly attendance was thirty-two, with only nine receiving communion. Signalling the importance of Holy Communion, he introduced a daily service. Discouragingly, as the months went by, he was almost always the only weekday communicant.[32]

On Sundays, the evening service continued to be better attended than the morning service. The church's pulpit was visible from the clergy house. When my grandfather was seen climbing up into the pulpit, my mother recalls, it was time for her to go to bed. However, as the novelty of the new curate-in-charge began to wear off, attendance at services declined too. By 1940, evening service attendance was down by half to an average of nineteen a week, with just fourteen attending the communion service in the morning.[33]

At the clergy house
in Binchester

Author's personal archives

In this rural mining village, the challenges were very different from the bustling inner-city parish in Glasgow. There were fewer candidates for running church activities. My grandmother stepped in and played her part, serving on the church committee, as well as running the Sunday school. In the absence of anyone suitably qualified, my grandfather served as treasurer.

Parish finances certainly needed attention. The curate was part-funded by a grant of £120 from a restricted fund administered by the Ecclesiastical Commissioners. However, by 1940 it was clear that action would need to be taken to raise more funds. The tin roof needed repairing, the caretaker was underpaid and the organist deserved reimbursement. At the annual meeting in 1941, the rector pointed out there was an obvious need for more regular and better giving. A plan was agreed at the meeting. Numbers on the electoral roll should be increased from the meagre twenty-eight members and regular giving should be sought from lapsed members and others who might be prepared to join the scheme. In less than a year, the plan yielded impressive results. There had been 'exceedingly satisfactory improvement in the finances of the church', the rector reported at the annual meeting. The electoral roll had risen from 28 to a staggering 141. Parishioners rarely attending Sunday worship were increasingly contributing via the Free Will Offering, collected each Monday. The caretaker got his pay-rise and the organist his honorarium. Thirty new hymnbooks were bought.[34]

The mood of the village itself had changed since the Nobbs' arrival in 1938. Great Britain had entered World War Two. Food was rationed. At the school across the road from the church, the children were served bread and syrup, with the meat ration going to the miners. Far from being protected by rural remoteness, Binchester and its surrounding coal mines were a target for German bombers. Wilkie, the family cat, had been born the day war was declared. When the air raid siren sounded in nearby Bishop Auckland, Wilkie always rattled the letterbox to come in. My mother and 'Granny' sheltered under the stairs. They all had good reason to take cover. There was a near miss when an incendiary bomb landed in the garden.

My grandfather had already been suffering from nervous exhaustion when the family left the demanding slum parish in Glasgow. Air raids around Binchester triggered stressful memories of the shelling and carnage of World War One. It was more than he could take. One afternoon, my 6-year-old mother looked out of the window to see him get off the bus, then collapse in the road. He was rushed to hospital in Newcastle and his condition seemed so serious that his family feared for his life. Yet somehow he rallied and gradually he resumed his parish duties. But it was clear a complete change was needed. A suitable opening appeared in the Lake District. The vicar of Mungrisdale had left to serve as an army chaplain and needed cover in his absence. The family moved in April 1942.

My father and his family had just moved too, to a neighbouring farm in Sussex. Prior to the move, John Norman had been observing World War Two with boyish interest. 'This morning the sirens went. We had some bombs on our farm' he writes aged 11 in his diary. 'One crater made a hole about 20 feet deep.' The insecurity of war seemed to be prompting an unusually high turnout at church. 'In the morning, my mother and I went to church. It was quite crowded. In the afternoon my mother and I went to have our gas mask fitted with a new filter.' On another occasion: 'It was so crowded that we nearly had to stand.' Going to church with his mother features routinely in his diary. 'In the morning my mother and I cycled to church. It was very windy. In the afternoon my mother and I rode our ponies. We had mud splashed over us.' On another Sunday: 'It was very cold'; and another 'We went through the fields'. Only once does he mention going to church with his father, in the evening once the cows had been milked. It seems his father's harrowing experience of World War One had left him dutiful without being especially devout.

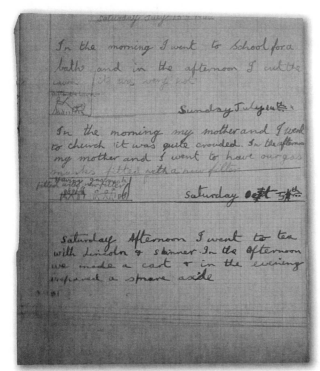

Sunday in wartime,
as recorded in my
father's diary

Author's personal archives

By then, both of William Norman's live-in in-laws had died. His father-in-law, Warden Gander, had lived at Heasewood Farm for fifty years and for all William and Amy's married life. Now William, Amy and John were free to make a fresh start. William's own father, who had also just died, had moved from Devon in 1896, with all his livestock. William's family now moved all their livestock the much shorter distance to Great Lywood Farm, Ardingly.

Ardingly is a small village in mid-Sussex. It is also the site of an Anglican boarding school, Ardingly College. My grandmother had inherited her father's share of the proceeds from the dairy in Haywards Heath, mostly invested in property. She decided some of it should go towards her son's education. Thus began the family's long association with Ardingly College.

The College is a red brick complex on a magnificent site, overlooking the valley of the River Ouse and, in the distance, a railway viaduct with thirty-seven arches. There is now a reservoir in the valley too. The school is just twenty miles from the Channel coast, which put it in a precarious position at the beginning of World War Two, with the high risk of invasion by Germany. A decision was nonetheless taken not to evacuate the school. 'In the event of a sudden emergency, Upper School Boys could have been trusted either to fight or to get themselves home.'[35] In 1942, when my father started there, the threat of invasion by Germany had receded. The war nonetheless cast its shadow. Several of the playing fields had been dug up to grow parsnips, carrots, swedes, turnips, beetroot, leeks, onions, potatoes and cabbages. The windows were blacked out at night, for good reason. A German Dornier XVII had been shot down on my father's farm. In Ardingly village, the rector had been shocked to receive five dead bodies at the Rectory, casualties of a bomb landing on cottages beside the allotment gardens.[36] With war an ever-present reality, the boys at Ardingly College trained as army cadets twice a week.

The school had been founded in 1858 by a remarkable Anglican clergyman, Nathaniel Woodard. By the time of his death, he had founded eleven schools. He had hoped to establish even more. His vision was to provide affordable Christian education for the middle classes. In the mid-nineteenth century, there were church schools for the poor, such as the primary school in Ardingly village. There were public schools for the rich, with a renewed Christian emphasis, thanks to the reforming work of Thomas Arnold at Rugby School. But there was little on offer for tradesmen, clerks and farmers. This had been brought home to Woodard when he served as curate in the harbour parish of Shoreham-by-Sea. As tradesmen shipped coal from the Tyne, timber, grain and other goods to the Baltic, Woodard was struck by their lack of education, with many of them illiterate.[37]

Woodard saw Christian education for the middle classes as crucial for the well-being of a nation in the throes of industrialisation. He set out his vision in a twenty-page tract, *A Plea for the Middle Classes* and conducted a tireless campaign of lobbying and fundraising. Supporters included the future prime minister, William Gladstone. Woodard's plan was to create a three-tier system of schools. The Upper Tier would provide education for sons of gentlemen, officers and clergy. The Middle Tier was for sons of more affluent tradesmen, clerks and farmers. The Lower Tier was for sons of small shopkeepers, mechanics and poorer clerks and farmers. In Sussex, the Upper Tier College would be at Lancing, the Middle Tier at Hurstpierpoint and the Lower Tier at Ardingly. Despite being Lower Tier, Ardingly College was Woodard's 'Jewel in the Crown'.[38]

The chapel would be at the heart of the school. This had been one of the innovations of Thomas Arnold at Rugby. Arnold himself, as headmaster, had preached each week. At a time when headmasters tended to be clergy, Woodard insisted that each of his schools should have its own chaplain whom he, as Provost, would appoint. Moreover, the Christian ethos would be Anglo-Catholic. Though raised as an evangelical Anglican, Woodard had been deeply influenced by the Oxford Movement when studying at Oxford in the 1830s. He was appointed curate in Bethnal Green, the Anglo-Catholic heartland of slum parishes, where my grandfather would begin his ministry as a lay person decades later. Under the wary eye of his bishop, Woodard ran into trouble. In one of his sermons, he seemed to promote 'confession' to a priest as necessary for full assurance of God's forgiveness. Bishop Blomfield of London removed him from his post and this was what lay behind his move to Sussex.

Woodard's churchmanship was in contrast to that of the public schools, which tended to be uneasy about Anglo-Catholicism. The year before Ardingly was founded, *Tom Brown's Schooldays* had been published. Based on the author's experience as a pupil in Thomas Arnold's Rugby, it strongly emphasised team sports as a means of character building. It contributed to the rise of 'muscular Christianity'. In some ways, this was seen as an antidote to the asceticism and 'unmanly' characteristics of the Oxford Movement, which some saw as 'sapping the vitality of the Anglican Church'.[39]

By the time my father started at Ardingly College, the Anglo-Catholic ethos had fused with the muscular Christianity of the public schools. Its headmaster, Canon Ernest Crosse, had been an army chaplain in World War One. He was one of the chaplains who had been awarded the Military Cross. A courageous man, he had also been mentioned three times in dispatches.

'The belief of Ardingly', he explained, 'is that the vital factor in all education is the spiritual one, by which I mean quite simply that the things which matter most at school are the training of character, the learning to work—if possible even the learning to enjoy hard work—and the playing of games hard and in the right spirit.'[40] In the school magazine, he writes 'The present generation of Ardinians is perhaps not aware of the fact that it was because of its Cricket that Ardingly first became known to the outside world. We have recently been reminded of this by the death of W. Newham, who was captain of the county club in 1890, 1891 and 1892. His record of a seventh wicket stand of 344 with the famous K. S. Ranjitsinhji still stands.'[41]

My father's diary in 1944 is mostly filled with daily references to sport. 29 January: 'Played football. . . . Lost 14-1. Scored the goal.' On the day before his fifteenth birthday: 'PT. Went on steeplechase practice. Watched boxing. Fight between Smith and Trower was absolute massacre.' 'Played cricket in B league against D. Lost. I scored 1 run.' Chapel occasionally features in the diary too. 'Tilt gave a sermon.' 'Cleaned chapel brass.' On 19 March: 'I was confirmed today by the Bishop of Chichester.' 1 October: 'We had the lights on in Chapel for the first time. Canon Crosse switched them on.' 8 October: 'Harvest Festival Hymns "Harvest home", "We plough the fields and scatter".' 'Harvest home' would become one of my father's favourites in his future years as a dairy farmer. Later that month, he notes the singing of the patriotic hymn so closely associated with boarding schools. 31 October: 'Had a Commemoration Service. Hymns "Abide with me", "Jerusalem".'

Only two items of national news are noted in my father's diary of 1944. 6 June: 'Allies invaded France.' 30 October; 'Archbishop of Canterbury, William Temple, died last Thursday.' After thirteen years as Archbishop of York, in 1942 Temple had finally taken over from Cosmo Lang as Archbishop of Canterbury. The conservative Prime Minister, Winston Churchill, defended his endorsement of this socialist Archbishop. He was the only 'half-crown article in a penny bazaar'.[42] Given Temple's reputation, it was all the more shocking that he should die after just two years in office. It is nonetheless a mark of very different times to today's that the death of an Archbishop of Canterbury should make it into the diary of a 15-year-old farmer's son.

William Temple had been a public school headmaster. So had his father, Frederick Temple, who also became Archbishop of Canterbury. William Temple's successor, Geoffrey Fisher, had also been a public school headmaster. In fact, of the eight Archbishops of Canterbury serving between 1862 and 1961, six had been public school headmasters. The Anglican microclimate of independent schools, of which Ardingly's was a variant, can be seen as a significant contributor to the leadership ethos of the Church of England for a hundred years. During that time, 183 of the 225 bishops studied at public schools. Half of them studied at the ten most prestigious schools.[43] Bearing this in mind, we shall be returning to public school spirituality in the next chapter, having already noted its connection to team sports and character building. For now, our attention turns to a different kind of Anglican boarding school: a girls' school run by Anglican nuns. The Oxford Movement's impact on education is not limited to Woodard's schools. With the Oxford Movement came the revival of religious communities. Education was to be one of the fruits of their renaissance.

Death of an Archbishop: one of the few national news items recorded in my father's diary   *Author's personal archives*

When my mother and her parents left County Durham, they were moving to a remote rural parish in the Lake District. Most of the parishioners were farming families. There was, however, a military family living in the parish. Brigadier Watkins was on active service, after a career in the Indian Army. His wife Sybil quickly got on well with my grandmother, Margaret. She suggested my mother might follow her own children to a boarding school run by Anglican sisters. My grandfather was enthusiastic, my grandmother less so. A decision was taken. Anna Norman was enrolled at St Hilda's, a remote boarding school on grouse moors, thirty miles away. She was 7 years old.

St Hilda's was run by Anglican nuns from the Order of the Holy Paraclete.[44] The order had been founded by an enterprising sister, Margaret Cope, who began her vocation with another Anglican religious community, the Society of St Peter. Margaret Cope was the daughter of a railway clerk employed by the Great Western Railway. Attending Dudley High School at the turn of the twentieth century, she went on to train as a teacher at Oxford University. Women were not eligible for degrees at Oxford, but Margaret Cope achieved a distinction in the University Secondary Teachers' Diploma. While in Oxford, she became deeply religious. She began to consider serving as a missionary in India, but at twenty-two was regarded as too young. Instead, she went to Yorkshire, to a small Anglican community of sisters near Wakefield.

The Society of St Peter, Horbury, had been founded in 1858. It was dedicated to serving women from congested mill town slums who were casualties of poverty and crime. Their community at Horbury was a refuge, known as the House of Mercy. At Horbury, the Society of St Peter had also opened a day school, St Hilda's, in 1875. One of Margaret's fellow students in Oxford, Katherina Rein, was put in charge of the school in 1908. In 1909, she invited Margaret to join her as second mistress. A year later, Margaret Cope took over as head, when Katherina Rein was accepted as a postulant in the society. In 1912, Margaret herself became a postulant and then a novice. She continued to run the school, but some within the community began to wonder whether education was a distraction from their main calling to serve vulnerable women.

When World War One began, a decision was taken to close the school. This placed Margaret Cope in a quandary. She felt her call was to teaching. In its last term at Horbury, she boldly proposed moving the school and starting a new order. With one of her fellow teachers, she visited possible premises in Whitby, the coastal town associated with St Hilda. They managed to take over the lease of Sneaton Castle, intended as a boys' boarding school before war broke out. Five of the teachers moved from Horbury to this new site in Whitby.

Margaret Cope's new order would be dedicated to the Holy Spirit. It would need the blessing of the Archbishop of York. So three days after the school opened, with its thirty-two pupils relocated from Horbury, Sister Margaret travelled to York to meet Archbishop Cosmo Lang.

Cosmo Lang had developed a reputation of being somewhat intimidating. Once, when looking at his recently completed portrait by Sir William Orpen, he remarked in earshot of Hensley Henson, 'They say I look proud, pompous and prelatical'. Henson supposedly murmured 'And may I ask your grace to which of these epithets your grace takes exception?'[45] When Sister Margaret explained her plans to Archbishop Lang, he suggested that at 28 she might be rather young to be founding a new Order. Standing her ground, she retorted that some said he was rather young to be Archbishop. She might have been pushing her luck, but the Archbishop was clearly impressed. He licensed the chapel and after two years formally accepted the new Order of the Holy Paraclete, becoming its first Visitor.

By the time of World War Two, the Order had set up houses in eight locations in Lancashire, Newcastle-upon-Tyne, North Yorkshire and West Africa, with thirty-four sisters in profession. Whitby had been one of the towns shelled by German battleships in World War One. In wartime, a school on the coast was far too exposed, so it was decided the pupils at St Hilda's would be split between two safer locations. Most would go to Canada. The remainder would form the nucleus of a relocated St Hilda's school, at a former shooting lodge near Middleton-on-Tees. A year after St Hilda's moved to the grouse moors, my mother joined the ten juniors (aged 9 and under) and the twenty-six senior girls.[46]

The regime was tough on a 7-year-old. The standard school day was: 7am rising bell. 7.20am chapel. 8am breakfast, followed by bed making. Lessons in forty minute periods started at 9.15am, and after a break for milk and an oatmeal biscuit, continued until 1pm lunch. The afternoon was divided into two periods, after which they changed out of school uniform into their own clothes for tea. From 4.45pm to 6pm was supervised prep (homework). Supper was at 6.30pm and 7.30pm was bedtime. The children were kept busy most of the day and free time was limited. Lessons were timetabled on Saturday mornings too. No school work was done on Sundays. Scripture, with Bible stories from the Old Testament, was taught by the chaplain during the week. On Sunday, the children attended Sung Mass, Matins and Evensong. There was plainsong and incense.[47]

Some children were content enough, but my mother found it hard to endure. Catching mumps was the last straw. After a term, it was clear she was not going to thrive there. So, her parents agreed they should come up with an alternative. One option was the school next door to the rectory, run singlehandedly by Miss Blanch Bott, the daughter of a vicar. In its only classroom, she taught thirty children from 5 to 14 years old. My grandmother decided home schooling would be preferable to this. So she tried it for a year. Despite being in a class of one, it was not a lonely existence for my mother. Evacuees came to stay in the rectory. There were two girls from Newcastle and two boys from Liverpool. At one point a family from Lancashire took over the top floor. Overall, being at home suited my mother much better.

At St Hilda's, she had nonetheless encountered the fruit of dynamic female leadership in the Church of England, fifty years before women would be ordained. Her own godmother, 'Auntie Birdie', would go on to join a religious order once World War Two was over.

⳨

In this chapter, we have encountered the exercise of women's ministry in religious orders and also in the Church Army, through the experience of my grandmother. For ordained ministers, we have seen further evidence of the bias towards those from privileged and well-educated backgrounds, despite the challenges posed to this during World War One. In parish ministry, we have seen the outworking of practical commitment to the local community in Scotland and England. We have noted the costliness of this in deprived areas such as Glasgow and have seen some of challenges in areas where Anglicans are a minority or resources are scarce. We have seen the scope for enterprise and for co-operation with Anglican agencies, such as the Missions to Seafarers and the Church Army. We have also witnessed the energising effect of different traditions, especially in caring for the vulnerable, in education, in outreach and in refocusing corporate worship. Once again, we have noticed how churchmanship can sometimes destabilise, in the Anglo-Catholicism of Nathaniel Woodard or the Rector of St Bride's Glasgow and in the modernism of the Bishop of Durham. We have noted that a distinctive Anglican ethos is not simply found in parish churches. We have observed it in boarding schools, religious communities and mission agencies, such as the Church Army.

All this has largely been a combination of time-honoured Anglican emphases and of Anglican innovations dating back to the nineteenth century. As we anticipated at the start of this chapter, this has generally amounted to holding a steady course. In observing the late 1920s, 1930s and early 1940s, we have not come across any major attempts at reform or renewal in Anglican life, despite changing times and the outbreak of another world war. We turn now to the years following World War Two, to see whether 'steady as she goes' was still a viable option.

3

Parsons, Schools and the Conversion of England

As WORLD WAR TWO drew to a close, Harry, Margaret and Anna Nobbs were firmly established in the Lake District, along with Granny and Wilkie the cat. Harry Nobbs had spent two years standing in for the vicar in Mungrisdale, who was still serving as a military chaplain. It was his first real taste of the life of the country parson. The white-washed parish church was smaller than the vicarage which stood opposite it. During Sunday services, sheep jumped up on to the stone wall outside the church, then peered in through the clear glass windows, as my mother recalls. The area was sparsely populated, so my grandfather took services in surrounding villages as well. These he conducted in the waiting room of Troutbeck railway station and the Quaker Meeting House in Mosedale. The setting was altogether too rural for my grandmother's taste. She was grateful for the companionship of Sybil, the home-alone wife of the Brigadier, whose children were faring better than my mother had done at St Hilda's School on the grouse moors. The Watkins family were dedicated churchgoers. Brigadier Watkins would go on to be Ecclesiastical Secretary to the Lord Chancellor when he retired from the army, with an office at 10 Downing Street.

The church at Mungrisdale was dedicated to St Kentigern, a reminder that the Christian presence in Cumbria pre-dated the arrival of Augustine from Rome. Kentigern was the sixth-century bishop responsible for founding Glasgow, the site of his monastery. In time he was driven from Scotland by the local ruler and headed south. He is said to have spent time in Cumbria while in exile, quite possibly at Mungrisdale. The clue is in the name. St Kentigern was also known as St Mungo, 'the well beloved'. In recent years, St Mungo has gained new prominence with the novels of J. K. Rowling and St Mungo's Hospital for Magical Maladies and Injuries. In Mungrisdale there is a well bearing the saint's name, traditionally used for baptisms.

Celtic reminder: Mungrisdale parish church, dedicated to St Kentigern
Photo © Simon Ledingham, visitcumbria.com, reproduced by permission

The parish church of Mungrisdale is one of many signs of Anglican identification with the deep Christian roots of Northern England. Others can be found close to my grandfather's previous parish. A few miles along the river from Binchester church, Escomb Church was built in the seventh century using stones from Binchester Roman fort. It is one of the oldest Saxon churches in the country and is still used for Anglican worship. Downstream, the city of Durham was founded as the burial spot of St Cuthbert, the seventh-century missionary from Iona who brought Christianity to much of northern England, ahead of Roman Catholic endeavour. The monks of Lindisfarne Island had hastily moved Cuthbert's remains inland when the Vikings invaded. Also buried at Durham Cathedral is the Venerable Bede, seventh-century monk and historian. His carefully-researched *Ecclesiastical History of the English People* has ensured that the Celtic missionaries are honoured among the heroes of the faith in England.

From Mungrisdale linked to St Mungo, the Nobbs family moved to Bassenthwaite, a parish whose 'bijou' church is dedicated to another Celtic Christian. St Bega's Church, Bassenthwaite, would inspire the art critic Melvyn Bragg to write his saga of Saxon Christianity, *Credo*. Its picturesque setting on the shore of Lake Bassenthwaite inspired Tennyson in writing his *Le Morte D'Arthur* and the legend of Excalibur. For my grandfather, St Bega's symbolised something more prosaic: the full acceptance of his ministry in the Church of England. No longer was he simply a curate, with permission to officiate granted for a fixed term by the Archbishop. He was a rector, with cure of souls for a parish. Sixteen years had passed since Archbishop Davidson had dismissed him as trained too little and too late for ministry in the Church of England.

St Bega's Church on the shore of Lake Bassenthwaite, when my grandfather was Rector

Author's personal archives

The village of Bassenthwaite had been founded as a Viking settlement by the lake. Down the centuries, it had been very much an agricultural community, but in the Victorian era it had gained new prominence with the advent of rail travel. It became fashionable to travel to the Lake District for vacations. In the school holidays, Thomas Arnold, headmaster of Rugby, used to decamp with his family to their second home in the Lake District. The poet William Wordsworth, as well as Tennyson, used to stay at Mirehouse, in Bassenthwaite parish.

St Bega's picturesque lakeside location may have charmed famous writers, but it was a long walk from where most of the parishioners lived. In the fifteenth century, they petitioned to build a chapel-of-ease. One was built at the crossroads outside the village and was used for several centuries. In 1878 a larger church, St John's, was built in the village, funded by local families from Armathwaite Hall and Bassenfell Manor. The chapel-of-ease became the church rooms and still stands.

When Harry Nobbs was inducted as Rector in 1944, the population of the parish was three hundred. His was a ministry of taking services and pastoral visiting. He used to cycle from the vicarage to St John's (half a mile) and St Bega's (three miles), with the rest of the family following on foot. My grandmother ran the Sunday school, rewarding the children who attended with stickers. During the week, homeschooling was no longer necessary, as the school bus stopped outside the rectory, en route to Keswick. Instead, Margaret Nobbs busied herself with fostering children, referred by a social agency of the Church of England, the Moral Welfare Council. One 2-year-old lad, Freddie, arrived with rickets. He was in such a poor state that he did not talk at all. Yet gradually his condition improved and he went on to be adopted by a local farmer.

To supplement the rector's meagre stipend, the Nobbs used to take in lodgers. The garden was huge, so my grandfather decided to raise further funds by selling daffodil bulbs. For several years he advertised in the *Church Times*. One of his regular customers was the rector of a parish in Essex, Percy Openshaw. After a while, Percy Openshaw came up with a proposition: swapping parishes. At the age of 63, the Lake District seemed rather attractive. For less obvious reasons, Essex appealed to the 61-year-old Harry Nobbs too, and the patrons, which included Brasenose College Oxford, had no objections. In 1948, the family moved to Weeley, a few miles inland from Clacton-on-Sea. Wilkie the cat, by then aged 9, made the journey in the back of the removals van, escaping from his basket en route.

Weeley parish was unmistakably rural, if not as isolated as Bassenthwaite or Mungrisdale. St Andrew's Church is still surrounded by fields and accessed via a farm road. Next to the church is a duck pond. My grandfather used to keep a stick in the hedge to defend himself against the belligerent geese. Without realising it, when he became Rector of Weeley, he would be entering the last days of the classic country parson.

Harvest Festival in Weeley's unmistakeably rural parish church

Author's personal archives

For the Church of England nationally, there had been high hopes of change a few years earlier, as World War Two drew to a close. These had been fuelled by the appointment of William Temple as Archbishop of Canterbury. Intelligent, engaging and mould-breaking, he was respected by those in authority and regarded warmly by ordinary people as their advocate and friend. He had been a leading champion of what would become the welfare state. Along with the Archbishop of York, Cyril Garbett, he promised major reform of the Church of England once the war was over. 'Never had an appointment to the archbishopric of Canterbury been so universally acclaimed as that of William Temple and, because expectations were so high, it is understandable that his death was viewed in catastrophic terms'.[1] This helps explain why my father recorded it in his schoolboy diary. Temple's successor, Geoffrey Fisher, had succeeded him as Headmaster of Repton School thirty years earlier. But he was a very different kind of prelate. Fisher's main gift was administration. 'He lacked charisma, theology or ideology', observes one church historian laconically. '"Commonsense" was his favourite expression.... His considerable intellectual powers he exercised chiefly upon *The Times* crossword.'[2]

While Temple had been Archbishop of Canterbury, a commission had been set up 'to survey the whole problem of modern evangelism', with the endorsement of the Church Assembly. Temple delivered the introductory address at the commission's first meeting. 'We cannot separate the evangelisation of those without from the rekindling of devotion within', he stressed. The spiritual life of the church needed strengthening.[3] Temple is remembered for being a social reformer and an ecumenist, yet he had a strongly evangelistic emphasis too. 'If we have to choose between making men Christian and making the social order more Christian, we must choose the former. But there is no such antithesis.'[4] This evangelistic motivation is seen in his leading of university missions. At one mission to Oxford University, he stopped the singing of the hymn 'When I survey the wondrous cross' before the last verse. He invited the students to read the words first and 'if you mean them with all your heart, sing them as loud as you can. If you don't mean them at all, keep silent. If you mean them even a little, and want to mean them more, sing them very softly.' Two thousand voices whispered:

> *Were the whole realm of nature mine,*
> *That were an offering far too small*
> *Love so amazing, so divine,*
> *Demands my soul, my life, my all.*[5]

The Commission on Evangelism, when it presented its report *Towards the Conversion of England*, dedicated it to William Temple, who had died the previous year. The report was generally well received and much discussed. 'The vast majority of the English people need to be converted to Christianity', it asserted. What's more, 'most of the worshipping community are only half-converted'. A major emphasis of the report was training and mobilising the laity, recovering 'the Apostolate of the whole church'. It quoted William Temple on this:

> The evangelisation of England ... is a work that cannot be done by the clergy alone; it can only be done to a very small extent by the clergy at all. There can be no widespread evangelisation of England unless the work is undertaken by the lay people of the Church. ... The main duty of the clergy must be to train lay members of the congregation in their work of witness.[6]

The report proposed a change of mindset, of both laity and clergy. 'There have always been special occasions (such as preparation for a parochial mission) when, in a well-run parish, lay co-operation with the clergy has reached a high level. What would strike the average layman as novel would be the idea of evangelism being a *normal* Christian duty.' There must be a 'call to the clergy for renewal'.[7] 'In view of the immense opportunities open to parochial evangelism, it is alarming to discover how few of the clergy have been given any training in the work of an evangelist, such as in the art of preaching or of personal dealing with enquirers.'[8]

There are echoes here of the Archbishops' reports in World War One. Unlike these earlier reports, *Towards the Conversion of England* did stimulate some renewed evangelistic endeavour, such as a mission to London. However, the report had its critics and, amongst other things, it under-emphasised the social dimension of the Church's witness and engagement. Crucially, it failed to achieve the pervasive change of mindset it argued for. The Church Assembly's rejection of its proposal for a permanent Council on Evangelism was symptomatic of this. As one church historian concludes, 'Faced with the rather dreary reality of post-war England, the Church of England as an institution sat tight, tied on every side by its venerable customs, pastoral amateurishness, and immensely complex separation of powers.'[9]

One of the problems was demography and deployment of clergy. Whether in Bassenthwaite or Weeley, my grandfather's situation was typical of Anglican clergy. 'Most of the parsons were in the countryside shivering in their unheated rectories, most of the people were in the towns. But at least in the villages they were, more or less, wanted and knew what to do.'[10]

Harry Nobbs undoubtedly felt he knew what to do in Weeley and his ministry was appreciated. Weeley parish had a population of 900. During the wars against Napoleon's France, it had risen briefly to over 6,000, thanks to a garrison of soldiers and their families on what is still called Barracks Field. As a result, in 1804 the rector had to conduct 173 baptisms. Ironically, not so long ago, there had been a French congregation in the neighbouring parish of Thorpe. When Protestant worship was suppressed in France in 1685, Huguenot refugees had flooded to England. Some were directed to Essex and secured the Bishop of London's blessing to build their own church. Help for the minister's stipend came from the Royal Bounty for refugee Protestants and the first service was held on 4 March 1688. At least thirty-nine families of Huguenots ended up living in Thorpe, with others settling in neighbouring villages. But by the time English soldiers were camping in Weeley and having their children baptised, the French church had been demolished. The last French minister died in 1726, by which time 'most of the French congregation were instructed in the English tongue sufficiently to attend Divine service in the parish church'.[11]

Unlike Napoleonic times, in 1949 there was just a handful of baptisms for the rector to conduct in Weeley. The parish was still small enough for the rector to visit everyone, which he did diligently, on his bicycle. It was a ministry which suited him well, for he stayed on till retirement, three times longer than any other post he had held. The churchwarden in 2013, Pearl Byfield, remembered meeting him on the bus just after he was appointed. 'That's the new Rector', said her mother. My grandfather promptly offered her a doughnut, knowing how to win a child's heart when rationing was still in place. A Methodist at the time, Pearl Byfield soon joined the choir and has been a loyal member of St Andrew's Weeley ever since.

Towards the Conversion of England had various suggestions for rural ministry, such as looking after the rectory garden. 'A parson's garden run to seed is a stumbling block to his flock.'[12] But the report was largely content to reaffirm classic patterns of ministry in the village. 'Owing to the traditional and steady routine of country life, George Herbert's *The Country Parson* still holds good as one of the best expositions of what a village ministry demands. Are the parson and his wife loving and amicable people, and such as villagers can grow to love, respect and trust? If so, the first great step towards a "converted village" has been achieved.'[13]

George Herbert was Rector of Bemerton near Salisbury in the seventeenth century. He wrote poetry and hymns and visited all his parishioners, however poor or wealthy they might have been. He was in post for less than three years. Yet his kindly and prayerful low-key approach to ministry has been upheld as quintessentially Anglican ever since. There were around 200 in his parish, so my grandfather's ministry in Bassenthwaite was certainly able to follow this model. Even in Weeley, with its larger population of 900, it was still a viable pattern of ministry. However, for more densely populated urban parishes, this kind of ministry had always been hard to sustain, as my grandfather had experienced in Glasgow.

Towards the end of my grandfather's time in Weeley, forty-two percent of the Church of England's clergy were serving eleven percent of the population living in rural areas.[14] This imbalance had been compounded by a shortage of curates. Compared with 1938, there were fewer than half the number of curates in 1948. In 1938 there had been 4,554 curates, but in 1948 there were only 2,189.[15] The situation in Binchester illustrates how the system was buckling under the strain. After Harry Nobbs left for the Lake District, the Vicar of Byers Green appealed for a replacement curate to serve his mission church in Binchester. He knew full well that curates were in short supply during the war. Yet the combined electoral roll of the three churches in the parish was 541. 'My sudden collapse has made it abundantly clear that I cannot carry on single handed', he wrote desperately to the bishop's assistant in 1943, 'and if a Priest is unobtainable in the near future I will have to consider some other form of help, a Church Army Captain or a stipendiary lay-leader.' He wanted to know if the fund set aside for a curate could be used in that way. No curate was forthcoming and reassigning the curate's fund was not a straightforward matter. Reporting at the annual meeting in 1945, the Rector 'longed to see an improvement in the duty of worship'. At the annual meeting two years later, 'the Rector regretted there was no present prospect of an assistant curate. In consequence the spiritual work, particularly at the mission churches, was not as satisfactory as it might be if there were a resident priest.' Overwhelmed by the challenges, yet recognising that sights needed to be raised, he 'spoke of the Report on Evangelism. With no hope of an assistant curate being found for some time he asked for a greater effort in the spiritual cause.' It would be another eight years before the Ecclesiastical Commissioners found a way of releasing the Binchester curate's fund to finance a Church Army worker. Sister Ridden eventually arrived in 1955 and lived in a caravan in the churchyard until 1960.[16]

In Weeley, the Rector's accommodation was somewhat grander than Sister Ridden's caravan. It had twenty-two rooms and a vast garden, which was used for the parish fete and meetings of the Girl Guides. Harry Nobbs' predecessor but one, Marcus Morris, turned the garden and the glebe land attached to it into a market garden. This was not quite what was expected of a country parson. 'The villagers thought I was mad', he admitted. He kept a goat, a cow called Flossy and a pig which the local butcher slaughtered for him. He formed a youth club, whose members helped with the garden. His wife was an actress, so they performed plays in the garden too. However, his use of the garden was not primarily designed as a form of outreach, or even as a contribution to the war effort. It was a means of supplementing his stipend. Even that was not enough. He took a job in a local factory for a while. A concerned friend understandably worried that this might detract from his calling. 'You cannot possibly have time for much serious reading, to prepare yourself for a bigger job.' For a while, Marcus Morris did manage to supplement his stipend with activity more obviously connected to his priestly ministry, by teaching divinity at a Church of England training college in Hockerill. But after two years of restless activity, he felt it was time to move on.

Marcus Morris was mould-breaking in many ways, but he was also archetypal, in that he continued the clergy tradition of enterprising pastimes. He left Weeley to take up the post of Rector of St James' Birkdale, a suburb of Southport. While there, he rebranded the parish magazine as *The Anvil,* intending to make it accessible to non-churchgoers, complete with cartoons. As circulation widened, funding was an issue, so he sent a copy to the Archbishop of Canterbury, hoping for a commendation. He also promoted it as means of carrying forward the recommendations of *Towards the Conversion of England,* which had called for 'monthly periodicals . . . which would interest and challenge the casual reader who purchased them at the railway bookstall'. Despite strenuous fundraising efforts and sales of 3,650 copies, Morris was forced to sell the pace-setting publication. It was bought by the *Church Times.* He was to be more successful with his next publication, the *Eagle* comic, which became a national institution as the first science-fiction comic, with iconic characters such as Dan Dare, pilot of the future.[17]

Marcus Morris thus continued the longstanding tradition of Church of England clergy combining modest parish responsibilities with pastimes that contributed to the public good. Many of Morris' forebears were spared his financial struggles. Bill Bryson, the travel writer, has described such clergy as 'a class of well-educated, wealthy people who had immense amounts of time on their hands'.[18] He lists a range of innovations owed to such clergy: quick-drying cement, the first dictionary of Icelandic, the power loom, aerial photography, the first scientific description of dinosaurs, Bayes' theorem (mathematical probability), the first novel to feature a werewolf (by the hymn-writer who penned 'Onward Christian Soldiers') and a new crossbreed of terrier (thanks to the Revd Jack Russell).

Charles Darwin, off the coast of South America on the HMS *Beagle,* reflected wistfully on the life of the country parson for which, up until then, he had himself been preparing. 'To a person fit to take the office, the life of a Clergyman is a type of all that is happy: and if he is a Naturalist...ave Maria;'[19] Some of these 'happy' and inventive clergy lived in Essex, such as the gardening vicar, the Revd Adam Buddle, responsible for the flowering buddleia.[20] But my grandfather, already in his sixties, would not be added to their illustrious ranks. Despite being successor to Marcus Morris, comic-strip pioneer and market-gardener, my grandfather was content to devote his time to parish ministry, aided by his wife, without grand projects of his own. He taught in the village school, referring frequently to his experiences in Canada. He joined the village whist drives, though was strict about not buying raffle tickets, so as not to promote gambling. My grandmother re-started the Sunday school, scheduling it at 2.30pm on Sunday afternoons. Exceptionally, she stepped in to cover routine pastoral work. When her husband was recovering from a serious cycling accident, she and my mother, then sixteen, met with couples wanting to get married in church. Active lay involvement was encouraged too. Alan Byford, now churchwarden of a neighbouring parish, found his niche as a youngster by pumping the church organ, there being no electricity. As my grandfather reflected towards the end of his time at Weeley, 'I recall with happy memories the support of a nucleus of faithful people who, for over 11 years, have been the backbone of the spiritual life of the parish centred around the parish church.'[21]

The year after their arrival in Weeley, the national movement to give celebration of Holy Communion greater prominence was launched. The Parish and People Movement aimed to establish Holy Communion as the main Sunday service in every parish, normally starting at 9am. It proved to be remarkably successful. Harry Nobbs needed no persuading about the importance of Holy Communion. While he no longer celebrated Holy Communion daily in church, as he had done in Binchester, he offered two services of Holy Communion each Sunday. Holy Communion without music was at 8.30am and Choral Eucharist was at 9.45am. This was followed by morning prayer (matins) at 11am and evensong at 3.15pm. Yet despite his best efforts, matins continued to be the most popular service.

The finances of the church were helped by the generosity of the son of a former Rector of Weeley. Having served in Southeast Asia during World War Two, he was married back at Weeley, with Harry Nobbs conducting his wedding. He went on to be a successful businessman in the plantations of Malaya and continued to support St Andrew's Weeley financially. This however did not enhance the rector's stipend. The Nobbs did not resort to digging up the four-acre rectory garden as the Morrises had done. But they did break convention in a different way. The rector's wife took up employment: as a cleaner. This raised eyebrows in the parish. It foreshadowed the kind of syndrome popularised in Joanna Trollope's 1991 novel, *The Rector's Wife*, where Anna Bouverie takes a job in the local supermarket to help pay the bills.[22]

The Church of England was making an attempt to address clergy stipends nationally at this time, encouraged by its administrator-Archbishop, Geoffrey Fisher. In 1949, the Pastoral Reorganisation Measure provided for the merging of smaller parishes. 'A very large number of parishes have an endowment income of less than £400, which is not a living wage', explained the bishop of a neighbouring East Anglian diocese, when the measure was considered in the House of Lords. 'In my diocese there are 149 parishes where the endowment income is less than £400.'[23] Harry Nobbs' stipend was £300.

The Pastoral Reorganisation Measure added to a succession of recent measures addressing clergy housing.[24] The days of the rambling vicarage were numbered. In Ardingly, where my father's family was worshipping, the rectory had just been demolished. Its bricks had been used to build the new rectory, with plenty to spare for building another new house in the village. The old rectory had been financed in 1875 by the Rector, James Bowden. It had seven bedrooms. His successor, John Brack, was Rector during both world wars. His staff had included a cook, a butler pantry-man, a maid and two jobbing-gardeners.[25] Despite this impression of wealth, he struggled with the expense of the rectory. The Bracks took in lodgers, but often the bedrooms were empty.

In Weeley, the rectory had also been built in the nineteenth century. It had been financed by a loan of £1,000 from Queen Anne's Bounty, one of the funds which would be merged to form the Church Commissioners under the watchful eye of Archbishop Fisher. The cost was more than three times that of the mission church in Binchester. The coach house had capacity for two coaches and four horses. With its turret, the main house formed a grand backdrop to parish fetes. In my grandfather's time, it was used for choir practice and church meetings. My mother remembers feeding red squirrels on the window sill. In many ways it was an ideal centre of operations for the rector. However, spurred on by the Pastoral Reorganisation Measure, the bishop decided it should be sold. Seven years after moving to Weeley, the Nobbs moved into a purpose-built box house much nearer the church. To ensure a positive spin was put on this downsizing, the bishop was present to bless the new rectory.

Farewell to grand old rectories, the time-honoured setting for parish fetes. *Below left:* Harry Nobbs (left) Anna Nobbs (centre right) *Below right:* Harry and Margaret Nobbs (right of centre)

Author's personal archives

By this time, my mother had left home and was earning her own living. She was nineteen and had heard about an opening the previous year at a school in Sussex. She was duly appointed junior matron at Ardingly College Junior School. The Junior House (JH), as it was known, was concentrated in one of the wings of the H-shaped redbrick complex. The chapel and some of the other facilities were shared with the senior school. Anna's tasks were to supervise the 8 to 13-year-old boys at mealtimes and bedtimes, to take care of them when they fell ill and to mend their clothes.

The Junior School had its own headmaster, but the overall tone of the school was set by the headmaster of the Senior School, George Snow. Like all his predecessors, he was an Anglican clergyman. His son, Jon Snow, went on to become a Channel 4 news presenter. 'My father, as headmaster, was God', Jon Snow recalls. 'He was an enormous man, six feet seven in his socks, and at least sixteen stone. To me he was strict, dependable and at times remote.'[26] George Snow conjures up stereotypes of devout yet austere Victorian clergy. 'Our family gathered for prayers at the start of every day. Adamson the butler, his wife the cook...and Nanny Rose would join us three boys, my mother and the eternal conductor of this solemn moment.... This formal, ordered start to the day, which included the collect and a brief reading from the

Bible, was part of the absolute security and order amid which I grew up. From the moment I could stand, I was in that line for prayers at eight in the morning, prompt.'[27]

George Snow was a high-achieving headmaster. His father had been a Lieutenant General and it showed. He was well-acquainted with public schools, having been a pupil at Winchester, on the staff at Eton for twelve years and chaplain at Charterhouse for ten years. At Ardingly, he brought renewed discipline, recruited a new generation of staff, strengthened the 'house' system and oversaw the building of a science block, a sanatorium and new tennis courts. Such an imposing figure might seem unpromising material for nurturing Christian faith in the pupils. Yet his efforts were surprisingly effective here too. The Christian life of the college was undoubtedly a priority for him. His first building project was the transformation of the Crypt chapel into an intimate place of worship. Once it was completed, the boys organised night prayers there. The main chapel was also gradually improved. The year my mother started as matron, a new oak lectern was made in the college carpentry shop. The following year, two new windows were installed in chapel. The inscription on one seemed to have bored schoolboys and their roving eyes in mind. It was 'in memory of R. C. Foster, a noted big game hunter, killed by a lion in the Congo in 1919, the eldest of four brothers at Ardingly'.

Alongside these physical improvements, he welcomed a wide cross-section of guest preachers to chapel. In 1954, these included six local clergy, a bishop from West Africa and three visiting headmasters.[28] His relationships with his own chaplains could be difficult. Chaplains in Woodard schools were not the headmaster's appointment, so there was scope for friction. One chaplain in the 1950s, John Gardner, did not see eye to eye with his headmaster and only lasted four terms.[29] Yet he respected the headmaster's 'deep insight into Scripture. His crypt addresses on Friday evenings on diverse subjects were superb and were appreciated by a very wide audience.'[30]

There was more fruitful collaboration with Gardner's predecessor, Nip Exon, who had previously served as an English teacher and housemaster at Ardingly. In February 1955 my mother was coping with an influenza epidemic which 'swept through J.H. like a tornado', with ninety boys bed-ridden.[31] In the senior school, the number was even higher: one hundred and sixty. As the epidemic passed, the school prepared itself for a week-long mission in Lent. The Missioner would be Jack Winslow, chaplain of Lee Abbey.

Lee Abbey had been founded by an evangelical clergyman, Roger de Pemberton, in 1945. Jack Winslow, an Anglo-Catholic former missionary, was one of its first trustees. Both de Pemberton and Winslow had been on the Commission which produced *Towards the Conversion of England*. Lee Abbey, a former hotel on the rugged North Devon coast, would operate as a centre for evangelism. It had now been running evangelistic holidays for ten years, with Jack Winslow becoming chaplain in 1948.[32] Prior to his appointment, he had been chaplain at Bryanston School. Before that, he had been a missionary in India, supported like my grandfather by SPG. He was an inspired choice as missioner for an Anglo-Catholic boarding school. 'One of the most moving moments our chapel has experienced', wrote the chaplain after the mission, 'was the sound of a large number of voices quietly renewing their dedication to the service of our Lord.'[33] A Christian Fellowship was formed, with meetings held in the headmaster's drawing room. Initial attendance averaged fifteen boys and a few masters. A guest speaker at an early meeting was David Sheppard, a Sussex county cricketer and ordination student at Ridley Hall.[34] He had taken time out from his studies the previous year to captain the England team against Pakistan. We will encounter him again as Bishop of Liverpool.

The Lent mission illustrates how nurturing Christian faith in an Anglican boarding school could entail more than compulsory attendance at chapel services. 'What gives me more pleasure than anything else' wrote the chaplain in the school magazine, 'is the help I have, I think, been able to give some of you in your own private prayer life.'[35] This emphasis at Ardingly coincided with a wider phenomenon in public schools after World War Two. The headmaster of Winchester, Spencer Leeson, had been chairman of the Headmasters' Conference from 1939 to 1945. He was a persuasive advocate for making Christianity in public schools 'the essence of the place'. At the heart of this was the appointment of full-time chaplains, following the example set in Woodard schools. In the post-war years, the Anglican boarding school was 'probably the most important surviving bastion of the Church of England', according to one church historian. 'It seems likely that this was an area in which all in all the Church of England gained effective strength in these years.'[36]

That is not to say that every schoolboy warmed to the mandatory religion that was prescribed. A 1957 edition of the Ardingly school magazine captures the range of reaction. On the one hand, there is a schoolboy's sardonic commentary 'On Going to Church':

> *Some go to church just for a walk*
> *Some go there to laugh and talk*
>
> .   .   .   .

Some go there to wake a passion
Some go there because 'tis fashion.
Some go to see and to be seen,
Some go there to say they've been.
Many go to doze and nod
But few go there to worship God.[37]

On the other hand there is another schoolboy's powerful evocation of the call to discipleship, written at Pentecost:

Imagine Galilee,
A flat, soft, tingling space of water,
A thin, rippling, thinking sea,
Thinking, curling her lip
And sighing to the One who wrought her

. . . .

No catch.
Just the clear water to praise when they return.
They unload their fruitless nets.
Their boats scratch at the shingle and the faint surge
Knocks at their legs.
Then a shining White meets them . . .
'Come,' He says
'And follow me'
And they forsake all,
In that quiet evening, electric dusk.
And they follow Him.
Their boats are still knocking and their nets still waiting,
If they dare turn back.[38]

Ardingly was given an opportunity to proclaim its confidence in its Christian vision in 1958. It would be a hundred years since it had been founded by Nathaniel Woodard. George Snow aimed high for the centenary celebrations and hit three targets. He launched a successful appeal to complete the chapel tower. Queen Elizabeth II and the Duke of Edinburgh paid a visit during the summer term, having visited Gatwick Airport, recently opened, earlier in the day. Five days later, the Prime Minister Harold Macmillan opened the Centenary Pavilion overlooking the main cricket pitch.

In his speech, Macmillan proffered three purposes of education: to know when a man is talking rubbish; to learn the things of practical value; and to preserve the Ancient Faith and strengthen it in successive generations.[39] On the playing fields of Ardingly, it looked very much as though the Church of England remained at the heart of the nation's life. The following decade, when I was born, would expose a very different reality.

Meanwhile, riding high on the euphoria of the Queen's visit, my mother accepted a tennis invitation. An Old Ardinian, who was a local farmer, had invited the bursar's two daughters for mixed doubles. One of them dropped out, in favour of an invitation to the opera at Glyndebourne. Anna Nobbs agreed to stand in. So it was that she met John Norman, whose farm was just a mile from the college. After leaving Ardingly, my father had spent a year at the local agricultural college in Plumpton. Now he had more or less taken over the farm from his father, William Norman, who was 66 years old. His family were still regular churchgoers, attending St Peter's church in Ardingly. John and Anna would be married there in October 1959. Harry Nobbs, aged 72, would officiate.

In front of Ardingly College chapel (my mother is on the left)

Author's personal archives

My mother remembers vividly when she first admitted to my father she was a parson's daughter. They were in Brighton, on their first date, crossing the road. He stopped in his tracks. In some ways, however, it was my father's parents who would take more getting used to. They still lived at Great Lywood Farm. As newly-weds, my parents would share the farmhouse with them.

The world into which I was born in 1963 was unmistakeably rural England. It was also cold. In the rectory garden in the village, a large snowman lasted three months before melting. At the farm, before rushing to hospital, my mother was unfreezing the pipes to the milking parlour. My brother, Paul, was two by then. There would be a curious symmetry in our future working lives. He would follow my paternal grandfather, William Norman, as well as my father, and become a farmer. I would follow my mother's father, Harry Nobbs, eventually, and become a priest.

A dairy farm was a wonderful playground for two boys. Treehouses to build, haystacks to climb in, mud to get stuck in, go-carts to build and push down the hill from the cow stalls. The Elizabethan farmhouse was a rival to the most characterful and ill-heated rectory. The only reliably warm rooms were the kitchen, with its solid fuel stove, and the bathroom, with its un-lagged airing cupboard. As soon as we were old enough, there were chores to do, such as collecting the eggs and feeding the numerous farm cats. Sometimes we accompanied my father around the farm, messing around in the fields while he mended the fences. Haymaking was always a highlight, with picnics in the field and tunnels made out of hay bales. The farm was populated by kind and colourful characters: Cyril, the chirpy cowman; Mrs Daley, with her smoker's cough, who helped clean the house and babysat; Mr Simmons, the elderly gardener; and Miss Scott, our stone-deaf neighbour, who lived to 105 with her two maids, Ethel and Phoebe.

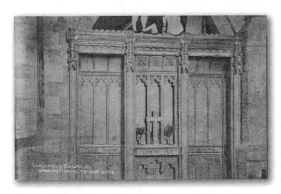

War memorial to 'our boys' at Ardingly Church, which I helped my grandmother decorate for Christian festivals

Author's personal archives

My grandfather, William Norman, died when I was one, forty-five years after his World War One homecoming. My grandmother, Amy, continued to live with us until I was nine. She was a strong character and a pillar of the local community. At church, she was responsible for decorating the war memorial for Christian festivals. I remember helping her gather the holly from the farm, then hanging around in church when she combined decorating the church with child-minding. My father had to milk the cows most Sundays, but we still made it to church for the morning service. When my father was on sides-person's duty, my brother and I would help to hand out the hymnbooks. When we were old enough for the evening service, we would ensure my father stayed awake during the sermon, knowing he had been up at 5.30am to milk the cows.

St Peter's Church had a varied succession of rectors. When my parents started their married life, it was George Parsons. He was a jovial pastor who was widely regarded as a 'people's parson'. He wore full vestments: colourful cope, stole, and chasuble. Disputes about the lawfulness of such 'Catholic' vestments were finally laid to rest by legislation introduced in the slipstream of Fisher's canon law reform.[40] Parsons was followed by Christopher Phillipson, who favoured the more conventional black cassock, white surplice and black preaching scarf. Phillipson came from India and was gifted musically. He used to join choir practices and lead the choir carol-singing round the village. His son went on to play county cricket for Sussex. His successor, Rupert Studd, also had cricketing connections, albeit indirect. He was great nephew of the famous England cricketer and missionary to China, C. T. Studd. More evangelical than his immediate predecessors, he made an impression with his 'clear and lucid bible-based sermons', along with his dry sense of humour.[41]

St Peter's, Ardingly

Author's personal archives

Services were conducted according to the 1662 *Book of Common Prayer* and experimental rites for communion services (Series 2 and 3, as they were known), which replaced 'thee' and 'thou' with you. At the start of each service, the choir processed in, followed by the rector. The red robes worn by female choir members had been introduced by George Parsons. Oblivious to political correctness, he liked to refer to his 'scarlet women'.[42] Strictly speaking the robes were illegal, as red was the colour reserved for royal choirs. A photo taken in the 1860s shows the choir (all male) dressed in dark jackets and starched collars. Over the intervening century, choir and congregation sang from the same hymn book, *Hymns Ancient and Modern,* the staple Anglican hymnbook first published in 1861. At St Peter's, Ardingly, it was only in 1972 that a new hymnbook was introduced, *The Anglican Hymn Book*. The new copies of the 1662 Prayer Book that accompanied them were given in memory of my grandmother, who had just died. We always dressed in our 'Sunday best' to go to church. The older women who faithfully attended matins were affectionately dubbed the 'hat and coat brigade'.

Harvest Festival was always a popular service and it was our family that provided the sheaves of corn to decorate the church. The Harvest Festival service was a Victorian innovation which quickly became a standard feature of Anglican worship. Robert Stephen Hawker of Morwenstow, a parish in Cornwall, is credited with introducing it. He was an eccentric parson. All his cats and dogs accompanied him to church. He disliked black, so he wore a blue fisherman's pullover with a small red cross woven into the side. Yet he won the hearts of parishioners by burying shipwrecked sailors whose decaying bodies were washed up on the beach. He covered the expenses from his own pocket. At St Peter's, Rupert Studd felt that the Revd Hawker's Harvest innovation was an opportunity for building Christian fellowship. During the Harvest Festival week, he reintroduced a Harvest Supper.

For us boys, the annual church fete was always a highlight. Often dogged by poor weather, so sometimes held in the village hall, there were plenty of games to compete in and second-hand toys to buy with pocket money. Both my brother and I attended the village school, one hundred metres from the church. It had been founded in 1848 'to train children to fear God, to obey their parents, and to live according to the Faith in Christ as true members of His Body, the Church'.[43] It was linked to the National Society for Promoting the Education of the Poor in the Principles of the Established Church in England and Wales, whose president was the Archbishop of Canterbury. According to its code of rules, children 'must be diligent in their studies. They must be very quiet and serious during prayers and when at Church.'[44] The 1944 Education Act had distinguished between church schools that were part-funded by the church and those funded by the local authority. St Peter's school was one of the latter, a 'controlled school'. Links with the church were nonetheless strong and we used to walk across to the church for services. Our ex-navy headmaster, Mr Teesdale, ensured we were suitably serious during prayers.

During my second year at primary school, my grandfather Harry Nobbs died, aged 83. He had retired as Rector of Weeley aged 75. Archbishop Randall Davidson might have thought 38 was too old for him to be ordained, but he had served for thirty-six years before retiring. The same year my grandfather retired, 1961, Archbishop Geoffrey Fisher had retired too. He reflected with satisfaction that the main achievement of his time as Archbishop was the comprehensive reform of canon law. Church finances had also been reformed, rectories had been sold and smaller parishes had started to be grouped together. The Church of England could believe itself to be in good shape. A report issued soon after this confidently predicted continued growth in the number of clergy.[45]

Yet that was the 1960s. Clergy numbers, far from increasing, declined. As the decade of the Beatles got underway, it became increasingly clear that the Church of England was struggling to keep pace with society. The year I was born, 1963, saw the publication of *Honest to God,* by an Anglican bishop, John Robinson.[46] The Church of England's optimism in the 1950s had given way to anxiety. Like the chaplains in the trenches forty years earlier, Bishop John Robinson encountered the 'all but total alienation of the urban working class from the institutional church'.[47] For most people, the bishop explained, 'what matters to them most in life seems to have nothing to do with God'.[48] His solution was to reframe Christian faith, with help from the German theologians Bonhoeffer, Bultmann and Tillich. His book was an instant best-seller, but responses were polarised. Some saw it as just what was needed in a scientific age. Others felt it undermined basic Christian belief.

The year my grandfather died, at the end of the decade, our next door neighbour Miss Lily Scott died too. She had been an active Anglican through-out her 105 years. At one time she worked for Lindfield parish church as a district visitor. With her two maids, she seemed to live in the same world in which she had grown up in the 1860s. In some respects, the Church of England gave the impression of living in this world too, at least in the coun-tryside. Church music might have changed and services might have become more elaborate, with increased prominence given to Holy Communion. But in many ways it was business as usual. The country parson was still in demand.

Yet even the countryside was not immune from changes to wider society. Two years after Harry Nobbs died, hitchhikers from all round the country started arriving in Weeley, along with passengers on nineteen special trains running from London's Liverpool Street station. A rock festival was being staged in the fields surrounding St Andrew's Church. It would attract 130,000 people over a long weekend, to hear performers such as Rod Stewart. It was an exuberant challenge to the Church of England's settled ways. The Bishop of Colchester, Roderick Coote, rose to this challenge. Under his supervision, a 'Jesus Tent' was set up and staffed by clergy and other helpers. St Andrew's Church stayed open throughout the festival. The new rectory, vacant during an interregnum, was used as the police headquarters.[49]

At the start of the 1970s, new efforts for engaging with those outside the church were called for. For some, it meant taking their lead from Bishop John Robinson by reframing the Christian message in ways that took modern thinking seriously. For others, it meant adopting a more missionary mindset, like Bishop Roderic Coote in Weeley. Rupert Studd, Rector of Ardingly, took the latter approach, as might be expected of a descendent of eminent missionaries. He hosted men's meetings in one of the village pubs, The Gardeners Arms. He and his wife visited every household in the village. They hosted 'open house' meetings and discussions in the rectory after morning prayer. As a result of these evangelistic efforts, numbers of the congregation at morning and evening services increased significantly.[50]

✠

Observing the three decades following World War Two, we have seen how a Church identifying with Saxon missionaries showed scant sign of adopting a missionary approach in modern times. Instead it largely stuck with familiar pastoral patterns, only sporadically heeding William Temple's challenge to rekindle the devotion of those nominally associated with the Church of England. Twenty-five years after the publication of *Towards the Conversion of England,* there were signs that its perspectives were now beginning to be acknowledged. For urban bishop and country parson, the Church's task could no longer be regarded as simply pastoral care of an extended Christian community. That 'Christendom' notion was fast becoming obsolete. In certain pockets, such as Woodard schools, identification with what Prime Minister Harold Macmillan called 'the Ancient Faith' could still be taken for granted by the Church of England. But would even that be sustainable as the 1970s progressed? A month after the Weeley Festival, thanks to money set aside by my grandmother, Amy Norman, I would find out first hand. Following in the footsteps of father, mother and brother, in 1971 I started at Ardingly College, aged 8, as a dayboy.

Access to compulsory
chapel services: the archway
at Ardingly College

4

Enthusiasm and the Unexpected

WHATEVER WAS HAPPENING elsewhere in the 1970s, at Ardingly College, I discovered, Anglican religion was still buoyant. In the Junior School, evening prayer was as much part of the daily routine as football, lessons, roller skating in the playground and visits to the tuck shop. There were now two chaplains, one of whom, Nick Waters, concentrated on the Junior School. Most of us were prepared for confirmation by him. It was 'opt out' rather than 'opt in'.

The outside world occasionally intruded. There were miners' strikes, for example, which meant power cuts. In our divinity class, we had all been asked to memorise a Bible story by the headmaster. I was poised to begin the story of Moses and the Exodus when the class was plunged into darkness. Since we were all relying on memory, I was instructed to continue regardless. In 1973, we debated the merits of Britain joining the European Common Market in geography lessons, with our teacher belatedly declaring his support. But mostly it was a protected environment, with its own subculture. All the teachers had nicknames. There was 'Grovel', the headmaster (surname Grove-Smith); 'Domo', the bald geography teacher with a commanding presence; 'Piggy', the knowledgeable history teacher who used to bolt his food. Dayboys like myself would join in with evening activities, eager to see James Bond films screened from crackly projectors and act in school plays such as *The Happiest Days of Your Life*. When it came to move up to the Senior School, aged 13, I was keen to become a boarder, so as not to miss out, despite living only a mile away. Thanks to a scholarship, my wish was granted.

In the Senior School, there was a service after breakfast every weekday morning, a choral Eucharist on Sundays, and sometimes choral evensong. Ardingly had a strong choral tradition, dating back to 1872 and to one of its earliest chaplains, Arthur Lewington, after whom my house was named.[1] Most Sunday services had an anthem, as well as classic Anglican hymns. For a short period I served as a rather inept sacristan, helping in the vestry with preparations for Sunday services. I gladly switched to singing bass in the choir. I shall never forget the thrill of singing Handel's *Zadok the Priest* to mark the Queen's Silver Jubilee. Nathaniel Woodard would have been gratified to see the Anglo-Catholic outworking of the Oxford Movement in all our services. Choral music, for example, had long been associated with cathedrals, but it was the Oxford Movement that led to its introduction in school chapels and in parish churches, with choirs processing in to sit prominently in choir stalls.[2]

Before then, choirs in parish churches were typically located at the back of church, on a gallery, together with a band of village musicians. Only gradually had even hymn singing become a feature of Sunday services. For three centuries, the singing of psalms was all that was officially sanctioned. Parishes started breaking the mould in the eighteenth century, linked to the so-called evangelical revival.[3] Things came to a head in 1820, when a vicar in Sheffield was taken to court by parishioners objecting to hymn singing. In a landmark ruling, the court judged that, while hymns were strictly speaking illegal, they had been legitimated by custom. The Archbishop of York promptly sanctioned their use, ushering in their widespread use in the Church of England.[4] At Ardingly College 150 years later, our hymnbook was *The New English Hymnal*. It was another product of Anglo-Catholic piety, containing hymns with a more 'Catholic' emphasis than *Hymns Ancient and Modern*. The whole school practised hymns every Friday morning after the daily service, which meant our repertoire was extended well beyond the favourites requested on BBC TV's *Songs of Praise*.

The chapel was a vast red-brick edifice, with a soaring roof. At the east end was the altar, up ten steps. Whenever we recited the creed, those of us in the choir stalls would turn and join the rest of the congregation facing this distant altar. In communion services, when it came to the eucharistic prayer, those not wishing to receive the bread and the wine left. The rest of us climbed up the steps to the altar and gathered round in a circle. The celebrant stood behind the communion table, facing towards the main body of the church. This practice was quite rare before World War Two.[5] In most churches, the priest would have stood to the side of the communion table, facing north. The Oxford Movement reintroduced the practice of facing east, with the priest's back to the congregation.[6] This had been my grandfather's preferred practice. In pre-war days, every pupil at Ardingly stayed for the whole service. It would surely have taken a brave chaplain to conduct a service with his back to four hundred schoolboys.

Alongside services in the chapel there were other activities for the more committed. In the Crypt Chapel, there were early morning weekday communion services, for the faithful few. After George Snow had dedicated the crypt for worship in 1947, it had been adorned by fourteen stations of the cross, depicting Jesus' final hours on carved slate tablets. There was also the Christian Union. Its origins can be traced back to the Jack Winslow's 1955 Lent mission and the meetings afterwards in George Snow's drawing room. 'This group will only serve its proper purpose in the school', wrote the chaplain at the time, 'if it becomes in reality what it is in name, a Fellowship—a body of Christian people who are determined to allow themselves to be moulded by the Holy Spirit into a real fellowship of friends so that the unity of the Spirit which is evident in these meetings will spread outward.'[7] However, it took two decades for this vision to be realised. 'The Forum' had been established for older boys in 1960, but this was short-lived. A Bible Reading Fellowship Group started in 1972. Only in 1974 was the Christian Union formed.[8]

One pupil at that time was Ian Hislop, who went on to edit *Private Eye*. 'Unlike most people who had to sit through compulsory chapel,' he recalls, 'I was not either bored or irritated—I always found it quite interesting.'[9] Recognising that this attitude was the exception, with most pupils voting with their feet when it came to receiving communion, the chaplain, Derek Laughton, was beginning to consider weekday alternatives, such as streaming according to age groups.[10] Missions had continued to be a feature of college life since the 1950s, as a means of raising the spiritual temperature. Speakers had included Trevor Huddleston, the anti-apartheid campaigner, and Geoffrey Fisher, after retiring as Archbishop of Canterbury. In the 1970s, a rather different kind of mission was conducted by two former schoolboys, William Ansah and Syd Birrell.[11] I was still in the Junior School, but my brother Paul was in the Senior School and remembers it as 'quite something'. Ian Hislop recalls it vividly:

Two old boys came back—a black guy who'd played football for the First XI, and his mate; they'd joined some Christian organisation and they were very, very cool. Christian Union membership went up from about 11 to about 300 (which was almost the entire school), and we had a full-blooded, charismatic evangelical revival. Boys who were supposed to be reading the lesson would suddenly start witnessing, American-style, and there were huge prayer meetings for hours after lights out. It was extraordinary, in a closed community, feeling that you were the Early Church, and the staff had no idea what to do about it. Most of them were good Christian men and the headmaster was a former monk, and although they were inclined to think that it was just schoolboy enthusiasm, part of them was paralysed by the terrifying thought that it might be the real thing.[12]

Another pupil, Glen Hocken, looks back to the mission as a formative influence on his life. 'The Chapel music and liturgy were traditional', he reflects. 'Eucharist in old language to Merbecke, sung compline, confession. . . . Sunday and weekday Chapel services were compulsory, but although far from universally popular I was attracted by the practice of religion.' After one of the mission meetings, he writes, 'I remember walking up the Farm Hill afterwards and saying to the Lord, "Here I am if you want me."' He was eventually ordained and served as a prison chaplain for many years.[13]

The headmaster wrote about the mission in the school magazine, evidently trying to keep things steady. 'Instead of religion, I prefer to think of God,' he wrote, 'and as for revival, He is doing it all the time.'[14] A geography teacher attending for interview the following year found the headmaster 'at a loss' as to how to steer the ongoing effects of the mission.[15] By the time I moved up into Senior School, eighteen months after the mission, the school's attention had shifted elsewhere. But there were older boys who were unashamed to be counted as committed Christians. Staff and pupils were jointly organising the Christian Union, with well-attended meetings on Thursday evenings in the Centenary Cricket Pavilion that Harold Macmillan had opened.

The Christian Union had close links with Scripture Union camps for young people. While non-denominational, they had been founded in the 1930s by an Anglican clergyman, Eric Nash, universally known as Bash. 'He has done more to change the face of the Church of England than anyone this century', a diocesan bishop once said of him.[16] His vision, which some found uncomfortably elitist, was to invest in future leaders by targeting public schools. Converts, in his strategy, could be 'multiplication tables'.[17] His formula was simple: summer activity holidays for boys recruited from the top thirty public schools. Their enjoyable holiday would be combined with a clear presentation of the Christian gospel. It would be followed by mentoring and leadership training which would continue through university years. Its impact was astonishing. In the second half of the twentieth century, many of the most influential evangelical clergy would trace their Christian commitment to these camps and their offshoots. Perhaps the best known is John Stott, who served as Rector of All Souls Langham Place in London. One of his sparring partners, David Edwards, Provost of Southwark, described him as 'the most influential clergyman in the Church of England during the twentieth century', apart from Archbishop William Temple.[18] An Archbishop of Canterbury, Robert Runcie, paid Stott a similar tribute.[19]

As a lower tier Woodard school, Ardingly did not qualify as one of Bash's top thirty public schools. But Lymington Holidays, based at a boarding school in Hampshire, was very much part of the Bash camp family. I first attended one of these camps the year I moved to the Senior School, along with a couple of school friends. For a teenager, the camps were fun, full of canoeing, zany games and impromptu table tennis. The leaders came across as caring but not too intense. Some were school teachers, many were students, and all of them seemed to be enjoying themselves. The overall leader was an Anglican clergyman. Students were recruited for practical tasks too, as 'senior campers'. Around this time, the future Archbishop of Canterbury, Justin Welby, would be serving as a senior camper on one of these Bash camps.

Prayers at the start and the end of the day would include a short talk, always with a visual aid, together with some choruses. The choruses were Christian truths and exhortations, set to catchy tunes, rather than the more devotional style of choruses that were just beginning to emerge in charismatic churches. 'The stone was rolled away, from where the Saviour lay' was a favourite, as was the jaunty 'When the road is rough and steep, fix your eyes upon Jesus'. Two thirds of the way into the holiday, there was always an invitation to Christian commitment ('The Way' talk), clearly presented without being pressurised. Knowing that many of us already had some kind of Christian background, we were invited to 'go over in ink what we may have written in pencil'. That certainly struck a chord with me.

These camps played a significant part in the renaissance of evangelicalism in the Church of England after World War Two. The century leading up to World War One has been described as the evangelical century in the Church of England, despite the growing influence of the Oxford Movement.[20] Yet by World War Two evangelicals in the Church of England were a beleaguered minority. Their story can be traced back to the eighteenth century, when evangelicals emerged as a global phenomenon. It was the century when England and Wales experienced the 'Evangelical Revival' while North America had its 'Great Awakening'. In these related movements, two of the most prominent leaders were Anglican clergy: John Wesley and George Whitfield. Fired by renewed Christian commitment, they regarded the world as their parish. They horrified their clerical peers by preaching to thousands in the open air. The spiritual malaise besetting the eighteenth-century Church of England has sometimes been overstated, with absentee clergy presented as incontrovertible proof of a moribund church.[21] Nonetheless, the evangelical revival undoubtedly represented 'a quickening of the spiritual tempo in Britain and beyond'.[22] The enthusiasm that went with it was often shunned. After all, as one historian wryly observes, 'its seventeeth-century version had killed a king'.[23] The Established Church in England could hardly forget how religious zealotry had led to the execution of King Charles I and the abolition of bishops in Oliver Cromwell's time. Even the *Book of Common Prayer* and the Archbishop of Canterbury had been condemned as inimical to 'true religion' and eliminated.

A century after bishops and the Prayer Book were reinstated, some of their successors refused to have clergy with evangelical leanings in their dioceses. The prolific hymn writer and converted slave trader, John Newton, initially found himself blocked in this way. 'I have not been able to purge myself from a suspicion of Enthusiasm,' wrote the author of 'Amazing Grace' to a friend, 'and I am rejected as an improper if not a dangerous person.'[24] Nevertheless, the impact of religious 'enthusiasm' on the Church of England and beyond would be far-reaching. As two church historians explain, 'the international evangelical awakening of the eighteenth century gave a renewed boost to the flagging Protestantism of the Reformation and converted many millions to a gospel message that claimed to transform lives, communities, cultures'.[25] Its features included a strong commitment to studying the Bible, an emphasis on conversion (of which John Newton was a well-publicised example), proclaiming Jesus' death on the cross, and activism, especially in relation to spreading the faith.[26] In the Church of England, it led to a proliferation of hymn singing, well before it was formally sanctioned by the church authorities. Among the most prolific evangelical hymn writers were Charles Wesley (over 6000 hymns) and John Newton (281 hymns), in tandem with his hymn-writing friend, William Cowper.[27]

By the end of the eighteenth century, there were an estimated 500 evangelical clergy in the Church of England, but little support in high places for evangelicalism.[28] Fifty years later, there were 6,500 evangelical clergy, around third of the total number of clergy. There was even an evangelical Archbishop of Canterbury, J. B. Sumner. The missionary movement, largely inspired by evangelicals, was well underway, the Church Missionary Society having been founded at the turn of the century. And evangelicals in England were among the movers and shakers in politics, business and the aristocracy. They were the pace-setters in philanthropy and social reform. In the opinion of the Liberal Prime Minister William Gladstone, their emphasis on preaching improved its standard throughout the church.[29]

Yet in the second half of the nineteenth century, the momentum started to slow. For evangelicals, the ritualism emanating from the Oxford Movement 'touched a raw nerve', as my grandfather would encounter much later in Drumheller in the dispute over candles.[30] Evangelicals became increasingly alarmed. 'The Reformation and the works of our Reformed Church is denounced by the Ritualist as mutilated, Antichristian, and a pestilential heresy', protested the future evangelical Bishop of Liverpool, J. C. Ryle in a tract distributed in the 1870s. 'In fact, the Ritualists are merely reintroducing the ceremonies and dogmas which our fathers cast off as idolatrous and superstitious.'[31]

Evangelicals were put further on the defensive by scholarly criticism of the Bible and Charles Darwin's theory of evolution. As the twentieth century arrived, Anglican evangelicals were in disarray over these twin academic challenges. With his usual acid wit, Hensley Henson dismissed them as 'an army of illiterates generalled by octogenarians'.[32] Those seeking to engage with academic scholarship found themselves being disowned by more wary evangelicals. Even the Church Missionary Society split.[33] Increasingly, Victorian-style evangelicals became an introverted and declining element in the Church of England.[34] Yet after World War Two, the fortunes of Anglican evangelicals started to change. This is when Bash camps started to bear fruit with their evangelical ordinands. There were also renewed efforts to engage with scholarship, as seen in the founding of Tyndale House in Cambridge to promote biblical studies.

While Harry Nobbs was ministering to the parishioners of Weeley, an American evangelist was addressing crowds in Harringay football stadium, day after day, for months. One rainy day, my father was among the 1.3 million who attended Billy Graham's London rallies in 1954. On another occasion, a party of sixth formers from Ardingly College travelled to the stadium.[35] At the end of the three month 'crusade', Archbishop Geoffrey Fisher sat beside Billy Graham in Wembley Stadium, as 120,000 people heard him speak.[36] Thirty years later, I would hear the veteran evangelist address a crowd at Aston Villa football stadium, and witness a school friend from Ardingly respond to his appeal, as many had done in 1954.

By the 1970s, there may not have been many evangelical bishops. But there were a fast-growing number of parishes being led by evangelical clergy, thanks to Bash camps, Billy Graham and renewed evangelical enterprise. John Stott, the ringleader of evangelical Anglicans, was urging fellow clergy to get involved in the structures of the Church of England.[37] Some of the old animosity between evangelicals and Anglo-Catholics was beginning to wane too.[38] At Ardingly College, evangelical and Catholic influences both contributed to its Christian life.

It would be an exaggeration to say that chapel and the Christian Union dominated life at Ardingly College, even for those of us who counted ourselves committed Christians. We were, after all, teenagers and there were plenty of other outlets for our enthusiasm, such as playing soldiers in the Combined Cadet Force, cricket, film club and kayaking on the reservoir. But like it or not, Anglican religion and Anglican clergy were on everyone's radar. In 1977, a new chaplain was appointed, Alan Cole. He quickly made an impression on pupils with his Australian accent, frizzy hair, leather jacket and decision to introduce incense into Sunday services. On the first Sunday we had incense, there was an outbreak of loud coughing around the chapel. Not easily embarrassed, Father Cole soon experimented with off-beat means of engaging with us from the pulpit, notably through his fictional character, Throsbuckleherbertson. As chapel prefect in my final term, I discovered his flair for engaging with sixth formers, especially over Aussie concoctions at his home on Sunday evenings.

As well as being chapel prefect, my final term was given over to the Oxford University entrance exam. Like several of my friends, I was planning to study maths at university, thanks to an inspirational maths teacher. Michaelmas term 1980 would also cover the last months my family would live at Great Lywood Farm. It felt like the end of an era. My brother had already left home and was studying at agricultural college. But my parents were as embedded as ever in village life, with my father serving his second term as churchwarden at St Peter's Church. They had no desire to uproot. However, joining the European Common Market had been tough for British dairy farmers, whatever my geography teacher may have concluded when we debated its merits in Junior School. Milk production had been capped ('the milk quota'), while the price of animal feed had soared. The advice of my father's accountant left no option: sell the cows and move.

Once term was over, we prepared to leave our Elizabethan farmhouse for a bungalow in Steyning, sixteen miles away and coincidentally close to the upper tier Woodard school, Lancing College. As boxes were being packed, there was much rejoicing when a letter arrived offering me a place at University College, Oxford. Beyond the move, my attention could now focus on finalising plans for my gap year. While my father was getting used to not milking the cows twice a day, I would be working in a bank in Paris. Up until then, my experience of paid work had been on the farm: driving the tractor, helping with bale-carting and painting gates. Working in an office would be a new experience. Functioning in French would make it even more alien. I would be working at the prestigious International Westminster Bank. The location, Place Vendôme, would become a household name years later, when Princess Diana left its Ritz Hotel for her fateful final journey.

Accommodation would be with a member of St Michael's, a church for English speakers in Paris. He had been recommended by a former chaplain of St Michael's, Eric McLellan, who had stayed with us on the farm while helping during an interregnum at St Peter's. St Michael's proved to be the perfect counterpoise to my demanding office hours in the bank. With school-boy French, I was just managing to hold down my job on the service desk, responding to enquiries and taking wealthy investors to inspect their valuables in the vault. Coming up for air in an English-speaking environment was a life-saver. St Michael's was walking distance from Place Vendôme and close to Place de La Concorde at the foot of the Champs Elysées. The Victorian Gothic church had been replaced by a multi-room church centre five years earlier. It acted as a magnet for English speakers in Paris, many of them my age. There were plenty of ways to get involved. I joined the choir and started practising for Duruflé's *Requiem*. I took minor parts in the church pantomime, *Snow White and the Seven Dwarfs*. I joined a home group.

There were meals out and cinema trips, yet there was a vibrancy to church life which made it much more than a social club. A few weeks after my arrival, a young oil executive helped arrange for a missionary to join us for a week and deliver a series of addresses. That young oil executive was Justin Welby, future Archbishop of Canterbury. Three years earlier, he had helped co-ordinate a visit to Cambridge by this extraordinary missionary, Jackie Pullinger.[39] Yet however impressive Justin Welby may have found her in Cambridge, my staunch evangelical landlord, Jim Colley, was much more wary. He had heard she was a divisive figure, insisting everyone should 'speak in tongues'. When she came to St Michael's, I was consequently on my guard.

Jackie Pullinger had served as a missionary since 1966 in the notorious Walled City of Hong Kong. She spoke disarmingly to us about her ministry amongst drug addicts, prostitutes and triad gangsters in this no-go area for the police. It was breathtaking. Many of us bought copies of her international bestseller, *Chasing the Dragon,* to learn more.[40] Some years later, the TV presenter Alan Whicker profiled her work for *Whicker's World*. He was clearly dumbfounded by her courage and the impact of her work. She made such an impression on him that he made a point of meeting her again in 2013 for his *Journey of a Lifetime* TV series, revisiting the highlights of his career.

As she spoke to us in Paris, she told stories of hardened criminals and hopeless addicts who had become Christians. To mark the beginning of a radically new way of life, they all seemed to have prayed in an unfamiliar language. Her talks were followed by an invitation to be more open to the work of the Holy Spirit. It was my first encounter with this kind of charismatic renewal, where individuals speak in a strange language and, after a pause, others offer an interpretation in English. During the Sunday morning service, Jackie Pullinger sang a message in a 'tongue'. It was Justin Welby who provided an interpretation. 'You could have heard a pin drop', recalls the chaplain's wife, as Jackie Pullinger expounded the interpretation further.[41]

Yet the exercise of these so-called spiritual gifts was not what struck me most. Rather, it was Jackie Pullinger's bold and uncompromising faith, and the sense that God had honoured this. By comparison, my own faith seemed half-hearted. She enlarged my vision of what it could mean to be a Christian and prompted me to rededicate my own life to God.

That same year, the Church of England was trying to assess the charismatic movement of which Jackie Pullinger was a celebrated member. A report was being prepared for debate by General Synod in the autumn.[42] The report noted that so-called charismatic renewal had begun to appear in the early 1960s in the Church of England. From that point, the report observed delicately, 'the Anglican public at large became vaguely aware that something new and extraordinary—something not quite British and certainly not quite Anglican—had found a home within the Church of England'.[43] One of its leading advocates, Michael Harper, had been a curate at John Stott's church in central London. Stott was initially sceptical of the charismatic emphasis on being 'baptised in the Holy Spirit', publicly rejecting it at a conference in 1964.[44] Other evangelical parishes proved more receptive, such as St John's, Harborne in Birmingham and St Mark's, Gillingham in Kent, where John Collins, future Rector of Holy Trinity Brompton, was serving.[45]

'The Charismatic Movement caught the Evangelical Armada like a cross wind as it sailed towards its conquest of the Church of England', observed one of the first Anglo-Catholic enthusiasts for charismatic renewal, John Gunstone.[46] To a lesser extent, the breeze of charismatic renewal would spread to parishes of Gunstone's churchmanship. As the Church of England report noted, it was the Anglo-Catholic Bishop of Pontefract, Richard Hare, who so far was the only 'card-carrying' charismatic bishop in the Church of England.[47] By 1978, however, there were enough charismatic bishops elsewhere in the Anglican Communion for a retreat to be held for them in Canterbury prior to the Lambeth Conference, with South Africa, the USA,

Australia and South East Asia represented.[48] 'There is a great hunger among Christians and non-Christians in Singapore for deeper knowledge of God the Holy Spirit and experience of the spiritual gifts in our lives both personally and corporately', explained Joshua Chiu Ban It, a former lawyer consecrated Bishop of Singapore in 1966.[49]

The Holy Spirit and so-called gifts of the Spirit were the key features of charismatic renewal noted by the Church of England's report. These gifts included healing and the more common gifts of music and art, with 'an insistence that "gifts" are for the good of the "body", to build it up in Christ'.[50] This emphasis was accompanied by a distinctive style of worship. 'The general "loosening" of public worship which has come with modern language services and modern hymns has often led to a new freedom in Sunday worship amongst charismatics, with new styles of music', it noted.[51] What is commonplace today was a novelty then. This included 'a thoroughgoing *use of the body*. Hands may be lifted into the air in praise. . . . The 1978 conference at Canterbury before the Lambeth Conference became famous for the dance of the bishops round the main table in Canterbury Cathedral at the close of the three-hour eucharist.'[52] All this was pushing at the boundaries of what was acceptable in the Church of England. 'The freedom desired and experienced goes light years beyond the gentle loosening up and relaxing which the liturgical movement has brought.'[53] There was nonetheless a sense that the Church of England had 'powerful lessons' to learn from the charismatic movement, especially in the area of openness. 'All Christians should be more open to each other—in small groups, in "prayer counselling", in the ministry of healing and in all forms of sharing themselves with each other. . . . There are important questions about the transcendence and the immediacy of God, which the charismatic movement has precipitated in a new way. In particular there is a need for the whole Church, nationally and locally, to exhibit a much greater "openness" to God—so that he can do with us what he wills.'[54]

Many of these distinctive features of charismatic renewal became evident in the life of St Michael's, Paris, though Sunday services remained faithfully within the liturgical framework of the recently authorised *Alternative Service Book*. They exposed me to a new variant of evangelical Anglicanism, which I was to encounter further when I began as an undergraduate later that year. When I returned to England in the summer, I joined another of the Lymington Holidays summer camps in Hampshire. I was asked to share something of my spiritual journey that year with sixth formers and fellow school-leavers. I struggled with what I was going to say, but to my surprise found the words flowing freely. As I sat down afterwards, a thought struck me for the first time: maybe I was being called to ordination in the Church of England.

As I made the requisite preparations for being a student, such as buying a kettle, I received a letter from a second-year medical student. He was writing on behalf of the University College Christian Union, welcoming me to his college, offering some practical advice and introducing the Christian Union. He mentioned a house-party before the start of term, which I decided to attend. Thus began my contact with the Christian life of Oxford University. Oxford has long had a pivotal role in the life of the Church of England, although not always for the good. Archbishop Thomas Cranmer, architect of the *Book of Common Prayer,* was sentenced to death in the University Church, then burnt at the stake a few minutes' walk from there. For generations, studying at Oxford or Cambridge Universities was normally a pre-requisite for ordination in the Church of England. When John Newton, the converted slave trader, felt called to ordination in 1759, his lack of an Oxbridge education was as much of an obstacle as his suspected enthusiasm.[55] It was in Oxford that Anglo-Catholicism was incubated in the nineteenth century, following John Keble's Assize sermon on national apostasy. 'Scoundrels must be called scoundrels!' he expostulated from the pulpit of the University Church, protesting against the British government's interference in church affairs in Ireland.[56] Even in the 1950s, Oxford had been a rallying point for Anglican ministry. At the end of that decade, there were no fewer than 160 Anglican clergy engaged in active ministry to 'town and gown'.[57]

What about in the 1980s? To give a short answer to that question, among the students I got to know during my three years as an undergraduate, I can name thirty who went on to become Anglican clergy. Amidst all the larking around, rowing, parties, plays and late-night essay writing, there was an intensity and seriousness to student Christian life. We saw ourselves as missionaries to our peers, and a surprising number of them endured our irrepressible enthusiasm and discovered a living faith for themselves. All Christian denominations were evident, but the Church of England was the most prominent. As such, these student days were played out in an important arena for Anglican life.

I had applied to University College without knowing very much about it. Unlike a few of my fellow students, whose parents and grandparents had been to 'Univ', neither of my parents had been to university, so there were no family ties. 'The college is traditionally claimed to date from Alfred the Great (872), which is complete nonsense', jeered the Cherwell Guide. 'In fact it was endowed by William of Durham in 1249. Statutes were drawn up in 1280, which makes it one of the three contenders for the "oldest college" title.'[58] It was situated on the High Street, across the road from the University Church where Cranmer's fate had been sealed. By Oxford standards, it was a medium-sized college, which meant it had a friendly feel to it. Most of its buildings dated from the seventeenth century, apart from the 1960s Goodhart block in which many of us first years had our study bedrooms. Its twentieth-century alumni included Stephen Hawking, who would soon publish *A Brief History of Time* while suffering from motor neurone disease; and C. S. Lewis, whose time at Univ had been interrupted by service in the trenches of World War One.

The chaplain aimed to memorise the photos of all first years before we arrived. Going by the name of Bill Sykes, this affable pastor could not have been more different from the Dickensian thug of the same name. 'His warm smile and his kindness made him a much-loved figure', recalled one of my contemporaries in his obituary. 'He and the Head Porter, Bill Warren—The "Two Bills", waged a good-natured campaign of banter against each other.'[59] A statue of a former student reminded us how the religious ethos at Univ had not always been as good-natured. Near the Porter's Lodge, a marble sculpture of a drowned body commemorated the poet Percy Shelley. As a student at University College, he had been expelled in the nineteenth century for writing a paper on 'The Necessity of Atheism'.

True to Oxbridge stereotype, the first few weeks were a frenzy of activity. In fact, the pace hardly seemed to slow throughout my three years as an undergraduate. At Freshers' Fair, the stall-holders hawked membership of a dizzying array of societies. I opted to join the Kodály Choir and agreed to try out the Fabian Society with some of my left-leaning fellow first years. By what seemed an overly expensive Oxford Union Society, we were invited to one free debate. The President, William Hague, later to be Foreign Secretary, was in the chair. General Sir John Hackett and the Rt Hon. John Nott, Secretary of State for Defence, argued in favour of the motion: 'This House believes that increased defence spending and the maintenance of a nuclear deterrent are essential safeguards of freedom.' E. P. Thompson, the socialist historian and peace campaigner, and Lord Soper, the Methodist pacifist, spoke against. Back at Univ, there were yet more activities on offer. I joined the rowing club, bracing myself for chilly outings on the river before breakfast.

Then there were the Christian activities. Services geared towards freshers were offered at the city centre churches, of which St Aldate's and St Ebbe's were the best attended. Near the start of term, the Archbishop of Canterbury, Robert Runcie, preached to hundreds of us at St Aldate's. In future terms,

St Aldate's would welcome the Bishops of Oxford, Lewes and Singapore, as well as David Sheppard, Bishop of Liverpool, Richard Hare, the charismatic Bishop of Pontefract, and Stuart Blanch, Archbishop of York. There was plenty of student enthusiasm at St Aldate's, yet it was firmly connected to mainstream Anglican life.

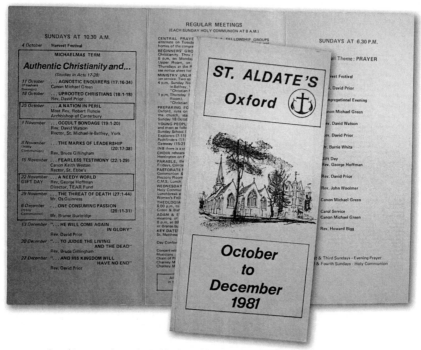

Preaching to students: the Archbishop of Canterbury, Robert Runcie and two Anglican evangelists — David Watson and Michael Green *Author's personal archives*

As I had already met members of the college Christian Union (CU) at their house-party, it was easy to join in with their welcome activities and settle into the pattern of a weekly evening meeting with Bible study. On Saturday evenings, we joined several hundred members of other college CUs for a Bible exposition at the Northgate Hall, premises in central Oxford owned by the Oxford Intercollegiate Christian Union (OICCU). The speakers lined up for the year read like a 'who's who' of the Anglican evangelical world, interspersed with Baptist and other Free Church ministers. Among them were the occasional bishop, such as Bishop John Taylor of St Albans and Bishop Maurice Wood of Norwich.

College CUs and chaplains sometimes had an uneasy relationship. Happily, this was not true at Univ. Several CU members were in the chapel choir, including the organ scholar. On Sunday evenings, most CU members joined the chaplain for sherry between evensong and dining at Formal Hall. The chaplain's weekday speciality was reflection groups. He had collected thought-provoking quotations on a wide range of themes, which he later published.[60] Up to four students would sit quietly in his study reflecting on a few selected topics, then discuss them together. It was a non-threatening way for 'astonishing numbers of Univ men and women' to reflect on the great questions of life, as those of us at his memorial service in the packed University Church were reminded thirty years later.[61] Quite a few CU members joined one of the chaplain's reflection groups at some point too, including myself.

There was one Christian group I had not expected to join. 'Christians and Politics' was run by a student who had also worshipped at St Michael's Paris, Charles Davey. As term began, he hosted a tea party for 'ex-Paris-ites' like myself and persuaded me to try out his society. In the first week of term, the Speaker of the House of Commons, Lord Tonypandy, was guest speaker at a meeting jointly hosted by Christians and Politics and the Oxford Union. 'How my Christian beliefs affect my political views' was his subject, speaking as a politician who unashamedly 'did God'. The following week's guest speaker, Jim Punton, tackled the topic of Christianity and class. These were new topics for me, but they sparked an interest.

As term progressed, I was thriving on the activities and social life, but was finding maths dull and demanding. My gap year had awakened an interest in the wider world. Five weeks into term, I went to a book sale at Blackwell's bookshop. I came away with a stack of discounted books on politics and social problems. As I got back to my room, it struck me that these were topics I would like to explore properly. An idea came to me. Why not change subject from Maths to Politics, Philosophy and Economics (PPE)? I began to discuss the idea with fellow students and within a week, it was agreed in principle. For someone whose A-levels had been in maths and physics, studying brand new topics and learning to write essays was quite daunting. The Univ PPE students were an impressive bunch. One would go on to be a philosophy professor, two would become MPs and another would play a key role in the British government's privatisation programme. At St Aldate's Church that Sunday, a reassuring paragraph in the notice sheet caught my eye. St Aldate's was gently embracing charismatic renewal and was open to the possibility of prophetic utterance. A few sentences were addressed to those seeking guidance. 'Do not be concerned that I might lead you where you do not desire to go', I remember reading. 'I will lead you to the perfect place for you, where you are stretched.'

After the service, I went across as usual with a mass of students for lunch in the Rectory Rooms. I sat next to a chemistry student from St Hugh's College I had already met. 'You'll never guess what happened to me during the service', I said to her. I went on to explain how the words on the notice sheet had confirmed my sense that a change of subject was right. 'That's funny' she responded. 'It did pretty much the same for me. I'm changing from chemistry to theology.' Priscilla went on to be one of the first women ordained priest in the Church of England.

By the end of my frenetic first term, I was exhausted but starting to prepare for thinking new thoughts and being stretched as a PPE student. Along with other members of the CU, I was also beginning to prepare for the student mission. Every three years, the OICCU would run a week-long university-wide mission. In February 1982, its theme would be *Is Anyone There?*—the title of a book written by the main speaker, David Watson.

I had heard David Watson speak a few months before at the Greenbelt Arts Festival, and again at St Aldate's. 'He was the best UK evangelist of the day', judged Michael Green, our Rector at St Aldate's and himself a well-known evangelist. Michael Green admired David Watson's combination of 'charm, humour, biblical teaching, illustrative stories and challenge in a way that brought hundreds to Christ in university and town missions'.[62] They had first met as junior leaders on Bash camps and they were both quick to acknowledge the grounding they had received on these camps. 'I was given a marvellous training', explains Michael Green: 'how to give an attractive talk, how to lead an inductive Bible study and how to do basic pastoral work.'[63] David Watson echoed this. 'It was the best possible training I could have received....I went to no less than thirty-five of these camps....I learned, until it became second nature, how to lead a person to Christ, how to answer common questions, how to follow up a young convert, how to lead a group Bible study...how to prepare and give a talk...how to teach others to pray... and also, most important, how to laugh and have fun as a Christian.'[64] This was precisely the kind of training that the reports commissioned during the two world wars felt was lacking amongst clergy. With this training put into practice, David Watson's church in York, St Michael le Belfry, had seen impressive growth in numbers, having been rescued from redundancy. It had also become a pace-setter in charismatic renewal and a resource for other churches. Its members offered workshops on lay ministry, evangelism, youth and children's work, and use of music, drama, dance and other creative arts.[65] It had a professional drama group, Riding Lights, which would come with David Watson to Oxford.

For the University mission, the CU in each college would be joined by two assistant missioners, most of whom were Church of England clergy, deaconesses or ordinands. Univ was allocated Nick McKinnell, a young curate who would become Bishop of Crediton and June Osborne, a deaconess who went on to become Dean of Salisbury Cathedral. The main talks were given by David Watson at the Union Debating Hall and at the Sheldonian Theatre, where degrees were awarded. We all plucked up courage and invited our fellow students along. Many accepted the invitation and the venues were packed. *Is Anyone There?* became a major talking point in college and the Assistant Missioners found themselves having in-depth conversations with plenty of students. There was a real sense of excitement, as students realised that God might indeed be alive and interested in them. 'What struck me', said a chemistry student on my staircase, 'was the speaker saying "Jesus is" rather than "Jesus was"'. We had arranged a discussion group for those who wanted to take things further, which I agreed to co-lead with a fellow CU member and an ordinand from Wycliffe Hall, the theological college up the road. We had plenty of takers.

With microeconomics, the politics of the Soviet Union and philosophical logic to master, it was a full term. When the vacation came, I was pleased to join 120 students from St Aldate's for a working party at Lee Abbey. This was the centre in North Devon whose chaplain, Jack Winslow, had led the Lent mission at Ardingly College, twenty-five years earlier. We arrived by coach to discover a stunningly beautiful setting. The woods surrounding the buildings and fields had been devastated by storms, so our job was to chop logs. It was still very much a centre for evangelism, especially in the summer. But for us, it was a place of retreat and refreshment, where we received exercise and Christian teaching in beautiful surroundings, and could digest what we had been receiving during the term. I had agreed to take over the leadership of the College CU, so it was a useful preparation for that too.

Once back in Oxford, I met regularly with the ordinand I had led the discussion group with, Iain Broomfield. Despite my new responsibilities as CU rep, I somehow managed to pass my exams.

In the days of student grants, there was less pressure to find paid employment in the long vacation. We therefore tended to do voluntary work and travel. With the boundless energy of youth, I filled the summer months painting a youth club in inner city London, serving as a leader on Lymington holidays, helping run holidays in Surrey for disabled adults and then in Northern Ireland for prisoners' wives and their families, at Corrymeela Community. For light relief, I joined a reading party of PPE students and tutors in the French Alps, in a remote chalet owned by Univ. What stands out, though, was a two-week mission in Huddersfield, organised by St Aldate's. After five training sessions during the summer term, sixty students descended on the town. We were hosted by Anglican, Methodist and United Reformed churches, each of which had organised events for us to take part in. Michael Green would deliver evangelistic addresses in the evenings. It was an opportunity for us to do all kinds of things for the first time. It was my first time preaching in a parish church and—following in the footsteps of my grandmother—in the open air.

Huddersfield parish church was the venue for my first ever sermon, at a poorly attended evening service. It over-ran, so by the time the service was finished, crowds had started to gather outside for the day's main guest event, also at the parish church. The charismatic Bishop of Pontefract, Richard Hare, would take part, but as usual the main address would be given by Michael Green. I was due to meet up beforehand with a fellow first-year at Univ, an engineering student. Pete lived up the road from Huddersfield and agreed to come to one of the evening meetings, as quite a few of us from Univ would be there. We used to play squash together and had suffered a crushing defeat in a darts match against a superior team from a women's college. He was not a committed Christian, though he had been to hear David Watson and had gamely attended a concert where Cliff Richard discussed his faith in between songs. But he didn't seem to be that interested, so I wasn't altogether surprised when there was no sign of him in the mêlée before the meeting began. At the end of his address, Michael Green invited those wishing to commit themselves as Christians to come to the front of church, following the pattern set by Billy Graham. As people starting moving forward, I saw Pete appear at the back of church. I assumed he had just arrived and became anxious he might inadvertently get swept up to the front. To my discomfort, he did indeed proceed forward. But he knew what he was doing. Afterwards he explained that he had only arrived a little late. Quite unexpectedly, as Michael Green spoke, he had a powerful sense that God was calling him to commit himself. Pete explains:

> I became a Christian in October 1982 at a mission in Huddersfield where Michael Green spoke from Revelation 3 on the subject of the church in Laodicea and being lukewarm.... That I should do so was surprising for a number of reasons. My friend Andy Norman who was on my landing at University College in our first year had been evangelising me repeatedly. I can remember being taken to several events by him, featuring some well-known names.... So having been impervious to all this I headed off on vacation to the safety of my home.

I arrived late at St Peter's . . . I sat alone in the gallery looking down on proceedings. I sensed a warmth there, and I was outside of it. I couldn't see the speaker who spoke about how being lukewarm was no good, unpalatable and a waste of time. This was me, and there was a warmth there that I wanted. I responded to the challenge and became a Christian that night.[66]

Others committed themselves as Christians that fortnight too. During one evening meeting, we were invited to talk to those around us. I spoke with a woman, Catherine, who shared her concern for unemployed young people in her neighbourhood. They simply 'sat on the wall all day, like blackbirds'. She urged us to try to engage with them. The only remaining slot in the programme was after lunch on the final Sunday. We were all worn out by then and quite relieved when it seemed too rainy for an outdoor engagement. Then a patch of clear sky appeared, so we summoned up energy and went to the recreation ground, ready to perform dramatic sketches and chat to the young people. But no-one was there. It seemed like we had wasted our time. Three months later, we would return to Huddersfield for a reunion. To our surprise, the same woman, Catherine, would be invited onto the stage. She would speak of how, on that last Sunday, she had attended the closing service at the parish church and committed herself as a Christian. It was our concern for her 'blackbirds' that had prompted her to go.

Re-motivated in evangelism, we returned from the Huddersfield mission to the start of a new academic year. Most students on the St Aldate's mission were also actively involved in their College CUs and the inter-collegiate Christian Union. However, the OICCU was very clear about its aims and theological underpinning and at times these could be strictly interpreted. 'I found the intransigent attitudes of the OICCU leadership rather trying when I was appointed Rector of St Aldate's in 1975', Michael Green recalls.[67] His invitation to lead the OICCU mission had been rescinded when he became rector of a church regarded as theologically suspect at the time. He nonetheless sought to work in partnership with the Christian Union. 'It seems to me undeniable', he reflected, 'that the best people to get alongside students are their peers. As a church leader in a student setting, therefore, I always encouraged students to get involved in the Christian Union, because it gives them unique opportunities for mission.'[68]

For students willing to take up these mission opportunities, there was an obvious danger to guard against. With so many Christian meetings and services, it was possible to live in a Christian bubble, thereby undermining the evangelistic aspirations of the CU. The OICCU Executive Committee did what it could to discourage this. Saturday evening Bible readings were moved to an earlier time, to allow students to go on to parties afterwards. For those of us at Univ, the strong community life of the college meant there was contact with a cross-section of fellow students, especially if you lived in the college itself. In my case, I decided to join the Modern Pentathlon Club too. I had given up rowing when I changed subject to PPE and was ready for some decent exercise. It seemed a good way to immerse myself in a different social group. As a farmer's son and former cadet, I knew how to ride and shoot. I was not a fast swimmer, but a passable runner. I would need to learn to fence.

Studying was another means of moving out of a Christian comfort zone. In my first year, I had come into direct contact with the Enlightenment, through studying the philosopher David Hume. As a movement in philosophy, the Enlightenment has shaped everyday thinking and been a major influence on the Church of England. I learnt about its origins and the philosopher Descartes' quest for clarity about what can be known. He famously locked himself in an oven and went through a ruthless mental exercise, eliminating everything he could not be absolutely certain about. In the end, the only thing he could be sure of was the fact that he was doubting and therefore thinking: 'I think, therefore I am'. It would lead to a new emphasis on the questioning individual as the starting point for what we know. Tradition or the Church no longer dictated what was true. As a mindset, it would encourage scientific enquiry, of which we are beneficiaries. But for religion, it would lead to scepticism, and the sense that religious belief comes a poor second to scientific knowledge. Accounts of miracles would be treated as deeply suspect. In my final year, I found myself being invited to debate with the chaplain of another college whether we can still believe in miracles. Only at the end of my time as an undergraduate did I discover Lesslie Newbigin, with his penetrating critique of Enlightenment assumptions. As a former bishop of the Church of South India, he argued for a missionary approach to Western culture. He felt the Church had too easily let Enlightenment thinking set the terms.[69]

A similar *cri de coeur* came from a popular writer who worshipped at St Aldate's and led well-attended seminars. Os Guinness' plea was for students to develop 'a Christian mind'. He was not opposed to doubt, arguing in a book on the subject that it could be positive, if it led to thinking things through more thoroughly.[70] However, as a sociologist, he was adamant that 'privatised' faith was the occupational hazard of Western—including Anglican—Christianity. By this, he meant that Christians kept their Christian views in a separate compartment from much of their everyday life.[71] He worked closely with John Stott, who also advocated the development of a Christian mind, having just set up his London Institute for Contemporary Christianity. The challenge was to keep your faith in mind during your studies. So, in my case, when it came to writing essays for moral philosophy, I did my best to argue a line that was compatible with my faith. As I was still learning the ropes, my efforts lacked sophistication, but I felt it was right to try to be consistent.

The Archbishop of Canterbury provided further encouragement for us to engage as Christians with philosophical ideas. Robert Runcie was one of the speakers at the Chaplains' Mission in February 1983. Like the CU mission, the Chaplains' Mission came round every three years. Though not officially endorsed by the OICCU, CU members promoted the Chaplains' Mission and we encouraged our friends to go to the events. Robert Runcie spoke on two occasions. In one of his addresses, he engaged with logical positivism. Unfortunately, as a philosophical approach, it was a bit of a spent force by then. Its main advocate, A. J. Ayer, had admitted as much on the BBC TV series, *Men of Ideas*. 'It must have had real defects', the interviewer, Bryan Magee, suggested politely to his guest. 'What do you now, in retrospect, think the main ones were?' 'Well,' responded A. J. Ayer, 'I suppose the most important of the defects was that nearly all of it was false'.[72]

The Archbishop may have picked the wrong target, but at least he was encouraging his hearers to engage with philosophical trends in a way that was consistent with Christian faith. Yet the show was stolen in this Chaplains' Mission by a speaker describing faith as more than an intellectual exercise. 'The only Christ is the Living Christ!' boomed Metropolitan Anthony of Sourozh, head of the Russian Orthodox jurisdiction in Britain. He was speaking in the University Church, where Keble had delivered his Assize sermon and Thomas Cranmer had been tried for heresy.

The University Church was also where the OICCU held their annual carol service. It was around this time that I was asked to join the Executive Committee of the OICCU, as Prayer Secretary. It was a time commitment, but felt like an honour. Church leaders we looked up to, such as N. T. Wright, later to become Bishop of Durham, had once served on the OICCU Exec. My main job was to drum up prayer for student evangelism and for the world church. There were daily lunchtime prayer meetings ('DPMS') with the best attended being Saturday lunchtime. There were also termly prayer letters to former OICCU members, which often elicited encouraging responses. 'It's nearly thirty years since I came to know Christ as my Saviour at St John's', wrote one recipient. 'I know for a fact the Lord switched the whole direction of my life along a path that I would not have taken if left to myself. So I thank the Lord for what he is doing in Oxford now.'[73] There were also twenty-two prayer groups for countries around the world. I decided to join the India prayer group. I had been given the opportunity to travel to India the coming summer and felt I should pray for the country. It would be my first experience of travel outside Europe.

✠

In charting these youthful encounters in the 1970s and 1980s, what is emerging about 'being Anglican'? Several threads can be identified. First, while society changes radically, we see Anglican life continuing to thrive in 'micro-climates' which have already established themselves as influential in the Anglican story. In particular, we see this in an Anglican independent school and at Oxford University. Second, in both these settings, as well as in Paris, we see how traditional Anglican patterns of worship are supplemented by an emphasis on nurturing personal faith. Third, we have noted that enthusiasm and religious zeal are not always welcome in Anglican circles and can sometimes be divisive. Fourth, we have paid particular attention to the fluctuating fortunes of the evangelical movement, noting characteristics of evangelical Anglican activity, including its capacity for working with non-denominational organisations in youth and student work. Fifth, we have observed ways the Anglican worship tradition has evolved, including hymns, choral singing and choruses. Sixth, we have registered the advent of charismatic renewal and ways in which it caught the Church of England and even evangelicalism by surprise. Seventh, we have encountered historical criticism and philosophical thought, acknowledging their potential to be accepted unthinkingly in the life of the Church or, alternatively, rejected outright. Linked to this is the syndrome of Christian beliefs being kept in a separate compartment from everyday life.

Some of these themes re-emerge as we move now beyond the shores of England, to India and then to West Africa.

5

Not Just the White Man's God

I NDIA WAS A FASHIONABLE travel destination for British university students and school leavers in the early 1980s. In my second summer vacation at Oxford, I followed the trend and flew to India, in the company of Jim Colley, whom I lodged with in Paris, Sam Sharpe—a fellow member of the OICCU Executive Committee and former co-leader of Univ CU—and a cello. It was a grand tour, taking in the major cities of Delhi, Hyderabad, Madras, Bombay and Calcutta (as they were then called), as well as the Sikh temple in Amritsar, the Hindu Temple in Madurai and the former hill station of Simla. We even visited the troubled region of Kashmir, before it became closed to tourists.

It was more than a sightseeing trip. We made a point of visiting church workers and development projects. Sam had been a Voluntary Service Overseas (VSO) worker in India in his gap year, so we revisited where he had served. He ended up living in Delhi with his family, overseeing the British government (DfID) aid programme in India. As an 18-year-old VSO worker, he had been located at a church-based agricultural project near Hyderabad, in South India, and then at the Oxford Mission to Calcutta.

It was Sam's links with the Oxford Mission to Calcutta that accounted for the cello being a travelling companion. We had arranged to drop it off in Delhi. Soon after landing at Delhi International Airport, the three of us, plus cello, walked up from our hotel to the bustling taxi-rank in front of the Red Fort, intending to take a 'tuk-tuk' auto-rickshaw to the Cambridge Mission to Delhi. To our embarrassment, it turned out that a very determined cycle-rickshaw rider had triumphed in the haggling. So the three of us, plus cello, were transported through the back streets of Delhi by one impressively fit cycle-rickshaw rider.

From Oxford to India:
following precedent

Photos © Andrew Norman

The Cambridge Mission to Delhi and the Oxford Mission to Calcutta were sister missions, dating back to the end of the nineteenth century. They were unusual in being university missions. Their initial focus was deliberately academic: engaging with educated Indians. The Cambridge Mission, founded in 1877, owed its origins to the Cambridge Professor of Divinity, B. F. Westcott, who went on to precede Handley Moule and Hensley Henson as Bishop of Durham. He in turn had been inspired by an energetic Anglican missionary, Thomas Valpy French, known as 'the seven-tongued padre'. French served in India with the Church Missionary Society (CMS), the Anglican agency founded in 1799 at the start of the missionary movement.[1] When the Cambridge Mission was launched, he was Bishop of Lahore. His neighbouring colleague, the Bishop of Calcutta, soon followed suit in his own diocese. Following the model of the Cambridge Mission, he appealed to Oxford University for young men to talk with educated Bengalis about the Christian religion. In 1881 the Oxford Mission to Calcutta was founded.[2]

Both the Cambridge and Oxford missions set up religious orders to take forward their work. This work soon diversified. The Oxford Brothers established hostels and schools, acted as chaplains to hospitals and engaged in pastoral visiting in Christian villages south of Calcutta. By the time Sam Sharpe went to Calcutta as a VSO worker, the Oxford Mission was running an orphanage in the southern outskirts of Calcutta, at Behala. Every boy had the chance to learn a musical instrument, hence the need for a cello.[3] It was viewed as an important part of the mission's work. 'Sam Sharpe, who is here as a V.S.O., is a simply SPLENDID young man', Father Theodore Mathieson enthused to his sister. 'At the moment he is burning midnight oil reforming the whole music library. This evening he conducted the 12 first violins and six cellos of our Nursery Orchestra, while I had an agonising two hours making 16 or more second violins play D major (one octave only) in tune one by one.'[4]

This musical emphasis might sound like an eccentric Western imposition, yet for talented orphans it was a means of securing future employment. Many of the boys went on to find employment in the Indian film industry. Later in the year, I would hear one of the Mission's alumni, Anup Kumar Biswas, perform at the Festival Hall in London.

The Oxford and Cambridge Missions were latecomers to Anglican missionary work in India. However, it would be wrong to assume that Anglican missionaries had simply arrived in India with the first British traders. It was only in 1858 that the British government assumed direct control of India. For the previous hundred years, British commercial interests had been looked after by the East India Company. The East India Company had its own locally recruited army (sepoys) and was anxious not to provoke unrest. Missionaries were seen as potentially destabilising. For several decades, Anglican clergy went to India to act as chaplains for Europeans, but were expected to abstain from missionary work amongst non-Europeans. A few broke ranks, such as Henry Martyn, the brilliant linguist who translated the *Book of Common Prayer* and New Testament into Urdu. But it would take mass lobbying of Parliament and a petition with half a million signatures before the East India Company finally relaxed their policy in 1813. William Wilberforce, the anti-slave trade campaigner, had taken up the cause twenty years earlier. But in 1793, Wilberforce had failed in his efforts to persuade Parliament to modify the East India Company's charter. Now, as it came up for renewal again, Wilberforce's cause finally prevailed and the so-called 'pious clause' was inserted. Missionaries would henceforth be permitted in India, so long as they had a licence from the East India Company. In addition, the East India Company would be required to fund three archdeacons and a bishop, based in Calcutta.[5]

By the time of our visit, Anglicans in India had merged with other denominations to form 'United Churches'. The Church of North India and the Church of South India were not just the fruit of Anglican missionary activity. They were the product of Methodist, Presbyterian, Lutheran and other non-Anglican missionary work too. In rural India, we visited the incongruously gothic Medak Cathedral. It had once been a Methodist church. Bishop Lesslie Newbigin, whose critique of the Enlightenment I had found so helpful, had been a Presbyterian missionary before becoming a bishop of the Church of South India. The cathedral and Newbigin both testified to a non-negotiable aspect of Anglican identity: bishops, whose seat or 'see' (cathedral) corresponds to their authority within geographical areas. When the Church of South India was formed in 1947, Anglicans were clear that bishops would be required in the 'United Church'. What that meant for clergy who had not already been ordained by bishops was hotly contested, especially by Anglo-Catholics. Should they be re-ordained? They were not. It was only in 1998 that these United Churches became full members of the Anglican Communion, by which time all active clergy had been ordained by bishops.[6]

Visiting India, at the age of twenty, had been my first direct encounter with Anglican life outside Europe, even if technically the Indian churches had not yet become fully Anglican again. It whetted my appetite for more. As I returned to Oxford for my final year before graduating, the question of 'what next?' loomed. Ordination in the Church of England seemed increasingly likely, but I felt I needed more life experience. In any case, the Church of England tended to discourage fresh graduates from going straight to theological college, according to the advice I received. I formulated a plan of taking another gap year, prior to starting as a graduate trainee in industry. In my first summer vacation at Oxford, I had narrowly missed trekking to West Africa across the Sahara Desert. To cultivate a diocesan link with Nigeria, the Youth Officer for Chichester Diocese had come up with an audacious plan. He would lead a convoy of Land Rovers overland to Nigeria. I had joined a post-Christmas training weekend in Herefordshire, sleeping in an eerily empty turkey shed. But I withdrew from the trip. It was the year I changed subject to PPE and the timing seemed wrong. In the end, the convoy made it no further than Algeria. Afterwards I kept in touch with the organiser and he suggested a second attempt might be made. I made my mind up to go to Nigeria after graduating, one way or another.

As a result, I opted to study the politics of sub-Saharan Africa in my final year. The hyperactivity of the year was compounded by applying for jobs in industry ('the milkround') and joining a dramatic production of the Book of Isaiah, by yet another Christian group, the Christian Arts and Drama Society (CADS). Lacking much acting talent myself, I nonetheless witnessed the missionary potential of drama in student settings and more widely in the church. During the Easter break, I joined a team from CADS for a mission to a group of parishes in Wiltshire. Our repertoire included contemporary sketches and excerpts from medieval mystery plays, all of which proved to be talking points for those on the fringes of church life. These dramatic sketches seemed appropriate not just in parish churches and church halls. During Holy week, we performed in Salisbury Cathedral, finding they suited a cathedral setting too.

After this Spring interlude, exams ('finals') soon came and went. There was the customary May Ball and then undergraduate days were over. I had failed to secure a job in industry with a deferred start date. I decided to go for two gap years. The first year would revolve around a trip to Nigeria. The second would combine a church-based post in England with applying for jobs in industry.

I would finally leave for Nigeria in March the following year. The idea of travelling across the Sahara was abandoned, but there was still money to be raised and background research to be done. I secured a short-term job in London, conveniently working in the East and West Africa Department of the Overseas Development Administration (ODA), the predecessor of DfID, my Indian travelling companion's future employer. This was the time of the 1984 famine in Ethiopia. Michael Buerk's BBC news footage of starving children had led to a public outcry. Bob Geldoff's Band Aid single 'Do they know it's Christmas?' and his Live Aid Concert would follow. An audience of 1.9 billion people would watch the concert live in 150 nations and £150 million would be raised.

The public had been roused and Africa was on people's minds. My job was to respond to letters to the British government about the Ethiopia famine. Members of the public would write to the Prime Minister, Mrs Thatcher, or the Minister of State, Malcolm Rifkind. They would receive a reply from me, a low-grade civil servant, acknowledging their concern and explaining how the British government was responding to the crisis. In the aftermath of this heart-rending tragedy, *News out of Africa: Biafra to Band Aid* was published. It noted how media coverage of humanitarian crises in Africa was changing public perception in the West. Positively, there was an increased sense of responsibility for development in Africa. More questionably, media coverage was creating the impression that Africa was no more than a patchwork of famines, oppressive regimes and game parks. 'Only the spectacular, the bizarre or the truly horrific tend to reach our screens, thus reinforcing our stereotypes of Africa and Africans.'[7]

My objective in going to Nigeria was to get beneath the stereotypes. It was Nigeria that had generated the first televised African famine, during its

'Biafran' civil war in 1967–70. But Nigeria was also known as the African Giant, with a population of around 80 million in 1985. It had extensive natural oil reserves. The South was predominantly Christian, the North mostly Muslim. There were more Anglicans in Nigeria than in any other country, apart from England.

My particular interest was the extent to which Christianity had taken root on Nigerian soil. 1985 marked twenty-five years since Nigeria's independence from colonial rule. In Oxford, the OICCU was still continuing its long tradition of promoting missionary work. In addition to its international prayer groups, there was a target of eighty former OICCU members becoming missionaries in the 1980s. But times had changed. Discomfort about European missionary activity was widespread. Books such as *The End of an Era: Africa and the Missionary* took seriously the call for a moratorium on European missionaries.[8] 'The continuation of the present missionary movement is a hindrance to the selfhood of the Church', John Gatu, Moderator of the Presbyterian Church of East Africa, had proclaimed in 1971. 'The imperialist attitude of the West, that you have something to share with your fellow man, must also be challenged.'[9] Conscious of this ambivalence about the missionary enterprise, I wanted to see how far the Christian gospel had been owned in Nigeria and whether there were lessons to be drawn for the Church in the West.

The project was not limited to the Anglican Church, but my programme would include plenty of contact with Anglicans in Nigeria. I would travel with my former room-mate at Oxford, Nick Polge, an agriculturalist. We would try to take account of the country's agricultural, political and economic development as we observed the life of the church.

Unlike India, Nigeria was not a popular destination for independent travellers. There was plenty of revenue from oil reserves but virtually no tourism. Some advised us not to go. In 1983 there had been a military coup, justified by the need to tackle corruption and crime. Now, through its 'War Against Indiscipline', Major-General Buhari's government was resorting to heavy-handed tactics. Its secret police, the NSO, was widely feared. Stiff jail sentences were being delivered by military tribunals for offences that included cheating in exams, tampering with mail and illegally exporting produce.[10]

Two British engineers had been accused of illegally servicing an aircraft and sentenced to seven years each. Some put this down to damaged diplomatic relations between Britain and Nigeria. This was linked to the Dikko affair. Umaru Dikko, Transport Minister in the ousted regime, stood accused of embezzling millions of dollars. His drugged body had been discovered in a crate at Stanstead Airport, marked 'Property of Nigeria'. The kidnappers had been given jail sentences of up to fourteen years. With Dikko not brought to account, this seemed like rough justice and in Nigeria it caused outrage.[11] It did not bode well for two British students wanting to travel around the country.

Initially we were only granted a three-week visa. We flew to Lagos, hoping to extend to the full three months. At that time, Lagos was the capital. Originally a coastal trading station, it is in the south-western corner of the country. Nigeria's civil war had been the product of tensions between ethnic groups in different parts of the country. A new capital, Abuja, was therefore being constructed in the bush, right in the middle of the country. Although hundreds of languages were spoken, the dominant ethnic groups were the Yoruba in the west, Ibo in the east and Hausa in the north.

Our first three weeks were in the largely Yoruba area. During that time, we travelled eighty miles north from Lagos to Ibadan. This 150-year-old city was where the Anglican archbishop was based. On the day we arrived at his residence, he was at the ancient city of Ife. We travelled with his wife and joined him at a funeral. It was our first taste of Nigerian Anglicanism. The funeral was a great celebration, as the person who had died had lived to a ripe old age. We returned with the archbishop to Ibadan and stayed at his guest house.

Archbishop Timothy Olufosoye was the first Nigerian Archbishop. The Anglican Church in Nigeria had only been formed as a separate province six years earlier. Prior to that, Nigeria had come under the jurisdiction of the Anglican Province of West Africa. The autonomous province of West Africa had been formed in 1951, ahead of the political independence of Nigeria, Sierra Leone, Ghana and its other constituent countries. To be viable, an Anglican province must have at least four dioceses. By 1978 there were sixteen in Nigeria, so it more than qualified. This would rise exponentially in the years to come. At the time of our visit, there were sixty. By 2013, there would be one hundred and sixty-seven.

Back in Lagos, we had lunch with the Provost of the Anglican cathedral. Most of our contact in Lagos, however, was with para-church organisations and non-Anglican churches. Through involvement in Scripture Union camps in England, we had openings with Scripture Union in Lagos and joined an Easter youth conference. Scripture Union was clearly a vibrant presence in schools and among young people. Its growing influence could be traced back to the Biafran War, when Scripture Union groups proliferated, especially in the East of Nigeria.[12] 'New groups were now to be found here, there and everywhere,' an Anglican lay worker with SU wrote towards the end of the war, 'in villages, churches of all denominations, ammunition factories, hospitals, army camps and refugee camps.'[13] The work of Scripture Union in schools was matched by the work of NIFES (the Nigeria Fellowship of Evangelical Students) in universities, linked to the Christian Union network in England. As in England, the African university Christian Union movement had strong Anglican links. The founder of the umbrella organisation, Tony Wilmot, had been a senior colonial administrator and a lay Anglican.[14] One of its general secretaries, David Gitari, would go on to serve as a distinguished Archbishop of Kenya.[15] In Lagos, we joined a NIFES conference and student meetings at the University of Lagos (Unilag). Both Scripture Union and NIFES groups were characterised by Bible study, fervent intercessory prayer and exuberant singing.

Cathedral Church
of Christ in Lagos

Photo © Andrew Norman

In Lagos, we also encountered Pentecostalism. One popular form of Pentecostalism had grown out of work amongst young people. On one Sunday, we joined the Deeper Life Ministries for worship at their fellowship centre in Gbagada, Lagos. There were three services on a Sunday morning. We joined the middle one, so witnessed those leaving the first service and arriving for the third. We were told 24,000 attended each Sunday and that seemed about right. The church's leader, William Kumuyi, had started a small group for prayer and Bible study when he was a maths lecturer at Unilag. Later, this led to large conferences, especially over Easter and Christmas. In 1978, over two thousand people were drawn each week to his Monday Bible study.[16] By the time of our visit, there were seven hundred home Bible study groups.

We also attended worship at a Pentecostal church originating outside Nigeria. The Foursquare Gospel Church was founded in Los Angeles in 1927 by Sister Aimee. By the end of the century, there would be 60,000 Foursquare Gospel churches in 164 countries. The Foursquare church in Yaba, Lagos, was popular with Unilag students. On Easter Day, we joined their service at the tail-end of a retreat. It would be our first direct encounter with the supernatural worldview that pre-dated Christianity in Nigeria. Participants in the retreat had been urged to surrender their 'juju' charms. At the end of the service, there was a bonfire where rejected charms were burnt.

On another occasion, we joined tens of thousands of Nigerians in Tafawa Balewa Square for a 'miracle-healing' crusade. It was led by Archbishop Benson Idahosa, an Assemblies of God pastor with an international ministry. I would hear him speak again the following year in Liverpool Cathedral. The tone of the rally was different to that of the SU and NIFES groups. 'Do you want to be healed?', Archbishop Idahosa kept asking, with resoundingly positive responses. Buckets were filled with money and there was more than a trace of 'name it and claim it' prosperity theology.

Emphasis on healing was also a feature of the so-called Aladura churches. Their origins can be traced back to the worldwide influenza epidemic in 1918 encountered by my grandfather in the trenches, and the perceived faithlessness of other Christians. 'By and large, the adherents of the Aladura are not fresh converts from paganism, but deserters from the 'orthodox' and African churches from which they had derived no religious satisfaction or spiritual consolation', explains the Nigerian church historian, E. A. Ayandele.[17] He speaks of 'the satisfaction enjoyed by the Aladura Christian believers that witches have no power over them, that they enjoy serenity of mind which eludes Christians outside the Aladura fold who clandestinely resort to other sources and forces in the search for freedom from fear'.[18]

Not surprisingly, these Aladura churches, Pentecostal churches and youth organisations were raising serious questions for Nigerian Anglicans, as we would discover when our visas were finally extended and we moved east. We travelled the seven-hour journey by coach. The dual carriageway was heavily pot-holed, so at times the coach driver would simply switch to the opposite carriageway and play 'chicken' with oncoming traffic. Eventually, we arrived safely at Onitsha, to be greeted by a CMS missionary attached to the Anglican Diocese on the Niger.

Onitsha itself is on the great Niger River, after which Nigeria is named. The Niger River was the conduit of the first missionary venture by Anglicans in what is now Nigeria. The expedition was backed by the British government. However, it did not quite fit the notion that missionaries were the 'running dogs' of self-interested British imperialism.[19] Motives were mixed, but at the heart of the enterprise was an overdue commitment to social justice. The primary motivation of the 1841 Niger Expedition was the long-term abolition of slavery.

Only gradually had it dawned on Anglicans that slavery was abhorrent. SPG, the mission agency that supported my grandfather in Canada, had even owned a slave plantation in the Bahamas.[20] However, first-hand reports of horrors of the slave trade, from the likes of John Newton, had galvanised a committed group of Anglicans to press for its abolition. William Wilberforce led the campaign.

In 1807, Wilberforce and his allies finally succeeded in abolishing the slave-trade in the British Empire, after twenty years of dogged campaigning. Two years earlier, the British had defeated the French fleet at the Battle of Trafalgar. Britannia now ruled the waves. From 1808, Royal Navy warships patrolled the coast of West Africa, intercepting slave ships.[21] Freed slaves were taken to Freetown in Sierra Leone and then given a missionary education by the CMS. Having abolished the slave trade, the next step was to abolish slavery itself. Again Wilberforce campaigned with the abolitionists, now nicknamed 'the Saints'. As Wilberforce's health deteriorated, the cause was taken up by another Parliamentarian, Thomas Fowell Buxton, who has been featured on the English £5 note.[22] A parliamentary bill was finally passed in 1833. But Buxton felt that this was not enough. The slave trade needed to be cut off at source. Substituting legitimate commerce for slavery seemed the only means of securing a lasting solution. His *The African Slave Trade and its Remedy* was widely read.

'It is the Bible and the plough that must regenerate Africa' was one of his slogans. His vision was for an expedition up the River Niger. It would lead to the founding of model agricultural settlements, managed by Africans. The venture would be financed by the British government, partly in reparation for the wrongs of the slave trade. So in 1841, three ships left England for West Africa, with agriculturalists, scientists, doctors and missionaries on board. After calling in at Sierra Leone to collect more crew members, they left for the River Niger on 1 July 1841. Three months later, of the 145 Europeans, 130 had contracted malaria and 40 had died. They had made it up the Niger River to Lokoja and managed to drop off a small group to start up a model farm. But even this had to be abandoned.[23]

The Africans on the Niger Expedition proved more resistant to disease than the Europeans. Among them was a young catechist, Samuel Ajayi Crowther. He had been rescued from a slave ship in 1821 and then received a missionary education in Sierra Leone. Reflecting on the disastrous outcome of the Niger Expedition, the CMS decided it should concentrate on sending Africans like Crowther to evangelise their homelands. They established a training college in Sierra Leone and ordained Crowther in 1843. He returned to Yorubaland in 1846 and had the satisfaction of seeing his mother become one of the first converts to Christianity in 1846.[24] By 1854, quinine was being used by Europeans as protection against malaria. Another expedition was planned for the Niger and Crowther joined it. It was much more successful than the 1841 expedition and another was planned for 1857.

Shortly after our arrival in Onitsha, the Bishop of Asaba arrived to collect us and take us back over the River Niger to his diocese. It would be the first of four Anglican dioceses we would visit in Eastern Nigeria. In Asaba, we stayed in the guest house in the Bishop's compound. Littered around the compound was the rusting wreckage of armoured vehicles from the Biafran civil war. Bishop Roland Nwosu spent the next ten days taking us round his diocese. Visits to a textile factory, a palm-oil mill and a college of agriculture gave us an impression of the local economy. As we visited churches, we encountered a variety of church groups. There was the uniformed Boys' Brigade, youth fellowships and the Girls' Guild. And there was the Mothers' Union, one of the mainstays of the Anglican Church in Nigeria. Often we would be treated to traditional dancing. Always, there were speeches and presentations.

Anglican life in Nigeria: *(clockwise from top left)* the Girls' Guild; the Mothers' Union; the Boys' Brigade; relics of the Biafran conflict in the Bishop of Asaba's compound   *Photos © Andrew Norman*

From Asaba, we crossed the River Niger once more and travelled to Bishop Crowther Junior Seminary, where we would stay for the next ten days. The school's name bore witness to Samuel Crowther's lasting influence in the region. In the year of the 1841 Niger Expedition, the CMS appointed a new Secretary, Henry Venn, who remained in post for thirty-one years. Venn developed further the plan for West Africa to be evangelised by Africans. He came up with his famous 'three-self' principle. CMS should establish churches that were self-governing, self-supporting and self-extending. As an outworking of Venn's principle, Crowther took over the Niger Mission shortly after the third Niger Expedition, setting up a mission station in Onitsha. 'The Committee repose entire confidence in you as Head and Director of the Niger Mission', Venn told him in 1858.[25] He was soon proposing that Crowther be appointed a missionary bishop.[26] In 1864, Samuel Ajayi Crowther was consecrated in Canterbury Cathedral, 'Bishop of Western Equatorial Africa beyond the Queen's dominions'.

Anglican schools: at the heart of missionary endeavour in southern Nigeria

Photo © Andrew Norman

Until the 1880s, the Niger Mission, based at Onitsha, was staffed entirely by Africans.[27] Bishop Crowther Junior Seminary, where we stayed, was a reminder not just of Crowther's episcopal oversight of this mission. It also represented his preferred method of evangelisation: schools. 'He introduced the mission into new places by getting rulers and elders interested in the idea of having a school of their own', explains J. F. A. Ajayi.[28] Before the advent of mission schools 'there was no organised system of written education and the population was almost entirely illiterate'.[29] This raises a question at the heart of Anglican identity. Here was an African overseeing the introduction of European-style schools. To what extent was Anglican Christianity an alien European imposition, undermining local culture?

During our time at Bishop Crowther Junior Seminary, we saw plenty of signs of traditional culture. We visited traditional rulers. It was masquerading season, when men in colourful masks and costumes parade dramatically, and with an air of menace. Masqueraders feature in one of Africa's most famous novels, *Things Fall Apart,* where villagers impersonate ancestral spirits.[30] The author, Chinua Achebe, is described by Nelson Mandela as 'the writer in whose company the prison walls fell down'.[31] Achebe tells the story of the gradual unravelling of traditional taboos as missionaries arrived in villages, built their churches on cursed ground and survived. In one incident epitomising the threat to the old order, nine masqueraders ('egwugwu') confront a resolute missionary.

Masquerading: cultural backdrop to Anglican missionary endeavour

Photo © Andrew Norman

There was undoubtedly a profound mistrust of traditional culture among European missionaries. This was linked to rejection of anything perceived as idolatry.[32] It was also fuelled by instances of what was regarded as barbaric superstition. As *Things Fall Apart* recounts, twins were understood to be cursed and were automatically left out in the forest to die. The year before our visit, a British television documentary was made to mark the centenary of the arrival in West Africa of Presbyterian missionary, Mary Slessor of Calabar. Mary Slessor is remembered locally as 'the Great Mother' for rescuing hundreds of twins. The first day the film makers arrived in Southeast Nigeria, they were astonished to find 3,000 women gathered there for the All Nigeria Women's Conference, each wearing a special dress celebrating Mary Slessor's arrival.[33]

Mistrust of traditional culture was not simply a knee-jerk reaction to rival religious beliefs and practices regarded as inhumane. It was also driven by the widespread belief in the benefits of so-called 'civilisation'. This was connected to the conviction associated with the Enlightenment, that human progress was inevitable and self-evidently manifested in Western society.[34] 'For most of the nineteenth century, British Christians believed that the missionary was called to propagate the imagined benefits of western civilisation alongside the Christian message', explains the historian of missionary endeavour, Brian Stanley.[35] Freed slaves in Sierra Leone had been beneficiaries of European education and were generally convinced of its value. This attitude continued into the twentieth century. A Nigerian Anglican scholar makes this observation about part of Asaba Diocese. 'Through its missionaries—pastors, catechists and schoolmasters—the church had close contact with the people, entering their villages and their homes, educating their children and burying their dead. Christianity was linked with enlightenment and civilisation and economic advancement. That was why thousands of Ukwuani citizens rushed into the church during the first three decades of this century.'[36]

Crowther was more willing to affirm aspects of local culture than some of his European counterparts, despite his promotion of Western education. He saw in the notion of a supreme being Chukwu, for example, a foundation for presenting a Christian notion of God. The grounds for this 'fulfilment' attitude is explained in *Things Fall Apart*. A villager tells a Christian, 'We make sacrifices to the little gods, but when they fail and there is no-one else to turn to we go back to Chukwu. We approach a great man through his servants. But when his servants fail to help us, then we go to the last source of hope.'[37]

When he had been bishop for more than ten years, it is ironic that it would be European missionaries who would question Crowther's emphasis on education. Towards the end of the nineteenth century, CMS recruited an increased number of graduates as missionaries. 'Able, young, zealous, impetuous, uncharitable and opinionated' is Ajayi's oft-quoted description of the new wave of missionaries who began arriving in Eastern Nigeria.[38] More interested in primary evangelism than the longer-term strategy of a European education, they adopted a different approach in the northern reaches of Crowther's jurisdiction. 'CMS missionaries in the Niger Mission at the end of the 1880s adopted the dress and title of the recognised Muslim teachers of the Hausa country—the mallam—and followed the Hausa diet and lifestyle. By living alongside the people on totally equal terms, they were confident that the power of the indwelling Christ would be transparently evident to the Hausa.'[39] This radical approach paradoxically combined accommodation to local practices with rejection of African missionaries. It was stopped in its tracks by disease. Its only survivor, Archdeacon Dobinson, ended up apologising for displacing African missionaries and he urged them to take the work forward instead.[40]

However much missionary attitudes towards local culture may have varied, the Anglicanism we encountered in Eastern Nigeria seemed remarkably like its English antecedent. Services were taken from the *Book of Common Prayer* and translated into Ibo. Even the optional canticles would sometimes be included. Hymns were sung dutifully from *Hymns Ancient and Modern*, to familiar English tunes. They were led by a choir robed in a remarkably similar fashion to the one at St Peter's, Ardingly, albeit in purple rather than red. In one church dedication service, we sang eleven English-style hymns. The only point at which a distinctly un-English feature was introduced was when the collection was taken. Singing African choruses, members of the congregation would cheerfully dance up the aisle to present their offering.

Scripture Union groups, their vibrancy causing Anglicans to rethink engagement with young people

Photos © Andrew Norman

As noted earlier, there were signs that the form of worship handed on by the missionaries was under strain. There was the challenge of the exuberant spirituality of young people. And there was the challenge from Pentecostal and Aladura churches, with their emphasis on healing and supernatural assistance against malevolent forces. With 1985 proclaimed as International Youth Year, the Diocese on the Niger took the opportunity to strengthen its connection with young people. It launched the Year of the Young for Christ Crusade. Some of its main protagonists were young Anglican clergy who were themselves products of the SU Movement. But not all clergy were convinced it was right to welcome the SU style of spirituality. One minister we spoke to was a great supporter of the Anglican Prayer Book. To his bewilderment, his church was packed with young people involved in the SU movement. It seemed to him that God was above all a God of order. Another Anglican minister, by contrast, defended the 'rough and ready' style of worship of the young.

There were also signs that Anglicans were starting to accommodate the Pentecostal and Aladura emphasis on healing and protection from supernatural forces. One example was the Anglican Healing Home in Igbo-Ukwu. Its Director, Nelson Kwulunebe, explained to us how he felt called to help people who in some way believed themselves to be plagued by evil spirits. He was also pastor of St Barnabas' Anglican Church, adjacent to the healing home. Its congregation exercised a disciplined ministry of prayer and fasting for the benefit of those convalescing in the home. As at Foursquare Gospel Church in Lagos, 'juju' charms had been surrendered. Those praying believed that some of the charms had previously been responsible for several deaths. 'While the traditional religious sanctions may stand in jeopardy, while reverence for the ancient cults may fade and certain customary rites disappear, belief in evil spirits (especially the fear of witchcraft and the use of charms to counter their harmful effects) is on the increase', observed Emmanuel Okolugbo elsewhere in the region.[41]

However, for the Christians in Nigeria to take culture seriously, traditional beliefs were by no means the full picture. 'We are Nigerians in a way different from how our ancestors who did not pass through Western influences were Nigerians. We are Westerners in a way different from how Westerners who did not go through traditional African cultures are Westerners. If this unique experience makes us hybrid, then we should see it as an opportunity for a synthetic viewpoint, rather than a loss of authenticity.' That was a view expressed at the time of our visit in a conference of Nigerian Catholic theologians.[42] A Baptist writer made a similar point when he referred to 'cultural flux' in Nigeria.[43] He saw this exemplified by Chinua Achebe's second great novel, *No Longer at Ease*.[44] The central character is a young Nigerian who is sent to London to be educated. He returns home, only to find himself caught between two worlds. In the words of the title, he is 'no longer at ease'.

We ended our stay in Eastern Nigeria with a visit by boat to Bonny Cathedral, on the Niger Delta. 'Things fell apart' in Bonny when Crowther finally persuaded the king of Bonny to renounce the worship of monitor lizards on Easter Day, 1867.[45] We were accompanied by a CMS missionary, Elisabeth Leicester. As an unmarried female missionary, she was a reminder of nineteenth-century examples of women's ministry in the Church of England. In the heyday of the missionary movement, in 1899, twenty-six percent of CMS missionaries were unmarried women.[46] From the oil-drilling region of the Niger Delta where Elisabeth Leicester worked, we set off with some Presbyterian missionaries for Northern Nigeria.

Nigeria came into existence as a country in 1914, the year my grandfather joined the Cinque Ports Battalion to fight on the Western Front. Events leading up to its formation reflected the haphazard way in which the British Empire developed. At the time of the 1841 Niger Expedition, none of what is now Nigeria had been annexed by Great Britain. Forty years later, during the European 'scramble for Africa', what is now Nigeria was declared as a British zone of influence. To the North was a French zone, to the East a German one. To protect against incursion from these rival European powers, a trading company was given a Royal Charter in 1886. The Royal Niger Company played this monopoly to its own advantage, but by the end of the century it was clear it was struggling in its mandate and provoking local unrest.[47] Northern Nigeria had unexploited tin-mining potential, which the French were eyeing up. The British decided to revoke the charter of the Royal Niger Company and annexe its zone of influence. But there were neither the funds nor the troops to impose direct rule. The head of the British forces, Lord Lugard, therefore proposed 'indirect rule'. The British would administer a protectorate by enhancing the authority of the Muslim emirs in the North.

This imperial chain of events impacted the development of missionary activity. Prior to the formation of the Royal Niger Company, Bishop Crowther and his fellow African missionaries had developed strong links with local traders, in the spirit of Buxton's 'Bible and the plough' anti-slavery strategy. The Royal Niger Company saw this as a threat to commercial interests, so distanced themselves from missionaries. As the Royal Niger Company pressed north, they made trading treaties with Muslim rulers which often included an undertaking not to permit missionary activity. Things had moved on since Buxton's days of humanitarian motives as a driving force for commerce, despite the fact that slave trading still existed in the North.[48] When the protectorate of Northern Nigeria was formed in 1900, Lord Lugard was committed to strengthening the emirs. 'Whatever threatened the Muhammedan religion threatened the authority of the Emirs and so imperilled the organisation of "indirect rule"', a government directive later proclaimed.[49] Crowther's strategy of missionary schools could not simply be extended to the British protectorate of Northern Nigeria.

In the twenty-first century, northern Nigeria has become renowned for the extremist activities of the Islamist group, Boko Haram. Indiscriminate killings in the name of Boko Haram have been accompanied by abductions, including the notorious kidnapping of over two hundred schoolgirls from a secondary school in Borno State. Boko Haram translates as 'Western education is forbidden'. During the colonial era, restrictions on missionary schools in northern Nigeria meant that Western education was much less freely available than in southern Nigeria. The north–south disparity of educational level was one of the contributory factors to the civil war from 1967 to 1970.[50]

But there was never a total ban on missionary schools in the north. Prior to the formation of the British protectorate, not all of the North was uniformly Muslim. In the nineteenth century, there had been a Muslim Jihad under Usman dan Fodio which extended Muslim influence beyond the cities. By the beginning of the twentieth century, there were three categories of areas: Muslim rulers in a Muslim area; Muslim rulers in a pagan area; pagan rulers in a pagan area. In the third category, missionaries were allowed to set up schools without the sanction of Muslim leaders. In practice, the take-up was patchy. Not all missionaries were convinced of the value of missionary schools, as we have seen. Missionaries from non-denominational 'faith' missions outnumbered CMS missionaries and only gradually were they persuaded of the long-term benefit of mission schools.

Travelling from the Niger Delta region in the South, we arrived on the Jos Plateau in the North. It is an island of granite masses enjoying a much more temperate climate than the plains of most of Northern Nigeria. When Northern Nigeria became a protectorate, the Jos Plateau was an area without a strong Muslim presence, so missionary activity had been relatively unimpeded.[51] We stayed in a hostel owned by the Church of Christ in Nigeria (COCIN), a denomination that had grown out of the non-denominational Sudan United Mission (SUM). It was one of the largest denominations in Northern Nigeria, as was the Evangelical Church of West Africa (ECWA), formed out of the Sudan Interior Mission (SIM).

One of our first engagements on the Jos Plateau was to be a lunch with SIM missionaries serving with ECWA. We never made it. Calling in first to another appointment, we were told the secret police (the 'NSO') wanted to see us. Without knowing why, we found ourselves escorted to the police headquarters. We were detained and questioned for three days. 'We don't like educated people travelling round our country with nothing much to do', we were told by one of our questioners. There was talk of us being transferred to Kirikiri, the high security prison in Lagos, where an English businessman had recently been incarcerated. The SUM's eventual acknowledgement of the value of mission schools fortunately worked in our favour. Another missionary we were due to visit had been headmaster at Gindiri School. He took our case up with a senior police official who had been one of his pupils. We were released, but our passports were retained. We were forbidden to leave Plateau State until authorisation had been given for the return of our passports.

Despite being called 'the suspects', we had been treated courteously and imprisoned in an office rather than a cell. Relieved nonetheless to be free, we were disappointed not to be able to proceed to the great Muslim cities of Kano and Zaria in the North. In particular, we had been looking forward to going to Zaria, one of the most effective zones of Anglican influence in the North. With finite resources, the missionary societies had divided up the north into such zones of influence and had tended not to stray onto one another's patches. Anglicans, under the CMS, had relatively few zones.[52]

Anglican activity in Zaria demonstrated that Lord Lugard's policy of exclusion was not absolute. If the emir welcomed missionaries, that was fine. A CMS missionary doctor, Walter Miller, had joined an expedition to Northern Nigeria at the time the Northern protectorate was first formed. A proficient Hausa speaker, he won the respect of the local emir, who invited him to set up a mission in the city of Zaria. Lugard was impressed with Miller too.[53] He was permitted to found a school, attended by Muslims. For a long time, this was the only mission school in the Muslim areas. For about thirty years, CMS work in Zaria was the only missionary work in the traditional Hausa Muslim Emirates. 'The missionaries lived as much as possible like the people among whom they worked and were friendly and accessible at all times.'[54] Here we have yet another variation in the combination of Western education and attitude to local culture.

Miller was clear that the mission's efforts should draw local people to Christianity, even when the British authorities became increasingly uneasy about this.[55] A major breakthrough came in 1913 when two representatives of the Isawa people walked thirty-five miles to see him. 'Isa' is the Arabic form of Jesus. They spoke of many scattered families who were awaiting the full teaching of Jesus.[56] Miller learned how a nineteenth-century Arabic scholar living in Kano, Malam Ibrahim, had been fascinated by references to Jesus. 'I determined to make a careful study right through the Koran and collect all references to the Prophet Jesus. Who is this of whom our own Prophet writes?' Malam Ibrahim gathered a group around him and began to encounter opposition from Emir Bello of Kano. Continuing undeterred, Malam Ibrahim was eventually seized, taken to Kano market and impaled on a stake. Anticipating trouble, he had urged his followers to flee, prophesying that God would reveal the true faith to them later on. 'These people knew no Christians', Miller wrote, 'and nothing of the Christian religion: they had remained Moslems, performing all the Moslem ritual and holding to all their religion and law, with some slight deviations, enough to make them non-conformists while essentially Moslems.'

Following the visit, some of the Muslim converts to Christianity went out to preach to them. It was decided that it would be good if these scattered Isawa people could come and live together as a community. The Emir of Zaria was reluctant at first to support this, but eventually made a plot of land available. One hundred and twenty Isawa people came to live at Gimli, baptisms took place and another school was opened. An Anglican clergyman from the Caribbean came to work with them and started sugar-crushing as a means of livelihood.

A number of leading public figures would come from this Christian community at Gimli in future years, including a Federal Commissioner, the first Nigeria Vice-Chancellor of Ahmadu Bello University, the first Northern woman to become a State Commissioner and Yakubu Gowon, the Head of State during the Nigerian Civil War.[57] Yakubu Gowon was ousted as President in a bloodless coup in 1976, while he was at a conference in Kenya. 'All the world's a stage', he reflected in a press conference, quoting Shakespeare, 'And all the men and women merely players; they have their exits and their entrances.'[58] He moved to England and studied for a doctorate at Warwick University in West African economic history. The year before our visit, he was appointed a lay selector for Church of England ordinands.[59]

Sadly, the NSO's travel restriction ruled out our planned visit to this significant Anglican centre in Northern Nigeria. We contented ourselves with visiting an Anglican agricultural project on the edge of the Jos Plateau and a festival of song at St Piran's Anglican Church, the former expatriate church, visited by Queen Elizabeth II in 1956. We were able to visit plenty of non-Anglican churches and projects on the Jos Plateau, but when our passports were finally returned to us, our visas had almost expired. We flew down to Lagos, to discover that our airline had grounded its only plane, with no alternative arrangements. We had no desire to overstay our visa and clash with the authorities again, but nor did either of us have a credit card. We somehow managed to phone home from the crowded bookings desk of British Caledonian Airways and persuade one of our parents to buy us a ticket home.

A month after we returned to England, Major General Buhari's government was ousted in a coup. One of the main reasons reported was the unrestrained activities of the NSO.[60] Thirty years later, Buhari would become head of state once again, this time as an elected President. His no-nonsense track record as a Muslim military ruler would appeal to voters aghast at the abduction of school children and the massacres perpetrated by the Islamist group, Boko Haram.

⚜

Despite our unnerving brush with Buhari's over-zealous secret police, our dominant experience had been of outgoing Nigerian hospitality. Aided by Nigerians and Western missionaries, we had received an unforgettable induction into Christianity in Nigeria. In spite of the heavy casualty rate among European missionaries in the so-called 'White Man's Grave', the so-called 'White Man's God' had undoubtedly been recognised as the God of many Nigerians too. Anglicans had played a leading role in this missionary enterprise, especially in Southern Nigeria. African Anglicans, under Samuel Crowther, had been trail-blazers.

Yet the Anglican Church in Nigeria had retained many of the trappings of English Anglicanism. Under pressure from young people and other more Pentecostal forms of Christianity, it was beginning to take steps to adapt further to its context. This meant taking traditional culture more seriously, especially in relation to fears about malevolent forces and hopes for physical healing. It also meant moving with the times, as Nigeria moved forward with a hybrid culture of the old and new.

In both the old and the new there were dangers to guard against. In one direction was pressure to resort to traditional religious practices in time of crisis. In the other direction were new pressures from uneven economic development, the loss of traditional sanctions and the prevalence of corruption. In both directions we encountered Anglican efforts to counter these pressures. Yet, as one Anglican commentator reflected, there was an underlying question of whether the Christianity brought by the missionaries had matched the scope of the worldview it was replacing. For Christians in mission-founded churches, was all of life viewed from a religious point of view, or was Christian practice limited to Sunday worship and other self-contained compartments of life?[61] Had Western Christians exported a privatised faith?

The introduction of Anglican Christianity had been closely associated with British imperial efforts. However, the relationship had been uneven. Initially, humanitarian efforts had brought missionaries and government together, in the first Niger Expedition and its aftermath. In time, however, missionary efforts would be resisted by imperial agents, whether it be the Royal Niger Company or Lord Lugard in his policy of indirect rule in the North. In the south, the British government was content to rely mostly on missionaries to provide education which did not require government funding. In post-independence Nigeria, Western education seemed to be greatly valued, even if there would be a belated backlash from the extremist Islamist group, Boko Haram, more than fifty years after independence. Limiting Western education in Muslim-dominated Northern Nigeria had created a disparity in the years following independence and this had contributed to the Biafran civil war. In India, I had noticed how even Western classical music could be valued in post-colonial times.

Nigeria had witnessed varied Anglican encounters with other religious systems. In common with the missionary movement more generally, there had been strong objections to idolatry. This had sometimes been tempered by a willingness to discern aspects of traditional beliefs that were consistent with Christianity. Engagement with Islam, while constrained by government, had unashamedly hoped for conversion. It had nonetheless been respectful, but had not led to the kind of scholarly engagement that the Cambridge and Oxford Missions had been founded to provide in India. As far as other churches were concerned, the Anglican missionaries were content to leave large tracts of Nigeria to other missions, especially in the North. In more recent times, there had been a growing sense of competition with other churches, especially the newer Pentecostal churches. By contrast, in India Anglicans had integrated their activities with other churches, in the formation of the United Churches.

In Nigeria, the sense of estrangement from other parts of the Anglican Communion was yet to come. But we were repeatedly asked how a Bishop of Durham who did not believe in the resurrection could have been appointed. David Jenkins had been consecrated Bishop of Durham the previous year at York Minster. Three days later, the minster had been struck by lightning. Some were quick to interpret this as a sign of God's displeasure.[62] It was not the only symptom of unease in the Church of England. The Church's engagement in urban areas was also raising concern, as I would find out first hand in the months ahead.

6

Urban Life, Civil Strife and Anglican Heritage

'THE WATERFRONT WAS a magical mixture of textiles and spice, tar and soot, ropes and rigging, sails and smokestacks, horses and carriages, kegs, casks and barrels and ships flying the flags and colours of every nation.'[1] That was Liverpool when Buxton's ships were setting sail for the first Niger Expedition and Liverpool was the second largest port in the British Empire. In 1985, it was a very different story. 'The 1980s was one of the bleakest decades in the long and colourful history of the city of Liverpool', laments one local historian.[2]

On my return from Nigeria, most of the following year would be spent in Liverpool. I travelled up to Liverpool in October to meet with the team rector of the parish I would serve in as a lay assistant. A Channel 4 News reporter joined us for lunch. The Church of England had just published its report, *Faith in the City*.[3] A Conservative cabinet minister had scornfully dismissed it as 'pure Marxist theology'.[4] Neville Black, a dynamic inner city priest, was being asked for his views.

Looking back, twenty-five years later, the church historian Adrian Hastings was clear that *Faith in the City* could not be brushed aside so easily. 'It seems likely that ... the two most significant events in English church history in the 1980s will be the Pope's visit to Canterbury and the publication of *Faith in the City.*'[5] Liverpool was heavily implicated in both these events. Together they provided fresh impetus for the Church's response to what *Faith in the City* described as 'Urban Priority Areas' (UPAs).

The Pope's visit to Canterbury in 1982 was combined with his visit to Liverpool, a city with a troubled history of tensions between Catholics and other Christians. The Catholic and Anglican cathedrals are connected by the appropriately named Hope Street. Liverpool's Anglican bishop and Catholic archbishop accompanied Pope John Paul II as he walked down Hope Street. This symbolised renewed co-operation in addressing the social deprivation besetting the once-great city of Liverpool.

Faith in the City had been the Church of England's response to another of the twentieth century's wake-up calls. The same summer when Britain had celebrated Prince Charles' marriage to Lady Diana Spencer, petrol bombs had been hurled at police in London, Birmingham and Liverpool. These urban riots had started in London, when plain clothes police resorted to heavy-handed tactics to stop street crime in Brixton.[6] In Liverpool, they erupted in Toxteth. One Friday in July, a young man on a motorbike was being chased by police. When he fell off his bike, local people came to his aid and started to assault the police officers. As more police cars arrived, they threw stones and bottles. Rioting continued into the night and flared up again the following evening. Police cars were captured and aimed driverless at police lines. Fire engines were smashed. A cinema and a men's club were burnt. Looters moved in. Four weeks later, there was more rioting. But this time the police were ready. They had helmets and shields. They charged the rioters in vans. For the first time on the English mainland, tear gas was used.[7]

Initial conclusions were quickly drawn about the causes of the rioting: unemployment, government spending priorities and urban decay. In Liverpool, the Anglican bishop and Catholic archbishop quickly emerged as community leaders. Michael Heseltine was appointed Minister for Merseyside. Nationally, Archbishop Robert Runcie commissioned the working group that would produce *Faith in the City*. The Anglican Bishop of Liverpool, David Sheppard, would join eighteen specialists and clergy on the working party. This was the same David Sheppard who had been England cricket captain and had visited the group set up at Ardingly College after Jack Winslow's mission in the 1950s. 'We are deeply disturbed by what we have seen and heard' reported the working group.[8] They offered thirty-eight recommendations to the Church of England and twenty-three to the nation. Much of what the report was advocating was reflected in the priorities of the parish in which I was now due to serve.

The Parish of St Luke in the City was formed in 1981, the year of the riots. It covered part of Toxteth and much of the centre of Liverpool, including both cathedrals. It combined three distinctive churches and their congregations. St Stephen's was a red-brick church, with a strong Anglo-Catholic ethos. It shared a patch of land with the lone survivor of a Victorian terrace,

The Oxford pub. St Bride's Church looked like a Greek temple, in the classical Palladian style that would go out of fashion soon after it was built in 1830. Its tradition was more evangelical. St Michael's, down the hill from the Anglican cathedral, had been built on the site of an older church that had been bombed during World War Two. Flat-roofed and functional, it served the multi-ethnic area that encompassed Chinatown and part of the docklands. Again, its tradition was more evangelical. The church of St Luke, after which the parish was named, had also been bombed. Its ruins were left as an open space for the people of Liverpool.

Liverpool: *(clockwise from top left)* St Luke's bombed-out church; St Bride's, with its Palladian-style architecture; St Luke's from the shopping centre; St Stephen's, sharing its turf with the Oxford pub *Photos © Andrew Norman*

'Grey walls, littered streets, boarded up windows, graffiti, demolition and debris are the drearily standard features of the districts and parishes with which we are concerned', the writers of *Faith in the City* grimly reported.[9] This certainly applied to parts of the parish of St Luke in the City, though efforts were now underway to renew housing in several corners of the neighbourhood. Crime was another feature of UPAs, as I would experience a week after my arrival in Liverpool. I returned to my flat to discover the door into the hallway eerily open. Inside, the kitchen window had been prised open. My camera and radio were missing, along with potatoes and Branston pickle.

After effects of the Toxteth riots, five years on

Photo © Andrew Norman

Housing around St Bride's Church, where my flat was located, bore witness to more affluent times. The grand Georgian terraces were reminiscent of Sherlock Holmes' London. One of them, Rodney Street, is where a future prime minister, William Gladstone, had been born. Now they had mostly been taken over by hostels and housing associations, with petty crime commonplace. Two of the streets were part of the city's kerb-crawling red-light district. 'Are you looking for business?' I would be asked cheerily as I walked to church.

The parish also bore witness to Liverpool's past as an international port. There was a Swedish church, a German church and a Chinese fellowship. Changes in international shipping had made a major contribution to Liverpool's economic decline. Since the 1970s, the introduction of container shipping had massively reduced the need for labour on the docks. The city's plight had been worsened by factories closing down. Alarming levels of unemployment had followed. *Faith in the City* proposed that each UPA parish should carry out an audit, to gain a better understanding of its local community. That was one of the tasks the team rector set me. It meant going down to the City Planning offices and collecting data from the 1981 census. The parish of 13,000 residents could be subdivided into forty-one enumeration districts. Some of these encompassed Liverpool's notorious high-rise flats, so the districts could be geographically small. In one tower block, sixty-one percent of males available for work were unemployed. The unemployment average for the parish (male and female) was thirty-five percent. Less than four percent of houses were privately owned.

Combined church attendance at the three churches was around 120 each Sunday. In the case of St Michael's, only six of the forty worshippers lived in the parish. The rest had moved away from the area, but chose to travel back each Sunday to where they used to live. In some streets around St Bride's, a third of the households contained one pensioner living alone. St Bride's therefore tended to attract the elderly, along with young families and a few international students. One of my tasks was to be the bingo caller at the pensioners' lunch club, offering prizes of tinned food. Another was to help run the children's group at St Bride's each Sunday. Of the twenty children who attended, almost all came from single parent families. We organised outings for young and old, with the help of a coach owned by the parish. A camping weekend in the Lake District was a completely new experience for the children. A coach trip for pensioners to the seaside town of Rhyl was more familiar to its participants. One of them, Mabel, decided to liven it up by wandering off. After raising the alarm, we eventually found her charming the staff at the local hospital.

Lunch club, before
the bingo started

Photo © Andrew Norman

Faith in the City judged that 'for the vast majority of people in the UPAS the Church of England ... is seen as irrelevant'.[10] In a parish of 13,000 where 120 people attended Church of England services in three places of worship, it was not hard to see how that conclusion was reached. It was echoing the Archbishops' reports in World War One. *Faith in the City* stressed the need to relate more effectively to each UPA neighbourhood and estate. It also recommended collaboration with 'the best experiences of local life' in order to contribute to the transformation of life in UPAS.[11]

This was very much the approach in St Luke in the City. Efforts were made to be present where people naturally gathered. There were forty pubs in the parish. St Stephen's had particularly close links with The Oxford pub, working together to raise money for children's holidays. The churchwarden at St Bride's was involved in the Caribbean Club. Collaborative relationships were developed with the police, victim support, the probation service and housing agencies. Time was also invested in the schools, including a Church of England primary school. St Bride's Church was reordered to create offices around the nave of the church. One of these was used by the Manpower Services Commission to provide office skills to job seekers.

Another of the offices in St Bride's was occupied by the Evangelical Urban Training Project (EUTP), whose patron was Bishop David Sheppard. This non-denominational organisation was addressing another of the issues identified by *Faith in the City:* 'It is the consistently middle class presentation of the gospel and style of church life which creates a gulf between it and most working class people.'[12] *Faith in the City* judged that the Church of England had generally failed to engage contextually in urban settings. '[T]he UPA Church must be sensitive to the *local cultures and life-styles* in its leadership, worship and manner of operating.'[13] The EUTP needed no convincing and sought to develop resources and approaches to learning for those 'who can read but don't'. These insights were carried across to a diocesan leadership programme, GUML (Group for Urban Ministry and Leadership), spearheaded by the Team Rector, Neville Black. GUML emphasised small group learning and sought to be sensitive to the context from which local leaders were drawn. A GUML group was set up at St Michael's. A leading figure was a retired electrician.[14]

One way in which the Church of England had responded to the challenge of cities in earlier times was by building churches. 'Until the great programme of Anglican church building in 1830s, there was little effective Anglican presence in cities' noted *Faith in the City*. Often these churches were funded by private individuals, as in the case of St Bride's. One benefactor of Liverpool churches who lived near St Bride's was William Gladstone's father. A merchant benefitting from slavery, John Gladstone was opposed to William Wilberforce's campaign but was nonetheless an ardent Anglican. He funded two churches.[15] The Liverpool church building tradition reached its apex with the construction of the two cathedrals. Construction of the Anglican cathedral commenced in 1904. Its completion in 1978 was celebrated in the presence of the Queen. It is the largest cathedral in the world after St Peter's Rome. Commanding the Liverpool skyline, it conveys a presence that has never been matched by grassroots commitment. Completed three years before the Toxteth riots, it could all-too-easily be seen as representing 'an era and a grandiosity of ecclesiastical aspiration long passed, a product not of the seventies but of late Victorianism'.[16] Our clergy team meetings were held in the cathedral and I enjoyed attending musical events and gatherings with guest speakers, such as Archbishop Benson Idahosa, whose healing crusade I had experienced in Lagos. However, it seemed unclear how a building of that scale could serve the UPAs on its doorstep.

The Roman Catholic cathedral had been completed twenty years earlier. There was a strong Roman Catholic presence in the parish, with residents of the Chatsworth Estate being predominantly Catholic. *Faith in the City* argued that UPA parishes should be local, outward-looking and participating, with an ecumenical bias.[17] In Liverpool, Bishop David Shepherd provided a strong ecumenical lead. In St Luke's Parish, this was mirrored by involvement with Catholic organisations such as St Vincent's primary school and the charitable order, the Knights of St Columba. In Toxteth, there were no fewer than forty-seven Christian groups meeting for worship, of which just nine were Anglican. For Anglicans to have acted as if they were the sole Christian presence would have been ludicrous. In St Luke in the City there were seven congregations in addition to the parish churches, plus the cathedrals. *Faith in the City* was not simply advocating symbolic ecumenical Christian presence in UPA parishes. It was adamant that 'the most urgent task facing the Church is nurturing...common belief in God towards an authentic Christian faith'.[18] In the parish of St Luke in the City, the challenge seemed as immense as the Anglican cathedral. 'If the Church of England is committed to staying and growing in UPAs...it will have to change.'[19]

It was somewhat surreal living in a parish of such high unemployment while applying for graduate jobs. After being judged ill-suited to the worlds of biscuits, clothes and freight distribution, I was finally given the choice between soap powder and banknotes. Working for a security printers would mean guaranteed overseas travel, so that tipped the scales. After rounding off my time in Liverpool with a church-run street party, I prepared to start as a business trainee with Thomas De La Rue. I would end up working for this unusual company for six years. During that time, as a by-product, I was introduced to Anglican life in yet more locations.

De La Rue is a British-based company, founded in 1838. Its main offices were in Basingstoke, in Hampshire. Basingstoke had been a market town until the 1970s. Major redevelopment took place at that time, with communities relocated from the East End of London. A commercial area was developed, attracting businesses such as IBM and MacMillan Publishing. The location suited De La Rue well, as it gave ready access to Heathrow Airport. St Mary's

Eastrop, the church I started attending, was on the edge of the business area and contained the 1970s flat-roofed housing of the Riverdene Estate. The church building was tiny, but its multiple congregations encompassed many, such as myself, who lived outside the parish. An evangelical church, it had a strong emphasis on evangelism and discipleship. Twelve home groups formed the backbone of church life during the week. For those in their twenties, there was a popular group which met after church on Sunday evenings, providing a means of quickly getting to know people.

My first year with De La Rue was spent on three-month placements. Half the time was in Basingstoke and half the time at other locations. De La Rue printed banknotes for about a hundred countries and issuing authorities around the world. The notes were printed in factories in England, New Zealand, Hong Kong, Singapore and Malta. Graduate trainees were required to spend three months working on the factory shop floor. This would have been problematic in the heavily unionised printing factories in England, so we were dispatched to Malta for three summer months instead. The factory operated twenty-four hours a day. No matter which eight-hour shift you were on, you could happily spend part of the day on the beach.

Malta had been a strategic Mediterranean island for the British navy. It had served as a refuelling point en route to the Suez Canal and India. There was therefore a residual Anglican presence. The spire of the Anglican cathedral forms part of the iconic view of the capital, Valetta. It is the Church of England that unwittingly stopped Malta becoming a county of England. In June 1955, Dom Mintoff became Labour Prime Minister of Malta. Educated at Oxford University, his aim was to integrate Malta with the United Kingdom.[20] The British government approved the principle of integration and convened a roundtable. A proposal granting Malta three seats in the House of Commons was agreed. However, the Roman Catholic hierarchy in Malta judged that the established Church of England risked compromising the Catholic character of the island. A referendum in 1956 was therefore boycotted by supporters of the pro-Catholic Nationalist Party and Mintoff's aspirations were sunk. Ironically, Anglicans had always been careful not to undermine the Catholic presence in Malta. When setting up a bishopric to cover the southern Mediterranean, Gibraltar was chosen over Malta in 1842, to avoid the impression of competing with the Catholic Bishop of Malta.[21] By the time I was printing banknotes by night and sunning myself by day, the Labour Party had been in power continuously for sixteen years, aligning the country with Libya. Elections were held while I was there, with the Catholic Church still openly backing the Nationalist Party. Violence was forecast and expatriates were advised to stay at home on election day, which we dutifully did. English Anglicans were no longer implicated in Malta's political calculations. Malta had moved to full independence in 1964.

Election victory in Malta, with the spire of St Paul's Anglican Cathedral in the background

Photo © Andrew Norman

Yet there were two thriving Anglican congregations on the island. In addition to the cathedral in Valetta, there was Holy Trinity, Sliema, fifteen minutes' walk from my apartment. It offered Anglican worship to expatriates and tourists. Among the regulars in the congregation were a retired British Army major, an English teacher and her Maltese husband. Our annual church fete was hosted at the residence of the British High Commissioner. Apart from the guaranteed sunshine, this fundraiser felt very much like the archetypal Church of England depicted in the second-hand Agatha Christie novels on sale there.

On returning to England's more bracing climate, further placements in Basingstoke led into my first major assignment. I would be moving to the North East of England, to a banknote printing factory in Gateshead. My initial job was to programme the printing of 45 million notes a week, armed with a pencil, an eraser and a healthy respect for shop floor managers. I opted to live in Newcastle upon Tyne, a twenty-minute drive north. Knowing my posting would last no more than two years, it made sense to join a church where I could settle quickly and make friends. I therefore headed for Jesmond Parish Church. Five hundred people attended each Sunday and I soon found myself co-leading a house group and an enquirers' group. As with St Mary's Eastrop in Basingstoke, there was a social group for 20 and 30-year-olds, appropriately called Meeting Point. It was a valuable means of developing a social life in an unfamiliar city.

It was just as I moved to Newcastle that one of the sadder episodes in the life of the twentieth-century Church of England took place. Up until then, it had been the custom for the annual address list of all Church of England

clergy to be preceded by an anonymous preface. The 1987 *Crockford's* preface
had contained pointed criticism of the current Archbishop of Canterbury,
Robert Runcie. 'He has the disadvantage of the intelligent pragmatist: the
desire to put off all questions until someone else makes a decision', the author
ventured. '... [T]he Archbishop is usually to be found nailing his colours to
the fence.' When it came to senior appointments, the Archbishop displayed
'a distaste for those who are so unstylish as to inhabit the clerical ghettos of
Evangelicalism and Anglo-Catholicism', favouring 'men of liberal disposition
with a moderately Catholic style which is not taken to the point of having
firm principles'.[22] It was clearly the work of a church insider, so the hunt
was on to uncover their identity. The culprit, Garry Bennett, initially denied
he had penned it. When it was clear he would be identified, he committed
suicide, killing his beloved cat first.

Garry Bennett had been a prominent Anglo-Catholic who himself had not
been offered a senior appointment. This had led, many were sagely concluding,
to a lack of objectivity in his analysis. But the shocked reaction included some
who felt Bennett's critique was not that wide of the mark. They included the
vicar of Jesmond Parish Church, David Holloway. He was a member of the
influential Policy Sub-Committee of the General Synod, as Garry Bennett
had been too. The Sub-Committee met with Archbishop Runcie very soon
after Bennett's suicide. At the end of the meeting, David Holloway made a
separate statement to the press, saying he had 'not been allowed to raise in
the sub-committee points concerning the contents of the preface', and he
believed Bennett had been 'speaking a word of prophecy'.[23] Despite David
Holloway's efforts to engage fully in the synodical life of the church, he was
becoming increasingly frustrated by what he saw as the marginalisation of
the concerns of evangelical Anglicans. This would lead to his helping found
the controversial pressure group, Reform, six years later.

In the meantime, after my first year worshipping at Jesmond Parish Church,
one of David Holloway's colleagues started to talk with me about my own sense
of calling within the Church of England. Knowing I would move every two
years and might be posted overseas after Gateshead, he suggested this could be
the right time to explore ordination more seriously. That meant meeting with
the Diocesan Director of Ordinands of Newcastle Diocese, Kenneth Gill, a
former bishop in the Church of South India. By the time De La Rue came up
with my next assignment, I was already being lined up for a selection conference.

My next posting proved not to be overseas, but back to Basingstoke. I would
leave the field of banknote printing and join De La Rue Identity Systems.
Customers were still mostly overseas governments, but what they were offered

were identity cards, national registration systems and help with elections. Whatever the outcome of my forthcoming selection conference for ordination, I felt it only right that I should see this two-year posting through. So I needed to decide where to live. One option was to live in London and commute to Basingstoke. The other was to live in Basingstoke. I decided to discuss this with the vicar of St Mary's Eastrop. After church one Sunday, I laid my cards on the table, naively enquiring whether there might be ways I could become more fully involved in the life of St Mary's while I was pursuing ordination. 'Why don't you come to supper?' Clive Hawkins suggested, deftly spotting an extra pair of hands, 'and we can discuss it further'. On the night, I was somewhat surprised to find others had been invited too. By the end of the meal, I had agreed to co-lead a teenage confirmation class with a young marketing executive working for MacMillan Publishing. By default, I would be staying in Basingstoke.

Five months later, my co-leader and I were engaged. By the end of the summer, Amanda and I were married. In the meantime, I had attended my selection conference. This was the standard means of selection introduced at the end of World War Two. After three days of interviews and group exercises, I was recommended for training in the Church of England.

My adventures with De La Rue were not over though. This was 1991, two years after the Berlin Wall had come down. With the ending of the Cold War, multi-party democracy was breaking out around the world. In Angola—in South-West Africa—the Cuban troops had returned home. There had been a ceasefire between the Soviet-backed government (MPLA) and the rebel forces (UNITA). A timetable for elections had been agreed in the Bicesse Peace Accord. Yet Angola's infrastructure was in a terrible state after sixteen years of civil war and 350,000 deaths. For elections to take place in line with the peace accord, the whole population would need to be registered and issued with identity cards, in record time. Two of us travelled to Angola for a two-week feasibility study. As I got off the plane, I was mistaken by the British military attaché for a landmine clearance specialist. Angola's massive landmine problem would be publicised by Princess Diana a few years later, when she visited Angola for herself and called for an international landmine ban.[24] Angola is a fertile country, rich in natural resources such as oil and diamonds, but in 1991 the after-effects of war were evident in countryside and cities alike. There were just two international hotels in the capital, Luanda, and the one we stayed in had no hot water and frequent power cuts.

As we travelled around the war-torn country, meeting with officials and witnessing electioneering in the bush, it was clear that there was a longing for lasting peace. Following our study, De La Rue was awarded the contract, so I spent much of the year travelling back and forth to Angola. In the face of much scepticism, the five million Angolans were registered and issued with ID cards in just four months. De La Rue was asked to assist in the logistics of the elections too, supplying all the polling stations.[25] The United Nations Special Representative, Margaret Anstee, worked valiantly to keep the elections on track. During the two days of polling, there was a ninety-two percent turnout. 'I therefore have the honour', pronounced Margaret Anstee, 'in my capacity as Special Representative of the Secretary General, to certify that, with all the deficiencies taken into account, the elections held on 29/30 September can be considered to have been generally free and fair.'[26] Tragically, the rebel leader, Jonas Savimbi, was unable to accept the result. Civil war broke out again and continued for another ten years. 'Whole cities were reduced to ruins, hundreds of thousands of people were killed or died from war-related deprivation and disease, and millions were displaced'.[27]

Post-Cold War Africa, with the UN involved in reconstruction and peace-keeping, would be the context for much of the Anglican Communion in the coming decade. In Angola, the Anglican presence had been too small to make a major contribution to nation-building in 1991. In fact, only six years earlier, its very existence had caught Anglican mission agencies by surprise. An Angolan, Alexander Domingos, turned up at Selly Oak College in Birmingham. He announced he was from the Anglican Church in Angola.[28] Angola had been a Portuguese colony until 1975, with longstanding resistance to foreign missionary activity. Despite this official policy, in 1922, an Anglican lay reader from Toxteth had slipped into Northern Angola and built a school. Archibald Patterson witnessed thousands of conversions and trained his converts to use the *Book of Common Prayer*. He was finally expelled in 1961, leaving behind many trained evangelists. Under Alexander Domingos, many of the converts remained firmly Anglican in the troubled decades which followed.[29]

Two years before the Angolan elections, a bishop from Mozambique, another Portuguese-speaking country, had visited Angola. Bishop Dinis Sengulane encountered a community of 10,000 Anglicans. He ordained Domingos as priest and other leaders as deacons. The number of Anglicans in Angola would grow to 25,000 over the next fifteen years. Their church life would be animated by choirs using locally composed tunes in their worship.[30]

If Anglicans were in no position to make a major contribution to peace-building in Angola, the same was not true in Mozambique. Achieving its independence from Portugal in 1975, the same year as Angola, Mozambique had also experienced years of civil war. Its peace accord would be signed in 1992, the year of Angola's elections. Anglican leaders would play a crucial role in bringing the warring factions together. As early as 1982, prompted by the Anglican Diocese of Lebombo, the Christian Council of Mozambique (CCM) met with the President of Mozambique and began to discuss ways of ending the war. His successor, Joaquim Chissano, proved more receptive, as Catholic bishops stepped up their own call for peace talks. A task force was set up, with two Catholic bishops and two representatives from the CCM. One of them was Bishop Dinis Sengulane. Their strategy was to work with the Kenyan government to arrange a meeting with the rebel group, Renamo. Travelling to Kenya, the group met with the Permanent Secretary for Foreign Affairs, Bethuel Kiplagat, an active member of the Anglican Church. He brokered a meeting with Renamo leaders in Kenya, sitting in on the meeting himself.[31] This was a year in which Anglicans would be visible for their political involvement in his own country. The Bishop of Mount Kenya East, David Gitari, had exposed election-rigging and narrowly missed being killed by thugs as a result.[32] This was the Kenyan bishop who had once been the General Secretary of the Pan African Fellowship of Evangelical Students, whose Nigerian outworking (NIFES) I had encountered in 1985.

The group of four from Mozambique reported back to their President and met again in Kenya, this time with the leader of Renamo, Afonso Dhlakama. Further shuttle diplomacy led to direct peace talks in Rome in 1990. These were hosted by the Catholic lay community, Sant'Egidio, which had been involved in Mozambique in humanitarian work since the 1970s. They too had forged links with the Mozambique government and Renamo, having negotiated the release of missionaries held hostage by Renamo in 1982.[33] Their involvement in Mozambique would generate strong links with Anglicans too, as I would experience for myself in later years. In 1992, ecumenical co-operation would lead to Mozambique's peace accord being signed, with the United Nations committing monitors and peace-keeping troops. It would prove more enduring than Angola's. Bishop Sengulane continued to contribute to reconciliation, through founding the Transforming Arms into Tools programme. Encouraged by this scheme, an estimated 600,000 weapons would be exchanged for books, bicycles, building materials and sewing machines. Bishop Sengulane started wearing a crucifix made from parts of surrendered weapons.[34] He arranged for 'The Tree of Life', a sculpture made from surrendered weapons by Mozambican artists, to be put on display in the British Museum.

Anglicans forging peace in Mozambique: the 'Tree of Life', made of surrendered weapons, on display in the British Museum   *Photos © Andrew Norman*

A year into married life, I prepared to exchange post-Cold War Africa for an English theological college. Amanda and I decided to take the kind of holiday that would be unaffordable once I started training for ordination. We spent three weeks in China and Thailand, armed with our Lonely Planet Travel guide. Not realising what was in store after ordination, I assumed this would mark the end of my globe-trotting days. On our return from the Far East, we moved to Cambridge.

As I was still under thirty, I would spend the full three years training for ordination, at Ridley Hall theological college. Amanda secured a new appointment as marketing manager for a Cambridge-based publishing company. She would also train to be a Church of England reader, concentrating full-time on this in my final year.

Ridley Hall is just a few minutes' walk from King's College, Cambridge, with its picture-postcard scenes of punting on the River Cam. Opened in 1881, Ridley's red-brick buildings match those of its neighbour, Newnham College, where Margaret Anstee, UN Special Representative to Angola, would shortly be appointed honorary fellow. Like Westcott House, also in Cambridge, Ridley Hall was founded to train clergy. In its early years, it would take graduates, most of whom had already studied in Cambridge. Rather like a PGCE teacher training course, it would add up to a year's training, concentrating on courses that would complement earlier studies. Before it was founded, relatively few clergy were trained at theological colleges. Clergy were more likely to have studied classics than biblical studies. In the immediate aftermath of World War One, only five serving diocesan bishops had been to theological college. Cosmo Lang, enthroned as my grandfather moved from Canada to Scotland, was the first Archbishop of Canterbury to study at theological college. His successor, William Temple, never went to theological college and Geoffrey Fisher, who followed him, only spent a very short time at Wells Theological College, while Headmaster of Repton School.[35] Nevertheless, Ridley Hall and other theological colleges would shape the ministry of many Church of England clergy, with global consequences for the development of Anglicanism. Before Ridley Hall's first Principal left to become Bishop of Durham in 1899, he oversaw the training of 514 ordinands. Of these, 117 became missionaries and a further 76 served overseas in posts such as colonial chaplaincies.[36]

By the 1990s, the norm was for stipendiary (paid) clergy to train for an undergraduate award in theology, even if they already had an undergraduate award in another subject, as I did. After World War One, the Church of England had started providing its own means of academic assessment, through the General Ordination Exam (GOE) and then, after 1978, the General Ministerial Exam (GME). Exams were taken in Holy Scripture, Doctrine, Church History and Worship, with Ethics added in 1963 and Pastoral Studies as a latecomer in 1978. But since the mid-1960s, colleges could submit their own programmes for recognition, some of which were validated by a local university and some by a national body. By 1984, only eleven percent of students in colleges were taking the GME. The GME had lost its credibility.[37]

A new approach was adopted in 1987. It was designed to rationalise the existing ad hoc arrangements by devolving responsibility to theological colleges and non-residential training courses. Known as ACCM 22, it required colleges and courses to answer a fundamental question: What ordained ministry does the Church of England require? They then each needed to elaborate an educational programme that would equip ordinands for this ministry, with appropriate assessment. ACCM 22 demanded rigour while allowing flexibility to respond to changing times. It would be overseen by the Committee for Theological Education, but this was no top-down approach. There was no centrally regulated syllabus. The senior selection secretary at the time, Graham James, went on to become chairman of the body which succeeded it, Ministry Division, while Bishop of Norwich. Addressing a meeting I attended twenty-three years later, Bishop Graham James observed, 'The application of ACCM 22 was on individual institutions rather than the Church itself. It was a catholic concept implemented in a protestant way.'[38] Colleges and courses were, in effect, being granted a franchise, with scope for customising their own product.

During my time at Ridley Hall, this 'licensed provider' model was challenged unsuccessfully by a more interventionist approach. As noted in Chapter Two, the Church Assembly had been launched soon after World War One, to enable the Church to take greater responsibility for its own affairs. After fifty years of operation, it was reformed to create General Synod in 1970.

During my first term at Ridley, *Theological Training: A Way Ahead* was published and presented to General Synod.[39] Known as the Lincoln Report, it was not well-received. Unusually, Synod refused even to 'take note'. The report saw itself as grasping a nettle. It 'comes at a time when theological training is under pressure both from changes in educational practice and from the financial problems caused by reduced numbers of students'.[40]

In the 1960s, the number of clergy ordained each year had steadily risen to nearly six hundred. 'The church may not therefore, as was once feared, face an actual shrinkage of men in the active ministry, but rather an increase', is what the Paul Report had concluded optimistically in 1964.[41] In practice, just three years later, the number of clergy ordained started to fall. By 1972, it was down to 361, including 21 of the new non-stipendiary (unpaid) ministers (NSM). The year I began training, this had dropped further to 320, including 59 NSM clergy. As NSM clergy were not trained in residential colleges, there was overcapacity. The Church of England owned none of the colleges. Each had its own distinctive ethos and was governed by trustees. The Lincoln Report proposed 'withdrawing recognition for training' for three of the colleges. It also endorsed 'the desirability... of a balance of Church traditions'.[42] The colleges losing their franchise spanned the three main Church traditions: Anglo-Catholic (Mirfield); Central (Salisbury and Wells); Evangelical (Oak

Hill). Though other factors were at play, it seemed as though an even-handed political correctness was at work, rather than an evaluation of the particular merits and sustainability of individual colleges.

A complicating factor was the shift in balance of churchmanship amongst ordinands. Not all ordinands shared the church tradition of their college, but the majority did. By 1991, more than half were being trained at evangelical colleges.[43] Following the frosty reception of the Lincoln Report, the House of Bishops hastily commissioned a follow-up. Our Principal advised us that 'all sponsored ordinands entering theological college this year have only provisional places', pending revised recommendations.[44] In the event, it was two non-evangelical colleges that had recognition for training withdrawn: Salisbury and Wells (central tradition) and Chichester (Catholic). Lincoln closed of its own accord, leaving eleven colleges.[45] Three were central, two were Anglo-Catholic and six evangelical. The 'licensed provider' model, responding to consumer demand, was the one that prevailed. Further attempts to implement a more centralised approach would come a decade later.

Five years after ACCM 22 was introduced, I would experience its outworking at Ridley Hall. For the first two years, I would study for a course taught and supervised by the Divinity Faculty of Cambridge University ('Theology Tripos'), with more practical training fitted around it. My final year would fill in any remaining gaps.

Ridley Hall had been part of the Cambridge Theological Federation for twenty years. It had been a founder member, along with another Anglican college, Westcott House, and a Methodist college, Wesley House. As an ecumenical venture, the Federation owed its origins to plans for organic union between Methodists and Anglicans. Despite sixteen years of discussions and the Church of South India serving as a precedent, organic union was rejected. The Church of England's General Synod failed to muster the required seventy-five percent majority.[46] The Federation came into being anyway and soon welcomed the United Reformed Church to this Anglican–Methodist venture. For courses taught by theological college staff, teaching would be shared across the Federation. Each college nonetheless retained its distinctive ethos, functioning as a microclimate in the ecology of the Federation.

Ridley Hall's ethos was evangelical Anglican, as stipulated by its Deed of Trust. It was named after Bishop Nicholas Ridley, an Anglican Reformer burnt at the stake for his Protestant beliefs.

In 1992 Ridley Hall regarded itself as 'evangelical, scholarly, practical and comprehensive'.[47] When I arrived, its long-serving Principal, Hugo de Waal, had just been installed as Bishop of Thetford. With the appointment of his successor, one of the questions being asked was how 'comprehensive' Ridley would be.

Ridley's new Principal was David Watson's successor at St Michael le Belfry in York. Graham Cray minted his currency in a college lecture. Ridley's ethos would be 'roots down, walls down'. At Ridley, ordinands could become more deeply rooted in core evangelical Anglican convictions, while engaging non-defensively with other traditions.

Over the years, Ridley had not shied away from scholarly engagement, even if much of the evangelical world had regarded academic theology with suspicion. Evangelical ordinands were often wary of what they would encounter at theological college. David Watson, who had led the OICCU mission so powerfully when I was at Oxford, looked back rather sheepishly on his attitude to theological study at Ridley Hall in the 1950s. 'I rejected any teaching that I considered remotely liberal'; though some of his lecturers impressed him, such as 'the saintliness of Professor Charlie Moule that shone radiantly through his lectures'. 'The staff were patient with my spiritual arrogance and critical attitudes, and I am sure now that I would have grown in my knowledge of God far more had I been a little more humble and positive in my approach. I have since met many students at theological colleges and seminaries of all traditions who are as critical and defensive as I was, digging in behind their own convictions for safety and not being open to other ways in which God may be at work within his worldwide church. Much of this is the inevitable mark of immaturity.'[48]

However, scholarly engagement was not simply a question of welcoming academic rigour. Since the 1960s, academic theology had been playing a different tune to the popular theology of many English parish churches. Its tone had been inspired by Bishop John Robinson's desire to reconnect with those who found Christianity incomprehensible. His *Honest to God* had made a lasting impact.[49] By 1967, it had sold over a million copies.[50] It had been followed by other works which radically challenged Christian doctrines such as the incarnation. Theologians contributing to *The Myth of God Incarnate,* published in 1977, were convinced that conceptions of Jesus 'as God Incarnate, the Second Person of the Trinity' were a 'mythological or poetic way of expressing his significance for us'. We were on much safer ground seeing him as 'a man approved by God for a special role within the divine purpose', in their view.[51]

By the late 1970s, according to Rowan Williams, the authority of *Honest to God* was beginning to wane. 'More theologians were turning back to

Barth for inspiration' he observed, alluding to Karl Barth's emphasis on God the Father sending his Son to the 'far country' of this world.[52] 'By the early 1980s, *Honest to God* seemed a museum piece.'[53] Nonetheless, it retained 'iconic status as crystallising some of the intellectual self-doubt of 1960s Christianity'.[54]

For an ordinand such as myself training in the 1990s, the challenge was for scholarly engagement to provide confidence for future ministry, rather than intellectual self-doubt. I would study the German theologians who had inspired John Robinson. But I would also study other German theologians who conveyed greater confidence in God's capacity to reveal himself intelligibly in human history, such as Karl Barth, Wolfhart Pannenberg and Karl Rahner. One of the debates pre-dating John Robinson was the extent to which the Christ of faith could be informed reliably by the Jesus of history. So-called quests for the historical Jesus had often simply reflected the presuppositions of writers. Then in the heyday of *Honest to God,* attempts to 'demythologise' the New Testament seemed to clinch the view that little about Jesus could be known for sure. Yet by the 1990s, there was renewed interest in the Jewish and Roman world in which Jesus lived. E. P. Sanders and N. T. Wright provided ample grounds for not dismissing the historical basis of the gospel accounts too hastily.[55] A few minutes' walk from Ridley Hall was Tyndale House, one of the best biblical studies libraries in the world and a magnet for scholarly research. Through its scholarship, there were now many more resources for those with evangelical convictions to engage with the tough questions of academic scholarship.

Commemorated on the walls of King's College Cambridge: the pub where the Church of England's future reformers imbibed Luther's teaching

Photo © Andrew Norman

Cambridge is closely associated with the biblically-grounded Reformation of the sixteenth century. Many of its leading players were attached to the university. The pub was where groups met together to discuss the subversive teaching associated with Martin Luther. The White Horse Tavern, next to King's College, became known as 'Little Germany'. As Luther's ideas gradually took hold, these academics went on to make their mark in the first four rounds of the Reformation in England.

Round one, during the reign of King Henry VIII, began with the break with Rome, to enable the king to marry Anne Boleyn. In 1534 he was declared 'the only supreme head in earth of the Church of England'. Thomas Cranmer, who had spent thirty years in Cambridge, was head-hunted by the king to become Archbishop of Canterbury. Henry VIII, an able theologian, was opposed to many of the Lutheran ideas. Nonetheless, under guidance from Cranmer and the King's fixer, Thomas Cromwell, there were modest attempts at reform, such as a royal decree requiring a Bible in English in every parish. More drastically, the king shut down the monasteries and commandeered their property.

Henry VIII keeping a watchful eye over the site of the White Horse Tavern, where academics discussed Lutheran Reforms

Photo © Andrew Norman

King Henry's death in 1547 sounded the bell for *round two,* under the sickly young Edward VI. Though only a child, Edward VI was much more receptive to Protestant ideas, abetted by his advisers in the Privy Council. During his six-year reign, comprehensive reform of the church took place, still under the guidance of Cranmer. Now Cranmer was aided by the 'White Horse Tavern' circle, including Nicholas Ridley, who was promptly appointed Bishop of Rochester and Hugh Latimer, formerly Bishop of Worcester.[56] Clergy were allowed to marry, which suited Cranmer well as he was already married. Images in churches were dismantled. Stone altars were replaced by wooden communion tables. Liturgy in English was developed, with the first Prayer Book published in 1549 and a more obviously Protestant version replacing it in 1552. An original copy of the 1549 Prayer Book was available for students to inspect at Ridley Hall. Doctrinal parameters were set out in Forty-Two Articles of Religion in 1553.

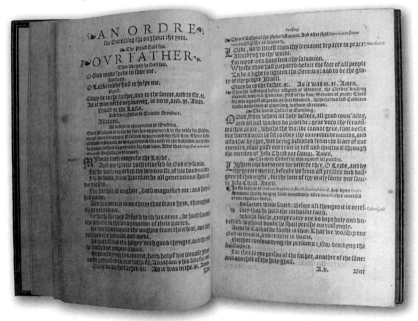

Liturgy in English: Ridley Hall's copy of Cranmer's first Prayer Book, published in 1549
Reproduced by kind permission of Ridley Hall, Cambridge; photo © Dona McCullagh

Edward VI's death that year abruptly halted this programme of reform and terminated round two. Mary Tudor was crowned as his successor. Her right to the throne depended on the legitimacy of her mother's marriage. It was Henry's determination to declare it invalid that led to the break with Rome. That meant she had to side with the Catholic Church, which she did with enthusiasm. During her reign *(round three)*, the Church in England became Catholic again. A Roman Catholic, Reginald Pole, was appointed Archbishop of Canterbury. Many of the bishops and clergy fled to the Continent. The White Horse Tavern circle was dangerously out of step with the new regime. Cranmer, Ridley and Latimer were burnt at the stake for not falling into line. The jailer's invoice for their prison expenses can be inspected in the library of Corpus Christi College, and includes a bill for the 'faggotts' used to burn them. Their deaths, depicted graphically in *Foxe's Book of Martyrs,* would provide iconic figures for future Anglicans, as Ridley Hall's name exemplifies. 'Be of good comfort, Master Ridley, and play the man', Latimer is reported to have said, as the firewood was stacked around them. 'We shall this day light such a candle, by God's grace, in England, as I trust shall never be put out.'[57]

Round three came to an end after five turbulent years, when Queen Mary died, probably of cancer. Elizabeth, her half-sister, knelt down in the grass when envoys delivered the news, exclaiming in Latin, 'This is the Lord's doing and it is marvellous on our eyes'. She was crowned queen in 1558.[58] Like Queen Mary, Elizabeth's right to the throne obliged her to take sides. Her mother was Anne Boleyn, whose marriage to King Henry had not been recognised by Rome. There was no way Elizabeth could side with the Pope and keep England Catholic, even if she wanted to. Conveniently for her, the Catholic Archbishop Pole died the same day as Queen Mary. She could now appoint an Archbishop of Canterbury to preside over a more lasting break with Rome. She went for someone she knew she could work with. Another member of the White Horse Tavern circle, Matthew Parker, had been her mother's chaplain. A mild-mannered scholar, he had thrived as Master of Corpus Christi College and he was hoping to end his days in Cambridge. Reluctantly, he complied with the Queen's request.

Paying the price: prison expenses for Thomas Cranmer, Nicholas Ridley and Hugh Latimer, including the faggots they were burnt with   *Reproduced by kind permission of The Master and Fellows of Corpus Christi College, Cambridge*

With Parker's co-operation secured, Elizabeth pressed on with *round four*. Conscious of her precarious position as Queen, national unity and stability were overriding concerns. At one extreme, she had those who had willingly reverted to Catholicism under Queen Mary. At the other, she had the bishops and clergy who had returned from their exile, fired up with the reforming teaching they had imbibed in Geneva, Strasbourg and other European cities. What she needed was a formula that would hold these together in one church. By the 1559 Act of Supremacy, she accepted the title 'Supreme Governor of the Church of England'. Cranmer's 1552 Prayer Book was re-introduced, with some significant changes to the text. At the administration of communion, for example, words from the 1549 Prayer Book were tagged on, providing greater latitude for beliefs about the presence of Christ in the communion service.

Elizabeth's 'settlement', as it became known, has been celebrated as the deftly constructed foundation of the Anglican *via media,* the middle way between Protestantism and Catholicism. However, it is misleading to see the settlement as simply an exercise in 'studied ambiguity'.[59] Archbishop Parker, who entered into the spirit of round four, was determined to provide clarity, not vagueness. The Forty-Two Articles prepared in round two were reworked into thirty-nine.[60] If you go to the library of Corpus Christi College, you can see Parker's annotations and crossings-out.[61]

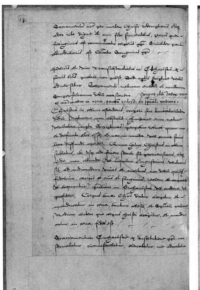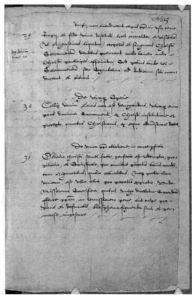

From 42 to 39: unwanted Articles deleted, preserved in the college where Archbishop Matthew Parker was Master   *Reproduced by kind permission of The Master and Fellows of Corpus Christi College, Cambridge*

Far from being vague, the Thirty-Nine Articles can be quite pointed, show-ing where the Church of England stood in the debates of the time. 'The Romish Doctrine concerning Purgatory, Pardons, Worshipping and Adoration, as well of Images as of Reliques, and also the invocation of Saints, is a fond thing vainly invented, and grounded upon no warranty of Scripture' (Article 22). On the subject of the Lord's Supper, for which Cranmer had been burnt at the stake, it rejected the prevailing Catholic view about the bread and the wine. 'Transubstantiation [the change of the substance of the Bread and Wine] in the Supper of the Lord, cannot be proved by holy writ; but it is repugnant to the plain words of Scripture, overthroweth the nature of the Sacrament and hath given occasion to many superstitions' (Article 28).

However, there was much the Articles left unsaid. The Church is not equated with a particular institutional structure, yet there is no mention of the Protestant notion of an 'invisible' church of true believers either. Instead, the visible Church of Christ is defined broadly as 'a congregation of faithful men in which the pure Word of God is preached, and the Sacraments be duly ministered according to Christ's ordinance' (Article 19). As the preamble to the Articles puts it, the purpose in what they explicitly affirm is 'for the avoiding of diversity of opinions and for the establishing of consent touching true religion'.[62] In what they do not explicitly affirm, diversity is permitted. 'They are minimal in their specifications', sums up the Anglican theologian and Reformation historian, Alister McGrath. 'The Articles do not commit the Reformed English Church to anything other than an affirmation of the main points of the catholic faith, allowing a considerable degree of freedom in relation to areas of division.'[63]

As well as the annotated Forty-Two Articles, the library at Corpus Christi College contains some of the oldest manuscripts in England. These include the sixth-century New Testament now used for swearing oaths at the enthrone-ment of Archbishops of Canterbury. This remarkable collection is the result of Matthew Parker's assiduous salvaging of manuscripts while Archbishop of Canterbury. His main motive was to demonstrate the pedigree of the Church of England. Whatever the Pope might say about the Church of England's credentials, Parker believed that his collection could be used to trace the continuity of the Church of England back to the early church. The Church of England could establish its lineage through the Celtic Christians and even to the alleged visit of Joseph of Arimathea to England.[64] These efforts were supplemented by John Jewel, who had been a fellow of Corpus Christi College when Matthew Parker was Master. As Bishop of Salisbury, four years into round four, Jewel published his persuasive *Apologia ecclesiae*

Anglicanae. 'From the primitive church, from the apostles, and from Christ, we have not departed', he argued. As for the Roman Catholic Church, 'Let them compare our churches and theirs together, and they shall see that themselves have most shamefully gone from the apostles, and we most justly have gone from them.'[65]

Yet, by the time I was studying at Ridley Hall, the terms set for the Church of England by these reformers from Cambridge were receding from view. Following round four and the Elizabethan Settlement, all Church of England clergy had been required 'willingly and from my heart to subscribe to the Thirty Nine Articles of Religion'.[66] They were now permitted to keep them much more at arm's length. In 1865, the wording had been softened to 'I assent to the Thirty Nine Articles. . . . I believe the doctrine . . . as therein set forth, to be agreeable to the word of God'.[67] The publication of *Honest to God* provided renewed pressure to revisit the Church of England's classic doctrinal formulations. The Archbishops' Doctrine Commission was set to work. It ruled out revision. 'The most practicable method of avoiding giving distress to those who are happy to assent to the Articles as they stand while at the same time easing the consciences of those who cannot at the present make the required subscription without mental reservation is to modify the formula of assent.'[68] In 1975, the newly established General Synod approved a revised Declaration of Assent, to be incorporated into the Church of England's canons. 'Led by the Holy Spirit,' the preface proclaimed, 'she has borne witness to Christian truth in her historic formularies, the Thirty Nine Articles of Religion, the *Book of Common Prayer* and the Ordering of Bishops, Priests and Deacons. In the declaration you are about to make,' clergy would be asked from now on, 'will you affirm your loyalty to this inheritance of faith as your inspiration and guidance under God in bringing the grace and truth of Christ to this generation . . . ?'[69] No longer were clergy required to say 'I assent to the Thirty-Nine Articles'. Instead they would be asked to affirm them as a source of inspiration and guidance.[70]

In this climate of rethinking, the need for all ordinands to engage with academic scholarship was obvious. Yet, this could not be to the exclusion of pastoral training, both practical and theoretical. For me, it included a course in bereavement counselling with the secular agency CRUSE, followed by meetings with a 'client'. It also meant leading marriage preparation in the parish to which I was attached. On the theory side, it involved a project on healing in the life of the church.

The Church of England was also waking up to the need to place greater emphasis on mission. The year I started at Ridley Hall, the new Advisory

Board for Ministry (ABM) produced *Order and Diversity,* which set out to map the present state of ordained ministry in the Church of England. 'This will be based in part on the call from the Lambeth Conference for 1988 for a "shift to a dynamic missionary emphasis going beyond care and nurture to proclamation and service".'[71]

This 'shift to a dynamic missionary emphasis' had been strongly encouraged by the African and Asian bishops at the Lambeth Conference and had led to a resolution to designate the 1990s 'The Decade of Evangelism'. This was welcomed at Ridley Hall, where mission and evangelism already featured prominently in the training mix. We were all required to go on a week's 'mission', which in my case was based in an affluent parish in Surrey. Our term-time church attachment could also have an evangelistic dimension. One of my responsibilities was to lead a course in 'sharing your faith' at the village church to which I was attached. I was also exposed to renewed efforts at church planting in the parishes. Daughter churches had long been a feature of parish life in urban and industrial settings, as we have seen through my grandfather's experiences. Parishes were now 'planting' congregations in housing estates, where they would meet in schools and community centres. On a month-long placement in Ipswich, I experienced a church that had planted two congregations from its parish church.

✠

In this chapter, we have observed an assorted selection of ways in which 'being Anglican' has been influenced by changing times. We have seen churches with large congregations in towns and cities welcoming those who move frequently because of their work, as well as being a platform for outreach. We have also seen the Church of England reflect soberly on urban deprivation, acknowledging yet again its struggle to connect with the vast majority of those who live in cities. In response, it has advocated changes to liturgy and leadership style, and encouraged parishes like St Luke in the City to work in partnership with other agencies in the local community. We have seen how the Church has been prepared to criticise British government policy, as well as facilitate constructive ways forward. We have seen this mirrored in Africa, in even more acute circumstances. We have observed Anglicans campaigning against election rigging in Kenya and helping to broker peace in Mozambique. We have been reminded how the Church of England was closely integrated with political life from the outset, recalling its changing fortunes in the first four rounds of the English Reformation. In Malta, we have seen how politics and Anglican–Catholic relations could still be intertwined, four hundred years later. We have seen signs of increased ecumenical co-operation, in urban settings, in theological training and in peace-making initiatives. We have encountered obstacles to overcoming denominational divisions, in the defeat of plans for organic union between Anglicans and Methodists. Within the Church of England, we have noted shifting dynamics between its constituent traditions.

We have observed varied ways in which the Church of England revised its approach to equipping its clergy for a changing society, not all of which were uniformly welcomed. These have included exposure to fresh emphases in academic theology, increased flexibility over the Thirty-Nine Articles and a more structured approach to pastoral care. In addition, training institutions have been empowered to devise courses that keep pace with the changing demands of ministry. They have begun to include an explicit emphasis on mission. This has been influenced by bishops of the wider Anglican Communion and their call for a shift to a greater missionary emphasis. The story of Angola reminded us how a missionary emphasis is part of the DNA of Anglican life in countries outside England, without necessarily being connected to British imperialism. We turn next to another area where other parts of the Anglican Communion were taking a lead: the ordination of women.

Up-to-date in its time:
Cranmer's first prayer
book 'in a language
understanded of the people'

7

Aggiornamento: 'Bringing Up to Date'

MY SECOND YEAR at Ridley Hall was a landmark in the history of the college and of the Church of England. For the first time, women ordinands were starting their training in the knowledge they would be ordained priest. 'It was fascinating arriving at theological college in 1993', recalls Maggi Dawn, well known at the time as a Christian musician and songwriter. 'The first women were to be ordained in the spring; some of them had already served for years as deaconesses and then as deacons, and there was something joyful about joining the long line of women who had blazed this trail.'[1]

The number of women sponsored for training had already been boosted over the previous six years, following the Church of England's decision to ordain women as permanent deacons. Women had served as deaconesses in the Church of England since 1862. But that was not the same as being a deacon, according to the Anglican understanding of ordained ministry. 'It is evident unto all men diligently reading holy Scripture and ancient Authors, that from the Apostles' time, there have been these orders of Ministers in Christ's Church; Bishops, Priests and Deacons.' So went the preface of the ordination services crafted by Thomas Cranmer and used in the Church of England for hundreds of years. Deacons were ordained by the bishop laying his hands on the head of each candidate. Their job description was set out in what the bishop asked them to do 'gladly and willingly'. It included pastoral work, instructing the youth and assisting the priest in the conduct of worship.

So much for deacons. Anglican deaconesses were authorised exclusively for pastoral work and there was no mandatory laying on of hands, at least initially.[2] They were a model of ministry inspired by the Lutheran Church in Germany. Elizabeth Ferrard, who would become the first Anglican deaconess, visited Kaiserswerth, where Lutheran deaconesses were living together in community and serving their parish. On her return, Elizabeth Ferrard was licensed by Archibald Tait, Bishop of London, who went on to become Archbishop of Canterbury. She set up the residential Community of St Andrew to serve the poor of London's parishes.[3]

This innovation for Anglicans was regarded as having precedent from New Testament times. It caught on. It was seen as a reinstating of the ministry exercised by Phoebe, who is greeted by the Apostle Paul in his Letter to the Romans (Romans 16:1). Romans 16 was the reading specified when deaconesses were admitted to their office in London Diocese.[4] Twenty-five years after it was introduced, the deaconess movement diversified beyond residential communities and became more parish-based, under the leadership of a newly licensed deaconess, Isabella Gilmore. By 1920, it was on the agenda for the bishops gathering from around the world for the Lambeth Conference. The bishops resolved that the form and manner for the 'making of deaconesses' should now include 'prayer by the bishop and the laying on of hands'. But they were still clear this did not make deaconesses the same as deacons. 'The order of deaconesses is for women the one and only order of ministry which has the stamp of apostolic approval, and is the only order of ministry which we can recommend and that our branch of the Catholic Church should recognise and use.'[5]

In 1924 the Church of England duly introduced a form of ordination for deaconesses involving the bishop laying on hands. In the decades that followed, the role of deaconess gradually expanded to include leading worship and preaching. The gap continued to close between what deaconesses and deacons were authorised to do. Eventually in 1986, the Church of England General Synod voted to ordain women as deacons. By June the following year, there were 750 women deacons in the Church of England.[6] The ratio of female to male sponsored students at Ridley Hall immediately rose to one in six.[7]

It was during my first term at Ridley Hall that the Church of England's General Synod voted to ordain women as priests. A journalist from *The Independent* newspaper joined us the week before the synod debate. Rosie Eager, a first-year student like myself, told him how she had completed a careers questionnaire at university. 'You put down all your interests and perceived strengths and the computer came up with a list of suggestions', she recalled. 'It obviously didn't realise I was a woman. It said I should become a minister of religion.'[8]

There was no guarantee that Synod would vote in favour of women priests. 'In Ridley and in the Federation there will be people who hold very different views from one another', we had been reminded as we started the term. 'As a community, we need to make a special effort to understand each other's views and to be sensitive to each other's feelings.' We were provided with a reading list, two box files of short articles and sessions to discuss the issues. While Synod met, there was a prayer vigil in chapel.[9]

Synod needed a two thirds majority in each of its three houses. When the votes were cast, the House of Bishops and the House of Clergy comfortably secured their majority. In the House of the Laity, it was a narrow margin in favour.[10] 'Two votes. It was two votes, that's all', wrote another first-year student, Peter Owen Jones, a former advertising executive who has since become a TV personality. 'I sat in front of the telly crying like a baby. I then drove like a maniac into college and insisted on hugging every woman I could find.... I have immense sympathy for those who feel they are unable to continue.... What a momentous day.'[11] For supporters and opponents alike, it was indeed a momentous day. 'After the General Synod of November 1992', Maggi Dawn recalls, 'and after a personal journey that involved much reading, talking and prayer, I sat alone on an English beach where the Atlantic tides wash in, looking out across the sea, and agreed with myself and God that I would accept the Church's call to become a priest.'[12]

Yet despite it being a momentous day in England, the Church of England was by no means leading the way in the Anglican Communion. During World War Two, an Anglican deaconess, Florence Li Tim-Oi, had been ordained priest in Macau by the Bishop of Hong Kong, as an emergency measure. This generated a strong reaction at the first Lambeth Conference after the war in 1948, so she voluntarily withdrew from priestly ministry. It took twenty years for women's ordination to be back on the Lambeth Conference agenda. At that same 1968 Conference, the bishops agreed that the Anglican Communion's business could not wait until they gathered every ten years. The Anglican Consultative Council (ACC) was thus established.

The ACC would meet every three years and be served by a Secretary General, based in London. Member churches were asked to feed in perspectives on women's ordination to its first meeting in 1971. At this first ACC meeting in Limuru, Kenya, the delegates considered whether Hong Kong should build on the precedent of Florence Li Tim-Oi. With a slender majority, their advice to the Bishop of Hong Kong was determined: 'if he decides to ordain

women to the priesthood, his action will be acceptable to this Council'.[13]
Later that year, two women deacons, Jane Hwang and Joyce Bennett, were
legally ordained as priests in Hong Kong.

As the 1970s progressed, women began to be ordained as priests in other
provinces: in the USA in 1974, in Canada in 1976 and in New Zealand in
1977.[14] In the case of the USA, the first ordinations were illegal. The Episcopal
Church (USA) had ordained its first women deacons in 1971, sixteen years
ahead of the Church of England. But during the preceding debate in its
General Convention, there had been strong opposition to the ordination
of women as priests. In defiance of this, eleven of the women deacons were
ordained priest in Philadelphia in 1974, by three retired bishops and others
'firmly committed to the principle of equal rights for women'.[15] One of the
deacons, Suzanne Hyatt, had been a prime mover. The intention was to force
the hand of the General Convention of the Episcopal Church by creating a
'fact on the ground'. Sure enough, when General Convention met two years
later, their ordinations were regularised.[16]

In the 1980s, women started to be ordained priest in Africa too, beginning
with Uganda in 1983 and Liberia in 1987.[17] At the 1988 Lambeth Conference,
women bishops were now on the agenda, since women were beginning to be
nominated as candidates in the Episcopal Church (USA).[18] A commission was
set up, the first of several major commissions to be chaired by Robin Eames,
Archbishop of Armagh. A few weeks after the 1988 Lambeth Conference,
Barbara Harris was elected bishop in the Episcopal Church. In the wake of
the 1988 Lambeth Conference, the ordination of women as priests was also
approved in Tanzania and Kenya.[19]

Although the ordination of women in the Church of England lagged
behind several other Anglican provinces, women had gradually been authorised to serve in other ways in the Church of England. In addition to serving
as deaconesses and, more recently, deacons, women exercised ministry in
religious orders and the Church Army, as we have observed in earlier chapters.
At the time of the 1992 synod vote, my mother was serving as churchwarden
in her parish church in Sussex, in Chichester Diocese. The office of churchwarden dates back to the thirteenth century in England. By the fifteenth
century, churchwardens were chosen annually by all parishioners. They were
the bishop's representative. By the end of the nineteenth century, women were
serving as churchwardens in dioceses such as Chichester and Salisbury. This
was when Parochial Church Councils (PCCs) were introduced to 'quicken the
life and strengthen the work of the church'. At the time, the bishops decided
that women were not eligible for election to PCCs, despite 'an appreciable

number' being churchwardens in at least one diocese. Some bishops spoke against this decision. There were immediate protests from lay people, beginning with a petition signed by 1,100 women.[20] Sixteen years later, as World War One was breaking out, women were finally authorised to be elected to PCCs as well as to serve as churchwardens.[21]

World War One saw the temporary introduction of women to another authorised role in the Church of England. My wife, Amanda, was following in their footsteps while we were at Ridley Hall, by training to be a reader. My grandfather, Harry Nobbs, had first gone to Canada in 1911 to serve as a lay reader, sponsored by the mission agency, SPG. While he and my other grandfather were serving in the trenches, there was a shortage of male clergy in England and Canada. As a result, female lay readers were licensed in twenty-two dioceses in England and one in Canada. They were called 'Bishop's Messengers'. Once World War One was over, the experiment was terminated. But fifty years later, it was restarted as a permanent arrangement.

This new wave of female lay readers in 1969 corresponded to increased pressure for extending the ministry of women in the Church of England. Four drivers were noted in the 1966 report *Women and Holy Orders*.[22] Two came from trends in wider society and two from the Church of England itself. From society came the twin pressures of the emancipation of women and of new insights awakened by the spirit of the times, such as the discrediting of biological and psychological assumptions about the unsuitability of women for certain roles. Within the Church, pressure came from the shortage of clergy and from its failure to provide adequate opportunities for women to exercise ministry in ways commensurate with their gifts.

Fuelled by developments elsewhere in the Anglican Communion, there were further Church of England reports in 1972, 1978, 1984, 1987 and 1988. The process was accelerated by a motion proposed by the Bishop of Oxford, Kenneth Woollcombe, at General Synod in July 1975. At the first ACC meeting in Limuru, which led to Hong Kong ordaining women priests, a request had been issued to each Anglican province for their views on ordaining women as priests. In order to produce an informed response from the Church of England, English dioceses had been asked whether they had 'fundamental objections'. Thirty of the forty-three said no. So the Bishop of Oxford proposed a motion: 'This Synod considers there are no fundamental objections to the ordination of women to the priesthood'. It was passed and 'no fundamental objections' became a fixed point of reference in further debates.[23] By 1992, the measure to ordain women to the priesthood received the necessary two thirds majority in Synod.

But was that the end of the matter? Not really. In 1993, the House of Bishops issued a statement which acknowledged that 'differing views can continue to be held with integrity within the Church of England'. Synod's vote was described as 'part of a wider process within the Church of England, within the Anglican Communion and within the universal Church in which the question of the women's ordination to the priesthood is being tested'. There were caveats, in other words. The Church of England's canons would be changed. Synod's decision 'expresses the mind of the majority of the Church of England, in so far as this can be ascertained'.[24] But provisions would be made for those unable to accept the ministry of women priests, because the Church of England was continuing its process of discernment. Parishes could therefore vote to restrict the ministry of women in their parishes. And, in an Act of Synod proclaimed in 1994, Provincial Episcopal Visitors ('flying bishops') could offer episcopal care to those unable to receive the ministry of women priests. There should be no discrimination against candidates for ordination or for senior appointments on the basis of their views about the ordination of women to the priesthood. All this signified a principle known as 'open reception'.[25] As Maggi Dawn explains, 'Reception offers a way to move forward on an issue over which opinion is divided, allowing for provisional decisions to be made and acted on, subject to later review. A decision made in this way continues to be provisional until such time as the church reaches a consensus on whether to ratify or rescind that decision.'[26]

The first women were ordained priest in the Church of England in March 1994. The following year, my final year before ordination, Amanda and I would spend four months in the Anglican province that had been a prime instigator for ordaining women: the Episcopal Church (USA). We would spend a semester at Virginia Theological Seminary, whose dean was a woman priest.

We arrived in Washington DC in January 1995. It was even colder than Cambridge. Virginia Theological Seminary (VTS) was in suburban Alexandria, a few Metro stops from the Pentagon. Its grassy eighty-two acres had been the site of a seminary since 1823. During the American Civil War, it had been transformed into a hospital. It served as a reminder that Anglican Christianity had taken root outside England many generations ago. Virginia had parishes and churchwardens as early as 1630. From 1634, parishes were under the authority of the Bishop of London, with clergy being ordained in England. John and Charles Wesley had operated within this framework in 1735, when they came to America as Anglican clergy.

In 1776, when America declared its independence, two thirds of the signatories were Anglicans, including the first President, George Washington.[27]

But Anglican church life could not continue uninterrupted. For many clergy, it was a matter of conscience and patriotism. They had taken the oath of allegiance to the British Crown when they were ordained. Half the total number of clergy left for Canada. In Virginia, churches were closed.[28] Who would consecrate new clergy? Bishops were needed.

A candidate was identified in Connecticut and dispatched to England. But the Archbishop of Canterbury was reluctant to interfere in American affairs. An alternative plan was needed, so the Scottish bishops were approached. They proved willing to oblige and in 1784 Samuel Seabury became the first bishop of the Episcopal Church in America. When two more bishops were elected, the American minister in London spoke with the Archbishop of Canterbury. The American diplomat assured the Archbishop he would not be committing a political *faux pas* if he consecrated these bishops. An Act of Parliament was duly implemented, removing the need for an oath of allegiance. In 1790, the first Bishop of Virginia was consecrated in Lambeth Palace by the Archbishop and two of his fellow bishops. Bishops with no formal connection to the state were now a part of the extended Anglican family in Scotland and the USA.

Virginia Theological Seminary: serving the Episcopal Church since 1823

Photo © Andrew Norman

On the snowy campus of VTS, we were given a warm welcome by staff and students. Formally known as the Protestant Episcopal Theological Seminary of Virginia, its ethos had originally been evangelical. As we settled in, it was clear that things had moved on since then. Only a handful of the staff owned this label. The evangelical mantle had passed to Trinity School for Ministry in Pittsburgh. VTS was simply regarded by students as 'low church' in its worship. 'Snake-belly low' is how one student described it. Yet by English standards, its attention to liturgical detail made it seem more 'middle of the road'. There was meticulous compliance to the rubric of the American Prayer Book introduced in 1979.

In a course on liturgy, as one of my assignments I made a study of Holy Communion rites in the 1979 American Prayer Book. It was clear that the liturgy had departed significantly from Thomas Cranmer's Prayer Book. There had been three earlier versions in the Episcopal Church. But this one differed markedly from its immediate predecessor, authorised in 1928. In part, this reflected the emphasis of the Liturgical Movement in England, especially the work of Gregory Dix, an Anglican priest and Benedictine monk. In 1945, Dix's *Shape of the Liturgy* had proposed ways of being more faithful to the practices of the early church. It drew on *The Apostolic Tradition,* an early Christian work that had been rediscovered in the nineteenth century. Dix championed a classic 'shape' of the liturgy, comprising four actions: offertory, consecration, fraction and communion. This shape did not quite match Cranmer's liturgy and adjustments had already been made in formulating the liturgy for the Church of South India.

One of the anomalies, according to Dix's 'shape', was Cranmer's Prayer of Humble Access. 'We are not worthy so much as to gather up the crumbs under thy table' was felt to be out of place when communicants were about to receive the bread and the wine. To the crafters of the 1979 American Prayer Book, the sentiment of the prayer seemed to contradict the logic, sequence and theology of the Eucharist. As a result, in the modern-language rite, Cranmer's 'Prayer of Humble Access' no longer featured as communicants prepared to receive the bread and wine.[29] This coincided with a diminished emphasis on penitence and unworthiness throughout the service, compared with Cranmer's Prayer Book. Such language 'clashed loudly with contemporary values and emerging images of God's relationship with the faithful', explains one American liturgist.[30] On the other hand, there was increased emphasis on other themes in the liturgy, such as creation and the cosmos. One of the eucharistic prayers came to be nicknamed the 'Star Wars' liturgy, with its evocative references to 'interstellar space' and 'this fragile earth, our island home'.

We were able to experience the liturgy in practice, not just in the chapel of VTS. Accompanying fellow students, we attended Sunday worship in a range of local parishes, including a black majority Episcopalian church. All students were required to be attached to a church for 'field education'. I was attached to Church of the Apostles. It combined Anglo-Catholic ritual with charismatic spirituality. Its rector, David Harper, was chairman of SOMA, the body responsible for leading the retreats before Lambeth Conferences for bishops engaged in charismatic renewal. We also attended Falls Church several times, a vast church on the edge of Washington DC, modelled on All Souls Langham Place, where John Stott had been rector. In both churches, services were normally preceded by adult Sunday school. This corresponded to a strong emphasis on Christian discipleship. One weekend, Amanda joined a women's retreat led by Church of the Apostles and I attended a men's retreat led by Falls Church. Both, coincidentally, were at the same venue in Chesapeake Bay, in different wings. Ten years later, these two thriving churches would secede from the Diocese of Virginia, in the dispute over sexuality.

My understanding of the Episcopal Church was aided by more than a study of liturgy and local church involvement. Two courses I took helped me to understand its engagement in social action. One, on urban ministry, introduced me to the Episcopal Church's increasing emphasis on civil rights and concern for the marginalised. In the 1960s, rioting in Detroit and New Jersey had led the Presiding Bishop, John Hines, to propose a $9 million programme for empowering the nation's poorest citizens. As a result, the General Convention Special Program (GCSP) was launched in January 1968.[31] John Hines would remain Presiding Bishop for another six years, during which time he would continue to champion engagement with radical social issues.[32]

Another course, 'Christianity, Politics and the State', allowed me to re-connect with my undergraduate degree and consider the context in which political influence was exercised by Episcopalians in the USA. Given the location of VTS, it was impossible not to be conscious of politics. The White House with its 'West Wing' was just a bus and Metro ride away. The niece of one of the students worked for the First Lady, Hillary Clinton. At the men's group retreat I attended with Falls Church, my small group included the speechwriter for a well-known senator.

As part of our course, we were required to select a lobbying group to visit in Washington DC. I chose the Ethics and Public Policy Center, an ecumenical agency which now numbers amongst its fellows Roger Scruton, a philosopher who has recently written a personal history of the Church of England. Such pressure groups were an attempt to articulate religious viewpoints in a society where the place of religion in public life is hotly contested. The Anglican sociologist Os Guinness, based in Oxford when I was an undergraduate and now worshipping at Falls Church, called this an 'uncivil war' in a book he had recently published on the subject, which I reviewed for the course.[33] Secularists took their lead from a letter published in a Massachusetts newspaper in 1802 by the third President of the United States, Thomas Jefferson. In his application of the First Amendment to the US Constitution, Jefferson referred to a 'strict wall of separation between church and state'. However, within the Episcopal Church, Jefferson's formula has not led to the Church opting out of public life altogether. The Episcopal Church has had a strong tradition of contributing towards a moral vision for the nation as a whole.

Our course on 'Christianity, Politics and the State' tackled the relative merits of close co-operation with civil authorities—the Church of England's historic approach—as opposed to providing a separate prophetic witness, advocated, for example, by the Mennonite John Howard Yoder.[34] I was introduced to the work of Richard Neuhaus, a Roman Catholic theologian, whose vote was for overtly Christian engagement in public affairs. In his *The Naked Public Square,* Neuhaus argued that banishing religious values from public discourse was dangerous, leaving the public square exposed to exclusively secular assumptions. 'Because government cannot help but make moral judgments of an ultimate nature,' he wrote, 'it must, if it has in principle excluded identifiable religion, make those judgments by "secular" reasoning that is given the force of religion.'[35]

VTS was part of a consortium of colleges, which meant it was possible to engage directly with Catholic theologians. I duly signed up for a module at the Catholic University of America. I was the only non-Catholic in a class studying the far-reaching implications of the Second Vatican Council. At the time John Robinson was writing his *Honest to God,* the Catholic Church was embarking on its own programme of 'bringing up to date' ('aggiorna-mento'). John XXIII had been elected Pope at the age of seventy-seven. Far from being an elderly 'night watchman', keeping things ticking over for a younger successor, he surprised everyone by announcing a second Vatican Council, just ninety days after becoming Pope. The first Vatican Council had been cut short in 1870 by the Franco-Prussian war. The powers of the Pope had been defined more fully, but other matters had been left hanging. These would now be picked up in three years of discussions in the 1960s, to which thousands would contribute. Its aim, according to Pope John XXIII, was to renew the Church, to define more fully the nature of the Church and the role of the bishop, to restore unity among all Christians, including seeking pardon for Catholic contributions to separation, and to start a dia-logue with the contemporary world. 'The ecumenical council will reach out and embrace under the widespread wings of the Catholic Church the entire heredity of our Lord Jesus Christ', he boldly proclaimed.[36]

Discussions were held between 1962 and 1965. They yielded far-reaching changes, some of which belatedly reflected the priorities of Protestant reformers. Mass would be celebrated in the vernacular. There would be greater emphasis on reading the Bible. Communion would be received by the laity in both kinds. There was a renewed emphasis on the Church as the People of God, rather than as an institution. The unity of all Christians was prioritised. For Anglo-Catholics, Vatican II was quite disorientating. As Anglo-Catholic charismatic John Gunstone put it, 'the compasses of Anglo-Catholics all went crazy'.[37] The contemporary Roman Catholic Church had been a frame of reference for practices espoused by Anglo-Catholics, along with the early church. Some of these practices were now being repudiated by the Roman Catholic Church itself.

Vatican II was enormously significant for all Anglicans, not just for Anglo-Catholics. This was inevitable, when Anglican identity was so closely linked to the break with Rome. 'I grew up with an inbred opposition to anything that came from Rome', admitted Geoffrey Fisher, Archbishop of Canterbury. 'I objected to their doctrine; I objected to their methods of reasoning; I objected to their methods of operation...and I saw no reason for differing from that opinion as the years went by.'[38] Yet a year after Pope John XXIII was elected, Archbishop Geoffrey Fisher decided to pay him a visit. It would be the first time an Archbishop of Canterbury had met the Pope since the fourteenth century.[39] It would be the third stop on an ecumenical pilgrimage that began with Jerusalem and Constantinople. There would be no official photo and no press release. Yet the meeting clearly demonstrated that things were changing. The Pope read the Archbishop a passage which referred to 'the time when our separated brethren should return to Mother Church'. The Archbishop gently objected. 'Your Holiness, not return.... None of us can go backwards. We are each now running on parallel courses; we are looking forward until, in God's good time, our two courses approximate and meet.' The Pope paused then responded. 'You are right.'[40]

In the Decrees of Vatican II, the 'communions' which separated from Rome at the time of the Reformation are considered, and Anglicans are given a special mention. 'Among those in which some Catholic traditions and institutions continue to exist, the Anglican Communion occupies a special place.'[41] This was a clear signal to renew efforts at improving relations between Anglicans and Roman Catholics. By the time the Council ended, Pope John XXIII had died and Geoffrey Fisher had retired. But their successors both proved willing to take things forward. In 1966, it was the turn of Archbishop Michael Ramsey to visit Rome. This time it would be an official visit. An Anglican Centre in Rome would be dedicated by the Archbishop. In the Sistine Chapel, Pope Paul VI applauded the Archbishop's efforts. 'You are rebuilding a bridge, which for centuries has lain fallen, between the Church of Rome and the Church of Canterbury: a bridge of respect, of esteem and of charity. You cross over this yet unstable viaduct, still under construction, with spontaneous initiative and safe confidence....'[42] Later in the visit, the Pope and the Archbishop signed a Common Declaration, launching a formal theological dialogue between Anglicans and Catholics. The closing service was at St Paul's Outside-the-Walls, said to be the site where St Paul was buried. After the service, on the steps of the church, the Pope caught the Archbishop by surprise. He took off his Episcopal ring and placed it on the right finger of the Archbishop's hand. A new era in Anglican–Roman Catholic relations was sealed and the ARCIC (Anglican–Roman Catholic International Commission) dialogues soon followed.

Studying Vatican II at the Catholic University of America enabled me to observe 'being Anglican' in settings I would not have expected. It would lead to my accompanying Archbishop Michael Ramsey's successor to Rome, to celebrate the fortieth anniversary of the groundbreaking 1966 visit. In 2006, amidst a packed programme of meetings, lectures, visits and services, Archbishop Rowan Williams would return to the Sistine Chapel and spend time with Pope Benedict XVI. They would commit to a further round of theological dialogue and renewed co-operation. The Archbishop would wear that same ring given to Michael Ramsey by Pope Paul VI. But the interest in Roman Catholic relations sparked in Washington would be fanned into flame long before then. It would prove an important feature of my curacy. As the cherry blossom in Washington came and went, it was time to return to Ridley Hall, with my curacy now on the horizon. My first post as an ordained Anglican would not exactly be typical. It would be in Paris. Fellow students at VTS eagerly promised to come and visit us there.

My sponsoring diocese, the Diocese of Newcastle, had been unable to offer me a suitable first appointment. I was therefore obliged to explore possible curacies on the open market. As is still the case, details of unfilled curacies would be circulated to theological colleges for us to peruse. In those pre-internet days, unplaced ordinands would pay regular visits to the library, to see if any new vacancies had been added to the box.

The idea of serving a curacy in France had emerged just as I was about to enter my final year at Ridley Hall. Amanda and I had spent most of the summer break in France. I had been intrigued by a throwaway line in a booklet on Christian renewal in Europe by Bishop Graham Dow, then Bishop of Willesden. He observed that 'the Anglican Church does not have churches in Europe attended by nationals from the countries of mainland Europe, with services in their own languages.... There is an understanding with the Roman Catholic church that Anglicans will keep things this way.'[43] This was now 1994, the year that Mrs Thatcher and President Mitterrand opened the Channel Tunnel. France was renowned for its secularism. It had been depicted as a 'mission field' by the Catholic writer Henri Godin, as early as 1943.[44] According to the missiologist David Bosch, Godin's *La France: Pays de Mission?* 'was the first serious study to have destroyed the "geographical myth" of mission: it proved that Europe too was a "mission field"'.[45] All this added up to a persuasive case for investigating whether an Anglican 'hands off' policy towards French-language ministry had passed its sell-by date. As times had changed, had this high-minded policy inadvertently become an abdication of responsibility?

This line of enquiry ran counter to the prevailing orthodoxy. Anglican ministry to French nationals sounded embarrassingly un-Anglican and un-ecumenical, especially in a new era for relations between Anglicans and Roman Catholics. Yet the great ecumenist, Anglican scholar and missionary bishop, Stephen Neill, encouraged me not to capitulate too easily. His credentials as an ecumenist were impeccable. He had been Associate General Secretary of the World Council of Churches, Professor of Missions and Ecumenical Theology at the University of Hamburg, and Anglican Bishop of Tinnevelly in South India. For years, his book on Anglicanism was a core text in Anglican studies. In it, he pointedly challenged the limited scope of Anglican activity in continental Europe:

> The Church of England has always taken the line that in nominally Christian countries it is not a proselytising church—it is there to care for its own children only. It is for this reason that services have been held usually in English, and in no other language; and many of the chaplains have been almost aggressively uninterested in the existence of other forms of Christianity in the area in which they ministered. But it is becoming increasingly doubtful whether this rigid attitude can be maintained.[46]

That was in 1958, and it seemed to me that nearly forty years later maintaining this rigid attitude was even more doubtful, especially in France. There were, after all, nearly two million French-speaking Anglicans elsewhere in the world.[47] Was it defensible to have none in France itself?

So in July 1994, to probe this topic further, Amanda and I embarked on a two-month *tour de France,* in our fittingly French Peugeot 205. During that time, we covered 5,500 miles on French roads, taking in visits to Lille, Paris, Normandy, Bordeaux, Toulouse, Montpelier, Aix-en-Provence, Valence, Grenoble, Burgundy and Strasbourg. We interviewed over one hundred people, including priests from Roman Catholic and Orthodox churches; pastors from Reformed, Lutheran, evangelical and Pentecostal churches; Anglican bishops, chaplains and church members; theology lecturers; leaders of youth organisations; members of religious communities including the so-called 'new communities', Taizé and the Benedictine Abbey of Bec; ordinands (Catholic and Protestant); missionaries; official representatives of various denominations; and lay members of a variety of churches.

The findings from this fascinating field study were distilled into a 100-page report, 'Anglican Mission en France'.[48] Not long after our return, we discussed these findings with the Church of England Bishop in Europe, Bishop John Hind. Energised by our encounters, I enquired whether curates would one day be taken on in France. To my surprise, the bishop spoke enthusiastically about this prospect. He was keen that the Diocese in Europe should function as a 'proper' Church of England diocese. The problem, he lamented, was that the Diocese in Europe had a very modest budget. As a result, any curates would need to be funded by the local Anglican church ('chaplaincy') where they served. A chaplaincy would need to be willing to take on a newly ordained person in the place of a more experienced assistant chaplain. As few chaplaincies could afford an assistant chaplain, the likelihood of something emerging that year was regrettably remote.

In spite of this, having both spent time living and working in France, Amanda and I found ourselves strongly attracted to the possibility of a curacy in France. We dutifully explored possible curacies in England, visiting parishes in Worthing, Canterbury, Cheltenham and inner city Bristol. But France still seemed to beckon. At one point, we explored a madcap possibility of a split curacy. The chaplain at Chantilly, to the north of Paris, was up for it. The future Bishop of London, Richard Chartres, then Bishop of Stepney, gamely offered to help find a parish in South East England willing to take a curate for part of each year. Yet after a while, common sense prevailed and the impractical idea of a twin-centre curacy was dropped.

Worryingly, when we left for the semester at Virginia Theological Seminary in January of that final year, there was still no curacy in place. We knew we could only afford to pay an air fare for one return visit to a possible training parish. By February, we were on the point of booking a flight to visit a parish in Sheffield when a fax arrived from Ridley Hall. They had received a letter from St Michael's, Paris. 'It appears they might have an opening for a deacon.'

So it was that I 'served my title' in Paris, at the church where I had worshipped in my gap year, fourteen years earlier. The France-wide focus of 'Anglican Mission en France' would be an important strand during the four and a half years that lay ahead. But the epicentre of those intensive years would be the dynamic life of a long-established and cosmopolitan city centre church.

How did this church come to occupy a prime site a few minutes' walk from the iconic Place de La Concorde and evolve into a thriving church centre? St Michael's is the nearest church of any kind to the Elysées Palace, official residence and centre of operations for the French President. It is closer still to the prestigious British Embassy, also on the boutique-lined rue du Faubourg St Honoré.

The answer can be traced back to the process of 'bringing up to date' which began in the nineteenth century. It conveniently opens the shutters to Anglican engagement in continental Europe, church–state relations and local church adaptation in changing times, as we shall now see. It reveals part of the Anglican story that is seldom told, despite the fact that the diocese in which I would serve as a curate, the Diocese in Europe, was a formidable size, spanning a landmass of 8,400 miles, and St Michael's was one of its flagship churches. So imagine yourself sitting down in a Parisian bistro with a café crème and let the story begin.

St Michael's owes its origins to a freelance bishop, Matthew Luscombe, who was concerned about Anglican congregations in France. Anglican worship had been provided in what is now France since the time of the Reformation. This continued the pre-Reformation provision of services for English subjects across continental Europe. Anglican worship had been conducted in English-controlled Calais, for example.[49] In 1633 all European congregations were placed under the jurisdiction of the Bishop of London, along with congregations in America, as already noted. This reflected London's significance as the chief port of England.[50] Congregations on the Continent were typically linked with English ambassadors and their chaplains. France was no exception. One such Embassy chaplain in seventeenth-century Paris, William Wake, went on to become Archbishop of Canterbury.[51] A successor in the eighteenth century, William Beauvoir, recorded how congregations could be small, with just fifteen to sixteen people attending weekly services in the ambassador's residence in 1715.[52]

It was in the aftermath of the Napoleonic wars that Anglican congregations began to proliferate throughout France, serving British workers and tourists.

Anglican churches duly began to be built, such as in Nice in 1822.[53] Another constructed in Boulogne could hold 1,000 worshippers and in 1829 was reported as being generally full in the summer.[54] In other locations, such as Dieppe, Anglican worship was initially held in a French Protestant chapel.[55]

This growing number of Anglicans in France and neighbouring countries needed improved episcopal care; that is what lay behind the consecration of Matthew Luscombe. He had been ordained twenty years earlier, spending much of his ministry as the first headmaster of Haileybury School. But in 1819, he moved with his family to Normandy and then on to Paris, two years later. What he encountered led him to press the Bishop of London, the Home Secretary and the Foreign Secretary for the appointment of a bishop, based in France, to assist the Bishop of London. The proposal was given serious consideration, but turned down for fear it would be seen as 'a serious intrusion and cause of suspicion, if not difficulties of a more serious kind'.[56] Given the history of animosity, it was understandably considered impolitic for the English to upset the French or for Anglicans to upset the Catholic Church.

Repeating what happened in the USA after independence, Luscombe turned to the bishops of the Scottish Episcopal Church, prompted by the advocacy of a former pupil at Haileybury, Revd Walter Hook. Luscombe wrote to the senior bishop (Primus) of the Scottish Episcopal Church in 1824, setting out the case for a bishop based in France. It was at this point he indicated his own willingness to be considered for the post, if no-one more suitable were found. The Primus consulted his fellow bishops, who agreed the proposal had merit. To test its viability, they would need to seek approval both from the Archbishop of Canterbury and from the British government. The Archbishop of Canterbury was uneasy about the idea, but let the government have the last word. Having already considered the earlier proposal, the Home Secretary, Robert Peel, and the Foreign Secretary, George Canning, had a common mind on the matter. They would not oppose the measure.[57]

Matthew Luscombe was therefore consecrated in Stirling on Palm Sunday in 1825, by three Scottish bishops. The Deed of Consecration explained he was being sent to the Continent of Europe 'not as Diocesan Bishop...but for the purpose similar to that which Titus was left by St Paul in Crete "that he may set in order the things that are wanting" among such natives of Great Britain and Ireland as he shall find there'. The 'natives' in mind were those 'professing to be members of the United Church of England and Ireland and the Episcopal Church of Scotland'.[58] They were, in other words, what we would now call Anglicans.

Luscombe moved to Paris. The initiative was predictably controversial and his former pupil, Walter Hook, was obliged to defend him back home for two years in the correspondence columns of the church press. A measure of recognition was nonetheless offered by the Bishop of London, who appointed Luscombe as his Commissary, one step down from being his 'suffragan'. Setting to work immediately, in 1825 Luscombe confirmed 120 candidates in Paris and 550 from seven congregations he visited along the Channel coastline.[59]

By 1828, Bishop Luscombe was also serving as chaplain to the British Embassy in Paris. The following year he reported weekly attendances of 350 at the Embassy and 400–500 at the Protestant Oratoire. Given these numbers, he started lobbying for a dedicated Anglican centre of worship.[60] No funds were forthcoming, so in 1833 he took it upon himself to finance the construction of a church close to the British Embassy, in rue d'Aguesseau.[61] It was to be known as the British Embassy Church for well over a century, only being dedicated to St Michael in 1969. This, then, is how St Michael's came to be located on such a prestigious site.

But how did it go on to flourish as a cosmopolitan church centre? And how was Bishop Luscombe's vision taken forward? When Bishop Luscombe died in 1846, his successor bought the church. It was a perfectly satisfactory arrangement for the eleven years Revd William Chamier served as chaplain. This, however, was no long-term solution and when he retired the church was put up for sale. The British Ambassador, Earl Cowley, almost succeeded in getting the Foreign Office to buy it. Unfortunately, the House of Commons took a dim view of this, and refused to vote the purchase money, contending that the British community should take responsibility for it. It was at this point that another significant player in the life of this church entered the scene. The Colonial and Continental Church Society stepped in, empowering the Bishop of London to offer £9,000 for the building. The British community in Paris contributed £2,000 towards this and Queen Victoria chipped in with £100, no doubt 'pour encourager les autres'.[62]

The Colonial and Continental Church Society (CCCS), known today as the Intercontinental Church Society (ICS), still owns the church. ICS and its antecedents have supported ministry amongst English speakers since 1823. Initially it was active in Canada and Australia. So when my grandfather began his second year training for ordination in Canada in 1922, twenty-four of the thirty-three candidates in training were sponsored by CCCS.[63] However, its activities had extended to continental Europe in 1839. From 1884, it funded the bishop finally appointed to take forward Luscombe's vision by assisting the Bishop of London in his oversight of continental churches. It also funded the purchase of numerous churches in continental Europe. But the church I would serve in as curate was not the one built by Bishop Luscombe. Nor was it any longer referred to as the Embassy Church. Luscombe's building had witnessed some prestigious occasions, such as the memorial services for King Edward VII in 1910, King George VI in 1952 and Winston Churchill in 1965, each attended by senior representatives of the French government.[64] In the early part of the twentieth century it was seen as a 'centre of earnest work among the British colony and of active "parochial" organisations'.[65] It weathered two world wars, the second of which saw it closed for four years, during the German occupation of Paris. But in the decades following World War Two, as English speakers were increasingly drawn to Paris, its limitations became all too evident.

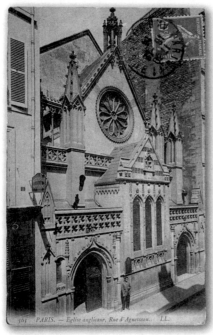

Bishop Luscombe's
Embassy Church,
later to become
St Michael's, Paris

Author's personal archives

The Embassy Church lacked any meeting rooms and toilets. As early as the 1890s, the chaplain had tried unsuccessfully to acquire a neighbouring building. By the 1960s, relying on the chaplain's flat for church activities became increasingly impractical and unpopular with the chaplain's longsuffering neighbours. The Anglican church at the other end of the Champs Elysées, St George's, was facing similar challenges. At the same time, the councils of both churches were facing up to the shifting demography of British residents in Paris. Increasingly, expatriates were choosing to live in the less expensive suburbs. A proposal emerged to consolidate assets. The Embassy Church and St George's would share the same site.

This kind of rationalisation inevitably required the involvement of the Embassy. Lord Soames, Winston Churchill's son-in-law, had been appointed British Ambassador in 1968. A committed Anglican, he immediately played an active part in the life of the Embassy Church, along with his wife. Shortly after his appointment, the congregation voted unanimously to dedicate the church to St Michael. Lord Soames supported this and in 1969 the Embassy Church was formally consecrated as St Michael's Church by the Archbishop of York, Donald Coggan. Two things followed shortly afterwards. First, the proposal for housing St Michael's and St George's on the same site began to be considered in earnest. Second, a new chaplain was appointed in 1970, having been advised of this proposal. Revd Eric McLellan was the candidate proposed by CCCS. It was he who had lodged briefly with us in Ardingly and assisted in finding accommodation for my gap year in Paris. Unfortunately, Lord Soames was not convinced he was suitable. The wardens re-interviewed him, and remained satisfied that his track record as a preacher and pastor made him a suitable candidate for the appointment. But a fault line between church and embassy was beginning to emerge.

In April 1972, the Bishop of London's suffragan, John Satterthwaite, preached at St Michael's. He conveyed episcopal support for the merger, so long as sixty percent of the congregation were in agreement. Just a few weeks earlier, St Michael's had hosted a congregational meeting to discuss the proposal, with Lord and Lady Soames present. Lord Soames had announced he was in favour, only to be opposed somewhat discourteously by a young student. While saying nothing at the time, it seems he was affronted that no efforts to offer an apology had been made by his chaplain, Eric McLellan. The following day, he wrote an aggrieved letter to the wardens, informing them that from 30 April 1972, the name of the British Embassy Church should no longer be used in correspondence.[66]

This parting of the ways might have been inevitable, had St Michael's moved to join St George's in common premises. But as things turned out, the merger was blocked. St George's voted unanimously, but St Michael's was four percent short of the required sixty percent. That left both churches with the problem of inadequate buildings, along with the severing of historic ties between St Michael's and the Embassy. What is more, the congregation of St Michael's had been shaken by the experience, with some of its members choosing to worship elsewhere.

The church council, in agreement with cccs, decided it was necessary to go for an equally bold course of action. Business as usual was no longer an option. They would redevelop the site to include offices, a place of worship, meeting rooms and an apartment for the chaplain. cccs would retain a forty-nine percent share. The plan went ahead, but in the event it was rather a botched job. Poor visibility on the balcony was symptomatic of a poorly conceived design. To make matters worse, the contractors went bankrupt during construction and left a legacy of shoddy workmanship. Yet, for all its deficiencies, when consecrated by the Bishop of London on 29 November 1975, the building provided sufficient facilities for St Michael's to thrive as a centre of hospitality and multiple activities, at the heart of one of the world's great cities.

That, then, provides the backstory to a thriving city-centre Anglican Church in a European capital. But the 'bringing up to date' didn't end with the open-ing of the new church in 1975, because times continued to change, even as I joined its clergy team. By the time I was appointed assistant chaplain, twenty years later, St Michael's had outgrown its facilities once again. The chaplain was no longer living in an apartment in the church centre. Bedrooms had become offices for a staff team comprising a chaplain, assistant chaplain, music director, secretary and pastoral assistant. Living rooms had become meeting rooms, used daytime and evenings, seven days a week. The chaplain lived in rented accommodation fifteen minutes' walk away. As assistant chaplain, there was no question of my living on site. Instead, Amanda and I would live in an apartment near the business district, La Défense. That would mean a daily thirty-minute commute to the church centre via Saint Lazare railway station, a modest travelling time by Paris standards.

In the Church of England, each diocese usually arranges for its candidates to be ordained together in June, around St Peter's Day. However, as I was something of a guinea pig, the Diocese in Europe had no such routine arrangement. It was therefore decided that I should move over the summer, but not be ordained until September. So the day before St Michael's Day, at St Michael's Church, Paris, I was ordained deacon by the Bishop of Gibraltar in Europe, Bishop John Hind.

The Church of England has always been clear that the ministry of deacon is an integral part of the Anglican understanding of ministry. In the preface to its ordination services, it asserts that the threefold ministry of deacon, priest (or presbyter) and bishop has its origins in the early church.[67] This is supported by strong ecumenical consensus that this threefold pattern became established as the pattern of ministry throughout the church by the second and third centuries.[68] Justification for the ministry of deacon can also be found in the New Testament, where it is repeatedly cited as a separate order of ministry. Yet the role of deacon can seem a little opaque. In part, this is because it has had an untidy history since New Testament times. Across church traditions, it has proved the most malleable of ministries.

Getting started: ordained deacon by the Bishop in Europe, John Hind

Author's personal archives

It was in the nineteenth century that the Church of England developed the notion of transitional deacons serving as apprentices to experienced priests. In 1995, when I was ordained deacon, there were two forms of authorised ordination service. One dated back to Thomas Cranmer in 1556. It had been the only authorised ordination service until 1980. The other was contained in the *Alternative Service Book* (ASB), approved in 1980. This newer version was based on the ordinal prepared for the ill-fated Anglican–Methodist unity scheme in 1968. In the ASB ordinal, the questions asked of deacons and priests were virtually identical. Yet, compared with the ordination of priests, the bishop set out a fairly scanty job description for deacons. The emphasis was on caring for the needy, preaching the word of God, searching out the indifferent and assisting the priest in leading worship.

These would all be features of my ministry as a transitional deacon in the coming year. The impression given in the ordinal was of priest and deacon doing most of their respective work singlehandedly, with the deacon doing 'such pastoral work as is entrusted to him'. Yet the reality would be of harnessing the gifts of the laity, with a strongly evangelistic dimension to church activities. When the ordinal was revised again in 2006, it would catch up with these emphases on every member ministry and mission.

However incomplete the role description may have been, I was required to affirm my sense of calling, prior to the bishop laying hands on me and praying for God to 'send down the Holy Spirit' on me. During the ordination service, the bishop also asked about the well-springs of my faith. I affirmed my willingness to accept the Holy Scriptures as revealing all things necessary for eternal salvation and to expound the Christian faith as the Church of England has received it. I vowed to be diligent in reading Scripture and prayer, and to fashion my life according to 'the way of Christ'. I pledged to accept the discipline and authority of the Church and to promote unity and love among all Christian people.

The ordination service at St Michael's was preceded by a private ceremony, where I was asked to make the Declaration of Assent. This required an affirmation of loyalty to the Anglican inheritance of faith. The Declaration of Assent must be made whenever someone is ordained and each time Church of England clergy take up a new appointment. More prominently than in the ASB ordination service for deacons, there is an emphasis on mission. Assent is given in the context of bringing 'the grace and truth of Christ to this generation'.

These were all weighty vows, linked to a lifetime's calling. But the overriding sense was of getting started and launching into bringing the 'grace and truth of Christ' to a generation living at the close of the second millennium in a bustling European city.

✠

In this chapter, we have observed a variety of ways in which, to borrow Pope John XXIII's watchword, there has been a 'bringing up to date' (aggiornamento) of Anglican life, in varied contexts and successive generations. We have seen this in relation to the ordination of women to the priesthood. Alongside this, we have seen the development of other forms of authorised ministry and lay leadership roles, especially in the Church of England. This has included deaconesses, deacons, readers, churchwardens and the institution of parochial church councils.

In the USA, we have seen how Anglican life has sought to keep pace with political and social developments. This has included the introduction of a distinctive form of church polity in the Episcopal Church, including General Convention and bishops with no formal link to the state in the USA or in England. We have seen Anglican liturgy evolve in the USA, taking account of scholarly insights and prevailing cultural norms. In Paris, we witnessed pressure to bring church buildings up to date, to allow for diversified church activities. Both in the USA and Europe, we have seen signs of growing cross-fertilisation between churches that would comprise what we now call the

Anglican Communion. In particular, we have seen the Episcopal Church in Scotland assist in ensuring bishops were consecrated to oversee Anglican congregations in the USA and continental Europe. We have witnessed the emerging role of the Lambeth Conference in providing guidance for innovation in individual Anglican provinces. We have also noted how this forum for discernment came to be supplemented by a consultative council that meets more frequently, the ACC.

As 'being Anglican' has been brought up to date in successive generations, locally and internationally, we have seen differing relations to political authority. We have noted how American independence presented clergy with conflicting political loyalties. We have seen how the British parliament complied with the desire for the Archbishop of Canterbury to consecrate bishops for America. We have seen Secretaries of State taking the lead in approving the unconventional provision of oversight to European Anglican congregations by Bishop Matthew Luscombe. We have also seen how congregations associated with British Embassies could lose their formal link, as happened to St Michael's in Paris.

We have also noted how changes in other churches have sometimes provided the impetus for Anglican *aggiornamento*. This was the case when the German Lutheran Church established its deaconess community in Kaiserswerth. It was true in a more far-reaching way when Pope John XXIII called a second Vatican Council, and Anglicans needed to take a fresh look at how they related to Roman Catholics. Yet, we have also acknowledged that non-Anglican churches have sometimes inhibited 'bringing up to date'. This is the case for the ordination of women to the priesthood, where the process of 'reception' takes account of the fact that other parts of the 'catholic' Church are not persuaded that this is acceptable. It is a reminder that 'bringing up to date' can be a controversial process. We have seen attempts to justify innovations as more than simply going along with the 'spirit of the times'. Bishop Tait, for example, justified the licensing of deaconesses on the grounds that this was a renewal of a New Testament order.

We turn next to observe grassroots experience of Anglican life in a context that is both similar and different to the parishes in which my grandparents lived as Anglicans. We join St Michael's for the *Rentrée*. This is when Paris comes alive after the interlude when any self-respecting Parisian has headed for the coast or countryside, for their annual down-time with the family.

Catholic neighbours:
L'Eglise de La Madeleine,
a few minutes' walk
from St Michael's

_____

Photo © Alf van Beem,
available under the Creative
Commons CC0 1.0 Universal
Public Domain Dedication

8

Chez Nous in Continental Europe?

IT WAS THE RENTRÉE, the time of year when Parisians are back from their month-long summer holiday and new people arrive in Paris. As usual, English-speaking students and au pairs gravitated towards St Michael's, along with Commonwealth diplomats, expatriate business people, English teachers and musicians. St Michael's had long grown accustomed to a high turnover of its members each year. In some ways it was like a bath with both taps running and the plug taken out.

Not everyone was transient though. Some had married French nationals or were children of bicultural families. Others just liked Paris and had chosen to make it their permanent home, perhaps because they worked in the fashion industry or for a French multinational. Their numbers were swelled by those whose employment brought them to Paris for more than a brief period. Remarkably quickly, such people became assimilated into the 'core' membership of St Michael's.

As might therefore be expected, there were some familiar faces from my time at St Michael's in my gap year. They included two couples sharing the name of John and Claudia. These were pillars of the church, two of them serving as churchwardens during my time. Of these three Americans and one Briton, one was an accountant, one a lawyer, one a PR executive and one a full-time mother. By this time, they had five children between them. Then there was David, an Englishman who had worked his way up through a French bank and was now married. Hede, a German, had become the leading figure in St Michael's prison-visiting ministry. Jim, an English agricultural economist with the OECD—and my former landlord—was still running the thriving St Michael's Christian bookstall. Connie, the Canadian organist was now the Music Director and Church Administrator.

These were some of the 'long-termers' amidst three hundred and fifty people worshipping each Sunday at St Michael's. The main morning service was fairly standard Church of England 'low church' fare of the time, with the choir typically singing an anthem. It attracted families from central Paris and the suburbs, with a lively Sunday school for the children and an 'all-age' service once a month. The evening service was more informal, with a music group accompanying the singing. Most of its congregation were under 35 and the service was followed by a gathering of the 18–25s group, Square One.

The congregation had become much more international since 1981. On a typical Sunday, there were forty different nationalities. Not all of these were from the British Isles, North America and English-speaking Commonwealth countries. They included worshippers from non-Anglophone countries such as Vietnam, Iran and Hungary. Many different denominations were represented too, from Lebanese Maronite to Southern Baptist.

Thanks to the church centre, hospitality was a central feature of church life. After the morning service, Sunday lunch was offered upstairs in 'the Salle' for up to sixty people. After the evening service, food was provided for the young people's group, Square One. During weekdays, there was food after lunchtime services, afternoon teas for the Toc H senior citizens group and hot meals before evening meetings. As might be expected in Paris, there was plenty of hospitality in people's homes too. Home groups were often preceded by a meal. Dinner parties were constantly being hosted by those church members who had suitably-sized accommodation. The custom in Paris was to eat late and not be too strict about arrival time, given the potential for transport hold-ups. The record arrival time for one of our dinner party guests was 10.25pm.

There was no escaping the fact that this curacy was in Paris. Just two months after my ordination, all the transport workers went on strike, in reaction to moves to raise the train drivers' retirement age above 55 years. Delaying retirement was something to do with the logic of no longer needing to shovel coal, but the proposal sparked mayhem. Paris was gridlocked for much of November. Yet despite this idiosyncratic context, my France-based curacy shared much in common with its counterparts in England.

Somewhat implausibly, for example, there was cricket, even if there was no clergy league. In 1957, Queen Elizabeth II had opened the British Standard Athletic Club in the Paris suburbs. It was now customary for the assistant chaplain at St Michael's to be offered complimentary membership of the Standard Athletic cricket team. During my first year as curate, I duly signed up to play. I was informed by a team-mate that the only person to have hit a six over the poplar tree was a former assistant chaplain, Revd Stephen Wookey. Not being a former Oxford University cricket blue myself, I failed dismally to be the trump card the team no doubt had hoped for.

Also in common with English clerical life were civic events. St Michael's was no longer the British Embassy Church; France modelled an even stricter separation between church and state than the USA. But we still rallied for days of national importance. There was a Remembrance Day service, for example, organised by the British Legion in Paris. It was in Notre Dame Cathedral, with St Michael's clergy and choir taking a leading part. Processing out with the organ resonating was one up on the standard tourist experience. We had a Battle of Britain service too, which was held in St Michael's itself. We needed to be mindful that St Michael's was no longer a church just for the British, so did our best to be sensitive to other nationalities. This was not a matter of being politically correct, but of being internationally astute. One year, for example, a young Japanese opera singer agreed to sing the anthem at the Battle of Britain service. For the British war veterans present, it powerfully symbolised commitment to peace and reconciliation.

Most features held in common with English parish life had a distinctive twist to them. There was an annual church sale, for example. But as St Michael's was entirely self-financing, with a sizeable staff team, the sale needed to yield more than your average church fete. So one Saturday in November each year, the chairs were stacked away and the church turned into a bazaar. It attracted impressive crowds from around Paris, lured by its stock of Christmas puddings, second-hand books in English and cast-offs from the fashion trade. Typically, it would raise £15,000, an amount comfortably exceeding the curate's stipend.

There were business lunches too. By custom, clergy from St Michael's were treated to a free lunch once a month at the prestigious Cercle Interalliée club, next to the British Embassy. The 'quid pro quo' was to say grace. The British Luncheon had its origins in World War One, when senior members of the British Community met to discuss which British residents should be conscripted into the army. It had subsequently become a congenial social club for British business people in Paris. With my own business background, and enjoying a good meal, I was more than pleased to take my turn as the clergy representative. I rather misjudged what was required though. I thought it would be a good idea to weave some topical item into each grace, such as the horrific shooting of sixteen schoolchildren in Dunblane in March 1996. One of the stalwarts of St Michael's was tasked with gently requesting that the eager young curate keep his graces a bit shorter.

As so-called 'occasional offices' are *de rigeur* for curacies, there were fortunately quite a few weddings and baptisms, as well as the occasional funeral. The major difference was that most of them had to be conducted bilingually. My imperfect French was put to the test two months into the curacy. It was my first wedding, and both the bride and groom were French. In the case of funerals, it was sometimes quipped that the only English speaker was in the coffin. Baptism and marriage preparation frequently needed to be conducted bilingually. Another difference came from the separation of church and state in France. There was no chapel at the crematorium at Père Lachaise Cemetery, for example. Similarly, at wedding services, there was no need for legal formalities, unlike in England. Since 1792, all marriages in France had been conducted as civil ceremonies. So by the time the church ceremony took place, the bride and groom were usually already legally married. However, that did not stop us using the authorised Church of England marriage service. Taking our lead from the Catholic Church in France, we treated the marriage service as though it were the point at which a couple really did become formally married, rather than simply treating it as a service of blessing. At times, when one of the couple was Catholic, the marriage was a joint celebration, combining Anglican and Catholic liturgy, with both Anglican and Catholic clergy officiating.

As would be true for busy parishes in England, St Michael's had plenty of courses and midweek activities for church members. In my first year, we ran the Alpha course in Christian basics and a course on developing prayer life. We also launched the 'Dovetail' initiative, to help church members relate their faith to the challenges of the workplace. One of our guest speakers was a banker who had just published a book, *Serving God, Serving Mammon*.[1] He went on to become chair of HSBC and Minister of Trade. Another speaker was my former ethics tutor at Ridley Hall, Richard Higginson, who directed the God on Monday project. By coincidence, a 'faith in the workplace' assignment I produced for him as a student had examined a francophone setting. It was a study of archetypal approaches to work, based on characters from *Les Misérables*.

In the midst of the hectic round of courses, social activities and services, it was heart-warming to see Christian faith awakened and deepened. People used to say with justification, 'Lost in Paris? Find Christ at St Michael's'. There was a real appetite for Christian teaching and a sense that time invested in sermon preparation would yield long-term results. On one occasion, St Michael's was visited by a member of the church Amanda attended as a teenager in Frinton-on-Sea. Maurice Rowlandson had been the national organiser for three of Billy Graham's missions to England. He told me the story of a lunch he hosted for his senior assistants from each of these three missions. None of these assistants had met each other before. He decided to ask them in turn to tell their Christian stories. The first began by saying, 'Well, I became a Christian at St Michael's, Paris'. The other two both looked stunned and exclaimed 'So did I!'

There was no shortage of acute pastoral problems at St Michael's. Paris seemed to attract people with complex back-stories, such as a mother whose son had just been murdered in Singapore. When misfortune struck, English speakers in need would make their way to St Michael's, whether or not they were churchgoers. Those already worshipping at St Michael's were not immune from the pressures of ill-health and relationship difficulties themselves. Not being in their country of origin, however, they tended not to have the usual support structures and therefore relied more heavily on the church. The congregation often rallied round marvellously, such as when one young Bulgarian businessman developed a malignant brain tumour and his English wife was diagnosed with cancer shortly afterwards.

In common with churches in England, St Michael's also attracted plenty of homeless people. Some of these *sans abri,* as they are known in France, simply wanted help getting home. Others, such as Eamon, seemed content staying in Paris and joined our congregation. We could refer people to hostels and provide food and practical support. We even had a fund dedicated to supporting 'the poor of rue d'Aguesseau', evoking the street characters of *Les Misérables.* We had a policy of no financial handouts. But we did sometimes help with return travel to England. We also attracted asylum seekers and did what we could to ensure they received a fair hearing. In one rare instance, we even managed to facilitate the emigration of a young refugee family to the USA.

Ecumenical relations were rather different from those of an English parish. Our nearest Protestant neighbour was a reformed congregation, *L'Eglise Réformée du St Esprit.* The Church of England was involved in an ecumenical dialogue with the French Reformed (ERF) and Lutheran churches at the time. The pastor of St Esprit, Jean-Arnold de Clermont, was an official delegate in these 'Reuilly Conversations'. This was indicative of the goodwill that existed between St Michael's and St Esprit. Their place of worship, rendered as *temple* in French, was a good deal bigger than St Michael's. We therefore made use of it for our annual carol service. It was a high point in the year for our choir and was preceded by a family-friendly variant at St Michael's the day before. Together the services attracted nine hundred French and English speakers and we took the opportunity to invite everyone back to St Michael's after the main service for mulled wine and minced pies. There is no French culinary equivalent to minced pies. We got round this by inviting everyone for *tartes traditionelles anglaises,* having imported all nine hundred from England in the back of our car.

We cultivated informal links with a range of French-speaking Protestant congregations. These included *L'Eglise Réformée de Belleville,* in the multi-ethnic and less prosperous district of the 20ᵗʰ Arrondissement. Its pastor was an ordained Anglican, Charlie Cleverly, who went on to become Rector of St Aldate's in Oxford, where I had worshipped as an undergraduate. As for Catholic relations, informal links included involvement by members of our congregation in the so-called new communities, such as Chemin Neuf. Our nearest Catholic neighbour was the parish of *L'Eglise de la Madeleine.* Just off the Place de la Concorde, the Madeleine is a famous Paris landmark, looking much more like a Greek temple than the *temple* of *L'Eglise Réformée du St Esprit.* The building was commissioned by Napoleon as a temple to the glory of the Great Army. After Napoleon's defeat, Louis xviii decreed it would become a church, but in 1837 it was nearly selected as Paris' first railway terminal. Finally it was consecrated as a church in 1842, dedicated to St Mary Magdalene.

Our main contact at the Madeleine was a retired South African priest, Canon Arnold Smit. As a diplomat before his ordination, he had been posted to Paris and had practised the organ in the old St Michael's. Relations were cordial; he preached at St Michael's and we enjoyed North African cuisine at the Presbytery, fifty metres from the church. During my first year at St Michael's, a new priest-in-charge of the Madeleine was appointed. I agreed to represent St Michael's at the installation of the curé. Robed in my white cassock alb and stole, I was indistinguishable from the bevy of Catholic clergy I processed in with. They were rather taken aback when I explained I was Anglican.

Of the two Church of England chaplaincies in central Paris, it was more common for St George's to be associated with Roman Catholicism. 'More Roman than the Catholics' is how it is described in the memoirs of a British Embassy official in the 1990s, Sherard Cowper-Coles.[2] St Michael's is described equally undiplomatically by him. Yet it is nonetheless true that St George's did tend to be described, with affection, as *'Plus catho que les catholiques'.* It was well placed for nurturing relations between Anglicans and Roman

Catholics in France. Its senior chaplain, Martin Draper, was the Archdeacon for France. He had been appointed in 1984 and took the lead role for Anglican ecumenical relations in France. He followed a succession of enterprising predecessors. Roger Greenacre (1965–75) had played an influential role in nurturing Anglican relations with the French Catholic Church, as commissioned by the Archbishop of Canterbury. Frederic Cardew (1907–34) had developed a missionary congregation for the five hundred or so young English women working on the Paris stage. In a more cynical age, the photo of Father Cardew playing the piano at the Theatre Girls Hostel, surrounded by dancers, would have been a gift for satirists at *Private Eye*.

St George's is located a few minutes' walk from the Arc de Triomphe, at the opposite end of the Champs Elysées to St Michael's. A church was first built on that site in 1887 to replace an earlier building, the Chapel Marboeuf, which had been demolished with the widening of avenues in central Paris. After the unsuccessful attempt to bring St Michael's and St George's together in 1972, St George's opted for a similar solution to St Michael's and redeveloped its own site. There were therefore Anglican churches of differing traditions at either end of the Champs Elysées, each with a busy church centre. I was pleased as part of my post-ordination training to spend the run-up to Easter at St George's, under the tutelage of Father Martin Draper. Easter being during the school holidays, I had not witnessed a distinctive Anglo-Catholic observance of Holy Week as a schoolboy. Some of the symbolism took quite a bit of explaining, but other aspects were straightforward and powerful, such as prostration before the cross on Good Friday. The Easter vigil, with the church plunged in darkness then bathed in light with bells ringing, was something I encountered again the following year in Crete, when Amanda and I celebrated Easter in an Orthodox Church.

Midway between St George's and St Michael's was another Anglican Church, the American Cathedral. Established for American Episcopalians, it had been consecrated as Holy Trinity Church in 1886. In 1922, it became a pro-cathedral and seat for an American bishop responsible for American churches in Europe. There were thus parallel Anglican jurisdictions in continental Europe. This was regarded as an anomaly by Anglican bishops at Lambeth Conferences.[3] But for Anglicans wishing to distance themselves from their own province, it has in recent times been appealed to as a precedent for the controversial notion of overlapping jurisdictions.[4] As a step towards integration, bishops of the Diocese in Europe and the American Convocation of Churches were assistant bishops in one another's jurisdictions. It was, for example, the American bishop Jeffery Rowthorn who licensed Amanda as reader at St Michael's.

At the end of my first year at St Michael's, I could already look back on a great deal of rich and varied exposure to Anglican life in this privileged setting. Amanda and I had learnt to savour the sense of satisfaction at the end of a busy Sunday, when we would drive out of the underground car park and set off down the glittering Champs Elysées, homeward bound. The time had come for me to be ordained priest. The ordaining bishop would be Bishop Henry Scriven, suffragan bishop in Europe. He later confided it was his first ordination. His subsequent experience illustrates how overlapping jurisdictions are indeed a live issue for the Anglican Communion. From being suffragan bishop in Europe, he moved to the United States to be assistant bishop in the Diocese of Pittsburgh. His senior colleague in the diocese, Bishop Bob Duncan, ended up leaving the Episcopal Church and became the Archbishop of the Anglican Church in North America, the rival jurisdiction to the Episcopal Church (USA). Bishop Henry Scriven moved to England to run the South American Missionary Society.

Once again, the ordination took place at St Michael's. Before returning to the vows made when I was ordained deacon, the bishop set out the nature of a priest's ministry. In contrast to the description of a deacon's role, the priest is described as shepherd. In his interactive sermon, the bishop asked for suggestions as to what that might mean. The metaphor evokes the charge given to church elders (presbyters) in the New Testament. The Apostle Paul, in his tearful parting from the elders in Ephesus, tells them to 'be shepherds of the church of God' (Acts 20:28). The ordination service emphasises serving the flock and building up their faith through teaching. The priest is 'to proclaim the word of God, to call his hearers to repentance and in Christ's name to absolve and declare forgiveness of sins'.

In practice, the two things I would be able to do as priest which I could not do as deacon were presiding at Holy Communion and declaring sins absolved. This difference can sometimes give the impression that, for Anglicans, the essence of being a priest is those two things. Yet it is significant that, at the time of the Reformation, Thomas Cranmer withdrew the practice of giving newly ordained priests a chalice and patten during the ordination service. From that point onwards, they have been given a Bible instead. It was therefore a Bible I received. The emphasis in the ordination service is emphatically a ministry of both Word and sacrament.

The term 'priest' might nonetheless suggest precedence should be given to the liturgical role of the priest in celebrating Holy Communion. It conjures up Old Testament imagery of sacrifice and altars. However, the ASB Ordinal tellingly describes the service as 'The ordination of Priests (also called presbyters)'. The New Testament uses the term 'priest' in describing Christ as the 'Great High Priest' (Hebrews 4:14). It rarely applies it to church ministers and never uses it to define their distinctive office. On one occasion the Apostle Paul engages in the 'priestly duty' of proclaiming the gospel of God (Romans 15:16). Elsewhere it is made clear that all Christians are priests (1 Peter 2:5,9). Reference to the 'priesthood' of all Christians is embedded in the prayers of the ASB Ordinal. But in the New Testament, the Church's ministers are presbyters (or elders), deacons and bishops, rather than priests.

'Receive the power to offer sacrifice to God.' Those were the bishop's words when the chalice was handed to the candidate for ordination, in the pre-Reformation Sarum rite.[5] This model of a sacrificing priesthood was roundly condemned by the Protestant reformers, Cranmer included. It was bound up with the notion that the Mass could be said on your behalf, by a priest, to lessen your time in purgatory. The charging of fees for this ('indulgences') was what Luther railed against in the Ninety-Five Theses that triggered the Reformation. In Cranmer's liturgy for Holy Communion, Jesus Christ's death on the cross is the only sacrifice that ultimately counts. He 'made there (by his one oblation of himself once offered) a full, perfect, and sufficient sacrifice, oblation and satisfaction, for the sins of the whole world'.[6] Any sacrifice that the rest of us offer is in grateful and humble response to God's initiative. 'Accept this our sacrifice of praise and thanksgiving' is what worshippers pray after receiving communion. In Cranmer's 1552 ordinal, reference to any kind of sacrificing priesthood is conspicuously absent. And when an eirenic attempt was made to find common ground with Catholics in the late nineteenth century, through offshore discussions between a French Catholic and an English Lord, it was precisely this omission that caused the exercise to backfire. In 1896, Pope Leo XIII declared Anglican orders 'absolutely null and utterly void'. The 1552 ordinal of Thomas Cranmer 'omitted reference to the Eucharist as sacrifice and the relationship between sacrifice and the priesthood', the papal bull declared.[7]

So why did Cranmer's ordinal use the term priest and presbyter interchangeably, when the medieval notion of 'priest' had been discredited? Here is the answer: in medieval English, 'priest' was the English word used to translate presbyter. In the Latin version of Cranmer's Prayer Book and ordinal, the word for presbyter was used. But in the English version, presbyter was translated as priest, because that was the English word commonly used at that time.[8] For reformers wishing to distance themselves from the way the role of 'priest' had come to be understood in the medieval Catholic Church, this was problematic. The conundrum was tackled by Richard Hooker, as he tried to make sense of the Church of England in the sixteenth century. Hooker had no problem in principle with using the term priest. But he conceded that it could conjure up unhelpful connotations and so saw the advantages of referring to presbyters instead.

> I would rather the one sort presbyters than priests, because in a matter of so small moment I would not offend their ears to whom the name of priesthood is odious, though without cause.... Seeing then that sacrifice is now no part of church ministry, how should the name of priesthood be thereunto applied? Wherefore, whether we call it a priesthood, a presbytership, or a ministry, it skilleth not: although in truth the word presbyter doth seem more fit, and in propriety of speech.[9]

For Anglicans, the term priest has stuck, despite Protestant reservations. And it has come to be cherished, pointing to the way ordained clergy represent and animate the common priesthood of all Christians. But it need not imply priority should be given to celebrating communion, rather than the ministry of the Word. In France, there are additional linguistic challenges if you are ordained as an Anglican. Do you describe yourself as *prêtre* or *pasteur?* To French Protestant ears, *prêtre* can sound as though you are distancing yourself from the Reformation origins of the Church of England. In French Catholic circles, *prêtre* can sometimes prompt an uneasy response too—especially if you are accompanied by your wife, until you hastily explain you are Anglican and entitled to be married. Yet elsewhere Anglicans have become accustomed to calling their clergy priests, as reflected in the ARCIC international dialogues launched by Archbishop Ramsey and Pope Paul VI in 1966. Downplaying this in a predominantly Catholic country would be a denial of efforts to find common ground, even if Anglican priesthood is officially judged 'null and void' by the Catholic church.

Evangelical Anglicans have sometimes gone to extremes in downplaying the importance of Holy Communion, in reaction to the legacy of the Oxford Movement.[10] I have been at services where communion has felt like a rushed epilogue to the main service. The undervaluing of communion is not an inevitable feature of evangelical Anglicanism. This is illustrated well by Charles Simeon, the influential Cambridge-based evangelical whose example inspired the founding of Ridley Hall. Writing of his conversion at an Easter Day communion service at King's College, he says, 'at the Lord's table in our Chapel I had the sweetest access to God through my blessed Saviour'.[11] Undervaluing Holy Communion was not a feature of St Michael's, Paris either. Anglican liturgical celebration of Holy Communion was accessible to those of Protestant and Catholic backgrounds. Once ordained priest, I found it deeply moving to see believers from so many nations and church backgrounds gather round the Lord's Table.

As with the service for deacons, the emphasis on harnessing the gifts of all believers and mobilising the people of God in mission was barely discernible in the ordination liturgy. But the bishop drew this out admirably in his interactive sermon. One thing the liturgy did stress was that 'you cannot bear the weight of this ministry in your own strength but only by the grace and power of God'. Little did I realise how much this would be put to the test in my remaining time at St Michael's.

For the *Rentrée* in 1996, Paris welcomed a new British Ambassador, Sir Michael Jay, who would go on to be Head of the Diplomatic Corps. Sir Michael and his wife had moved into their historic residence in July. The building had been bought by the Duke of Wellington from Napoleon's sister. Queen Victoria had used its ballroom as her throne room. Margaret Thatcher had received the news of her downfall when staying there for the summit to celebrate the end of the Cold War. As the Jays settled in, it was evident that there was no trace of the awkwardness that had accompanied the rupture with St Michael's under Lord Soames. St Michael's clergy were welcomed as guests in their magnificent residence and, at Christmas, our choir sang carols in the ballroom. In the summer, we would be invited to the 'QBP', the annual Queen's Birthday Party. At one memorable QBP, we would witness the Regimental Band of The Royal Welsh marching up and down the ambassador's garden, obediently accompanied by the regimental goat.

Lady Sylvia Jay entered enthusiastically into her role as ambassador's spouse. As guest of honour at the British Luncheon Christmas dinner, she spoke of being one of a dying breed of 'two-fors'. This, she explained, was the 'two-for-the-price-of-one' package. It was no longer possible to assume, she explained, that if an ambassador is appointed their spouse will automatically work full-time in support. It resonated with our own reflections on the role of the clergy spouse. Amanda was pleased to play an active role in the life of St Michael's. But she also worked four days a week, teaching English to business people. And her main formal contribution to St Michael's was as a reader, not as a clergy spouse. It was a different pattern to that followed by my grandmother.

It was by no means all pomp and ceremony at St Michael's. This second year at St Michael's witnessed a significant break with its English-speaking tradition, as it sought to accommodate the needs of refugees. A service for Tamil speakers was launched.

The very first week after I had been ordained deacon, a Sri Lankan Tamil had come to see me. John Princely Croos had once been a Roman Catholic seminarian, but had subsequently been drawn to independent charismatic fellowships. Princely explained how large numbers of Tamils had come to Paris to flee the civil war in Sri Lanka. Though most were Hindu, some were demonstrating a genuine interest in Christian faith and were joining independent charismatic fellowships. Unfortunately, there had been problems with leaders of these fellowships. Princely's proposal was that St Michael's become the base for a Tamil speakers' fellowship. He argued that the Anglican Church was known and trusted in Sri Lanka. He felt that St Michael's could provide the right blend of accountability and openness to charismatic spirituality.

I discussed this with my senior colleague and we agreed that the first step should be for us to get to know Princely over the next twelve months. The church could then judge whether it might be right to proceed. A year later, the church council agreed we should try out what Princely had proposed. So in December, the Tamil Fellowship was launched, with a colourful Christmas party. Monthly services then began on Sunday afternoons. Before long these became weekly. Princely was the anchor person, with St Michael's clergy taking it in turns to preach and officiate. When the children were present, translation was into both Tamil and French, as the older ones were at French schools. Sixteen years later, the fellowship is still going strong and Princely has been ordained.

The launching of the Tamil service compounded the sense that the church centre was in need of remedial attention. With so many activities, it was manifestly unfit for purpose. The council had set up a working group earlier in the year to oversee re-ordering of the premises. Using the former chaplain's apartment as offices had turned the place into a rabbit warren. The annexe at the back of church, where coffee was served, was shabby and poorly equipped. A phased development programme was therefore conceived.

On the surface, St Michael's was thriving. But a crisis was looming. My senior colleague was much appreciated for his pastoral skills, but there was an increasing sense that running such a busy church did not play to his strengths. Unlike clergy in England, he was on a fixed term contract. After much deliberation, the churchwardens decided not to renew it. This proved to be a very painful decision. When it became public, feelings ran high. Church members took sides. Meetings of protest were convened. As a chronicler of St Michael's notes, there was a very real risk of a split.[12] Even the church council was divided over the decision.

Nonetheless, near the end of my second year at St Michael's, my colleague moved on to another appointment. It was agreed that a lengthy interregnum was needed, to allow time for the church to come to terms with this destabilising move. I found myself appointed Acting Chaplain, supported by my experienced non-stipendiary colleague, Anthony Brown. In addition, Bishop John Hind appointed a pastoral consultant, the retired Bishop of St Albans, John Taylor. He was familiar with St Michael's, as he had been guest speaker at a church weekend the previous November. His first assignment would be to lead a retreat for the divided church council in September.

At the end of a busy and stressful year, with some challenging months ahead, Amanda and I needed a good holiday. We booked two weeks travelling across the Pyrenees, ending up at a holiday home owned by a member of St Michael's. The holiday clashed with the Pope's visit to Paris for a youth congress. But we were more than happy to let Anthony Brown represent St Michael's at the open air mass at the Longchamps racetrack. In the event, Anthony was rewarded by being one of the select few presented to Pope John Paul II from the 500,000 worshippers.

As our holiday in South West France drew to a close, we decided to drive across the border to Spain for Sunday worship. We had not been to Barcelona before and we knew there was a lively Anglican chaplaincy there. The journey took slightly longer than we expected, and we were ten minutes late. Thankfully, when we arrived, the service was only just starting. At the end of the service, over coffee, we were asked where we were from. 'Paris' provoked an outburst. 'Isn't it terrible?!' We had missed the announcement that had delayed the start of the service. Princess Diana had just been killed; in Paris.

Members of St Michael's appeared on French national television that fateful day, as the French press scrambled to find people to interview. It was Martin Draper from St Georges who had been summoned to the hospital by the ambassador in the middle of the night. Accompanied by Sir Michael Jay, he said the traditional commendatory prayers from the 1928 Prayer Book. There were no last rites. Before any priest had access to her, she was pronounced dead.[13] To the inexperienced Acting Chaplain at the former British Embassy Church, who could easily have been telephoned instead, it felt like a narrow escape. I was shocked, but relieved to be the one on holiday. Martin Draper deserved his subsequent OBE.

When we returned to Paris, we started to field sympathy calls from Parisian well-wishers. A few metres away from St Michael's, queues to the Ambassador's residence trailed down the road for days, with members of the public waiting their turn to write in the condolence books. As plans for the Westminster Abbey funeral service progressed, it became clear that a memorial service would be needed in Paris too. St George's had held a solemn requiem on the eve of the funeral, broadcast by the BBC World Service. But a more representative service was needed. Gone were the days when such memorial services were held in the former Embassy Church. Instead, it would be in the Madeleine. Sir Michael convened a planning group with representatives from the English-speaking churches. Canon Arnold Smit was point person for the Madeleine; Anthony Brown represented St Michael's. The preacher would be Bishop John Taylor, conveniently travelling to Paris for the council retreat. Used to associating with the royal household, as former Queen's Almoner, he was eminently well-suited to the task.

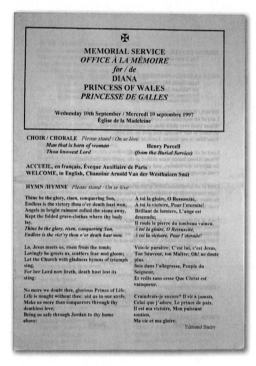

MEMORIAL SERVICE
OFFICE À LA MÉMOIRE
for / de
DIANA
PRINCESS OF WALES
PRINCESSE DE GALLES

Wednesday 10th September / Mercredi 10 septembre 1997
Église de la Madeleine

CHOIR / CHORALE   Please stand / On se lève
Man that is born of woman   Henry Purcell
Thou knowest Lord   (from the Burial Service)

ACCUEIL, en français, Éveque Auxiliaire de Paris
WELCOME, in English, Chanoine Arnold Van der Westhuizen Smit

HYMN / HYMNE   Please stand / On se lève

Thine be the glory, risen, conquering Son,   À toi la gloire, O Ressuscité,
Endless is the victory thou o'er death hast won;   À toi la victoire, Pour l'eternité!
Angels in bright raiment rolled the stone away,   Brillant de lumière, L'ange est
Kept the folded grave-clothes where thy body   descendu;
lay.   Il roule le pierre du tombeau vaincu.
Thine be the glory, risen, conquering Son,   À toi la gloire, O Ressuscité,
Endless is the vict'ry thou o'er death hast won.   À toi la victoire, Pour l'eternité!

Lo, Jesus meets us, risen from the tomb;   Vois-le paraître; C'est lui, c'est Jesus,
Lovingly he greets us, scatters fear and gloom;   Ton Sauveur, ton Maître; Oh! ne doute
Let the Church with gladness hymns of triumph   plus.
sing,   Sois dans l'allégresse, Peuple du
For her Lord now liveth, death hast lost its   Seigneur,
sting: Et redis sans cesse Que Christ est
   vainqueur.
No more we doubt thee, glorious Prince of Life;
Life is nought without thee: aid us in our strife,   Craindrais-je encore? Il vit à jamais,
Make us more than conquerors through thy   Celui que j'adore, Le prince de paix.
deathless love;   Il est ma victoire, Mon puissant
Bring us safe through Jordan to thy home   soutien,
above: Ma vie et ma gloire;
                     Edmond Budry

Singing 'Thine be the glory' in French and English, as the world mourned the death of a princess

Four days after the funeral at Westminster Abbey, 1,300 people gathered in the Madeleine to express their grief at this tragic event. The French authorities were represented by the Health Minister, the Mayor of Paris and the Prefect of Police. The lessons were read by Sir Michael Jay and a senior representative of the French Red Cross. A French translation of the sermon was provided with the order of service. At the end of the service, as the clergy processed out onto the steps, we were greeted with a barrage of flash photography from the discredited paparazzi.

Two days later, St Michael's church council gathered with some trepidation in Versailles, to confront its differences over the brief tenure of the outgoing chaplain. The venue was a centre run by the Deaconesses of Reuilly, whose unpronounceable name had been given to the formal conversations between the Church of England and the French Reformed and Lutheran churches. Bishop John Taylor began the residential with a 24-hour retreat, focussing on passages from the Book of Isaiah. This was followed by opportunities for council members to express views on the decision not to renew the chaplain's contract. The General Director of ICS, Canon John Moore, helped to facilitate these exchanges. A stroll round the grounds of the Chateau of Versailles helped to relieve the intensity of the discussions. As the council returned to Paris, there was a genuine sense of improved understanding and shared commitment to working together for the healing and future wellbeing of St Michael's.

Two strands would emerge later as significant in helping St Michael's to move on. The first was the recognition that the role of priest in the Church of England was not 'one-size-fits-all', despite the prevalence of this view. This was aided by research carried out in the USA on the relationship between clergy responsibilities and size of congregation, made available to council members. In smaller 'family' and 'pastoral' sized churches, clergy can concentrate on direct one-to-one pastoral relationships. Once congregations rise above about 150 members, senior clergy need to adopt a much more supervisory and facilitating approach. They need to be more selective in their pastoral engagement, empowering lay church members and others in their staff team. St Michael's, with its three hundred and fifty worshippers each Sunday, multiple activities and high turnover of membership, needed a senior pastor who thrived on the demands of this kind of 'programme'-sized church.[14]

A second strand related to how best to approach the interregnum. The received wisdom was not to implement major changes pending the arrival of a new incumbent. However, there was a lengthy interregnum ahead, along with a sense of forward momentum in various aspects of the life of St Michael's. It was therefore agreed that St Michael's should continue to press ahead with initiatives, to help it 'move on' and to pave the way for a new chaplain. It was felt that judicious support from Bishop John Taylor would ensure this was not too reckless an approach.

This meant progressing with the building project, amongst other things. However, in this regard, the interregnum opened up a new opportunity. In order to vacate the chaplain's apartment in the church centre, rented accommodation had been provided for the chaplain. Given rental levels in central Paris, this placed a heavy burden on the annual budget. Could we purchase an apartment for the new chaplain? After the trauma of the previous year, there was a renewed sense of seriousness within the congregation. But it was not at all clear whether the congregation was in a fit state to rise to this challenge. The church council agreed to read a book about another church's efforts to renew their buildings against the odds. It was *The Church in the Market Place,* by George Carey. Council members were initially sceptical about the practical relevance of a book by the current Archbishop of Canterbury. Yet the story of St Nicholas' Church, Durham succeeded in fuelling their sense of what might be possible in a venture of faith.[15]

Sufficient funds to purchase an apartment were duly donated, raised and pledged later that year. An offer was accepted on a characterful apartment a few minutes' walk from St Michael's, across the road from the Madeleine Presbytery. Meanwhile, plans progressed for reordering the church centre itself. With funds in place, stage one was implemented. The annexe containing the coffee area and bookstall at the back of church was given a complete 'makeover'. All this was a great boost to faith and morale, and to the sense of moving on.

Another innovation during the interregnum related to French-language ministry. It was, of course, interest in this issue that had led to my coming to Paris as a curate in the first place. During my first two years in post, the church council had begun to consider increasing activity amongst French speakers, as had other Anglican chaplaincies in France. It seemed a natural step to conduct an experiment during the interregnum, by running the Alpha Course in French. In the event, the pilot course demonstrated clearly that there was demand for this. There were forty-nine participants, with an average weekly attendance of thirty. Eleven of the participants were French-speaking spouses of English-speaking church members.[16]

Nine months earlier, I had flown to Nice for the annual synod of the Archdeaconry of France. It was January, but lemons were on the trees and the weather was mild. My lodgings were along the coast from Nice, overlooking the Mediterranean, in the home of one of the members of St John's, Menton, a chaplaincy founded in 1863.[17]

At the previous year's synod in Paris, our bishop, John Hind, had proposed that the theme of the 1997 synod be taken from my project report, 'Anglican Mission en France'.[18] Copies of the report were circulated beforehand to all the chaplaincies and I was asked to facilitate discussions. In my introductory comments, I reported the lukewarm reaction of one chaplaincy council. 'Put it this way,' the person facilitating the discussion had told me, 'out of the four words, 'Anglican Mission en France', the council had difficulty with three of them. And 'en' is not a very big word!'

Synod members in Nice were therefore invited to consider the three bigger words. To what extent are members of chaplaincies conscious of being Anglican? And what is distinctive about being Anglican anyway? What do we understand by mission? And what about France? On what grounds should we limit our mission to English speakers? Anglicans have prided themselves on their 'no proselytism in continental Europe' track record. But was it right to curtail evangelistic activity amongst French speakers, especially when Anglicans were well integrated with local communities?

Nice itself bears witness to Anglicans being rooted in local communities in France. In the early 1820s, about a hundred English families were coming to Nice for the winter. Holy Trinity Church was duly opened for Anglican worship in 1822. That year, a severe frost had killed large numbers of orange trees in the Nice area, with a devastating effect on the local economy. Holy Trinity's chaplain, the Revd Lewis Way, persuaded British residents to provide employment by funding the construction of a coastal road. It came to be known as the 'Promenade des Anglais', now one of the best-known vistas of the French Riviera.[19] Practical commitment to the welfare of the local community has of course been a classic feature of Anglican parish life in England. So was it defensible to limit the outreach of an Anglican chaplaincy in France to English speakers alone?

The seventy delegates of the synod were provided with a range of discussion questions to explore this further. These included questions about grassroots opportunities for supporting the mission activities of other churches in France. Delegates were then invited to vote on two recommendations. The first was that church councils be encouraged to set targets for developing involvement in French-language mission activity over the next eighteen months. The second was that one or more chaplaincies be designated a resource centre for French-language activity. 'Straw poll' support for these two recommendations was overwhelming.

As follow-up to the synod, each chaplaincy was sent a questionnaire. One section covered French-language activities that had already been carried out or might be selected as a target for the next eighteen months. Eighteen possible activities were suggested, ranging from bilingual Sunday schools and weddings to French-language study groups and joint hosting of guest events with other churches. Another section covered French-language resources, ranging from translations of wedding and funeral services to bilingual baptism preparation material, French-language study course materials and French translations of hymns and songs.

Data from these questionnaires was collated and presented at the next archdeaconry synod in January 1998. This one was held just north of Paris in

Chantilly, at a former Jesuit training centre. We were joined by the Bishop in Europe, John Hind, and the Bishop of the American Convocation, Jeffery Rowthorn. Bishop Henry Scriven, who had ordained me as priest four months earlier, had sent his apologies at the last minute. Rather shockingly, he was in Milan to conduct the funeral of its chaplain who had been murdered the previous week.

Once again, much of the synod was devoted to 'Anglican Mission en France'. Twenty-one of the twenty-four chaplaincies had completed the questionnaire distributed after the Nice synod. These were supplemented by written reports, which included comments on French-language engagement. Of those responding, baptism services had been conducted bilingually in all but two of the chaplaincies. A similar proportion had conducted weddings bilingually or in French. In eight cases, children's Sunday school was conducted bilingually, ranging from chaplaincies in the Paris area to those on the Cote d'Azur, in the Pas de Calais and in Strasbourg. Activities had been offered in French for teenagers in Lyons, Strasbourg, Paris and Versailles.

The Strasbourg chaplain explained that 'a significant amount of our pastoral work is done among people whose first modern European language is French and of them a small number are native French speakers'. French speakers in the congregation were mainly from Madagascar and Rwanda, including a Rwandan Anglican bishop.[20] Eighteen of the twenty-one chaplaincies said they organised guest events, such as carol services, that are 'French friendly'. Fourteen chaplaincies listed French-friendly guest events as one of their targets for the next eighteen months. Four chaplaincies indicated they had hosted Bible study groups and courses for enquirers either bilingually or in French.

The questionnaires also revealed that a strong ecumenical sensibility accompanied acknowledgement of these pastoral and evangelistic openings. Sixteen out of twenty-one claimed active local links with both Catholics and Protestants and had jointly hosted guest events with them. When invited to set targets for French-language ministry for the following eighteen months, fifteen opted for developing links with local Catholics and fourteen for developing links with local Protestants. Twelve included support for French mission causes, both financially and through volunteers. In the written reports, disavowal of 'proselytism' surfaced once again.

Several speakers had been primed to offer their reflections. One chaplain expressed guarded support for increased use of the French language in chaplaincy life. It was tempered by opposition to any notion of 'mission to the French', which he felt would be an ecumenical disaster. Another chaplain spoke of his chaplaincy's experience of running the Alpha Course bilingually 'because of popular demand, particularly from French relatives or friends of members of the congregation'. Another observed that some members of his chaplaincy found it hard to break out of the community of English speakers. A representative from the American Cathedral, the Revd George Hobson, spoke of efforts to develop the cathedral's francophone ministry. This included laying on seminars, study days and a course at the Institut Catholique on the nature of Anglicanism. A Roman Catholic ecumenical observer, Suzanne Martineau, observed that 'witness' *(témoignage)* might be a more helpful term than 'mission' in a French setting.

Synod delegates then split up into small groups to discuss four questions. The first was whether the new Church of England prayer book, once ready, should be translated officially into French. Three of the ten groups thought not, but a motion was carried expressing support for a French translation of at least some of what would come to be called *Common Worship*. The second question was around improving effectiveness in French-language activity, which led to an almost unanimous endorsement of a motion affirming that chaplains should receive French language training, with financial implications addressed. Bishop John commented that he had introduced a condition that new chaplains should have a knowledge of French or be willing to learn. The third question was around improved support for families, in particular those where one partner is French or children were in the French school system. This prompted wide-ranging discussions about enabling French speakers to feel at home in an Anglican setting. A motion was passed proposing the setting up of a website with details of French-language resource materials. The final question raised the possibility of wider ownership of an increased emphasis on French-language engagement. Should this topic be on the agenda of the Lambeth Conference due to take place later in the year? There was some resistance to this coming from the archdeaconry, so instead it was referred to the meeting the following month in Madrid of the four Anglican jurisdictions in Europe.

Reflecting on all this, the American bishop Jeffery Rowthorn suggested the discussion be recast as 'Being Anglican in France today'. He noted that in Paris there were now Anglican services in Taiwanese (at the cathedral), Malagasy (at St George's) and Tamil (at St Michael's). He wanted to leave one thought. 'There is a slowly evolving constituency of indigenous French-speaking Anglicans: a few here, a few there, gradually increasing in numbers. We are being challenged by the Holy Spirit', he suggested, 'to discover what it means to be Anglican today in France.' Bishop John Hind then added his thoughts. While generally appreciative of the discussions, he stressed that any moves proposed as a result of the synod's discussion must be in an ecumenical context. He applauded the 'excellent' non-proselytising presence in France and was pleased that some Roman Catholic churches remained open only because there were Anglicans worshipping there, with the approval of the local Roman Catholic bishop. He preferred the terms 'ministry' or 'outreach' to mission, and sounded a note of caution about the bewildering diversity of Anglicanism.

Back at St Michael's, busy months brought the arrival of a new chaplain closer. As springtime arrived, Paris prepared for all eyes to turn its way. This was 1998, the year France hosted the World Cup. The chaplaincies made optimistic plans for welcoming the influx of football supporters. ITV decided it wanted Sunday worship to be broadcast from Paris on the day of the final. The American Cathedral was felt to be the most sympathetic setting. So an ecumenical planning group was put together. When it came to deciding who would preach, the youngest member of the planning group was volunteered. So it fell to me to preach on St Paul's example of 'pressing on towards the goal'.

The service was pre-recorded several weeks before being broadcast. Far more memorable was the night of the *Coupe du Monde* finals itself. It was a Sunday and we had decided to screen the match in the church centre, immediately after the evening service. France beat Brazil 3–0. By the time we set out to leave, the Champs Elysées was filling with jubilant hordes. Amanda and I drove down the back streets to the Arc de Triomphe and on down the Avenue de la Grande Armée, with a tide of joyous Parisians surging towards us.

We chose the *Coupe du Monde* as the theme for a youth camp in the Loire Valley a month later. This camp was the fruit of one of the recommendations of 'Anglican Mission en France'. The idea was to run a youth camp in France along the lines of the Scripture Union camps I had helped to lead for many years. The difference was that everything would be done bilingually. The theory was that French parents would be attracted by the prospect of their children speaking English for a week. English young people would be attracted by a camp in France. Children in chaplaincies would fit perfectly into the bilingual setting. Running it under the umbrella of an Anglican organisation, CPAS, should help reassure any French parents wary of religious sects. In its first year, leaders were recruited from St Michael's and those I had led camps with in the UK. Sixteen years later, three bilingual camps would be running each summer.

The new chaplain for St Michael's, Anthony Wells, was inducted in the autumn. By that stage, St Michael's had travelled quite a distance since the troubled departure of the previous chaplain. Amanda and I would stay at St Michael's a further year, before returning to England. When we did so, it was by Eurostar. We were accompanied by our first daughter, Sophie, who had been born in the British Hospital six weeks earlier. It was three days before the new millennium, so most Eurostar travellers were travelling in the opposite direction to us, to join the spectacular celebrations in Paris.

✠

As the millennium drew to a close, so too did four extraordinary years in Paris. 'It had been the best of times and the worst of times', to quote Charles Dickens' Paris-based novel, *A Tale of Two Cities*. Or, to misquote a Punch cartoon from 1895, it had been a curate's egg: a mixture of good and bad, with much that was excellent.[21] We had witnessed a vibrant expression of Anglicanism at St Michael's. But the church had been severely tested by internal tensions, not for the first time in its recent experience. I had served as an apprentice in a European setting that was a short train ride from England, where familiar features of Anglican parish life were applied and reinterpreted. We had come to appreciate more fully the unique opportunities open to Anglicans of varying traditions in France. And we had witnessed a cautious willingness to entertain new ways of being Anglican in France, constrained by respect for other churches in France. Yet as we left France, there was a sense of unfinished business. Anglicans had an impressive history of enterprising outreach to English speakers in France. But there was still a reluctance to heed Stephen Neill's 1958 challenge.[22] Anglicans still seemed to be holding back from their classic holistic commitment to the local community, to avoid being guilty of 'proselytism'. It would be something I would take up again in an MPhil thesis, seven years later. But for now it indicated once again how reticent Anglicans can be about changing the status quo, even on the threshold of a new millennium.

Christ Church Clifton:
landmark of a trading city,
now replicated in Shanghai

9

Act Local, Think Global

C LIFTON WAS A DELIGHTFUL place to be moving to as a young family. Best known for its suspension bridge, spanning the River Avon, it rises above Bristol city centre. Its crescent-shaped terraces and Georgian squares bear witness to Bristol's prosperity as Britain's second port. Like Liverpool, which eventually upstaged it, it was heavily implicated in the slave trade. By the time the slave trade was finally abolished, slaving ships would routinely be fitted out in Bristol, ready to exchange their cargo for Africans on the coast of West Africa. Having transported this human cargo across the Atlantic, they would return laden with sugar, rum, tobacco, rice and cotton. Following World War Two, when Bristol experienced major bomb damage, the docks were moved seven miles downstream, to accommodate bigger ships. By the turn of the millennium, Bristol's economy had diversified, incorporating the aerospace industry, information technology and the arts, including the Oscar-winning creators of Wallace and Gromit. There were two thriving universities. A Navigation School founded in 1595 for the British Society of Merchant Venturers had become the University of the West of England (UWE) in 1992. Bristol University, founded in 1909, had established itself as one of the country's leading universities.

We moved into one of Clifton's tall and thin terraced town-houses. At one point, we were asked if the TV series, *Casualty*, could be filmed from our house, as they wanted to stage a fall from an upper storey window. Unlike in Paris, but in common with most clergy, I worked from home, a few minutes' walk from church. I was Associate Vicar in a clergy team with a senior colleague and curate, along with seven lay staff. Christ Church Clifton, across the grass from the suspension bridge, was a familiar landmark in Bristol, with its tall spire. Ten years later, it would be used as the model for a church built in mainland China, outside Shanghai.[1] Like other parish churches, it served the local community. Its meeting rooms in the crypt were used for mums and toddlers groups, lunches for international students and coffee mornings for senior citizens. The parish had no shortage of elderly residents, so there were plenty of funerals.

Yet Christ Church was hardly a typical parish church. Each Sunday, we would have a thousand adult worshippers. Some, especially at the evening service, were students from the two universities. But all age groups were represented. Thirty attended the quiet 8am service of Holy Communion using the 1662 *Book of Common Prayer*. The 9.30am service was packed with young families. At 11am, a more traditional service was attended by a cross-section of ages. At 6.30pm, with seven hundred attending, students were joined by young professionals and representatives of all ages. There were 951 on the electoral roll.

Like Falls Church in Virginia, Christ Church had developed in the 1980s as a church modelled on John Stott's All Souls Langham Place. John Stott would be one of the many guest preachers during my time at Christ Church, aged nearly 80. There was a strong emphasis on preaching, just as there was at All Souls. Sermon preparation was expected to be a priority, especially if you were preaching to seven hundred. Under its latest vicar, Andrew Dow, Christ Church had developed into a church which encompassed the growing variety of emphases within evangelical Anglicanism. Its staff team included a former youth worker from the charismatic Holy Trinity Brompton, who ran the Alpha Course, and a female lay worker from a non-charismatic conservative evangelical background, who ran the follow-up course to Alpha. A ten-person staff team might seem extravagant, but with over nine hundred on the electoral roll and many midweek activities, we were overstretched and spread thinly. Initially, my two main responsibilities were student work and home-groups, but it soon became evident that this was not sustainable. A lay student minister was appointed a year later, releasing me to concentrate on home groups and the everyday demands of priestly ministry.

I inherited thirty-one home groups. About a third of those on the electoral roll were members. There were fifty-three home group leaders, but many had been in post for years and there was a feeling that the whole system was jaded. My main mandate, when appointed, was to overhaul these home groups. There was an impressive record of lay involvement at Christ Church. There were, for example, fifty on the pastoral care team, subdivided into teams for the sick, the bereaved, the elderly and those with more general needs. Nonetheless, it soon became apparent to me that in a mega-church like Christ Church, it was all too easy for worshippers to take a back seat, relying on the staff and faithful enthusiasts to run activities. I discovered a quote which seemed rather apposite from the preacher D. L. Moody: 'I would rather put a thousand people to work than do the work of a thousand people.' I tried it out in a sermon to a packed church on mobilising the people of God.

For worshippers to be more than consumers, it seemed clear that they needed to relate to a smaller group of people. Theorists of church dynamics talked of the benefit of worshippers experiencing church life at the 'cell' level (such as home groups), the 'congregation' level (a larger group where they could nonetheless get to know a cross-section of people) and the 'celebration' level (an uplifting gathering where many will be strangers to one another).[2] At Christ Church, extra attention was needed at both 'cell' and 'congregation' level.

In the overhaul, home group leaders were given permission to stand down, and many did. New home group leaders were recruited and given initial training. I was expected to prepare customised study material each week, so on Sunday afternoons I offered ongoing training for those leading the week's Bible study. Equal numbers of home groups were scheduled on three evenings each week. 'Congregation'-sized groups were formed by clustering each evening's home groups together in pastorates. Each pastorate would meet together midweek once a month in its 'congregation'-sized group and spend a weekend away together on a residential house party.

Despite wanting to build up its common life in this way, Christ Church regarded itself as a 'sending church', as had long been the case. Resources devoted to teaching, leadership training and all kinds of lay ministry were seen as an investment. It was expected that many church members would migrate elsewhere. The aim was for them to be better equipped to play an active part in local church life. Yet this strategic vision for Christ Church was not obviously shared by the wider diocese. There was an uneasy feeling that the exceptional Sunday attendance at Christ Church must somehow be at the expense of other churches. Christ Church was not openly affirmed as a resource for teaching, training and evangelism.

This was most evident when it came to money. When I joined the staff team, Christ Church faithfully paid to the diocese whatever was asked of it. As a result it paid £279,000 a year to the diocese, forty percent of its budget. This represented over five percent of the total diocesan budget. It was hard not to treat Christ Church as a 'cash cow', as the Diocesan Secretary conceded to Christ Church's PCC when she met with them. In exchange for this quota, the diocese paid the stipend for the three clergy, with the parish providing the housing. When Christ Church's curate approached the end of his time, the diocese proposed he should not be replaced. In exchange for its £279,000 quota, Christ Church would be receiving just two stipends along with pension payments.

Since World War Two, parishes had been assuming increasing responsibility for financing the Church's ministry. The Church of England's historic assets were now administered by the Church Commissioners, formed in 1948 by the merger of two funding bodies: Queen Anne's Bounty, set up in 1704 for the relief of poor clergy and the Ecclesiastical Commissioners, established in 1836. The financial burden of clergy pensions had meant that less and less Church Commissioners funds were available for clergy stipends. This had not been helped by unwise investment in property. Some of the Church Commissioners' property investments had brought excellent returns, such as the retail centre down the road from the banknote printing factory where I had worked in Gateshead. But a staggering £500 million had been lost in mismanaged property speculation, according to an exposé by a *Financial Times* journalist in 1992.[3] This had triggered a major review of the way the Church of England managed its historic resources and set its policy. 'There is a cat's cradle of autonomous and semi-autonomous bodies with distinctive, but sometimes overlapping functions', observed the working party set up to address this question.[4] Their recommendations, in the Turnbull Report, led to a new body at the heart of the national life of the Church of England: The Archbishops' Council. It was designed to bring asset management and policy making closer together. With the two Archbishops as chair and vice-chair, it would balance consultation with leadership. Serving as an executive, it would analyse issues and propose strategies for dealing with them.[5]

Wiser investments led to the Church Commissioners building up its funds again. Yet the fact remained, an increasing financial burden was being placed on parishes. In order to maintain clergy cover, parishes with more income were subsidising those with less. In the case of deserving UPA parishes, that seemed only fair. However, at grassroots level, there was growing dissatisfaction. Churches whose members gave sacrificially were increasingly uncomfortable about subsidising churches whose members were content with a few coins in the collection plate. Churches wishing to develop the scope of their activities by, say, appointing a youth worker, could find themselves held back by the quota. The matter had come to a head with the formation of Reform in 1993, when certain churches opted to 'cap' their quota.[6] Christ Church had not yet chosen that route, but there were clearly conversations to be had. Other dioceses, such as London Diocese, were pioneering formulae for parish contributions which encouraged, rather than dampened, entrepreneurial activity and targeted giving.

My own exposure to the workings of the wider Church of England, not just in the area of finance, would be extended by my election to Diocesan Synod. The formation of General Synod in 1970 had been accompanied by changes at diocesan and deanery level too. Diocesan synods have a long history. They pre-date the formation of the Diocese of Bristol in King Henry VIII's reign. However, they were discontinued at the end of the seventeenth century. Assemblies of clergy and laity in dioceses were revived in the nineteenth century and then turned into diocesan conferences at the end of World War One when the Church Assembly was formed. Like the Church Assembly itself, they were unwieldy, with up to nine hundred members. When General Synod was formed in 1970, diocesan assemblies were slimmed down to synods of up to 270 members, half of whom were lay. Synods were introduced at deanery level at the same time.[7]

As members of Diocesan Synod, we would consider matters referred from General Synod. We could also raise matters for discussion at General Synod. On my watch, there was not much that was controversial. Debates about the ordination of women to the priesthood were long past and it would be another ten years before diocesan synods would discuss women bishops. The most controversial item came from our own bishop. The issue was the requirement for children to be confirmed before they could receive communion. He wanted the canons to be amended, so it would become the norm for baptised children to receive communion before they were confirmed.[8]

As well as issues of national significance, we discussed diocesan matters. We were expected to advise the bishop. One item before us was a proposed Diocesan Strategy. As far as I could see, it was not really a strategy at all, but a wish list compiled after consulting clergy. There was no real analysis of context and resources and certainly no discussion of the place of resource churches like Christ Church. Whatever our views on this or other matters, Synod members were not able to dictate policy to the bishop. The bishop had an effective veto over any decisions of Diocesan Synod. When diocesan synods in Canada voted to approve rites for same-sex blessings a year or two later, bishops would be seen exercising that right of veto, with one notable exception, as we shall see.

Deanery synods were expected to discuss matters referred by Diocesan Synod. This was a two-way arrangement, so they could also raise matters for discussion at Diocesan Synod. The appetite for policy discussions was not always great. At my first Deanery Synod meeting in Bristol, the Area Dean introduced Deanery Synod as 'a meeting waiting to go home'. He was only half-joking. Deanery synods were also intended to discuss local matters of common concern. In the years ahead, dioceses would increasingly look to deaneries to come up with joined-up mission strategies for their locality.

One topic which General Synod had been discussing for some time was liturgy. Authorisation to use the *Alternative Service Book* expired during my first year in Bristol. Much attention had been given to what would replace it. 'One book or many?' was a key issue. 'Many' would be the outcome. The core texts for Sunday services would be introduced in 2000. Other texts would follow. At Christ Church, *Common Worship* liturgy was now the basis for three of our four services, the other service being led according to 1662 *Book of Common Prayer.*

One of the aims of *Common Worship* was to take seriously the concerns of *Faith in the City.*[9] Experimental resources had been published in 1989 as *Patterns for Worship.*[10] These included 'services of the Word' and Eucharistic prayers that would were felt to be better adapted to liturgical needs of Urban Priority Areas. They were generally well-received and drawn on for *Common Worship.*[11] Also published in 2000 was *Common Worship: Pastoral Services.*[12] This would provide a range of healing services for the first time, catching up with the heightened emphasis on healing that had accompanied charismatic renewal. It also contained revised services for marriages and funerals. The wedding services now enabled the congregation to respond to declarations by the couple. The funeral service allowed for a eulogy by one of the mourners, something that had been a prominent feature of Princess Diana's funeral three years earlier. The liturgies published in 2000 would be followed by others over the next eight years, including *Times and Seasons,* with liturgical material for use around Christmas and Easter.

Draft 'experimental' liturgies had been tried out by eight hundred par-ishes.[13] The approved services allowed for much greater flexibility and variety in Anglican worship than their predecessors. Liturgies were available elec-tronically, allowing services to be customised and printed out or projected on screens. The Service of the Word set out structure more than content. Overall, *Common Worship* was a marked departure from Cranmer's principle of uniformity, whereby 'all the whole realm shall have but one use'.

I felt it was important to make time for involvement in the life of the wider church. In practice, the activities of an understaffed 900-member church were all-consuming. Seventy hour working weeks took their toll, with only a day and an evening off. The hours were similar to my curacy in Paris, but this time I had a young family. For a spell, I found it difficult to sleep. The outside world did nonetheless break in, occasionally at least. One Tuesday in September, Amanda telephoned home and urged me to turn on the television. On the live news coverage, smoke was billowing from one of the twin towers in New York. It was 9/11.

The following Sunday, I was leading the evening service. It was a youth service, so Neil, the youth worker, was responsible for parts of it. After the intercessions, with prayer for the aftermath of the terrorist attacks, there was an unnerving interruption. A bearded young man, wearing a kaftan, was at the back of the church with its seven hundred worshippers. He started walking down the aisle, calling out in an accusatory manner. He had a backpack. My first thought was the youth team had planned it as an impromptu (and poorly judged) part of the service. I looked at Neil and he shook his head. The only option was to engage with this rather menacing heckler. After an exchange, I attempted to address some of his concerns in an extemporary prayer. He grudgingly withdrew. What remained was a grim sense that we were now living in a changed world, after the events of 9/11.

Another opportunity to be reminded of the wider world was a talk advertised in a neighbouring parish church, All Saints Clifton, on Anglican ecumenism. It was being given by the Archbishop of Canterbury's Assistant Secretary for the Anglican Communion and Ecumenism. I put the date in my diary. I discovered later that Herman Browne, a Liberian priest, rarely accepted invitations to speak. By the time he arrived at All Saints, I had applied for his job. The advert in the church press had caught my eye. After attending for interview at Lambeth Palace, the job was offered to someone else. But the preferred candidate withdrew. Following further interviews, Archbishop George Carey offered me the job.

So it was that one Sunday evening in April, I drove in through the gates of Lambeth Palace, to begin my new appointment. Lambeth Palace could surprise even the most seasoned London cab driver. Its fifteenth-century gatehouse, Morton's Tower, is a familiar enough backdrop for news briefings from the BBC religious affairs correspondent. Behind the gates, however, is a hidden world. Just across the Thames from the Houses of Parliament, it contains the second biggest private garden in London, upstaged only by the garden at Buckingham Palace. Some of its buildings date back to the thirteenth century, when the Archbishop of Canterbury first started to have a London base. We would be privileged to live on this historic site, in the converted stables. For now, arriving alone, I would be staying in a guest room in the main Palace building.

As I made my way to the main building, I was greeted by the Chief of Staff, who had been expecting me. 'We're just off to pay our respects to the Queen Mother', explained Bishop Richard Llewellin, in his typically friendly manner. 'The queues have finally died down. Would you like to come with us?' So I left my bags in the car and walked back across Lambeth Bridge, with Bishop Richard and his wife Jennifer. We joined the ranks of the thousands who had already filed passed the Queen Mother's body, lying in state in Westminster Hall. It was an early sign that life at Lambeth Palace was going to place me frequently at the intersection of church activities and public life.

Lambeth Palace was officially regarded as one of the 'national church institutions' ('NCIS'), along with the Church Commissioners and Church House, whose departments were now under the oversight of the newly created Archbishops' Council. The designation 'national church institution' was actually a little misleading, when applied to Lambeth Palace. The ministry of the Archbishop of Canterbury is not merely a subset of the life of the Church of England. The Archbishop's ministry is global. He is first among equals of the eight hundred Anglican bishops worldwide. He is regarded as an instrument of communion, a focus of unity. In a globalised world, the Archbishop of Canterbury is one of very few Christian leaders with an international profile. Unlike staff in the other so-called NCIS, Lambeth Palace staff resisted having email addresses which mentioned the Church of England. To church leaders elsewhere in the world, it would have suggested that the Church of England still saw itself pulling the Archbishop's strings, clinging on to its colonial past.

My first assignment made the international scope of the Archbishop's ministry abundantly clear. I joined the senior bishops and archbishops of the Anglican Communion in Canterbury. Archbishop George Carey was hosting a Primates' Meeting in the cathedral precincts, at the newly completed International Study Centre. Unlike Primates' Meetings in years to come, the Archbishop of Canterbury welcomed 'primates' from almost all the thirty-eight Anglican provinces. No-one stayed away on principle. The longest serving Archbishop preached at the Sunday service in Canterbury Cathedral. It was Archbishop David Gitari, who had courageously opposed election-rigging in Kenya a decade or so earlier.

This would be Archbishop Carey's last Primates' Meeting, as he had announced his intention to retire by the end of the year. While in Canterbury, the primates were able to offer their views on his successor to the Joint Secretaries of the Crown Appointments Commission. In the event, the 104th Archbishop of Canterbury was already present, as Archbishop of Wales. During the Primates' Meeting, Rowan Williams presented a paper on the Church and her mission in the world, as did the Primate of Canada. 'These broke fresh ground in relation to the possibility of developing new ecclesial structures so as to free the Churches of the Communion for more effective mission in the context of a rapidly changing world', according to the official report of the Meeting. 'Reflection in these papers highlighted the need for Primates to be open to the development of new patterns of ministry within the inherited framework of our tradition.'[14] It was a sign of things to come. 'Fresh expressions of church' would become a priority for Rowan Williams when he became Archbishop of Canterbury.[15]

Reflection of this kind was the activity intended to be at the heart of Primates' Meetings when they were first introduced. Since 1867, the bishops of the Anglican Communion had met together every decade for the Lambeth Conference. By 1978, attendance at the Lambeth Conference had grown to nearly five hundred. The formation of new provinces had accelerated, as nations emerged from colonialism and proclaimed political independence. By then there were twenty-four provinces, each with a senior bishop or archbishop. So at the 1978 Lambeth Conference, Archbishop Donald Coggan, the successor to Michael Ramsey, proposed that the most senior bishops of each province should assemble reasonably often for 'leisurely prayer, thought and deep consultation'.[16] At the four Primates' Meetings I would attend, prayer and thought turned out to be anything but 'leisurely'.

Leisurely or not, the Primates' Meeting became the fourth 'instrument of unity' in the Anglican Communion. It complemented the work of the other three instruments: the Archbishop of Canterbury, the Lambeth Conferences and the Anglican Consultative Council (ACC), launched following the 1968 Lambeth Conference, as noted earlier in the story of women's ordination.

The Archbishop of Canterbury was a common element in all these four instruments.[17] He hosted two, was President of the third and was himself the fourth. The mandate of the ACC Secretary General was enlarged to serve all four instruments. As Archbishop's staff members, our job was to supplement this by supporting the Archbishop personally. It meant collaborating with the vast range of people implicated in the Archbishop's ministry. For me, the Primates' Meeting in 2002 was mostly an induction exercise, getting to know the business and personalities of the Anglican Communion and acquainting myself with the role of the Archbishop. I was coached in this by Herman Browne, the Liberian priest I had met in Clifton, who was now the Archbishop's senior Anglican Communion Officer.

The primates reflected together on an impressive array of topics. These included Christian–Muslim relations in the aftermath of 9/11, with news of a newly launched dialogue between the Anglican Communion and the prestigious al-Azhar University in Cairo. There was a report on canon law, proposing forty-four common features of canon law within the global Anglican Communion. Should canon law be regarded as a fifth instrument of unity, the primates wondered? They reflected on efforts to combat HIV/AIDs in Africa. They responded to the challenge to develop a clear strategy for improving the theological education of clergy and laity. Its outworking would become an important strand of my own work over the next six years.

All this hinted at the breadth of the Archbishop's engagement in the Anglican Communion. But the Anglican Communion was only one of the arenas Herman Browne bequeathed to me through his promotion. The other was ecumenism. An analysis of the role of Archbishop of Canterbury had been carried out the previous year, to help set the terms for Archbishop Carey's successor. Douglas Hurd, former British Foreign Secretary, chaired the working group. The resulting Hurd Report cited Randall Davidson, the Archbishop who had written to my grandfather in Canada. The job of Archbishop was 'an impossible job for one man', Davidson once said, but, he added, it was a job only one person could do.[18] The Hurd Report unravelled six strands in the role of Archbishop of Canterbury. In addition to his Anglican Communion and ecumenical roles, supported by my post, the Archbishop had a growing interfaith role, a national role as Primate of All England, a local role as diocesan bishop in Canterbury and a regional role as Metropolitan of the Southern Province and its thirty dioceses.

Another Archbishop of Canterbury, William Temple, was said to be doing 'the work of a Prime minister with the staff of a headmaster', the report recalled.[19] As one of the former headmaster Archbishops, Temple would have smiled at the comparison. I returned from Canterbury to Lambeth Palace to join the rest of the current Archbishop's staff team. I would be one of ten 'principals', each responsible for supporting particular aspects of the Archbishop's multi-stranded role. We would meet together each week, to discuss issues that required joined-up thinking. Once a month we would be joined by the Archbishop, but the rest of the time the Chief of Staff, Bishop Richard, would oversee our common enterprise. By 3pm every Friday, a written brief would need to be ready for every meeting and engagement in the Archbishop's diary the following week. Sometimes these would be courtesy calls from bishops and visiting politicians. Often they would be visits, church services, lectures or meetings, which we would arrange in advance. One of the principals would accompany the Archbishop for the meeting or event, overseeing practicalities and recording significant features, especially those requiring follow-up. As well as events, there was also a vast amount of correspondence, only some of which the Archbishop could answer personally. There was also the need for policy advice, which meant cultivating links with specialists and key players.

As I found my bearings in this new world, my family, which now included a second daughter, was getting used to this 'secret garden' in the heart of London. In the early months, most of my work was UK-based. My first overseas trip came in July. I would learn the ropes for an Archbishop of Canterbury's overseas visit, again under the guidance of Herman Browne. We would be crossing the Atlantic with the Archbishop and his wife Eileen, to visit two dioceses in the Episcopal Church.

Our party of four was greeted at Houston Airport by the Bishop of Texas, Claude Payne. We were driven by security personnel to a palatial villa, owned by one of Houston's oil magnates, where we would stay. Over the next four days, in Houston's humid climate, the Archbishop and Mrs Carey would engage with the dynamic life of the Anglican Diocese of Texas.

Our first engagement was a breakfast meeting, with forty civic and business leaders. Among them was the person responsible for bid for the 2012 Olympics. The verdict had just been announced, to his disappointment, but it would be three more years before London's bid was accepted. On another day, breakfast was in the shady cloistered courtyard of Palmer Memorial Church. Pancakes were served to recovering addicts and homeless people. Afterwards we proceeded to St Luke's Episcopal Hospital, founded by a former Bishop of Texas. It was an unashamedly Christian hospital, grounded in prayer and the faith of its staff, with the current bishop chair of the board. It was one of the top thirty-eight hospitals in the USA for patient care. Its heart institute, celebrating its fortieth birthday, had achieved the first successful heart transplant in the USA.

We moved on to a 'box-lunch' at Houston's Episcopal High School, in a balloon-decked sports hall. Since term was over, lunch was an open event, attended by four hundred members of the Diocese. The Archbishop broke the ice by noting that 'Episcopal' was an anagram of Pepsi Cola. He then fielded questions from the floor. These ranged from personal questions ('What is the most spiritually challenging event of your life?') to questions about the Archbishop's ministry ('What did you discuss when you met the Pope?') to church matters ('How can different styles of music be accommodated in church life?').

The Archbishop responded to further questions at a meeting of the diocese's two hundred and fifty clergy. Topics ranged from Islam, the Middle East, the legacy of the 'Honest to God' debate, blessings for same-sex couples and his retirement plans. At a Texas-style dinner, with over six hundred attending, the Careys were each presented with cowboy boots. Giving and receiving gifts was an integral part of overseas visits. After a closing Eucharist, attended by 2,500 worshippers, we headed for the airport, with gifts crammed into the suitcases. Our next destination was the Diocese of Pittsburgh, for a briefer visit.

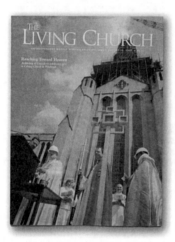

Lift high the cross:
Archbishop George Carey at
Calvary Episcopal Church,
Pittsburgh, reported
by *The Living Church*

---

*Reproduced by kind
permission of*
The Living Church
www.livingchurch.org

The Sunday service the following day was at Calvary Episcopal Church, Pittsburgh. With no air-conditioning and temperatures well above ninety degrees outside, the church was swelteringly hot. Undeterred, the Archbishop preached energetically on the subject of 'living stones', anticipating what would follow. At the end of the service, we processed out into the sunshine, to install a new cross on top of the stone steeple. The Archbishop donned a hard hat, ready to bless the cross, but there were no spares for his chaplain (me), who stood beside him with his primatial cross. I watched warily as the iron cross was winched up, swaying, then placed on top of the steeple. 'This has been so uplifting', someone quipped. 'It doesn't get much better than this', beamed the Rector.

The next day, the Bishop of Pittsburgh, Bob Duncan, hosted an event for the diocesan clergy. This was followed by a visit to an inner city parish and a church-funded training centre for inner city youth, Manchester Craftman's Guild. At one of several press encounters, the Archbishop gave a TV interview, speaking of the distinctiveness of Anglicanism, the homosexuality debate, September 11 and Islam. The visit ended with an evening lecture on 'The contribution of the Anglican Communion to the Mission of God'. As we headed for home, George Carey's successor was announced. During Rowan Williams' time as Archbishop, many members of the Diocese of Pittsburgh would leave the Episcopal Church and join a new body, 'the Anglican Church in North America' (ACNA). The departing Episcopal Bishop of Pittsburgh, Bob Duncan, would be its Archbishop.

It would be another eight months before Rowan Williams was enthroned in Canterbury Cathedral as Archbishop. When the day finally arrived, I joined staff colleagues in looking after the guests from other churches. During the televised service, my job was to introduce some of these guests to the Archbishop's wife, Jane, during the Peace. The morning after the enthronement, each representative from another church was presented to the Archbishop in his Canterbury residence, the Old Palace.

This was 2003. Three weeks after the enthronement, Iraq was invaded. George Carey had counselled against military action on his final Sunday as Archbishop. Rowan Williams now raised his own concerns in a private meeting with the Prime Minister, Tony Blair. He made a joint statement with the Catholic Archbishop of Westminster, urging continued engagement with the United Nations. 'Doubts still persist about the moral legitimacy' of military action, they warned in unison.[20] Later that year, Archbishop Rowan would be interviewed on the *Today* radio programme. 'Was it immoral?' insisted John Humphries, in an exchange that was never broadcast. The Archbishop paused for twelve seconds, according to *The Guardian*. 'You hesitated a very long time before you answered that, Archbishop', his interviewer is quoted as commenting. 'Immoral is a short word for a very, very, long discussion', the Archbishop is said to have replied.[21]

When Iraq was invaded, the Archbishop was already committed to going to the Middle East. He was due to be in Qatar, for the next Christian–Muslim dialogue in the 'Building Bridges' series inaugurated by George Carey. With the Middle East unstable and local Christians feeling vulnerable, the idea of a pastoral visit to Jerusalem started to take shape. Families of diplomats in Jerusalem had been sent home, so security advice was needed. What emerged was a trip to Jerusalem over the Palm Sunday weekend. The Archbishop would be based exclusively at the compound of St George's Cathedral in Jerusalem, to minimise the security risk. Two of us would accompany him: his press secretary, Jonathan Jennings, and myself.

I had visited St George's Cathedral once before, during my time at Ridley Hall. Amanda and I had been on a self-drive pilgrimage in 1993, at a time of renewed hope. While we were in Galilee, the Oslo Peace Accord was signed on the White House Lawn by Yasser Arafat and Yitzhak Rabin. As we drove down the Jordan Valley past Jericho, we saw Palestinian flags raised for the first time. In Jerusalem, we had tea in the St George's compound, described in the Lonely Planet Guide as 'an oasis' and 'a piece of the British mandate seemingly frozen in time'. The tower of the cathedral was said to have been modelled on Magdalen College Oxford. Now, however, ten years after this earlier visit, St George's was unmistakably at the heart of a Palestinian diocese, whose members made a valiant contribution to their troubled land. There were just thirteen Anglican parishes in the Holy Land. Yet the diocese ran seven schools and nurseries, four hospitals and clinics, a community centre and home for the elderly and a centre for disabled children. The diocese had also been doggedly engaged in reconciliation initiatives, such as the Alexandria Process which George Carey had been instrumental in moving forward, with its commitment to peace from senior Muslim, Jewish and Christian leaders.[22]

Archbishop Rowan William's party arrived at Tel Aviv airport on Saturday afternoon. We were met by the British Consul General, Bishop Riah (of the Anglican Diocese in Jerusalem) and his chaplain. Hordes of excited schoolgirls were there too, but it turned out they were waiting for a Brazilian pop star, not the Archbishop. We proceeded to Jerusalem in the Consul General's bullet-proof BMW and Bishop Riah's Mercedes, protected equally effectively by its well-known diocesan flag.

Once at St George's, it was not long before the Heads of Churches began to arrive for the evening reception. Over dinner, Archbishop Rowan addressed them and read out his pastoral letter. One of the Patriarchs responded. As the event drew to a close, an Anglican priest from Galilee serenaded the distinguished guests with Palestinian and English choruses.

'Have you ever been to the Church of the Holy Sepulchre?', Archbishop Rowan asked us afterwards, at Bishop Riah's residence. 'Well no, actually', admitted my colleague, Jonathan Jennings. 'Let's see what we can do then.' At 8am the following morning, with the connivance of Bishop Riah, we paid an impromptu visit to the site associated with Jesus' burial. Bishop Riah drove us to the Jaffa Gate of the Old City and we proceeded on foot to the church. A Greek Orthodox Archbishop, known to Archbishop Rowan from university days, was on hand to escort us. The church was alive with the simultaneous Palm Sunday celebrations of the various denominations which uneasily co-exist there. We embarked on a private tour, pausing for brief devotions and to greet the occasional patriarch passing by in full procession. After a strong cup of Greek coffee, we made our way back down the near-deserted streets. We walked past a donkey laden with barrels, symbolically appropriate on this Palm Sunday morning.

We arrived back at the St George's compound in time to robe for the Palm Sunday service. Clergy and congregation assembled outside in the sunshine with palm fronds and palm crosses, providing a perfect photo opportunity for the press. We processed into the cathedral for a service of Holy Communion. It was predominantly in Arabic, but based on the Church of England's time-expired *Alternative Service Book* liturgy from 1980. Hymns were from the *New English Hymnal,* which we had used at Ardingly College. Archbishop Rowan's sermon was translated into Arabic and took as its starting point Jesus standing at the gates of a turbulent city. It held out the hope that the city gates could somehow become a gateway to the garden of Eden, borrowing a phrase from a soul-searching book by an Israeli journalist.

The Consul General joined us for lunch and escorted us to the airport. After a delay due to a bomb scare, we were back in England.

Archbishop Rowan's first summer in post would be anything but quiet. Six weeks after his return from Jerusalem, the Diocese of New Hampshire would elect an openly homosexual priest to be its bishop. The reverberations from this new 'fact on the ground' would dominate Rowan Williams' time as Archbishop over the next ten years. In the weeks running up to this seismic event, my own work took me back to themes I had explored during my curacy. The topic was Anglican Mission in Europe. I would travel to Madrid for a 'Partners in Mission' (PIM) consultation. This kind of consultation had become a standard stepping stone in the formation of new provinces in the Anglican Communion. The presence of four overlapping Anglican jurisdictions in Europe had repeatedly been judged an anomaly through Lambeth Conference resolutions from 1968 to 1998.[23] The time had come to conduct a strategic evaluation of Anglican mission opportunities and challenges, to see if greater integration made sense. All four jurisdictions were represented: the Diocese in Europe, the American Convocation in Europe, the Spanish Episcopal Reformed Church and the Portuguese Lusitanian Church all provided delegates.[24] So too did non-Anglican churches in continental Europe, such as the Roman Catholic Church, and churches 'in communion' with Anglicans, such as the Old Catholic Church and the Lutheran Church of Sweden. The Archbishop of Canterbury was Metropolitan of the Spanish and Portuguese churches, so I took part as his representative.

The consultation identified 'converging and diverging' understandings of the Anglican presence in Europe.[25] There was a shared openness to all people 'who find their spiritual home in our churches'. At the same time, there was no real consensus about ministry in languages other than English. Two of the jurisdictions already used only non-English languages (Spanish and

Portuguese). We were reminded of this when we gathered for Sunday worship at the Spanish Episcopal Reformed Church's Cathedral of the Redeemer. When the consultation statement was drafted, proselytism was once again firmly rejected. But there was no clear sense of what constituted 'proselytism' in a Europe no longer neatly divided into the denominational zones of Christendom. A letter from Cardinal Kasper, President of the Vatican's Council for Christian Unity, seemed to concede that it was no longer appropriate for Anglican witness to be confined to English speakers.[26] Further work on the subject was therefore invited. By this time, I had started my MPhil thesis on this very topic.

Two Anglican mission agencies were represented at the PIM Consultation in Madrid: CMS and ICS, the successor to CCCS and owner of St Michael's, Paris. A few weeks later, I would join another Anglican mission agency for their own strategic review. As Archbishop's representative, I joined Anglicans from all over the world at the International Study Centre in Canterbury. At this iconic location for the Anglican Communion, we would be considering the future of the oldest Anglican mission agency. It was none other than the agency that had secured a Rolls Royce for my grandfather in Canada, USPG.

The 'U' in USPG (United Society for the Propagation of the Gospel) had been introduced in 1965, when SPG merged with the Anglo-Catholic mission agency, UMCA. The Universities Mission to Central Africa (UMCA) was a relative late-comer to missionary enterprise. It was founded in 1857, in response to a plea by the missionary explorer, David Livingstone. Back in 1840, just before the ill-fated Niger Expedition, Livingstone had been stirred by Thomas Buxton's advocacy of Christianity and commerce. The slave trade was continuing unabated in East Africa, overseen by Arab traders. Livingstone was convinced that Buxton's formula of Christianity and commerce was urgently needed to stop slavery in East Africa. 'I beg to direct your attention to Africa', he pleaded with his audience in the Cambridge Senate House. 'I go back to Africa to make an open path for commerce and Christianity; do you carry out the work which I have begun?'[27] UMCA did just that. Its activities would be spearheaded by bishops, reflecting the society's high view of the place of bishops. This would contrast to CMS, whose activities were ultimately overseen from London, despite the groundbreaking consecration of Bishop Crowther for West Africa.

Unease at mission activities being controlled from London lay behind the USPG Consultation I joined. USPG had already seen an evolution in its own role as a mission agency. Initially concentrating on ministry to colonists, it had lagged behind CMS in missionary outreach to non-Europeans. As we have noted, it was drawn into missionary outreach in India, as the East India Company succumbed to pressure to relax its restrictions. Soon afterwards, SPG sent missionaries to South Africa. By the 1860s, it was sending missionaries outside the British Empire to China and Japan. In the twentieth century, as autonomous Anglican provinces began to be created, the emphasis was more on 'partnership' with these local churches. The term 'Partnership in Mission', as used in the Madrid Consultation, was coined at the ACC's meeting in 1973. This set the terms for the coming decades for all the Anglican mission agencies. Yet by the turn of the twenty-first century, even this was beginning to look dated. The 'Heirs Together' Consultation helped articulate a more nuanced approach. 'Like most mission agencies, USPG has tried to leave behind the colonial "North to South" role in favour of "Mission from Everywhere to Everywhere", exploring how all our worldwide partners—Anglican provinces and Dioceses—can be "Heirs Together" of SPG and UMCA.' That's how its General Secretary, Michael Doe, summed it up.[28]

The sense that Anglican provinces should run their own affairs without interference from England would be a crucial strand in the Episcopal Church's handling of the election of Gene Robinson as Bishop of New Hampshire. 'Bonds of affection' had held together the Anglican Communion, in addition to its four instruments of unity. These bonds could be stretched to breaking point by unilateral activities of individual provinces. When a practising homosexual was elected as an Anglican bishop, there was an urgent need for conferring. The Archbishop called for an emergency meeting of the primates, to take place in October.

Meanwhile, it was the Archbishop's turn to bring the affairs of continental Europe into focus. At the end of June, he set off for the fiords of Norway, accompanied by the same pair who had travelled to Jerusalem with him. The Conference of European Churches (CEC) was holding its General Assembly in Trondheim. CEC had been formed in the 1950s, as a means of bringing together the churches of Europe during the Cold War. Five decades later, it still brought together Protestant and Orthodox churches from Eastern and Western Europe. Anglicans had been prominent members from the outset. In the 1990s, its President had been the Dean of Durham Cathedral, John Arnold.

The common mission of the churches in Europe was at the heart of the 12th CEC Assembly in Trondheim. A shared commitment to mission in Europe had been signed both by CEC and a body with a similar acronym, the Roman Catholic Council of European Bishops' Conferences (CCEE). The Charta Oecumenica, as it was called, provided guidelines for cooperation among the churches in Europe. 'The most important task of the churches in Europe', its signatories agreed, 'is the common proclamation of the gospel, in both word and deed, for the salvation of all.' The Charta also affirmed the responsibility of 'the whole people of God to communicate the gospel in the public domain', which meant commitment to social and political issues.[29] Norway itself was not in the European Union, but the Church's role within the EU was a topical feature of this Assembly. Brussels was working on its European Constitution, which included a clause mandating dialogue with the churches (Article 51). Among those present was the policy adviser at the European Commission for dialogue with religion and the churches.

Soon after arrival in Trondheim, Archbishop Rowan met with the Church of England delegation, headed by the Bishop of London. Most of the Archbishop's time was spent in meetings with leaders from other churches from across Europe. These included Orthodox delegates from Russia, Serbia, Greece, Romania, Albania and the Ecumenical Patriarchate. They also included Protestant delegates from France, Denmark, Norway and Germany. It was an efficient way of making contact with a wide cross-section of churches at the start of his time as Archbishop. A meeting with the European Commission's policy adviser on religion, Dr Michael Weninger, was an unexpected bonus. A cumulative effect of these meetings was a strong sense that greater Anglican involvement in European affairs would be warmly welcomed. For Archbishop Rowan, this would lead to a number of European visits, engagements and initiatives in the months ahead. It would for me too.

Archbishop Rowan's main public engagement at the Assembly was preaching during the closing service. The imposing cathedral where we assembled had once been the seat of the bishop responsible for the Isle of Man. From Nidaros Cathedral, the mixed denomination procession set off downhill to the temporary platform beside the river, and a trilingual service began. After a pause, to allow two Norwegian fighter jets to complete their circuit, the Archbishop preached on Jesus' encounter with the Samaritan woman at the well. The water theme continued afterwards as Orthodox delegates blessed water samples from around Europe, then poured them into the river.

We returned to England, impressed by the sense of Europe entering a new phase. On arrival, we were immediately reminded of old Europe. The new Italian holder of the EU Presidency had just committed an extraordinary gaffe, by 'ironically' accusing a German colleague of acting like a Nazi Commandant. The European project would never be straightforward.

Soon afterwards, several of the Archbishop's staff travelled to York for the Church of England's General Synod. While there, we witnessed a thirty minute interruption, when gay rights campaigner Peter Tatchell walked on stage with six young supporters. 'Church of hate—stop crucifying queers' proclaimed the banners accusingly. It was an act of protest against the controversial withdrawal of the gay—but now celibate—priest, Jeffrey John, as candidate for Bishop of Reading. Internationally, the next instalment in the Anglican dispute about homosexuality would be three months later. The Anglican primates would gather at Lambeth Palace in October, ahead of the scheduled consecration of Gene Robinson.

✠

In this chapter, we have considered the dynamics of an Anglican megachurch. We have detected signs of ambivalence in the Church of England about such churches, in spite of the potential scope of their ministry. We have noted increased financial pressure on parishes, with question marks about the automatic redistribution of funds donated by a particular congregation. We have witnessed efforts to restructure the national institutions of the Church of England, in response to adverse publicity about the investment of historic funds. We have also noted the place of local synods in the life the Church of England, at diocesan and deanery level.

We have started to look more closely at the demands made of an Archbishop of Canterbury, both nationally and internationally. We have increased our familiarity with the Episcopal Church (USA), by joining an Archbishop on his travels to Texas and Pittsburgh. We have encountered the Primates' Meetings and begun to appreciate the range of challenges faced by Anglicans across the world. In continental Europe, we have seen signs that Anglicans should be less reticent in playing a full part in European affairs, along with other churches. We have seen efforts to promote a more coherent Anglican presence in Europe, through better integration of Anglican jurisdictions. The 9/11 terrorist attack and the invasion of Iraq have been a new reminder that the context for all Anglicans is global and not just local. We have witnessed efforts to foster mutual support in this changing global setting, by the Archbishop of Canterbury, other Anglican primates and a long-established mission agency, SPG. Yet in this globalised world, we have seen how Anglicans are no longer held together by a virtually identical liturgy. *Common Worship,* as we have noted, allows for much greater variety in the Church of England's worship than Cranmer's Prayer Book or the 1980 ASB. In doing so, it seeks to respond to the local context, including the urban settings addressed in the 1980s by *Faith in the City.* In the next chapter, we will be considering other new facts of our era.

Entente cordiale:
ecumenical encounter
at the Abbey of Bec
in Normandy

Photo © Andrew Norman

10

New Facts of our Era

'WE HAVE STRUGGLED at great cost with the issues before us', the primates reported at the end of their emergency meeting at Lambeth Palace. There were two presenting issues. The first was the election of a priest in a committed same-sex relationship to the office and work of a bishop; the second was the authorisation by a Canadian diocese (New Westminster) of a public rite of blessing for those in committed same-sex relationships; the bishop had not exercised his right of veto. 'These actions threaten the unity of our own Communion as well as our relationships with other parts of Christ's Church, our mission and witness, and our relations with other faiths.' For the primates, these new departures were not just the private business of individual Anglican provinces. 'We recognise the sensitive balance between provincial autonomy and the expression of critical opinion by others on the internal actions of a province.' Yet the fact remained, these actions 'do not express the mind of the Communion as a whole and...jeopardise our sacramental fellowship with each other'.

The primates emphasised the importance of the Bible in the current dispute, despite differences in interpretation. 'We reaffirm our common understanding of the centrality and authority of Scripture in determining the basis of faith. Whilst we acknowledge a legitimate diversity of interpretation that arises in the Church, this diversity does not mean that some of us take the authority of Scripture more lightly than others. Nevertheless, each province needs to be aware of the possible effects of its interpretation of Scripture on the life of other provinces in the Communion.'

The archbishops and senior bishops also underlined the landmark resolution on human sexuality endorsed by the majority of their fellow bishops at the Lambeth Conference five years earlier. They reaffirmed it 'as having moral force and commanding the respect of the Communion as its present position on these issues'. The resolution (1:10) reaffirmed traditional teaching on abstaining from homosexual practice, while calling for pastoral sensitivity towards homosexual people and more active listening to their experience, assuring them 'that they are loved by God'.[1]

The primates felt themselves to be within weeks of a radical change to what it meant to be Anglican. If Gene Robinson were to be consecrated as a bishop, 'the future of the Communion itself will be put in jeopardy'. It will 'tear the fabric of our Communion at its deepest level'. These projected outcomes were in part due to the significance of bishops for Anglicans. 'The ministry of this one bishop will not be recognised by most of the Anglican world, and many provinces are likely to regard themselves as out of communion with the Episcopal Church (USA).' Picking up on a request made at the 1998 Lambeth Conference, the primates finished their time together by asking the Archbishop of Canterbury to establish a commission to consider situations where 'grave difficulties arise', including 'urgent and deep theological and legal reflection' on the dangers they had been discussing.

Two weeks later, the Archbishop of Canterbury announced the membership and terms of reference of this commission, which would be chaired by the Primate of All Ireland, Robin Eames, who had also chaired the working group on women bishops. 'He had an extraordinary gift of summing up the heart of an argument, and he carried huge moral weight', Rowan Williams explained later, reflecting on the 'appallingly difficult job' given to the Archbishop of Armagh. 'He also had an immensely genial presence.... He was somebody not identified with an agenda, and therefore people trusted him to a very remarkable degree.'[2] Four days after the announcement, Gene Robinson was consecrated bishop. What would end up being called the Windsor Process, named after this Lambeth Commission report, was now underway. It would go to the heart of what it means to be Anglican in the twenty-first century.

Another international working group began its work at about the same time. Its focus was theological education, as requested by the primates at their meeting in Canterbury the previous year. This had been given renewed impetus by Archbishop Rowan, for whom theological education was a major priority. Theological Education in the Anglican Communion (TEAC) would be a significant element of my own work in the support of the Archbishop over the next five years. I would be on the Steering Group for TEAC and join its consultations in St Albans, Bristol, Johannesburg, Cuddesden and Singapore. I would also be a member of the TEAC subgroup examining 'the Anglican Way'. Its task was to promote a shared global understanding of what it means to be Anglican. The first four-day TEAC meeting took place the week after Gene Robinson's consecration.

In the months that followed, we all waited to see whether the Anglican provinces in North America would inadvertently trigger a re-definition of what it means to be Anglican. In the meantime, I would encounter ways of being Anglican that were far removed from Western experience. The Archbishop would visit the Province of Melanesia in 2004. Herman Browne and I travelled there several months beforehand, to co-ordinate preparations. This was my first 'recce' for an overseas visit.

Archbishop Rowan inherited the pattern of two major visits to Anglican Communion provinces each year. They would typically last just over a week. They were a means of encouraging the life and witness of an individual province and connecting its members with the wider Anglican Communion. On occasion, it would lead to follow-up initiatives. Geoffrey Fisher had been the first Archbishop of Canterbury to act as an 'instrument of unity' in this way, as air travel became easier. Relying on sea travel would have made such a role impossible. Even travelling by air took up scarce diary space. Travelling the Archbishop's route in advance, it took Herman and myself thirty-three hours to travel from London to the Solomon Islands.

We landed on Guadalcanal, the main island in the archipelago of three hundred and fifty inhabited islands. Anglican origins in the Solomons go back to the mid-nineteenth century and Bishop Selwyn, first Bishop of New Zealand. Thanks to a clerical error—in his letters patent—Bishop Selwyn's jurisdiction included all the Pacific Islands.[3] With characteristic enterprise, the bishop rose to the challenge, founding the Melanesian Mission in 1849. He was convinced that Melanesian Anglicanism should be 'clothed in Melanesian forms'. The Pacific islands should therefore be evangelised by their own inhabitants. European missionaries were there to train and support. To implement this vision, he founded a Melanesian school near Auckland in New Zealand, raised money to buy a ship, the Southern Cross, and recruited a young Oxford graduate, John Coleridge Patteson. 'Use Melanasians. . . . I have no intention of taking any more [clergy] from England, Australia or New Zealand', Patteson would later proclaim. 'They cost about ten times as much as Melanesians (literally) but a very small portion do the work as well.' A gifted linguist, Patteson became the first Bishop of Melanesia in 1861. He was clubbed to death ten years later on the beach of one of the islands, but the work of the

Melanesian Mission progressed all the more, stirred by his example.[4] By the time of our preparatory visit, 220,000, or forty percent, of the islanders were Anglicans.

In between meetings with church and government officials, we found ourselves addressing several hundred pupils in a church school. As in Africa, schools had been one of the wellsprings of the church's growth. Leaving the capital, Honiara, we went by road to another source of the Church of Melanesia's expansion. Next to the Church's main theological college, at the foot of Pentecost Mountain, is the headquarters of the Melanesian Brotherhood. This remarkable Anglican community was founded in 1925 by a Solomon Islander, Ini Kopuria. A baptised Anglican from birth, he had attended Anglican schools and then joined the native police force in the service of the British colonial government. Once, while making an arrest, he seriously injured his knee. When in hospital, he experienced a vision of Christ and a call to missionary activity. He wrote to the bishop, describing a sense of call 'to declare the kingdom of God among the heathen'.[5]

Anglican schools: still active on the Solomon Islands

Photo © Andrew Norman

In consultation with the bishop, he founded a brotherhood dedicated to evangelism. The gospel would be taken and lived out in the remotest islands and villages. He sent the Brothers in pairs. They arrived with no food, possessions or weapons.[6] Even in the 1930s, the islanders were among the world's most hostile people, with killing, cannibalism and skull worship central elements of traditional culture. Vestiges of this violent past could be seen in the ferocity of the traditional warrior welcomes that would greet Archbishop Rowan. If the brothers were welcomed by the chief of a village, they would stay. The chapel at the Brotherhood's headquarters kept spears and shields on the wall, to remind them what the brothers had faced in those early years.

When taking their vows, the Brothers were required to climb Pentecost, a steep mountain, then spend the night in prayer on the summit. In common with many religious orders, they promised poverty, chastity and obedience. Unlike most orders, they took only temporary vows. The Brothers we met were young men. Their singing was captivating. During World War Two, there was fierce fighting in the Solomons, depicted graphically in the movie *Thin Red Line*. The film soundtrack includes the Brothers' singing. 'I have waited all my life to hear this', said the French sound recorder from Los Angeles. 'For the place where I found harmony', he wrote in the Brotherhood's visitors' book.

Anglican martyrs: the graves of seven Melanesian Brothers killed in 2004 while working for peace

Photo © Andrew Norman

In recent times, the Melanesian Brothers have been identified with a different sort of harmony. The year before our visit, six of them had been killed in peacekeeping efforts. We saw their freshly dug graves and arranged for Archbishop Rowan to plant a tree beside them. The Solomons had only just emerged from four years of civil war. Placards proclaiming 'This is a weapons-free village' were a common sight as we travelled round. Law and order had been restored over the previous six months by a regional intervention force of two thousand troops and police.

At the height of the conflict, only members of religious communities were allowed freedom of movement by the opposing factions. The Brothers commissioned a team to work directly for peace. They moved into the no-man's land between the road blocks and camped between the enemy lines for four months. They circulated amongst militants on both sides, challenging alarmist rumours and praying with combatants. They visited camps where training was taking place and prisoners were being held and tortured. The Melanesian Sisters were also active, trying to get supplies through roadblocks to families and children.

When eventually a peace agreement was signed, the Brothers' work continued. They were seen as guarantors of safety. Qantas Airlines refused to land without the Brothers present.[7] In 2002, they agreed to help in collecting weapons, calling for all guns to be returned. The following year, a key militant leader, Harold Keke, was still refusing to lay down arms. A brother who knew Keke well, Nathaniel Sado, took him a letter from the Anglican Archbishop, trying to open up dialogue. It would lead to chain of events which culminated in his murder and that of five other Brothers who had set out to find him.

From our meetings, it was evident that the Anglican Church of Melanesia had grown in stature through the conflict. It had ended up as virtually the only significant institution still functioning, with its active members generally not perpetrators of violence and often prominent in peace-making. The distinguished role of church women in peace-making was recognised by AUSAID. We were told the Australian government had broken with precedent to channel Australian government funds through the Church of Melanesia, to empower women to contribute to rebuilding society.

The Archbishop of Canterbury's visit would involve island-hopping. Anticipating this, I flew by light aircraft to the island of Malaita, landing on a coral runway. I learnt from the Bishop of Malaita that he oversaw thirty-nine parishes, with over four hundred Anglican churches, parishes and institutions. Most worshippers were in rural areas, living by fishing, hunting and subsistence farming. Anglican spirituality combined Anglo-Catholic orthodoxy with traditional Malaitan elements, such as faith healing, music, drama and dance. A striking illustration of this kind of Melanesian Anglican blend was evident in the communion service, with the Bible carried on a canoe for the gospel reading. This would be a feature of the opening service of the Lambeth Conference, in Canterbury Cathedral, four years later.

Anglican witness through drama: the Prodigal Son, Melanesian-style, performed beneath portraits of 18th-century archbishops at Lambeth Palace

Photo © Lambeth Palace

Well before then, in October 2004, three hundred bishops gathered in Lagos for the first African Anglican Bishops' Conference. 'We have come to celebrate the coming of age of the Church in Africa', the bishops announced.[8] It was nearly twenty years after I had arrived in Lagos as a recent graduate to see how far Christianity had taken root on African soil. Since then, the Anglican Church in Nigeria had become all the more conscious of its African identity. A new Prayer Book had been issued in 1996, which included 'ministration to the sick' with provision for choruses and extempore prayer. A revised ordination service had been produced which required ordinands to renounce membership of secret cults.[9] Now the province was hosting a groundbreaking conference for African bishops, opened by the Nigerian President, Chief Olusegun Obasanjo. In the homeland of the first African Anglican bishop, Crowther's successors would discuss poverty, disease, corruption, church–state relations, youth issues and Anglican identity. The conflict in the Darfur region of Sudan would also feature, with an update from the Primate of Sudan, Archbishop Joseph Marona.[10]

Planned two years earlier, this first African Anglican Bishops' Conference turned out to be well-timed. A year after the Primates' Meeting hurriedly convened to discuss Gene Robinson's election, the commission chaired by Archbishop Robin Eames had just published its findings. The African bishops were well placed to study it together and give their initial reactions. 'We believe that the Windsor Report offers a way forward that has the potential to be marked with God's grace', they cautiously concluded at the end of their conference.[11] This was more positive than the earlier response of the President of their gathering, Peter Akinola, Archbishop of Nigeria. 'After an initial reading, it is clear to me that the report falls far short of the prescription needed for this current crisis', he had judged. 'It fails to confront the reality that a small, economically privileged group of people has sought to subvert the Christian faith and impose their new and false doctrine on the wider community of faithful believers.'[12]

Across the Atlantic, the Canadian Bishop of New Westminster, Michael Ingham, offered his own initial response. 'We should pay careful attention to the Report and study it with open hearts and minds. It contains a serious rebuke not merely for our decision to authorise the blessing of same-sex unions but more particularly for doing so in advance of agreement on this matter across the Church as a whole. We are judged to have acted unilaterally and to have breached the bonds of affection that hold our worldwide communion together.'[13] The Presiding Bishop of the Episcopal Church (USA), Frank Griswold, voiced his own immediate reaction too. 'My first reading shows the Report as having in mind the containment of differences in the service of reconciliation. However, unless we go beyond containment and move into some deeper place of acknowledging and making room for the differences...we will do disservice to our mission.' He added a pastoral statement for homosexual members of the Episcopal Church. 'Given the emphasis of the Report on difficulties presented by our differing understandings of homosexuality, as Presiding Bishop I am obliged to affirm the presence and positive contribution of gay and lesbian persons to every aspect of the life of our church and in all orders of ministry.'[14]

The Windsor Report did not limit itself to the issue of homosexual practice. Rather, it addressed the way the Anglican Communion functions as a global family of churches. It identified weaknesses in the way that the Instruments of Unity were able to resource the common life of the Communion. It also challenged the idea that provinces should be free to develop as they saw fit, without reference to the views of other provinces. The model proposed for provinces by the Windsor Report was 'autonomy in communion'. There was no right of interference in the life of an 'autonomous' province. But each province should take into account possible repercussions of their own actions, as a consequence of belonging to a 'communion'.

By moving beyond the presenting issue of homosexual practice, the Windsor Report was moving into uncharted territory. It proposed reform of the very instruments that were needed to deal with this crisis, rebranding 'Instruments of Unity' as 'Instruments of Communion' with the Archbishop of Canterbury a focus of unity. A high level of trust and co-operation would be needed if this complex exercise were to move ahead. 'It is an invitation to the entire Communion to reflect on our life together', explained the Primates' Standing Committee, which met in London to receive the report in October. The Windsor Report would be discussed by all the primates four months later, in the light of feedback from each province. They would meet in Northern Ireland, in Dromantine, as guests of Archbishop Robin Eames.

Almost all the primates were present for this, along with staff members such as myself. We met in the aftermath of the tsunami that had devastated communities on the rim of the Indian Ocean. After hearing reports from the region, prayers were offered for the victims and for the ongoing relief work being carried out in the Provinces of South East Asia, South India, the Indian Ocean and the Church of Ceylon. It was a reminder that the interdependence of Anglicans had much practical benefit.

The majority of the week in Dromantine was devoted to discussing the Windsor Report. The primates welcomed the 'general thrust of the Windsor

Report as offering a way forward for the mutual life of our Communion'. They were satisfied that the report offered 'an authentic description of the life of the Anglican Communion'. Noting that the report spoke of 'the central place Anglicans accord to the authority of scripture' and of 'autonomy in communion', the primates pointedly requested all provinces to consider whether they were willing to be committed to the interdependent life of the Anglican Communion as set out in the report.

The primates welcomed most of the Windsor Report's recommendations for developing the Instruments of Unity. These included the proposal for an Anglican Covenant, which they felt should be taken forward before the next Lambeth Conference in 2008. However, they were wary about any increase to the authority of the Archbishop of Canterbury.

The Windsor Report made specific requests of the Anglican provinces in North America. In particular, they were requested to offer expressions of regret for their actions and put the brake on similar actions. Primates recognised that time would be needed for the consideration of these requests. With this in mind, they requested that the Episcopal Church (USA) and the Anglican Church in Canada voluntarily withdraw their members from the Anglican Consultative Council (ACC) for the period leading up to the next Lambeth Conference. They also recommended that the ACC organise a hearing at their meeting later that year, during which representatives of these North American churches would be able 'to set out the thinking behind the recent actions of their Provinces'.[15]

Two other important aspects of the Windsor Report were addressed. One was the situation facing groups in serious theological dispute with their bishops or provinces. The primates committed themselves 'neither to encourage nor to initiate cross-boundary interventions'. They should not encroach on one another's provinces, in other words. Rather, the Archbishop of Canterbury should set up a Panel of Reference to supervise the adequacy of pastoral provisions for groups in dispute. The other aspect addressed was renewed commitment to the resolution on human sexuality passed at the last Lambeth Conference (Lambeth 1.10). This included pastoral care and support of homosexual people and led to a request to the ACC to initiate a process of listening to those of homosexual orientation.[16]

As the primates returned to Belfast Airport to fly back to their provinces, they had moved forward a process that would have four main foci. First, there was the question of whether the churches in North America would accept the requests for moratoria and expressions of regret, in relation to consecrating those in same-sex unions and blessing those in same-sex relationships. Second, there was the question of cross-border interventions and care for traditionalist groups out of sympathy with their bishops or provinces. Third, there was the need to strengthen and reform global Instruments of Communion, notably through establishing an Anglican Covenant. Finally, there was the task of engaging with those of homosexual orientation. All this would constitute 'The Windsor Process'.

It was at this time that my two senior colleagues at Lambeth Palace moved on to other appointments. There was scope for reorganisation and it was proposed that an international team be formed, which I would lead, retaining involvement in both Anglican Communion and Ecumenical Affairs. I saw the logic of providing more integrated support of the Archbishop's international ministry. However, I was uneasy about the expanded workload. I could see it would involve much more international travel, and I had two daughters, aged 5 and 3. I decided to explore alternatives and applied for another post in the Diocese in Europe. I was told I was within 'a cigarette paper' of being offered the job. Somewhat unexpectedly, the experience gave Amanda and me a stronger sense of assurance that it was right to stay on at Lambeth Palace after all. I accepted the appointment, Amanda secured a part-time job with a relief and development agency and we employed a Polish nanny.

I was not wrong about the amount of overseas travel. That year, moving alphabetically through the destinations, I visited Belgium twice, Burundi twice, France three times, Germany once, Italy four times, Kenya three times (briefly), and once each to Northern Ireland, Norway and Pakistan. Within two weeks of starting in my new position, Pope John Paul II died and I was off to Rome with the Archbishop for the Pope's funeral. Seated outside St Peter's Basilica, my prime position placed me directly opposite President Bush. There was plenty of chance to survey the world leaders (seated in alphabetical order). The United Kingdom (Prince Charles) was next to Zimbabwe (President Mugabe), which presented a diplomatic challenge when it came to exchanging the peace. We hitched a ride back in Prince Charles' jet, to ensure the Archbishop returned safely for the royal wedding. Neatly demonstrating how much times had changed since Henry VIII's royal wedding to Anne Boleyn, this royal wedding had been postponed a day, to allow Prince Charles—the future Supreme Governor of the Church of England—to attend the Pope's funeral. Two weeks later we were back in Rome for the inauguration of Pope Benedict XVI. Sandwiched between the two Rome visits was a week-long meeting of the Design Group for the 2008 Lambeth Conference, which I took part in. Anglican–Roman Catholic relations would sit neatly with my brief for Anglican Communion Affairs.

At that time, the fate of the Anglican Communion and the Windsor Process was the dominant issue from the Vatican's point of view.

Yet the Archbishop of Canterbury's engagement with Roman Catholicism was not limited to set-piece visits to the Vatican and dialogue about difficulties. For a start, it involved contact with Catholic religious communities. That summer, religious communities would be in the news when the founder of Taizé, Brother Roger, was stabbed to death by a mentally-ill Romanian woman. Based in Burgundy, Taizé drew thousands of young people each year, as I experienced for myself ten years earlier when researching for 'Anglican Mission en France'. Taizé had caught the imagination of Anglicans and its simple choruses were often sung in English parish churches. But, to the surprise of some, Taizé is a Protestant community. It would be a Catholic religious community in France that Archbishop Rowan visited during the month following Pope Benedict's inauguration. It was the Abbey of Bec Hellouin, provider of three Archbishops of Canterbury in Norman times, including Anselm, the great theologian. When Michael Ramsey visited the Abbey in 1967, accompanied by a delegation from the British Embassy Church, it was the first visit of an Archbishop of Canterbury to France since 1520.[17]

We travelled to Normandy by car and Eurotunnel, arriving in time for supper. With their historic link with Canterbury, the white-habited Brothers and Sisters regarded praying for Anglicans as part of their vocation. At the time of the visit, members of St George's, Paris were on retreat there. The Mass the following day was presided over by the Bishop of Evreux. The visit was a sign of the strength of Anglican relations not just with the community of Bec but also with the Catholic Church in France. Two months earlier, I had attended a meeting further north in France, in Lille, which brought together the committees responsible for nurturing relations between Anglicans and Catholics in France, Belgium and England.

The 104th Archbishop of Canterbury visits the Abbey of Bec Hellouin in Normandy, whose 12th-century abbots became the 35th and 36th Archbishops of Canterbury   *Photos © Andrew Norman*

With ecumenical relations so manifestly strong in France, it was no accident that the Anglican Alpha Course had been enthusiastically adopted by the Catholic Church there. It would not be long before two thirds of Catholic dioceses in France ran the Alpha Course, promoting it as one of their chief means of evangelisation.[18] Initially, the Alpha Course had been offered in French at chaplaincies such as St Michael's, Paris and in French Protestant churches. But its potential for the Catholic Church in France began to open up in 1997, when a French expatriate banker, Marc de Leyritz, attended an Alpha Course in London at Holy Trinity Brompton. Through a tenuous link with one of the French Catholic charismatic communities, *L'Emmanuel,* and a conversation in Paris while stranded in a snow storm, he was invited to train seven hundred leaders of the *L'Emmanuel.* He was then approached by the founder of the Chemin Neuf Community and invited to train all eight hundred Chemin Neuf members at their twenty-fifth anniversary assembly in Savoie. De Leyritz became increasingly convinced that the support of the Catholic bishops in France was needed if Alpha were to be an effective tool in France. In September 1999, he was able to meet with Cardinal Lustiger in Paris, by which time 3,000 French facilitators of Alpha had been trained, including five hundred Catholic priests. The Cardinal immediately proposed setting up an ad hoc committee of the French Bishops' Conference, to report to the annual bishops' assembly two months later. At this assembly in Lourdes, it was decided that Alpha should be introduced on an experimental basis for a year, in any dioceses wishing to run it. Nothing heretical was identified in the course, though concerns were raised about various points of emphasis. At the end of the following year, a new version of the course text was proposed. But after numerous discussions, it was finally agreed that the version used by all confessions should be used after all.[19] By the time Archbishop Rowan visited the Abbey of Bec, the Alpha Course was receiving accolades from bishops all over France. 'For the French Church, Alpha is a great opportunity for our time', proclaimed the Archbishop of Lyon, Cardinal Philippe Barbarin. 'It is a wonderful gift we have received from England'.[20]

From Bec, we took the road to Charles de Gaulle Airport, pausing en route to bid farewell to our escort of local gendarmes. We were bound for Assisi, to join another ecumenically-minded community. Though we would stay at a Franciscan hostel, it was not the community founded by St Francis of Assisi that had invited the Archbishop. It was L'Arche, with its worldwide households for those with learning disabilities. One of my contemporaries at Oxford, by then an Anglican priest in Toronto, had been a community member in Canada for many years. It was the international meeting of L'Arche that was being held in Assisi.

We linked up in Rome with Cardinal Walter Kasper, head of the Vatican's Council for Christian Unity (PCPCU) and proceeded together to Assisi. The Cardinal and Archbishop Rowan were billed as a double-act, speaking on 'The mission for L'Arche today'. At one point, the Cardinal and the Archbishop joined the L'Arche team for the chorus 'Jesus' love is very wonderful', complete with actions. They later headed off for an ice cream in the back streets of Assisi. It was a relaxed and joyful assignment, indicative of the 'spiritual ecumenism' that Cardinal Kasper was warmly promoting.[21]

Spiritual ecumenism at Assisi: Cardinal Kasper, Rowan Williams and Jean Vanier at the L'Arche Community International Meeting

Photo © Andrew Norman

In the autumn, the Archbishop would return to mainland Europe, initially to encounter yet another ecumenically-minded community. This time it was Sant'Egidio, the lay community that played an active part in peace-making in Mozambique at the time I was with De La Rue, organising elections in Angola. Sant'Egidio had worked with the Anglican Bishop of Mozambique at the time. Since then, they had worked assiduously in cultivating links with Anglicans. The church they used in Rome, St Bartholomew's, was dedicated to commemorating Christian martyrs. The Anglican Archbishop, Janani Luwum, murdered in Idi Amin's Uganda, was among those commemorated. When Archbishop Rowan returned to Rome the following year, they would host a service to commemorate the six Melanesian Brothers who had so recently lost their lives.

It was Sant'Egidio's International Meeting for Prayer and Peace that we would attend in Lyons. The Archbishop would be joining Catholic, Muslim, Jewish and Protestant religious leaders for roundtable discussions on 'Faiths in Dialogue after September 11'. Events in London two months earlier cast a sombre shadow over this interfaith encounter. At the opening ceremony, the Archbishop recalled the 'cruel ironies' of his programme that day.

My diary for the seventh of July involved a very early start from London in order to travel to the North of England. I was due to meet a number of Muslim leaders in West Yorkshire....We had almost arrived...when a message came through on my chaplain's mobile phone that the London underground had been closed because of what looked like a terrorist attack....I was able to make a first, unscripted statement on television, directly in front of one of the largest Muslim institutions in Northern England, to speak not only of the shock and condemnation which I wanted to express but of the revulsion of those who stood around me at this indiscriminate and brutal violence....It was a day of cruel ironies.... [T]he substance of our discussions was the prospects for more and better co-operation between Christian and Muslim communities in the work of urban regeneration.[22]

I was in London myself that day, with my daughters at school a few minutes' walk from one of London's main underground stations, the terminus of their daily bus trip, and mobile phones jammed. I later learned that one of my student contemporaries from Oxford, John Valentine, found his parish at the epicentre of the terrorist attacks. He was thrust into the guise of a World War One chaplain on the front line, as casualties were evacuated from the Underground station.

Against this disturbing backdrop, the Archbishop was also able to articulate more of his own thinking on the place of religion in Europe as the Sant'Egidio meeting got underway. 'Europe is, historically speaking, an unusual experiment', he began. Power is now exercised in a secular framework, yet this framework benefits from its religious foundations much more than is often acknowledged, he suggested. In the present context, 'the presence of Islam within Europe, whether in the shape of significant minorities or through the presence of a majority Muslim state, need not be seen as an insoluble problem for what a Christian might see as the European identity. Islam, in such circumstances, is invited to become, along with the historic religious communities of Christian Europe, the critical friend of the modern state, asking awkward questions, forming partnerships. This does suggest the challenge to Islam to continue formulating new ways of understanding itself in a non-Muslim environment'.[23]

Europe would continue to be a focus for the Archbishop in the days and weeks following the Sant'Egidio meeting. We would fly from Lyons to Germany to join the clergy conference of the Diocese in Europe, celebrating twenty-five years since the founding of the diocese. Then the following month we would travel to Norway. Since 1992, Anglicans in England, Wales, Scotland, Ireland and continental Europe have been in full communion with the Lutheran Church of Norway. Under the Porvoo Agreement, the same applies to Anglican relations with six other Lutheran churches in Scandinavia and the Baltics. This means that in Norway, Sweden, Finland, Lithuania, Estonia, Iceland and Denmark, Anglican priests can minister in Lutheran churches and vice versa. As part of this agreement, the archbishops of the so-called Porvoo churches meet together every two years. En route to the Porvoo Primates' Meeting, Archbishop Rowan would visit the Church of Norway, playing his part in making this relationship of 'full communion' more than just a contractual convenience.

A month afterwards, in November, the Archbishop would be back in Europe. This time, it was Brussels. Two years earlier, at the CEC General Assembly in Norway, there had been strong encouragement for Anglicans to become more actively engaged in continental Europe, with all churches being invited to contribute to dialogue about EU policy. This visit to Brussels was an opportunity to test that further. It was also a chance to take forward a project that had been taking shape in the intervening time: appointing an Anglican representative to the European Institutions. The idea was to base the post at the Anglican chaplaincy in Brussels, Holy Trinity. It would combine pastoral care with shaping European policy.

The Archbishop's visit began with addresses at three contrasting Sunday services at Holy Trinity: a morning service with a cross-section of nation-alities, an exuberant afternoon service comprised mostly of Africans, and an informal evening service for young people, the majority working with lobbying groups in the European institutions. It was followed the next day by a public lecture at the European Policy Centre, on religion and shaping the new Europe. 'Recent discussions about the admission of Turkey to the EU have brought into the open all sorts of concerns about the historic Christian identity of Europe', was his opening salvo.

> Sociologists writing about religion in Europe have taken lately to referring to the 'European exception': everywhere in the world except in Europe, the public visibility of religion has increased and is increasing. The picture, popular a few decades ago, of a universal drift towards secularisation (i.e. the virtual disappearance of religious belief as a significant factor in either personal com-mitment or public policy) has had to be modified. This may be deplorable to the self-consciously progressive Western mind.... The solution requires us to retell the history of Europe.

This he proceeded to do, with the aim of rehabilitating the place of reli-gion in European public life, with implications for an Islamic country such as Turkey. It was a substantial address, published later in his *Faith in the Public Square*.[24]

It was matched by a series of substantial meetings and conversations. One with lay members at Holy Trinity illustrated the strength of connections between the chaplaincy and the European institutions, with several senior office holders being members of Holy Trinity. Staying at the residence of the UK representative to the European Institutions provided ample opportunity for conversations about the British government's perspective on European issues. The Archbishop met with the President of the European Commission, José Barroso, the President of the European Parliament, Josep Borrell Fontelles, the High Representative for Common and Security Policy, Javier Solana and various MEPs. There were also meetings with representatives of other denominations and Christian bodies relating formally to the European institutions, including CEC.

The net result was to give increased impetus to the plan to appoint an Anglican representative to the European Institutions. Funding would be an issue, as there was no money available from the Archbishops' Council budget. However, Church House, Lambeth Palace and Holy Trinity Brussels finally came up with a workable package, with funding extracted from several sources. Two years later, the Revd Dr Gary Wilton would be appointed to this pioneering post, taking forward the Church of England's tradition of contributing to public life, but extending it beyond Westminster to continental Europe. In order to anchor it in the life of the Church of England, Gary Wilton would relate to Church House, Lambeth Palace and the recently formed House of Bishops' Europe Panel. Five years later, the post would be part-funded by the British Foreign Office, signalling renewed interest in religion and the public square.

These various European encounters reinforced my enduring sense that Anglicans needed to see their presence in Europe with fresh eyes. I was inching forward with my MPhil thesis on Anglican mission in France. It seemed increasingly evident that Anglicans needed to regard themselves as genuine players in continental Europe, rather than guests on someone else's patch. With such a strong ecumenical track record, there was no need for anxiety that Anglicans would be trespassing provocatively on someone else's territory. Rather, in a supposedly secular Europe, where there were new challenges and opportunities for religion, Anglicans should lose some of their reticence. 'Proselytism' was rightly condemned if it meant sheep-stealing or resorting to dubious methods to secure conversions. But operating as a lively and outgoing Christian presence should not be subject to the same censure. None of the other denominations in Western Europe played by those rules. Nor were they advocated by ecumenical statements on proselytism, which instead speak of 'the priority of the announcement of the gospel' and opposition to 'sheep stealing', self-sufficiency, malevolent or unfair criticism, psychological pressure and violation of human rights.[25]

My wider Anglican Communion activities that year reinforced this sense that Anglicans needed to be more proactive in European life, moving beyond the pastoral care of English speakers. African trips provided evidence that French-speaking Anglicanism was already well-established in that great continent, so why not in Europe too? Pakistan provided a reminder that Islam needs to be encountered as a global phenomenon. Continental Europe is part of that equation. In the eyes of non-Western Muslims, Christianity is often closely associated with European policy. Turkey joining the European Union might help subvert unhelpful aspects of that association, if it was prepared to pay the price of increased religious freedom within its own borders. Anglicans, with their Western and global credentials, undeniably had a stake in debating European policy. They needed to be at the table.

It was a landlocked francophone country in East Africa that the Archbishop visited in July 2005, in the midst of his various European trips. Burundi was among the five poorest countries in the world. In 2005, it was emerging from years of civil war. Over 250,000 had been killed and 300,000 displaced. Like its neighbour, Rwanda, it had witnessed genocide, with Tutsi murdering Hutu (1972) and Hutu massacring Tutsi (1993). Anglicans comprised about ten percent of the population. They spoke French because this had not been a British colony. After World War One, Belgium took it over from Germany. Anglican missionaries only arrived in the 1930s, setting up hospitals and schools at three principal sites. They were emissaries of the CMS Ruanda Mission, inspired by what came to be known as the East Africa Revival. This 'revival' began at a similar mission station in Belgian Ruanda (now Rwanda). At Gahini Mission Hospital, forty miles from Kigali, African staff became convinced of their need to acknowledge, confess and renounce behaviour they felt was out of step with their Christian faith. As the revival movement spread to other parts of East Africa, there was a fresh emphasis on holy living, evangelism and God's empowering through the Holy Spirit.[26] In Burundi (then known as Urundi), the majority of missionaries were Roman Catholic when the first Anglicans arrived. By the time of Archbishop Rowan's visit, sixty years later, there were 600,000 Anglicans, with 170 clergy.

In the year preceding the visit, peace agreements had been signed with all but one of the warring factions. The United Nations stepped in to assist civil reconstruction in June 2004. A series of elections were being held, but in contrast to Angola, twelve years earlier, there would be provision for power-sharing, instead of 'winner takes all'. There were high hopes that lasting peace would be achieved, and churches were being encouraged to play their part. Church schools had been nationalised in the 1970s. Now the church was being invited to take them back. Already six primary schools and ten secondary schools had been returned to the Anglican Church. The state paid staff salaries and the church was responsible for governance and maintenance. Many of the schools were in a poor state of repair and it was hoped that the Archbishop's visit would act as a catalyst for external funding to be secured from governments and NGOs. It would be one of the main priorities for the Archbishop of Canterbury's recently appointed Secretary for International Development, who took part in the Archbishop's visit.

We arrived in the capital Bujumbura, in time for the enthronement of the newly elected Archbishop of Burundi, Bernard Ntahoturi. By coincidence, he had trained for ministry at Ridley Hall. The service was held in the football stadium and attended by 4,000, including archbishops from neighbouring African provinces. It was broadcast on national radio, in the slot usually reserved for a Roman Catholic service. The reception afterwards was held on the shore of Lake Tanganyika.

Post-conflict Burundi: the enthronement of its Anglican Archbishop in 2005

Photo © Lambeth Palace

The characteristically packed programme included a lecture to students and university staff on 'The role of the university in post-conflict society'. This was followed by a radio interview in French. Protected by a truckload of teenage soldiers, the Archbishop travelled upcountry to Matana, site of one of the original CMS mission stations. The former church hospital was still located there, along with schools and the province's main theological college. Its library was just a few shelves of books. Many of Burundi's clergy

were obliged to go to Uganda to train. To enable us to stick to schedule, the
UN provided one of their helicopters to fly us back to the capital.

The Church and the
UN, both active in post-
conflict reconstruction:
Burundi in 2005

Photo © Lambeth Palace

Officials we met included the current President and the Minister for Good
Governance, who would later be elected President. The minister's parents
had been Anglican and he spoke appreciatively of his education at Anglican
primary and secondary schools. Archbishop Rowan's wife, Jane, was able
to engage with another Anglican contributor to civil society, the Mothers'
Union (MU). In a settlement of internally displaced people, near the border
with the Congo, she visited one of the sites for the MU literacy programme.

The return journey involved a stopover in Kenya. To profit from this, an
Anglican roundtable had been organised on 'The Role of the Church in
Post-Conflict Reconstruction in the Great Lakes Region'. It was attended by
Anglican primates from Congo, Sudan, Rwanda, Kenya and Burundi, and
representatives of NGOs active in the region.

While Anglicans in Africa applied themselves to post-conflict reconstruction,
the Church of Pakistan faced rather different challenges. I flew to Islamabad to
set up the Archbishop's forthcoming visit to Pakistan, with my veteran travelling companion, Jonathan Jennings, Archbishop's Press Secretary. Accompanied
by the Bishop of Lahore, the senior bishop in the Church of Pakistan, we
trail-blazed a visit designed to affirm the Church of Pakistan and promote
interfaith harmony. Over the past few years, there had been a well-publicised
rash of terrorist attacks in Pakistan, with churches and church institutions
targeted, as well as the President himself. In 2002, for example, six people
had been gunned down at the Murree Christian School in the foothills of
the Himalayas. Founded in 1956 to educate the children of missionaries in
Pakistan, and now catering for Pakistani as well as expatriate children, its main
school building was a former garrison church, originally providing Anglican

worship for soldiers in the hill station of Murree. During our weeklong visit, one of the alleged ringleaders of the terrorist attacks on the President, the Libyan Al Qaeda leader, Abu Faraj al-Libbi, was captured in Pakistan. We witnessed the kind of security protection offered to high profile visitors when a carcade overtook us as we travelled in the bishop's car to the North-West Frontier. It was the Hollywood 'Tomb Raider' star Angelina Jolie, en route to an Afghan refugee camp.

The Bishop of Lahore's diocese had been carved out of the Anglican Diocese of Calcutta in 1877 to serve the Punjab and Kashmir. spg contributed to its endowment, as did the Colonial Bishoprics' Fund. Its first bishop was Thomas Valpy French, who was translated from being rector at St Ebbe's Church in Oxford and had inspired Westcott in founding the Cambridge Mission to Delhi.[27] By contrast, the Diocese of Raiwind, which included the capital of Pakistan, Islamabad, had less obvious Anglican credentials. It was formed in 1970 from a predominantly Methodist area of missionary activity. Like the Church of South India and the Church of North India, the Church of Pakistan is a 'United Church'. It was created by merging the 'LAMP' churches: the Pakistan Lutheran Church (L), the Anglican Dioceses of Lahore and Karachi (A), the United Methodist Church (M) and the Scottish Presbyterian Church (P). In 2005, it had an estimated 800,000 members, mostly drawn from the poorer strata of society. The majority traced their origin to Anglican mission activity in rural areas. However, with the mechanisation of farming, a rural exodus was increasingly bringing unskilled labour to the cities.

Although the Church of Pakistan was a full member of the Anglican Communion, there were traces of its multi-denominational past from the colonial era. Property ownership was still linked to the original denominations. In Peshawar, Archbishop Rowan would preach at St John's Cathedral. Its pews still had the rifle racks from its time as a garrison church at the foot of the Khyber Pass. On the wall was a plaque commemorating the Royal Sussex Regiment, in which my grandfather had served in Europe and which had been stationed in Peshawar. The remodelled sanctuary, where shoes were removed to receive Holy Communion, only partially overcame its character as an Anglican church of the British Raj. By contrast, in the heart of the city, the architecture of All Saints Peshawar made it seem more like a mosque than a church, a far cry from the European churches of parent denominations on which so many Pakistani churches were modelled. Despite this, it would be targeted by suicide bombers eight years later, in protest against us drone attacks in Pakistan. Seventy-eight would be killed and one hundred and thirty injured.

A visit to All Saints Peshawar with the Archbishop of Canterbury's Press Secretary, eight years before a terrorist attack killed 78 and injured 130

Photo © Andrew Norman

'Avoid places of worship', advised the travel advice website of the British Foreign and Commonwealth Office in 2005. The Archbishop of Canterbury was not exactly in a position to heed this on his visit. He would need to rely on the government's protection. Applying President Musharraf's philosophy of 'enlightened moderation', the government were making efforts to uphold the religious freedom of Christians. They routinely provided armed guards at churches for Sunday worship. Yet Christians repeatedly protested about unjust treatment. Archbishop Rowan summed up the nub of the problem in a press interview during his visit. 'I think it is widely recognised the abuse of the blasphemy laws is a major problem which this country has to tackle; the problem is not so much the idea of a law against blasphemy as about a law whose penalty is so severe and whose practice gives so much scope for allowing people to settle private scores.... I was able to speak directly to the President about this.' He was also able to discuss protection of religious minorities with the Minister for Religious Affairs and Minorities, Mr Muhammad Ijaz-ul-Haq. The meeting took place just after the so-called Sangla Hill incident, when 3,000 militants attacked Christians in Sangla Hill over allegations of violations of blasphemy laws by a Pakistani Christian. The militants destroyed Roman Catholic, Salvation Army and United Presbyterian churches. Two days later, at a seminar in Lahore for Christian and Muslim leaders, the Minister for Religious Affairs and Minorities issued an apology.[28]

The Archbishop's visit would be an opportunity to affirm the Church of Pakistan not only in its campaign for civil liberties. 'For us, gathering as a small church in the middle of a society that is mostly not Christian', he told a congregation at Christ Church Rawalpindi, 'we think "what can we do and what can we give?"'[29] As in Burundi, there would an opportunity to affirm its work in education. Church schools in Pakistan would mirror the Cambridge Mission's vision for educating India's elite. Despite the low social status of many Pakistani Christians, flagship church colleges and schools still educated future leaders and professionals, many of whom were Muslim. In Lahore, the Archbishop's wife, Jane, would address students at Kinnaird College, Pakistan's leading women's college, founded by missionaries. In Peshawar, on the North-West Frontier, the Archbishop would lay a foundation stone for a new building at Edwardes College.

The visit would also be a chance to encourage the Pakistani bishops, after a troubled saga following a contested bishop's election. In 1997, much publicity had been given to objections about the Bishop of Karachi's election. The case ended up in the High Court, where it was proposed that the Archbishop of Canterbury set up a commission. Archbishop George Carey duly complied and his commission's recommendations were accepted in 2001 by the court.[30] It proved a traumatic and divisive saga for the bishops, with complex repercussions. During his visit, Archbishop Rowan would lead the bishops in retreat, supporting them in their efforts to move forward together in renewed episcopal collegiality.

Promoting harmony between faiths, and not just within the Church, was a major strand of Archbishop Rowan's visit. At the Islamic University in Islamabad, after addressing Muslim students on 'What is Christianity?', he would speak with Muslim academics on dialogue between faiths. 'Dialogue is not debate. I am not out to secure agreement, but understanding.'[31] In Lahore he visited a strict Muslim Madrassa school, addressing a mass gathering of male students. 'When we enter into interfaith dialogue, it is so we can see each other's face and see each other's heart. In Britain there are many places where Christians and Muslims work together for the good of the whole community.... When we work together like this we see in each other a face and a heart that is marked by compassion.' He continued this theme the following day, talking with Muslim intellectuals on Muslim–Christian dialogue in Britain and beyond.[32]

'The great new fact of our era' is how the 98th Archbishop of Canterbury described the world ecumenical movement in 1942, preaching in Canterbury Cathedral.[33] The formation of the United Churches in Pakistan, India and Bangladesh represented an attempt to take forward the ecumenical vision that became inextricably part of being Anglican in the twentieth century. In 2006, the programme of the 104th Archbishop would express Anglican ecumenical identity in three other significant spheres: participation in the World Council of Churches, engagement with the Church in China and celebration of forty years of formal theological dialogue with the Roman Catholic Church. Seldom far from view would be the turbulence within the Anglican Communion and efforts to bring greater coherence and stability.

✠

This chapter has touched on other new facts of our era, in addition to ecumenism. For Anglicans, the Windsor Report and what lies behind it counts as one of these new facts. As we have followed the unfolding 'Windsor Process', we have observed the challenge of maintaining coherence in the face of controversy. We have seen the Anglican Instruments of Unity at work, having noted the Windsor Report's verdict that they urgently needed developing if they were to be 'fit for purpose'. Once again, we have seen how European opportunities may be a new fact of our era for Anglicans. Through the Archbishop's travels, we have seen further signs that Anglicans would be pushing at an open door if they became more active and vocal in continental Europe. We have encountered grassroots Anglican life in the Pacific, East Africa and South Asia. Post-conflict reconstruction and engagement with Islam can both be seen as new facts of our times in such places. We have admired the way religious communities can make a heroic contribution in such settings. We have also noted the potential for religious communities to engage with new facts of our time through ecumenical cooperation. The Archbishop of Canterbury himself can act as a catalyst for Anglicans in responding to all these new facts, as we will observe further in the next chapter.

A token of the shifting
demography of world
Christianity: the 45 millionth
Bible printed in Nanjing

Photo © Lambeth Palace

11

Unchanged by what is Happening?

A 'RED-EYE' 72-HOUR round trip to Brazil delivered us to the General Assembly of the World Council of Churches, the first of the Archbishop of Canterbury's three major ecumenical assignments in 2006. The World Council of Churches (WCC), when it was founded in 1948, had merged the two main highways of the ecumenical movement. The Archbishop of Canterbury whose death had been marked in my father's wartime diary—William Temple—had been a driving force in both of these. Other Anglicans, such as Bishop Charles Brent of the Episcopal Church, had also been groundbreakers. Following these pioneers, Anglicans would be committed members of the WCC, joining Protestant and Orthodox Christians in a common effort to achieve practical co-operation and visible unity for the Church. On the 'Life and Work' track, churches laboured together for the benefit of wider society. The 'Faith and Order' track was where churches attempted to bridge their disagreements about beliefs and church organisation and work round obstacles to closer union.

In the years that followed, Anglicans had been among those who criticised the functioning of the WCC. Some regarded it as top-heavy, remote from ordinary church members and prone to speaking for the churches with insufficient consultation.[1] Others, notably evangelical Anglicans, felt it promoted an imbalanced approach to mission. The birth of the ecumenical movement is generally traced back to the International Missionary Conference in Edinburgh in 1910. Yet in the years following World War Two, commitment to evangelism seemed to have been overtaken by a 'social gospel' in the WCC's priorities. John Stott was invited as an official adviser to the fourth WCC General Assembly in Uppsala. In one plenary session he addressed this perceived imbalance head-on. 'The Assembly has given its earnest attention to the hunger, poverty and injustices of the contemporary world. Rightly so. ... But I do not find a comparable compassion for the spiritual hunger of man. ... If the report retains this mood (which manifests little or no compassion for the unevangelised) I for one will feel obliged to say that the World Council of Churches does not seem to care much for them.'[2]

The work of the WCC was fuelled by General Assemblies, taking place every seven years or so. In February 2006, Archbishop Rowan would be a keynote speaker at the ninth General Assembly, one of several indicators of the continuing prominence of Anglicans in the life of the WCC. During the Assembly, a member of the Church of England, Mary Tanner, would be elected as one of the WCC presidents. The following year, a Canadian Anglican, John Gibaut, would be appointed Director of the Faith and Order Commission.

The topic the Archbishop was invited to address was one of the new facts of our era that we have already noted: 'Christian Identity and Religious Plurality'. All churches were needing to reassess how they related to adherents of other faiths. Archbishop Rowan was emerging as a leading voice in this field, with his unrivalled engagement with representatives of other faiths around the world and in Britain. It meant that Anglicans were not simply at the forefront of ecumenical relations. They were also on the leading edge of Christian engagement with Islam and other religions.

It would have been a long way to travel just to deliver a keynote address. The Archbishop's day or so in Brazil was therefore packed with other meetings and engagements. It was, of course, a convenient opportunity to meet with senior leaders of other churches, such as the Armenian Catholicos, Aram I, from Lebanon. It was also a chance to spend time with Assembly delegates from the various Anglican provinces. The crisis within the Anglican Communion was reverberating through Anglican ecumenical relations around the world. It was also affecting the internal life of provinces, including the Anglican province where the Assembly was taking place. Before leaving for the airport, the Archbishop was able to meet with the bishops of the Anglican province of Brazil. One of their number had been deposed the previous year, generating much publicity.

The name of the province, the Anglican Episcopal Church of Brazil, bears witness to its origins. The missionaries who founded the province mostly came from the Episcopal Church (USA). The first two arrived in 1889 from Virginia Theological Seminary, where I studied on exchange. The Province of Brazil has therefore retained close links with the Episcopal Church. In 2004, the Bishop of Recife took part in the kind of cross-border intervention the Windsor Report subsequently condemned. He joined retired bishops for a confirmation service in Ohio, since parishioners objected to the theological stance of their own bishop. This triggered a complex chain of events, in which the Bishop of Recife was deposed. The neighbouring Province of the Southern Cone had been drawn into the dispute, so it was no longer an internal issue for the Province of Brazil. It was an opportune time for a meeting with the Archbishop of Canterbury.[3]

This packed 72-hour round trip to Brazil was upstaged later that year with a packed 72-event trip to China. It was the most ambitious visit I would oversee during my time with the Archbishop. The invitation had come when Chinese church leaders met the Archbishop at Lambeth Palace in 2003. Since then, I had paid two ten-day visits to China and organised an unusually large number of briefing sessions for the Archbishop, involving a fascinating array of so-called China Hands. The aim of the visit was to gain a deeper understanding of the Church in China and its context, strengthen relationships and engage with issues of global concern.

Anglican survivors: Bishop K. H. Ting, consecrated as an Anglican and in 2006 the one remaining bishop in the post-denominational Church in China (above); Holy Trinity Cathedral in Shanghai, a cinema during the Cultural Revolution (right)

Photos © Lambeth Palace (above) and Andrew Norman (right)

The visit began in Shanghai. The Maglev train from the airport catapulted the Archbishop's party into the reality of China's high-speed development, at 150 km/h. In the lee of glittering high-rise offices, we visited the former Anglican cathedral, Holy Trinity. During the Cultural Revolution, when every church was closed, the cathedral had been turned into a cinema. Now it had been handed back to the Church and was being gradually refurbished, with the banks of cinema seats removed. In Nanjing, we would meet the one remaining bishop consecrated as an Anglican in mainland China, the legendary Bishop K. H. Ting. 'Ah—*Anglican World*', he said when given a copy of the magazine by Archbishop Rowan. 'I've been grateful for this over the years. It has many readers in China.' But in reality, the 90-year-old bishop was no longer part of the 'Anglican world' himself.[4] In the 1950s Anglicans had been obliged to merge with all Protestant churches under a 'post-denominational' arrangement. Borrowing the approach espoused by Henry Venn of the Church Missionary Society, they came under the umbrella of the 'Three-Self Patriotic Movement' (TSPM). TSPM churches would be self-governing, self-propagating and self-financing. In a communist China, any hint of interference from the West was repudiated.

Anglican antecedents: 7th-century Christian pagoda in China (left), built around the same time that Escomb Saxon Church (above) was built from the ruins of Binchester Roman Fort

Photos © Andrew Norman

There had in fact been Christians in China since the sixth century. Testament to this was a wax rubbing of a three metre high Nestorian tablet, hung in a corridor of Lambeth Palace. It had been presented as a gift to Archbishop Robert Runcie by Bishop Ting. Archbishop Rowan Williams would be able to touch the cold stone of the sixth-century tablet for himself during his visit, in a museum in Xi'an, the city famed for its terracotta warriors. Sadly there was insufficient time for the Archbishop's party to visit the site where the tablet was discovered, an hour's drive from Xi'an. During the preparatory visit, I had made the trip and seen for myself what else had survived the ravages of time at that site: a seventh-century Christian pagoda, constructed at a similar time to the Saxon church at Escomb, near where my grandfather served in Binchester. Christianity in China could not simply be dismissed as a Western import, even if it was an Anglican vicar's son who had rediscovered the Da Qin pagoda in 1998.[5]

Yet its association with Western imperialism is all too understandable. China was opened up to missionaries on the back of the Opium Wars, when Britain insisted on its right to sell opium in exchange for tea. 'We have triumphed in one of the most lawless, unnecessary, and unfair struggles in the records of history', lamented the Anglican social reformer, Lord Shaftesbury, in 1842. 'It was a war on which good men could not invoke the favour of heaven.'[6] Many Christians agreed. 'The missionary movement was unequivocal in its condemnation of the opium trade', according to the historian, Brian Stanley. Yet mission agencies regarded the establishment of five treaty ports as a providential opening for missionary work, as they did later concessions after the Second Opium War. 'God had turned the evil of human design to the good of his purposes.'[7] The first CMS missionaries set sail for China in 1844. That same year, the Episcopal Church appointed William Jones Boone to be Bishop of the American (Episcopal) Church Mission in China. The first Chinese priest, Huang Kuang-ts'ai, was baptised in 1846 and ordained in 1861.[8]

By the time Bishop Ting was consecrated in 1955, there were thirteen Anglican bishops, all Chinese. Compared with other denominations, Anglicans were always a minority in China. Shortly after Bishop Ting's consecration, when denominations were abolished under communism, no more than 80,000 of China's four million Christians were Anglican.[9] After the formation of the TSPM in the 1950s, things soon deteriorated for all China's Christians, however liberated they might have been from Western influence. This was when the Cultural Revolution (1966–76) saw visible church life banned altogether. Bishop Ting was placed under house arrest and many other Christians fared far worse.[10] Yet in the aftermath of the Cultural Revolution, Anglicans would quickly develop strong relations with China's post-denominational church, where Bishop Ting became a senior figure.

In 1983, just four years after the end of the Cultural Revolution, the visit to China of the Archbishop of Canterbury, Robert Runcie, was almost at the level of a State visit. Nine years later, when Archbishop George Carey visited, the reception was more muted, against the backdrop of the British handover of Hong Kong and international tensions over the killing of students in Tiananmen Square. By the time Archbishop Rowan visited, Church and government in China were ready to host a high-profile visit once again. It would include visits to five Chinese provinces, numerous encounters with local

Christians, meetings with senior government officials, engagement with environmental initiatives and events in universities. It would also include meetings with representatives of the four other recognised religions in China: Islam, Daoism, Buddhism and—somewhat jarringly for ecumenists—Catholicism, as a distinct religion to Protestantism.

It was an unforgettable trip and it is tempting to re-live it day-by-day in this account: services in packed churches, visits to the Daoist Monastery on Wudang Mountain, to the Great Mosque in Xi'an (the Imam remembered welcoming Archbishop Runcie), to the Buddhist temple in Beijing and to the 90-year-old Catholic Bishop of Shanghai, who had spent 9,900 days of his life in detention. However, for our purposes, we need to concentrate on what the visit revealed about being Anglican as times change. Let me offer four insights.

Firstly, it was abundantly clear that Anglican ecumenical engagement must reach beyond the familiar historic churches, to include Chinese Christians. At the end of the visit, Archbishop Rowan referred to 'the astonishing and quite unpredictable explosion in Christian numbers in recent years'.[11] Accurate figures were hard to come by, especially as millions of Chinese Christians chose not to associate with the registered TSPM churches. In a briefing provided for the 2008 Beijing Olympics, the Chinese government had reported a figure of 21 million Christians. While very much lower than estimates provided by bodies such as the Global China Center, this official estimate was nonetheless a fifty percent increase on figures provided by the Chinese government ten years earlier.[12] 'China is moving towards having the largest Christian population in the world', Archbishop Rowan observed on his return, in a lecture at Chatham House. 'Today, 50–80 million Protestants in China may be a safe guess.'[13] Two years later, the Chinese Academy for Social Sciences was estimating 29 million. By 2010, the Pew Foundation, drawing on a range of sources, would estimate 58 million Protestants and 9 million Catholics.[14]

Whatever the actual figures, the authorities were openly acknowledging that Christianity was a force to be reckoned with in China. 'The Chinese Government now repeats regularly that religion is essential to the "harmonious society" it aims to create,' Archbishop Rowan informed readers of *The Times*, 'the sort of statement unthinkable ten or fifteen years ago.'[15] Relating to this growing body of Christians, in the world's most populous nation, should be a priority for ecumenically-minded Anglicans.

The second feature of 'being Anglican' which the visit highlighted was the significance of the Archbishop of Canterbury as a widely recognised world church leader and spokesperson. In the Great Hall of the People in Tiananmen

Square, at the Beijing Mayor's Office, at the State Environmental Protection Agency, over sumptuous dinners and other striking settings, Archbishop Rowan was able to discuss common concerns and human rights issues with the most senior government officials. 'We had a long discussion on the environmental challenges of modern China', he told journalists gathered in the British Ambassador's residence. 'We raised a number of specific cases of reported harassment of religious personnel, Roman Catholic and Protestant, and of lawyers defending them', he went on to comment. 'We raised some particular half dozen cases that had been brought to my attention before leaving, which applied to both registered and unregistered Christian personnel.' This included the case of Pastor Chai, arrested and imprisoned for 'illicitly trading Bibles', despite the millions of Bibles printed in Nanjing each year. During our visit to the printing factory, the Archbishop had been presented with its 45 millionth Bible.[16]

Moving on to the third insight, the visit revealed renewed significance for Anglican commitment to academic scholarship. The Archbishop's visit included encounters with the growing number of Chinese academics studying Christianity and its potential benefit to society. Sometimes called 'cultural Christians', they were the product of what has been labelled another 'opium war'.[17] Rather than dismissing religion as the opium of the people, deadening their senses, academics were reappraising Christianity as a source of social virtues. At Wuhan University, the Archbishop met with academics to discuss the Church's influence on British Society. 'It came as something of a surprise that the philosophy faculty had so much expertise in the history of the Church of England', observed one of the Anglican bishops accompanying the Archbishop. In Beijing, at the Chinese Academy for Social Sciences, the bishop was similarly impressed when theological developments in England were discussed. 'Around 20 of China's top academics working in this field gathered for a first rate discussion.'[18] As follow-up to the visit, the Archbishop was able to invite Chinese academics to Lambeth Palace for series of roundtables with British academics.

The fourth insight revealed about 'being Anglican' is this: Anglicans were able to strengthen their relations with the Church in China, thanks to the changing demographic within the Anglican Communion. The Anglican provinces in South East Asia and Hong Kong already had close ties with the Church in China. However, there was real interest in seeing how Anglicans in the Global South were making Christianity authentically their own, rather than regarding it as the religious component of Western imperialism. This was a feature of discussions with both church leaders and government officials. The year after the Archbishop's visit, ten Anglican primates from the Global South made a week-long visit to the Church in China, following it up with another in 2011.[19] Tectonic plates were shifting in Anglican ecumenical relations.

After returning from this marathon visit to China, the Archbishop set off a few weeks later for his third major ecumenical engagement of 2006. He was bound for Rome, to more familiar terrain for Anglican ecumenism. With Pope Benedict, he would celebrate forty years since the historic visit of his predecessor, Michael Ramsey, and the launching of the formal theological dialogue between Anglicans and Roman Catholics (ARCIC). He would also celebrate forty years since the founding of the Anglican Centre in Rome, of which I was a Governor.

The Second Vatican Council, which I had enjoyed studying at the Catholic university in Washington, had been a game-changer for relations between the Roman Catholic Church and non-Catholics. The idea of an Anglican Centre in Rome had been proposed by one of the Anglican observers at the Council, Bernard Pawley. Archbishop Michael Ramsey supported the idea, and plans were taken forward to buy a suitable property, funded by Anglicans in Canada, the USA and Australia. As things turned out, this would not be necessary. A ten-room apartment was offered in the prestigious Palazzo Pamphilj, enabling the Anglican Centre to be opened in 1966, with a library, accommodation and facilities for seminars. The Doria Pamphilj family, who made this possible, had a colourful family history. Prince Filippo and his Scottish wife, Gesine, had been defiantly anti-fascist during World War Two and as a result were banished by Mussolini to Southern Italy. When Italy was liberated, Prince Filippo was appointed Mayor of Rome. His daughter, Orietta, joined the Catholic women's league and helped run canteens for the Allied forces. She met and later married Lieutenant Commander Frank Dobson. The Doria Pamphilj family turned into long-term supporters of the Anglican Centre, offering a larger apartment in 1998 on the Piazza Collegio Romano side of the Palace. When Archbishop Rowan visited in 2006, his programme included a reception in the Doria Pamphilj Gallery, surrounded by paintings by Caravaggio and other renaissance artists.

Much ground had been covered in forty years of dialogue since the Anglican Centre was opened. Strenuous efforts had been made to get behind the language of polemic and disagreement to find points on which the two churches could agree. 'Your method has been to go behind the habit of thought and expression born and nourished in enmity and controversy,' observed Pope John Paul II in 1980, 'to scrutinise together the great common treasure, to clothe it in a language at once traditional and expressive of an age which no longer glories in strife but seeks to come together in listening to the quiet voice of the Spirit.'[20] The Final Report from the first round of dialogue was issued in 1981, covering ministry, the Eucharist and authority.[21] It would not, however, be endorsed on both sides. The co-chairs wrote to the Pope and the Archbishop of Canterbury, asking two questions:

- Are these Agreed Statements and their Elucidations consonant in substance with the faith of the Catholic Church and the Anglican Communion?
- Does the Final Report offer a sufficient basis for taking the next step towards reconciliation?

Pope John Paul II referred the Final Report to the Congregation for the Doctrine of the Faith (CDF), to make a doctrinal examination of the report. Cardinal Ratzinger, as Prefect of the CDF, wrote to the Catholic co-chair of ARCIC. He described the Final Report as a significant step towards reconciliation, but not 'an agreement which is truly substantial'. The Final Report was then released to Catholic bishops' conferences, along with the CDF's *Observations*. The Anglican response was to send the Final Report to Anglican provinces first, then collate responses for the 1988 Lambeth Conference. When they voted, the bishops were satisfied that the Agreed Statements and their Elucidations are 'consonant in substance with the faith of Anglicans' and that 'this agreement offers a sufficient basis for taking the next step towards the reconciliation of our two Churches'.[22] Three years later, the Catholic Church published its own formal response. 'It is not yet possible to state that substantial agreement has been reached on all the questions studied by the Commission.'[23] It was not just Anglicans who were dismayed. The French Episcopal Commission signalled its 'astonished' disappointment.[24]

Despite this discouraging outcome, ARCIC dialogue had not been on hold. When John Paul II visited England in 1982, with his symbolic walk down Hope Street in Liverpool, he and Archbishop Runcie announced the next round of ARCIC dialogue. ARCIC II would begin by looking at salvation and the Church (1987) and the Church as communion (1991). It would go on to consider ethics (1994), authority in the church (1999) and Mary (2005). Individual Anglican provinces considered these reports as they saw fit, but this time there was no attempt to provide Communion-wide endorsement through the Lambeth Conference.

In the light of the mixed reception of ARCIC statements, a joint meeting of Anglican and Catholic bishops was held in 2000 in Canada, at Mississauga. The convenors were the Archbishop of Canterbury, George Carey, and the

President of the Pontifical Council for Promoting Christian Unity (PCPCU), Cardinal Cassidy. The bishops came in pairs from thirteen countries. Their discussions were animated by a Roman Catholic Sister, Donna Geernaert, and Mary Tanner, the Anglican ecumenist elected President of the World Council of Churches at Porto Alegre, six years later. The aim of this millennial gathering was to consider advances made by ARCIC, to review grassroots relations and to consider what the next step might be. In other words, the purpose was to consider how best to harvest the work of ARCIC in order to make a practical difference. What resulted was a working party of Catholic and Anglican bishops (IARCCUM).[25] Its aim was to distil the essence of the ARCIC agreements, noting outstanding areas of disagreement, yet highlighting scope for increased practical co-operation. IARCCUM's report would be published following Archbishop Rowan's 2006 visit to Rome as *Growing Together in Unity and Mission.*[26]

Vespers in the Vatican with Pope Benedict in 2006: 40 years of Anglican–Roman Catholic dialogue   *Photo © Lambeth Palace*

Cardinal Ratzinger, who as head of the CDF had conveyed the ambivalent response to ARCIC's agreed statements, was now Pope Benedict XVI, receiving the Archbishop of Canterbury at the Vatican. 'There are many areas of witness and service in which we can stand together', Pope Benedict and Archbishop Rowan affirmed in their Common Declaration. 'We also commit ourselves to inter-religious dialogue through which we can jointly reach out to our non-Christian brothers and sisters.' Yet they were frank about the new challenges posed by developments within the Anglican Communion:

'in renewing our commitment to pursue the path towards full visible communion in the truth and love of Christ, we also commit ourselves in our continuing dialogue to address the important issues involved in the emerging ecclesiological and ethical factors making that journey more difficult and arduous.'[27]

This, in part, was code for the Windsor Process and the issues it was seeking to address. We turn now to plot the trajectory of this process. Not long after the bishops on IARCCUM had begun harvesting ARCIC, their work had been stalled. Immediately following the consecration of an actively gay bishop in the Episcopal Church in 2003, the President of PCPCU and the Secretary General of the Anglican Communion issued a joint statement. The work of IARCCUM would be 'put on hold in the light of ecclesiological concerns raised as a consequence of these events'.[28] There would be a delay of two years before the full working group gathered again. I joined IARCCUM for this closing meeting in 2005 at the stunningly located Villa Palazzola, overlooking Lake Albano, just south of Rome.

By then, the Primates' Meeting had taken place at Dromantine and the Windsor Report had been broadly endorsed. The following year, in sweltering hot conditions, in Nottingham (not the Tropics), the Anglican Consultative Council made its own response. Inadequate air-conditioning was not the only reason the two-week meeting was uncomfortable. As requested by the primates, North American provinces had withdrawn their representatives. Instead of normal participation, they would provide a spirited defence of their controversial actions, in a hearing. 'A gathering like this always attracts a degree of media attention,' the Archbishop of Canterbury observed drily in his presidential address, 'and we can guess already what the pattern of this is likely to be—"The Communion is in great trouble; conservatives and liberals are going to split from one another."'[29] As it turned out, this would be one of a series of events where there was no media scoop about formal schism. Instead, by a narrow margin, the ACC endorsed the recommendations of the primates at Dromatine, citing the primates' reaffirmation that 'the standard of teaching on matters of human sexuality is expressed in the 1998 Lambeth Resolution 1.10, which should command respect as the position overwhelmingly adopted by the bishops of the Anglican Communion'. This was the resolution that upheld a traditional line about homosexual practice, while urging improved pastoral responses to those of homosexual orientation. In a separate resolution, passed unanimously, the ACC voted to establish a means of listening to the experiences of homosexual persons and local churches' reflections on sexuality in the light of 'Scripture, Tradition and Reason'.[30]

A report was also given to members of the ACC about the next Lambeth Conference. At previous meetings, the ACC had hoped it might be possible to combine the Lambeth Conference for bishops with a congress for a wider cross-section of Anglicans. There had been three previous 'pan-Anglican' Congresses: in London (1908), Minnesota (1954), and Toronto (1963). The 1963 Congress in Toronto had left an indelible mark on global Anglican dynamics, by advocating 'mutual responsibility and interdependence' (MRI).[31] 'In our time the Anglican Communion has come of age', the 1963 Congress had proclaimed. 'Our professed nature as a world-wide fellowship of national and regional churches has suddenly become a reality—all but ten of the 350 Anglican dioceses are now included in self-governing churches.... It is now irrelevant to talk of giving and receiving churches. The keynotes of our time are equality, interdependence, mutual responsibility.'[32]

Since its 1987 meeting in Singapore, the ACC had been advocating another Congress, outside Europe or North America. By 1999, costings had been put together for hosting it in Jordan, Hong Kong or South Africa. At ACC 11, Archbishop George Carey suggested it be held in association with the Lambeth Conference. In 2002, this had been narrowed down to an Anglican Gathering followed by the Lambeth Conference in Cape Town, endorsed at ACC 12. In 2004, I had joined the Design Group set up for these paired events, along with bishops and members of the ACC. But insufficient funding was in place for the congress. Without a congress, there were no economies of scale to make a Lambeth Conference in Cape Town affordable. So by ACC 13, in Nottingham, plans were maturing to host Lambeth 2008 in Canterbury.[33]

The aim of the 2008 Lambeth Conference, explained Archbishop Rowan to ACC delegates, was twofold. It would help bishops be 'better equipped for mission', while not 'avoiding the issues' associated with the Windsor Report. 'Invitations will be sent at the end of 2007', said Bishop James Tengatenga of Malawi, a member of the Design Group.[34] With American delegates currently excluded from the ACC, this would clearly be a delicate issue. Would Gene Robinson be invited, for example? Would any American bishops be invited?

Over the following year, while the Lambeth Conference Design Group continued its work, eyes were turned to the Episcopal Church (USA), to see how it would respond to the recommendations of the Windsor Report. The bishops of the Episcopal Church had pressed the pause button on blessing same-sex unions. 'We pledge not to authorise any public rites for the blessing of same-sex unions, and will not bless any such unions, at least until the General Convention of 2006' they covenanted.[35] Now, as the 75th General Convention of the Episcopal Church (USA) approached, tension mounted, and not just in Lambeth Palace. How would the Windsor Report be received? Would its vision for interdependence ('autonomy in communion') be endorsed? Would there be expressions of regret for breaching bonds of affection by consecrating someone whose lifestyle contradicted the teaching of Lambeth 1.10? Would there be a block on bishops living in same-gender unions 'until some new consensus in the Anglican Communion has emerged'? Would there also be a moratorium on public rites of blessing for same-sex unions?

The authority of the General Convention of the Episcopal Church needs to be understood in the light of its origins. It was a pivotal part of the polity formed in 1789, after American independence. It reflected the democratic and egalitarian ideals of the American Revolution itself.[36] Within this polity, the voice of the laity was prized. The 75th General Convention was held in Columbus, Ohio. Its delegates were clear they had no intention of opting out of the Anglican Communion. They reaffirmed 'the abiding commitment of The Episcopal Church to the fellowship of churches that constitute the Anglican Communion', commending the Windsor Report as a means of deepening commitment to 'interdependent life in Christ'.[37] They even supported the development of an Anglican Covenant.[38] But what about bishops? On the very last day, the presiding bishop, Frank Griswold, proposed resolution B033. It embraced 'the Windsor Report's invitation to engage in a process of healing and reconciliation', calling for the exercise of restraint 'by not consenting to the consecration of any candidate to the episcopate whose manner of life presents a challenge to the wider church and will lead to further strains on communion'.[39]

There was also mention of 'the agonising position of those who do not feel able to receive appropriate pastoral care from their own bishop', along with a call to respect historic boundaries of dioceses and provinces. 'No cross-border interventions, please', in other words. But there was no explicit mention of public rites of blessing for same-sex unions. The previous General Convention had resolved 'that we recognise that local faith communities are operating within the bounds of our common life as they explore and experience liturgies celebrating and blessing same-sex unions'.[40] It was therefore not clear where things now stood.

A small working group was set up to assess these responses and report to the Instruments of Communion. February 2007, when the primates next met, would be its first opportunity. In the meantime, Archbishop Rowan offered a commentary on Anglican identity and what was at stake in the current crisis. 'There is no way in which the Anglican Communion can remain unchanged by what is happening at the moment', he warned. In his 'The Challenge and Hope of Being an Anglican Today', he addressed all bishops, clergy and faithful of the Anglican Communion.[41] 'The debate in the Anglican Communion is not essentially a debate about the human rights of homosexual people', he argued, reflecting the wider terms of reference of the Windsor Report. It is about how Anglicans deal with such issues 'in our own terms'.

The debate, in his view, went to the very heart of what it meant to be Anglican, from a global perspective. 'Institutionally speaking, the Communion is an association of local churches, not a single organisation with a controlling bureaucracy and a universal system of law. So everything depends on what have generally been unspoken conventions of mutual respect. Where these are felt to have been ignored, it is not surprising that deep divisions result.' Without necessarily realising it, the Episcopal Church (USA) had been reckless and had undermined Anglican polity, jeopardising its own good standing in the Communion. 'No member church can make significant decisions unilaterally and still expect this to make no difference to how it is regarded in the fellowship. . . . Actions believed in good faith to be "prophetic" in their radicalism are likely to have costly consequences.'

Even without the international dimension, questions needed to be raised. 'The decision of the Episcopal Church to elect a practising gay man as a bishop was taken without even the American church itself (which has had quite a bit of discussion of the matter) having formally decided as a local church what it thinks about blessing same-sex partnerships.'

He went on to present a theological framework for this common Anglican life. 'We do have a distinctive historic tradition—a reformed commitment to the absolute priority of the Bible for deciding doctrine, a catholic loyalty to the sacraments and the threefold ministry of bishops, priests and deacons.' To flourish within this framework as a global family of churches, without become 'tightly centralised', new ways of expressing mutual commitment were called for. The most promising way forward, in his view, was a 'covenant', where local freedoms might be limited for the sake of a wider witness. It might lead to a two-tier communion, if some churches felt unable to opt in. But it would be 'a positive challenge for churches to work out what they believed to be involved in belonging to a global sacramental fellowship'.

By the end of the year, a design group would be in place to work on an Anglican Covenant. Our first meeting, in January 2007, took us to an exotic beachside location. We met in the Bahamas, hosted by our chair, Archbishop Drexel Gomez of the West Indies. His province had been self-governing since 1883, so it was a fitting place to consider how Anglican provinces should relate to one another. The other members of the Design Group came from South East Asia, the USA, West Africa, Ireland, Canada, the Seychelles and the UK. Given the diversity of these provinces, it seemed unlikely we would make much headway in this first meeting. At one stage, we took time out to visit a hotel that featured in one of the James Bond movies. It had a water slide that went through a shark pool, which led to macabre comparisons with our own perilous assignment. Yet by the end of our week, to our surprise and relief, we had completed our first draft. We had been given a head start by draft Covenants already prepared by the Anglican Church in Australia, the Anglican mission commission (IASCOME), a working group of Global South Anglicans and the Lambeth Commission which had produced the Windsor Report.

This 'Nassau draft' sought to distil the essence of what Anglicans held in common, drawing heavily on established formulae, such as the Lambeth Quadrilateral and the Five Marks of Mission.[42] In doing so, it was signalling the potential of the Covenant to be much more than a device for dealing with disputes.

The draft Covenant was expressed as a series of affirmations and commitments. In the closing section, the issue of controversy was tackled head-on. 'Each church commits itself... in essential matters of common concern, to have regard to the common good of the Communion in the exercise of its autonomy.' Protocols for dealing with controversial issues were then set out. 'Some issues, which are perceived as controversial or new when they arise, may well evoke a deeper understanding of the implications of God's revelation to us; others may prove to be distractions or even obstacles to the faith: all therefore need to be tested by shared discernment in the life of the Church.' Matters in serious dispute should be referred to the Primates' Meeting. 'In the most extreme circumstances, where member churches choose not to fulfil the substances of the covenant... we will consider that such churches will have relinquished for themselves the force and meaning of the covenant's purpose.'

The next stage was for the Nassau draft to be considered at the Primates' Meeting the following month. At the same meeting, the primates would consider the response of the North American churches to the Windsor Report. The trouble was, it was far from clear whether the primates would even agree to sit down together to discuss them. A few months earlier, the primates of the Global South had met together in Rwanda, describing themselves as 'a growing fellowship of primates and leaders of churches in the Global South, representing more than 70 per cent of the active membership of the worldwide Anglican Communion'. They had visited the genocide museum and 'wept at the mass grave of 250,000 helpless victims'. While heartened by the Covenant project, they were discouraged by the response of General Convention to the requests of the Windsor Report, according to their formal statement. Then it became personal. They were unimpressed with the newly elected Presiding Bishop, who 'holds to a position on human sexuality—not to mention other controversial views—in direct contradiction of Lambeth 1.10 and the historic teaching of the Church.... At the next meeting of the Primates in February 2007, some of us will not be able to recognise Katharine Jefferts Schori as a Primate at the table with us.'[43]

I arrived in Tanzania in advance of the Archbishop, a few days before the Primates' Meeting was due to start. It would be my second beachside location that winter: this time, the White Sands Hotel on the outskirts of Dar es Salaam. Media interest was high, with dire predictions of the imminent collapse of the Anglican Communion and of boycotts or walkouts by Global South primates. Yet most of the Global South primates had already arrived and were meeting separately before the main meeting. Journalists were also starting to arrive—like circling vultures, someone quipped—including religious correspondents from the *Guardian* and the *Telegraph*. They would stay in the public part of the hotel, kept from the delegates' section by a security cordon, supervised by a burly South African.

The Primates' Standing Committee and Anglican Consultative Council met immediately before the Primates' Meeting too. Archbishop Rowan would join them part-way through, as was his custom. I travelled to Dar es Salaam airport to meet him. He was greeted by the Archbishop of Tanzania, two children with a bouquet of flowers and Reuters press agency. We travelled down the busy airport road, passing the University of Dar es Salaam, cyclists with stacks of eggs and an open-back lorry with convicts. Thus began an intensive and difficult week, with a lot of sitting around tables in earnest discussion. 'An agonising time', is how the Nigerian primate, Peter Akinola, described it.[44] In the end, there was no walkout. But nor was there a group photo of smiling primates. Eventually, at midnight on the final day, there was an agreed communiqué, and no front page news of a split.

The primates did occasionally come up for air. During the coffee break one morning, a message was received to say that the Tanzanian President wished to see the Archbishop of Canterbury. Accompanied by the Tanzanian and Pakistani primates, we set off in a carcade later that day, with the police outrider intimidating oncoming vehicles onto the verge. At the President's, we were joined by the British High Commissioner, as is usual for the Archbishop's meetings with heads of state. Then on the Sunday, almost all the primates took the boat to Zanzibar. Archbishop Rowan presided at a service at the historic Anglican cathedral, built out of coral.

Time out from the Primates' Meeting in Dar Es Salaam: meeting the President of Tanzania (above); outside the coral stone cathedral in Zanzibar, on the site of the former slave market (right)

Photos © Anglican Communion Office

On a predominantly Muslim island, the cathedral was built at the end of the nineteenth century, on the site of the former slave market. When the missionaries of UMCA heeded Livingstone's call to bring Christianity, civilisation and commerce to Africa (the three 'c's), the cathedral would become their launching point for mission on the mainland. Later, it became the see of one of the most influential Anglo-Catholic bishops in the twentieth century, Frank Weston. Weston was a staunch critic of Hensley Henson and his attempts to restate the doctrines of the Church of England.[45] Henson, he argued, had strayed into heresy. Henson in turn retorted that the Bishop of Zanzibar's 'natural home is in the Roman Catholic Church and not ours'.[46] Yet Weston was a staunch advocate for adapting Anglican liturgy to make it more in tune with the local context, echoing Henson's call for cultural relevance. He would oversee the development of Swahili liturgy that incorporated more indigenous customs than most other parts of Africa, albeit with more Catholic theology than the *Book of Common Prayer*. CMS missionaries would also be active in parts of what became Tanzania at independence. Given the differing churchmanship, coming up with a common prayer book for

Tanzania in 1995 would prove quite a challenge.[47] This was the liturgy used when the primates gathered for worship in 2007.

At the service in Christ Church Cathedral, the Archbishop admitted the new Anglican Observer at the United Nations, Mrs Helen Wangusa from Uganda, a reminder that Anglicans were not only concerned about their internal tensions but were committed to the Millennium Development Goals. Lunch after the service was in the presence of the President of Zanzibar, with waves lapping up to the side of the restaurant. Afterwards, the primates returned to the cathedral, to view the cells in which slaves were held before the cathedral was built. This coincided with the 200th Anniversary of the abolition of the slave trade in the British Empire. The Arab slave trade run from Zanzibar would continue for another ninety years after this, hence Livingstone's plea in 1857 to stop it at source with the three c's, along similar lines to Buxton's efforts in Nigeria. The Archbishop of York, John Sentamu, was attending the Primates' Meeting for the first time. He and Archbishop Rowan recorded a film after visiting the slave cells, to mark the 200th Anniversary. 'How could you put 75 men and women in that tiny room?' the Ugandan-born Archbishop exclaimed. The site would be in the media spotlight seven years later, when Islamic militants bombed the main entrance to the cathedral.[48]

Whatever the Global South primates may have said in Rwanda, the communiqué hammered out at the White Sands Hotel was generally positive about the Episcopal Church's response to the Windsor Report. The primates took their lead from the working group set up immediately after the meeting of General Convention in Ohio the previous June.[49] However, the Episcopal Church needed to go further, in their view. 'There remains a lack of clarity about the stance of the Episcopal Church in relation to rites of blessing for those living in same-sex relationships.' Much of the communiqué was devoted to those referred to in the Windsor Report as 'dissenting groups' in the Episcopal Church. The Primates' Meeting had been joined by three bishops of the Episcopal Church, where concerns had been aired. One of them was the Bishop of Pittsburgh, whose diocese I had visited with Archbishop George Carey. The primates acknowledged that the estrangement of dissenting groups had led to 'recrimination, hostility and even to disputes in the civil courts'. But interventions by bishops of other provinces, 'against the explicit recommendations of the Windsor Report, however well-intentioned, have exacerbated the situation'.[50] As an alternative to interventions, the primates proposed a 'pastoral scheme' which respected the polity of the Episcopal Church while taking seriously the concerns of dissenting groups. It was based on the so-called

'Camp Allen principles', drawn up by a small group of Episcopalian bishops. 'We are Communion-committed bishops' they had stressed, 'and find the option of turning to foreign oversight presents anomalies which weaken our own diocesan families and places strains on the Communion as a whole.'[51] The primates also gave the green light to the Nassau draft of the Covenant. It was commended for study, with provinces invited to send in comments by the end of the year. A revised draft would be discussed at the Lambeth Conference.

The primates' communiqué was not well received in the Episcopal Church (USA). Meeting the following month, its bishops expressed 'significant concerns' about what they perceived to be 'an unprecedented shift of power towards the Primates'. They declined to participate on the proposed pastoral scheme, believing it to contravene the canons and constitution of the Episcopal Church. Come and talk to us instead, was the invitation.[52]

It was in Canada, two months later, that the Archbishop confirmed his acceptance. 'My aim is to try and keep people around the table for as long as possible on this', he explained at a press conference. It was my first visit to Canada, the country where my grandfather had been ordained priest. We were not as far west as Calgary, though. We were in unseasonably cold Toronto, having left Heathrow on an unseasonably warm spring Sunday afternoon. After a lecture delivered by the Archbishop at Wycliffe College, we headed for the Retreat Centre at Niagara Falls. The next morning revealed grey skies over the famous Falls in one direction, just a few hundred yards away, and casinos and high-rise hotels in the other. The Archbishop was there to lead the Canadian bishops in retreat.

Fascination with Anglican politics: media interest in Toronto
Photo © Lambeth Palace

They were gathering shortly before their General Synod, when it would be Canada's turn to respond further to the recommendations of the Windsor Report. It was not the only challenge facing the Anglican Church in Canada. As the Primate, Andrew Hutchison, would remind Synod representatives, the Anglican Church in Canada was making reparations for the tragic saga of abuse in residential schools set up for aboriginal students. Individuals accused of sexual and physical abuse included those serving at the residential school on Blood Reserve Indian settlement, adjacent to the town of Cardston, where my grandfather had served his curacy.[53]

Since the 1870s, residential schools had been run as a joint venture between the Canadian government and Anglican, Catholic, Presbyterian and United Churches. The government's ultimate goal was the assimilation of educated native peoples into the non-aboriginal world. Anglican dioceses around the country had contributed to a $25 million settlement fund by June 2007, Archbishop Hutchison reported. As well as enabling payments to be made to individuals, the fund would help finance a Truth and Reconciliation Commission, whose work would begin later in the year.[54] The following year, the Canadian Prime Minister would offer a full apology on behalf of the Canadian people. 'The government now recognizes that the consequences of the Indian Residential Schools policy were profoundly negative and that this policy has had a lasting and damaging impact on Aboriginal culture, heritage and language', Prime Minister Stephen Harper acknowledged. 'While some former students have spoken positively about their experiences at residential schools, these stories are far overshadowed by tragic accounts of the emotional, physical and sexual abuse and neglect of helpless children.... The Government of Canada sincerely apologizes and asks the forgiveness of the Aboriginal peoples of this country for failing them so profoundly.'[55]

Despite this spectre of shared culpability in a national tragedy, it was the Windsor Report that would be the main agenda item at the General Synod in 2007. Archbishop Hutchison asked delegates to obey their conscience 'and with it the ethic of respect for the conscience of those who disagree with your own' when deciding what he called 'one of the most difficult items for our discernment' — the issue of whether the church should allow the blessing of same-sex unions. In the event, a motion to authorise dioceses to permit the blessing of such unions was narrowly defeated by the order of bishops (it was passed by the orders of clergy and laity).[56]

Over the next few months, Archbishop Rowan would take time out to write his book on Dostoevsky and I would finish my MPhil thesis on Anglican engagement in French-language ministry. In September, it was time to join the bishops of the Episcopal Church. They were meeting in New Orleans. It was just two years after Hurricane Katrina. The Archbishop would visit 9th Ward, most of which had been devastated by flooding. We would worship in the Ernest Morial Convention Center, a 'shelter of last resort' during the hurricane. Thousands had taken refuge there for several days, without power, food, medical supplies or proper sanitation. In the chaotic days that followed, the Diocese of Louisiana would be at the forefront of efforts to bring relief.[57]

In the neighbourhood of the House of Bishops meeting: a mobile clinic in a New Orleans still recovering from Hurricane Katrina

Photo © Anglican Communion Office

The House of Bishops of the Episcopal Church gave careful attention to the primates' request for greater clarity in their response to the Windsor Report. On the question of blessing of same-sex unions, the bishops pledged 'not to authorise for use in our dioceses any public rites of blessing of same-sex unions until a broader consensus emerges in the Communion, or until General Convention takes further action'. While rejecting the pastoral scheme proposed by the primates, they recognised a useful role for 'communion-wide consultation with respect to the pastoral needs of those seeking alternative oversight', encouraging their presiding bishop to explore this further, in ways compatible with the canons and constitution of the Episcopal Church. At the same time, they called for 'an immediate end to diocesan incursions by uninvited bishops', as requested by the Windsor Report.[58] This, they asserted, was consistent with 'statements of past Lambeth Conferences and the Ecumenical Councils of the Church'.

The bishops' discussions over-ran their allotted time, which meant that the members of the Joint Standing Committee (JSC) were not able to meet together to discuss the bishops' final statement.[59] However, the JSC finalised its report a few days later and made it public. Overall it was positive about the increased clarity provided by the Episcopal Church bishops. It was also sympathetic to calls for 'an end to diocesan incursions by uninvited bishops'. It underlined support for this from ecumenical councils, citing the Councils of Nicaea (325), Constantinople (381), Chalcedon (451) and the Western Council of Sardica (343), whose canons stipulated that 'a bishop do not pass from his own province in which there are bishops; unless, perchance, he has been invited by his brethren'. It also spelt out the support from Lambeth Conference Encyclicals and Resolutions in 1878 ('bishops should not cross boundaries'), 1888, 1897 (Resolution 24), 1908 (Resolutions 22 and 23), 1988 (Resolutions 72 and 46) and 1998 (v.13).[60]

But there were dissenting voices, as soon as it was published. The first was that of the Bishop of Egypt, Mouneer Anis, a member of the JSC, who issued a separate statement, dismissing the Episcopal Church's response as 'superficial'. By December, the Archbishop of Canterbury was noting that, among the primates, there was 'no consensus about the New Orleans statement'. [61] In his Advent letter to the primates, he attempted to sum up where things stood: '... it is historically an aspect of the role of the Archbishop of Canterbury', he reminded them, 'to "articulate the mind of the Communion" in moments of tension and controversy, as the Windsor Report puts it.... [A]ll of us will be seriously wounded and diminished if our Communion fractures any further.' In his view, 'most if not all of the bishops present in New Orleans were seeking in all honesty to find a way to meet the requests of the Primates'. Any further elucidation is 'practically impossible to imagine'.

What concerned the Archbishop was that moratoria would be in place 'until General Convention provides otherwise'. For him, this raised 'a major ecclesiological issue.... [T]here seems to be a gap between what some in the Episcopal Church understand about the ministry of bishops and what is held elsewhere in the Communion.' Bishops in the Episcopal Church seem reluctant to take a lead in relation to doctrine and the Church's teaching, in other words.[62] This led him to reflect on expectations for the Lambeth Conference, when Anglican bishops from the around the world would assemble for three weeks in Canterbury.

He tackled head-on the suggestion that the Conference was designed to avoid addressing difficult issues. The Conference should be viewed as 'a meeting of the chief pastors and teachers of the Communion, seeking an authoritative common voice'. Discussions would be aided by the work of the Covenant Design Group and a new group, set up to maintain the momentum of the 'Windsor Process'. However, the Conference should not be viewed as a 'canonical tribunal'.[63] In his letter of invitation, sent out six months earlier, he had reminded the bishops that the Lambeth Conference had never been a formal Synod or Council of Bishops. The Archbishop of Canterbury 'exercises his privilege of calling his colleagues together, not to legislate but to discover and define something more about our common identity through prayer, listening to God's Word and shared reflection'.[64]

In the run-up to the Conference, the Archbishop explained how this shared reflection and discernment would nonetheless break with precedent. 'We have listened carefully to those who expressed their difficulties with Western and parliamentary styles of meeting, and the Design Group has tried to find a new style.... At the heart of this will be the *Indaba* groups. *Indaba* is a Zulu word describing a meeting for purposeful discussion among equals. Its aim is not to negotiate a formula that will keep everyone happy, but go to the heart of an issue.'[65]

Previous Conferences had been characterised by their many resolutions, debated in plenary with an increasingly unwieldy number of bishops. One history of Lambeth Conferences reads as a commentary on how well Archbishops chaired them:

1867:	'not much of a chairman'
1878:	'goodish chairman, but he wanted to press his views more forcibly' than a good chair should
1888:	'bad chairman, but chose an excellent manager' to run the meeting
1897:	'dictator'
1908/1920:	'top-class', 'quiet and wise'
1968:	'went to sleep in the chair', yet still quite good[66]

Some of the resolutions passed were received as an authoritative indicator of the mind of the bishops. Many, however, sank without trace. At the 1998 Lambeth Conference, there were a total of 347 resolutions. Twenty percent of these were beyond the Communion's remit, such as those calling on all governments and people of goodwill to work for peace and reconciliation. Another thirty-seven percent had no specific aim, such as welcoming the peace process in Northern Ireland. As an alternative to passing such resolutions, at the 2008 Lambeth Conference, bishops would discuss topics in smaller Indaba groups. Their views would be fed back to a communications group by rapporteurs, and synthesised into a common report. Issues to do with strengthening Anglican identity would be interspersed with themes relating to mission.

The Indaba principle had been proposed by a member of the Lambeth Conference Design Group, Thabo Makgoba, who was Bishop of Grahamstown in South Africa at the time. The Design Group had members from Africa, the

Pacific, the UK, Hong Kong, Latin America and the USA. We met regularly for four years before the Lambeth Conference. Our meetings were usually held in London, to ensure the Archbishop of Canterbury could offer his perspectives and engage with proposals emerging from the group. For our last full meeting before the Conference, in April 2008, we travelled to a different location: Cape Town. This enabled us to be present for the installation of Thabo Makgoba as Archbishop of Cape Town.

Working together for four years: the Design Group of the 2008 Lambeth Conference

Photo © Anglican Communion Office

Archbishop Thabo's illustrious predecessors included one of the most cele-brated Anglicans of the twentieth century, Desmond Tutu. 'If you are neutral in situations of injustice,' warned Tutu, 'you have chosen the side of the oppressor.'[67] Practising what he preached with disarming ebullience, Tutu had campaigned relentlessly against apartheid and its racial segregation. 'We face a catastrophe in this land and only the action of the international community can save us.... I call upon the international community to apply punitive sanctions against this government to establish a new South Africa—non-racial, democratic, participatory and just.'[68] When Mandela was released after twenty-eight years in custody, he and his wife Winnie spent their first night of freedom at Tutu's residence. The first press conference, for two hundred journalists, was on Bishopscourt lawn the next morning.[69] Mandela would ask Tutu to chair the Truth and Reconciliation Commission, which oversaw public hearings for alleged victims of gross human rights violations.

Respect for the office of Archbishop of Cape Town meant that the instal-lation of Thabo Makgoba in the cathedral was a high profile national event. The service began with a fanfare of kudu antelope horns. The President of South Africa, Thabo Mbeki, contributed later in the service, joking about which Thabo had the tougher job.

The South African setting was a reminder that Anglican concerns extended far beyond disputes about same-sex relations. Human and social justice would be one of the daily themes on the Lambeth Conference programme being finalised by the Design Group in Cape Town. So too would the environment and mission and evangelism. Each of these daily themes would be addressed under the heading of 'equipping bishops for God's mission'. The bishops would be given the opportunity to reaffirm their commitment to an understanding of mission which spanned these daily themes and was reflected in a formula described as a 'benchmark' for Anglicans by an international commission on mission: the 'Five Marks of Mission'.[70] Their predecessors had endorsed them at the 1988 Lambeth Conference.

The Five Marks of Mission had been developed by the Anglican Consultative Council. They provided Anglicans with an understanding of Christian mission which included the call to personal conversion but embraced the whole of life:

The mission of the Church is the mission of Christ:
- to proclaim the good news of the kingdom of God
- to teach, baptise and nurture new believers
- to respond to human need by loving service
- to seek to transform the unjust structures of society
- to strive to safeguard the integrity of creation, and sustain and renew the life of the earth.[71]

At the 2008 Lambeth Conference, the bishops would encounter these 'Five Marks of Mission' in the draft Anglican Covenant they would consider. The Covenant Design Group had judged that this formula was sufficiently widely accepted by Anglicans to serve as a rallying point.[72]

Although the 2008 Lambeth Conference was planned collegially through its Design Group, it was the Archbishop of Canterbury who actually hosted Lambeth Conferences. That meant it was Archbishop Rowan Williams who issued invitations. Almost all the North America bishops would be invited. The exceptions would be Gene Robinson, Bishop of New Hampshire, and bishops consecrated expressly for 'cross-border oversight'. Some of the larger African provinces felt unable to go along with this, especially those who had consecrated bishops for cross-border oversight. Thus the Church of Uganda announced that its bishops would not be attending the Conference. 'This decision has been made to protest the invitations extended by the Archbishop of Canterbury... to TEC bishops whose stand and unrepentant actions created the current crisis of identity and authority in the Anglican Communion.'[73] The Church of Nigeria similarly announced its intention not to attend. Most Kenyan and Rwandan bishops would not attend either. Yet while around 230 bishops declined the invitation, 650 attended, including African bishops from the Provinces of Central Africa, the Sudan, Burundi, West Africa, Congo, the Indian Ocean and Southern Africa.

The absent bishops would instead meet in Jerusalem six weeks before the Lambeth Conference. At the Global Anglican Future Conference (GAFCON) they would be joined by bishops who would also be attending the Lambeth Conference, as well as lay people and clergy. Though not an initiative of the Global South, participants came mainly from churches in the southern hemisphere—Africa, Asia, Australia and South America—with a contingent from the US, Canada and England. Out of the Conference came a statement on 'the Global Anglican Future', and what became known as the Jerusalem Declaration. The statement described GAFCON as a spiritual movement 'to preserve and promote the truth and power of the gospel of salvation in Jesus Christ as we Anglicans have received it'. The GAFCON movement was thereby launched as a fellowship of 'confessing' Anglicans, with the Jerusalem Declaration as a basis of fellowship. 'We cherish our Anglican heritage and the Anglican Communion and have no intention of departing from it.'

The alleged structuring of the Lambeth Conference to avoid hard decisions was given as one of the four justifications for GAFCON. Added to this was 'the acceptance and promotion within certain provinces of a different gospel; the declaration by provincial bodies in the Global South that they are out of communion with bishops and churches promoting this false gospel; and the 'manifest failure' of Communion instruments to exercise discipline in the face of 'overt heterodoxy'.

The Jerusalem Declaration proposed fourteen tenets of orthodoxy. It also addressed the question of territorial jurisdiction. It recognised the desirability of territorial jurisdiction, 'except where churches and leaders are denying the orthodox faith'. Actions of primates and dioceses offering 'orthodox oversight to churches in false leadership' were therefore affirmed and described as 'courageous'. A Primates' Council was proposed to oversee the GAFCON movement and 'authenticate and recognise confessing Anglican jurisdictions'.

The immediate response of the Archbishop of Canterbury was to affirm 'much that is positive and encouraging about the priorities of those who met for prayer and pilgrimage'. He pointed out that the tenets of orthodoxy were shared by the vast majority of Anglicans. At the same time, he observed that a self-selected Primates' Council could not offer legitimacy to Anglican jurisdictions, noting that crossing provincial boundaries was theologically and practically problematic. He urged instead the renewal of existing structures, rather than improvising solutions.[74]

In Canterbury to confer:
650 bishops gather for the
2008 Lambeth Conference

*Photo © Anglican
Communion Office*

In the face of GAFCON's counsel of despair, the Lambeth Conference was to see progress made on the renewal of existing structures and the strengthening of Anglican identity. Six hundred and fifty bishops travelled from all corners of the globe to Canterbury, accompanied by their spouses. Lambeth Palace had long been too small for this once-every-ten-years gathering, so in 2008 they would once again be billeted on the campus of the University of Kent, overlooking the cathedral. After a two-day retreat in the cathedral precincts, the bishops settled into a pattern of examining daily themes. By the end of two weeks, the challenges facing the Anglican Communion had been discussed at length. This included careful consideration of the Anglican Covenant. A second draft had been prepared by the Covenant Design Group, in the light of feedback from the provinces of the Communion. The bishops were now able to provide detailed comments on this latest 'St Andrew's draft'. The main opportunity to do so, however, came near the end of the

Conference. That meant the discussion on the Covenant was preceded by the two-day retreat, followed by ten days of discussion on aspects of Anglican identity and on the bishop's responsibility in mission.

A key resource for discussions about Anglican identity was the document produced by the TEAC working group on the Anglican Way, of which I had been a member for the past four years. Taking a global perspective, it offered four signposts for Anglican identity: formed by Scripture; shaped by worship; ordered for Communion, directed by God's mission. By studying this document together first, bishops were able to discuss their shared Anglican identity without getting caught up prematurely on the small print of the Covenant document. Alongside this, the bishops were able to deepen their understanding of one another's contexts, as they discussed daily themes in their Indaba groups, such as mission and evangelism, the environment and relations with other world religions. In the afternoons, there were 'self-select' sessions, which included hearings on aspects of the Windsor process.[75] At the beginning, middle and end of the conference, the Archbishop sought to capture the essence of the Conference as it unfolded, in presidential addresses.

The outward-looking 'mission' dimension of the Conference was reinforced by the time-honoured 'London day'. As usual, the bishops would have lunch at Lambeth Palace, where the first Lambeth Conferences were held, and finish the day with a garden party hosted by Queen Elizabeth at Buckingham Palace. My job at the garden party was to be a grabber, identifying bishops and spouses to be introduced to the Duke of Edinburgh. Unlike at previous Lambeth Conferences, the day would begin with a walk of witness, with leaders of other faiths. It would signal a shared commitment to the relief of poverty and the Millennium Development Goals. It would conclude at Lambeth Palace with an address by the British Prime Minister, Gordon Brown.

'In the morning, we watched the splendid sight of hundreds of purple-clad bishops on their Walk of Witness march from Westminster to Lambeth Palace', recalled the Prime Minister's wife, Sarah Brown. 'Gordon follows the Archbishop of Canterbury on to an outdoor platform to address an audience of bishops. He speaks at his finest—just a very powerful piece of oratory, with no notes, perhaps not much different from a minister's style, giving a call for all faiths to continue the work to reduce poverty. ... He cites the vision of Isaiah in the Bible—"to undo the burden of debt and let the oppressed go free"—and the words of Amos, that "justice will flow like water and righteousness like a mighty stream" to declare there is nothing we cannot do for justice if we do it together.'[76] It was Helen Wangusa, the Ugandan who had been licensed in Zanzibar as Anglican Observer at the UN, who thanked the Prime Minister, suggesting he might have a future vocation as a preacher. It was filmed live on BBC NEWS 24.

Campaigning to reduce poverty: the British Prime Minister joins the Lambeth Conference London Day

Photos © Anglican Communion Office

Had the wives of nineteenth-century Prime Ministers Benjamin Disraeli or William Gladstone attended the first Lambeth Conferences, they would not have been impressed by purple-clad bishops. In 1867 and 1878, Anglican bishops largely wore black cassocks. Few had pastoral staffs.[77] None wore mitres or pectoral crosses. These outward symbols of the bishop's authority would only become commonplace at the end of the nineteenth century. It was only in 1888 that Bishop Edward King of Lincoln paved the way for bishops wearing mitres, when objectors from the evangelical Church Association were defeated in court.[78]

With experiences such as the London day contributing to a renewed sense of shared vocation, the now purple-clad bishops made genuine progress in their discussion of the more controversial matters. Sixty representatives of other churches and faiths contributed their own insights to the full range of topics. Plenary addresses were given by Cardinal Diaz, from the Vatican's Congregation for the Evangelization of Peoples, Brian McLaren, a leading figure from 'emerging church' in the USA and Rabbi Jonathan Sacks, offering Jewish perspectives on Covenant.

The Conference ended with a service in Canterbury Cathedral. The service was not triumphalistic. Nonetheless, accompanied by music from the Melanesian brothers, it was deeply moving. 'At the end of our time together,' reflected the Archbishop of Canterbury shortly afterwards, 'many people, especially some of the newer bishops, said they had been surprised by the amount of convergence they had seen'.

On the questions posed by the Windsor Report, which GAFCON expected the Lambeth Conference to duck, there was a discernible outcome. 'A strong majority of bishops present agreed that moratoria on same-sex blessings and on cross-provincial interventions were necessary.' More generally on human sexuality, 'there was a very widely held conviction that premature or unilateral local change was risky and divisive, in spite of diversity of opinion expressed on specific questions. . . . There was no appetite for revising Resolution 1:10 of Lambeth 1998, though there was also a clear commitment to continue theological and pastoral discussion of the questions involved.' Inspired by the experimental format of the Lambeth Conference, 'there was a general desire to find better ways of managing our business as a Communion'.[79]

✠

The 2008 Lambeth Conference would signal the end of my work assisting the Archbishop in 'managing the business of the Communion'. I would be moving on from Lambeth Palace at the end of the year. During six and a half years of Anglican Communion and ecumenical work, my understanding of Anglican identity had been enlarged by perspectives from all over the world. I would now be refocusing on the life of the Church of England. I had been appointed Principal of one of its theological colleges. I would return to Cambridge, to Ridley Hall, where I had begun my own ordination training sixteen years earlier.

Bishops' spouses at the 2008 Lambeth Conference, with Canterbury Cathedral in the background   *Photo © Anglican Communion Office*

12

Today's Church, Tomorrow's Ministers

'RIDLEY HALL is in very good heart, you know', I was repeatedly told once my appointment as Principal was made public, especially by bishops sidling up to me at the Lambeth Conference. As I took up the reins, part-way through an academic year, I could see for myself that they were right. The only way is down, I found myself imagining. Fortunately, three years later, the formal inspection of Ridley Hall would prove that wrong. Ridley is 'in very good heart and a vibrant learning, worshipping and praying community', the inspectors concluded in 2011. Benefitting from Cambridge's rich academic and ecumenical environment, they observed, it provides 'exciting opportunities' for contributing to the mission of the wider church.[1]

Ridley Hall's ecumenical environment had diversified since my time as an ordinand. The Cambridge Theological Federation now included a Roman Catholic women's college, an Orthodox institute and a centre for relations between Christians, Jews and Muslims, in addition to its Methodist and Anglican founder-members and its earliest recruit from the United Reformed Church. Ridley Hall's ethos suited this ecumenical setting, echoing the strapline my former Principal, Graham Cray, had come up with. 'Roots down, walls down' signalled Ridley's desire to help its students become rooted in evangelical Anglicanism, while engaging directly and openly with other traditions. To this couplet Graham Cray's successor, who went on to become Bishop of Coventry, had added 'bridges out'.[2] Ordinands were not being trained to be functionaries in an ecclesiastical twilight zone, remote from contemporary society. The emphasis was outward-looking, recognising that the Church of England needed to forge new links with local communities and wider society.

Graham Cray, having been appointed Bishop of Maidstone by Archbishop George Carey, had emerged as a leading proponent of 'fresh expressions of church'. From 2002 to 2004, he had chaired the working group that produced the influential report *Mission-Shaped Church*. This report called for a fundamental change of mindset. 'The Church of England bases a significant part of its identity on its physical presence in every community, and on a "come to us" strategy', it observed. Changing times, it argued, call for a 'go to them' approach.[3] 'What is taking place is not merely the continued decline of organised Christianity, but the death of the culture that formerly conferred Christian identity upon the British people as a whole', it pointed out, quoting the social historian Callum Brown.[4] 'We believe the Church of England is facing a great moment of missionary opportunity', wrote Graham Cray in the introduction. 'The report is subtitled "church planting and fresh expressions of church in a changing context", reflecting our ongoing and shared calling to embody and inculcate the gospel in the evolving contexts and cultures of our society', he explained. 'Church has to be planted, not cloned' in a 'mixed economy' of church life which still includes traditional parish churches.[5]

The publication of *Mission-Shaped Church* coincided with the commitment of Archbishop Rowan Williams to fresh expressions of church. 'I think if there is one thing I'd like to be remembered for in the Church of England', he said near the end of his time as Archbishop of Canterbury, 'it's putting my shoulder behind fresh expressions.'[6] While Archbishop of Wales, Rowan Williams had supported innovative forms of church life and commended them at the Primates' Meeting I attended in Canterbury in 2002. 'In order that we might participate effectively in God's mission,' he had written in the foreword to the Church in Wales report, *Good News in Wales* (1999), 'we need to consider seriously the possibilities that there are ways of being church alongside the inherited parochial pattern.'[7] Writing the foreword to *Mission-Shaped Church* five years later, he applied this to England too. Alongside inherited patterns of ministry, 'there are many ways in which the reality of "church" can exist.... [W]e are going to have to live with variety...so that everyone grows together in faith and in eagerness to learn about and spread the good news.'[8]

With funding from the Lambeth Partners, benefactors for the Archbishop's projects, Rowan Williams gave an archiepiscopal shove to the agenda of

Mission-Shaped Church. In partnership with the Archbishop of York, he set up the Archbishops' Fresh Expressions initiative, as a joint venture with the Methodist Church. Its aim was 'to help Christians of any denomination think about ways of starting and growing fresh expressions of church in their area', where a fresh expression is defined as 'a form of church for our changing culture, established primarily for the benefit of people who are not yet members of any church'.[9] I attended the commissioning of the first Team Leader of Fresh Expressions, Steven Croft, formerly Warden of Cranmer Hall theological college in Durham. When he became Bishop of Sheffield in 2009, Graham Cray would be appointed to succeed him. It is probably no accident they were both former theological college principals. Being principal of a theological college, as I would discover, forces you to look ahead and imagine the kind of church your students will serve in as their ministry progresses.

By the time of my appointment to Ridley Hall, fresh expressions had already become 'part of the bloodstream of the traditional, mainstream Church's life [in England]', according to Archbishop Rowan. Addressing General Synod in 2007, he explained that 'the Fresh Expressions programme is not simply about a kind of scattered set of experiments; it's about that gradual, but I think inexorable shift, in the whole culture of our Church that has been going on in the last few years and which will undoubtedly continue to grow and develop'.[10] Giving institutional support to fresh expressions, General Synod duly passed the legislation for Bishops' Mission Orders, enabling bishops to support the development of new Christian communities cutting across parish boundaries.[11]

This did not mean that inherited patterns of church life were now obsolete. The phrase 'mixed economy church' had been coined by Rowan Williams when he was Archbishop of Wales. It was increasingly being used as shorthand in the Church of England to describe the blend of inherited patterns of parish life and fresh expressions.[12] Ridley Hall and its sister college in Cambridge, Westcott House, were committed to preparing future clergy for this mixed economy. A practical outworking of this was a joint staff appointment to resource the training of pioneer ministers. Recognising that developing fresh expressions required entrepreneurial gifts, the Church of England had come up with a new category of priest in 2005: the Ordained Pioneer Minister (OPM). Of the seventy students training for ordained ministry at Ridley Hall each year, the number of OPMs would rise to ten over the next five years. The rest were being prepared for a Church of England where a pioneering mentality would increasingly be required.

Even with the 'both–and' approach of the mixed economy, not everyone was convinced that fresh expressions would be beneficial for the Church of England. A colleague at Westcott House, Andrew Davison, co-authored a book which sounded alarm bells. *For the Parish* was wary of developing communities for the like-minded. Fresh expressions could turn out to be a recipe for segregation, it warned. 'Throughout Christian history', the authors argued 'the Church has struck a balance between being enculturated and being mixed.... If taken too far, the Church will fragment and segregate on the basis of micro-cultures: skateboarders, affluent young accountants, Goths of a particular variety in their twenties, the long-term unemployed and so on.'[13] Fresh expressions cannot simply be a pragmatic response to empty churches, in other words. When the book was first published, it prompted lively discussions between Andrew Davison and the OPM students in the Cambridge Theological Federation, in the classroom and in the pub.

Whatever the risks involved in fresh expressions, the Church of England was increasingly coming to terms with the fact that 'business as usual' was no longer viable. Not long after I started, theological college principals received a paper prepared by the Ministry Division of the Church of England. A chronic shortage of ministers was calmly forecasted. Forty percent of paid ('stipendiary') clergy were due to retire over the next ten years. At the current rate of ordination of new clergy, within twenty years there would be twenty-five percent fewer stipendiary clergy. Yet the problem was not simply one of vocations. Shortage of funds could well place a glass ceiling on the number of clergy. Dioceses were already struggling to fund enough curacies to offer posts to all those being trained. In 2009, five ordinands had remained unplaced. The number of those training for ministry would therefore need to be capped, the paper argued.[14] Two years later, General Synod voted to cap the training budget and this was translated into a cap on the numbers in training.

The Church of England was therefore coming to terms with three related pressures: the need to engage effectively with those unconnected with church life, declining numbers of paid clergy, and limited finances. At the opening of General Synod in November 2010, Archbishop Rowan set out three priorities for the next five years:

Three main themes have emerged with absolute clarity. We are called—

(i) To take forward the spiritual and numerical growth of the Church of England—including the growth of its capacity to serve the whole community of this country;

(ii) To re-shape or re-imagine the Church's ministry for the century coming, so as to make sure that there is a growing and sustainable Christian witness in every local community; and

(iii) To focus our resources where there is both greatest need and greatest opportunity.

With this challenge laid out to the Church nationally, we decided that Ridley Hall and Westcott House should host a roundtable for bishops on 'What kind of clergy do we need?' By facilitating discussion, we would be able to listen in to perspectives from the dioceses and map the kind of patterns that were emerging. By hosting the twenty-four hour event as a joint initiative between two colleges of different traditions, it would clearly be a non-partisan event. All bishops were invited. Twenty-three took part, from dioceses all over the country.

The bishops were agreed that 'the core shift in our society is that the Christian story is no longer widely told or understood'. Yet there was also 'a residual—and indeed burgeoning—"post-secular" interest in religion and spirituality'. According to the roundtable report, 'a confident and coherent vision of "the clergy we need"' did indeed emerge. 'Adaptability and willingness to experiment' was a clear strand within that vision. The church must continue to train its clergy to act as priests, yet it needs to move away from a 'one-size-fits-all' approach to ministry. 'The mixed economy of the church requires that we train those at all points on the inherited/new spectrum to work together, while being able to pursue ministries to which they are best suited.' Clergy will increasingly be required to exercise collaboration, enablement and the gifts of oversight. They must be visionaries, forming whole Christian communities in the work of ministry, enabling them to function as schools of discipleship. 'The clergy must prioritise a mission focus, understood in the widest sense, so as to include social transformation.' They must also be ecumenically rooted. Undergirding all this is the pre-requisite of deep spirituality and discipleship. 'Before people can be engaged in the work of the Kingdom, they need to be fired up about God. . . . In order to equip others to be heralds of the Gospel, clergy must first have been gripped and formed themselves by the good news.' To inhabit this vision, clergy will need 'a spirit of adventure, a stability of character and a delight in relating to others'.[15]

To observe how this vision related to grassroots experience in England, I decided to revisit some of the locations that have featured earlier in this narrative. With times changing, how did 'being Anglican' now look in parishes in County Durham, the Lake District, Essex, Cambridgeshire, Sussex, Hampshire, Bristol, Liverpool and Newcastle-upon-Tyne?

I visited Binchester, south of Durham, on the day of Margaret Thatcher's funeral at St Paul's Cathedral. In his funeral sermon, the Bishop of London recalled 'the storm of a life lived in the heat of political controversy'. As the nation recalled strong emotions about confrontation with coal miners and the closure of uneconomic pits, I walked round a former mining village whose mines had long ceased to function. The tin church, beside which my grandfather had collapsed of nervous exhaustion at the outbreak of World War Two, had been demolished. Only the churchyard remained. The other mission church, in Newfield, had also been knocked down.

Byers Green, in whose parish both mission churches had been located, had recently welcomed a new vicar. She had been inducted by a newly appointed Bishop of Durham, Justin Welby. Her predecessor in the 1940s had pleaded with the diocese for a curate or Church Army worker to replace my grandfather, finally resulting in the appointment of Sister Ridden, who had lived in her caravan in the churchyard. Mining might have ceased in the parish since then, but new housing estates had been built, for commuters to Durham and surrounding towns. Yet the new priest-in-charge would have no curate or Church Army worker. In fact, she was not even paid herself. The arrangement was 'house for duty'. Down the road, Binchester Roman fort, owned by the Church of England, had been opened as a tourist attraction. In 2007 the Church Commissioners had purchased Binchester Hall, to be used as a visitor centre for the fort.[16] But the Diocese of Durham could not appeal to the historic assets of the Church to fund its routine ministry. It was facing major financial challenges. Its new bishop, before becoming Archbishop of Canterbury, had boldly told parishes to pay what they could, rather than fall into arrears. Byers Green had dropped its parish contribution from £10,700 to £6,000.[17] Few of the congregation were wage earners. With one exception, the weekly congregation of twenty-two at Byers Green was over 55. The organist had just retired, aged 87, replaced by the one member of the congregation under 55 and an iPod. The choir had disbanded in the 1970s.

After Binchester's tin church was demolished, worshippers used to travel to Byers Green for Sunday services. Now no-one came from Binchester. There was still some residual support for the church though. The Free Will offering, given a boost in my grandfather's time, still had nine faithful contributors from Binchester. It was early days for the new incumbent, but there was no doubt that she would need to find new ways of connecting with the local community and to do so while holding down paid employment elsewhere.

Across the Pennine mountains in the Lake District, the parish of Bassen-thwaite had been joined with eight other parishes. The Team Rector, Tricia Rogers, oversaw worship in ten churches, including the three located in Bassenthwaite. Over the past ten years, the Diocese of Carlisle had seen a twenty percent reduction in clergy and was expecting a further twenty percent reduction by 2020. A radical overhaul of diocesan life was underway. As the twenty-first century began, 'the whole idea of mission was not on the radar of the diocese', its bishop, James Newcome, had explained to me.[18] But things were starting to change, after widespread consultation and presentations to 1,600 people around the diocese. The vision for the future was ecumenical. Anglicans would join forces with Methodist and United Reformed churches, 'three churches journeying as one', to develop congregations grouped together in forty ecumenical mission clusters. Each congregation would have a recognised leader, lay or ordained. Each cluster would usually have an ordained, stipendiary 'leader in mission'. Currently there were 145 stipendiary ministers across the three denominations, with five in pioneering work. The plan was to reduce the total number of stipendiary ministers to 110, but increase the number in pioneering ministry to up to 40. The number of self-supporting ministers would be increased from 50 to 150. The number of lay ministers would increase from 350 to 500.[19]

There would be a much stronger emphasis on both mission and disciple-ship: 'God is for all, Church is by all' summed up the strategy for ministry. The Diocese of Carlisle would be emphasising five marks of discipleship: maturity in faith; prayer and worship that is expectant and lively; community engagement; evangelism and quality of relationships. It suggested what might constitute signs of progress in each mission cluster, such as an adult Christian basics course; a variety of styles of worship; at least one fresh expression; a strategy for making the most of special occasions; improved use of church buildings in the local community; all church members equipped to tell others about their life as a disciple of Jesus; trained welcomers in each church.[20] For finance, the approach was similar to Durham Diocese: 'parish share' had been replaced by 'parish offer'—pay what you can.

Tricia Rogers had only been in post in Bassenthwaite for two years, but she was fully behind the diocesan strategy. Her cluster included one Methodist church along with the ten Anglican churches. In Bassenthwaite itself, Sunday worship alternated between an Anglican venue and the Methodist church. St Bega's, by the lake, was used for special occasions. The rector's team included a team vicar, a curate, one self-supporting minister and three readers. She was clear that new ways of relating to the local community were needed. There

were no Sunday schools in any of the ten churches. In her view, Sunday mornings were no longer the optimum time for children's groups. Instead, with
six church schools in her patch, the plan was to start up after-school clubs.
Meanwhile she had launched a group for mothers which met in the village
hall, attracting thirty to forty mothers. With the encouragement of the bishop,
she was also exploring ways of engaging with the seasonal influx of tourists.
She was making contact with campsites, guesthouses and hotels, with plans
for hosting 'Songs of Praise' services on the larger campsites.

Moving South to Essex, as my grandparents had done, I met with David
Newman, the priest responsible for St Andrew's Weeley. His home was not
the purpose-built rectory into which my grandparents had downsized. That
had been sold thirty-four years ago. He was now living in Little Clacton and
was responsible for the church there as well as St Andrew's, Weeley. When
I visited St Andrew's, still surrounded by fields, I was accompanied by one of
the churchwardens, Pearl Byfield. It was she who had been given a doughnut
on the bus by my grandfather when he first arrived in 1948. She showed
me a tapestry in the side chapel, which my grandmother had designed and
sewed 'in her spare time', according to the caption. It had taken her five
years. Since then, the population of the village had quadrupled to 4,300. As
in my grandfather's time, the church benefitted from what he had called 'a
nucleus of faithful people'.[21] Yet it was encouraging to hear that there was
a viable Sunday school. There was also a well-attended family service held
once a month. There were fifty-two on the electoral roll.

One of the 'faithful people' at St Andrew's
Weeley: the churchwarden, Pearl Byfield,
who started worshipping there
when my grandfather was Rector

Photo © Andrew Norman

The Bishop of Chelmsford, however, was clear there was no room for complacency in the diocese in which Weeley was situated. His diocese comprised
500 parishes, 500 clergy and 50,000 adult church members. 'We know we
need to change', he stressed. '47% of our stipendiary clergy will have retired in

ten years' time. This alone should concentrate our thinking. Change is going to come whether we like it or not.'[22] A key priority should be to 'reimagine the way we minister so that...each individual Christian discovers their part in God's ministry'.[23] Alongside this should be efforts to encourage 'a much greater biblical and theological literacy'. There should also be a much stronger emphasis on evangelism. 'For too long the Church of England has either considered evangelism something other churches do...or simply waited till people come through the door.'[24]

In the neighbouring Diocese of Ely, it was interesting to see how the ministry of Histon parish church had developed since the early 1990s, when I had spent three years attached to the church while training at Ridley Hall. As a church rooted in a large village on the outskirts of Cambridge, St Andrew's remained well-integrated in community life, with a flourishing congregation of all ages. Though the vicar from the 1990s had been appointed Archdeacon in the diocese, there were still plenty of familiar faces. Yet the church had been breaking new ground. 'Essence' had been set up as a fresh expression for young mums. 'Soccer Sunday' had been introduced by a youth worker who was now training for ordination at Ridley Hall. This was an attempt to engage with teenage boys hanging around Tesco's. The format was Sunday soccer matches, with a Christian talk at half-time, together with involvement in community projects. 'Third Space' was run in the local pub, with an emphasis on faith stories. In the 1990s, the Parish Rooms on the High Street had been inhospitable and under-used. Now, twenty years later, the congregation of St Andrew's had finally raised £1 million to refurbish the halls and turn them into a church-resourced centre for the community, providing a much-needed coffee-shop for a village lacking Starbucks or Costa Coffee.[25]

Moving further south to Sussex, Ardingly parish church still had a thriving congregation. However, the pattern of worship had changed. The weekly evening service, so convenient for my father after milking the cows, had been discontinued. On Sundays, there were just two morning services in the church: a 1662 communion at 8am, using the prayer books donated in memory of my grandparents; and a 10.15am Holy Communion, using *Common Worship,* on all but the first Sunday. There was still a robed choir, but it had finally fallen into line, exchanging the illicit red robes for blue ones. There were still bell-ringers and brass-rubbers. But on one Sunday a month there was worship of a different sort, Sunday@thecentre. The primary school I had attended had moved to new premises in 1987. The congregation of St Peter's Church had bought the old buildings and were using them for fresh expressions of church. On the first Sunday of the month, the main morning service was now 'café church'. Worshippers sat round tables, rather than in rows. Coffee was served from 10am, with worship beginning at 10.15am. Issues of faith were discussed around tables in the hall where I had endured school dinners. Children's activities were run in the classrooms where I had learned to read and write. Another kind of fresh expression had just been trialled on weekdays in the same venue. 'Messy Church' had become popular nationwide as a form of worship for all ages, with 'hands-on' activities such as baking, painting and craft work. What St Peter's was trying out began as an experiment in an Anglican Parish in Portsmouth in 2004. A Messy Church website was now providing details of over 2,300 locations for Messy Church.[26]

Moving west to Basingstoke, in Hampshire, St Mary's Eastrop still had the same vicar, Clive Hawkins, who had introduced me to my future wife and paired us up to run a teenage confirmation class. The staff team had expanded from rector, curate and part-time administrator to six staff engaged in teaching, pastoral work and evangelism, plus two administrators. Community engagement now included links with the local mosque. Evangelistic activity focussed more on constant small-scale courses than on infrequent large events of the kind Amanda and I had helped to organise. The organ, which no-one could play, had been sold to a Welsh church. Music was now provided by a band. It advertised itself as a seven-days-a-week church for all ages. On its website, it said:

> Come as you are. We don't have a dress code. Please feel free to wear whatever you feel most comfortable in. Jeans or suits—it's up to you. Most dress casually. NO COLLECTION IS TAKEN AT ANY SERVICES. Our regulars contribute to the running of the church so our guests don't have to.[27]

On most Sundays, there were four services. Once a month, like St Peter's, Ardingly, it was running café church.

Continuing westwards to Bristol, Christ Church Clifton had witnessed some changes. Since I left in 2002, the Diocese of Bristol had harnessed the church's potential in new ways. In Easter 2007, forty members of Christ Church left with my successor as associate vicar to start a church plant, making use of the new Bishops' Mission Orders. Emmanuel Bristol church plant was now meeting weekly at Red Maid's School (Sunday mornings) and Bristol City College (Sunday afternoons), with combined services for Holy Communion once a month. For Sunday afternoon services, a meal was provided afterwards for children, so that parents could stay behind too. A second church plant had been started five years later, again led by one of the clergy from Christ Church. This time forty members of Christ Church were grafted onto a church in the neighbouring parish of Bishopston that risked closure, following a similar pattern to church plants in London initiated by Holy Trinity Brompton. Sunday morning activities included a communion service, an all-age service and children's groups. Once a month there was an evening service, using Taizé-style worship.

I travelled by train to the city that had once upstaged Bristol as England's second port. Arriving at Liverpool Lime Street Station, I walked up the hill to the parish of St Luke in the City, where I had served as lay assistant in 1986. I called in to the bombed-out church of St Luke's, still set aside as a place of rest and tranquillity by the City Council. Inside the ruined church, an Anglican priest was leading two people in what I later learned were Qigong exercises. A notice advertised a service of commemoration in the afternoon for those who had died as a result of substance abuse. In this public place, the church was clearly trying to find creative ways of engaging with the local community.

'Creativity' was one of the hallmarks of the rebranded St Bride's Church, my next destination. I carried on up the hill, noting there were more coffee shops than there used to be amidst the faded glory of this city-centre residential location. At St Bride's, the church that looked more like a Greek temple, I was welcomed by Guy Elsmore, the Rector of St Luke's Parish. We had overlapped at Ridley Hall as ordinands, but this was the first time I had seen him since then. It was food bank day, and church members were serving lunch in St Bride's to the beneficiaries of food parcels, who included refugees from Syria, Iran, Eritrea and Afghanistan.

Guy recounted how St Bride's had fared since my sojourn. Things had not gone well for much of the intervening time. By 2005, the Sunday congregation had declined to six. The children's group I had helped with and taken on outings had been discontinued several years before. It was 'do or die' and the bishop was open to more experimental use of St Bride's. As a result, it was relaunched in 2007 as 'St Bride's, Liverpool's creative, progressive, inclusive church'. Now it had a committed core of members and ran a range of activities on Sunday and during the week. 'City centre churches need a strong sense of identity', explained the rector. In St Bride's case, its own identity made sense because the parish included a burgeoning creative arts area in former dockland warehouses. One of the rector's colleagues, Ruth Stock, was designated Minister for Mission Development. Her role included reaching out to those from New Age backgrounds, hence the Qigong meditation she was leading at St Luke's. The following month, she would lead an evening service at St Bride's advertised as 'Ruach' sacred movement drawing together Qigong and Christian mysticism. Even the children's work was labelled 'progressive'. Part of the church building was set aside for 'Godly play', an approach to children's work becoming increasingly popular in Anglican parishes. 'Our children's space "The Greenhouse" is a place which values children's spirituality, creativity and questions.'[28]

Sunday evenings at St Bride's saw a rotation of monthly services for different congregations. These included the 'Sacred Silence' Christian meditation group and 'The Well' Celtic worship group. It also included the 'Open Table' lesbian, gay, bisexual and transgendered (LGBT) worship community. 'We're offering something radically different from most mainstream churches', St Bride's explained on its website. 'If a community whose life is centred around LGBT, multifaith, meditation, music, arts, peace work & ecology sounds like fun then come along.'[29] Yet despite its 'radically different' character, the rector was insistent that they must work within the official parameters of the Church of England.

This approach was nonetheless a far cry from the recommendations of the 1985 *Faith in the City* report.[30] Since my time in St Luke's parish, Liverpool had seen much urban regeneration. The docklands area had been transformed. The high rise blocks in the parish had been demolished. Yet parts of the parish remained unmistakably Urban Priority Areas. This was true where St Michael's was situated, near the China Town area. The independent Chinese fellowship there attracted 350 worshippers each Sunday and had strong links with the parish. St Michael's itself typically had no more than thirty people at its main service, many of whom had moved away from the area but retained their church links. Rather than change the form of worship that existing worshippers were used to, the Minister for Mission Development had started a fresh expression aimed at young families in the area. While the longstanding members worshipped in familiar ways, families met in the church centre for a cross between Messy Church and café church. This drew up to twenty-four children each Sunday. At the other end of the parish, there were plans for an Anglo-Catholic fresh expression. Dry rot had finally got the upper hand at St Stephen's Church, which had shared its patch of land with The Oxford pub. The building had been demolished, but a new building had been constructed on another site.

A few minutes' walk from St Bride's, at the cathedral, I met up with the curate, Tim Watson. His appointment represented a new twist to the ecumenical approach pioneered by the former bishop of Liverpool, David Sheppard, with his Catholic counterpart, Archbishop Derek Worlock. Tim Watson was an Anglican member of Chemin Neuf, one of the Catholic charismatic communities I had encountered when at St Michael's Paris. He had been appointed by the former Dean of Liverpool Cathedral, Justin Welby. Shortly afterwards, Justin Welby had been appointed Bishop of Durham. Tim Watson's appointment was symptomatic of Justin Welby's determination to bring a creative approach to the life of the cathedral. *Mission-Shaped Church* had identified the importance of cathedrals in complementing the work of parish churches.[31] Justin Welby argued that the cathedral should be for the whole diocese, not just those who enjoyed a particular liturgical and musical tradition. He therefore established a fresh-expression, Zone 2, meeting at the same time as the main service in the cathedral. The cathedral would model the 'mixed economy church'.

By the time of my visit, Zone 2 had become established as a regular weekly event, under Justin Welby's successor. Its format was 'café church', using *Common Worship's* Service of the Word. Resources prepared week by week were made available on the website for use around the diocese.

What the parish of St Luke in the City and the Anglican cathedral illustrated was that the Diocese of Liverpool was steadily moving towards being a 'mixed economy' diocese. The following day, I met with the Diocesan Secretary, Mike Eastwood, whose offices were in the cathedral precincts. He explained to me how fresh expressions were an important strand in the bishop's 'growth agenda'. Bishop James Jones, whose farewell service had taken place earlier that week, had posed three questions at his diocesan synod in 2009. How can we grow numerically? How can we kindle our love for God and neighbour? How are we serving our local community? Out of this had come a plan for responding to thirty years of decline in church attendance in the diocese. The average age of church members in the diocese was 61. Clergy numbers were declining and it would no longer be possible to have one stipendiary priest per parish. 'How do you create an appropriate sense of urgency?' was one of the key questions. One response was to classify parishes according to their vibrancy and viability, as follows:

1. What next
2. Emerging signs
3. Treading water
4. Cause for concern
5. Category 5.

There were now emerging signs throughout the diocese, notably in the area of fresh expressions. A survey had been carried out the previous year. It revealed there were seventy-eight fresh expressions in the diocese, representing thirty-eight percent of ecclesial communities. A quarter were in Urban Priority Areas. Twenty-one percent of the total were just for adults. The rest were all-age or strongly geared towards children. Of the 2,900 involved in fresh expressions each week, 1,700 were adults and 1,200 children. Eighty-eight percent of these had not been churchgoers prior to their involvement. Before catching the train home, I met with the former rector of St Luke's, Neville Black, who had recruited me as lay assistant. Now retired, he was still active in the life the diocese. He confessed to being wary of too much emphasis on attendance at acts of worship as an indicator of the health of the diocese. Yet the fact remained: without worshipping communities, there would be no Christian presence in deprived areas.

In Liverpool, there were no large and established city centre congregations like Christ Church Clifton. The same could not be said of Newcastle-upon-Tyne, which I also revisited. I had worshipped at Jesmond Parish Church (JPC) when working in Gateshead in the 1980s at the banknote printing factory. It was one of the clergy at JPC who had convinced me it was time to offer myself as a candidate for ordination. Sunday church attendance had been around five hundred in those days. Now it was over a thousand. The evening service at JPC was broadcast on the church's own 24-hour internet TV channel. At Christmas time, 5,000 people attended its carol services. It was not unusual for six hundred people to sign up for Christianity Explored courses.[32] JPC employed thirty-eight staff. Its rector, David Holloway, had now been in post for forty years.

However, despite the scale of its activities, JPC could not really be regarded as the jewel in the Diocese of Newcastle's crown. JPC had declared itself in a state of impaired communion with its diocesan bishop, as a result of his views on sexual ethics.[33] It also had an uneasy relationship with Durham Diocese, following its planting of two congregations south of the River Tyne. David Holloway, who had served for fifteen years on General Synod, had come to the conclusion that conflict was inevitable if 'slow death' was to be avoided in the Church of England. In his view, there were three strategies for confronting slow death. 'Don't rock the boat', 'active exit' or 'deep change'. The first two made no impact. The third, 'deep change' was likely to mean breaking ranks, sooner or later. To do so need not mean being un-Anglican. For him, as for the body he helped to found, Reform, the essence of being Anglican is located in one of the Church of England's canons. 'The *Church of England (Worship and Doctrine) Measure 1974* underlines as the "canon of canons", Canon A5', he argues. 'The doctrine of the Church of England is grounded in the Holy Scriptures,' Canon A5 asserts, 'and in such teachings of the ancient Fathers and Councils of the Church as are agreeable to the said Scriptures. In particular such doctrine is to be found in the Thirty-nine Articles of Religion, the Book of Common Prayer, and the Ordinal.'[34] The Thirty-Nine Articles, according to David Holloway, do not insist that the diocese is paramount. Rather, they define the visible Church of Christ as 'a congregation of faithful men, in which the pure word of God is preached, and the Sacraments be duly ministered'.[35]

This circuit of England, ending back in the North-East, reinforced the picture that had emerged from the roundtable for bishops on 'What kind of clergy do we need?' Throughout England, clergy were playing their part in developing a mixed economy church of inherited modes of ministry and fresh expressions of church life. In rural and urban settings, in north and south, clergy were generally exhibiting the kind of adaptability and willingness to experiment the bishops were calling for. Some were more ecumenically rooted than others, with Carlisle Diocese being a striking example with its 'three churches journeying together as one'.

The circuit encompassed a range of settings and geographical locations. But one context not represented was parishes with many adherents of non-Christian faiths. That's not to say that non-Christian faiths had no impact on these parishes. Two years after my visit to Weeley, St Andrew's hosted a funeral service for one of the 130 victims of the Paris terrorist attacks by Muslim extremists. Nick Alexander, killed at the Bataclan concert hall where he was selling merchandise, had worshipped at St Andrew's regularly since childhood and last attended the month before his death.[36] Yet such tragic pastoral circumstances were not the kind of challenge facing the increasing number of clergy whose parishes were populated by adherents of non-Christian faiths.

Back in 2005, I had been joined at Lambeth Palace by a new interfaith adviser, Guy Wilkinson. Formerly Archdeacon of Bradford, he had just spearheaded a national assessment of the Church of England's engagement in multifaith settings. In 2006, his report, *Presence and Engagement,* was considered by General Synod and set the tone for the years that followed.[37] It pointed out that sixty-two parishes had more than fifty percent of their population as people of faiths other than Christianity (¶70) and nine hundred parishes had more than ten percent (¶67). 'What did it mean for the parish church to be "there" for all the people, when in some parishes more than 50% of the people belonged to communities of faith other than Christian?', it asked.[38] Clergy serving in multifaith parishes were asked to rank four possible priorities in multifaith parishes. The report noted: '"Maintaining a worshipping Christian presence" and "Learning and building mutual trust" were generally in either first or second place. "Sharing in promoting the common good" was largely a third priority' (¶160).

It was noteworthy that 'across all dioceses and churchmanships, these churches virtually without exception placed "Mission" in fourth place' (¶160). In part, these priorities reflected a sense of being ill-prepared for such settings. 'To a certain extent clergy and lay leadership have made bricks without straw in their responses to contexts which have mainly happened around them. Most clergy were not called to ministry amongst people of other Faiths; most had not had previous experience of such ministry; most lay people have not received appropriate training' (¶193). The report called for long-term strategies to support 'presence and engagement' in multifaith areas. 'We are clear that there is much to be done to facilitate local churches to explore and share their experiences in multi Faith neighbourhoods in relation to Christian scripture and theology' (¶192).

Each year, ordinands at Ridley Hall were coming from parishes with multifaith neighbourhoods. I decided to visit one of these parishes, in the Diocese of Birmingham. St Christopher's Springfield is located in the south-east of Birmingham, next to a mosque attracting hundreds of worshippers, many with strong family links to Kashmir. The church centre hosted the Springfield Project, a community project started in 1999. Its primary purpose was to provide support and activities for the community, encouraging access by all members and age groups. It set out to form bridges between the various social and cultural groups within the Springfield area. Its means of doing so included a nursery, a play-and-stay group, out-of-school clubs and a family support team, with a major focus on children under five and their families.

I learned that St Christopher's is linked with a neighbouring parish, Christ Church Sparkbrook, whose population is ninety-eight percent Muslim. To add to the challenges, a freak tornado rendered Sparkbrook's Victorian church unsafe in 2005. Now there were no Sunday services in Sparkbrook parish. Instead, a 'missional community' gathered midweek. Between Springfield and Sparkbrook is Sparkhill. The Faithful Neighbourhoods Centre was opened in Sparkhill in 2011. It is part of the Near Neighbours programme, which was awarded £5 million from the British government. The programme was designed to bring together people who were near neighbours in religiously and ethnically diverse communities. The idea was for them to get to know each other better, build relationships of trust and collaborate together on initiatives that improved their local community. The national initiative was overseen by the Church Urban Fund, which was set up following the *Faith in the City* report in the 1980s. In Sparkhill, the Faithful Neighbourhoods

Centre was not simply an Anglican initiative. It was established in partnership with Birmingham Churches Together.

The Diocese of Birmingham Director of Interfaith Relations, Dr Andrew Smith, was nonetheless based in the Faithful Neighbourhoods Centre. So too was The Feast, an initiative he had set up in association with Scripture Union. In his current role he continued as chair of trustees. The Feast described itself as a Christian charity which promotes community cohesion between Christian and Muslim young people. When it began in 2008, it was supported by the Springfield Project at St Christopher's Springfield, which provided offices and rooms for meetings and youth events. 'The way we work is to build good relationships with groups of Christian and Muslim young people and then invite them to "encounter" events where they can meet one another', its website explained. The topics discussed were ones of concern to young people aged 11–18, such as faith and fashion.[39]

Ground rules for youth encounters included:

- Listen to what everyone has to say.
- Be honest in what we say.
- Speak positively of my own faith, rather than negatively about other people's.
- Respect other people's views, even if I disagree.
- Don't treat people as a spokesperson for their faith.
- Don't tell others what they believe, but let them tell me.
- Acknowledge similarities and differences between our faiths.
- Don't judge people here by what some people of their faith do.
- Don't force people to agree with my views.

The Birmingham Faithful Neighbourhoods Centre and The Feast are both examples of the changing contours of the Church of England's ecumenical co-operation, as Christians of different denominations work together in a multifaith and multi-ethnic setting. The multi-ethnic nature of British society is changing the Christian landscape in England in other ways too. In revisiting parishes around England, we have already noted the presence of a large Chinese fellowship in the parish of St Luke in the City in Liverpool. More numerous than Asian ethnic churches in England are 'Black Majority' churches. Of Britain's ten largest megachurches, five are led by Nigerians.[40] The Pentecostal churches I encountered when I visited Nigeria in 1985 have now spawned offshoots in the UK. Deeper Life Ministries, whose 24,000 strong morning services I attended in Lagos, began establishing churches in England that same year. What started as a Bible study fellowship in the

University of Lagos in 1973 had, by the year 2000, led to congregations all over London and in Watford, Leeds, Newcastle, Huddersfield, Nottingham, Manchester and Birmingham.[41] There was now even a Deeper Life congregation within walking distance of Ridley Hall in Cambridge.

Back in 1985, I had worshipped on Easter Day in Foursquare Gospel Church in Lagos. A Nigerian pastor, Matthew Ashimolowo, left Foursquare in 1992 to start Kingsway International Christian Centre (KICC) in London.[42] KICC began with rented accommodation in Holloway and eventually moved to a warehouse in Hackney, with an auditorium seating 4,000. It now had its own television station and had planted congregations elsewhere, including in West Africa. More widespread than KICC in England was the Redeemed Christian Church of God (RCCG), another network of churches originating in Nigeria. I met with one of its senior pastors, Babatunde Adedibu, who was studying for his second doctorate, through the Cambridge Theological Federation. He discussed the vigorous church planting programme of the RCCG. The first RCCG church was planted in Britain in 1988. By 2010 there were over 440 congregations ('parishes'), with 85,000 members.[43] By 2014, its website listed 589.[44]

These kinds of churches were posing fresh challenges for 'being Anglican'. The Church of England had tended to be more active in cultivating relations with long-established denominations than with newer Pentecostal and evangelical churches. When on the Archbishop's staff, I was responsible for organising the annual meeting of 'ecumenical bishops'. These were Church of England bishops who took a lead in ecumenical relations with particular families of churches, such as the Methodist Church, the Roman Catholic Church and the Orthodox Churches. As a sign of the times, David Hawkins was appointed Church of England lead bishop for relations with Black Majority churches in 2007. He had previously served as a CMS mission partner in Nigeria. It was he who was asked to represent the Archbishop of Canterbury in a global initiative that had been set up in recognition of the worldwide growth of Pentecostal and evangelical churches. The Global Christian Forum was a joint initiative by the World Council of Churches and the Roman Catholic Church. It was designed to draw in churches that had so far remained on the fringes of the ecumenical movement.

This brings us back to the international arena. While my primary focus at Ridley Hall was on the British context, I was thankfully not expected to turn my back on the world church. Our college community included visiting scholars and church leaders from around the world, many of whom were beneficiaries of our bursary programme. The ultimate beneficiaries were our own students, who had the opportunity to learn from high calibre church leaders from the Global South.

With Ridley's international programme in mind, in my second year as Principal I took part in a congress in South Africa. The event signalled the growing importance of Pentecostal and evangelical churches in world church dynamics, including for Anglicans. Four thousand evangelicals and Pentecostals from two hundred nations gathered for a week in Cape Town in 2010, shortly after the football World Cup. It was the Third International Congress on World Evangelization. Known as the Lausanne Congress, it took its name from the first congress, held in Lausanne, Switzerland. This landmark congress was organised in 1974 at the instigation of the evangelist Billy Graham. However, it had been Anglicans who had been the most influential participants, notably John Stott, who was the main architect of the document emerging from the congress, the Lausanne Covenant.[45] In 2010 Anglicans were still prominent, but this time it was Anglicans from the Global South. In the main conference hall, all 4,000 of us were randomly allocated to 'table' groups, for discussion and Bible study. My table group facilitator was an Anglican bishop from Sudan. The closing communion service was presided over by Archbishop Henry Orombi of Uganda with the liturgy from the Anglican Church of Kenya prepared when David Gitari was Archbishop.

My own role was to oversee the invitation and participation of observers. Both the Vatican and the World Council of Churches sent six-person delegations, illustrating how engagement with Pentecostals and evangelicals was becoming an ecumenical priority beyond the Anglican Communion. Compared with the first congress, there were relatively few British participants of any denomination, reflecting the shift in the numerical centre of gravity of world Christianity. However, several keynote speakers were insistent there was no place for complacency in the Global South. The Anglican Dean of Kigali, Antoine Rutayisire, was perhaps the most eloquent:

> I come to you as a Christian and a preacher and also as a member of the National Unity and Reconciliation Commission established in the aftermath of the Rwandan genocide of 1994.... The fastest growing churches are now in Africa, South America and South East Asia: regions that have witnessed wars, ethnic clashes, even genocides. How do we reconcile the joy of fast-growing churches with this history? Most countries with a dominant Christian presence in Africa are deeply wounded. If they look normal and healthy, then the healing is only superficial, with wounds underneath festering like a volcano ready to explode.... My plea is for a rediscovery of 'the gospel of reconciliation'.... We need to re-examine the evangelisation and discipleship of our own nations.[46]

The church in the West was not let off lightly either. The impression was given that Western Anglicans had forfeited much of their authority, by too much accommodation with Western culture. An optional session on the Anglican Communion drew an audience of several hundred. During question time, I found myself challenging from the floor the rather bleak picture being painted of the Church of England. It seemed overly pessimistic and dismissive of the ways the Church of England was responding to the challenges it was facing.

Immediately after this optional session, members of the Catholic delegation expressed their alarm to me at the way the overall health the Anglican Communion had been portrayed. Presenters of this session had included Anglican primates and former members of the Episcopal Church (USA). Since the Lambeth Conference in 2008, the Anglican Church in North America (ACNA) had been formed. It had brought together a coalition of those who felt estranged by the Episcopal Church's prevailing ethos, epitomised by its approach to human sexuality. Its Archbishop was Bob Duncan, the former Bishop of Pittsburgh who had hosted Archbishop George Carey when I accompanied him in 2002. Following the Lambeth Conference, the primates had met in Alexandria in February 2009. They reached no consensus about the ACNA, called for gracious restraint on all fronts and for a move to 'communion with autonomy and accountability'. However, later that year, two Canadian dioceses authorised the blessing of same-sex unions. Then the following year, a few months before the Lausanne Congress, the Episcopal Church consecrated its second bishop in an active same-sex relationship, Mary Glasspool. It seemed as though the formal processes of the Anglican Communion were being blithely ignored. This rejection of 'gracious restraint' and 'communion with autonomy and accountability' was further undermining the credibility of the Anglican Communion's capacity to order its affairs.

Hosted by Ridley Hall, the Covenant Design Group finalise the Ridley–Cambridge draft

Photo © Dona McCullagh

Nonetheless, at this point, the Anglican Covenant process was still moving forward as a means of bringing greater coherence to Anglican life globally. The Covenant Design Group had gathered in Ridley Hall in March 2009 and prepared the Ridley–Cambridge draft. At the meeting of the Anglican Consultative Council in Jamaica, two months later, most of the draft was approved. A final version was agreed later that year and the process for ratification in member provinces inaugurated. By the time the Church of England considered the Covenant in its diocesan synods, it had been approved in the West Indies, Myanmar, South East Asia, Mexico and Ireland.

Once back in England from the Lausanne Congress, I was invited to explain the Covenant to clergy chapters and deanery synods. I encountered widespread mistrust. There seemed little understanding of the Anglican Communion, let alone what might be needed to help it function more effectively. At the same time, a national campaign had been mounted to oppose the Covenant. The group's website, 'No Anglican Covenant: Anglicans for Comprehensive Unity' offered 'ten reasons why the proposed Anglican Covenant is a bad idea'. One was that it 'would transform a vibrant, cooperative fellowship of churches into a contentious, centralised aggregation of churches designed to reduce diversity and initiative'. Another was that the 'centralisation of authority envisioned by the proposed Covenant is cumbersome, costly and undemocratic'.[47]

This contrasted with the primates' perception at their meeting in Alexandria. 'We welcome the Covenant Design Group's intention to produce a Covenant text which has a relational basis and tone', they agreed in their communiqué. 'It is about invitation and reconciliation in order to lead to the deepening of our koinonia in Christ, and which entails both freedom and robust accountability.' At their meeting, they had been asked by the Windsor Continuation Group, on which I had served, whether the Anglican Communion suffers from an 'ecclesial deficit'. In other words, 'do we have the necessary theological, structural and cultural foundations to sustain the life of the Communion?' What did the primates conclude? 'We need "to move to communion with autonomy and accountability"', with the development of the Anglican Covenant an important step in that direction.[48]

At the Church of England's General Synod the following year, Archbishop Rowan Williams had addressed objections to the Covenant head on. 'It does not invent a new orthodoxy or a new system of doctrinal policing or a centralised authority, quite explicitly declaring that it does not seek to override any province's canonical autonomy. After such a number of discussions and revisions, it is dispiriting to see the Covenant still being represented as a tool of exclusion and tyranny.' To claim that no change was needed was to misjudge the situation gravely, he went on to explain. 'It is an illusion to think that without some changes the Communion will carry on as usual, and a greater illusion to think that the Church of England can somehow derail the entire process. The unpalatable fact is that certain decisions in any province affect all. We may think they shouldn't, but they simply do. If we ignore this, we ignore what is already a real danger, the piece-by-piece dissolution of the Communion and the emergence of new structures in which relation to the Church of England and the See of Canterbury are likely not to figure significantly.'[49]

The Church of England's diocesan synods did not heed their Archbishop. By March 2012, more than half had voted against the Anglican Covenant. As a result, there was no vote taken at General Synod. The Church of England did not adopt the Anglican Covenant. Nor would the Scottish Episcopal Church, where a resolution to adopt it in principle was defeated three months later. Yet by the time the Church of England's verdict was clear, seven of the thirty-eight provinces had approved or subscribed to the Covenant, the Secretary General of the Anglican Communion reported. Undeterred by the Church of England, other provinces continued to give formal consideration to the Covenant. Southern Africa and Hong Kong adopted it in full in 2013, Aotearoa, New Zealand and Polynesia subscribed to the first three sections and Australia, Melanesia, Canada and Korea committed to further study. The Episcopal Church, at its 2012 General Convention, declined to take a position.

A few days before the Church of England's response to the Covenant was finalised, Archbishop Rowan Williams declared his intention to resign at the end of the year. But this did not mean freewheeling for the remainder of his time as Archbishop. Another major issue was working its way through the Church of England's diocesan synods. The Church of England was paving the way for women bishops. We kept pace with this at Ridley Hall by organising study days with guest speakers. In preparing for women bishops, the Church of England was lagging behind some of the other Anglican provinces, just as it had done in ordaining women to the priesthood. By 2012, Anglicans had women bishops in the USA, Canada, Australia and New Zealand. Back in 1988, the bishops of the Lambeth Conference had resolved that 'each province respect the decision and attitudes of other provinces in the ordination and consecration of women to the episcopate'. Then in 1998, the bishops at the Lambeth Conference called on the provinces of the Anglican Communion 'to affirm that those who dissent from, as well as those who assent to, the ordination of women to the priesthood and the episcopate are both loyal Anglicans'.[50]

As discussions progressed in the Church of England, the aim was to make space for differing views within the Church of England itself, and not just the wider Anglican Communion. In July 2000, the General Synod had requested a thorough theological study on the question of women bishops. This led to a succession of reports. The second of these was discussed by General Synod in February 2005. In July that year, Synod members resolved that 'the process for removing the legal obstacles to the ordination of women to the episcopate should now be set in train'. Twelve months later, after yet another report, General Synod passed a series of motions which acknowledged majority support for women bishops in the House of Bishops, while reaffirming that you could dissent from this and still be a loyal Anglican, just as the bishops had declared at the 1998 Lambeth Conference. Other motions set out practical steps for removing legal obstacles while continuing theological debate at grassroots level.

Those objecting to women bishops were appealing to a number of considerations. For some, it was a straightforward matter of biblical interpretation. 'The Biblical principle of male headship and female submission needs to be upheld as a way of ordering relationships within marriage and the church', explained Carrie Sandom to one of the working parties on women bishops. 'The feminist agenda tells us that equality of being necessitates the removal of all gender distinctions and insists on identical roles for men and women. God's word demands a complementarity of roles that has its roots in the Godhead itself.'[51]

For others, from a more Anglo-Catholic point of view, there was a question of faithfulness to the Church's practice down the centuries. If bishops are an indispensable means of connecting the Church to its origins at the time of the apostles, you need to be cautious about changing the person profile. What's at stake, from this Anglo-Catholic point of view, is the effectiveness of the Church's sacraments: 'by their continuity "from the Apostles' time", [bishops] offer assurance of the authenticity of the sacraments they mediate'.[52] This unwillingness to sanction women bishops was linked to ecumenical considerations. What makes Anglicans so sure they are right to break ranks with other historic denominations? 'The idea that the Anglican Communion or the C/E can act on its own in matters such as having women bishops questions the whole claim of our Church to be part of the One Holy Catholic and Apostolic Church, when the greater part of Catholic Christendom does not yet agree with this move.'[53]

This wider ecumenical context led Archbishop Rowan to invite Cardinal Kasper to address the House of Bishops in May 2006. Given my ecumenical responsibilities at Lambeth Palace, I was present when he spoke. The Cardinal emphasised the bishop as an 'office of unity'. He noted the steady progress made in relations between Anglicans and Roman Catholics since Archbishop Michael Ramsey had met with Pope Paul VI in Rome, forty years earlier. 'But then the growing practice of the ordination of women to the priesthood led to an appreciable cooling off. A resolution in favour of the ordination of women to the episcopate within the Church of England would most certainly lower the temperature once more.' He acknowledged that women bishops had already been consecrated in other Anglican provinces. 'These developments already stand as a major obstacle in Anglican–Catholic relations. But the Catholic Church has always perceived the Church of England as playing unique role in the Anglican Communion: it is the church from which Anglicanism derives its historical continuity and with whom the divisions of the sixteenth century are most specifically addressed.'[54]

Cardinal Kasper's address prompted a 'spectrum' of responses from Church of England bishops, according to the report published afterwards.[55] Nevertheless, with the motions passed in General Synod two months later, the process moved forward. By July 2008, Synod was affirming that 'the wish of its majority is for women to be admitted to the episcopate', along with special arrangements 'for those who as a matter of theological conviction will not be able to receive the ministry of women as bishops or priests'. This was the same month the 2008 Lambeth Conference was held in Canterbury. Once again, Cardinal Kasper was invited to offer his thoughts, this time to bishops from around the Anglican Communion; once again, I was present. 'What I am about to say, I say as a friend', he said as he began in a crowded lecture hall. 'It is a strength of Anglicanism that even in the midst of difficult circumstances, you have sought the views of your ecumenical partners, even when you have not particularly rejoiced in what we have said.'

He went on to the special mention given to the Anglican Communion in the Second Vatican Council's decree on ecumenism. He celebrated the fruit of ecumenical dialogue, before returning to the theme of women bishops. This he set in the context of the wider search for coherence in the Anglican Communion, in the midst of tensions about sexuality and the possibility of fragmentation. 'It is our overwhelming desire that the Anglican Communion stays together, rooted in the historic faith which our dialogue and relations over four decades have led us to believe that we share to a large degree', he reaffirmed. 'Anyone who has ever seen the great and wonderful Anglican cathedrals and churches the world over, who has visited the old and famous Colleges in Oxford and Cambridge, who has attended marvellous Evensongs and heard the beauty and eloquence of Anglican prayers, who has read the fine scholarship of Anglican historians and theologians, who is attentive to the longstanding contributions of Anglicans to the ecumenical movement, knows well that the Anglican tradition holds many treasures.'[56]

Four years later, back in Cambridge with its 'old and famous colleges', we awaited the outcome of General Synod's consideration of proposals that would remove all remaining obstacles to women bishops in the Church of England. Some of those opposed to women bishops had left the Church of England by then, accepting Pope Benedict's surprise invitation in 2011 to join his 'Ordinariate'. Meanwhile, forty-two out of forty-four dioceses had approved the proposed legislation. The vote was taken one Tuesday in November, after a day of debating at Church House. It happened to coincide with one of the fortnightly acts of worship attended by staff and students in the Cambridge Theological Federation. In the closing hymn, the news was being picked up on mobile phones. The motion had not received its two-thirds majority in the General Synod's House of Laity. Objections had been raised about provisions for those not in favour of women bishops. Tony Baldry, the Conservative MP responsible for speaking for the synod in parliament, said it would be 'extremely difficult if not impossible' for him to explain to MPs what had happened.[57]

Two months later, I was in Canterbury, as a member of the College of Canons. I was there for the formality of electing the new Archbishop, Justin Welby. Rowan Williams had retired as Archbishop of Canterbury and just moved to Cambridge, as Master of Magdalene College. On Justin Welby's watch, revised proposals for women bishops would be voted through, with the help of 'five guiding principles' to accommodate the diversity of views.[58] Two months after electing Justin Welby, I was back in Canterbury once more, for his enthronement on the marble Chair of St Augustine, the ancient 'seat' that symbolises the authority and teaching office of the 'seat'/'see' of Canterbury and its Archbishop.[59] Ten years had passed since I was introducing ecumenical guests to the Archbishop's wife during the Peace at the previous enthronement. The 105th Archbishop of Canterbury set out his three main priorities from the very beginning: prayer, reconciliation and evangelism. All three priorities anticipated that things would continue to change.

'If we want to see things changed,' explained the newly enthroned Archbishop, 'it starts with prayer. It starts with a new spirit of prayer, using all the traditions, ancient and modern. When it comes, it will be linked to what has gone before, but it will look different—because it is a new renewal for new times.'[60] Signalling his commitment to prayer, he would invite members of the Chemin Neuf Community, the Roman Catholic community originating in France, to be based at Lambeth Palace. He would go on to set up the Community of St Anselm, a community of prayer for young people, whose first Prior would be a recent graduate from Ridley Hall.

Inauguration of the ministry of the 105th Archbishop of Canterbury, Justin Welby
Photos © Andrew Dunsmore / Picture Partnership / Lambeth Palace

Despite a poor turnout at the 2011 Primates' Meeting, almost all the Anglican primates attended Justin Welby's enthronement. 'Reconciliation doesn't mean we all agree,' Archbishop Justin observed as his new ministry began. 'It means we find ways of disagreeing—perhaps very passionately—but loving each other deeply at the same time, and being deeply committed to each other.'[61] During his first eighteen months in post, the new Archbishop would visit all thirty-eight primates, as an outworking of this commitment to reconciliation. As Ugandan and Nigerian governments considered legislation penalising anyone engaging in same-sex practice, he would write to their presidents and to the primates of the Anglican Communion, recalling the primates' commitment at Dromantine to the support and pastoral care of everyone worldwide, regardless of sexual orientation.[62] When he eventually announced his first Primates' Meeting, he would be clear that other official statements about same-sex issues should be respected too. The Windsor Process would not be ignored. 'Our way forward must respect the decisions of Lambeth 1998, and of the various Anglican Consultative Council and Primates' meetings since then', he would explain to the primates in his letter of invitation. Nevertheless, he was adamant that reconciliation was compatible with disagreement. 'A 21st-century Anglican family must have space for deep disagreement, and even mutual criticism, so long as we are faithful to the revelation of Jesus Christ, together.'[63] For him, this was not simply pragmatism, an Anglican variant of realpolitik. 'How we live with our deepest differences is probably the fundamental challenge of our time—for the world as well as the Church', he had already put on record. 'If, as the body of Christ, we can work out a way of disagreeing without dividing, then we will have much to offer the world.'[64]

The primates who gathered in Canterbury in 2016 would somehow manage to heed this call. 'Over the past week the unanimous decision of the Primates was to walk together,' they reported, 'however painful this is, and despite our differences, as a deep expression of our unity in the body of Christ.' They condemned homophobic prejudice and reaffirmed their rejection of criminal sanctions against same-sex attracted people. They expressed 'profound sorrow' at the 'deep hurt' caused by ways Anglicans have often acted towards people on the basis of their sexual orientation. But they also explained how they had agreed to discuss the Episcopal Church's change to its marriage doctrine, with its elimination of any reference to marriage being between a man and a woman.[65]

The Episcopal Church's decision at its 2015 General Convention had taken disagreement to a new level, the primates concluded during their time together.

'It is our unanimous desire to walk together', they reiterated. 'However given the seriousness of these matters we formally acknowledge this distance by requiring that for a period of three years The Episcopal Church no longer represent us on ecumenical and interfaith bodies, should not be appointed or elected to an internal standing committee and that while participating in the internal bodies of the Anglican Communion, they will not take part in decision making on any issues pertaining to doctrine or polity.' Meanwhile, Archbishop Justin was asked to appoint a task group 'to facilitate the restoration of relationship, the rebuilding of mutual trust, healing the legacy of hurt, recognising the extent of our commonality and exploring our deep differences'.[66]

Archbishop Justin's quest for good disagreement would characterise his approach in his own province too. It included promoting facilitated conversations on same-sex issues in dioceses, as England legalised same-sex marriage but its Anglican bishops maintained that 'the Christian understanding and doctrine of marriage as a lifelong union between one man and one woman remains unchanged'.[67]

In a similar way, Archbishop Justin would be unrelenting in urging the Church of England to be more intentional in sharing the Christian faith. 'Making evangelism a priority is not simply a growth strategy, or a desperate attempt to fill empty churches. It is about faithfully and effectively witnessing to Jesus Christ, who is himself the principal agent of the good news. When the Church engages in evangelism imaginatively—through prayer, listening, proclaiming and responding—people become disciples of Jesus and churches grow.'[68]

With a new Archbishop in place, General Synod's so-called 'growth agenda' would therefore be given a new boost. A cluster of task groups would be set up the following year to take this agenda forward. One of them focussed on 'simplification'. 'The remit of the Simplification Task Group has been to identify hindrances to mission', explained its chair, Bishop Pete Broadbent. 'We asked bishops, archdeacons and dioceses—"What is it that prevents you from making changes that will enable parishes, churches and congregations to flourish and new initiatives to take shape?"'[69] Another task group addressed 'Resourcing Ministerial Education', which meant it related directly to our mandate at Ridley Hall. I made sure I was in the gallery when General Synod debated it. The Church of England is facing 'an existential crisis', the First Church Estates Commissioner, Andreas Whittam Smith, told us bluntly.[70] To offset the retirement of forty percent of stipendiary clergy over the next ten years, a fifty percent increase in numbers training for stipendiary ministry was being proposed by the Resourcing Ministerial Education task group.

'If we are to have an impact, we will not be able to do it from within the pockets that are currently available to us', the Finance Committee Chair of the Archbishops' Council, John Spence, had already warned. 'Out of all of this comes an application to the Church Commissioners for the potential for a significant but one-off piece of funding.' Backed by hastily conducted research, *Resourcing Ministerial Education* offered proposals ensuring that an injection of around £10 million a year would keep pace with increased numbers in training and make a real difference to the Church. Synod members raised quite a few questions and requested further consultation before proposals were finalised, to my relief. But I was even more relieved that the short-sighted policy of capping numbers in training might soon be replaced by a much more ambitious drive to equip the Church for the future.

✠

This change of key for the Church of England brings us full circle to the reasons set out for writing this book, as does the sideways glance at the wider Anglican Communion following the Lambeth Conference. In the twenty-first century, in a de-Christianised England and across the world, what does it mean to be Anglican as times change? In this chapter, we have seen varying ways in which Anglicans are seeking to engage with changing contexts in England. Classic Anglican commitment to the local community is having to come to terms with decreasing numbers of people identifying with their local parish church. For Anglicans, relations with non-Anglican churches continue to be important, but the ecumenical landscape is changing, especially with the growth of ethnic and Pentecostal churches. In the international arena, 'autonomy in communion with accountability' seems hard to achieve. The Church of England has objected to the Anglican Covenant, yet it is not clear how else the Anglican Communion will hold together. Disagreement is set to continue over the extent to which inherited ways of being Anglican are fit for purpose.

We come to the end of our box-set of Anglican episodes, with their mixture of soap opera, documentary and costume drama. In the final two chapters, we will see if we can somehow come up with a 'future-proof' frame of reference for Anglicans, in the light of what we have viewed. We move next to change itself, what has driven it and how its validity has been assessed by Anglicans. In the last chapter, we will consider what, in theory at least, should be immutable—forever Anglican.

Richard Hooker, regulating
Anglican polity since
1585 (Ridley Hall chapel
stained glass window)

Photo © Stephen Day

13

Letting Change Happen

As MY TWO GRANDFATHERS struggled through the ordeal of World War One, the Church of England was facing up to the need to change. Army chaplains felt they were peddling unmarketable goods. Reports commissioned by the Archbishops proposed changes to liturgy, decision-making processes and training of clergy, together with a much greater emphasis on actively nurturing Christian faith. Change did come to the Church of England, as we have seen, but only gradually and intermittently. In the meantime, there were major changes to the Anglican landscape worldwide, not always noticed by Anglicans in England.

Yet it would be a mistake to imagine that 'being Anglican' was somehow a fixed and unchanging experience prior to the wake-up call of World War One. In our 'Grand Tour' around Anglican settings, we have noted ways in which Anglican experience had already adapted and mutated since Henry VIII broke with Rome and his acolytes pressed for reform. Many of the changes had surfaced in the nineteenth century. Religious orders, monasteries and convents, eradicated under Henry VIII, were now replanted. Candlesticks became commonplace on Communion tables. Clergy started to wear dog-collars, bishops started to wear purple and don mitres. Choirs were kitted out in surplices, hymn singing became standard fare and organs replaced gallery bands. Diocesan assemblies of clergy and laity were established. Meanwhile, Anglicanism had turned into a truly global phenomenon. It now had the benefit of the *Book of Common Prayer* in 198 languages.[1]

Even before the nineteenth century, significant changes had already taken place. In Scotland and the United States of America, Anglican practice had developed without a formal church–state relationship or a carbon copy of the *Book of Common Prayer*. In England itself, the idea of a state-sponsored religious monopoly had long been abandoned. Increasing concessions had been made to non-Anglican 'dissenters' on the Church of England's home turf.

Despite this previous experience of change, for much of the twentieth century Anglican life seemed stubbornly resistant to further adaptation, notably in the British Isles and continental Europe. Church of England reports repeatedly called for fresh approaches. Yet as late as the 1950s little of substance had actually changed, apart from Holy Communion being given a more prominent place in parish life and the introduction of an unwieldy form of governance through the Church Assembly. Elsewhere in the world, Anglicans were on an increasingly independent trajectory, as host nations proclaimed their political independence from colonial rule. Even so, Anglican practice was remarkably similar in its diverse cultural settings, as if the Anglican Communion were an earlier version of Starbucks or McDonalds, with near-identical franchises from country to country. However, as the twentieth century progressed, this sense of a shared, inherited pattern came under mounting pressure. In the early years of the twenty-first century, 'business as usual' was starting to look unsustainable for Anglicans, even irresponsible. Each Anglican province—the Church of England included—was seeking to engage imaginatively and authentically in its local context, whether in the face of secular indifference, ethnic conflict, dynamic Pentecostalism or radical Islam. Collectively, the provinces stood accused of an 'ecclesial deficit', their archbishops and senior bishops conceded, as they addressed a crisis that had 'torn the fabric' of their common life together.

In this account of 'being Anglican as times change', the time has now come to consider these dynamics of continuity and change more thematically, to see how we might arrive at some fixed points of reference for the future. We will begin by surveying what has driven change in Anglican life and practice. We will then consider how Anglicans can assess whether particular changes are valid. In the final chapter, a frame of reference for 'being Anglican' will finally be offered. I end by setting out some challenges for Anglicans in what may lie ahead.

We proceed, then, by trying to detect what has prompted change in Anglican life and practice, based on what we have observed in the previous chapters. As will be apparent, change has been driven by an eclectic mix of forces, locally and globally.

Let's begin by returning to the trenches of World War One. What we have seen is that *traumatic circumstances* can serve as a catalyst for change for the Church. The war delivered 'a startling and vivid revelation of need and opportunity'.[2] Informed by the harrowing experiences of military chaplains, the Archbishops' reports called for a radical rethink. We have encountered this syndrome again in the Liverpool riots of the 1980s and the publication of *Faith in the City*. 'If the Church of England as an institution is committed to staying and growing in UPAS... it will have to change', the report asserted.[3] Traumatic circumstances can reveal an underlying reality. In both examples just cited, what they exposed was the failure of the Church of England to connect sufficiently well with individuals and their day-to-day lives. In another example, a publicised loss of £500 million by the Church Commissioners exposed a muddled organisational structure, where financial decisions were disconnected from policy making by the Church of England's recognised leaders. This traumatic revelation led to the Turnbull Report and the introduction of a new governance arrangement in the form of the Archbishops' Council.[4] 'Existential crisis' is how the Church of England's condition was described to its General Synod in 2015, by the senior office holder of the Church Commissioners, Andreas Whittam Smith. As First Church Estates Commissioner, he was arguing that the Church needed to inject emergency funds from its historic investments to support a comprehensive programme of renewal. His message was reinforced by John Spence, the Archbishops' Council member overseeing various task groups. 'In less than ten years, we could see a threat to the presence of the Church in communities across rural England, and the Church of England eliminated from its key essential role in promoting the risen Christ.'[5]

This brings us to another driver for change: *finance*. In an obvious way, financial resources can open up new possibilities, directly or indirectly. At grassroots level, finance can turn church buildings into thriving community centres with innovative ministries, as we have seen in Paris, Cambridgeshire and Sussex. At a national level, finance can facilitate creative approaches to mission and social engagement, as seen through the Archbishops' fresh expressions initiative and the establishment of the Church of England representative to the European Institutions. Moving beyond Europe, finance makes it possible for members of a world communion to meet one another, confer together and initiate change. Bringing hundreds of bishops to Canterbury every ten years costs money; so too does staging pan-Anglican Congresses, hence the missed opportunity of the 2008 Cape Town Gathering. Finance also enables Anglicans to engage ecumenically in the global arena. When

Anglican and Roman Catholic bishops met to discuss harvesting the works of ARCIC and co-operating more fully in mission, someone had to pay the airfares. In order for Anglicans to influence and benefit from the activities of the World Council of Churches or the Conference of European Churches, Anglicans must contribute their share of the costs. Finance can reshape the manner and scope of Anglican activity locally, nationally and globally.

The flipside of this is that shortage of finance can itself dictate change at all these levels, for good or ill. Lack of funds can constrain ministerial training and mean clergy are spread more thinly. Internationally, uneven financial resources influence the internal dynamics of the Anglican Communion. There is scope for both constructive partnership and for unequal relationships of dependency. In 1963, the Toronto Congress called for 'mutual responsibility and interdependence' in the Anglican Communion. At the time, 'large areas of the Anglican Communion were being underwritten by the American Church', observes Bruce Kaye, Australian founder editor of the *Journal of Anglican Studies*.[6] Forty years later, 'One of the greatest challenges facing the Anglican provinces of the Global South is the lack of financial resources at every level', the Singaporean Keith Chua reported on behalf of a Global South working group on economic empowerment; '...many of the Global South provinces and people are still very dependent on others (especially the West) for their survival.' As provinces declared themselves 'out of communion' with the Episcopal Church (USA) in disputes over sexuality, there were often financial repercussions. New partnerships were soon formed with the churches of the Anglican Church in North America (ACNA). By 2015, the Anglican Relief and Development Fund promoted by ACNA was reporting it had 'partnered with Anglican churches in thirty-four countries in Africa, Asia, Latin America and the Middle East to complete more than 139 high impact, sustainable development projects'.[7] However, Keith Chua's working group was thinking beyond realignment. It was urging a 'move from economic dependence to financial freedom', echoing a meeting of Global South primates the previous year.[8]

Linked to financial dependency is the fact that change can be driven by *global geopolitics*. The experience of colonialism is of particular relevance for Anglicans. In considering this, we must be careful not to write off Anglicanism as a biddable 'running dog' of imperialism. Anglican missionary activity was sometimes hampered by colonial authorities, such as in India and Northern Nigeria, as we have seen. We have also witnessed how Anglicans could be critical of colonial authorities, obliging the British government to be mindful of the humanitarian lobby. Yet Anglican clergy were chaplains to colonialists and shared many of their assumptions. And Anglicans undoubtedly worked largely with the groove of colonialism in their missionary expansion, seeing this as somehow providential in God's purposes, even after an Opium War. Anglican missionary enterprise radiated from the Western nations. Now, however, in the post-imperial era, there is no appetite at all for the Church of England—nor for prosperous North American provinces—to exercise quasi colonial oversight over autonomous Anglican provinces. Thus we have witnessed primates working collegially in their efforts to respond to divisive issues. Increased authority for the Archbishop of Canterbury was one of the few recommendations of the Windsor Report that the primates rejected at Dromantine in 2005. 'While we welcome the ministry of the Archbishop of Canterbury as that of one who can speak to us as *primus inter pares* about the realities we face as a Communion, we are cautious of any development which would seem to imply the creation of an international jurisdiction which could override our proper provincial autonomy.'[9] In 2005, the Anglican Church of Nigeria even removed 'communion with the See of Canterbury' from its constitution.[10]

The significance of this post-colonial experience is compounded by another driver for change: *the demographic shift in global Anglicanism.* As the twentieth century began, only one percent of Anglicans were African.[11] A century later, the percentage had risen to fifty-five percent, even allowing for a generous 23 million nominal Anglicans in England.[12] As Christian adherence declines in the United Kingdom and other Western countries such as Canada, the traditional authority of Western Anglicans is weakened further.

The Anglican demographic shift reflects a similar shift in world Christianity. This is a reminder that Anglicans do not operate in an ecclesiastical vacuum, oblivious to other denominations. *Non-Anglican churches* have prompted Anglicans to change in a variety of ways. In the seventeenth century, Anglicans in effect conceded their right to exist on English soil, loosening the connection between being Anglican and being an English subject. In the twentieth century, as we have seen, a 'great new fact of our era' was the ecumenical movement, with Anglicans playing a leading role. At grassroots level, non-Anglican churches have increasingly influenced Anglican life. Often this has meant moving from competition or coexistence to co-operation. 'Three churches journeying as one' in Carlisle Diocese is a recent example of this. Mutual respect between Anglicans and other denominations has opened up scope for Anglican activity in one of the few geographical zones considered largely off-limits: continental Europe. It is now possible to conceive of Anglican congregations worshipping in French and other European languages in mainland Europe, with the goodwill of local Catholics and Protestants.

The internal developments within non-Anglican churches have also been a catalyst for change. A classic example is the Roman Catholic Church and the 'aggiornamento' of Vatican II. Not only has this opened up new possibilities for relations between Anglicans and Catholics; it has obliged Anglicans, especially Anglo-Catholics, to recalibrate their understanding of the catholic nature of the Church.

This brings us to a major driver for change: *vibrant sectors within the Anglican Communion*. Those identifying with a particular churchmanship have championed particular causes, as we have repeatedly observed. Often this has constituted pressure for change. We have seen how changes associated with churchmanship can be hotly contested, as my grandfather discovered in the candles dispute in Drumheller. Yet the Oxford Movement and its offspring, for all the resistance encountered from other sectors, ended up shaping Anglican experience throughout the world, even where local churches would not regard themselves as Anglo-Catholic. 'Our duty is to save the Church of England from the strange transformation at the hands of its own members,' opined Hensley Henson on the influence of church parties, 'which if it proceed much further will leave it nothing Anglican but the name.'[13]

Sometimes *new paradigms* have generated change, without necessarily originating from a particular 'party' within the church. In recent times, we have seen this with the notion of the 'mixed economy church', combining fresh expressions of church with inherited patterns of church life. A few decades earlier, we have seen how a new paradigm influenced the shape of Anglican liturgy through the work of Gregory Dix. Going back further still, to the heyday of the missionary era, we have seen another example of a new paradigm in Henry Venn's three-self principle, applied in West Africa, then later appropriated by the 'Three-Self Patriotic Movement' Protestant church in China.

Another driver for change has been *intellectual challenges,* especially those linked to modernity, in the wake of the Enlightenment. Historical criticism and Darwin's theory of evolution challenged commonly held notions about the Bible and its assertions. It also led to rifts between Anglicans drawing different conclusions. At times, intellectual challenges have led to attempts to recast Anglican belief in ways felt to be more in tune with contemporary thinking, as seen in Bishop John Robinson's *Honest to God.*

More proactively, change has been driven by *a desire to combat injustice.* In West and East Africa, Anglican missionary activity—and the shape it took—reflected a commitment to stop the slave trade at source. The cocktail of trade, education and evangelism was the prescription offered to overcome this grave injustice, by the likes of Thomas Buxton and David Livingstone. More recently, the consecration of women as bishops is considered by some to be primarily a matter of justice: 'it is unjust to women, an infringement of their rights, if they are not allowed to be bishops, just as it would be an infringement of their rights if they were not allowed to be High Court judges, ministers of the Crown or the chief executives of businesses', runs the argument.[14] A similar approach is sometimes taken about the endorsement of same-sex partnerships, when they are justified on the basis of civil rights. Representatives of Changing Attitude objected to disputes about same-sex relationships being depicted as 'a disagreement between two strongly held but conflicting interpretations of the Bible'. In a letter to the *Church Times,* they argued that 'the majority of Anglicans have already moved well beyond these polarised arguments. For most it is a matter of Christian integrity, truth and justice'.[15] Yet Anglicans can sometimes disagree vehemently about what constitutes Christian justice, when applied to particular issues. William Wilberforce campaigned for nineteen years to abolish the slave trade and his bill was defeated eleven times. 'Let not parliament be the only body that is insensible to the principles of national justice', he cautioned as he came towards the end of a three and a half hour speech in the House of Commons.[16] Yet when his bill suffered its first defeat, church bells were rung in Bristol, a bonfire was lit in the city and a half-day's holiday was awarded to workers and sailors.[17] The rhetoric of justice has often won a hearing, but has not in itself guaranteed Anglican votes, either immediately or in the longer term. Nevertheless, a desire to combat injustice must undoubtedly be numbered amongst influential motivators for significant changes.

A perceived lack of spiritual vitality has been another driver for change. This has been a recurring refrain of Church of England reports for the past hundred years, after World War One exposed 'the grave fact that the instinct for worship has diminished in the people as a whole'.[18]

Recognition of missionary challenge and opportunity is a related change agent. We have seen this in England with the dawning realisation that numbers of churchgoers are declining and the rallying cry for the Church to become more 'mission-shaped'. Missionary challenge and opportunity were, of course, a powerful force in shaping nineteenth-century Anglican life. To take just one example from that era, we see it in Bishop Selwyn's setting up of the Melanesian mission in a way that suited the Pacific context.

Bishop Selwyn is also an example of how *pioneering leadership* has driven change. Often, this kind of pioneering leadership has been inspirational, 'up front' leadership. Still in the Pacific, we see it in Ini Kopuria's founding of the distinctive Melanesian Brotherhood. Back in England, we see it in Elizabeth Ferrard's pioneering of the deaconess movement, Nathaniel Woodard's establishing of boarding schools with a distinctive Anglo-Catholic ethos and in William Temple's leadership in the ecumenical movement. As well as high profile pioneering leadership, we have also encountered pioneering transformational leadership on the fringes of the church's institutional life. We have seen it in Bishop Luscombe's efforts to oversee congregations in continental Europe, in E. J. H. Nash's pioneering of youth camps for schoolboys and in Archibald Patterson's establishment of Anglican schools in colonial Angola, below the radar of the Portuguese authorities.

Often, change has been brought about not by the leadership of a lone individual, but by the concerted efforts of a like-minded group of people, typically in *voluntary associations*. We have seen this in the work of mission agencies such as CMS and UMCA. As we have observed, this has been one of the ways in which lay people have shaped the life of the church.

Fluctuations in clergy numbers have also led to change, at times highlighting the need for increased involvement of lay people in the life of the Church. The introduction of female lay readers during World War One is a case in point. When numbers of clergy have declined, we have seen how existing models of church life have been brought under pressure, such as George Herbert's archetypal country parson.

Inevitably, *popular culture* has been a major driver for change. This is strikingly evident when it comes to approaches to corporate worship. We have encountered this in Nigeria in the 1980s, for example, with Anglican youth groups preferring livelier forms of worship to *Hymns Ancient and Modern* and with the broad appeal of prayer for healing. We have seen it in Pakistan, when shoes are removed to receive the bread and wine at communion. The force of popular culture has also been evident when it comes to ethical issues. Where same-sex relationships have become increasingly accepted in wider society, and regarded as a matter of social justice, we have witnessed pressure for Anglicans to follow suit.

Another feature of wider society is a driver for change: *the presence of other religions*. In countries where non-Christian religions are dominant, such as Pakistan, Anglicans have had to adapt their life and witness accordingly, as we have seen. In traditionally Christian countries, such as England, with a growing number of adherents of other faiths, Anglicans have had to find new ways of expressing their Christian witness, through 'presence and engagement'.

As Anglican provinces have engaged with their respective local contexts, *increasing complexity* has brought pressure on the global status quo. How can

Anglicans keep in step with one another as they engage with their differing contexts in the USA and Nigeria? The Windsor Report, as we have seen, judged the Anglican Communion's instruments in need of an overhaul, exposing an 'ecclesial deficit' in Anglican life.

Finally, from time to time *unplanned developments* have driven change. Charismatic renewal is a vivid example of this. When it first surfaced in the Church of England, it was viewed warily, as we have seen. Yet charismatic renewal has influenced Anglican approaches to corporate worship and praying for healing, as well as giving a boost to the recognition of the gifts of the whole people of God. A recent Church of England report goes so far as to claim that 'the most significant changes in the Church over history have rarely emanated from official central structures—they usually originate on the edge where the Spirit of God inspires willing people to do things that others would not imagine'.[19] A similar point was made by the Bishop of the American Convocation of Churches in Europe, Jeffery Rowthorn, when reflecting on the case for Anglican ministry to French nationals. 'There is a slowly evolving constituency of indigenous French-speaking Anglicans: a few here, a few there, gradually increasing in numbers. We are being challenged by the Holy Spirit', he suggested in 1998 at the Chantilly Synod, 'to discover what it means to be Anglican today in France.'[20]

This claim that the Spirit of God instigates change brings us to the task of discernment. We have identified drivers for change at micro and macro levels of Anglican life. How can Anglicans assess whether embracing change is the right thing to do? As we have observed, change is by no means automatic for Anglicans. So when there is pressure for change, what authority is appealed to? Here are some possible candidates.

We begin with an obvious one, *Anglican formularies:* the *Book of Common Prayer,* the Thirty-Nine Articles and the Ordinal. Changes can be justified on the basis that they are sanctioned by these formularies or are a natural extension of their logic. When it comes to liturgical revision, for example, 'the Book of Common Prayer 1662 is the normative standard for liturgy', according to an international gathering of canon lawyers who compared the canons of Anglican provinces.[21] 'We uphold the Thirty-nine Articles as containing the true doctrine of the Church agreeing with God's Word and as authoritative for Anglicans today', proclaims the Jerusalem Declaration issued at GAFCON in 2008.[22] Yet there are problems with this approach. In practice the provinces of the Anglican Communion have not uniformly regarded these formularies as a final authority. As far back as 1888, the bishops of the Lambeth Conference agreed that 'newly constituted' churches 'should not necessarily be bound to accept in their entirety the Articles of Religion'. It would be sufficient to hold 'substantially the same doctrine as our own'.[23] Taking stock a century later, the Anglican theologian Stephen Sykes acknowledged that the Thirty-Nine Articles had 'lost status as an indication of the standpoint to which Anglicans are corporately committed'.[24] The authority of the 1662 *Book of Common Prayer* has been eroded too. As we have noted, liturgical revision has at times made significant changes to the shape of the liturgy, as in the case of the *American Book of Common Prayer* (1979). Even the Church of England has changed the way in which these formularies shape its life, as we have noted. *Common Worship* has deregulated the uniform liturgy of Cranmer's *Book of Common Prayer.* Church of England clergy are no longer required to state that they 'willingly and from the heart subscribe to the Thirty-nine Articles of Religion'. Instead, in the Declaration of Assent, a minister must simply 'declare my belief in the faith . . . to which the historic formularies of the Church of England bear witness'.[25]

Nevertheless, these formularies continue to occupy an honoured place for Anglicans, to be brought into the conversation when change is proposed. This was the line taken in the Anglican Covenant, in one of the sections that has received widespread endorsement from Anglican provinces. 'Each Church affirms . . . the catholic and apostolic faith uniquely revealed in the Holy Scriptures and set forth in the catholic creeds, which faith the Church is called upon to proclaim afresh in each generation. The historic formularies of the Church of England, forged in the context of the European Reformation and acknowledged and appropriated in various ways in the Anglican Communion, bear authentic witness to this faith.'[26]

An alternative to treating these Anglican formularies as final arbiter is to go back further in the Christian story. This is potentially compatible with taking the formularies seriously. There are two main strands here: *tradition,* understood principally in this context as the practices and beliefs of the early church, and *Scripture.* As we have seen, following the Church of England's break with Rome, efforts were made to trace the pedigree of the Church of England to the early church. We see this in Bishop John Jewel's 1562 *Apology for the Church of England.* 'Thus we have been taught by Christ, by the apostles and holy fathers; and we do faithfully teach the people of God the same things', he argues.[27] 'There can be nothing more spitefully spoken against the religion of God than to accuse it of novelty, as a new comen up matter. . . . [N]o man can now think our doctrine to be new, unless the same think either the prophets' faith, or the gospel, or else Christ himself be new.'[28] With a similar agenda, Archbishop Matthew Parker, with his impressive library of ancient books, was keen to establish a lineage which predated the sixth-century Roman Catholic mission to England. Via the Celtic Christians, the Church of England had its own independent line back to the era of the early church.

Yet these advocates were careful about the authority given to the Councils of the early church. 'The Church has erred and its Councils have erred', is one of the Thirty-Nine Articles signed off by Matthew Parker under Queen Elizabeth I. If *tradition* and *Scripture* are in conflict, these Reformation-minded apologists were in no doubt which trumps the other. The Articles commended by Parker contain numerous references to the unique authority of Scripture. To give just two examples: 'It is not lawful for the Church to ordain anything that is contrary to God's word written' and 'whatsoever is not written therein, nor may be proved thereby, is not to be required of any man, that it should be believed as an article of faith, or be thought requisite or necessary to salvation'.[29] Then in Jewel's words, 'We bring you nothing but God's holy word, which is a sure rock to build on, and will never flee or shrink'.[30]

In the nineteenth century, the Oxford Movement can be seen as pressing this logic about guiding principles further. By emphasising particular church traditions and practices, its proponents were arguing that the Church of England had at times misfired or over-reacted. If the Church of England aspired to be truly in step with the primitive church, it needed to place more emphasis on the apostolic calling of bishops and Holy Communion and also reinstate practices such as confession to a priest. The evangelical backlash to this was unleashed by concerns that the traditions of the church down the ages might be elevated above the teaching of Scripture. 'The Ritualists are merely reintroducing the ceremonies and dogmas which our fathers cast off as idolatrous and superstitious', Bishop Ryle protested.[31] What Anglo-Catholics and evangelicals held in common was their recourse to a higher authority than Anglican formularies in assessing whether proposed changes were acceptable for Anglicans: the teaching and practices of the early church.

Over the centuries, there were those on both wings who ended up concluding that, by appealing to this higher authority, the Church of England was hoist by its own petard. Oliver Cromwell, whose Puritan beliefs shared common ground with later evangelicals, joined the ceremonial ripping up of the *Book of Common Prayer* in Cambridge's Great St Mary's Church.[32] John Henry Newman had authored the first Tract of the Oxford Movement. He went on to promote Anglicanism as an ideal middle way ('via media') between Catholic and Protestant extremes.[33] But by the time he wrote the ninetieth and final Tract, trying earnestly to reconcile the Thirty-Nine Articles with 'old Catholic Truth', he confessed 'I was on my death-bed as regards my membership of the Anglican Church'.[34] Four years later he would become a Roman Catholic.

With nineteenth-century disputes about church tradition in full swing, the bishops of the Anglican Communion found themselves considering what to say about tradition and Scripture when engaging with non-Anglican churches. What was the bottom line? At the third Lambeth Conference in 1888, they rallied behind a formula already approved by the General Convention of the Episcopal Church (USA): the Chicago–Lambeth Quadrilateral. Thus they proclaimed that for Anglicans, non-negotiables were as follows:

A The Holy Scriptures of the Old and New Testaments, as 'containing all things necessary to salvation', and as being the rule and ultimate standard of faith.
B The Apostles' Creed, as the Baptismal Symbol; and the Nicene Creed, as the sufficient statement of the Christian faith.
C The two Sacraments ordained by Christ Himself—Baptism and the Supper of the Lord—ministered with unfailing use of Christ's Words of Institution, and of the elements ordained by Him.
D The Historic Episcopate, locally adapted in the methods of its administration to the varying needs of the nations and peoples called of God into the Unity of His Church.[35]

Since the Lambeth Conference in 1888, this Lambeth Quadrilateral has endured as a shared reference point for Anglicans. It is frequently quoted in ecumenical dialogue, a recent example being the attempt to harvest forty years of dialogue between Anglicans and Roman Catholics.[36] It is affirmed in full in the draft Anglican Covenant.

The Quadrilateral's minimalist approach to church tradition has not stopped Anglicans appealing to a wider spread of church tradition, when change is proposed. This has been especially true of Anglo-Catholicism. But it is true more generally. The Liturgical Reforms proposed by Dix, for example, appeal to early church traditions deduced from a document discovered in the nineteenth century. Resistance to cross-border interventions by bishops is also justified by appeal to traditions of the early church.[37]

The Quadrilateral is nonetheless clear that the Holy Scriptures are the ultimate rule and standard of faith, as John Jewel and Matthew Parker would have expected. When deaconesses were introduced by the Bishop of London two decades before the Quadrilateral was endorsed, it was the scriptural precedent of Phoebe that clinched the case for the bishop. Yet since the bishops' endorsement of the Quadrilateral, the notion that Scripture can be authoritative has taken quite a battering. As we have noted, the Enlightenment encouraged a critical approach to all forms of authority. Historical criticism and Darwin's theory of evolution raised fundamental questions about the trustworthiness of the Bible as God's self-revelation. To render the Bible intelligible to modernity, Anglican leaders have been among those proposing radical re-workings of scriptural understanding. As a result, the impression in some Anglican circles is that Scripture has lost its potency as a source of divinely-inspired authority.

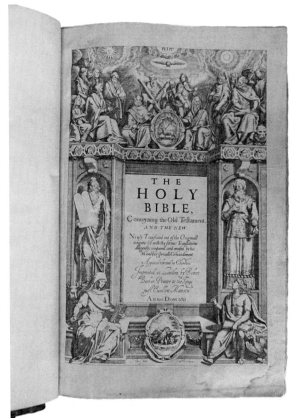

Established authority: the version of the Old and New Testament approved for use in the Church of England in 1611 (the King James Bible)

Reproduced by kind permission of Ridley Hall, Cambridge; photo © Dona McCullagh

Yet, Scripture still remains a primary source of authority for Anglicans.[38] This is undergirded by a track record of rigorous engagement with biblical scholarship. Anglicans disagree amongst themselves about the ways in which Scripture is interpreted, as we have seen in debates over sexuality and women bishops. Despite this, the Anglican Covenant, once again in a section widely endorsed by provinces, unashamedly invited the churches of the Anglican Communion to commit themselves 'to ensure that biblical texts are received, read and interpreted faithfully, respectfully, comprehensively and coherently, with the expectation that Scripture continues to illuminate and transform the Church and its members, and through them, individuals, cultures and societies'.[39]

As we have considered appeals to tradition and Scripture in assessing change, we have also encountered another possible authority for what counts as acceptably Anglican: *Anglican theorists.* Bishop John Jewel can be numbered among these theorists, with his *Apology for the Church of England.* Chief amongst the theorists is Richard Hooker (1554–1600), protégé of Bishop Jewel. In his set-piece disputes at the Temple Church in London with the Puritan Walter Travers, and in his later writings, Hooker is felt to have crystallised insights about Anglican authority and practice that have stood the test of time.

Michael Ramsey, 20th-century Anglican theorist, processing to the British Embassy Church in Paris

Photo © Gyles Longley

We have already heard Hooker think out loud about calling Anglican clergy 'priests', despite the linguistic mix-up. It is Hooker who is frequently regarded as the craftsman responsible for the three-legged stool of 'Scripture, tradition and reason'. In fact he is misunderstood on this point, if he is taken to be proposing that Scripture, tradition and reason are of equal authority. For him, as for his mentor John Jewel, Scripture was unquestionably the paramount authority. However, reason, which for him included intuition, was 'an instrument, without which we could not reap by the scripture's perfection that fruit and benefit which it yieldeth'.[40] As for tradition, he disagreed with the extreme Puritan view that any practice not explicitly warranted by Scripture should be abandoned. Customs 'confirmed by long use' could be retained. Church government could be regarded as something on which Christians could agree to differ, even if the scales were tipped in the direction of bishops, as far as he was concerned.[41]

Still influential: Richard Hooker and George Herbert
celebrated in Ridley Hall's chapel   *Photo © Stephen Day*

One prolific writer on Anglicanism, Mark Chapman, has lamented the declining influence of sixteenth- and seventeenth-century theorists in the Anglican Communion.[42] Yet such theorists are still appealed to. So too are theorists from more recent times. Like Hooker, they are seen as crystallising insights about what constitutes acceptable parameters for Anglicans. Michael Ramsey, Archbishop of Canterbury (1961–74), is one such twentieth-century theorist. He is often quoted as an authority for regarding the 'incompleteness' of the Anglican Church as a positive attribute. 'Its credentials are its incompleteness, with the tension and travail in its soul', he wrote in 1936.[43]

'It is clumsy and untidy, it baffles neatness and logic. For it is not sent to commend itself as "the best type of Christianity", but by its very brokenness to point to the universal Church wherein all have died.'[44] These theorists can sometimes offer a shortcut to assessments of change. Their authority comes from the wisdom they offer and the respect it has been afforded.

Church processes are a more robust form of authority, at least on the surface. These processes vary from province to province, but usually involve synods or conventions, meetings of bishops and specialist working groups. We have observed such church processes in operation in evaluating prayer book revision, the ordination of women, expanding French-language ministry in France and disputes over human sexuality. It might seem as though such processes, in the end, are a straightforward matter of democracy. Those authorised to vote, in other words, determine what it means to be Anglican. It is true that in some parts of the Anglican Communion the democratic ideal is so highly prized that there is a great reluctance to stand in its way. We have observed the House of Bishops of the Episcopal Church (USA), for example, feeling duty bound to defer to voting at General Convention and showing reluctance to claim areas of church life as their primary responsibility.[45]

Yet for changes to be accepted as legitimate, a straightforward vote may not be enough. Reasons given for the changes must have a persuasive force and be seen as compatible with values supposedly held in common. If this is not the case, the coherence of Anglicanism starts to unravel. In extreme cases, as we have seen, those unable to accept the changes can break away, protesting that they constitute the faithful remnant, as we have seen with the Anglican Church in North America. Provinces can distance themselves from one another, if they feel their sister provinces are sanctioning problematic innovations. 'Impaired communion' can be declared.

In addition, the credentials of those voting is important. *Bishops,* for example, have a particular responsibility for overseeing the church's teaching, in classic Anglican thinking, however 'locally adapted' their role may be.[46] In the order of service penned by Cranmer for consecrating bishops, the Archbishop asks, 'Are you ready, with all faithful diligence, to banish and drive away all erroneous and strange doctrine contrary to God's Word...?'[47] In the Church of England, this responsibility is still enshrined in the Church's canons. 'It appertains to [the bishop's] office to teach and uphold sound and wholesome doctrine, and to banish and drive away all erroneous opinions'.[48] Somehow this needs to be taken into account as issues are debated in synods and conventions. At the very least, canon law in the provinces of the Anglican Communion generally dictates that 'no new doctrinal formula may be approved by a central church assembly without the consent of the House of Bishops or equivalent collegial Episcopal body'.[49]

We should acknowledge here that bishops are seen as having intrinsic authority, as reflected in the Chicago–Lambeth Quadrilateral. We have noted how the Oxford Movement laid particular emphasis on the authority of the bishop in the life of the Church. The first of its tracts, written by John Henry Newman, stressed the independence of the Church under bishops standing in the succession of the apostles. Subsequent generations of Anglo-Catholics, one church historian wryly observes, 'combined high theoretical esteem for bishops with an uncanny ability to provoke the ones actually existing in the Church of England'.[50] Nathaniel Woodard's clash with the Bishop of London is a case in point. Nevertheless, for Anglo-Catholics and all Anglicans, bishops have authority to encourage or inhibit change in their dioceses, within the parameters set by canon law and their corresponding role as chief pastor.[51]

Church processes and diocesan bishops often find themselves responding to activities already emerging at grassroots level, rather than initiating them. In such circumstances, *experience* can operate as a form of authority. We have noted how hymn singing became a part of Anglican life in this way in 1820, when the church court judged that the practice had been legitimated by custom.[52] Experimentation, on the margins of what is authorised by the church, can force the church to take note of changes that are subsequently judged appropriate. In the Church of England, this has been characteristic both of Anglo-Catholic practice and of charismatic renewal. To take just one example, an approved liturgy for a service of healing was introduced long after such services had become commonplace in parish churches. Formal church authorisation can thus be behind the curve. The time-consuming nature of canon law reform and liturgical revision is one reason why this may be so. Some go so far as to say that deep change necessitates breaking the rules, given the natural inertia of the status quo.[53] We saw this being acted on in the Episcopal Church (USA), when women were first ordained as priests in the 1970s. There is, however, no guarantee that 'breaking the rules' in this way will be later legitimated.

Experience can be appealed to both before and after a matter is addressed formally through church processes. This brings us to the question of reception. In the Anglican Communion, the controversial question of women bishops is in a process of 'open reception'. As the Eames Commission explained:

> Once a Synodical decision has been made then that must necessarily be respected on all sides as a considered judgement of that particular representative gathering. However, it has always been recognised that councils not only may, but have,

erred. Conciliar and synodical decisions would still have to be received and owned by the whole people of God as consonant with the faith of the Church throughout the ages professed and lived today. In the continuing and dynamic process of reception, freedom and space must be available until a consensus one way or another has been achieved.[54]

As Maggi Dawn explains, the notion of reception can be linked to a story from the Acts of the Apostles. Gamaliel, a leading Pharisee, argues that if what we now call Christianity was of human origin, it would fail, whereas if it were of God, it would be unstoppable (Acts 5: 34–39). 'The "wisdom of Gamaliel" offers a principle whereby when new movements or new developments rise up, rather than stifling them in the name of integrity the best course is to allow them to develop, trusting God to ensure that what is good will grow, and what is vain and ephemeral will quickly wither.'[55] Yet once again, it is important to note that it can be problematic to assume that popular support alone guarantees something is right. In his *Apology for the Church of England*, John Jewel notes biblical warrant for this caution, when he warns that 'there was the greatest consent that might be amongst them that worshipped the golden calf, and among them which with one voice jointly cried against our Saviour Jesu Christ, "Crucify him."'[56]

Canon law can be in tension with an appeal to experience, when there is unauthorised experimentation. Yet it nonetheless functions as an authority where innovations are considered. Although canon law varies from province to province, the Anglican Communion legal advisors' network has identified one hundred principles of canon law held in common by the provinces of the Anglican Communion. Yet canon law cannot be the last word when changes are envisaged. Canon law can be revised in the light of higher authorities, as we have seen. 'The courts and tribunals of a church do not declare the doctrine or create new doctrine, but only state what the law is with regard to doctrine.' This is a common strand in the canon law of the provinces of the Anglican Communion.[57]

A form of authority becoming increasingly prominent is *mission* and the extent to which it is served by changes. In the Church of England, this is reflected in talk of 'mission-shaped' church.[58] 'Although mission is wider than evangelism, the mission of God is not being undertaken in all its fullness unless people are called to become disciples of Christ', according to a report presented to the Church of England General Synod in 2013. 'What is required is incremental and sustained cultural change throughout the whole Church, so that the business of making new disciples influences all it does.'[59] Mission sets the terms for change, in other words. This perspective lies behind the work of the four Church of England task groups set up in 2014. 'If the goals of mission and growth are to be realised, it is vital that all of the Church's activity is aligned with them', according to the Resourcing the Future Task Group.[60] 'The remit of the Simplification Task Group has been to identify hindrances to mission', explained its chair, Bishop Pete Broadbent. 'We asked bishops, archdeacons and dioceses—"What is it that prevents you from making changes that will enable parishes, churches and congregations to flourish and new initiatives to take shape?"'[61]

Another form of authority is *attitudes of other churches*. We have seen this at work in discussions about Anglican engagement in continental Europe. We have also seen how Cardinal Kasper was invited to address Anglican bishops about women bishops and the future development of the Anglican Communion. Recognising the authority of non-Anglican churches is the result of an ecumenical commitment to the unity of the Church. It is also the consequence of regarding the Anglican Communion as part of the catholic Church, as opponents of women bishops have pointed out.[62]

The remaining two sources of authority in this list belong together: *practical considerations* and *reason*. A pragmatic streak has long been discernible amongst Anglicans. Rowan Williams has even described Richard Hooker's approach as 'contemplative pragmatism'. Hooker, he contends, is pragmatic in the sense that he gives real weight in his thinking to the ways things have worked out in practice over time. Yet at the same time he is 'contemplative', in that 'his guiding principles are seen by him as received, not invented, as the uncovering of a pattern of wisdom in the universe'.[63] When Anglicans assess proposals for change, practical considerations combine with other guiding principles. Will provisions for those opposed to women bishops work in practice? When proposing new ways of being Anglican locally and globally, what are their financial considerations? When viewing the Anglican Communion, what are facts on the ground that cannot be changed? Are there genies that cannot be put back into the bottle?

Yet Hooker's understanding of the 'pattern of wisdom in the universe' encompasses more than practical considerations. It includes a broader understanding of what he calls 'reason'. As we have already noted, Hooker describes reason as 'an instrument, without which we could not reap by the scripture's perfection that fruit and benefit which it yieldeth'.[64] Reason adds to the scope of Scripture. 'What Scripture doth plainly deliver, to that the first place both of credit and obedience is due; the next whereunto is whatsoever any man can necessarily conclude by force of reason.'[65]

Two hundred years later, the European Enlightenment would unleash much debate about the nature of reason and its relationship to other sources of authority in the life of the Church.[66] But for Anglicans, reason has endured as a treasured asset. 'It is the divine gift in virtue of which human persons respond and act with awareness in relation to their world and to God', Anglican bishops were reminded at the 1988 Lambeth Conference.[67] Arguably, reason has been in the background in the exercise of all the other sources of authority we have noted, as it was for Hooker in his interpretation of Scripture. But it nonetheless merits a mention in its own right. When, for example, William Wilberforce used his oratory in the House of Commons to oppose the slave trade, he persistently deployed reason to persuade his fellow politicians to see slavery in a new light. Reason, then, will be included in our list of sources of authority for authorising change.

In considering change in Anglican life and experience, we have identified twelve possible sources of authority for regulating it:

1. Anglican formularies
2. tradition
3. Scripture
4. Anglican theorists
5. church processes
6. bishops
7. experience
8. canon law
9. mission
10. attitudes of other churches
11. practical considerations
12. reason.

These sources of authority are not of equal weight, but each have their part to play. Where, considering them all together, does God feature? If the Church is more than a human institution, how have Anglicans assessed whether change has divine approval? As we have seen, from the time of the Reformation, there has been much more to this than exercising common sense. Discerning God's perspective on change has not simply relied on guesswork or the assumption that God is happy to go along with whatever the Church decides. Taking Cranmer's lead, Anglicans have treasured the written legacy of the first followers of Jesus of Nazareth as an irreplaceable gift for understanding God's purposes, along with the Scriptures of the Jewish people. 'For the whole Scriptures (sayth St Paul) were given by the inspiration of GOD', Cranmer marvelled in one of the Homilies commended in the Thirty-Nine Articles. 'And shall we…think to learne the knowledge of GOD and of ourselves, in any earthly mans worke of writing, sooner or better than in the holy Scriptures, written by the inspiration of the holy Ghost? The Scriptures were not brought unto us by the will of man.'[68]

Yet belief in the divine inspiration of 'holy Scriptures' has not privileged Anglicans with fast-track access to God's mind on every issue. Some issues seem not to be addressed by Scripture, as Hooker pointed out when arguing for certain customs 'confirmed by long use'. There may be room for latitude. 'It is not necessary that Traditions and Ceremonies be in all places one, or utterly alike', Cranmer conceded reassuringly.[69] In 2009, the Bible in the Life of the Church Project was mandated by the Anglican Consultative Council 'to explore how we, as Anglicans, actually use the Bible', in the context of current controversies. Introducing its findings three years later, Archbishop David Moxon of New Zealand observed that 'in turning to Scripture for insights we have discovered that we reach different conclusions as to the way forward'.[70] This is hardly a new phenomenon. From the time of Cranmer, Jewel and Hooker onwards, Anglicans have engaged in lively debate about scriptural interpretation, among themselves and with representatives of other churches. 'As Anglicans, we discern the voice of the living God in the Holy Scriptures', asserts the Signposts document produced by the international working group I served on for four years. 'We read the Bible together, corporately and individually, with a grateful and critical sense of the past, a vigorous engagement with the present, and with patient hope for God's future.'[71]

It is in this context that the other sources of authority play their part in assessing whether particular changes might have God's sanction. From Cranmer's time onwards, Anglicans have acknowledged that God may be actively involved through these other sources of authority too. To take the example of church processes, the Thirty-Nine Articles accept that the Church has power to exercise authority 'in controversies of faith', as do General Councils of the kind convened in the early centuries of the Church's existence. However, there is no guarantee that God's purposes will prevail. Church processes may 'err' in 'things pertaining unto God' and do so by definition if they ordain anything 'contrary to God's Word written'. Those shaping policy may not necessarily be 'governed by the Spirit and Word of God'.[72]

Four hundred and fifty years later, the Virginia Report encouraged Anglican bishops to consider how God might be at work as they assessed controversial changes. 'In the matter of discerning the mind of Christ for the Church, under the guidance of the Holy Spirit, discernment, conciliar debate and decision-making, followed by a process of reception, all have a part to play.'[73]

One of the report's architects was Stephen Sykes, Bishop of Ely, former Regius Professor of Divinity at Cambridge and one of the twentieth century's leading experts on Anglicanism. 'By far the most considerable statement on authority in Anglicanism to be found in official Anglican documentation is contained in a section of the 1948 Lambeth Conference Report', he had written twenty years earlier.[74] He was still enthusing about this 'celebrated document' in 1995, the year I first heard him speak (while an ordinand at Ridley Hall), and as the Virginia Report was being drafted.[75] Not all of the twelve sources of authority identified above are explicitly mentioned in the 1948 statement. There is no direct mention of the sway of non-Anglican churches, for example. The ecumenical movement was, after all, still in its infancy in 1948. But the document covers most of the ten and confidently maintains that through this 'dispersed' authority God's perspective can be discerned by those with eyes to see:

> Authority, as inherited by the Anglican Communion from the undivided Church of the early centuries of the Christian era, is single in that it is derived from a single divine source, and reflects within itself the richness and historicity of the Divine Revelation, the authority of the Eternal Father, the incarnate Son and the life-giving Spirit. It is distributed among Scripture, Tradition, Creeds, the Ministry of Word and Sacraments, the witness of saints, and the *consensus fidelium,* which is the continuing experience of the Holy Spirit through his faithful people in the Church. It is thus a dispersed rather than a centralised authority having many elements which combine, interact with and check each other; these elements together contributing by a process of mutual support, mutual checking, and redressing of errors or exaggerations to the many-sided fullness of the authority which Christ has committed to his Church.[76]

✠

This Lambeth Conference statement brings us to the end of our examination of Anglican change agents and sources of authority for assessing possible changes. We turn now to those aspects of 'being Anglican' that might be considered fixed points in the pattern of Anglican life: the stars making up the night-sky constellation by which we can navigate. Some of these are in close proximity to the sources of authority we have considered, as we shall see. Others may hardly need pointing out at all as we view the Anglican story so far. Several shine more dimly. They are examples of the latent potential within Anglican life: features that have surfaced periodically, but that have at other times been obscured.

14

Forever Anglican

WHEN IT COMES TO being Anglican, 'unlike Coca-Cola, there is no secret formula protected in a head office', warns the Anglican theologian, Mark Chapman.[1] In the absence of that kind of patent-protected formula, readers may justifiably wonder whether what they are being offered is—in the words of a 1970s Coca-Cola advertising campaign—the real thing. In this final chapter, I am not pretending to disclose the full recipe for 'real thing' Anglicanism, resolving all speculation about its contested ingredients. But I am setting out what some of those ingredients might be, in the light of what we have observed in preceding chapters. They include certain items not commonly found in such lists; they omit others that are. The aim, as anticipated at the start of this book, is to provide a sense of what Anglicans should keep stocked in their store cupboard as we look to the future. These articles correspond to a richly flavoured Anglican past, albeit one that has not always been to everyone's taste.

We begin with an appetiser that is not often cited. *Anglicans accept the Church must change.* This may seem a curious place to start, given the inertia we have witnessed in our walk through the past one hundred years. Yet in our excursions across centuries and continents, we have discovered ample evidence of change, driven by the forces discussed in the previous chapter. Sometimes change seems only to be accepted as a last resort, in response, say, to long-term decline in church attendance. However, we can claim more positively that change is part of the essence of being Anglican, when we consider a second element of 'being Anglican'.

Change is inevitable because *Anglicans make worship accessible.* Again, this may not be a commonly recognised feature of 'being Anglican'. The demoralised World War One chaplains or the empty churches in urban Liverpool in the 1980s suggest a different reality. So too might the replica English-style churches encountered in Nigeria in 1985. Yet the break with Rome ushered in a form of church life which was destined to change, if it lived up to its ideals. Liturgy in the vernacular and a Bible in every church meant that worship would be made accessible. As Cranmer put it in the Thirty-Nine Articles, 'It is a thing plainly repugnant to the Word of God, and the custom of the primitive Church, to have publick Prayer in the Church, or to minister the Sacraments in a tongue not understanded of the people'.[2] In Cranmer's view, much of the Bible was readily understandable by everyone, whatever their education. In the Homilies, which he provided to supplement what could be learnt simply by hearing Scripture read, he underlines this point:

> For God receiveth the learned and the unlearned, and casteth away none, but is indifferent unto all. And the scripture is full, as well of low valleys, plain ways, and easy for every man to use and walk in; as also of high hills and mountains, which few men can climb unto.[3]

Anglicans making worship accessible: Solomon Islanders carrying the Bible on a canoe at the 2008 Lambeth Conference

Photo © Anglican Communion Office

To be true to itself, Anglican worship would need to continue to be accessible as times changed. We see this aspiration realised at the beginning of the nineteenth century with the authorisation of congregational hymn singing in England and the trend towards accessible preaching, promoted so assiduously by Charles Simeon. When Anglican worship was exported beyond the shores of the British Isles, change would become inevitable, if it were to be accessible in different cultural settings. The template offered by the *Book of Common Prayer* would in practice inhibit change to the essential liturgy of Anglican services. Only in 1958 did serious liturgical revision come onto the agenda of bishops at Lambeth Conferences.[4] But sung worship would evolve, making use of local idiom, as we have seen in Angola and the Solomon Islands. Local symbolism would be included in services, such as when the Bible is carried on a canoe for the gospel reading on a Pacific island. One of my favourite adaptations of Cranmer's Prayer Book canticles is the rendering of *Benedicite, Omnia Opera* in *A New Zealand Prayer Book:*

> *Dolphins and kahawai, sealion and crab,*
> *Coral, anemone, pipi and shrimp:*
> *Give to our God your thanks and praise*
>
> . . . .
>
> *All prophets and priests, all cleaners and clerks,*
> *Professors, shop workers, typists and teachers,*
> *Job-seekers, invalids, drivers and doctors:*
> *Give to our God your thanks and praise.*[5]

Making worship accessible has taken Anglicans beyond making cosmetic changes to a single format. The Church of England's *Common Worship* offers much more variety than Cranmer's *Book of Common Prayer,* in a society accustomed to novelty and creative engagement, from the school classroom onwards. There is room for improvisation alongside authorised liturgical texts. This is not just true of English liturgy. 'As Anglicans we offer praise to the Triune Holy God, expressed through corporate worship, combining order with freedom', concluded the international TEAC working group on the Anglican Way.[6]

This brings us to our next component of authentic Anglicanism. *Anglicans engage with their local context.* Through the parish system, engagement with local context has been an enduring feature of Anglican life. It is seen in Anglican schools, such as the primary school I attended in Ardingly. Across the world, Anglican missionary activity exemplified commitment to the local context, as illustrated by Crowther's schools in Nigeria and the Oxford Mission's orphanage outside Calcutta. The Indian and Nigerian contexts are a reminder that local contexts can include adherents of non-Christian faiths. Anglicans have attempted to engage in such contexts as good neighbours whose faith is attractive, even when faced with hostility from extremists.

Anglicans have combined this engagement with local contexts with a willingness to work collaboratively. An important aspect of this is that *Anglicans work with civil authorities.* When Henry VIII became Supreme Head of the Church of England, the die was cast for Anglican engagement with civil authorities. Anglicans could not act like Anabaptists, who distanced themselves from affairs of state to provide a distinctive Christian witness, as did their descendants the Mennonites. When British interests spread to other parts of the world, Anglicans continued to work with civil authorities. Sometimes there was direct partnership, as in the Niger Expedition or when my grandfather served as a Justice of the Peace in colonial Canada. At times this was compromising for the Church, sometimes severely so, as seen in the Indian residential schools in Canada. At other times the Church's interests were blocked by the authorities, as happened with the East India Company and Lord Lugard's indirect rule in Northern Nigeria.

Anglicans have a global track record in engaging with civil authorities, well beyond the ambiguous experience of the colonial era. In recent times, striking examples are Bishop Dinis Sengulane taking a lead in peace-making in Mozambique, and the Melanesian brothers doing likewise in the Solomon Islands. At times, Anglicans offer challenge or critique. Archbishops of Canterbury are uniquely placed to do this, as we have seen in Pakistan and China. The Church is an 'unreliable ally', observes Rowan Williams, when it comes to working with civil authorities.[7] Nowhere has this been more evident than in South Africa, when Archbishop Desmond Tutu campaigned relentlessly against apartheid. Even after apartheid's fall, Tutu proved himself an 'unreliable ally' of civil authorities, insisting on calling the African National Congress to account.[8] Yet this was in the context of Archbishop Tutu assisting the government by chairing the Truth and Reconciliation Commission. 'The presence of the churches and other recognised religious bodies within society today can often be seen as that of a "critical friend" — to use a favourite term', observed Rowan Williams to an audience of Chinese students and academics at Wuhan University.[9] With this perspective, fault-finding need not always be the default setting for Anglicans. 'How do you respond to those who say the poor will always be with us?' the UN Secretary General, Kofi Annan, asked Archbishop Rowan Williams. This was just before the G8 Summit where Millennium Development Goals would be discussed; '...my real motivation was to ask for spiritual guidance....I had been presented with the view that to make poverty history was impossible.'[10]

The fact that Anglicans engage with their local context and work with civil authorities together illustrate a more general feature of 'being Anglican'. *Anglicans contribute to the common good.* Borrowing a phrase from the Chinese government, they contribute to a 'harmonious society'. We have repeatedly encountered this. When my grandfather was appealing for woollies for shipwrecked sailors, he was continuing the long-standing Anglican tradition of practical caring in the parish. So too was the chaplain in Nice when he organised the building of the *Promenade des Anglais,* to create employment after the lemon tree blight. Wilberforce and Buxton, campaigning against slavery, were working for the common good on a grand scale. We have seen how in modern times Anglicans contribute to the common good all over the world: the Diocese of Jerusalem, with its disproportionate number of schools and hospitals; the Province of Burundi, taking back schools after years of neglect during civil war; the Episcopal Church in New Orleans, in the aftermath of Hurricane Katrina.

This commitment to the common good can be seen as a yet more general feature of 'being Anglican', using a term that has become increasingly prominent in Anglican discourse. *Anglicans mobilise for mission.* Over the past fifteen years, Anglicans have increasingly talked of the five marks of mission, as reflected in the draft Anglican Covenant. This reflects a holistic understanding of mission. It involves responding to human need by loving service, transforming unjust structures of society and safeguarding the integrity of creation, all of which could be regarded as aspects of the common good. It also entails proclaiming the good news and nurturing new believers: evangelism, in other words.

Evangelism has not been universally prominent in Anglican life. Yet the overwhelming majority of Anglicans can trace their lineage to Anglican evangelistic activity. Most Anglican provinces are the result of Anglican missionary activity. In the Western world, Anglicans have been obliged to embrace evangelism more fully in recent years. It was at the 1988 Lambeth Conference that African bishops challenged all Anglicans to relinquish a primarily pastoral mindset and become a movement for mission.[11] In the Church of England, it is only in the past decade that it has been common to speak across church traditions of the Church being 'mission-shaped'. This has been described as a 'quiet revolution'.[12] Faced with the declining church attendance we observed in my grandfather's former parishes, Anglicans are mobilising for mission. The Anglican Communion TEAC working party I served on was in absolutely no doubt that following the Anglican Way means mobilising for mission:

> As Anglicans, we are called to participate in God's mission in the world, by embracing respectful evangelism, loving service and prophetic witness. As we do so in all our varied contexts, we bear witness to and follow Jesus Christ, the crucified and risen Saviour. We celebrate God's reconciling and life-giving mission through the creative, costly and faithful witness and ministry of men, women and children, past and present, across the Communion.[13]

This mobilising for mission carries an implicit logic. *Anglicans nurture personal faith*. 'We cannot separate the evangelisation of those without from the rekindling of devotion within', insisted Archbishop William Temple in the 1940s.[14] This is another feature of 'being Anglican' that has at times been neglected, perhaps understandably where churchgoing was compulsory or the social norm. World War One army chaplains sounded the alarm on this point. Yet to neglect the nurturing of personal faith is to sell Anglicanism short. In Cranmer's words, 'the profession of our faith … must needs kindle a warm fire of love within out heart towards God, and towards all other for the love of God—a fervent mind to seek and procure God's honour, will and pleasure in all things'.[15] At the beginning of Morning and Evening Prayer, Cranmer invited worshippers to 'Rend your heart and not your garments, and turn unto the Lord your God'. The idea of 'allurement' can be seen to epitomise Cranmer's approach to nurturing personal faith in word and sacrament. 'Cranmer wanted a liturgy that promoted the alluring power of the Gospel in a culturally relevant manner', explains Ashley Null.[16]

Since Cranmer's time, Anglicans have increasingly recognised that nurturing personal faith cannot be restricted to church services, even in ostensibly Christian societies. This was reflected in *Towards the Conversion of England*, when it declared that 'most of the worshipping community are only half-converted'.[17] Soon afterwards, even schools set up to promote Christian faith, such as Ardingly College, were supplementing regular worship with missions and small group activity, as we have seen. Actively nurturing Christian faith, so indispensable on the mission field, was needing to become common practice in England too, in the face of declining church attendance. As the sociologist Grace Davie reflected more recently, the Church of England became accustomed to offering 'vicarious religion' to those who were not interested in deeper commitment but were happy to let an active minority pray in their stead.[18] Those who contributed to the free will offering in Binchester but never came to church fitted that pattern. But would this kind of symbiosis be sustainable for much longer? For the children of those born in the 1960s ('Generation Y'), concludes Grace Davie, 'Religion, vicarious or otherwise, is very largely an irrelevance in their day to day lives'.[19]

'The Church of England has not devoted a great deal of time and energy to reflection on the discipleship of the whole people of God in recent times', its General Synod was informed rather sheepishly in 2015. The mandate was nonetheless clear enough. 'Disciples are formed through the ancient discipline of catechesis, teaching the faith to those who are ready to learn more',

Synod was reminded. A local Anglican church should be 'a community which continually invites others to explore the Way of Faith'.[20] One that nurtures personal faith, in other words. Or, again, using classic Christian terminology, one that promotes 'holiness'. For the country parson, according to George Herbert, 'the character of his Sermon is Holiness. . . . [I]t is gained, first, by choosing texts of devotion. . . . Secondly, by dipping, and seasoning all our words and sentences in our hearts, before they come into our mouths.'[21] East African Christianity has been associated with holiness since the so-called East African revival of the 1930s which ignited in Rwanda.[22] When the Dean of Kigali called for a re-examination of 'the evangelisation and discipleship of our own nations' at the 2010 Lausanne Congress, he was appealing to a long-established Anglican tradition of nurturing personal faith and holiness.[23]

So what are the hallmarks of the personal faith and holiness that Anglicans might wish to see nurtured in the 'whole people of God'? The Lambeth Quadrilateral put down some markers on this. *Anglicans assent to historic creeds.* Sunday by Sunday, at services of Holy Communion, Morning Prayer or Evening Prayer, congregations recite one of two creeds: the Nicene Creed and the Apostles' Creed. As we have noted, it is common for Anglicans to turn and face East when reciting the creeds, reflecting a second-century practice where an adult candidate for baptism would face west to 'renounce the Devil and all his works', then turn to face east to pray. For Anglicans, reciting these creeds is intended to be both a symbolic statement and an articulation of their belief. In the words of the Lambeth Quadrilateral, the Nicene Creed serves as 'the sufficient statement of the Christian faith'; the Apostles' Creed, which covers less ground, is 'the baptismal symbol'. This understanding is generally reflected in the canon law of the provinces of the Anglican Communion.[24] When Anglicans seem to sit lightly to aspects of these creeds, there has often been an outcry. When Hensley Henson attempted to restate the doctrines of the Church of England to render them more intelligible, Archbishop Davidson requested written assurance that he still subscribed to the creeds.[25]

These two creeds are the result of General Councils of the early church, but for Anglicans their authority has not simply rested on this fact. General Councils 'may err, and sometimes have erred', according to the Thirty-Nine Articles. 'Wherefore things ordained by them as necessary to salvation have neither strength nor authority, unless it may be declared that they be taken out of holy Scripture.'[26] The creeds 'ought thoroughly to be received and believed: for they may be proved by the most certain warrants of holy Scripture'.[27] In the canon law of the provinces of the Anglican Communion, this understanding of the legitimacy of the creeds has stood the test of time: 'doctrinal formularies shall be consistent with the faith revealed in Holy Scripture, summed up in the creeds'.[28]

With the creeds characterised as subordinate to Holy Scripture, we return once again to Scripture as a defining feature of 'being Anglican'. We have already considered Scripture's credentials in acting as a source of authority in Anglican life. It serves, in the words of the Lambeth Quadrilateral, as 'the rule and ultimate standard of faith'. Borrowing a phrase from the TEAC 'Signposts' statement on the Anglican Way, *Anglicans are formed by Scripture.* 'Accepting their authority,' the TEAC statement goes on to say, 'we listen to the Scriptures with open hearts and attentive minds.'[29] In the ordination service, as we have noted, Cranmer introduced the giving of a Bible, in the place of a chalice and paten. With the examples of Henry Martyn in India and Samuel Crowther in West Africa, we have seen that translation of Scripture was a priority for Anglicans throughout the missionary movement. A key motivation in setting up mission schools was to enable people to read the Bible. For Anglicans, the Bible is not simply intended as a reference book, but something that nourishes personal faith. Queen Elizabeth I exemplified this, reading her Greek New Testament every day.[30]

Yet, as we have noted, Anglicans recognise that applying Scripture is not always straightforward. When it comes, say, to women bishops, there are sharp differences of interpretation. These take account of advances in biblical scholarship. They also keep in mind the traditions of the Church down the ages: both settled convictions and customary practices. As the TEAC 'Signposts' statement puts it: 'As Anglicans, we discern the voice of the living God in the Holy Scriptures, mediated by tradition and reason'.[31] This naturally brings us to two further features of 'being Anglican'. *Anglicans apply reason* and *Anglicans respect tradition.*

Let's take the first of these: *Anglicans apply reason.* As we have seen, Anglicans value scholarly engagement. Cardinal Kasper, discussing the 'many treasures' of the Anglican tradition, at the 2008 Lambeth Conference, numbered among them 'the fine scholarship of Anglican historians and theologians'.[32] B. F. Westcott's vision for the Oxford Mission in India in the nineteenth century was founded on Anglican commitment to scholarly engagement. 'Don't raise your voice, improve your argument', Desmond Tutu liked to say.[33] Back in the sixteenth century, Richard Hooker was clear that reason needed to be applied in order to reap the 'fruit and benefit' yielded by Scripture.[34]

We have also seen ways in which Hooker's contemporaries valued tradition. Jewel and Parker sought to anchor the practices of the Church of England in the pattern set by the early church, including the period immediately following New Testament times. We have witnessed countless ways in which *Anglicans respect tradition*. Their respect for the traditions of the wider church has provided many points of contact in ecumenical engagement. In Vatican II, Anglicans are awarded a special mention as 'separated brethren' of the Reformation where 'some Catholic traditions and institutions continue to exist'.[35] Anglicans respect their own traditions too. Positively, this can be seen in a treasuring of Anglican heritage. It can also be seen in a reluctance to break with precedent. Yet Anglicans are not required to be unquestioning when it comes to tradition. 'Traditions and Ceremonies...at all times...have been divers', according to the Thirty-Nine Articles, 'and may be changed according to the diversities of countries, times and men's manners'.[36] The bottom line is that traditions 'be not repugnant to the word of God'. According to the Thirty-Nine Articles, worshipping and adoration of 'images' and 'reliques' is a test case. In its medieval context, such practice is 'a fond thing vainly invented' and 'repugnant to the word of God'.[37] Some church traditions are 'stinking puddles', parish clergy reading Cranmer's Homilies would declare.[38]

This nuanced approach to tradition has led Anglicans to be cautious about officially designating church practices as sacraments. By the time of the Reformation, the Roman Catholic Church recognised seven sacraments. The Anglican reformers were not prepared to go that far. For them, just two sacraments were singled out as 'certain sure witnesses and effectual signs of God's grace'. The other five practices are treated differently, 'being such as have grown partly of the corrupt following of the Apostles, partly are states of life allowed in the Scriptures'.[39] Confession to a priest, for example, has never become mandatory for Anglicans. We have seen how Nathaniel Woodard, founder of Anglo-Catholic schools, came into conflict with his bishop when he seemed to suggest it should be. Similarly, Anglicans do not have a sacrament of sacred unction, to administer to the dying. This, as we have noted, put Anglican chaplains at a pastoral disadvantage in the trenches of World War One, compared with their Roman Catholic counterparts. When Princess Diana died in Paris, the Anglican chaplain could not have used an authorised Anglican rite for sacred unction, even if he had reached her in time.

Thus, taking their lead from Thomas Cranmer and Matthew Parker in the Thirty-Nine Articles, *Anglicans insist on 'two sacraments ordained by Christ himself'*. These are baptism and the Lord's Supper. They are the two sacraments specified in the Lambeth Quadrilateral. We have witnessed how the practice of baptism, especially of infants, has been a routine feature of parish ministry. We have also seen how the practice of Holy Communion is at the heart of Prayer Book worship and gained new prominence in the wake of the Oxford Movement. Anglicans still disagree amongst themselves about aspects of the theology of baptism and the Lord's Supper. They generally agree that baptism is a sign of regeneration or new birth, by which individuals are incorporated (or 'grafted') into the Church of Christ, including babies. This is one of the common strands in the principles of canon law throughout the Anglican Communion.[40] In addition to this, as a sacrament, baptism is more than just a symbol, it is somehow an 'effectual sign'. However, Anglicans have disagreed—sometimes sharply—about the extent to which faith is required for regeneration to take place. In nineteenth-century England, there was even a high profile court case on the matter, with the Bishop of Exeter threatening to excommunicate the Archbishop of Canterbury if he failed to back his position.[41]

There have been even more acrimonious disputes about the Lord's Supper. It was their views on this issue that led Cranmer, Latimer and Ridley to be burnt at the stake. On the question of the presence of Christ at Holy Communion, Hooker argued soon afterwards for a degree of latitude. 'Let it therefore be sufficient for me presenting myself at the Lord's table to know what there I receive from him, without searching or enquiring of the manner how Christ performeth his promise.... [W]hat these elements are in themselves it skilleth not, it is enough that to me which take them they are the body and blood of Christ.'[42] Yet despite differences of opinion, for Anglicans there are clear parameters about the way the Lord's Supper is celebrated. In the words of the Lambeth Quadrilateral, 'it must be ministered with unfailing use of Christ's words of Institution, and of the elements ordained by him'. It must only be celebrated using authorised forms of service, as stipulated in canon law throughout the Anglican Communion.[43]

For Anglicans, ordination does not formally qualify as a sacrament on a par with baptism and the Lord's Supper. Nevertheless, it can be said unequivocally that *Anglicans rely on ordained priestly ministry*. As we have noted, we need to be careful when discussing priesthood. As the former Archbishop of Canterbury, Michael Ramsey, explained to his ordination candidates:

> In the books of the New Testament the title priest is never given to the ministry: apostles or bishops or presbyters are never called priests. If they had been so described in the early days of Christianity, it might have suggested a kind of continuation of the Levitical priests of the old covenant, and that old order had been totally superseded by the new concept of priesthood in the person of Christ himself. Indeed, in the New Testament there are two uses of the word priest in relation to Christianity: Jesus Christ himself is priest and the whole Church is a priesthood.[44]

Using the English word 'priest' to translate 'presbyter' (or elder) in Cranmer's Ordinal was potentially misleading, when the Church of England was trying to distance itself from the medieval church's model of sacrificing priesthood. In Hooker's view, the nomenclature was nonetheless liveable with: 'whether we call it a priesthood, a presbytership, or a ministry, it skilleth not: although in truth the word presbyter doth seem more fit.'[45] Since then, Anglicans have acknowledged ways in which the term 'priest' is conveniently apt after all, denoting someone set apart to represent and animate the priestly ministry of the whole people of God. This is affirmed in the Final Report of the ARCIC dialogue with the Roman Catholic Church. 'The goal of the ordained ministry is to serve the priesthood of all the faithful.... It exists to help the Church to be "a royal priesthood, a holy nation, God's own people, to declare the wonderful deeds of him who called them out of darkness into his marvellous light." (1 Pet. 2.9).' By presiding at Holy Communion, those ordained priest are 'representative of the whole church in the fulfilment of its priestly vocation of self-offering to God as a living sacrifice (Rom. 12.1).'[46] In their ordination services, Anglicans have recognised ordained priestly ministry as part of a threefold order of ministry going back to the time of the early church. 'Since the ordained ministers are ministers of the Gospel,' the ARCIC report further affirms, 'every facet of their oversight is linked with the word of God.... By the preaching of the word, they seek to bring those who are not Christians into the fellowship of Christ. The Christian life needs also to be unfolded to the faithful.'[47]

This ordained priestly ministry, reflected back in the ARCIC report, has been at the heart of Anglican life since Cranmer's time. We have observed it in North America, West Africa, Scotland, France and many English parishes. However, this ministry has been exercised in a variety of ways. George Herbert's approach to being a country parson may have served as a suitable model for my grandfather in the Lake District and rural Essex. But it was not designed for urban settings or multi-activity churches with large congregations. In some ways it has more in common with the chaplains we have encountered at Ardingly College and University College Oxford. Clergy can continue to exercise this priestly ministry, according to the reformers, despite their imperfections. The 'unworthiness of the minister' does not hinder the effect of the sacrament, according to Article 26.[48] For certain kinds of 'unworthiness', there may come a point when church discipline is needed, as the same Article acknowledges. Yet we can discern a predisposition within Anglicanism for living with the foibles and eccentricities of its clergy.

At times, ordained priestly ministry has been treated as though it was the only Anglican activity that really counted. This was a criticism in the

Archbishops' reports in World War One and in *Towards the Conversion of England*. Yet viewed through the lens of the New Testament, as Michael Ramsey stressed in unison with the ARCIC report, ordained priests 'enable the Church to be indeed the Church of God and to fulfil its mission as the royal priesthood'.[49] This points to another feature of being Anglican. *Anglicans make room for lay initiative.* At the time of the Reformation, there was no choice. Lay people had their say because the Church of England was integrated with the state. Its supreme head—then governor—was a King or a Queen. Parliament authorised changes. Bypassing Parliament could be disastrous, as Archbishop Laud and Charles I discovered when they were both executed in the 1640s. Yet at parish level, successive generations of lay people in England tended to be passive recipients of a ministry provided by an ordained priest. Only a select few served as churchwardens and musicians, patrons and benefactors. However, in the nineteenth century more room began to be allowed for lay initiative. Lay people began to serve in new ways, such as in Sunday schools, religious communities and societies such as the Church Army.

We have noted a more explicit emphasis in recent decades on the place of the 'whole people of God' in the life of the Church of England. We have seen this, for example, in revisions to the Church of England ordinal with regard to the role of the deacon and the priest in harnessing the gifts of lay people. More room is being made for the laity when the Diocese of Carlisle stresses that 'Church is by all and for all' and when bishops reimagining ministry together agree that clergy increasingly need to work collaboratively. Meanwhile, outside England, we have seen room made for lay involvement in church governance in General Conventions and Synods and in the Anglican Consultative Council. We have also acknowledged the significant contribution made by lay women and men in missionary endeavour.

This brings us to another feature of 'being Anglican'. *Anglicans are fuelled by voluntary associations.* Time and again, we have seen how voluntary associations have given a significant boost to Anglican life and witness. Much of the Anglican Communion owes its existence to the endeavours of mission agencies such as SPG, UMCA and CMS. Other mission agencies have concentrated on a particular niche, such as ICS funding ministry to English speakers in continental Europe. Mission agencies have largely been associations of committed enthusiasts, funded by individuals who share the vision. As we have seen, church life and outreach have been enriched by voluntary associations such as the Church Army and theological colleges. In some ways, religious orders can be seen as fitting this pattern too. Anglicans also benefit from non-denominational voluntary associations in which they actively participate. We have noted this in the case of Scripture Union and its camps and the work of university Christian Unions and fellowships, in England and Nigeria. In the case of England, both have fuelled vocations to ordination, as we have seen.

The activities of voluntary associations illustrate a related feature of 'being Anglican'. *Anglicans accommodate pioneering leadership.* We have encountered pioneering leadership on numerous occasions. In Canada, we have seen my grandfather exercising pioneering ministry, carrying out pastoral visiting with his Rolls Royce. However, pioneering leadership is more than being resourceful. It means taking others with you. We have witnessed pioneering leadership in the activities of Henry Venn, Samuel Crowther and the Church Missionary Society; in the setting up of schools by Sister Margaret and Nathaniel Woodard; in Ini Kopuria's founding of the Melanesian Brotherhood and in Bishop Luscombe's activities in continental Europe. Pioneering leadership has often been exercised on the margins of Anglican institutional life. Much of the missionary movement, for example, was not directed by church authorities. Bishop Luscombe, in continental Europe, carved out a role because he saw a need, rather than being commissioned to do so. The recent emphasis on fresh expressions represents a move from the institutional church to make pioneering leadership a mainstream feature of Anglican life in England, under the direct oversight of the diocesan bishop.

This reminds us of another hallmark of 'being Anglican'. *Anglicans are overseen by bishops.* We have repeatedly encountered bishops exercising their ministry. For my grandfather in Canada, it was the Bishop who transferred his training from Vancouver to Winnipeg, who paid a pastoral visit during the dispute about candles and who blocked his move to another diocese. While missionaries tended to operate in advance of bishops, especially in the first half of the nineteenth century, we have observed Bishop Crowther directing missionary work in Nigeria, the Bishop of Calcutta appealing for educated missionaries in India and Bishop Selwyn directing missionary activity in Pacific islands. We have also noted how the Oxford Movement led to increased emphasis on bishops in the life of the Church, including its missionary endeavours, with Zanzibar emerging as a base for missionary activity in East Africa, overseen by a bishop. We have noted the significance of bishops conferring together at the Lambeth Conferences. We have seen the emphasis on a bishop as a leader in mission, highlighted at the 1988 Lambeth Conference and reflected in the programme for the 2008 Lambeth Conference. We have seen Church of England bishops exercising leadership in the face of declining church attendance and financial pressures. We have also noted the significance of the bishop as a focus for unity.

All these reflect an embedded understanding of the place of the bishop in Anglican life. According to the Lambeth Quadrilateral, Anglicans uphold the historic episcopate, 'locally adapted in the methods of its administration to the varying needs of the nations and peoples'. In canon law around the Anglican Communion, the bishop is the chief pastor and principal minister of word and sacraments, with authority to ensure the worthiness of public worship. The bishop has responsibility to teach and safeguard the faith and doctrine of the Church. The bishop also exercises leadership in the governance of the diocese.

The reference to the 'historic' episcopate in the Lambeth Quadrilateral is revealing. The wording was chosen with an eye to strengthening ecumenical relationships with Protestant churches. To insist that bishops were mandated by the New Testament would have alienated churches that had a different form of governance.[50] Anglicans have never agreed amongst themselves whether bishops are part of the 'being' of the church (the 'esse'), the 'well-being' of the church (the 'bene esse') or the 'fullness of being' of the church (the 'plene esse').[51] The Lambeth Quadrilateral therefore described bishops as 'historic', simply acknowledging that bishops have been around since New Testament times. Hooker would have approved, as he argued that church governance was a matter on which Christians could legitimately differ.

Archbishop Laud, for one, would not have been satisfied with this. For him, bishops were a divine institution, which put him on a collision course with the Puritans who believed the opposite and soon scrapped them altogether under Cromwell. Nineteenth-century Anglo-Catholics of course agreed with Laud, seeing bishops as indispensable. 'The Lord Jesus Christ gave His Spirit to His Apostles', Newman proclaimed in Tract 1 of *Tracts for the Times;* 'they in turn laid their hands on those who should succeed them; and these again on others; and so the sacred gift has been handed down to our present Bishops'.[52] Whatever the rationale for bishops, formal conversations with other churches would reflect the Lambeth Quadrilateral and take it for granted that bishops are non-negotiable for Anglicans. This was evident in the formation of the United Churches in India, Pakistan and Bangladesh.

This approach has enabled particularly strong ecumenical relationships with those churches that also have bishops, such as the so-called Porvoo Lutheran Churches. In the Porvoo Agreement, Anglicans and Lutherans cherish bishops as a sign and instrument of the apostolic credentials of the whole Church (its 'apostolicity'). They acknowledge bishops can sometimes fail the Church in this calling, but their shared commitment to bishops permits

Lutheran clergy from Scandinavia to minister to Anglican congregations and vice versa.[53] Churches that do not insist on bishops are not eligible for this interchangeability. So Anglican relations with Protestant churches in France or in Germany cannot attain this degree of communion.[54]

The Church of England's engagement with Protestant churches in Europe is an example of a more general feature of 'being Anglican'. *Anglicans develop their relations with other churches.* From the outset, Anglicans have seen themselves as only part of the catholic Church. They do not expect to have a starring role at all times and in all places. Well before the ecumenical movement, Anglicans saw themselves as complementing the life and witness of other churches outside England. In the early days, the continental Reformed churches had close ties with Anglicans. When Protestants were persecuted in France, Huguenot refugees were welcomed in England, as we encountered in Thorpe, the neighbouring parish to Weeley. The Lambeth Quadrilateral, as we have noted, was designed as a tool for forging closer links with Protestant churches in the nineteenth century. Meanwhile, Anglican missionaries were content to avoid regions covered by non-Anglican missionaries, such as in Northern Nigeria. Reflecting on this, they joined with other missionaries at the 1910 Edinburgh Conference and helped spark the ecumenical movement. Since then, Anglicans have invested heavily in developing relations with other churches, with new possibilities opening up after Vatican II.

This pattern of developing relations with other churches has sometimes led to extreme caution in regions where other churches are more numerous, as we have seen in France. In continental Europe, Anglicans have tended to take meticulous care not to overstep the mark, so have held back from offering ministry in local languages. Yet since the seventeenth century, Anglicans have increasingly taken the opposite approach in situations where they are more numerous themselves. In England, the Act of Uniformity in 1549 had established the *Book of Common Prayer* as the only legal form of worship. But since the Act of Toleration in 1689, Anglicans have ceased to claim exclusive Christian responsibility for any geographical area. Coexistence has gradually given way to collaboration with other churches, as we have seen. In the fresh expressions movement and in English diocesan strategies, we have witnessed efforts to develop grassroots ecumenical cooperation in mission. We have also seen Anglicans and Roman Catholics working together to harvest the fruit of theological dialogue in order to 'grow together in unity and mission' in practical ways.

Amongst themselves, however, Anglicans do carve up geographical areas, placing them under the jurisdiction of bishops. In other words, *Anglicans acknowledge territorial jurisdiction.* This applies not just at the level of the bishop and the diocese. It applies at the level of provinces. The notion of provincial autonomy lies at the heart of the recommendations of the Windsor Report. Anglican provinces are responsible for the oversight of Anglican ministry in the geographical area they cover. In the context of disputes about sexuality, bishops have intervened in other dioceses, without permission from the local bishop. However, even GAFCON statements acknowledge that this is anomalous.[55] Respect for territorial jurisdiction has been standard practice for Anglicans, undergirded by principles established in some of the earliest church councils. In continental Europe, the four overlapping Anglican jurisdictions have been repeatedly designated as anomalies at Lambeth Conferences.[56] Anglicans do not offer a free market in pastoral oversight. This respect for territorial jurisdiction corresponds to the notion of cure of souls at parish level. Bishops' Mission Orders in the Church of England acknowledge that the complexity of modern life may call for flexibility here. Yet initiatives that cut across parish boundaries are still required to be authorised by the bishop, in accordance with the principle of territorial jurisdiction.

Does that mean that Anglican life develops in silos? Not according to the Windsor Report. The Episcopal Church (USA) and the Anglican Church in Canada 'have not attached sufficient importance to the impact of their decisions on other parts of the Communion', the Windsor Report explained.[57] To act without taking due note of other Anglicans was to neglect a critical aspect of being Anglican, the report made clear. Anglicans belong to a communion of churches.[58] Within this global family, *Anglicans are obliged to promote communion.* 'Communion is all about... mutual relationships', the Windsor Report points out.[59] Borrowing the phrase coined at the Anglican Congress in 1963, it depicts 'Anglican life in communion' as 'mutual interdependence and responsibility in the Body of Christ'.[60] In official Anglican reports and ecumenical dialogues, the notion of communion or, to use the Greek equivalent, koinonia, is repeatedly offered as foundational in understanding what it means to be Anglican. This is true, for example, in the Virginia Report and in the ARCIC dialogues.[61] Anglicans do not worship in a patchwork of independent Christian fellowships. Nor do they simply belong to an impersonal institution. As we have seen, Anglicans are connected to one another. Bishops and synods matter. A bishop acts as a focus of unity in a diocese and a means of connection with the universal Church. Synods bring the voice of other clergy and laity into discernment and decision-making. Internationally, the Instruments of Communion by definition are intended to promote communion. The Windsor Report argued that they should be developed in order to do this and exercise their 'moral authority' more effectively.[62] Furthermore, it recommended that an Anglican Covenant be adopted to 'make explicit and forceful the loyalty and bonds of affection which govern the relationships between the churches of the Communion'.[63] As the Covenant drafts were later prepared, their aim was to intensify communion, despite fears that they represented a crude attempt to centralise authority.[64]

Anglican authority is dispersed rather than centralised, as we observed in the last chapter. 'We do not favour the accumulation of formal power by the instruments of unity, or the establishment of any kind of central "curia" for the Communion', the authors of the Windsor Report were careful to point out.[65] Long gone are the days when the sovereign could attempt to impose uniformity. Nevertheless, when it comes to promoting communion, the Archbishop of Canterbury retains a unique role, as 'first among equals' of the bishops. 'From the beginning,' the Windsor Report asserts, 'the Archbishop of Canterbury, both in his person and his office, has been the pivotal instrument and focus of unity; and relation to him became a touchstone of what it was to be Anglican.'[66] Must the Archbishop of Canterbury inevitably play this role? Not according to the Anglican Church in Nigeria, when it changed its constitution in 2005 to remove reference to the See of Canterbury.[67] However, such a challenge must contend with the ways that communion with the See of Canterbury is embedded in the life of the provinces throughout the Anglican Communion. Common principles of canon law include the definition of the Anglican Communion as 'a fellowship of churches...characterised by their historic relationship of communion with the See of Canterbury' and the recognition that 'the churches of the Anglican Communion are bound together...by mutual loyalty maintained through the instruments of Anglican unity as an expression of that communion'.[68] This upholds the bishops' view at the 1930 Lambeth Conference, where they agreed: 'The Anglican Communion is a fellowship, within the one Holy Catholic and Apostolic Church, of those duly constituted dioceses, provinces or regional Churches in communion with the See of Canterbury'.[69]

The contesting of the Archbishop of Canterbury's role in promoting communion brings us to another Anglican attribute. *Anglicans live with disagreement.* At the simplest level, this is inevitable if controversial issues are resolved through dispersed authority. As N. T. Wright and J. I. Packer explain, it is 'the unavoidable result of...Anglicanism's...desire to rule out no questions and clamp down on no discussions, but to give every viewpoint which claims, however freakishly, to be in line with Scripture and reason, opportunity to make its claim good'.[70] As we noted in the previous chapter, there are plenty of drivers for change in Anglican life. How to respond to these drivers for change can lead to disagreement, even conflict. At a local level, we have seen this in the candles controversy in Drumheller and plans for merging chaplaincies in Paris. At provincial and global level, we have seen this in disputes over liturgy, the ordination of women or the recognition of same-sex relationships.

Some of this disagreement can be contained within the 'comprehensiveness' of Anglican life. From Hooker's time onwards, there has been a degree of latitude over beliefs on controversial matters such as aspects of the Eucharist. In some instances, this has been linked to a notion of 'adiaphora', or 'matters regarded as non-essential, issues about which one can disagree without dividing the Church'.[71] Hensley Henson, assessing the Church of England at the time my grandfather moved to his diocese in County Durham, argued that Anglicans must generally resign themselves to doctrinal differences, as the price to be paid for proper theological reflection. 'The doctrinal incoherence of the Church of England, though it is unquestionably perplexing, practically embarrassing and not infrequently actually scandalous, has its roots in something far more respectable than an indolent acquiescence in undiscipline or a reprehensible indifference to truth. It reflects the reluctance of considering and responsible English Churchmen to thrust the rough hand of authority into the sphere of religious opinion.' In Henson's view, it made good sense to 'shrink from discouraging individual efforts to reconcile the theological tradition expressed in creeds and immutable in theory, sacrosanct by time, and the ever-growing knowledge of mankind'.[72]

However, as the Windsor Report observes, 'it has never been enough to say that we must respect or tolerate difference without further ado. Not all differences can be tolerated.'[73] In a benchmark review of Anglican 'comprehensiveness', Stephen Sykes points out that 'the Anglican Communion is not literally all-embracing. As a matter of fact it was unable to include many of those Protestants of the sixteenth or seventeenth centuries who felt the Anglican reformation had been incompletely faithful to the scriptures.' He then appeals to a statement in one of the 1968 Lambeth Conference reports:

> Comprehensiveness demands agreements on fundamentals, while tolerating disagreement on matters in which Christians may differ without feeling the necessity of breaking communion.... [I]t implies that the apprehension of truth is a growing thing: we only gradually succeed in knowing the truth.[74]

At times, as we have seen, Anglicans have in fact felt it necessary to declare impaired communion with other Anglicans who in their opinion have crossed an unacceptable line. In other instances, Anglicans have judged it necessary to leave the Anglican Communion altogether. As Mark Chapman observes, the so-called Anglican *via media* is not an eight-lane motorway, according to Sykes' road map.[75]

Yet sometimes when disagreement is fiercest, another feature of 'being Anglican' can be discerned. *Anglicans experience renewal.* As we have seen, Anglicans from time to time experience movements which bring renewed spiritual devotion. Often they bring controversy too. The evangelical revival renewed preaching, motivated social reform and unleashed the missionary movement. It was criticised for its enthusiasm and reckless open air preaching. The Oxford Movement led to a renewed sense of awe and mystery in worship, together with commitment to the integrity of the Church and its apostolic nature. It was opposed for reintroducing practices that were outlawed at the time of the Reformation. Charismatic renewal brought a fresh willingness to see God at work in daily experience, on God's own terms. It was commonly dismissed as being overly subjective and too disorderly. Although some have been strongly opposed to the ordination of women, many others have celebrated it as evidence of renewal. In so far as it is a product of the Reformation, the Anglican Communion is steeped in the conviction that the Church must be open to reform and renewal. The status quo, in other words, is no guarantee that the Church is as it should be. This brings us full circle back to the first of our features of 'being Anglican'. Anglicans accept the Church must change.

Here endeth a list of twenty-two features of being Anglican. The list is by no means exhaustive, so it is not a full recipe or, to use the navigation analogy, a complete inventory of every bright star in the Anglican constellation. Nor does it provide a simple checklist for assessing whether a particular innovation is Anglican. Rather, it offers a frame of reference. In some ways, it is a 'permission giving' list. Given that Anglicans have shown themselves resistant to change, it subverts some of the common assumptions about Anglican points of reference. Does being Anglican require the singing of particular types of hymn? Not necessarily. The framework invites an imaginative approach to what it means to be authentically Anglican. But it is not unboundaried, even if some of the boundary fences may seem to be languishing in a state of benign neglect. 'We need to learn enough about our own tradition to improvise', Archbishop Justin Welby remarked to a meeting of theological college staff I attended, echoing a theme from a leadership report by the Church of England's Faith and Order Commission.[76]

For a number of the features listed, I have spoken of the latent potential of Anglicanism, rather than universal practice. I could be accused of taking a cup half full approach, when really the cup should be regarded as half empty.

Anglicans do not always make worship accessible or mobilise for mission, to take two obvious examples. But here of course is where my own hand is revealed. I am convinced that the Anglican Communion has a great deal to offer, despite its faults and shortcomings. To realise this potential may call for changing mindsets, as we are witnessing in the Church of England in the renewed emphasis on mission. For the Anglican Communion to flourish as a distinctive family of churches, business as usual is not an option. Yet, I would argue, the features I have proposed provide the kind of circuitry required to generate vibrant Anglican activity across the world. This will require Anglicans to resist being parochial, in the sense of limiting their concern to their own immediate neighbourhood. It will also require Anglicans to reach back towards their inherited sources of authority and bring them into conversation with today's challenges. As we do so, we are not constrained by some of the factors that inhibited change in the past, such as an uncritical belief in the superiority of Western culture and a reluctance to tamper with the cherished liturgy of the *Book of Common Prayer*. 'You cannot go on indefinitely being just an ordinary, decent egg', warned C. S. Lewis, whose *A Grief Observed* inspired the title of this book. 'We must be hatched or go bad.'[77]

I leave you with ten challenges for Anglicans as times continue to change. How can Anglicans:

- mobilise for mission in a complex and interconnected world?
- adapt to local contexts without sell-out?
- build consensus on what Anglicans hold in common?
- combine order with space for disagreement and experimentation?
- relate constructively to the changing landscape of non-Anglican churches?
- be mindful of other Anglicans when changes are considered?
- flourish as a global family of churches without centralised control or bland uniformity?
- promote interdependence internationally without relationships being skewed by uneven finances?
- achieve continuity with Anglican heritage in faithful and imaginative ways?
- be attentive to God's purposes?

Put differently, these ten challenges can be seen as adding up to a single and abiding challenge. How can those who belong to the Anglican family of churches live out their shared vocation as members of one, holy, catholic and apostolic Church, as times change?

As members of *one* Church, Anglicans are obliged to promote communion, develop relations with other churches and live with disagreement. To be authentic members of a *holy* Church, Anglicans must nurture personal faith, insist on the two sacraments ordained by Christ himself, be formed by Scripture and experience renewal.

To live as members of the *catholic* or universal Church, Anglicans must remember the Church is global, engaged with local contexts in diverse settings and jurisdictions, making worship accessible. We must not forget this catholic Church has existed down the ages, with traditions inviting respect as well as rigorous critique.

And if an *apostolic* Church is what Anglicans aspire to be part of, we must embrace the permanent characteristics of the Church of the apostles.[78] These include mobilising for mission, recalling how the apostles were sent by Jesus, with the promise of the Holy Spirit. This does not just apply to religious professionals, however important bishops, priests and deacons may be. Nor does mobilising for mission boil down to institutional self-preservation. The apostles expected all members of the one Church to be enlisted in God's redemptive purposes for the world.

Thomas Cranmer invited Anglicans to reaffirm this last point every time they received the bread and wine at Holy Communion. 'And here we offer unto thee, O Lord, ourselves, our souls and bodies to be a reasonable, holy, lively sacrifice unto thee, that all we, who are partakers of this holy communion, may be fulfilled with thy grace and heavenly benediction.'[79] In Cranmer's day and now, in England, Canada, Nigeria, Pakistan, Scotland, Angola, the USA, Burundi, India, South Africa, France and the Solomon Islands, 'a lively sacrifice unto thee' is ultimately what Anglicans are called to be as times change.

Appendix

A. Questions for Reflection and Discussion

1. What was your earliest experience of 'being Anglican'?
2. In what ways has your understanding of 'being Anglican' changed since then?
3. As you have read *A Church Observed*, what has surprised you about Anglican life and practice?
4. What do you make of the various features of 'being Anglican' identified in Chapter 14 (see section C below)? Which do you think might be hardest to live up to in practice?
5. Can you give examples of what it might mean for Anglicans to 'act locally and think globally'?
6. If the Anglican Communion disintegrated, what do you think would be lost?
7. What might it mean for Anglicans to address any of the ten challenges set out at the end of Chapter 14 (section D below)?
8. If you were writing your own version of *A Church Observed*, what aspects of 'being Anglican' might you wish to emphasise?

B. Twelve Sources of Authority for Anglicans (from Chapter 13)

1. Anglican formularies
2. Tradition
3. Scripture
4. Anglican theorists
5. Church processes
6. Bishops
7. Experience
8. Canon law
9. Mission
10. Attitudes of other churches
11. Practical considerations
12. Reason

C. A Framework for Being Anglican (from Chapter 14)

Anglicans...

1. accept the Church must change
2. make worship accessible
3. engage with their local context
4. work with civil authorities
5. contribute to the common good
6. mobilise for mission
7. nurture personal faith
8. assent to historic creeds
9. are formed by Scripture
10. apply reason
11. respect tradition
12. insist on 'two sacraments ordained by Christ himself'
13. rely on ordained priestly ministry
14. make room for lay initiative
15. are fuelled by voluntary associations
16. accommodate pioneering leadership
17. are overseen by bishops
18. develop their relations with other churches
19. acknowledge territorial jurisdiction
20. are obliged to promote communion
21. live with disagreement
22. experience renewal.

D. Ten Challenges for Anglicans

How can Anglicans:

1. mobilise for mission in a complex and interconnected world?
2. adapt to local contexts without sell-out?
3. build consensus on what Anglicans hold in common?
4. combine order with space for disagreement and experimentation?
5. relate constructively to the changing landscape of non-Anglican churches?
6. be mindful of other Anglicans when changes are considered?
7. flourish as a global family of churches without centralised control or enforced sameness?
8. promote interdependence internationally without relationships being skewed by uneven finances?
9. achieve continuity with Anglican heritage in faithful and imaginative ways?
10. be attentive to God's purposes?

Notes

Introduction

1 Anglican Communion, 'Member Churches', *Anglican Communion* website <http://www.anglicancommunion.org/structures/member-churches> accessed 13.7.13.

2 Archbishops' Council, *The Church of England Yearbook 2012* (London: Church House Publishing, 2011), pp. 335, 367.

3 The European court of human rights (ECHR) ruled in January 2013 that a British Airways check-in worker's right to express her religion had been unfairly restricted when she was prevented from wearing a cross at work. By then, British Airways had changed their policy. See Owen Bowcott, 'Cross Ban Did Infringe BA Worker's Rights, Strasbourg Court Rules', *The Guardian* website, 15 January 2013 <http://www.theguardian.com/law/2013/jan/15/ba-rights-cross-european-court>, accessed 28.3.16.

4 Michael Ramsey, *The Gospel and the Catholic Church* (Peabody: Hendrickson, 2009), p. 188.

5 See W. Taylor Stevenson, 'Lex Orandi–Lex Credendi', in Stephen Sykes and John Booty, *The Study of Anglicanism* (London: SPCK, 1988), pp. 174–88.

6 Theological Education in the Anglican Communion (TEAC) was launched in 2003. See Anglican Communion, 'Education/Studies', *Anglican Communion* website <http://www.anglicancommunion.org/mission/theology/educationstudies> accessed 15.7.14.

7 C. S. Lewis, *A Grief Observed* (London: Faber & Faber, 1966), p. 5.

8 See e.g. Alan Billings, *Lost Church: Why We Must Find it Again* (London: SPCK, 2013) and Roger Scruton, *Our Church: A Personal History of the Church of England* (London: Atlantic Books, 2012).

9 See David Heywood, *Reimagining Ministry* (London: SCM Press, 2011), pp. 15–67.

10 For a brief survey of *missio Dei* in Protestant, Orthodox and Catholic theology see David Bosch, *Transforming Mission: Paradigm Shifts in Theology of Mission* (New York: Orbis, 1993), pp. 390–91.

11 Lambeth Conference, *The Lambeth Conference 1948: The Encyclical Letter from the Bishops Together with the Resolutions and Reports* (London: SPCK, 1948), p. 22.

Chapter 1   Conflict, Colonies and Home Truths

1 Royal Sussex Archive, 'Order of Service for Temporary Laying of Colours', RSR/MSS/11/23, Chichester, County Records Office, 1915 and 'Diary: An Account of the Proceedings of the 5th Cinque Ports Battalion: 18 February 1915–31 March 1919', RSR/MSS/5/72, Chichester, County Records Office, 1915–19, entry for 19 February 1915.

2 Royal Sussex Archive, 'Diary', entry for 4 April 1915.

3 Peter Hancock, *Aubers Ridge* (Barnsley: Pen and Sword, 2005).

4   Hancock, *Aubers Ridge,* p. 56; Royal Sussex Archive, extract from letter dated 14 May 1915 from Lt Col. Langham commanding 5th Royal Sussex Regiment, MS/5/79, Chichester, County Records Office, 1915; see also 'Aubers Ridge Battle / Memorial Service at Crowborough', report of 1933 memorial service at Crowborough in undated article from *Mid-Sussex Times* (author's collection).

5   *Eastbourne Gazette,* May 1915, as quoted in Out of Battle, 'Festubert 1915—5th Sussex in Action', entry for 17 July 2008 on *Out of Battle* blog <http://outofbattle.blogspot.co.uk/2008/07/festubert-1915-5th-sussex-in-action.html> accessed 24.2.14.

6   Royal Sussex Archive, 'Diary', entry for 30 July 1916.

7   Carole Lanoue (ed.), *Canadian Forces Medical Services: Introduction to its History and Heritage* (Ottawa: Director General Health Services, 2003), p. 6.

8   For the history of 8th Canadian Field Ambulance, 1915–1919, see J. Gunn, *Historical Records of No. 8 Canadian Field Ambulance* (Toronto: Ryerson Press, 1920).

9   Philip Byard Clayton, *Tales of Talbot House: Everyman's Club in Poperinghe and Ypres* (London: Chatto and Windus, 1919), p. 18.

10 Gunn, *Historical Records,* p. 9.

11 Clayton, *Tales of Talbot House,* p. 7.

12 Alan Wilkinson, *The Church of England and the First World War* (London: SCM Press, 1978), p. 145.

13 Clayton, *Tales of Talbot House,* p. 53.

14 Clayton, *Tales of Talbot House,* p. 61.

15 Clayton, *Tales of Talbot House,* p. 34.

16 Canadian Great War Project, 'Canadian War Diaries: Medical Units', *Canadian Great War Project* website <http://www.canadiangreatwarproject.com/warDiaryLac/wdLacP09.asp> accessed 29.4.13, entry for 2–3 June 1916, 8th Canadian Field Ambulance.

17 'Canadian War Diaries', entry for 15 October 1917, 8th Canadian Field Ambulance.

18 Siegfried Sassoon, 'Memorial Tablet', in Siegfried Sassoon, *War Poems* (Mineola: Dover Publications, 2004), p. 101.

19 'Canadian War Diaries', entry for 26 October 1917, 8th Canadian Field Ambulance.

20 'Canadian War Diaries', entry for 30 November 1917, 8th Canadian Field Ambulance, Appendix 1, 'With the Canadians in their Attack on Passchendaele Ridge', Sheet 3.

21 'Canadian War Diaries', entry for 30 November 1917, 8th Canadian Field Ambulance, Appendix 1, Sheet 9.

22 'Canadian War Diaries', entry for 30 November 1917, 8th Canadian Field Ambulance, Appendix 1, Sheet 8.

23 'Canadian War Diaries', entry for 26 October 1917, 8th Canadian Field Ambulance.

24 'Canadian War Diaries', entry for 18 February 1918, 8th Canadian Field Ambulance.

25 Gunn, *Historical Records,* p. 125.

26 J. G. Lockhart, *Cosmo Gordon Lang* (London: Hodder & Stoughton, 1949), p. 442.

27 Crawley Papers, 'World War One Correspondence', M126/F, Windsor: St George's House Archives, 1915–19, M126/F/38 (1915).

28 Aidan Crawley, *Leap Before You Look* (London: Harper Collins, 1988), p. 43.

29 Crawley Papers, 'World War One Correspondence', M126/F/40 (1915) and M126/F/211 (1916).

30 Crawley Papers, 'World War One Correspondence', M126/F/275 (1916).

31 S. Roberts, 'Summary Report of the Papers of Arthur Stafford Crawley (1878–1948) and Anstice Katharine Crawley (1881–1963) in the muniments of St George's Chapel Windsor', Historical Manuscripts Commission, GB-0260-M.126, p. 2, *National Archives* website, 1996 <http://www.nationalarchives.gov.uk/nra/lists/GB-0260-M.126.htm> accessed 10.7.13.

32 Crawley Papers, 'World War One Correspondence', M126/B/549 (1919).

33 Alan Wilkinson, *The Church of England and the First World War* (London: SCM Press, 1978), p. 31.

34 Wilkinson, *The Church of England,* p. 130.

35 Wilkinson, *The Church of England,* p. 129.

36 Crawley Papers, 'World War One Correspondence', M126/F/61 (1915).

37 Wilkinson, *The Church of England*, p. 144.

38 Crawley Papers, 'World War One Correspondence', M126/F/275 (1916).

39 See Wilkinson, *The Church of England*, p. 129.

40 Crawley Papers, 'World War One Correspondence', M126/F/53 (1915).

41 'Finis' by Donald Cox in Clayton, *Tales of Talbot House*, p. 109.

42 Crawley Papers, 'World War One Correspondence', M126/F/57 (1915).

43 Wilkinson, *The Church of England*, p. 140.

44 Crawley Papers, 'Italy Diary', M126/K/18, Windsor, St George's House Archives, 1918–19, 22 September, 1918.

45 Wilkinson, *The Church of England*, p. 81.

46 Archbishops' Committees of Inquiry, *Reports of the Archbishops' Committees of Inquiry* (London: SPCK, 1919), 'The Worship of the Church', p. 36.

47 Wilkinson, *The Church of England*, p. 83.

48 E. A. Corbett, *Henry Marshall Tory: A Biography* (Alberta: University of Alberta Press, 1992), pp. 138–57.

49 Gunn, *Historical Records*, p. 105.

50 'Twickenham—New Curate of All Saints', undated press cutting from 1929 (author's collection).

51 Anglican Theological College of Vancouver, 'Anglican Theological College Bulletin: 1923', Vancouver, Anglican Diocese of Vancouver Archives, 1923, p. 4.

52 Anglican Theological College of Vancouver, 'Anglican Theological College Bulletin: 1922', Vancouver, Anglican Diocese of Vancouver Archives, 1922, pp. 4–5.

53 Anglican Theological College of Vancouver, 'Student Body Minute Book', Vancouver, Anglican Diocese of Vancouver Archives, 1923, entry for 23 October 1923.

54 Laurence Wilmot, 'The St John's College Story: A Documentary', Winnipeg, St John's College, 2002, p. xxii.

55 Diocese of Calgary Archives, 'H. L. Nobbs Archive Materials', Calgary: University of Calgary, 1926–28, p. 19.

56 Diocese of Calgary Archives, 'H. L. Nobbs Archive Materials' (1926–28), p. 20.

57 SPG Archive (Society for the Propagation of the Gospel), 'SPG Reports', Oxford, Rhodes House Library, 1926–27, pp. 30–31.

58 Diocese of Calgary Archives, 'H. L. Nobbs Archive Materials' (1926–28), p. 20.

59 Diocese of Calgary Archives, 'H. L. Nobbs Archive Materials' (1926–28), p. 13.

60 See Jeff Sterr, 'Drumheller: From Coal to Cool', entry for 29 May 2013 on *Retroactive: Blogging Alberta's Historic Places* blog <http://www.albertashistoricplaces.wordpress.com/2013/05/29> accessed 8.2.16; and Government of Canada, 'Table 12: Population of Canada by provinces, counties or census divisions and subdivisions, 1871–1931' in Census of Canada, Ottawa, 1931, pp. 98–102, held by Statistics Canada.

61 Diocese of Calgary Archives, 'H. L. Nobbs Archive Materials' (1926–28), p. 17.

62 SPG Archive, 'SPG Reports', p. 29.

63 'It wasn't SPG practice to provide clergy with vehicles of any kind for parish work, let alone a Rolls Royce...but it was actually included in the 1927 Report on p. 31!' Email to author on 7 February 2015 from SPG archivist Catherine Wakeling.

64 Diocese of Calgary Archives, 'H. L. Nobbs Archive Materials' (1926–28), p. 17.

65 'Twickenham—New Curate of All Saints'.

66 See Diocese of Calgary Archives, 'H. L. Nobbs Archive Materials' (1926–28), pp 2–8, 13–14.

Chapter 2 Vision, Enterprise and Anglican Communities

1 Diocese of Calgary Archives, 'H. L. Nobbs Archive Materials', Calgary: University of Calgary, 1926–28, p. 9.

2 David L. Edwards, *Leaders of the Church of England 1828–1944* (London: Oxford University Press, 1971), p. 241.

3 Edwards, *Leaders of the Church of England*, pp. 10–11.

4 Stephen Ferns, 'Attendance at Bishops' Advisory Panels', London, Ministry Council, 2013, p. 2.

5 Robert Reiss, *The Testing of Vocation: 100 Years of Ministry Selection in the Church of England* (London: Church House Publishing, 2013), pp. 84–85.

6 Reiss, *The Testing of Vocation*, p. 328.

7 E.g. the Knutsford Test School. See Reiss, *The Testing of Vocation*, pp. 88–92.

8 Diocese of Calgary Archives, 'H. L. Nobbs Archive Materials' (1926–28), p. 12.

9 JCCC (Joint Committee of the Convocation of Canterbury), *The Position of the Laity in the Church* (London: Church Information Board, 1902), p. 56.

10 Helen Ball, *A Short History of St Bride's Episcopal Church, Glasgow* (Glasgow: Kirklee Books, 2004), p. 24.

11 'Twickenham—New Curate of All Saints', undated press cutting from 1929 (author's collection).

12 David O. McEwan, *Wings of Faith: A History of Saint Kiaran's Scottish Episcopal Church, Campbeltown* (Edinburgh: Scottish Episcopal Church, 2003), p. 128.

13 Kevin Ward, *A History of Global Anglicanism* (New York: Cambridge University Press, 2006), p. 30.

14 McEwan, *Wings of Faith*, p. 128.

15 Donald Lynch, *Chariots of the Gospel: The Centenary History of the Church Army* (Worthing: Walter Ltd, 1982), p. 41.

16 Lynch, *Chariots of the Gospel*, p. 53.

17 Diocese of Calgary Archives, 'H. L. Nobbs Archive Materials' (1926–28), p. 5.

18 John Shelton Reed, *Glorious Battle: The Cultural Politics of Victorian Anglo-Catholicism* (Nashville: Tufton Books, 1996), p. 148.

19 McEwan, *Wings of Faith*, p. 130.

20 Vinovium, 'Binchester: A Short History', *Vinovium* website <http://www.vinovium.org> accessed 4.3.13.

21 'Byers Green Parish' in *Kelly's Directory of Durham* (1890), quoted in Forebears, 'Binchester Genealogy & History', *Forebears* website <http://www.forebears.io/england/durham/byers-green/binchester> accessed 4.3.13. For a discussion of building costs for Victorian churches, see John Wolffe, 'The Chicken or the Egg? Building Anglican Churches and Building Congregations in a Victorian London Suburb', *Material Religion* vol. 9, iss. 1 (2013), 36–59, esp. 49.

22 Adrian Hastings, *A History of English Christianity, 1920–1990* (3rd edn, London: SCM Press, 1991), p. 66.

23 Robert Beaken, *Cosmo Lang: Archbishop in War and Crisis* (London: I. B. Tauris, 2012), p. 153.

24 Owen Chadwick, *Hensley Henson: A Study in the Friction between Church and State* (Norwich: Canterbury Press, 1994), p. 91.

25 Chadwick, *Hensley Henson*, p. 297.

26 Chadwick, *Hensley Henson*, p. 299.

27 Chadwick, *Hensley Henson*, p. 296.

28 Chadwick, *Hensley Henson*, p. 289.

29 Chadwick, *Hensley Henson*, p. 300.

30 Chadwick, *Hensley Henson*, p. 302.

31 See W. S. Baker (ed.), *The Parish Communion* (London: SPCK, 1944).

32 Durham Church Register, 'Byers Green St Peter Parish', EP/13–132, Durham, County Records Office, 1901–85, EP/BG 16 (1938).

33 Durham Church Register, 'Byers Green St Peter Parish', EP/BG 16 (1940).

34 Durham Church Register, 'Byers Green St Peter Parish', PCC Minutes, EP/BG 13 (1940–42).

35 Reginald Perry, *Ardingly, 1858–1946: A History of the School* (London: The Old Ardinians Society, 1951), p. 265.

36 Peter Simpson, *A Thousand Years of Village Christianity: A History of St. Peter's Church Ardingly, Sussex* (Ardingly: Ardingly History Society, 2008), p. 77.

37 David Gibbs, *A School with a View: A History of Ardingly College, 1858–2008* (London: James & James Ltd, 2008), p. 14.

38 Gibbs, *A School with a View*, p. 6.

39 Charles Kingsley (1819–1875), clergyman and Christian socialist, quoted in David Newsome, *Godliness and Good Learning: Four Studies on a Victorian Ideal* (London: Cassell, 1961), p. 207; see also Nick Watson, Stuart Weir and Stephen Friend, 'The Development of Muscular Christianity in Victorian Britain and Beyond', *Journal of Religion and Society*, vol. 7 (2005), 1–21. 'Men who were indifferent to the Victorian ideal of manliness, or repelled by it, found in Anglo-Catholicism an alternative to "muscular Christianity", one that tolerated, even encouraged, personal sensitivity and sometimes extravagant aesthetic expression.' John Shelton Reed, *Glorious Battle: The Cultural Politics of Victorian Anglo-Catholicism* (Nashville: Tufton Books, 1996), p. xxiii.

40 Perry, *Ardingly, 1858–1946*, p. 284.

41 Ardingly College, 'The Ardingly Annals: Number 224', Haywards Heath, Charles Clarke, 1944, p. 74.

42 John Kent, *William Temple: Church, State and Society in Britain 1880–1950* (Cambridge: Cambridge University Press, 1992), p. 190.

43 Leslie Paul, *The Deployment and Payment of the Clergy* (London: Church Information Office, 1964), p. 111.

44 For the full story see Rosalin Barker, *The Whitby Sisters: A Chronicle of the Order of the Holy Paraclete 1915–2000* (Whitby: OHP, 2001).

45 J. G. Lockhart, *Cosmo Gordon Lang* (London: Hodder & Stoughton, 1949), p. 290.

46 Barker, *The Whitby Sisters*, p. 6.

47 See Helen Espir, 'Wemmergill Hall—Memories of School Days During the Second World War, 1940–44', *Lunedale Heritage* project website (2007) <http://www.lunedaleheritage.org.uk/wemmergill_hall.htm> accessed 4.5.13.

Chapter 3   Parsons, Schools and the Conversion of England

1   Kenneth Hylson-Smith, *The Churches in England from Elizabeth I to Elizabeth II: Volume III, 1833–1998* (London: SCM Press, 1998), p. 224.

2   Adrian Hastings, *A History of English Christianity, 1920–1990* (3rd edn, London: SCM Press, 1991), p. 436.

3   Archbishop's Commission on Evangelism, *Towards the Conversion of England* (London: Board of the Church Assembly, 1945), p. ix.

4   Archbishop's Commission on Evangelism, *Towards the Conversion of England*, p. viii.

5   Adrian Hastings, *The Shaping of Prophecy: Passion, Perception and Practicality* (London: Geoffrey Chapman, 1995), p. 61.

6   Archbishop's Commission on Evangelism, *Towards the Conversion of England*, p. 36.

7   Archbishop's Commission on Evangelism, *Towards the Conversion of England*, p. 55.

8   Archbishop's Commission on Evangelism, *Towards the Conversion of England*, p. 45.

9   Hastings, *A History of English Christianity*, p. 437.

10 Hastings, *A History of English Christianity*, p. 438.

11 Ernest Wood, *A History of Thorpe-le-Soken to the Year 1890* (Thorpe-le-Soken: T. C. Webb, 1975), pp. 61–63.

12 Archbishop's Commission on Evangelism, *Towards the Conversion of England*, p. 85.

13 Archbishop's Commission on Evangelism, *Towards the Conversion of England*, p. 82.

14 Hastings, *A History of English Christianity*, p. 438.

15 Hastings, *A History of English Christianity*, p. 437.

16 Durham Church Register, 'Byers Green St Peter Parish', EP/13–132, Durham, County Records Office, 1901–85, correspondence concerning the curate's fund, EP/BG 122 and PCC Minutes, EP/BG 13 (1940–1956).

17 Sally Morris and Jan Hallwood, *Living with Eagles* (Cambridge: Lutterworth Press, 1998).

18 Bill Bryson, *At Home: A Short History of Private Life* (London: Doubleday, 2010), p. 17.

19 Adrian Desmond and James Moore, *Darwin* (London: Penguin Books, 2009), p. 168.

20 Bryson, *At Home,* pp. 16–20.

21 St Andrew's PCC, AGM minutes, Weeley, Weeley Parish Church, 1960.

22 Joanna Trollope, *The Rector's Wife* (London: Bloomsbury, 1991).

23 House of Lords Debates, 'Pastoral Reorganisation Measure', Hansard: 11 July 1949, vol. 163, cc1047-58, *Hansard* website <http://hansard.millbanksystems.com/lords/1949/jul/11/pastoral-reorganisation-measure-1949> accessed 8.2.16.

24 National Archives, 'Parsonage Measure 1938', *National Archives* website <http://www.legislation.gov.uk/ukcm/Geo6/1-2/3/contents> accessed 8.2.16 and 'Parsonages (Amendment) Measure 1947', *National Archives* website <http://www.legislation.gov.uk/ukcm/Geo6/10-11/3/contents> accessed 8.2.16.

25 Peter Simpson, *A Thousand Years of Village Christianity: A History of St. Peter's Church Ardingly, Sussex* (Ardingly: Ardingly History Society, 2008), p. 74.

26 Jon Snow, *Shooting History: A Personal Journey* (London: Harper Collins, 2004), p. 8.

27 Snow, *Shooting History,* p. 14.

28 Ardingly College, 'The Ardingly Annals: Number 254', Haywards Heath, Charles Clarke, 1954, p. 112 and 'The Ardingly Annals: Number 255', Haywards Heath, Charles Clarke, 1955, p. 5.

29 David Gibbs, *A School with a View: A History of Ardingly College, 1858–2008* (London: James & James Ltd, 2008), p. 83.

30 Nigel Argent, *Ardingly College, 1939–1990* (London: Autolycus Press, 1991), p. 140.

31 Ardingly College, 'The Ardingly Annals: Number 256', Haywards Heath, Charles Clarke, 1955, pp. 66, 95.

32 Richard More, *Growing in Faith: The Lee Abbey Story* (London: Hodder, 1982), p. 48.

33 Ardingly College, 'The Ardingly Annals: Number 256', p. 68.

34 Argent, *Ardingly College,* p. 81.

35 Ardingly College, 'The Ardingly Annals: Number 256', p. 68.

36 Hastings, *A History of English Christianity,* p. 440.

37 R. C. Radford, 'On Going to Church' in Ardingly College, in Ardingly College, 'The Ardingly Annals: Number 263', Haywards Heath, Charles Clarke, 1957, p. 179.

38 N. R. MacGibbon, 'Written at Pentecost 1957 and partly inspired by a very ordinary picture' in Ardingly College, 'The Ardingly Annals: Number 263', pp. 176–77.

39 Gibbs, *A School with a View,* p. 90.

40 House of Commons Debates, 'Vesture of Ministers Measure' Hansard: 30 July 1964, vol. 699, cc1865-935, *Hansard* website <http://hansard.millbanksystems.com/commons/1964/jul/30/vestures-of-ministers-measure> accessed 8.2.16.

41 Simpson, *A Thousand Years of Village Christianity,* pp. 84–86.

42 Simpson, *A Thousand Years of Village Christianity,* p. 119.

43 Gibbs, *A School with a View,* p. 31.

44 Peter Simpson, *St Peter's C. E. School Ardingly Then and Now: 1848–1998* (Ardingly: St Peter's C. E. School, 1998), p. 10.

45 Leslie Paul, *The Deployment and Payment of the Clergy* (London: Church Information Office, 1964), p. 22.

46 John A. T. Robinson, *Honest to God* (London: SCM Press, 1963).

47 John Bowden (ed.), *Thirty Years of Honesty: Honest to God Then and Now* (London: SCM Press, 1993), p. 53.

48 Bowden, *Thirty Years of Honesty,* p. 12.

49 Donald Brown, 'Weeley: Through the Ages', Weeley, Parochial Church Council, Weeley Parish Church, 1996, p. 93.

50 Simpson, *A Thousand Years of Village Christianity,* p. 87.

Chapter 4   Enthusiasm and the Unexpected

1   Nigel Argent, *Ardingly College, 1939–1990* (London: Autolycus Press, 1991), p. 325.

2   John Shelton Reed, *Glorious Battle: The Cultural Politics of Victorian Anglo-Catholicism* (Nashville: Tufton Books, 1996), p. 30.

3   John Wolffe, 'Praise to the Holiest in the Height: Hymns and Church Music', in John Wolffe (ed.), *Religion in Victorian Britain: Volume 5* (Manchester: Manchester University Press, 1997), pp. 59–99, pp. 61–62.

4   Wolffe, 'Praise to the Holiest in the Height', p. 63.

5   David W. Bebbington, *Evangelicalism in Modern Britain: A History from the 1730s to the 1980s* (London: Routledge, 1989), p. 204.

6   Reed, *Glorious Battle*, p. 16.

7   Argent, *Ardingly College*, p. 82.

8   Argent, *Ardingly College*, p. 82.

9   Ian Hislop, 'Atheist with Doubts: A C of E "Don't Know"' in Caroline Chartres (ed.), *Why I am Still an Anglican* (London: Continuum, 2006), pp. 99–107, pp. 100.

10   Argent, *Ardingly College*, p. 87.

11   Argent, *Ardingly College*, p. 79.

12   Hislop, 'Atheist with Doubts', pp. 100–101.

13   Glen Hocken, 'Recollections of Ardingly College' (2013), emailed to author 28.10.2013.

14   Argent, *Ardingly College*, p. 57.

15   Jonathan Perkin, email to the author, 19 July 2013.

16   John Eddison (ed.), *Bash: A Study in Spiritual Power* (Basingstoke: Marshall, Morgan & Scott, 1982), p. 69. In very recent times, Revd Nash's far-sighted vision has had negative publicity. This resulted from allegations that, fifty years after the camps were founded, a volunteer leader brutally abused boys he met on camps associated with this vision, when he invited them to his home. The leader in question was not involved in camps attended by pupils from Ardingly College. See Justin Welby, 'Statement on behalf of the Archbishop of Canterbury', *Archbishop of Canterbury* website, 1 February 2017 <http://www.archbishopofcanterbury.org/articles.php/5833/statement-on-behalf-of-the-archbishop-of-canterbury> accessed 12.6.17.

17   Eddison, *Bash*, p. 19.

18   David Edwards and John Stott, *Essentials: A Liberal–Evangelical Dialogue* (London: Hodder & Stoughton, 1988), p. 1.

19   Michael Green, *Adventure of Faith: Reflections on Fifty Years of Christian Service* (Michigan: Zondervan, 2001), p. 209.

20   David W. Bebbington, *Evangelicalism in Modern Britain: A History from the 1730s to the 1980s* (London: Routledge, 1989), p. 149.

21   For a more positive evaluation of 18th Century clergy, see David Hempton, *The Church in the Long Eighteenth Century* (London: I. B. Tauris, 2011), pp. 170–73.

22   Bebbington, *Evangelicalism in Modern Britain*, p. 21.

23   Bebbington, *Evangelicalism in Modern Britain*, p. 22.

24   D. Bruce Hindmarsh, *John Newton and the English Evangelical Tradition* (Michigan: Eerdmans, 1996), p. 91.

25   Hempton, *The Church in the Long Eighteenth Century*, p. 167.

26   See Bebbington, *Evangelicalism in Modern Britain*, pp. 2–17 for evangelical characteristics sometimes referred to as 'the Bebbington Quadrilateral'. See also Mark Hutchinson and John Wolffe, *A Short History of Global Evangelicalism* (Cambridge: Cambridge University Press, 2012), pp. 16–17.

27   Wolffe, 'Praise to the Holiest in the Height', p. 62 and Hindmarsh, *John Newton and the English*

Evangelical Tradition, p. 278.

28 Bebbington, *Evangelicalism in Modern Britain,* p. 106.

29 Bebbington, *Evangelicalism in Modern Britain,* p. 106.

30 Bebbington, *Evangelicalism in Modern Britain,* p. 146.

31 John Charles Ryle, 'The Teaching of the Ritualists not the Teaching of the Church of England', Church Association Tract 4, p. 1, *Church Society* (archived) website <http://archive.churchsociety.org/publications/tracts/CAT004_RyleRitualism.pdf> accessed 22.2.13.

32 Alister McGrath, *The Renewal of Anglicanism* (Harrisburg: Morehouse Publishing, 1993), p. 74.

33 Bebbington, *Evangelicalism in Modern Britain,* p. 218.

34 See Randle Manwaring, *From Controversy to Co-Existence: Evangelicals in the Church of England, 1914–1980* (Cambridge: Cambridge University Press, 1985) and Bebbington, *Evangelicalism in Modern Britain,* pp. 181–228.

35 Argent, *Ardingly College,* p. 83.

36 Adrian Hastings, *A History of English Christianity, 1920–1990* (3rd edn, London: SCM Press, 1991), p. 455.

37 For details of Stott's impact through the landmark 1967 National Evangelical Anglican Conference in Keele see Alister Chapman, *Godly Ambition: John Stott and the Evangelical Movement* (New York: Oxford University Press, 2012), pp. 95–97 and Roger Steer, *Inside Story: The Life of John Stott* (Nottingham: IVP, 2009), pp. 135–43; Stott's call for evangelical Anglicans to renounce a ghetto mentality set the tone for the 1970s and beyond.

38 See Christopher J. Cocksworth, *Evangelical Eucharistic Thought in the Church of England* (Cambridge: Cambridge University Press, 1993) and John Maiden, 'Evangelical and Anglo-Catholic Relations 1928–1983', in Andrew Atherstone and John Maiden (eds), *Evangelicalism and the Church of England in the Twentieth Century* (Woodbridge: Boydell, 2014), pp. 136–61.

39 Andrew Atherstone, *Risk-Taker and Reconciler: Archbishop Justin Welby* (London: Darton, Longman & Todd, 2014), pp. 38–39.

40 Jackie Pullinger and Andrew Quicke, *Chasing the Dragon* (Sevenoaks: Hodder & Stoughton, 1980).

41 Atherstone, *Risk-Taker and Reconciler,* p. 50.

42 General Synod, *The Charismatic Movement in the Church of England* (London: CIO Publishing, 1981).

43 General Synod, *The Charismatic Movement,* p. 7.

44 James H. S. Steven, *Worship in the Spirit: Charismatic Worship in the Church of England* (Oregon: Wipf & Stock, 2002), p. 14.

45 General Synod, *The Charismatic Movement,* p. 8; Steven, *Worship in the Spirit,* p. 17.

46 Steven, *Worship in the Spirit,* p. 13.

47 General Synod, *The Charismatic Movement,* p. 9.

48 General Synod, *The Charismatic Movement,* p. 11.

49 Michael Harper (ed.), *Bishops' Move: Six Anglican Bishops Share Their Experience of Renewal* (London: Hodder & Stoughton, 1978), p. 160.

50 General Synod, *The Charismatic Movement,* p. 35.

51 General Synod, *The Charismatic Movement,* p. 10.

52 General Synod, *The Charismatic Movement,* p. 36.

53 General Synod, *The Charismatic Movement,* p. 36.

54 General Synod, *The Charismatic Movement,* pp. 47–48.

55 Hindmarsh, *John Newton and the English Evangelical Tradition,* p. 90.

56 John Cornwell, *Newman's Unquiet Grave: The Reluctant Saint* (London: Continuum, 2010), p. 57.

57 Hastings, *A History of English Christianity,* p. 446.

58 Anthony Jennings and Harry Thompson (eds), 'The Cherwell Guide to Oxford', Oxford, Oxford Student Press, 1981, p. 16.

59 Robin Darwall-Smith, 'Revd W. G. D. Sykes, MA, Fellow and Chaplain', obituary on *University*

College Oxford website, 19 January 2015 <http://www.univ.ox.ac.uk/Billsykes> accessed 28.1.15.

60 Stephen Sykes, 'The Anglican Character', in Ian Bunting (ed.), *Celebrating the Anglican Way* (London: Hodder & Stoughton, 1996).

61 University College Oxford, 'Memorial Service for The Reverend William Sykes', *University College Oxford* website <http://univ.ox.ac.uk/univ-news/memorial-service-reverend-william-sykes> accessed 1.7.15.

62 Michael Green, *Adventure of Faith: Reflections on Fifty Years of Christian Service* (Michigan: Zondervan, 2001), p. 220.

63 Michael Green, *Compelled by Joy* (Nottingham: IVP, 2011), p. 21.

64 David Watson, *You are my God: An Autobiography* (Sevenoaks: Hodder & Stoughton, 1983), p. 39.

65 Teddy Saunders and Hugh Sansom, *David Watson: A Biography* (Sevenoaks: Hodder & Stoughton, 1992), p. 140.

66 Email to the author, 18 January 2015.

67 Green, *Adventure of Faith*, p. 54.

68 Green, *Compelled by Joy*, p. 94.

69 See Lesslie Newbigin, *The Other Side of 1984: Questions for the Churches* (Geneva: WCC, 1983) and *Foolishness to the Greeks: Gospel and Western Culture* (London: SPCK, 1986).

70 Os Guinness, *Doubt* (Oxford: Lion, 1983).

71 See Os Guinness, *The Gravedigger File* (London: Hodder & Stoughton, 1983).

72 Bryan Magee, *Men of Ideas* (Oxford: Oxford University Press, 1978), p. 107.

73 Letter to the author from former OICCU member, 13 May 1983.

Chapter 5 Not Just the White Man's God

1 Constance Millington, *Whether We Be Many or Few: A History of the Cambridge/Delhi Brotherhood* (Bangalore: Asian Trading Corporation, 1999), pp. 4–5.

2 Andrew Porter, *Religion Versus Empire?* (Manchester: Manchester University Press, 2004), p. 235.

3 Gillian Wilson (ed.), *Theodore: Letters from the Oxford Mission in India 1946–1993* (Romsey: The Oxford Mission, 1997), p. x.

4 Wilson, *Theodore*, p. 316.

5 Brian Stanley, *The Bible and the Flag* (Leicester: Apollos, 1990), p. 99.

6 Kevin Ward, *A History of Global Anglicanism* (New York: Cambridge University Press, 2006), p. 235; Colin Podmore, *Aspects of Anglican Identity* (London: Church House Publishing, 2005), pp. 89–91.

7 Paul Harrison and Robin Palmer, *News Out of Africa: Biafra to Band Aid* (London: Hilary Shipman, 1986), p. 82.

8 Elliott Kendall, *The End of an Era: Africa and the Missionary* (London: SPCK, 1978).

9 Kendall, *The End of an Era*, pp. 87, 108.

10 Toyin Falola and Matthew M. Heaton, *A History of Nigeria* (New York: Cambridge University Press, 2008), p. 214.

11 Falola and Heaton, *A History of Nigeria*, p. 213.

12 See Bill Roberts, *Life and Death Among the Ibos* (London: Scripture Union, 1970).

13 Roberts, *Life and Death Among the Ibos*, p. 79.

14 Lindsay Brown, *Shining Like Stars: The Power of the Gospel in the World's Universities* (Chorley: 10 Publishing, 2010), p. 104.

15 David Gitari, *Troubled But Not Destroyed: The Autobiography of Archbishop David Gitari* (McLean, Virginia: Isaac Publishing, 2014), p. 19.

16 For the history of Deeper Life Ministry see Alton Loveless, *A Look at Some of the World's Largest Churches* (Columbus: FWB Publications, 2015), pp. 11–13 and Alan Isaacson, *Deeper Life: The Extraordinary Growth of the Deeper Life Bible Church* (London: Hodder & Stoughton, 1990), esp. pp. 57, 66 for

Sunday attendance in the 1980s.

17 Ogbu Kalu (ed.), *Christianity in West Africa: The Nigerian Story* (Ibadan: Day Star Press, 1978), pp. 386, 388.

18 Kalu, *Christianity in West Africa,* p. 386.

19 Stanley, *The Bible and the Flag,* p. 15.

20 Tristram Hunt, *Ten Cities that Made an Empire* (London: Penguin, 2014), p. 89.

21 Stewart Brown, *Providence and Empire: Religion, Politics and Society in the United Kingdom 1815–1914* (Harlow: Pearson Education Limited, 2008), p. 41.

22 Brown, *Providence and Empire,* p. 41.

23 Brown, *Providence and Empire,* pp. 141–43.

24 Peter B. Clarke, *West Africa and Christianity* (London: Edward Arnold Publishers, 1986), p. 63.

25 Jacob Ade Ajayi, *Christian Missions in Nigeria: 1841–1891* (Evanston: North Western University Press, 1965), p. 184.

26 Ajayi, *Christian Missions in Nigeria,* p. 185.

27 Ajayi, *Christian Missions in Nigeria,* p. 208.

28 Ajayi, *Christian Missions in Nigeria,* p. 218.

29 Kalu, *Christianity in West Africa,* p. 101.

30 Chinua Achebe, *Things Fall Apart* (London: Heinemann, 1958).

31 Chinua Achebe, *There was a Country* (London: Allen Lane, 2012), back cover sleeve.

32 Stanley, *The Bible and the Flag,* pp. 63–64.

33 Ruth Wishart, 'It Seems I Only Know What I Think When I've Heard What I've Said', *The Guardian,* 21 November 1984.

34 Stanley, *The Bible and the Flag,* p. 161.

35 Stanley, *The Bible and the Flag,* p. 157.

36 Emmanuel Okolugbo, *The Ndosumili and The Ukwuani: A History of Christianity in Nigeria* (Ibadan: Daystar Press, 1984), p. 78.

37 Achebe, *Things Fall Apart,* p. 127.

38 Ajayi, *Christian Missions in Nigeria,* p. 250, quoted in Clarke, *West Africa and Christianity,* p. 67 and Kalu, *Christianity in West Africa,* p. 31.

39 Stanley, *The Bible and the Flag,* p. 166.

40 Kalu, *Christianity in West Africa,* p. 38.

41 Okolugbo, *A History of Christianity in Nigeria,* p. 78.

42 Andrew Norman, 'The White Man's God in the White Man's Grave', unpublished report, 1985, p. 71.

43 David Smith, 'The Communication of the Christian Faith in Africa', Emem Publications, 1983, pp. 85–89.

44 Chinua Achebe, *No Longer at Ease* (London: Heinemann, 1960).

45 Geoffrey Moorhouse, *The Missionaries* (London: Eyre Methuen, 1973), p. 107.

46 Steven Maughan, *Mighty England Do Good: Culture, Faith, Empire, and World in the Foreign Missions of the Church of England, 1850–1915* (Cambridge: Eerdmans, 2014), p. 467.

47 Falola and Heaton, *A History of Nigeria,* p. 99.

48 Kalu, *Christianity in West Africa,* p. 59.

49 Kalu, *Christianity in West Africa,* p. 66.

50 See Paul Anber, 'Modernisation and Political Disintegration: Nigeria and the Ibos', *The Journal of Modern African Studies,* vol. 5, iss. 2 (1967), 163–79 and Achebe, *There was a Country,* pp. 74–75.

51 Kalu, *Christianity in West Africa,* p. 74.

52 Kalu, *Christianity in West Africa,* p. 152.

53 Kalu, *Christianity in West Africa,* p. 131.

54 Kalu, *Christianity in West Africa,* p. 131.

55 Kalu, *Christianity in West Africa*, p. 102.

56 See Kalu, *Christianity in West Africa*, pp. 131–33 for the account that follows and Edward Hulmes, 'Walter Miller and the Isawa: An Experiment in Christian Muslim Relationships', *Scottish Journal of Theology*, vol. 41 (1988), 233–46.

57 Kalu, *Christianity in West Africa*, p. 134.

58 Anthony Kirk-Green and Douglas Rimmer, *Nigeria Since 1970: A Political and Economic Outline* (London: Hodder & Stoughton, 1981), p. 9.

59 John Clarke, *Yakubu Gowon: Faith in a United Nigeria* (London: Frank Cass, 1987), pp. 145–46.

60 See *West Africa Magazine*, 9 September 1985.

61 Peter John Dominy, 'Church and Change on the Jos Plateau, Nigeria', MLitt thesis, University of Aberdeen, 1983.

62 See Lauren Potts, 'Remembering the York Minster Fire 30 Years On', *BBC News* website <http://www.bbc.co.uk/news/uk-england-york-north-yorkshire-28112373> accessed 28.8.15.

Chapter 6   Civil Strife, Urban Life, and Anglican Heritage

1 Peter Aughton, *Liverpool: A People's History* (Lancaster: Carnegie Publishing, 2008), p. 173.

2 Aughton, *Liverpool*, p. 293.

3 Archbishop of Canterbury's Commission on Urban Priority Areas, *Faith in the City: A Call for Action by Church and Nation* (London: Church House Publishing, 1985).

4 John Campbell, *Margaret Thatcher: The Iron Lady* (London: Jonathan Cape, 2003), p. 390.

5 Adrian Hastings, *A History of English Christianity, 1920–1990* (4th edn, London: SCM Press, 2001), p. xxxviii.

6 Ian Hernon, *Riot! Civil Insurrection from Peterloo to the Present Day* (London: Pluto Press, 2006), p. 198.

7 Hernon, *Riot!*, pp. 201–9; See also Michael Leroy, 'Riots in Liverpool 8: Some Christian Responses', London, Evangelical Coalition for Urban Mission, 1983.

8 Commission on Urban Priority Areas, *Faith in the City*, p. xiii.

9 Commission on Urban Priority Areas, *Faith in the City*, p. 18.

10 Commission on Urban Priority Areas, *Faith in the City*, p. 27.

11 Commission on Urban Priority Areas, *Faith in the City*, p. 77.

12 Commission on Urban Priority Areas, *Faith in the City*, p. 66.

13 Commission on Urban Priority Areas, *Faith in the City*, p. 75. Italics original.

14 For GUML and Liverpool's response to *Faith in the City* see Neville Black, 'Two Years On: The Liverpool Perspective', *Anvil*, vol. 5, no. 1 (1988), 17–21.

15 Aughton, *Liverpool*, p. 107.

16 Adrian Hastings, *A History of English Christianity, 1920–1990* (3rd edn, London: SCM Press, 1991), p. 602.

17 Commission on Urban Priority Areas, *Faith in the City*.

18 Commission on Urban Priority Areas, *Faith in the City*, p. 66.

19 Commission on Urban Priority Areas, *Faith in the City*, p. 74.

20 Robert Holland, *Blue-Water Empire: The British in the Mediterranean since 1800* (London: Penguin, 2013), p. 315.

21 Henry Joseph Corbett Knight, *The Diocese of Gibraltar; A Sketch of its History, Work and Tasks* (London: SPCK, 1917), p. 42.

22 Humphrey Carpenter, *Robert Runcie: The Reluctant Archbishop* (London: Hodder & Stoughton, 1996), p. 346.

23 Carpenter, *Robert Runcie*, p. 358.

24 CNN, 'Princess Diana's Anti-Mine Legacy', *CNN* website, 10 September 1997 <http://edition.cnn.com/WORLD/9709/10/diana.angola/> accessed 17.12.15.

25 Margaret Joan Anstee, *Orphan of the Cold War: The Inside Story of the Collapse of the Angolan Peace Process, 1992-3* (Basingstoke: Macmillan Press, 1996).

26 Anstee, *Orphan of the Cold War,* p. 237.

27 Guus Meijer and David Birmingham, 'Angola from Past to Present', *Accord* online journal, iss. 15, 2004 <http://www.c-r.org/accord-article/angola-past-present> accessed 7.2.16.

28 See Angola London Mozambique Association, 'A Brief History of the Anglican Church in Angola', *ALMA Link* website <http://www.almalink.org/dioceses/bhistang.htm> accessed 7.7.13.

29 Adrian Chatfield, *Something in Common: An Introduction to the Principles and Practices of Worldwide Anglicanism* (Nottingham: St John's Extension Studies, 1998), p. 12.

30 Alastair Redfern, *Being Anglican* (London: Darton, Longman & Todd, 2000), p. 129.

31 Dinis Sengulane and Jaime Goncalves, 'A Calling for Peace: Christian Leaders and the Quest for Reconciliation in Mozambique', *Accord* online journal, iss. 3, 1998 <http://www.c-r.org/accord-article/calling-peace-christian-leaders-and-quest-reconciliation-mozambique> accessed 7.2.16.

32 See David Gitari, *Troubled But Not Destroyed: The Autobiography of Archbishop David Gitari* (McLean, Virginia: Isaac Publishing, 2014), pp. 243–51 and Graham Kings, 'The Most Revd Dr David Gitari', *Church Times,* 18 October 2013, also online at <https://www.churchtimes.co.uk/articles/2013/18-october/gazette/obituaries/the-most-revd-dr-david-gitari> accessed 28.3.16.

33 See Alex Vines, 'Sant'Egidio and the Mozambique Peace Process', *Accord* online journal, iss. 3, 1998 <http://www.c-r.org/accord-article/calling-peace-christian-leaders-and-quest-reconciliation-mozambique> accessed 7.2.16; George Carey, *Know the Truth: A Memoir* (London: Harper Collins, 2004), p. 436; Andrea Riccardi, *Sant'Egidio, Rome and the World* (Rome: St Pauls, 1996), pp. 80–93.

34 Bishop Dinis Sengulane would wear his cross made from former weapons when campaigning against gun violence in the USA too. See Peggy Eastman, 'Tears of God', *Living Church* website, 26 March 2013 <http://www.livingchurch.org/tears-god> accessed 17.12.15.

35 Robert Reiss, *The Testing of Vocation: 100 Years of Ministry Selection in the Church of England* (London: Church House Publishing, 2013), p. 37.

36 Andrew Porter, *Religion Versus Empire?* (Manchester: Manchester University Press, 2004), p. 248.

37 See Reiss, *The Testing of Vocation,* p. 274.

38 See Reiss, *The Testing of Vocation,* p. 275 n. 55.

39 Steering Group for Theological Courses, *Theological Training: A Way Ahead* (London: Church House Publishing, 1992).

40 Steering Group for Theological Courses, *Theological Training,* p. 1.

41 Leslie Paul, *The Deployment and Payment of the Clergy* (London: Church Information Office, 1964), p. 22.

42 Steering Group for Theological Courses, *Theological Training,* p. 86.

43 Steering Group for Theological Courses, *Theological Training,* p. 193.

44 Letter from Graham Cray to all students and staff at Ridley Hall, 20 January 1993 (author's collection).

45 Reiss, *The Testing of Vocation,* p. 278.

46 See e.g. Trevor Beeson, *The Church of England in Crisis* (London: Davis-Poynter, 1973), p. 9.

47 Steering Group for Theological Courses, *Theological Training,* p. 103.

48 David Watson, *You are my God: An Autobiography* (Sevenoaks: Hodder & Stoughton, 1983), pp. 36–38.

49 John A. T. Robinson, *Honest to God* (London: SCM Press, 1963).

50 Hugh McLeod, *The Religious Crisis of the 1960s* (Oxford: Oxford University Press, 2007), p. 84.

51 John Hick (ed.), *The Myth of God Incarnate* (London: SCM Press, 1977), p. ix.

52 Rowan Williams, *Anglican Identities* (London: Darton, Longman & Todd, 2004), p. 115.

53 Williams, *Anglican Identities,* p. 115.

54 Williams, *Anglican Identities,* p. 120.

55 On the quest for the historical Jesus, see Stephen Neill and Tom Wright, *The Interpretation of the New Testament 1861–1986* (Oxford: Oxford University Press, 1988), pp. 379–403.

56 Whether Cranmer himself had joined discussions in the White Horse Tavern is disputed. Stephen Neill is among those who believe he did; see *Anglicanism* (Middlesex: Penguin Books, 1958), p. 52. Cranmer's biographer, Diarmaid MacCulloch, is much more sceptical, believing he took longer to come round to Luther's ideas; see *Thomas Cranmer: A Life* (London: Yale University Press, 1996), p. 25.

57 Quoted in J. C. Ryle, *Five English Reformers* (Carlisle: Banner of Truth, 1960), p. 149.

58 Alison Weir, *Elizabeth the Queen* (London: Vintage, 2008), p. 1.

59 See Alister McGrath, *The Renewal of Anglicanism* (Harrisburg: Morehouse Publishing, 1993), p. 88.

60 For the changes proposed by Archbishop Parker see Martin Davie, *Our Inheritance of Faith: A Commentary on the Thirty Nine Articles* (Malton: Gilead, 2013), pp. 52–55.

61 See MS 121, pp. 233–66 on Corpus Christi College and the Stanford University Libraries, *Parker Library* website <https://parker.stanford.edu> accessed 8.2.16.

62 Church Assembly, *Book of Common Prayer: 1662 Version* (Oxford: Oxford University Press, 1965), p. 689.

63 McGrath, *The Renewal of Anglicanism,* p. 88.

64 Geoffrey Rowell (ed.), *The English Religious Tradition and the Genius of Anglicanism* (Oxford: Ikon Productions, 1992), p. 27; Paul Avis, *The Identity of Anglicanism: Essentials of Anglican Ecclesiology* (London: T&T Clark, 2007), p. 32.

65 Quoted in Richard H. Schmidt, *Glorious Companions: Five Centuries of Anglican Spirituality* (Michigan: Eerdmans, 2002), p. 19.

66 Davie, *Our Inheritance of Faith,* p. 75.

67 Davie, *Our Inheritance of Faith,* p. 76.

68 Quoted in Davie, *Our Inheritance of Faith,* p. 72.

69 See e.g. Stephen Sykes and John Booty, *The Study of Anglicanism* (London: SPCK, 1988), p. 141.

70 Davie, *Our Inheritance of Faith,* pp. 75–80.

71 Reiss, *The Testing of Vocation,* p. 263.

Chapter 7 *Aggiornamento:* 'Bringing Up to Date'

1 Maggi Dawn, *Like the Wideness of the Sea: Women Bishops and the Church of England* (London: Darton, Longman & Todd, 2013), p. 50.

2 See Henrietta Blackmore (ed.), *The Beginning of Women's Ministry: The Revival of the Deaconess in the Nineteenth Century Church of England* (Suffolk: Boydell Press, 2007), pp. 42–44. The 1868 Diocese of London service of admission in 1868 includes a prayer of blessing with the bishop laying on his hands.

3 Brian Heeney, *The Women's Movement in the Church of England 1850–1930* (Oxford: Clarendon Press, 1988), p. 68 and Dawn, *Like the Wideness of the Sea,* p. 12.

4 See Blackmore, *The Beginning of Women's Ministry,* p. 42.

5 For Lambeth Conference (1920) Resolutions 48 and 50 see Roger Coleman (ed.), *Resolutions of the Twelve Lambeth Conferences 1867–1988* (Toronto: Anglican Book Centre, 1992), p. 60.

6 General Synod, *Deacons in the Ministry of the Church* (London: Church House Publishing, 1988), p. 123.

7 Steering Group for Theological Courses, *Theological Training: A Way Ahead* (London: Church House Publishing, 1992), p. 197.

8 Jim White, 'Oh for a Dog Collar of our Own', *The Independent,* 6 November 1992, p. 17.

9 Ridley Hall, 'Ridley Hall College Handbook', Cambridge, Ridley Hall, 1992, no page numbers.

10 Votes cast were as follows: House of Bishops 39 Ayes, 13 Noes (75%); House of Clergy 176 Ayes, 74 Noes (70.4%); House of Laity 169 Ayes, 82 Noes (67.3%). See Colin Buchanan, *Taking the Long View: Three and a Half Decades of General Synod* (London: Church House Publishing, 2006), p. 173.

11 Peter Owen Jones, *Bed of Nails: An Advertising Executive's Journey Through Theological College* (Oxford: Lion Publishing, 1996), p. 35.

12 Dawn, *Like the Wideness of the Sea,* p. 2.

13 Bruce N. Kaye, *An Introduction to World Anglicanism* (Cambridge: Cambridge University Press, 2008), pp. 158–59 and Buchanan, *Taking the Long View*, p. 163. The ACC voted 24–22 in favour.

14 Buchanan, *Taking the Long View*, pp. 163–64.

15 David Hein and Gardiner Shattuck, *The Episcopalians* (New York: Church Publishing, 2004), p. 141.

16 Kaye, *An Introduction to World Anglicanism*, pp. 159–60.

17 See Esther Mombo, 'The Ordination of Women in Africa: A Historical Perspective', in Ian Jones et al. (eds), *Women and Ordination in the Christian Churches* (London: T&T Clark, 2008), pp. 123–43, p. 131.

18 For the 1988 Lambeth Conference resolution on women and the episcopate see Coleman, *Resolutions of the Twelve Lambeth Conferences 1867–1988*, p. 193.

19 Coleman, *Resolutions of the Twelve Lambeth Conferences 1867–1988*, pp. 132–33.

20 Heeney, *The Women's Movement in the Church of England 1850–1930*, p. 96.

21 Heeney, *The Women's Movement in the Church of England 1850–1930*, pp. 96–99, 104.

22 Archbishops' Commission on Women and Holy Orders, *Women and Holy Orders* (London: Church Information Office, 1966).

23 Buchanan, *Taking the Long View*, p. 163.

24 The Manchester Statement, quoted in House of Bishops, *Women Bishops in the Church of England?* (London: Church House Publishing, 2004), pp. 126–27.

25 House of Bishops, *Women Bishops in the Church of England?*, pp. 127–28.

26 Dawn, *Like the Wideness of the Sea*, p. 18.

27 Kevin Ward, *A History of Global Anglicanism* (New York: Cambridge University Press, 2006), p. 52.

28 Ward, *A History of Global Anglicanism*, p. 53.

29 See Lesley Northup, 'The Episcopal Church in the USA', in Charles Hefling and Cynthia Shattuck (eds), *The Oxford Guide to the Book of Common Prayer: A Worldwide Survey* (Oxford: Oxford University Press, 2006), pp. 360–68, p. 366.

30 Northup, 'The Episcopal Church in the USA', p. 366.

31 Northup, 'The Episcopal Church in the USA', pp. 136–38.

32 Ward, *A History of Global Anglicanism*, p. 62.

33 Os Guinness, *The American Hour* (New York: Simon and Schuster, 1988).

34 See e.g. John Howard Yoder, *The Politics of Jesus* (Michigan: Eerdmans, 1996).

35 See Richard Neuhaus, *The Naked Public Square: Religion and Democracy in America* (Michigan: Eerdmans, 1996), p. 82.

36 Address by Pope John XXIII to a group of Blessed Sacrament Fathers in June 1961 quoted in Archdiocese of Indianapolis, 'Pope Speaks of Unity and the Council', *The Criterion*, vol. 1, no. 40 (7 July 1961), p. 1, *Archdiocese of Indianapolis* website <http://www.archindy.org/criterion/local/1961/07-07-preview.html> accessed 17.12.15.

37 W. S. F. Pickering, *Anglo-Catholicism: A Study in Religious Ambiguity* (Cambridge: James Clarke & Co., 2008), p. 262.

38 As quoted in Adrian Hastings, *A History of English Christianity, 1920–1990* (3rd edn, London: SCM Press, 1991), p. 522.

39 Hastings, *A History of English Christianity*, p. 522.

40 Hastings, *A History of English Christianity*, p. 523.

41 Walter Abbott, *The Documents of Vatican II* (New York: Guild Press, 1966), p. 366.

42 Bernard Pawley and Margaret Pawley, *Rome and Canterbury Through Four Centuries* (Oxford: Mowbray, 1974), p. 336.

43 Graham Dow, *Christian Renewal in Europe: Lessons for Christians in Britain* (Nottingham: Grove Books, 1992), p. 24.

44 See Maisie Ward (ed.), *France Pagan? The Mission of Abbé Godin* (London: Sheed and Ward, 1949).

45 David Bosch, *Transforming Mission: Paradigm Shifts in Theology of Mission* (New York: Orbis, 1993), p. 10. See Henri Godin and Yvan Daniel, *La France: Pays de Mission?* (Paris: Éditions du Cerf, 1950).

46 Stephen Neill, *Anglicanism* (Middlesex: Penguin Books, 1958), p. 319.

47 By 2005, the estimated number of French-speaking Anglicans had risen to four million. See Anglican Communion, 'French-speaking Anglicans set Theological Education, Translation as Priorities', *Anglican Communion News Service* website, 10 August 2005 <http://www.anglicannews.org/news/2005/08/french-speaking-anglicans-set-theological-education,-translation-as-priorities> accessed 16.8.07.

48 Andrew Norman, 'Anglican Mission en France', self-published, 1994.

49 Jacques Grès-Gayer, 'Le culte de l'ambassade de Grande Bretagne à Paris au début de la régence (1715–20)', *Bulletin de Protestantisme,* vol. CXXX (1984), 29–45, 34.

50 Diocese in Europe, *Yearbook 2007* (London: Diocese in Europe, 2007), p. 7.

51 Roger Greenacre, *The Catholic Church in France: An Introduction* (London: Council for Christian Unity, 1996), p. 46.

52 William Beauvoir, 'William Beauvoir Papers', London, Lambeth Palace Library, 1715–20, MS1552, ff. 94–97.

53 Patrick Howarth, *When the Riviera was Ours* (London: Routledge and Kegan Paul, 1977), p. 16.

54 Fulham Papers, *Blomfield Papers,* vol. 65, 'Letters from Bishop Luscombe', London, Lambeth Palace Library, 1829, f. 38.

55 Fulham Papers, *Blomfield Papers,* vol. 65, f. 39 and vol. 38, 'Dieppe—Letter on Building a Church', London, Lambeth Palace Library, 1843, f. 77.

56 Edward Luscombe, *Matthew Luscombe: Missionary Bishop in Europe of the Scottish Episcopal Church* (Edinburgh: General Synod of the Scottish Episcopal Church, 1992), p. 5.

57 Luscombe, *Matthew Luscombe,* p. 6.

58 Luscombe, *Matthew Luscombe,* p. 7.

59 Luscombe, *Matthew Luscombe,* p. 8.

60 Fulham Papers, *Blomfield Papers,* vol. 65, ff. 10, 12.

61 Luscombe, *Matthew Luscombe,* p. 8.

62 British Embassy Church, 'The British Embassy Church', Paris, 1955, p. 2.

63 Brian Underwood, *Faith and New Frontiers: A Story of Planting and Nurturing Churches, 1823–2003* (Cambridge: ICS, 2004), p. 30.

64 Jetta S. Wolff, *The Story of the Paris Churches* (London: Cecil Palmer & Hayward, 1918), p. 195 and Guy Sancerres, *A Bridge Over Troubled Waters: The Story of St Michael's, an Anglican Church in the Heart of Paris* (Paris: Format B, 2011), pp. 199, 205.

65 Wolff, *The Story of the Paris Churches,* p. 196.

66 Sancerres, *A Bridge Over Troubled Waters,* p. 222ff.

67 The Church of England, 'Of Holy Orders in the Church of England', Canon C1, *The Church of England* website <http://www.churchofengland.org/about-us/structure/churchlawlegis/canons/section-c> accessed 21.12.15.

68 World Council of Churches, Faith and Order Commission, *Baptism, Eucharist and Ministry* (Geneva: WCC, 1982).

Chapter 8   *Chez Nous* in Continental Europe?

1   Stephen Green, *Serving God? Serving Mammon? Christians and the Financial Markets* (London: Marshall Pickering, 1996).

2   Sherard Cowper-Coles, *Ever the Diplomat: Confessions of a Foreign Office Mandarin* (London: Harper Press, 2012), p. 183.

3   'This Conference deplores the existence of parallel Anglican jurisdictions in Europe.' Lambeth

Conference 1968, Resolution 63, in Roger Coleman (ed.), *Resolutions of the Twelve Lambeth Conferences 1867–1988* (Toronto: Anglican Book Centre, 1992), p. 170.

4 See e.g. the open letter from Archbishop Peter Akinola to Archbishop Robin Eames, 16 October 2005, quoted in full in Christian Today, 'Archbishop Akinola Responds to Eames' Comments in Open Letter', *Christian Today* website, 19 October 2005 <http://www.christiantoday.com/article/4279> accessed 26.1.16.

5 Stephen Sykes and John Booty, *The Study of Anglicanism* (London: SPCK, 1988), p. 287.

6 Church Assembly, *Book of Common Prayer: 1662 Version* (Oxford: Oxford University Press, 1965), p. 313.

7 Quoted in Mary Reath, *Rome & Canterbury: The Elusive Search for Unity* (Maryland: Rowman & Littlefield, 2007), p. 30.

8 See Christopher J. Cocksworth and Rosalind Brown, *Being a Priest Today* (Norwich: Canterbury Press, 2002), p. 23.

9 Richard Hooker, *The Laws of Ecclesiastical Polity* (Nashotah: Nashotah House Press, 2012), VII.v.78.

10 See Christopher J. Cocksworth, *Evangelical Eucharistic Thought in the Church of England* (Cambridge: Cambridge University Press, 1993), esp. pp. 80–94.

11 Quoted in Philip Seddon, *Gospel and Sacrament: Reclaiming a Holistic Evangelical Spirituality* (Cambridge: Grove Books, 2004), p. 21.

12 Guy Sancerres, *A Bridge Over Troubled Waters: The Story of St Michael's, an Anglican Church in the Heart of Paris* (Paris: Format B, 2011), pp. 237–38.

13 Matthew Harrison, *An Anglican Adventure: The History of St George's Church, Paris* (Paris: St George's Anglican Church, 2005), p. 87.

14 See Steven Croft, *Ministry in Three Dimensions* (London: Darton, Longman & Todd, 1999), pp. 194–99 and Alice Mann, *The In-Between Church: Navigating Size Transitions in Congregations* (The Alban Institute, 1998), pp. 77–87.

15 George Carey, *The Church in the Market Place* (Eastbourne: Kingsway Publications, 1984).

16 Andrew Norman, 'Common Mission and the Case for Anglican Engagement in French Language Ministry in France', MPhil thesis, University of Birmingham, 2007, p. 52.

17 Patrick Howarth, *When the Riviera was Ours* (London: Routledge and Kegan Paul, 1977), p. 53.

18 Andrew Norman, 'Anglican Mission en France', self-published, 1994.

19 Howarth, *When the Riviera was Ours*, pp. 16–17.

20 James Barnett, report of the Strasbourg Chaplaincy Annual Archdeaconry Synod, author's collection, 1988.

21 The cartoon was published in *Punch* on 9 November 1895. See *The New Oxford Dictionary of English* (Oxford: Oxford University Press, 1998), p. 449.

22 Stephen Neill, *Anglicanism* (Middlesex: Penguin Books, 1958), p. 319.

Chapter 9   Act Local, Think Global

1 Bristol Post, 'Christ Church in Clifton Recreated in China' on *Bristol Post* website, 22 February 2015 <http://www.bristolpost.co.uk/Christ-Church-Clifton-recreated-China/story-26059370-detail/story.html> accessed 28.3.16.

2 See C. Peter Wagner, *Church Growth and the Whole Gospel: A Biblical Mandate* (New York: Harper and Row, 1981).

3 Monica Furlong, *The C of E: The State It's In* (London: Hodder & Stoughton, 2000), p. 172.

4 Archbishops' Commission on the Organisation of the Church of England, *Working as One Body* (London: Church House Publishing, 1995).

5 Archbishops' Commission on the Organisation of the Church of England, *Working as One Body*, p. 119.

6 David Holloway, 'Reform Discussion Paper No. 1', London, Reform, 1993, p. 1.

7　See Martin Davie, *A Guide to the Church of England* (London: Mowbray, 2008), pp. 42–47.

8　See Colin Buchanan, *Taking the Long View: Three and a Half Decades of General Synod* (London: Church House Publishing, 2006), p. 67 and Paul F. Bradshaw (ed.), *A Companion to Common Worship, Vol 1* (London: SPCK, 2001), p. 60.

9　Archbishop of Canterbury's Commission on Urban Priority Areas, *Faith in the City: A Call for Action by Church and Nation* (London: Church House Publishing, 1985).

10　Church of England Liturgical Commission, *Patterns for Worship: A Report by the Liturgical Commission of the General Synod of the Church of England* (London: Church House Publishing: 1989).

11　Buchanan, *Taking the Long View*, pp. 37, 77.

12　The Archbishops' Council, *Common Worship: Pastoral Services* (Cambridge: Cambridge University Press, 2000).

13　The Church of England, 'Liturgical Revision', *The Church of England* website <http://www.churchofengland.org/prayer-worship/worship/texts/introduction/litrevis.aspx> accessed 22.12.15.

14　Anglican Communion, 'Report of the Meeting of Primates of the Anglican Communion', *Anglican Communion News Service* website, 17 April 2002 <http://www.anglicannews.org/news/2002/04/report-of-the-meeting-of-primates-of-the-anglican-communion> accessed 4.6.13.

15　See Andrew Goddard, *Rowan Williams: His Legacy* (Oxford: Lion, 2013), pp. 49–61.

16　Lambeth Conference, *Lambeth Conference 1978 Report* (London: CIO Publishing, 1978), p. 123.

17　These four 'Instruments of Unity' would be reclassified in 2005 as three 'Instruments of Communion' and one 'Focus of Unity' (The Archbishop of Canterbury). See Anglican Consultative Council, *Living Communion: ACC 13* (New York: Church Publishing, 2006), p. 5 (Resolution 2).

18　Quoted in Archbishops' Review of the See of Canterbury, *To Lead and to Serve: The Report of the Review of the See of Canterbury* (London: Church House Publishing, 2001), p. 65.

19　Archbishops' Review of the See of Canterbury, *To Lead and to Serve*, p. 65.

20　Daniel Gover, *Turbulent Priests? The Archbishop of Canterbury in Contemporary English Politics* (London: Theos, 2011), p. 42.

21　Goddard, *Rowan Williams*, p. 248.

22　For details of the Alexandria Process launch, see George Carey, *Know the Truth: A Memoir* (London: Harper Collins, 2004), pp. 394–97 and David Smock, 'The Alexandria Process', *United States Institute of Peace* website <http://www.usip.org/programs/projects/alexandria-process> accessed 21.10.15.

23　See Lambeth Conference 1968, Resolution 63 in Roger Coleman (ed.), *Resolutions of the Twelve Lambeth Conferences 1867–1988* (Toronto: Anglican Book Centre, 1992), p. 170. See also Resolution V.6 in Lambeth Conference, *The Official Report of the Lambeth Conference 1998* (Harrisburg: Morehouse Publishing, 1999), p. 421.

24　The Spanish Episcopal Reformed Church and the Portuguese Lusitanian Church are two small indigenous churches. See John Hind, 'Why have an Anglican Church on Mainland Europe?', in Wingate et al. (eds), *Anglicanism: A Global Communion* (London: Mowbray, 1998), pp. 114–19, p. 115.

25　James M. Rosenthal, 'European Anglicans Set Common Goals at Madrid Consultation', *Anglican Communion News Service* website, 20 May 2003 <http://www.anglicannews.org/news/2003/05/european-anglicans-set-common-goals-at-madrid-consultation> accessed 5.6.13 and Anglican European Provincial Consultation, 'Europe Partners in Mission Consultation: Madrid, 16-18 May 2003', *Anglican European Provincial Consultation* website <http://europeconsultation.anglican.org/may03pimreport.html> accessed 5.6.13.

26　Letter from Cardinal Walter Kasper to Bishop Geoffrey Rowell, 13 May 2003 (Pontifical Council ref: 1347/2003/h), quoted in Andrew Norman, 'Common Mission and the Case for Anglican Engagement in French Language Ministry in France', MPhil thesis, University of Birmingham, 2007, p. 85.

27　Brian Stanley, *The Bible and the Flag* (Leicester: Apollos, 1990), p. 70.

28 Michael Doe, 'USPG and Theological Education', p. 3, *Rethinking Mission* website (2009) <http://www.rethinkingmission.org.uk/article_doe0609.html> accessed 3.6.13.

29 CEC (Conference of European Churches), 'Charta Oecumenica', Strasbourg, 2001, p. 6.

Chapter 10   New Facts of our Era

1 Resolution 1:10, *The Official Report of the Lambeth Conference 1998* (Harrisburg: Morehouse Publishing, 1999), pp. 381–82.

2 Alf McCreary, *Nobody's Fool: The Life of Archbishop Robin Eames* (London: Hodder & Stoughton, 2005), pp. 304–5.

3 Stephen Neill, *Anglicanism* (Middlesex: Penguin Books, 1958), p. 291.

4 Richard Anthony Carter, *In Search of the Lost: The Death and Life of Seven Peacemakers of the Melanesian Brotherhood* (Norwich: Canterbury Press, 2006), p. 14.

5 Carter, *In Search of the Lost,* p. 22.

6 Carter, *In Search of the Lost,* p. 23.

7 Carter, *In Search of the Lost,* p. 48.

8 Anglican Communion, 'African Bishops' Conference Now Opens in Lagos', *Anglican Communion News Service* website, 27 October 2004 <http://www.anglicannews.org/news/2004/10/african-bishop-conference-now-opens-in-lagos> accessed 26.1.16.

9 David Okeke, 'The Church of Nigeria: The Book of Common Prayer', in Charles Hefling and Cynthia Shattuck (eds), *The Oxford Guide to the Book of Common Prayer: A Worldwide Survey* (Oxford: Oxford University Press, 2006), pp. 302–3.

10 Anglican Communion, 'Communique from the African Anglican Bishops' Conference', *Anglican Communion News Service* website, 1 November 2004 <http://www.anglicannews.org/news/2004/11/communique-from-the-african-anglican-bishops-conference> accessed 3.5.13.

11 Anglican Communion, 'A Statement from the Primates Gathered at the First African Anglican Bishops' Conference', *Anglican Communion News Service* website, 28 October 2004 <http://www.anglicannews.org/news/2004/10/a-statement-from-the-primates-gathered-at-the-first-african-anglican-bishops-conference> accessed 3.5.13.

12 Peter J. Akinola, 'Statement on the Windsor Report 2004 from the Primate of All Nigeria', *Anglican Communion News Service* website, 20 October 2004 <http://www.anglicannews.org/news/2004/10/statement-on-the-windsor-report-2004-from-the-primate-of-all-nigeria> accessed 3.5.13.

13 Michael Ingham, 'Bishop of New Westminster Windsor Report Statement', *Anglican Communion News Service* website, 26 October 2004 <http://www.anglicannews.org/news/2004/10/bishop-of-new-westminster-windsor-report-statement> accessed 3.5.13.

14 Frank T. Griswold, 'Statement from the Most Revd Frank T. Griswold on the Windsor Report 2004', *Anglican Communion News Service* website, 18 October 2004 <http://www.anglicannews.org/news/2004/10/statement-from-the-most-revd-frank-t-griswold-on-the-windsor-report-2004> accessed 3.5.13.

15 Anglican Communion, 'The Primates' Meeting, February 2005 Communiqué', *Anglican Communion* website <http://www.anglicancommunion.org/media/68387/communique-_english.pdf>, p. 4, accessed 12.7.14.

16 Anglican Communion, 'The Primates' Meeting, February 2005 Communiqué'.

17 Owen Chadwick, *Michael Ramsey: A Life* (London: SCM Press, 1990), p. 323; Roger Greenacre, *The Catholic Church in France: An Introduction* (London: Council for Christian Unity, 1996), pp. 63–65; Guy Sancerres, *A Bridge Over Troubled Waters: The Story of St Michael's, an Anglican Church in the Heart of Paris* (Paris: Format B, 2011), p. 209.

18 Alpha International, *The Alpha Course in a Catholic Context* (London: Alpha International, 2006), p. 12;

Andrew Norman, 'Common Mission and the Case for Anglican Engagement in French Language Ministry in France', MPhil thesis, University of Birmingham, 2007, p. 59.

19 Marc de Leyritz, *Devine qui vient diner ce soir?* (Paris: Presses de la Renaissance, 2007), pp. 59–95.

20 Alpha International, *The Alpha Course in a Catholic Context*, p. 12.

21 See Walter Kasper, *A Handbook of Spiritual Ecumenism* (New York: New City Press, 2007).

22 Rowan Williams, 'Address at Opening Ceremony Sant'Egidio International Meeting of Prayer for Peace—Palais de Congress, Lyons', *Dr Rowan Williams: 104th Archbishop of Canterbury* website, 11 September 2005 <http://rowanwilliams.archbishopofcanterbury.org/articles.php/1289/> accessed 12.5.13.

23 Rowan Williams, 'Forum Debate: Is Europe at its End?—Sant'Egidio International Meeting of Prayer for Peace', *Dr Rowan Williams: 104th Archbishop of Canterbury* website, 12 September 2005 <http://rowanwilliams.archbishopofcanterbury.org/articles.php/1180/> accessed 12.5.13.

24 Rowan Williams, *Faith in the Public Square* (London: Bloomsbury, 2012), pp. 75–85.

25 See JWG (Joint Working Group of the World Council of Churches and the Roman Catholic Church), 'Common Witness and Proselytism', *Ecumenical Review*, vol. 23 (1970), 9–20, p. 28; JWG, 'The Challenge of Proselytism and the Calling to Common Witness', in Jeffrey Gros et al. (eds), *Growth in Agreement II* (Geneva: WCC Publications, 2000), pp. 891–99; and CEC (Conference of European Churches), 'Charta Oecumenica', Strasbourg, 2001. These are discussed in Andrew Norman, 'Common Mission and the Case for Anglican Engagement in French Language Ministry in France', pp. 78–85.

26 Gordon Hewitt, *The Problems of Success: A History of the Church Missionary Society, 1910–1942, vol. 1, Tropical Africa, the Middle East, At Home* (London: SCM Press, 1971), pp. 271–73; see also Kevin Ward and Emma Wild-Wood, *The East African Revival: History and Legacies* (London: Ashgate, 2012).

27 Eugene Stock, *An Heroic Bishop: The Life Story of French of Lahore* (London: Hodder & Stoughton, 1914), p. 29; Constance Millington, *Whether We Be Many or Few: A History of the Cambridge/Delhi Brotherhood* (Bangalore: Asian Trading Corporation, 1999), pp. 4–5.

28 Rowan Williams, 'Archbishop—Sangla Hills Apology "a hopeful sign"', *Dr Rowan Williams: 104th Archbishop of Canterbury* website, 27 November 2005 <http://rowanwilliams.archbishopofcanterbury.org/articles.php/1287/> accessed 26.1.16.

29 Rowan Williams, 'Archbishop's Visit to Pakistan', *Dr Rowan Williams: 104th Archbishop of Canterbury* website, 24 November 2005 <http://rowanwilliams.archbishopofcanterbury.org/articles.php/1288/> accessed 19.5.13.

30 George Carey, *Know the Truth: A Memoir* (London: Harper Collins, 2004), p. 383.

31 Williams, 'Archbishop's Visit to Pakistan'.

32 Williams, 'Archbishop—Sangla Hills Apology "a hopeful sign"'.

33 Quoted in F. A. Iremonger, *William Temple, Archbishop of Canterbury: His Life and Letters* (London: Oxford University Press, 1948), p. 387.

Chapter 11   Unchanged by what is Happening?

1 See e.g. Alec Vidler, *The Church in an Age of Revolution* (Harmondsworth: Penguin, 1961), p. 257.

2 Quoted in Timothy Dudley-Smith, *John Stott: A Global Ministry* (Leicester: IVP, 2001), p. 126.

3 See Church Society, 'Conflict in the Diocese of Recifé, Brazil', *Church Society* website <http://www.churchsociety.org/issues_new/communion/division/iss_communion_division_recife.asp> accessed 17.12.15.

4 Rowan Williams, 'Notes from China—Day by Day Highlights', *Dr Rowan Williams: 104th Archbishop of Canterbury* website, 23 October 2006 <http://rowanwilliams.archbishopofcanterbury.org/articles.php/628> accessed 11.9.08.

5 See Martin Palmer, *The Jesus Sutras: Rediscovering the Lost Religion* (London: Piatkus, 2001), pp. 11–38.

6 Brian Stanley, *The Bible and the Flag* (Leicester: Apollos, 1990), p. 106.

7   Stanley, *The Bible and the Flag*, p. 109.

8   Kevin Ward, *A History of Global Anglicanism* (New York: Cambridge University Press, 2006), p. 246.

9   Bob Whyte, *Unfinished Encounter: China and Christianity* (London: Fount Paperbacks, 1988), p. 200.

10 Bishop Ting was held under House arrest in Nanjing from 1966, according to Bob Whyte (note to the author, September 2006).

11 Rowan Williams, 'China—Press Conference, British Ambassadors' Residence, Beijing', *Dr Rowan Williams: 104th Archbishop of Canterbury* website, 24 October 2006 <http://rowanwilliams.archbishopofcanterbury. org/articles.php/748/> accessed 11.9.08.

12 Pew Research Centre, 'Religion in China on the Eve of the 2008 Beijing Olympics', *Pew Research Centre* website, 2 May 2008 <http://www.pewforum.org/2008/05/01/religion-in-china-on-the-eve-of-the-2008-beijing-olympics/> accessed 2.9.14.

13 Rowan Williams, 'Christianity in the Reinvention of China', Chatham House Lecture, *China Review* iss. 40 (2007).

14 Pew Research Centre, 'Regional Distribution of Christians', *Pew Research Centre* website, 19 December 2011 <http://www.pewforum.org/2011/12/19/global-christianity-regions/> accessed 2.9.14.

15 Rowan Williams, 'A Society that does not Allow Crosses or Veils in Public is a Dangerous one', *The Times*, 27 October 2006, available online at <http://www.globalsouthanglican.org/index.php/ blog/comments/a_society_that_does_not_allow_crosses_or_veils_in_public_is_a_dangerous_one> accessed 28.3.16.

16 Rowan Williams, 'China—Press Conference, British Ambassadors' Residence, Beijing'.

17 Daniel H. Bays, *A New History of Christianity in China* (Chichester: Wiley-Blackwell, 2012), pp. 199–202.

18 Quoted in Rowan Williams, 'Notes from China—Day by Day Highlights', pp. 10, 20.

19 Global South Anglican, 'Communiqué of the Global South Primates during their visit to China in September 2011', Global South Anglican website, 14 September 2011 <http://www.globalsouthanglican. org/index.php/blog/comments/communique_of_the_global_south_primates_during_their_visit_to_ china_in_sept> accessed 30.6.13.

20 See Frederick Bliss, *Anglicans in Rome: A History* (London: Canterbury Press, 2006), p. 154.

21 ARCIC (Anglican–Roman Catholic International Commission), *The Final Report* (London: SPCK, 1982).

22 Lambeth Conference 1988: Resolution 8 in Roger Coleman (ed.), *Resolutions of the Twelve Lambeth Conferences 1867–1988* (Toronto: Anglican Book Centre, 1992), pp. 202–4.

23 Christopher Hill and Edward Yarnold, *Anglicans and Roman Catholics: The Search for Unity* (London: SPCK, 1993), p. 156.

24 Hill and Yarnold, *Anglicans and Roman Catholics*, p. 173.

25 The International Anglican Roman Catholic Commission on Unity and Mission.

26 Anglican Consultative Council and Pontifical Council for Promoting Christian Unity, *Growing Together in Unity and Mission: Building on 40 Years of Anglican-Roman Catholic Dialogue* (London: SPCK, 2007).

27 Rowan Williams, 'Archbishop and Pope: "Our Churches Share Witness and Service"', *Dr Rowan Williams: 104th Archbishop of Canterbury* website, 23 November 2006 <http://rowanwilliams.archbishopofcanterbury. org/articles.php/1459/> accessed 25.5.13.

28 Quoted in Bliss, *Anglicans in Rome*, p. 174.

29 Rowan Williams, 'Archbishop of Canterbury's Presidential Address at ACC-13', *Anglican Communion News Service* website, 20 June 2005 <http://www.anglicannews.org/news/2005/06/archbishop-of-canterburys-presidential-address-at-acc-13> accessed 15.6.13.

30 Anglican Communion, 'Resolutions Passed Today At ACC-13', *Anglican Communion News Service* website, 22 June 2005 <http://www.anglicannews.org/news/2005/06/resolutions-passed-today-at-acc-13> accessed 15.6.13.

31 For the 1963 Toronto Congress and 'mutual responsibility and inter-dependence' (MRI), see

Bruce N. Kaye, *An Introduction to World Anglicanism* (Cambridge: Cambridge University Press, 2008), pp. 47–48 and IASCOME (Inter Anglican Standing Commission on Mission and Evangelism), *Communion in Mission and Travelling Together in God's Mission* (London: Anglican Communion Office, 2006), p. 43.

32 Quoted in Ian Douglas, 'Anglicans Gathering for God's Mission: A Missiological Ecclesiology for the Anglican Communion', *Journal for Anglican Studies*, vol. 2, iss. 2 (2004), 9–40, 35.

33 ACC 11: Resolution 14 and ACC 12: Resolution 35. See also Anglican Consultative Council, *Living Communion: ACC 13* (New York: Church Publishing, 2006), pp. 355–57 and Martyn Percy, Mark Chapman, Ian Markham and Barney Hawkins (eds), *Christ and Culture: Communion After Lambeth* (Norwich: Canterbury Press, 2010), pp. 168–71.

34 Anglican Communion, 'Lambeth Conference Set for Canterbury 2008', *Anglican Communion News Service* website, 28 June 2005 <http://www.anglicannews.org/news/2005/06/lambeth-conference-set-for-canterbury-2008> accessed 15.6.13.

35 Anglican Communion, 'House of Bishops adopts "Covenant Statement"', *Anglican Communion News Service* website, 16 March 2005 <http://www.anglicannews.org/news/2005/03/house-of-bishops-adopts-covenant-statement> accessed 15.6.13.

36 Colin Podmore, 'Two Streams Mingling: The American Episcopal Church in the Anglican Communion', *Journal of Anglican Studies,* vol. 9, iss. 1 (2011), 12–37, 14.

37 The Episcopal Church, 'Affirm Commitment to the Anglican Communion', Resolution A159 of the 75th General Convention, *The Archives of the Episcopal Church* website <http://www.episcopalarchives.org/cgi-bin/acts/acts_resolution-complete.pl?resolution=2006-A159> accessed 15.6.13.

38 The Episcopal Church, 'Support Development of an Anglican Covenant', Resolution A166 of the 75th General Convention, *The Archives of the Episcopal Church* website <http://www.episcopalarchives.org/cgi-bin/acts/acts_resolution-complete.pl?resolution=2006-A166> accessed 15.6.13.

39 The Episcopal Church, 'Exercise Restraint in Consecrating Candidates', Resolution B033 of the 75th General Convention, *The Archives of the Episcopal Church* website <http://www.episcopalarchives.org/cgi-bin/acts/acts_resolution-complete.pl?resolution=2006-B033> accessed 15.6.13.

40 The Episcopal Church, 'Consider Blessing Committed, Same-Gender Relationships', Resolution C051 (5) of the 75th General Convention, *The Archives of the Episcopal Church* website <http://www.episcopalarchives.org/cgi-bin/acts/acts_resolution-complete.pl?resolution=2003-C051> accessed 15.6.13.

41 Rowan Williams, 'The Challenge and Hope of Being an Anglican Today: A Reflection for the Bishops, Clergy and Faithful of the Anglican Communion', 27 June 2006 <http://rowanwilliams.archbishopofcanterbury.org/articles.php/1478/> accessed 15.6.13.

42 See Coleman, *Resolutions of the Twelve Lambeth Conferences 1867–1988,* p. 13 for the Lambeth Quadrilateral, and Missio (Anglican Communion Mission Commission), *Anglicans in Mission: A Transforming Journey* (London: SPCK, 2000), p. 20 for the Five Marks of Mission.

43 Global South Anglican, 'Global South Primates Kigali Communiqué, September 2006', *Global South Anglican* website, 23 September 2006 <http://www.globalsouthanglican.org/index.php/comments/kigali_communique/> accessed 15.6.13.

44 GAFCON Theological Resource Group, *Being Faithful: The Shape of Historic Anglicanism Today* (London: Latimer Trust, 2009), p. 76.

45 Owen Chadwick, *Hensley Henson: A Study in the Friction between Church and State* (Norwich: Canterbury Press, 1994), p. 148.

46 The Church Times, 'Hereford v. Zanzibar', 28 May 1915, republished in *The Church Times*, 29 May 2015, p. 12.

47 Charles Hefling and Cynthia Shattuck (eds), *The Oxford Guide to the Book of Common Prayer: A Worldwide Survey* (Oxford: Oxford University Press, 2006), p. 280.

48 Church of England Newspaper, 'Cathedral Bombed in Zanzibar', *Church of England Newspaper,* 14 March 2014, p. 5.

49 For the subgroup's report, see Anglican Communion, 'ACO: Report of the Communion Sub-Group', *Anglican Communion News Service* website, 15 February 2007 <http://www.anglicannews.org/news/2007/02/aco-report-of-the-communion-sub-group> accessed 15.6.13.

50 Anglican Communion, 'ACO: Primates' Meeting Communique', *Anglican Communion News Service* website, 19 February 2007 <http://www.anglicannews.org/news/2007/02/aco-primates-meeting-communique> accessed 15.6.13.

51 Anglican Communion, 'ACO: Primates' Meeting Communique'.

52 See The Episcopal Church, 'Bishops' "Mind of the House" Resolutions', *Episcopal News Service* website, 20 March 2007 <http://archive.episcopalchurch.org/79425_84230_ENG_HTM.htm> accessed 15.6.13 and 'House of Bishops: Message to God's People', *Episcopal News Service* website, 21 March 2007 <http://archive.episcopalchurch.org/78695_84233_ENG_HTM.htm> accessed 15.6.13.

53 Email to the author from Bernice Pilling, Diocese of Calgary archivist, 16 September 2014.

54 Anglican Church of Canada, 'Historical Sketch for Anglican Residential Schools', *Anglican Church of Canada* website <http://www.anglican.ca/tr/schools/> accessed 4.4.14.

55 Government of Canada, 'Statement of Apology to Former Students of Indian Residential Schools', *Indigenous and Northern Affairs Canada* website, 11 June 2008 <http://www.aadnc-aandc.gc.ca/eng/1100100015644/1100100015649> accessed 7.11.14.

56 Marites N. Sison, 'Primate Urges Synod Members to Embrace Ethic of Respect', *Anglican Journal* website, 20 June 2007 <http://www.anglicanjournal.com/articles/primate-urges-synod-members-to-embrace-ethic-of-respect-7318> accessed 7.11.14; Solange De Santis, 'Synod Narrowly Defeats Same Sex Blessings', *Anglican Journal* website, 24 June 2007 <http://www.anglicanjournal.com/articles/synod-narrowly-defeats-same-sex-blessings-7329> accessed 7.11.14.

57 See Courtney Cowart, *An American Awakening* (New York: Seabury, 2008).

58 Anglican Communion, 'Statement by the Secretary General', *Anglican Communion News Service* website, 26 September 2007 <http://www.anglicannews.org/news/2007/09/statement-by-the-secretary-general.aspx> accessed 17.12.15.

59 Anglican Communion, 'Statement by the Secretary General'.

60 The Episcopal Church, 'The Report of the Joint Standing Committee to the Archbishop of Canterbury on the Response of The Episcopal Church to the Questions of the Primates articulated at their meeting in Dar es Salaam and related Pastoral Concerns', *The Episcopal Church in Vermont* website <http://www.diovermont.org/archived-site/EpiscopalChurch/HoBNewOrleans/JSC%20Report%20on%20New%20Orleans%20071003.pdf> accessed 30.8.14.

61 Rowan Williams, 'The Archbishop's Advent Letter to Primates, 2007', *Dr Rowan Williams: 104th Archbishop of Canterbury* website, 14 December 2007 <http://rowanwilliams.archbishopofcanterbury.org/articles.php/631/> accessed 30.8.14.

62 On the polity of the Episcopal Church and the place of bishops, see Colin Podmore, 'A Tale of Two Churches: The Ecclesiologies of the Episcopal Church and the Church of England Compared', *International Journal for the Study of the Christian Church,* vol. 8, no. 2 (2008), 124–54 and Podmore, 'Two Streams Mingling'.

63 Rowan Williams, 'The Archbishop's Advent Letter to Primates, 2007'. <http://rowanwilliams.archbishopofcanterbury.org/articles.php/631/> accessed 30.8.14.

64 Rowan Williams, 'First Invitations Sent for "Reflective and Learning-Based Lambeth Conference"', *Dr Rowan Williams: 104th Archbishop of Canterbury* website, 22 May 2007 <http://rowanwilliams.archbishopofcanterbury.org/articles.php/1418/first-invitations-sent-for-reflective-and-learning-based-lambeth-conference> accessed 30.8.14.

65 Anglican Communion, 'Archbishop of Canterbury's Pentecost Letter to the Bishops of the Anglican Communion', *Anglican Communion News Service* website, 13 May 2008 <http://www.anglicannews.org/news/2008/05/archbishop-of-canterburys-pentecost-letter-to-the-bishops-of-the-anglican-communion>

accessed 30.8.14.

66 Owen Chadwick, 'Introduction' in Roger Coleman (ed.), *Resolutions of the Twelve Lambeth Conferences 1867–1988* (Toronto: Anglican Book Centre, 1992), p. ix.

67 As quoted on The Desmond Tutu Peace Foundation, *The Desmond Tutu Peace Foundation* website <http://www.tutufoundation-usa.org/exhibitions.html> accessed 30.8.15.

68 As quoted in John Allen, *Rabble Rouser for Peace: The Authorized Biography of Desmond Tutu* (London: Rider Books, 2006), p. 232.

69 Allen, *Rabble Rouser for Peace,* pp. 313–14.

70 See Lambeth Conference, 'Lambeth Indaba: Capturing Conversations and Reflections from the Lambeth Conference 2008', Lambeth Conference, 2008, p. 8. The Anglican Communion Mission Commission (Missio) suggested that other marks could be added to these, but its successor (IAS-COME) stuck with 'Five Marks of Mission' as the benchmark for Anglicans. See Missio, *Anglicans in Mission,* pp. 19–21; IASCOME (Inter Anglican Standing Commission on Mission and Evangelism), *Communion in Mission and Travelling Together in God's Mission* (London: Anglican Communion Office, 2006), p. 68.

71 Missio, *Anglicans in Mission,* p. 20.

72 See Anglican Communion, 'The Anglican Communion Covenant', pp. 4–5 (Section 2.2.2), *Anglican Communion* website <http://www.anglicancommunion.org/media/99905/The_Anglican_Covenant.pdf> accessed 14.4.13.

73 Anglican Communion, 'Statement from the Church of the Province of Uganda', *Anglican Communion News Service* website, 15 February 2008 <http://www.anglicannews.org/news/2008/02/statement-from-the-church-of-the-province-of-uganda> accessed 28.5.13.

74 Anglican Communion, 'Archbishop of Canterbury Responds to GAFCON Statement', *Anglican Communion News Service* website, 30 June 2008 <http://www.anglicannews.org/news/2008/06/archbishop-of-canterbury-responds-to-gafcon-statement> accessed 28.5.13.

75 Hearings on the Windsor process were facilitated by the Windsor Continuation Group. Chaired by Bishop Clive Handford, retired Bishop of Cyprus and the Gulf, this had been set up in 2008 to identify unanswered questions arising from the requests of the Windsor Report and to offer advice to the Instruments of Communion. I served as a staff member of this group. See Anglican Communion, 'The Windsor Continuation Group', *Anglican Communion* website <http://www.anglicancommunion.org/media/100354/The-Windsor-Continuation-Group.pdf> accessed 1.8.15.

76 Sarah Brown, *Behind the Black Door* (London: Ebury Press, 2011), pp. 197–98.

77 Owen Chadwick, *The Victorian Church: Part Two* (London: SCM Press, 1972), pp. 310–11.

78 Chadwick, *The Victorian Church,* pp. 353–54.

79 Anglican Communion, 'Archbishop's Pastoral Letter to Bishops of the Anglican Communion', *Anglican Communion News Service* website, 26 August 2008 <http://www.anglicannews.org/news/2008/08/archbishops-pastoral-letter-to-bishops-of-the-anglican-communion> accessed 3.6.13.

Chapter 12   Today's Church, Tomorrow's Ministers

1 Ministry Council, 'Ridley Hall Report: November 2011', *Church of England* website, 2012 <http://www.churchofengland.org/clergy-office-holders/ministry/ministerial-education-and-development/quality-assurance-in-ministerial-education/inspection-reports> accessed 2.5.12.

2 Christopher Cocksworth, Principal of Ridley Hall, 2001–2008.

3 Mission and Public Affairs Council, *Mission-Shaped Church* (London: Church House Publishing, 2004), pp. 11–12.

4 Mission and Public Affairs Council, *Mission-Shaped Church,* p. 11.

5 Mission and Public Affairs Council, *Mission-Shaped Church,* pp. xi–xiii.

6 As quoted in Andrew Goddard, *Rowan Williams: His Legacy* (Oxford: Lion, 2013), p. 49.

7 As quoted in Goddard, *Rowan Williams*, p. 52.

8 Mission and Public Affairs Council, *Mission-Shaped Church*, p. vii.

9 Fresh Expressions, 'What is a Fresh Expression?', *Fresh Expressions* website <http://www.freshexpressions. org.uk/about/whatis> accessed 13.7.13.

10 As quoted in Goddard, *Rowan Williams*, p. 57.

11 See George Lings, 'A History of Fresh Expressions and Church Planting in the Church of England' in David Goodhew (ed.), *Church Growth in Britain: 1980 to the Present* (Farnham: Ashgate, 2012), pp. 161–78.

12 Goddard, *Rowan Williams*, p. 52.

13 Andrew Davison and Alison Milbank, *For the Parish: A Critique of Fresh Expressions* (London: SCM Press, 2010), p. 79.

14 Ministry Division, 'Relating Recruitment to Deployment', London, Ministry Division of the Church of England, 2009.

15 Ridley Hall and Westcott House, 'Bishops' Roundtable Report: What Kind of Clergy Do We Need?', Cambridge, Ridley Hall, 2012.

16 See The Church of England, 'Church Commissioners' Annual Report 2007', p. 18, *Church of England* website <http://www.churchofengland.org/media/49938/2007report.pdf> accessed 8.2.16.

17 Conversation between the author and Jennifer Harbour, churchwarden, 17 April 2013.

18 Conversation between with the author and Bishop James Newcome, 16 April 2013.

19 Carlisle Diocese, 'Growing Together: Three Churches Journeying as one for God's Kingdom in Cumbria', Carlisle, Carlisle Diocese Church House, 2013, p. 11.

20 Carlisle Diocese, 'Growing Disciples: Vision and Strategy 2011–2020', Carlisle, Carlisle Diocese Church House, 2011, pp. 6–11.

21 St Andrew's PCC, AGM minutes, Weeley, Weeley Parish Church, 1959.

22 Chelmsford Diocese, 'Transforming Presence: Strategic Priorities for the Diocese of Chelmsford', Chelmsford, Chelmsford Diocese Church House, 2011, p. 3 n. 1.

23 Stephen Cottrell, 'A Message from Bishop Stephen' in parish vacancy document on *Halstead Area Team* website <http://www.halsteadchurches.co.uk/uploads/Halstead%20Area%20Team%20Profile. pdf>, p. 2, accessed 28.3.16.

24 Chelmsford Diocese, 'Transforming Presence', p. 5.

25 Email to the author from James Blandford Baker, Vicar of St Andrew's Histon, 3 July 2014.

26 Bible Reading Fellowship, *Messy Church* website <http://www.messychurch.org.uk/> accessed 6.4.14.

27 Email to the author from Clive Hawkins, Rector of St Mary's Eastrop, 25 November 2013; see St Mary's Basingstoke, *St Mary's Basingstoke* website <http://www.stmarys-basingstoke.org.uk> accessed 16.4.14.

28 'Progressive Sunday School' on *St Bride's* website <http://www.stbridesliverpool.co.uk/children> accessed 23.4.16.

29 'St Bride Liverpool' on *Inclusive Church* website <http://inclusive-church.org.uk/location/st-bride-liverpool> accessed 21.3.16.

30 Archbishop of Canterbury's Commission on Urban Priority Areas, *Faith in the City: A Call for Action by Church and Nation* (London: Church House Publishing, 1985).

31 See Mission and Public Affairs Council, *Mission-Shaped Church*, pp. 73–74; see also Paul Bayes and Tim Sledge (eds), *Mission-Shaped Parish* (London: Church House Publishing, 2009).

32 Jesmond Parish Church, 'Jesmond Parish Church: A History of God's Work—150th Anniversary', Newcastle-upon-Tyne, Clayton Publications, 2011, p. 14.

33 Alan Munden, *A Light in a Dark Place: Jesmond Parish Church* (Newcastle: Clayton, 2006), p. 229.

34 'Interpretation', in National Archives, 'Church of England (Worship and Doctrine) Measure 1974 (No. 3)', *National Archives* website <http://www.legislation.gov.uk/ukcm/1974/3/contents> accessed

21.3.16.

35 'Articles of Religion' on *Church of England* website <https://www.churchofengland.org/prayer-worship/worship/book-of-common-prayer/articles-of-religion.aspx>, XIX Of the Church, accessed 28.3.16. See also David Holloway, 'The Pastor and Church Growth', in Melvin Tinker (ed.), *The Renewed Pastor: Writings in Honour of Philip Hacking* (Fearn: Mentor, 2011), pp. 169–98, pp. 170–72.

36 See BBC, 'Funeral for British Victim of Paris Attacks', *BBC* website, 21 December 2015 <http://www.bbc.co.uk/news/uk-england-essex-35152849> accessed 8.1.16.

37 Lambeth Palace, 'Presence and Engagement: The Churches' Task in a Multi Faith Society', *Presence and Engagement* website <http://www.presenceandengagement.org.uk/presence-and-engagement-report> accessed 7.7.13.

38 Lambeth Palace, 'Presence and Engagement', Foreword, p. 3.

39 The Feast, *The Feast* website <http://www.thefeast.org.uk> accessed 3.6.13.

40 David Goodhew (ed.), *Church Growth in Britain: 1980 to the Present* (Farnham: Ashgate, 2012), p. 127.

41 Goodhew, *Church Growth in Britain*, pp. 111–13.

42 Goodhew, *Church Growth in Britain*, p. 114.

43 Goodhew, *Church Growth in Britain*, p. 130.

44 Redeemed Christian Church of God, 'Church Finder', *RCCG* website <http://www.rccguk.church/places/churches/> accessed 23.6.13.

45 See Roger Steer, *Inside Story: The Life of John Stott* (Nottingham: IVP, 2009), pp. 159–67.

46 Julia Cameron (ed.), *Christ Our Reconciler: Gospel–Church–World* (Nottingham: IVP, 2012), pp. 64–69.

47 No Anglican Covenant Coalition, 'Ten Reasons Why the Proposed Anglican Covenant is a Bad Idea', *No Anglican Covenant* website <http://noanglicancovenant.org/resources.html> accessed 23.4.16.

48 Anglican Communion, 'Deeper Communion; Gracious Restraint: A Letter from Alexandria to the Churches of the Anglican Communion', *Anglican Communion* website <http://www.anglicancommunion.org/media/68372/Pastoral-Letter.pdf> accessed 26.3.15.

49 Rowan Williams, 'Archbishop's Presidential Address—General Synod November 2010', *Dr Rowan Williams: 104th Archbishop of Canterbury* website, 23 November 2010 <http://rowanwilliams.archbishopofcanterbury.org/articles.php/919/> accessed 26.3.15.

50 Resolution III.2 in Lambeth Conference, *The Official Report of the Lambeth Conference 1998* (Harrisburg: Morehouse Publishing, 1999), pp. 394–95.

51 House of Bishops, *Women Bishops in the Church of England?* (London: Church House Publishing, 2004), p. 150.

52 House of Bishops, *Women Bishops in the Church of England?*, p. 144.

53 House of Bishops, *Women Bishops in the Church of England?*, p. 143.

54 House of Bishops, 'Women in the Episcopate? An Anglican–Roman Catholic Dialogue', London, General Synod of the Church of England, 2008, p. 20.

55 House of Bishops, 'Women in the Episcopate?', p. 1.

56 The Vatican, 'Address of Cardinal Walter Kasper at the Lambeth Conference, July 30, 2008', *Vatican* website <http://www.vatican.va/roman_curia/pontifical_councils/chrstuni/angl-comm-docs/rc_pc_chrstuni_doc_20080730_kasper-lambeth_en.html> accessed 7.7.13.

57 Lizzy Davies, 'Church of England Votes against Allowing Women Bishops', 21 November 2012, *The Guardian* website <http://www.theguardian.com/world/2012/nov/20/church-of-england-no-women-bishops> accessed 28.3.16.

58 The Church of England, 'House of Bishops' Declaration on the Ministry of Bishops and Priests', *Church of England* website <http://www.churchofengland.org/about-us/structure/general-synod/about-general-synod/house-of-bishops/declaration-on-the-ministry-of-bishops-and-priests> accessed 21.12.15.

59 See Matthew Reeve, 'A Seat of Authority: The Archbishop's Throne at Canterbury Cathedral', *Gesta*, vol. 42, no. 2 (2003), 131–42.

60 Quoted on Archbishops' Council, *Just Pray* website <http://www.justpray.uk/what/> accessed 27.1.16.

61 Justin Welby, 'Reconciliation', *Archbishop of Canterbury* website, <http://www.archbishopofcanterbury.org/pages/reconciliation-.html> accessed 27.1.16.

62 Justin Welby, 'Archbishops Recall Commitment to Pastoral Care and Friendship for All, Regardless of Sexual Orientation', *Archbishop of Canterbury* website, 29 January 2014 <http://www.archbishopof-canterbury.org/articles.php/5237/> accessed 8.2.16.

63 Justin Welby, 'Archbishop of Canterbury calls for Primates' Gathering', Archbishop of Canterbury website, 16 September 2015 <http://www.archbishopofcanterbury.org/articles.php/5613/> accessed 8.2.16.

64 Phil Groves and Angharad Parry Jones, *Living Reconciliation* (London: SPCK, 2014), p. xii.

65 Sharon Sheridan, 'General Convention Approves Marriage Equality', *Episcopal News Service* website, 1 July 2015 <http://episcopaldigitalnetwork.com/ens/2015/07/01/general-convention-approves-marriage-equality/> accessed 28.3.16.

66 Anglican Communion, 'Communiqué from the Primates' Meeting 2016', *Anglican Communion News Service* website, 15 January 2016 <http://www.anglicannews.org/features/2016/01/communique-from-the-primates-meeting-2016.aspx> accessed 28.3.16.

67 The Church of England, 'House of Bishops Pastoral Guidance on Same Sex Marriage', Church of England website, 15 February 2014 <https://www.churchofengland.org/media-centre/news/2014/02/house-of-bishops-pastoral-guidance-on-same-sex-marriage.aspx> accessed 28.3.16.

68 Anglican Communion, 'Archbishop Justin's Priorities', *Anglican Communion* website <http://www.anglicancommunion.org/structures/instruments-of-communion/archbishop-of-canterbury/justin-welby/archbishop-justins-priorities.aspx> accessed 25.10.15.

69 See Law and Religion UK, 'CofE Simplification Report—Key Recommendations', *Law and Religion UK* website, 15 January 2015 <http://www.lawandreligionuk.com/2015/01/15/cofe-simplification-report-key-recommendations> accessed 6.8.15.

70 Tim Wyatt, 'Cash Requested to Combat the "Doomsday Machine"', *Church Times,* 13 February 2015, p. 2.

Chapter 13   Letting Change Happen

1 Bruce N. Kaye, *An Introduction to World Anglicanism* (Cambridge: Cambridge University Press, 2008), p. 77.

2 Alan Wilkinson, *The Church of England and the First World War* (London: SCM Press, 1978), p. 81.

3 Archbishop of Canterbury's Commission on Urban Priority Areas, *Faith in the City: A Call for Action by Church and Nation* (London: Church House Publishing, 1985), p. 74.

4 Archbishops' Commission on the Organisation of the Church of England, *Working as One Body* (London: Church House Publishing, 1995).

5 Tim Wyatt, 'Cash Requested to Combat the "Doomsday Machine"', *Church Times,* 13 February 2015, p. 2.

6 Kaye, *An Introduction to World Anglicanism,* p. 48.

7 See Anglican Relief and Development Fund, 'Values', *The Anglican Relief and Development Fund* website <http://ardf.org/values/> accessed 10.8.15.

8 Global South Anglican, 'Economic Empowerment: Consultation, Networking and Partnership within Global South—May 2006', *Global South Anglican* website, 7 June 2006 <http://www.globalsouthanglican.org/index.php/blog/comments/economic_empowerment_within_global_south> accessed 12.7.14 and 'Third Trumpet: Communique from 3rd South to South Encounter', *Global South Anglican* website, 14 November 2005 <http://www.globalsouthanglican.org/index.php/comments/third_trumpet_communique_from_3rd_south_to_south_encounter/> accessed 12.7.14.

9 Anglican Communion, 'The Primates' Meeting, February 2005 Communiqué', *Anglican Communion*

website <http://www.anglicancommunion.org/media/68387/communique-_english.pdf> accessed 12.7.14.

10 See Evan Kuehn, 'Instruments of Faith and Unity in Canon Law: The Church of Nigeria Constitutional Reform of 2005', *Ecclesiastical Law Journal*, vol. 10, iss. 2 (2008), 161–73.

11 See pie charts 'Global Distribution of Anglicans' in World Christian Database, 'Pie Charts: Anglican Communion & The Episcopal Church', entry for 28 June 2008 on *God, Christ: Questions of Faith* blog site <http://www.one-episcopalian-on-faith.com/2008/06/pie-charts-angl.html> accessed 8.2.16, originally sourced from the World Christian Database (research version, May 2008).

12 World Christian Database, 'Global Distribution of Anglicans'.

13 Quoted in Mark Chapman, *Anglican Theology* (London: T&T Clark, 2012), p. 175.

14 House of Bishops, *Women Bishops in the Church of England?* (London: Church House Publishing, 2004), p. 72.

15 Colin Coward et al., 'Grace and Disagreement Guide to Conversations Lacks Personal Experience', letter to *Church Times*, 6 March 2015, p. 14.

16 Quoted in William Hague, *William Wilberforce: The Life of the Great Anti-Slave Trade Campaigner* (London: Harper Press, 2008), p. 183.

17 Hague, *William Wilberforce*, p. 227.

18 Wilkinson, *The Church of England and the First World War*, p. 81.

19 The Church of England, 'Making New Disciples: The Growth of the Church of England', GS Misc 1054, *Church of England* website <http://www.churchofengland.org/media/1783339/gs%20misc%20 1054%20-%20making%20new%20disciples.pdf> accessed 8.7.15.

20 Quoted in Archdeaconry of France, minutes of the Annual Archdiaconal Synod in Chantilly 30–31 January 1998, author's collection, 1998, p. 9.

21 Anglican Consultative Council, *The Principles of Canon Law Common to the Churches of the Anglican Communion* (London: Anglican Communion Office, 2008), p. 61.

22 GAFCON Theological Resource Group, *Being Faithful: The Shape of Historic Anglicanism Today* (London: Latimer Trust, 2009), pp. 2–9.

23 Roger Coleman (ed.), *Resolutions of the Twelve Lambeth Conferences 1867–1988* (Toronto: Anglican Book Centre, 1992), p. 16.

24 Stephen Neill and Tom Wright, *The Interpretation of the New Testament 1861–1986* (Oxford: Oxford University Press, 1988), p. 163.

25 See e.g. The Church of England, 'Main Volume: Authorization, Preface, and Declaration of Assent', *Church of England* website <http://www.churchofengland.org/prayer-worship/worship/texts/mvcontents/ preface> accessed 8.2.16.

26 Anglican Communion, 'The Anglican Communion Covenant', *Anglican Communion* website <http:// www.anglicancommunion.org/media/99905/The_Anglican_Covenant.pdf> accessed 2.3.10.

27 John Jewel, *The Apology of the Church of England* (London: SPCK, 1838), p. 32 (Apology III.2).

28 Quoted in Richard H. Schmidt, *Glorious Companions: Five Centuries of Anglican Spirituality* (Michigan: Eerdmans, 2002), p. 19.

29 Article 20 and Article 6. See Church Assembly, *Book of Common Prayer: 1662 Version* (Oxford: Oxford University Press, 1965), pp. 701, 694.

30 Quoted in Schmidt, *Glorious Companions*, p. 16.

31 John Charles Ryle, 'The Teaching of the Ritualists not the Teaching of the Church of England', Church Association Tract 4, p. 1, *Church Society* (archived) website <http://archive.churchsociety.org/ publications/tracts/CAT004_RyleRitualism.pdf> accessed 22.2.13.

32 John Schofield, *Cromwell to Cromwell: Reformation to Civil War* (Stroud, Gloucestershire: History Press, 2011), p. 178.

33 See John Henry Newman, *The Via Media of the Anglican Church* (Oxford: Clarendon, 1990) and a discussion of the 'via media' in Stephen Sykes, *The Integrity of Anglicanism* (London: Mowbrays,

1978), pp. 14–16.

34 Quoted in John Cornwell, *Newman's Unquiet Grave: The Reluctant Saint* (London: Continuum, 2010), p. 73.

35 See Coleman, *Resolutions of the Twelve Lambeth Conferences 1867–1988*, p. 13.

36 IARCCUM (International Anglican–Roman Catholic Commission for Unity and Mission), *Growing Together in Unity and Mission: Building on 40 years of Anglican–Roman Catholic Dialogue* (London: SPCK, 2007), p. 17.

37 See e.g. The Episcopal Church in Vermont, 'The Report of the Joint Standing Committee to the Archbishop of Canterbury on the Response of The Episcopal Church to the Questions of the Primates articulated at their meeting in Dar es Salaam and related Pastoral Concerns', *The Episcopal Church in Vermont* website <http://www.diovermont.org/archived-site/EpiscopalChurch/HoBNewOrleans/JSC%20Report%20on%20New%20Orleans%20071003.pdf> accessed 30.8.14. Ending cross-border interventions is justified by citing the Councils of Nicaea (325), Constantinople (381), Chalcedon (451) and the Western Council of Sardica (343).

38 See, e.g., Bible in the Life of the Church Project, 'What the Anglican Communion Has Said About the Bible 2: Themes and Principles', p. 9, *Anglican Communion* website <http://www.anglicancommunion.org/media/98270/22-Themes-Principles.pdf> accessed 28.8.15.

39 Anglican Communion, 'The Anglican Communion Covenant', Section 1.2.5, *Anglican Communion* website <http://www.anglicancommunion.org/media/99905/The_Anglican_Covenant.pdf> accessed 3.3.12.

40 Richard Hooker, *The Laws of Ecclesiastical Polity* (Nashotah: Nashotah House Press, 2012), III.viii.10.

41 Rowan Williams, *Anglican Identities* (London: Darton, Longman & Todd, 2004), p. 37 and Hooker, *The Laws of Ecclesiastical Polity*, VII.i.4.

42 Mark Chapman, *Anglican Theology* (London: T&T Clark, 2012), p. 173.

43 Michael Ramsey, *The Gospel and the Catholic Church* (Peabody: Hendrickson, 2009), p. 188, quoted in Paul Avis, *The Identity of Anglicanism: Essentials of Anglican Ecclesiology* (London: T&T Clark, 2007), p. 32; Ralph McMichael (ed.), *The Vocation of Anglican Theology* (London: SCM, 2014), p. 171; Colin Podmore, *Aspects of Anglican Identity* (London: Church House Publishing, 2005), p. 41.

44 Ramsey, *The Gospel and the Catholic Church*, p. 188.

45 See 'A Tale of Two Churches: The Ecclesiologies of the Episcopal Church and the Church of England Compared', *International Journal for the Study of the Christian Church*, vol. 8, no. 2 (2008), 124–54 and Colin Podmore, 'Two Streams Mingling: The American Episcopal Church in the Anglican Communion', *Journal of Anglican Studies*, vol. 9, iss. 1 (2011), 12–37.

46 See e.g. Lambeth Conference, *Lambeth Conference 1988 Report* (London: Church House Publishing, 1988), p. 61. 'Teacher and defender of the faith' is listed as one of ten distinguishing features of the bishop's ministry.

47 Church Assembly, *Book of Common Prayer: 1662 Version* (Oxford: Oxford University Press, 1965), p. 671.

48 Canon C18 (1). See The Church of England, 'Section C Ministers, their ordination, functions and charge', *Church of England* website <http://www.churchofengland.org/about-us/structure/churchlawlegis/canons/section-c.aspx> accessed 21.12.15.

49 Anglican Consultative Council, *The Principles of Canon Law Common to the Churches of the Anglican Communion* (London: Anglican Communion Office, 2008), p. 58.

50 John Shelton Reed, *Glorious Battle: The Cultural Politics of Victorian Anglo-Catholicism* (Nashville: Tufton Books, 1996), p. 64.

51 See Anglican Consultative Council, *The Principles of Canon Law Common to the Churches of the Anglican Communion*, pp. 47–48, for more on the bishop's authority according to the principles of canon law common to the churches of the Anglican Communion.

52 John Wolffe, 'Praise to the Holiest in the Height: Hymns and Church Music', in John Wolffe (ed.),

Religion in Victorian Britain: Volume 5 (Manchester: Manchester University Press, 1997), pp. 59–99, p. 63.

53 See David Holloway, 'The Pastor and Church Growth', in Melvin Tinker (ed.), *The Renewed Pastor: Writings in Honour of Philip Hacking* (Fearn: Mentor, 2011), pp. 169–98, pp. 193–94.

54 House of Bishops, *Women Bishops in the Church of England?* (London: Church House Publishing, 2004), p. 105.

55 Maggi Dawn, *Like the Wideness of the Sea: Women Bishops and the Church of England* (London: Darton, Longman & Todd, 2013), p. 19.

56 Jewel, *The Apology of the Church of England*, p. 36 (Apology III.7).

57 Anglican Consultative Council, *The Principles of Canon Law Common to the Churches of the Anglican Communion* (London: Anglican Communion Office, 2008), p. 60.

58 Mission and Public Affairs Council, *Mission-Shaped Church* (London: Church House Publishing, 2004).

59 The Church of England, 'Making New Disciples: The Growth of the Church of England'.

60 The Church of England, 'Report of the Task Force on Resourcing the Future of the Church of England', GS Misc 1978, *Church of England* website <http://www.churchofengland.org/media/2139976/gs%201978%20-%20resourcing%20the%20future%20task%20group%20report.pdf> accessed 8.7.15.

61 See Pete Broadbent, 'Simplicity Itself: The Future Shape of the Church of England…', *Fulcrum* website, 14 April 2015 <http://www.fulcrum-anglican.org.uk/articles/simplicity-itself-the-future-shape-of-the-church-of-england/> accessed 16.4.15.

62 House of Bishops, *Women Bishops in the Church of England?*, p. 143.

63 Williams, *Anglican Identities*, p. 38.

64 Hooker, *The Laws of Ecclesiastical Polity*, III.viii.10.

65 Hooker, *The Laws of Ecclesiastical Polity*, V. viii.2.

66 For an in-depth discussion of Anglican engagement with reason in the context of the Enlightenment, see Avis, *The Identity of Anglicanism*, pp. 237–344.

67 Lambeth Conference, *Lambeth Conference 1988 Report*, p. 102.

68 Thomas Cranmer, *Homilies* (Oxford: Oxford City Press, 2010), p. 301.

69 Church Assembly, *Book of Common Prayer*, Article 34, p. 708.

70 BILC (Bible in the Life of the Church), *Deep Engagement, Fresh Discovery* (London: Anglican Communion Office, 2012), p. 3.

71 Stephen Pickard and Duleep de Chickera, *The Anglican Way: Signposts on a Common Journey* (London: Anglican Communion Office, 2008), p. 4.

72 Church Assembly, *Book of Common Prayer*, Articles 20 and 21, pp. 701–2.

73 Lambeth Conference, *The Official Report of the Lambeth Conference 1998* (Harrisburg: Morehouse Publishing, 1999), p. 55.

74 Sykes, *The Integrity of Anglicanism*, p. 87.

75 Stephen Sykes, *Unashamed Anglicanism* (London: Darton, Longman & Todd, 1995), pp. 168–69.

76 Lambeth Conference, *The Lambeth Conference 1948: The Encyclical Letter from the Bishops Together with the Resolutions and Reports* (London: SPCK, 1948), quoted in Sykes, *Unashamed Anglicanism*, pp. 168–69.

Chapter 14   Forever Anglican

1 Mark Chapman, *Anglican Theology* (London: T&T Clark, 2012), p. 201.

2 Church Assembly, *Book of Common Prayer: 1662 Version* (Oxford: Oxford University Press, 1965), Article 24, p. 703.

3 Thomas Cranmer, *Homilies* (Oxford: Oxford City Press, 2010), p. 15 (First Homily, Part II).

4 See David Gitari (ed.), *Anglican Liturgical Inculturation in Africa: The Kanamai Statement 'African Culture and Anglican Liturgy'* (Nottingham: Grove Books, 1994), p. 17.

5 Charles Hefling and Cynthia Shattuck (eds), *The Oxford Guide to the Book of Common Prayer:*

A Worldwide Survey (Oxford: Oxford University Press, 2006), p. 339.

6 Stephen Pickard and Duleep de Chickera, *The Anglican Way: Signposts on a Common Journey* (London: Anglican Communion Office, 2008), p. 9.

7 *Faith in the Public Square* (London: Bloomsbury, 2012), p. 4.

8 John Allen, *Rabble Rouser for Peace: The Authorized Biography of Desmond Tutu* (London: Rider Books, 2006), p. 367.

9 Rowan Williams, 'China—Universities Have "Essential Role" in Public Life', *Dr Rowan Williams: 104th Archbishop of Canterbury* website, 13 October 2006 <http://rowanwilliams.archbishopofcanterbury.org/articles.php/1468/> accessed 11.10.15.

10 Kofi Annan with Nader Mousavizadeh, *Interventions: A Life in War and Peace* (London: Allen Lane, 2012), p. 228.

11 See George Carey, *Know the Truth: A Memoir* (London: Harper Collins, 2004), p. 106.

12 David Heywood, *Reimagining Ministry* (London: SCM Press, 2011), pp. 15–61.

13 Pickard and de Chickera, *The Anglican Way*, p. 17; see also Michael Doe, 'USPG and Theological Education', p. 3, *Rethinking Mission* website (2009) <http://www.rethinkingmission.org.uk/article_doe0609.html> accessed 3.6.13, on Anglicans and Mission.

14 Archbishop's Commission on Evangelism, *Towards the Conversion of England* (London: Board of the Church Assembly, 1945), p. ix.

15 Quoted in David Goodhew (ed.), *Towards a Theology of Church Growth* (Farnham: Ashgate, 2015), p. 198.

16 Goodhew, *Towards a Theology of Church Growth*, p. 207.

17 Archbishop's Commission on Evangelism, *Towards the Conversion of England*, p. 36.

18 Grace Davie, *Religion in Britain: A Persistent Paradox* (2nd edn, Chichester: Blackwell, 2015), pp. 5–6 and pp. 81–88.

19 Davie, *Religion in Britain*, p. 88.

20 The Church of England, 'Developing Discipleship', GS1977, *Church of England* website, pp. 3, 6 <http://www.churchofengland.org/media/2144200/gs%201977%20-%20developing%20discipleship.pdf> accessed 5.4.15.

21 Quoted in Geoffrey Rowell, Kenneth Stevenson and Rowan Williams (compilers), *Love's Redeeming Work: The Anglican Quest for Holiness* (Oxford: Oxford University Press, 2001), p. 174.

22 See Kevin Ward and Emma Wild-Wood, *The East African Revival: History and Legacies* (London: Ashgate, 2012) on the East Africa Revival and its legacy.

23 See Julia Cameron (ed.), *Christ Our Reconciler: Gospel–Church–World* (Nottingham: IVP, 2012), p. 64 for the Dean of Kigali (Antoine Rutayisire); and for Anglicanism and holiness see Ellen Charry, 'The Beauty of Holiness: Practical Divinity' in Ralph McMichael (ed.), *The Vocation of Anglican Theology* (London: SCM Press, 2014), pp. 196–243.

24 Anglican Consultative Council, *The Principles of Canon Law Common to the Churches of the Anglican Communion* (London: Anglican Communion Office, 2008), p. 58.

25 David L. Edwards, *Leaders of the Church of England 1828–1944* (London: Oxford University Press, 1971), p. 279.

26 Church Assembly, *Book of Common Prayer*, Article 21, p. 702.

27 Church Assembly, *Book of Common Prayer*, Article 8, p. 696.

28 Anglican Consultative Council, *The Principles of Canon Law Common to the Churches of the Anglican Communion*, p. 58.

29 Pickard and de Chickera, *The Anglican Way*, p. 3.

30 John Schofield, *Cromwell to Cromwell: Reformation to Civil War* (Stroud, Gloucestershire: History Press, 2011), p. 199.

31 Pickard and de Chickera, *The Anglican Way*, p. 4.

32 The Vatican, 'Address of Cardinal Walter Kasper at the Lambeth Conference, July 30, 2008', *Vatican*

website <http://www.vatican.va/roman_curia/pontifical_councils/chrstuni/angl-comm-docs/rc_pc_
chrstuni_doc_20080730_kasper-lambeth_en.html> accessed 7.7.13.

33 Allen, *Rabble Rouser for Peace,* p. 22.

34 Richard Hooker, *The Laws of Ecclesiastical Polity* (Nashotah: Nashotah House Press, 2012), III.viii.10.

35 Walter Abbott, *The Documents of Vatican II* (New York: Guild Press, 1966), Decree on Ecumenism III.13, p. 356.

36 Church Assembly, *Book of Common Prayer,* Article 34, p. 708.

37 Church Assembly, *Book of Common Prayer,* Article 22, p. 702.

38 Thomas Cranmer, *Homilies* (Oxford: Oxford City Press, 2010), 1st Homily, Part I, p. 10.

39 Church Assembly, *Book of Common Prayer,* Article 25, p. 703.

40 Anglican Consultative Council, *The Principles of Canon Law Common to the Churches of the Anglican Communion* (London: Anglican Communion Office, 2008), p. 67.

41 See Owen Chadwick, *The Victorian Church: Part One* (London: SCM Press, 1971), pp. 250–71 for the Gorham case; p. 263 for the Bishop of Exeter's threat to excommunicate the Archbishop of Canterbury.

42 Hooker, *The Laws of Ecclesiastical Polity,* V.lvii.12.

43 Anglican Consultative Council, *The Principles of Canon Law Common to the Churches of the Anglican Communion,* p. 70.

44 Michael Ramsey, *The Christian Priest Today* (revised edn, London: SPCK, 1987), p. 106.

45 Hooker, *The Laws of Ecclesiastical Polity,* VII.v.78.

46 ARCIC (Anglican–Roman Catholic International Commission), *The Final Report* (London: SPCK, 1982), pp. 33, 36.

47 ARCIC, *The Final Report,* p. 34.

48 Church Assembly, *Book of Common Prayer,* Article 26, pp. 704–5.

49 Ramsey, *The Christian Priest Today,* p. 109.

50 See J. Robert Wright (ed.), *Quadrilateral at One Hundred: Essays on the Centenary of the Chicago-Lambeth Quadrilateral, 1886/88–1986/88* (Cincinnati, Ohio: Forward Movement Publications, 1988), p. 142.

51 Archbishops' Group on the Episcopate, *Episcopal Ministry* (London: Church House Publishing, 1990), pp. 86–87. See also House of Bishops, 'Apostolicity and Succession', GS Misc 432, London, General Synod of the Church of England, 1994, p. 35 (2.6.9) and John Findon, 'Developments in the Understanding and Practice of Episcopacy in the Church of England', in Rupert Hoare and Ingolf U. Dalferth, *Visible Unity and the Ministry of Oversight* (London: Church House Publishing, 1996), pp. 79–92 for a fuller discussion.

52 See Cardinal Newman, 'Thoughts on the Ministerial Commission, Respectfully Addressed to the Clergy', *Newman Reader* website <http://www.newmanreader.org/works/times/tract1.html> accessed 15.12.15.

53 House of Bishops, 'Apostolicity and Succession', pp. 28–31.

54 See CCU (Council for Christian Unity), *Called to Witness and Service: The Reuilly Common Statement* (London: Church House Publishing, 1999).

55 See GAFCON Theological Resource Group, *Being Faithful: The Shape of Historic Anglicanism Today* (London: Latimer Trust, 2009), p. 9: 'We recognise the desirability of territorial jurisdiction for provinces and dioceses of the Anglican Communion except in those areas where churches and leaders are denying the orthodox faith or preventing its spread, and in a few areas for which overlapping jurisdictions are beneficial for historical or cultural reasons.'

56 See e.g. Roger Coleman (ed.), *Resolutions of the Twelve Lambeth Conferences 1867–1988* (Toronto: Anglican Book Centre, 1992), p. 170: 'This Conference deplores the existence of parallel Anglican jurisdictions in Europe' (Lambeth Conference 1968, Resolution 63). The four overlapping jurisdictions are the Diocese of Gibraltar in Europe, the Convocation of Episcopal Churches in Europe, the Spanish Episcopal Reformed Church and the Portuguese Lusitanian Church.

57 Lambeth Commission on Communion, *The Windsor Report* (London: Anglican Communion Office, 2004), p. 65.

58 Lambeth Commission on Communion, *The Windsor Report*, p. 21.

59 Lambeth Commission on Communion, *The Windsor Report*, p. 36.

60 Lambeth Commission on Communion, *The Windsor Report*, p. 21.

61 See Lambeth Conference, *The Official Report of the Lambeth Conference 1998* (Harrisburg: Morehouse Publishing, 1999), pp. 27–30 and ARCIC (Anglican–Roman Catholic International Commission), *ARCIC II: Church as Communion* (London: Church House Publishing, 1991).

62 ARCIC, *ARCIC II*, p. 57.

63 ARCIC, *ARCIC II*, p. 62.

64 See Anglican Communion, 'Deeper Communion; Gracious Restraint: A Letter from Alexandria to the Churches of the Anglican Communion', *Anglican Communion* website <http://www.anglicancommunion.org/media/68372/Pastoral-Letter.pdf> accessed 26.3.15. 'We welcome the Covenant Design Group's intention to produce a covenant text which has a relational basis and tone. It is about invitation and reconciliation in order to lead to the deepening of our koinonia in Christ, and which entails both freedom and robust accountability'. See also Paul Avis, *The Anglican Understanding of the Church: An Introduction* (London: SPCK, 2000), pp. 66–68 on Anglicans and 'koinonia'.

65 Lambeth Commission on Communion, *The Windsor Report*, p. 57.

66 Lambeth Commission on Communion, *The Windsor Report*, p. 55 and n. 39.

67 See Evan Kuehn, 'Instruments of Faith and Unity in Canon Law: The Church of Nigeria Constitutional Reform of 2005', *Ecclesiastical Law Journal*, vol. 10, iss. 2 (2008), 161–73.

68 Anglican Consultative Council, *The Principles of Canon Law Common to the Churches of the Anglican Communion* (London: Anglican Communion Office, 2008), p. 25.

69 Resolution 49 in Coleman, *Resolutions of the Twelve Lambeth Conferences 1867–1988*, p. 83.

70 J. I. Packer and N. T. Wright, *Anglican Evangelical Identity: Yesterday and Today* (Vancouver: Regent College Publishing, 2008), p. 167.

71 Lambeth Commission on Communion, *The Windsor Report*, p. 51.

72 Quoted in Paul Avis, *The Identity of Anglicanism: Essentials of Anglican Ecclesiology* (London: T&T Clark, 2007), p. 35.

73 Lambeth Commission on Communion, *The Windsor Report*, p. 52.

74 Stephen Sykes, *The Integrity of Anglicanism* (London: Mowbrays, 1978), p. 9.

75 Chapman, *Anglican Theology*, p. 176.

76 Address to theological college staff at Common Awards Conference, Durham on 6 July 2015. On 'faithful improvisation' see also The Church of England, The Faith and Order Commission of the Church of England, 'Senior Church Leadership: A Resource for Reflection', pp. 10–11, *Church of England* website, <http://www.churchofengland.org/media/2145175/senior%20church%20leadership%20faoc.pdf> accessed 8.2.16.

77 C. S. Lewis, *Mere Christianity* (Glasgow: Fount, 1977), p. 167.

78 'Apostolic Tradition in the Church means continuity in the permanent characteristics of the Church of the Apostles', World Council of Churches, Faith and Order Commission, *Baptism, Eucharist and Ministry* (Geneva: WCC, 1982), quoted in Paul Avis, *The Anglican Understanding of the Church: An Introduction* (London: SPCK, 2000), p. 70. See also pp. 65–73 for a discussion of catholicity, apostolicity and Anglican identity.

79 Church Assembly, *Book of Common Prayer*, p. 316.

Bibliography

Published Works

Abbott, Walter M., *The Documents of Vatican II* (New York: Guild Press, 1966)

Achebe, Chinua, *Things Fall Apart* (London: Heinemann, 1958)

—— *No Longer at Ease* (London: Heinemann, 1960)

—— *An Image of Africa, And, The Trouble with Nigeria* (London: Penguin Books, 1977)

—— *There was a Country* (London: Allen Lane, 2012)

Ajayi, Jacob Ade, *Christian Missions in Nigeria: 1841–1891* (Evanston: North Western University Press, 1965)

Allen, John, *Rabble Rouser for Peace: The Authorized Biography of Desmond Tutu* (London: Rider Books, 2006)

Alpha International, *The Alpha Course in a Catholic Context* (London: Alpha International, 2006)

Anber, Paul, 'Modernisation and Political Disintegration: Nigeria and the Ibos', *The Journal of Modern African Studies*, vol. 5, iss. 2 (1967), 163–79

Anglican Consultative Council, *Living Communion: ACC 13* (New York: Church Publishing, 2006)

—— *The Principles of Canon Law Common to the Churches of the Anglican Communion* (London: Anglican Communion Office, 2008)

—— and Pontifical Council for Promoting Christian Unity, *Growing Together in Unity and Mission: Building on 40 Years of Anglican-Roman Catholic Dialogue* (London: SPCK, 2007)

Annan, Kofi with Nader Mousavizadeh, *Interventions: A Life in War and Peace* (London: Allen Lane, 2012)

Anstee, Margaret Joan, *Orphan of the Cold War: The Inside Story of the Collapse of the Angolan Peace Process, 1992–3* (Basingstoke: Macmillan Press, 1996)

Archbishop of Canterbury's Commission on Urban Priority Areas, *Faith in the City: A Call for Action by Church and Nation* (London: Church House Publishing, 1985)

Archbishops' Commission on Christian Doctrine, *Subscription and Assent to the Thirty-Nine Articles* (London: SPCK, 1968)

Archbishop's Commission on Evangelism, *Towards the Conversion of England* (London: Board of the Church Assembly, 1945)

Archbishops' Commission on the Organisation of the Church of England, *Working as One Body* (London: Church House Publishing, 1995)

Archbishops' Commission on Urban Life and Faith, *Faithful Cities: A Call for Celebration, Vision and Justice* (London: Methodist Publishing House and Church House Publishing, 2006)

Archbishops' Commission on Women and Holy Orders, *Women and Holy Orders* (London: Church Information Office, 1966)

Archbishops' Committees of Inquiry, *Reports of the Archbishops' Committees of Inquiry* (London: SPCK, 1919)

Archbishops' Council, *Common Worship: Pastoral Services* (Cambridge: Cambridge University Press, 2000)

—— *The Church of England Yearbook 2012* (London: Church House Publishing, 2011)

Archbishops' Group on the Episcopate, *Episcopal Ministry* (London: Church House Publishing, 1990)

Archbishops' Review of the See of Canterbury, *To Lead and to Serve: The Report of the Review of the See of Canterbury* (London: Church House Publishing, 2001)

ARCIC (Anglican–Roman Catholic International Commission), *The Final Report* (London: SPCK, 1982)

—— *ARCIC II: Church as Communion* (London: Church House Publishing, 1991)

—— *ARCIC II: Life in Christ* (London: Church House Publishing, 1994)

Argent, Nigel, *Ardingly College, 1939–1990* (London: Autolycus Press, 1991)

Atherstone, Andrew, *Clergy Robes and Mission Priorities* (Cambridge: Grove Books, 2008)

—— *Archbishop Justin Welby: The Road to Canterbury* (London: Darton, Longman & Todd, 2013)

—— *Risk-Taker and Reconciler: Archbishop Justin Welby* (London: Darton, Longman & Todd, 2014)

—— and Maiden, John (eds), *Evangelicalism and the Church of England in the Twentieth Century* (Woodbridge: Boydell, 2014)

Aughton, Peter, *Liverpool: A People's History* (Lancaster: Carnegie Publishing, 2008)

Avis, Paul, *The Anglican Understanding of the Church: An Introduction* (London: SPCK, 2000)

—— *Anglicanism and the Christian Church* (Edinburgh: T&T Clark, 2002)

—— *The Identity of Anglicanism: Essentials of Anglican Ecclesiology* (London: T&T Clark, 2007)

—— *Reshaping Ecumenical Theology: The Church Made Whole?* (London: T&T Clark, 2010)

—— (ed.), *Seeking the Truth of Change in the Church: Reception, Communion and the Ordination of Women* (London: T&T Clark, 2004)

Baker, W. S. (ed.), *The Parish Communion* (London: SPCK, 1944)

Ball, Helen, *A Short History of St Bride's Episcopal Church, Glasgow* (Glasgow: Kirklee Books, 2004)

Barclay, Oliver R., *Whatever Happened to the Jesus Lane Lot?* (Leicester: IVP, 1977)

Barker, Rosalin, *The Whitby Sisters: A Chronicle of the Order of the Holy Paraclete 1915–2000* (Whitby: OHP, 2001)

Bayes, Paul and Tim Sledge (eds), *Mission-Shaped Parish* (London: Church House Publishing, 2009)

Bays, Daniel H., *A New History of Christianity in China* (Chichester: Wiley-Blackwell, 2012)

Beaken, Robert, *Cosmo Lang: Archbishop in War and Crisis* (London: I. B. Tauris, 2012)

Bebbington, David W., *Evangelicalism in Modern Britain: A History from the 1730s to the 1980s* (London: Routledge, 1989)

Bede, *Ecclesiastical History of the English People*, tr. Leo Sherley-Price (London: Penguin, 1990)

Bediako, Kwame, *Theology and Identity: The Impact of Culture upon Christian Thought in the Second Century and in Modern Africa* (Oregon: Wipf & Stock, 1999)

Beek, Huibert van (ed.), *Revisioning Christian Unity: The Global Christian Forum* (Oxford: Regnum Books International, 2009)

Beeson, Trevor, *The Church of England in Crisis* (London: Davis-Poynter, 1973)

Bell, G. K. A., *A Brief Sketch of the Church of England* (London: Student Christian Movement, 1929)

—— *Randall Davidson: Archbishop of Canterbury* (London: Oxford University Press, 1938)

—— *Christian Unity: The Anglican Position* (London: Hodder & Stoughton, 1946)

BILC (Bible in the Life of the Church), *Deep Engagement, Fresh Discovery* (London: Anglican Communion Office, 2012)

Billings, Alan, *Lost Church: Why We Must Find it Again* (London: SPCK, 2013)

Black, Neville, 'Two Years On: The Liverpool Perspective', *Anvil*, vol. 5, no. 1 (1988), 17–21

Blackmore, Henrietta (ed.), *The Beginning of Women's Ministry: The Revival of the Deaconess in the Nineteenth Century Church of England* (Suffolk: Boydell Press, 2007)

Bliss, Frederick, *Anglicans in Rome: A History* (London: Canterbury Press, 2006)

Borman, Tracy, *Thomas Cromwell: The Untold Story of Henry VIII's Most Faithful Servant* (London: Hodder, 2014)

Bosch, David, *Transforming Mission: Paradigm Shifts in Theology of Mission* (New York: Orbis, 1991)

Botting, Michael, *Fanning the Flame: The Story of Ridley Hall Cambridge: Volume 3, 1951–2001* (Cambridge: Ridley Hall, 2006)

Bowden, John (ed.), *Thirty Years of Honesty: Honest to God Then and Now* (London: SCM Press, 1993)

Bradshaw, Paul F. (ed.), *A Companion to Common Worship, Vol 1* (London: SPCK, 2001)

Bradshaw, Tim, *The Olive Branch: An Evangelical Anglican Doctrine of the Church* (Oxford: Latimer House, 1992)

Bragg, Melvyn, *Credo* (London: Sceptre, 2001)

Briden, Timothy (ed.), *Moore's Introduction to English Canon Law* (4th edn, London: Bloomsbury, 2013)

Brook, V. J. K., *A Life of Archbishop Parker* (London: Oxford University Press, 1962)

Brown, Lindsay, *Shining Like Stars: The Power of the Gospel in the World's Universities* (Chorley: 10 Publishing, 2010)

Brown, Sarah, *Behind the Black Door* (London: Ebury Press, 2011)

Brown, Stewart J., *Providence and Empire: Religion, Politics and Society in the United Kingdom 1815–1914* (Harlow: Pearson Education Limited, 2008)

—— and Nockles, Peter B., (eds), *The Oxford Movement: Europe and the Wider World, 1830–1930* (Cambridge: Cambridge University Press, 2012)

Bryson, Bill, *At Home: A Short History of Private Life* (London: Doubleday, 2010)

Buchanan, Colin, *Taking the Long View: Three and a Half Decades of General Synod* (London: Church House Publishing, 2006)

Bullock, F. W. B., *The History of Ridley Hall Cambridge: Volume 1, to the end of A.D. 1907* (Cambridge: Cambridge University Press, 1941)

—— *The History of Ridley Hall Cambridge: Volume 2, 1908–1951* (Cambridge: Cambridge University Press, 1953)

Bunting, Ian (ed.), *Celebrating the Anglican Way* (London: Hodder & Stoughton, 1996)

Burgoyne, Joan, *Weeley and Weeley Heath: A Pictorial History* (Weeley Heath: Millstone, 1999)

Cameron, Julia (ed.), *Christ Our Reconciler: Gospel–Church–World* (Nottingham: IVP, 2012)

Campbell, John, *Margaret Thatcher: The Iron Lady* (London: Jonathan Cape, 2003)

Carey, George, *The Church in the Market Place* (Eastbourne: Kingsway Publications, 1984)

—— *Know the Truth: A Memoir* (London: Harper Collins, 2004)

Carpenter, Edward, *Cantuar: The Archbishops in their Office* (3rd edn, London: Mowbray, 1971)

Carpenter, Humphrey, *Robert Runcie: The Reluctant Archbishop* (London: Hodder & Stoughton, 1996)

Carter, Richard Anthony, *In Search of the Lost: The Death and Life of Seven Peacemakers of the Melanesian Brotherhood* (Norwich: Canterbury Press, 2006)

CCU (Council for Christian Unity), *Called to Witness and Service: The Reuilly Common Statement* (London: Church House Publishing, 1999)

Chadwick, Henry et al., *Not Angels But Anglicans: An Illustrated History of Christianity in the British Isles* (Norwich: Canterbury Press, 2010)

Chadwick, Owen, *The Victorian Church: Part One* (London: SCM Press, 1971)

—— *The Victorian Church: Part Two* (London: SCM Press, 1972)

—— *Michael Ramsey: A Life* (London: SCM Press, 1990)

—— 'Introduction' in Roger Coleman (ed.), *Resolutions of the Twelve Lambeth Conferences 1867–1988* (Toronto: Anglican Book Centre, 1992)

——— *Hensley Henson: A Study in the Friction between Church and State* (Norwich: Canterbury Press, 1994)

Chandler, Andrew, *The Church of England in the Twentieth Century: The Church Commissioners and the Politics of Reform, 1948–1998* (Woodbridge: The Boydell Press, 2006)

——— and David Hein, *Archbishop Fisher, 1945–1961: Church, State and World* (Farnham: Ashgate, 2012)

Chapman, Alister, *Godly Ambition: John Stott and the Evangelical Movement* (New York: Oxford University Press, 2012)

Chapman, Mark, *Anglicanism: A Very Short Introduction* (Oxford: Oxford University Press, 2006)

——— *Anglican Theology* (London: T&T Clark, 2012)

——— (ed.), *The Hope of Things to Come: Anglicanism and the Future* (London: Mowbray, 2010)

Charry, Ellen, 'The Beauty of Holiness: Practical Divinity', in Ralph McMichael (ed.), *The Vocation of Anglican Theology* (London: SCM Press, 2014), pp. 196–243

Chartres, Caroline (ed.), *Why I am Still an Anglican* (London: Continuum, 2006)

Chatfield, Adrian, *Something in Common: An Introduction to the Principles and Practices of Worldwide Anglicanism* (Nottingham: St John's Extension Studies, 1998)

Church Assembly, *Book of Common Prayer: 1662 Version* (Oxford: Oxford University Press, 1965)

Church of England Liturgical Commission, *Patterns for Worship: A Report by the Liturgical Commission of the General Synod of the Church of England* (London: Church House Publishing: 1989)

Church of England Newspaper, 'Cathedral Bombed in Zanzibar', *Church of England Newspaper*, 14 March 2014, p. 5

Church Times, The, 'Hereford v. Zanzibar', 28 May 1915, republished in *The Church Times*, 29 May 2015, p. 12

Clarke, John, *Yakubu Gowon: Faith in a United Nigeria* (London: Frank Cass, 1987)

Clarke, Peter B., *West Africa and Christianity* (London: Edward Arnold Publishers, 1986)

Clatworthy, Jonathan, *Liberal Faith in a Divided Church* (Winchester: O Books, 2008)

Clayton, Philip Byard, *Tales of Talbot House: Everyman's Club in Poperinghe and Ypres* (London: Chatto and Windus, 1919)

Cocksworth, Christopher J., *Evangelical Eucharistic Thought in the Church of England* (Cambridge: Cambridge University Press, 1993)

——— and Brown, Rosalind, *Being a Priest Today* (Norwich: Canterbury Press, 2002)

Coleman, Roger (ed.), *Resolutions of the Twelve Lambeth Conferences 1867–1988* (Toronto: Anglican Book Centre, 1992)

Colson, Charles and Richard Neuhaus (eds), *Evangelicals & Catholics Together: Working Towards a Common Mission* (London: Hodder & Stoughton, 1996)

Corbett, E. A., *Henry Marshall Tory: A Biography* (Alberta: University of Alberta Press, 1992)

Cornwell, John, *Newman's Unquiet Grave: The Reluctant Saint* (London: Continuum, 2010)

Coward, Colin, et al., 'Grace and Disagreement Guide to Conversations Lacks Personal Experience', letter to *Church Times*, 6 March 2015, p. 14.

Cowart, Courtney, *An American Awakening* (New York: Seabury, 2008)

Cowie, Leonard and Evelyn Cowie, *That One Idea: Nathaniel Woodard and His Schools*. (Ellesmere: The Woodard Corporation, 1991)

Cowper-Coles, Sherard, *Ever the Diplomat: Confessions of a Foreign Office Mandarin* (London: Harper Press, 2012)

Cranmer, Thomas, *Homilies* (Oxford: Oxford City Press, 2010)

Crawley, Aidan, *Leap Before You Look* (London: Harper Collins, 1988)

Cray, Graham, Ian Mobsby, and Aaron Kennedy (eds), *Ancient Faith, Future Mission: New Monasticism as Fresh Expression of Church* (London: Canterbury Press, 2010)

Croft, Steven, *Ministry in Three Dimensions* (London: Darton, Longman & Todd, 1999)

Darwin, John, *Unfinished Empire: The Global Expansion of Britain* (London: Allen Lane, 2012)

Davie, Grace, *Europe the Exceptional Case* (London: Darton, Longman & Todd, 2000)

—— *Religion in Britain: A Persistent Paradox* (2nd edn, Chichester: Blackwell, 2015)

Davie, Martin, *A Guide to the Church of England* (London: Mowbray, 2008)

—— *Our Inheritance of Faith: A Commentary on the Thirty Nine Articles* (Malton: Gilead, 2013)

Davison, Andrew, *Why Sacraments?* (London: SPCK, 2013)

—— and Milbank, Alison, *For the Parish: A Critique of Fresh Expressions* (London: SCM Press, 2010)

Dawn, Maggi, *Like the Wideness of the Sea: Women Bishops and the Church of England* (London: Darton, Longman & Todd, 2013)

Dearmer, Percy, *The Parson's Handbook* (Milton Keynes: Dodo Press, 2009)

Desmond, Adrian and James Moore, *Darwin* (London: Penguin Books, 2009)

Dillistone, F. W., *Into All the World: A Biography of Max Warren* (London: Hodder & Stoughton, 1980)

Diocese in Europe, *Yearbook 2007* (London: Diocese in Europe, 2007)

Doe, Michael, *Saving Power: The Mission of God and the Anglican Communion* (London: SCM, 2011)

Doe, Norman, *An Anglican Covenant: Theological and Legal Considerations for a Global Debate* (Norwich: Canterbury Press, 2008)

Douglas, Ian T., *Fling Out the Banner! The National Church Ideal and the Foreign Mission of the Episcopal Church* (New York: Church Hymnal Corporation, 1996)

—— 'Anglicans Gathering for God's Mission: A Missiological Ecclesiology for the Anglican Communion', *Journal for Anglican Studies*, vol. 2, iss. 2 (2004), 9–40

Dow, Graham, *Christian Renewal in Europe: Lessons for Christians in Britain* (Nottingham: Grove Books, 1992)

Driver, Jeffrey W., *A Polity of Persuasion: Gift and Grief of Anglicanism* (Oregon: Cascade Books, 2014)

Dudley-Smith, Timothy, *John Stott: The Making of a Leader* (Leicester: IVP, 1999)

—— *John Stott: A Global Ministry* (Leicester: IVP, 2001)

Eddison, John (ed.), *Bash: A Study in Spiritual Power* (Basingstoke: Marshall, Morgan & Scott, 1982)

Edwards, David L., *Leaders of the Church of England 1828–1944* (London: Oxford University Press, 1971)

—— and Stott, John, *Essentials: A Liberal–Evangelical Dialogue* (London: Hodder & Stoughton, 1988)

Enahoro, Peter, *How to be a Nigerian* (Ibadan, Nigeria: Spectrum Books Limited, 1998)

Falola, Toyin and Matthew M. Heaton, *A History of Nigeria* (New York: Cambridge University Press, 2008)

Findon, John, 'Developments in the Understanding and Practice of Episcopacy in the Church of England' in Rupert Hoare and Ingolf U. Dalferth, *Visible Unity and the Ministry of Oversight* (London: Church House Publishing, 1996), pp. 79–92

Ford, David F., *The Future of Christian Theology* (Chichester: Wiley-Blackwell, 2011)

Franklin, William (ed.), *Anglican Orders: Essays on the Centenary of Apostolicae Curae, 1896–1996* (London: Mowbray, 1996)

Furlong, Monica, *The C of E: The State It's In* (London: Hodder & Stoughton, 2000)

GAFCON Theological Resource Group, *Being Faithful: The Shape of Historic Anglicanism Today* (London: Latimer Trust, 2009)

Gassman, Günther, 'From Reception to Unity: The Historical and Ecumenical Significance of the Concept of Reception' in Colin Podmore (ed.), *Community—Unity—Communion: Essays in Honour of Mary Tanner* (London: Church House Publishing, 1998), pp. 117–29

Gatiss, Lee and Peter Adam, *Reformed Foundations, Reforming Future: A Vision for 21st Century Anglicans* (Watford: Lost Coin, 2013)

Gavshon, Arthur, *Crisis in Africa: Battleground of East and West* (Middlesex: Penguin Books, 1981)

General Synod, *The Charismatic Movement in the Church of England* (London: CIO Publishing, 1981)

—— *Deacons in the Ministry of the Church* (London: Church House Publishing, 1988)

George, Carl F., *How to Break Growth Barriers: Capturing Overlooked Opportunities for Church Growth* (Michigan: Baker Book House, 1993)

Gibbs, David, *A School with a View: A History of Ardingly College, 1858–2008* (London: James & James Ltd, 2008)

Giles, Richard, *Always Open: Being An Anglican Today* (Cambridge: Cowley Publications, 2004)

Gitari, David, *Troubled But Not Destroyed: The Autobiography of Archbishop David Gitari* (McLean, Virginia: Isaac Publishing, 2014)

—— (ed.), *Anglican Liturgical Inculturation in Africa: The Kanamai Statement 'African Culture and Anglican Liturgy'* (Nottingham: Grove Books, 1994)

Goddard, Andrew, *Rowan Williams: His Legacy* (Oxford: Lion, 2013)

Goodhew, David (ed.), *Church Growth in Britain: 1980 to the Present* (Farnham: Ashgate, 2012)

—— *Towards a Theology of Church Growth* (Farnham: Ashgate, 2015)

Gover, Daniel, *Turbulent Priests? The Archbishop of Canterbury in Contemporary English Politics* (London: Theos, 2011)

Green, Michael, *Adventure of Faith: Reflections on Fifty Years of Christian Service* (Michigan: Zondervan, 2001)

—— *Compelled by Joy* (Nottingham: IVP, 2011)

Green, Stephen, *Serving God? Serving Mammon? Christians and the Financial Markets* (London: Marshall Pickering, 1996)

Greenacre, Roger, *The Catholic Church in France: An Introduction* (London: Council for Christian Unity, 1996)

Gres-Gayer, Jacques, 'Le culte de l'ambassade de Grande Bretagne à Paris au début de la régence (1715–20)', *Bulletin de Protestantisme*, vol. CXXX (1984), 29–45

Groves, Phil and Angharad Parry Jones, *Living Reconciliation* (London: SPCK, 2014)

Guinness, Os, *Doubt* (Oxford: Lion, 1983)

—— *The Gravedigger File* (London: Hodder & Stoughton, 1983)

—— *The American Hour* (New York: Simon and Schuster, 1988)

Gunn, J., *Historical Records of No. 8 Canadian Field Ambulance* (Toronto: Ryerson Press, 1920)

Guy, John, *Thomas Becket: Warrior, Priest, Rebel, Victim: A 900-Year-Old Story Retold* (London: Viking, 2012)

Hague, William, *William Wilberforce: The Life of the Great Anti-Slave Trade Campaigner* (London: Harper Press, 2008)

Hancock, Peter, *Aubers Ridge* (Barnsley: Pen and Sword, 2005)

Harper, Michael (ed.), *Bishops' Move: Six Anglican Bishops Share Their Experience of Renewal* (London: Hodder & Stoughton, 1978)

Harrison, Matthew, *An Anglican Adventure: The History of St George's Church, Paris* (Paris: St George's Anglican Church, 2005)

Harrison, Paul and Robin Palmer, *News Out of Africa: Biafra to Band Aid* (London: Hilary Shipman, 1986)

Hastings, Adrian, *A History of African Christianity, 1950–1975* (New York: Cambridge University Press, 1979)

—— *A History of English Christianity, 1920–1990* (3rd edn, London: SCM Press, 1991)

—— *The Church in Africa, 1450–1950* (Oxford: Clarendon Press, 1994)

—— *The Shaping of Prophecy: Passion, Perception and Practicality* (London: Geoffrey Chapman, 1995)

—— *A History of English Christianity, 1920–1990* (4th edn, London: SCM Press, 2001)

—— (ed.), *A World History of Christianity* (London: Cassell, 1999)

Hebert, A. Gabriel (ed.), *The Parish Communion* (London: SPCK, 1937)

Heeney, Brian, *The Women's Movement in the Church of England 1850–1930* (Oxford: Clarendon Press, 1988)

Hefling, Charles and Cynthia Shattuck (eds), *The Oxford Guide to the Book of Common Prayer: A Worldwide Survey* (Oxford: Oxford University Press, 2006)

Hein, David and Gardiner Shattuck, *The Episcopalians* (New York: Church Publishing, 2004)

Hempton, David, *The Church in the Long Eighteenth Century* (London: I. B. Tauris, 2011)

Henson, Herbert Hensley, *Ad Clerum* (London: SPCK, 1958)

Hernon, Ian, *Riot! Civil Insurrection from Peterloo to the Present Day* (London: Pluto Press, 2006)

Hewitt, Gordon, *The Problems of Success: A History of the Church Missionary Society, 1910–1942, vol. 1, Tropical Africa, the Middle East, At Home* (London: SCM Press, 1971)

Heywood, David, *Reimagining Ministry* (London: SCM Press, 2011)

Hick, John (ed.), *The Myth of God Incarnate* (London: SCM Press, 1977)

Hill, Christopher and Edward Yarnold, *Anglicans and Roman Catholics: The Search for Unity* (London: SPCK, 1993)

Hind, John, 'Why have an Anglican Church on Mainland Europe?' in Wingate et al. (eds), *Anglicanism: A Global Communion* (London: Mowbray, 1998), pp. 114–19

Hindmarsh, D. Bruce, *John Newton and the English Evangelical Tradition* (Michigan: Eerdmans, 1996)

Hislop, Ian, 'Atheist with Doubts: A C of E "Don't Know"' in Caroline Chartres (ed.), *Why I am Still an Anglican* (London: Continuum, 2006), pp. 99–107

Holland, Robert, *Blue-Water Empire: The British in the Mediterranean since 1800* (London: Penguin, 2013)

Holloway, David, 'The Pastor and Church Growth', in Melvin Tinker (ed.), *The Renewed Pastor: Writings in Honour of Philip Hacking* (Fearn: Mentor, 2011), pp. 169–98

Holman, Bob, *Woodbine Willie: An Unsung Hero of World War One* (Oxford: Lion Books, 2013)

Hooker, Richard, *The Laws of Ecclesiastical Polity* (Nashotah: Nashotah House Press, 2012)

Horton, Charles H., *Stretcher Bearer! Fighting for Life in the Trenches* (Oxford: Lion Books, 2013)

Hough, Brenda, *Times Past: Notes Towards a History of the Nikaean Club* (London: Church House Publishing, 2001)

House of Bishops, *Women Bishops in the Church of England?* (London: Church House Publishing, 2004)

Howarth, Patrick, *When the Riviera was Ours* (London: Routledge and Kegan Paul, 1977)

Hughes, Thomas, *Tom Brown's Schooldays & Tom Brown at Oxford* (Ware: Wordsworth Editions, 1993)

Hulmes, Edward, 'Walter Miller and the Isawa: An Experiment in Christian Muslim Relationships', *Scottish Journal of Theology*, vol. 41 (1988), 233–46

Hunt, Tristram, *Ten Cities that Made an Empire* (London: Penguin, 2014)

Hutchinson, Mark and John Wolffe, *A Short History of Global Evangelicalism* (Cambridge: Cambridge University Press, 2012)

Hylson-Smith, Kenneth, *The Churches in England from Elizabeth I to Elizabeth II: Volume II, 1689–1833* (London: SCM Press, 1997)

—— *The Churches in England from Elizabeth I to Elizabeth II: Volume III, 1833–1998* (London: SCM Press, 1998)

IARCCUM (International Anglican–Roman Catholic Commission for Unity and Mission), *Growing Together in Unity and Mission: Building on 40 years of Anglican–Roman Catholic Dialogue* (London: SPCK, 2007)

IASCOME (Inter Anglican Standing Commission on Mission and Evangelism), *Communion in Mission and Travelling Together in God's Mission* (London: Anglican Communion Office, 2006)

Ifere, Simeon E., *God's Response to Nigeria: The Story of NIFES* (Jos, Nigeria: NIFES Press, 1995)

Iremonger, F. A., *William Temple, Archbishop of Canterbury: His Life and Letters* (London: Oxford University Press, 1948)

Isaacson, Alan, *Deeper Life: The Extraordinary Growth of the Deeper Life Bible Church* (London: Hodder & Stoughton, 1990)

JCCC (Joint Committee of the Convocation of Canterbury), *The Position of the Laity in the Church* (London: Church Information Board, 1902)

Jenkins, Philip, *The Next Christendom: The Coming of Global Christianity* (Oxford: Oxford University Press, 2002)

—— *The New Faces of Christianity: Believing the Bible in the Global South* (Oxford: Oxford University Press, 2006)

Jenson, Michael P., *Sydney Anglicanism: An Apology* (Oregon: Wipf & Stock, 2012)

Jewel, John, *The Apology of the Church of England* (London: SPCK, 1838)

Jones, Ian, Janet Wootton, and Kirsty Thorpe (eds), *Women and Ordination in the Christian Churches* (London: T&T Clark, 2008)

JWG (Joint Working Group of the World Council of Churches and the Roman Catholic Church), 'Common Witness and Proselytism', *Ecumenical Review,* vol. 23 (1970), 9–20

—— 'The Challenge of Proselytism and the Calling to Common Witness', in Jeffrey Gros et al. (eds), *Growth in Agreement II* (Geneva: WCC Publications, 2000), pp. 891–99

Kalu, Ogbu (ed.), *Christianity in West Africa: The Nigerian Story* (Ibadan: Day Star Press, 1978)

Kasper, Walter, *That They May All Be One: The Call to Unity Today* (London: Burns & Oates, 2004)

—— *A Handbook of Spiritual Ecumenism* (New York: New City Press, 2007)

—— *Harvesting the Fruits: Basic Aspects of Christian Faith in Ecumenical Dialogue* (London: Continuum, 2009)

Kaye, Bruce N., *An Introduction to World Anglicanism* (Cambridge: Cambridge University Press, 2008)

—— *Conflict and the Practice of Christian Faith: The Anglican Experiment* (Oregon: Cascade Books, 2009)

Kendall, Elliott, *The End of an Era: Africa and the Missionary* (London: SPCK, 1978)

Kent, John, *William Temple: Church, State and Society in Britain 1880–1950* (Cambridge: Cambridge University Press, 1992)

Keulemans, Michael, *Bishops: The Changing Nature of the Anglican Episcopate in Mainland Britain* (Xlibris Publishing, 2012)

Kings, Graham, 'The Most Revd Dr David Gitari', *Church Times,* 18 October 2013

Kirk-Green, Anthony and Douglas Rimmer, *Nigeria Since 1970: A Political and Economic Outline* (London: Hodder & Stoughton, 1981)

Knight, Henry Joseph Corbett, *The Diocese of Gibraltar; A Sketch of its History, Work and Tasks* (London: SPCK, 1917)

Kuehn, Evan, 'Instruments of Faith and Unity in Canon Law: The Church of Nigeria Constitutional Revision of 2005', *Ecclesiastical Law Journal,* vol. 10, iss. 2 (2008), 161–73

Lambert, Tony, *China's Christian Millions* (Oxford: Monarch Books, 2006)

Lambeth Commission on Communion, *The Windsor Report* (London: Anglican Communion Office, 2004)

Lambeth Conference, *The Lambeth Conference 1948: The Encyclical Letter from the Bishops Together with the Resolutions and Reports* (London: SPCK, 1948)

—— *The Lambeth Conference 1958: The Encyclical Letter from the Bishops Together with the Resolutions and Reports* (London: SPCK and Seabury Press, 1958)

—— *Lambeth Conference 1978 Report* (London: CIO Publishing, 1978)

—— *Lambeth Conference 1988 Report* (London: Church House Publishing, 1988)

—— *The Official Report of the Lambeth Conference 1998* (Harrisburg: Morehouse Publishing, 1999)

Lanoue, Carole (ed.), *Canadian Forces Medical Services: Introduction to its History and Heritage* (Ottawa: Director General Health Services, 2003)

Lewis, C. S., *A Grief Observed* (London: Faber & Faber, 1966)

—— *Mere Christianity* (Glasgow: Fount, 1977)

Lewis, Donald M., *Christianity Reborn: The Global Expansion of Evangelicalism in the Twentieth Century* (Michigan: Eerdmans, 2004)

Lewis-Anthony, Justin, *If You Meet George Herbert on the Road, Kill Him: Radically Re-thinking Priestly Ministry* (London: Mowbray, 2009)

Leyritz, Marc de, *Devine qui vient diner ce soir?* (Paris: Presses de la Renaissance, 2007)

Lings, George, 'A History of Fresh Expressions and Church Planting in the Church of England', in David Goodhew (ed.), *Church Growth in Britain: 1980 to the Present* (Farnham: Ashgate, 2012), pp. 161–78

Lockhart, J. G., *Cosmo Gordon Lang* (London: Hodder & Stoughton, 1949)

Loveless, Alton, *A Look at Some of the World's Largest Churches* (Columbus: FWB Publications, 2015)

Luscombe, Edward, *Matthew Luscombe: Missionary Bishop in Europe of the Scottish Episcopal Church* (Edinburgh: General Synod of the Scottish Episcopal Church, 1992)

Lynch, Donald, *Chariots of the Gospel: The Centenary History of the Church Army* (Worthing: Walter Ltd, 1982)

MacCulloch, Diarmaid, *Thomas Cranmer: A Life* (London: Yale University Press, 1996)

McCreary, Alf, *Nobody's Fool: The Life of Archbishop Robin Eames* (London: Hodder & Stoughton, 2005)

McCrum, Michael, *Thomas Arnold, Head Master: A Reassessment* (Oxford: Oxford University Press, 1989)

Macdonald-Milne, Brian, *The True Way of Service: The Pacific Story of the Melanesian Brotherhood, 1925–2000* (Leicester: Christians Aware, 2003)

McEwan, David O., *Wings of Faith: A History of Saint Kiaran's Scottish Episcopal Church, Campbeltown* (Edinburgh: Scottish Episcopal Church, 2003)

McGrath, Alister, *To Know and Serve God: A Biography of James I Packer* (London: Hodder & Stoughton, 1977)

—— *The Renewal of Anglicanism* (Harrisburg: Morehouse Publishing, 1993)

McLeod, Hugh, *The Religious Crisis of the 1960s* (Oxford: Oxford University Press, 2007)

McMichael, Ralph (ed.), *The Vocation of Anglican Theology* (London: SCM Press, 2014)

Magee, Bryan, *Men of Ideas* (Oxford: Oxford University Press, 1978)

Maiden, John, 'Evangelical and Anglo-Catholic Relations 1928–1983', in Andrew Atherstone and John Maiden (eds), *Evangelicalism and the Church of England in the Twentieth Century* (Woodbridge: Boydell, 2014), pp. 136–61

Mann, Alice, *The In-Between Church: Navigating Size Transitions in Congregations* (The Alban Institute, 1998)

Manwaring, Randle, *From Controversy to Co-Existence: Evangelicals in the Church of England, 1914–1980* (Cambridge: Cambridge University Press, 1985)

Maughan, Steven, *Mighty England Do Good: Culture, Faith, Empire, and World in the Foreign Missions of the Church of England, 1850–1915* (Cambridge: Eerdmans, 2014)

Millington, Constance, *Whether We Be Many or Few: A History of the Cambridge/Delhi Brotherhood* (Bangalore: Asian Trading Corporation, 1999)

Missio (Anglican Communion Mission Commission), *Anglicans in Mission: A Transforming Journey* (London: SPCK, 2000)

Mission and Public Affairs Council, *Mission-Shaped Church* (London: Church House Publishing, 2004)

Mombo, Esther, 'The Ordination of Women in Africa: A Historical Perspective', in Ian Jones et al. (eds), *Women and Ordination in the Christian Churches* (London: T&T Clark, 2008), pp. 123–43

Moorhouse, Geoffrey, *The Missionaries* (London: Eyre Methuen, 1973)

More, Richard, *Growing in Faith: The Lee Abbey Story* (London: Hodder, 1982)

Morris, Sally and Jan Hallwood, *Living with Eagles* (Cambridge: Lutterworth Press, 1998)

Moule, Handley C. G., *Charles Simeon* (London: Inter-Varsity Fellowship, 1892)

Moynahan, Brian, *Book of Fire: William Tyndale, Thomas More and the Bloody Birth of the English Bible* (London: Abacus, 2010)

Munden, Alan, *A Light in a Dark Place: Jesmond Parish Church* (Newcastle: Clayton, 2006)

Murray, Paul (ed.), *Receptive Ecumenism and the Call to Catholic Learning: Exploring a Way for Contemporary Ecumenism* (Oxford: Oxford University Press, 2008)

Murray, Stuart, *Church after Christendom* (Milton Keynes: Pater Noster, 2004)

Neill, Stephen, *Anglicanism* (Middlesex: Penguin Books, 1958)

—— *A History of Christian Missions* (2nd edn, Middlesex: Penguin, 1986)

—— *God's Apprentice: The Autobiography of Bishop Stephen Neill* (Sevenoaks: Hodder & Stoughton, 1991)

—— and Wright, Tom, *The Interpretation of the New Testament 1861–1986* (Oxford: Oxford University Press, 1988)

Neuhaus, Richard, *The Naked Public Square: Religion and Democracy in America* (Michigan: Eerdmans, 1996)

Newbigin, Lesslie, *The Other Side of 1984: Questions for the Churches* (Geneva: WCC, 1983)

—— *Unfinished Agenda: An Autobiography* (London: SPCK, 1985)

—— *Foolishness to the Greeks: Gospel and Western Culture* (London: SPCK, 1986)

Newman, John Henry, *The Via Media of the Anglican Church* (Oxford: Clarendon, 1990)

Newsome, David, *Godliness and Good Learning: Four Studies on a Victorian Ideal* (London: Cassell, 1961)

Nicolson, Adam, *When God Spoke English: The Making of the King James Bible* (London: Harper Press, 2004)

Nigeria Church Union Committee, *Scheme of Church Union in Nigeria* (Lagos: The Nigeria Church Union Committee, 1963)

Noll, Mark A., *The Rise of Evangelicalism: The Age of Edwards, Whitefield and the Wesleys* (Leicester: Apollos, 2004)

Northup, Lesley, 'The Episcopal Church in the USA', in Charles Hefling and Cynthia Shattuck (eds), *The Oxford Guide to the Book of Common Prayer: A Worldwide Survey* (Oxford: Oxford University Press, 2006), pp. 360–68

O'Connor, Daniel et al., *Three Centuries of Mission: The United Society for the Propagation of the Gospel, 1701–2000* (London: Continuum, 2000)

Okeke, David, 'The Church of Nigeria: The Book of Common Prayer', in Charles Hefling and Cynthia Shattuck (eds), *The Oxford Guide to the Book of Common Prayer: A Worldwide Survey* (Oxford: Oxford University Press, 2006), pp. 298–304

Okolugbo, Emmanuel, *The Ndosumili and the Ukwuani: A History of Christianity in Nigeria* (Ibadan: Daystar Press, 1984)

Ostheimer, John, *Nigerian Politics* (New York: Harper and Row, 1973)

Oswald, Roy M., *Making Your Church More Inviting: A Step-by-Step Guide for In-Church Training* (The Alban Institute, 1992)

Owen Jones, Peter, *Bed of Nails: An Advertising Executive's Journey Through Theological College* (Oxford: Lion Publishing, 1996)

Packer, J. I. and N. T. Wright, *Anglican Evangelical Identity: Yesterday and Today* (Vancouver: Regent College Publishing, 2008)

Palmer, Bernard, *A Class of Their Own: Six Public School Headmasters Who Became Archbishop of Canterbury* (Lewes: The Book Guild, 1997)

Palmer, Martin, *The Jesus Sutras: Rediscovering the Lost Religion* (London: Piatkus, 2001)

Paul, Leslie, *The Deployment and Payment of the Clergy* (London: Church Information Office, 1964)

Pawley, Bernard and Margaret Pawley, *Rome and Canterbury Through Four Centuries* (Oxford: Mowbray, 1974)

Percy, Martyn, *The Ecclesial Canopy: Faith, Hope, Charity* (Farnham: Ashgate, 2012)

—— Chapman, Mark, Ian Markham and Barney Hawkins (eds), *Christ and Culture: Communion After Lambeth* (Norwich: Canterbury Press, 2010)

Perry, Edith Weir, *Under Four Tudors: Being the Story of Matthew Parker, Sometime Archbishop of Canterbury* (London: George Allen & Unwin, 1964)

Perry, Reginald, *Ardingly, 1858–1946: A History of the School* (London: The Old Ardinians Society, 1951)

Pickard, Stephen and Duleep de Chickera, *The Anglican Way: Signposts on a Common Journey* (London: Anglican Communion Office, 2008)

Pickering, W. S. F., *Anglo-Catholicism: A Study in Religious Ambiguity* (Cambridge: James Clarke & Co., 2008)

Podmore, Colin, *Aspects of Anglican Identity* (London: Church House Publishing, 2005)

—— 'A Tale of Two Churches: The Ecclesiologies of the Episcopal Church and the Church of England Compared', *International Journal for the Study of the Christian Church*, vol. 8, no. 2 (2008), 124–54

—— 'Two Streams Mingling: The American Episcopal Church in the Anglican Communion', *Journal of Anglican Studies*, vol. 9, iss. 1 (2011), 12–37

—— (ed.), *Community—Unity—Communion: Essays in Honour of Mary Tanner* (London: Church House Publishing, 1998)

Pollock, John, *Billy Graham: The Authorised Biography* (London: Hodder & Stoughton, 1966)

—— *Wilberforce* (Tring: Lion Publishing, 1977)

Porter, Andrew, *Religion Versus Empire?* (Manchester: Manchester University Press, 2004)

Porter, Muriel, *Sydney Anglicans and the Threat to World Anglicanism: The Sydney Experiment* (Farnham: Ashgate, 2011)

Pullinger, Jackie and Andrew Quicke, *Chasing the Dragon* (Sevenoaks: Hodder & Stoughton, 1980)

Radano, John A. (ed.), *Celebrating a Century of Ecumenism: Exploring the Achievements of International Dialogue* (Geneva: WCC Publications, 2012)

Ramsey, Michael, *The Christian Priest Today* (revised edn, London: SPCK, 1987)

—— *The Gospel and the Catholic Church* (Peabody: Hendrickson, 2009)

Raven, Charles (ed.), *The Truth Shall Set You Free: Global Anglicans in the 21st Century* (London: Latimer Trust, 2013)

Reath, Mary, *Rome & Canterbury: The Elusive Search for Unity* (Maryland: Rowman & Littlefield, 2007)

Redfern, Alastair, *Being Anglican* (London: Darton, Longman & Todd, 2000)

Reed, John Shelton, *Glorious Battle: The Cultural Politics of Victorian Anglo-Catholicism* (Nashville: Tufton Books, 1996)

Reeve, Matthew, 'A Seat of Authority: The Archbishop's Throne at Canterbury Cathedral', *Gesta,* vol. 42, no. 2 (2003), 131–42

Reiss, Robert, *The Testing of Vocation: 100 Years of Ministry Selection in the Church of England* (London: Church House Publishing, 2013)

Riccardi, Andrea, *Sant'Egidio, Rome and the World* (Rome: St Pauls, 1996)

Roberts, Bill, *Life and Death Among the Ibos* (London: Scripture Union, 1970)

Robinson, John A. T., *Honest to God* (London: SCM Press, 1963)

Routley, Erik, *A Short History of English Church Music* (London: Mowbray, 1977)

Rowell, Geoffrey (ed.), *The English Religious Tradition and the Genius of Anglicanism* (Oxford: Ikon Productions, 1992)

——, Stevenson, Kenneth and Rowan Williams (compilers), *Love's Redeeming Work: The Anglican Quest for Holiness* (Oxford: Oxford University Press, 2001)

Rowse, A. L., *Robert Stephen Hawker of Morwenstow: A Belated Mediaeval* (Cornwall: Elephant Press, 1975)

Russell, Anthony, *The Clerical Profession* (London: SPCK, 1984)

—— *The Country Parish* (London: SPCK, 1986)

—— *The Country Parson* (London: SPCK, 1993)

Ryle, J. C., *Five English Reformers* (Carlisle: Banner of Truth, 1960)

—— *Knots Untied: Being Plain Statements on Disputed Points in Religion from the Standpoint of an Evangelical Churchman* (Cambridge: James Clarke & Co., 1977)

Sancerres, Guy, *A Bridge Over Troubled Waters: The Story of St Michael's, an Anglican Church in the Heart of Paris* (Paris: Format B, 2011)

Sassoon, Siegfried, *War Poems* (Mineola: Dover Publications, 2004)

Saunders, Teddy and Hugh Sansom, *David Watson: A Biography* (Sevenoaks: Hodder & Stoughton, 1992)

Schmidt, Richard H., *Glorious Companions: Five Centuries of Anglican Spirituality* (Michigan: Eerdmans, 2002)

Schofield, John, *Cromwell to Cromwell: Reformation to Civil War* (Stroud, Gloucestershire: History Press, 2011)

Scruton, Roger, *Our Church: A Personal History of the Church of England* (London: Atlantic Books, 2012)

Secor, Philip B., *Richard Hooker and the Via Media* (Bloomington, Indiana: Author House, 2006)

Seddon, Philip, *Gospel and Sacrament: Reclaiming a Holistic Evangelical Spirituality* (Cambridge: Grove Books, 2004)

Sheppard, David, *Bias to the Poor* (Sevenoaks: Hodder & Stoughton, 1983)

—— *Steps Along Hope Street: My Life in Cricket, the Church and the Inner City* (London: Hodder & Stoughton, 2002)

—— and Worlock, Derek, *Better Together: Christian Partnership in a Hurt City* (Sevenoaks: Hodder & Stoughton, 1988)

Shortt, Rupert, *Christianophobia: A Faith Under Attack* (London: Rider, 2012)

Simpson, Peter, *St Peter's C. E. School Ardingly Then and Now: 1848–1998* (Ardingly: St Peter's C. E. School, 1998)

—— *A Thousand Years of Village Christianity: A History of St. Peter's Church Ardingly, Sussex* (Ardingly: Ardingly History Society, 2008)

Snow, Jon, *Shooting History: A Personal Journey* (London: Harper Collins, 2004)

Spencer, Stephen, *Anglicanism* (London: SCM Press, 2010)

Stanley, Brian, *The Bible and the Flag* (Leicester: Apollos, 1990)

—— (ed.), *The World Missionary Conference, Edinburgh 1910* (Michigan: Eerdmans, 2009)

Steer, Roger, *Church on Fire: The Story of Anglican Evangelicals* (London: Hodder & Stoughton, 1998)

—— *Inside Story: The Life of John Stott* (Nottingham: IVP, 2009)

Steering Group for Theological Courses, *Theological Training: A Way Ahead* (London: Church House Publishing, 1992)

Stephenson, Alan, *The Rise and Decline of English Modernism* (London: SPCK, 1984)

Steven, James H. S., *Worship in the Spirit: Charismatic Worship in the Church of England* (Oregon: Wipf & Stock, 2002)

Stevenson, W. Taylor, 'Lex Orandi–Lex Credendi', in Stephen Sykes and John Booty, *The Study of Anglicanism* (London: SPCK, 1988), pp. 174–88

Stock, Eugene, *An Heroic Bishop: The Life Story of French of Lahore* (London: Hodder & Stoughton, 1914)

Stott, John, *Christian Mission in the Modern World* (London: Falcon, 1975)

Stubbs, John, *Donne: The Reformed Soul* (London: Penguin Books, 2006)

Swanson, R. N. (ed.), *Unity and Diversity in the Church* (Oxford: Blackwell, 1996)

Sykes, Stephen, *The Integrity of Anglicanism* (London: Mowbrays, 1978)

—— *Unashamed Anglicanism* (London: Darton, Longman & Todd, 1995)

—— 'The Anglican Character', in Ian Bunting (ed.), *Celebrating the Anglican Way* (London: Hodder & Stoughton, 1996), pp. 21–32

—— and Booty, John, *The Study of Anglicanism* (London: SPCK, 1988)

Sykes, William, *Visions of Faith: An Anthology of Reflections* (Oxford: BRF, 1996)

Tinker, Melvin (ed.), *The Renewed Pastor: Writings in Honour of Philip Hacking* (Fearn: Mentor, 2011)

Tomlin, Graham, *The Widening Circle: Priesthood as God's Way of Blessing the World* (London: SPCK, 2014)

Trollope, Joanna, *The Rector's Wife* (London: Bloomsbury, 1991)

Turner, Barry, *The Victorian Parson* (Stroud, Gloucestershire: Amberley Publishing, 2015)

Underwood, Brian, *Faith and New Frontiers: A Story of Planting and Nurturing Churches, 1823–2003* (Cambridge: ICS, 2004)

Vidler, Alec, *The Church in an Age of Revolution* (Harmondsworth: Penguin, 1961)

Wagner, C. Peter, *Church Growth and the Whole Gospel: A Biblical Mandate* (New York: Harper and Row, 1981)

Wainwright, Geoffrey, 'Is Episcopal Succession a Matter of Dogma for Anglicans? The Evidence of Some Recent Dialogues' in Colin Podmore (ed.), *Community—Unity—Communion: Essays in Honour of Mary Tanner* (London: Church House Publishing, 1998), pp. 164–79

Wallis, Arthur, *The Radical Christian* (Eastbourne: Kingsway Publications, 1981)

Walls, Andrew F., *The Missionary Movement in Christian History: Studies in the Transmission of Faith* (New York: Orbis Books, 1996)

Ward, Kevin, 'The Development of Anglicanism as a Global Communion', in Andrew Wingate et al. (eds), *Anglicanism: A Global Communion* (London: Mowbray, 1998), pp. 13–22

—— *A History of Global Anglicanism* (New York: Cambridge University Press, 2006)

—— and Stanley, Brian (eds), *The Church Mission Society and World Christianity, 1799–1999* (Michigan: Eerdmans, 2000)

—— and Wild-Wood, Emma, *The East African Revival: History and Legacies* (London: Ashgate, 2012)

Ward, Maisie (ed.), *France Pagan? The Mission of Abbé Godin* (London: Sheed and Ward, 1949)

Ward, Robin, *On Christian Priesthood* (London: Continuum, 2011)

Warner, Robert, *Reinventing English Evangelicalism, 1966–2001: A Theological and Sociological Study* (Oregon: Wipf & Stock, 2007)

Watson, David, *You are my God: An Autobiography* (Sevenoaks: Hodder & Stoughton, 1983)

Watson, Nick, Stuart Weir and Stephen Friend, 'The Development of Muscular Christianity in Victorian Britain and Beyond', *Journal of Religion and Society*, vol. 7 (2005), 1–21

Webster, Peter, *Archbishop Ramsey: The Shape of the Church* (Farnham, Surrey: Ashgate, 2015)

Weir, Alison, *Elizabeth the Queen* (London: Vintage, 2008)

Wells, Samuel, *What Anglicans Believe: An Introduction* (London: Canterbury Press, 2011)

White, Jim, 'Oh for a Dog Collar of our Own', *The Independent*, 6 November 1992, p. 17

Whyte, Bob, *Unfinished Encounter: China and Christianity* (London: Fount Paperbacks, 1988)

Wilkinson, Alan, *The Church of England and the First World War* (London: SCM Press, 1978)

Williams, Rowan, *Anglican Identities* (London: Darton, Longman & Todd, 2004)

—— 'Christianity in the Reinvention of China', Chatham House Lecture, *China Review* iss. 40 (2007)

—— *Faith in the Public Square* (London: Bloomsbury, 2012)

Wilson, Gillian (ed.), *Theodore: Letters from the Oxford Mission in India 1946–1993* (Romsey: The Oxford Mission, 1997)

Wingate, Andrew et al. (eds.), *Anglicanism: A Global Communion* (London: Mowbray, 1998)

Wishart, Ruth, 'It Seems I Only Know What I Think When I've Heard What I've Said', *The Guardian*, 21 November 1984

Wolff, Jetta S., *The Story of the Paris Churches* (London: Cecil Palmer & Hayward, 1918)

Wolffe, John, *God & Greater Britain: Religion and National Life in Britain and Ireland, 1843–1945* (London: Routledge, 1994)

—— 'Praise to the Holiest in the Height: Hymns and Church Music', in John Wolffe (ed.), *Religion in Victorian Britain: Volume 5* (Manchester: Manchester University Press, 1997), pp. 59–99

—— 'The Chicken or the Egg? Building Anglican Churches and Building Congregations in a Victorian London Suburb', *Material Religion* vol. 9, iss. 1 (2013), 36–59.

Wood, Ernest, *A History of Thorpe-le-Soken to the Year 1890* (Thorpe-le-Soken: T. C. Webb, 1975)

World Council of Churches, Faith and Order Commission, *Baptism, Eucharist and Ministry* (Geneva: WCC, 1982)

Wright, J. Robert (ed.), *Quadrilateral at One Hundred: Essays on the Centenary of the Chicago-Lambeth Quadrilateral, 1886/88–1986/88* (Cincinnati, Ohio: Forward Movement Publications, 1988)

Wyatt, Tim, 'Cash Requested to Combat the "Doomsday Machine"', *Church Times*, 13 February 2015, p. 2.

Yates, Nigel, *The Oxford Movement and Anglican Ritualism* (London: The Historical Association, 1983)

Yates, Timothy, 'The Idea of a "Missionary Bishop" in the Spread of the Anglican Communion in the Nineteenth Century', *Journal of Anglican Studies*, vol. 2, iss. 1 (2004), 52–61

Yoder, John Howard, *The Politics of Jesus* (Michigan: Eerdmans, 1996)

Electronic Sources

Akinola, Peter J., 'Statement on the Windsor Report 2004 from the Primate of All Nigeria', *Anglican Communion News Service* website, 20 October 2004 <http://www.anglicannews.org/news/2004/10/statement-on-the-windsor-report-2004-from-the-primate-of-all-nigeria> accessed 3.5.13

Anglican Church of Canada, 'Historical Sketch for Anglican Residential Schools', *Anglican Church of Canada* website <http://www.anglican.ca/tr/schools/> *http://www.anglican.ca/relationships/schools*accessed 4.4.14

Anglican Communion, 'A Statement from the Primates Gathered at the First African Anglican Bishops' Conference', *Anglican Communion News Service* website, 28 October 2004 <http://www.anglicannews.org/news/2004/10/a-statement-from-the-primates-gathered-at-the-first-african-anglican-bishops-conference> accessed 3.5.13

—— 'ACO: Primates' Meeting Communique', *Anglican Communion News Service* website, 19 February 2007 <http://www.anglicannews.org/news/2007/02/aco-primates-meeting-communique> accessed 15.6.13

—— 'ACO: Report of the Communion Sub-Group', *Anglican Communion News Service* website, 15 February 2007 <http://www.anglicannews.org/news/2007/02/aco-report-of-the-communion-sub-group> accessed 15.6.13

—— 'African Bishops' Conference Now Opens in Lagos', *Anglican Communion News Service* website, 27 October 2004 <http://www.anglicannews.org/news/2004/10/african-bishop-conference-now-opens-in-lagos> accessed 26.1.16

—— 'Archbishop Justin's Priorities', *Anglican Communion* website <http://www.anglicancommunion.org/structures/instruments-of-communion/archbishop-of-canterbury/justin-welby/archbishop-justins-priorities.aspx> accessed 25.10.15

—— 'Archbishop of Canterbury Responds to GAFCON Statement', *Anglican Communion News Service* website, 30 June 2008 <http://www.anglicannews.org/news/2008/06/archbishop-of-canterbury-responds-to-gafcon-statement> accessed 28.5.13

—— 'Archbishop of Canterbury's Pentecost Letter to the Bishops of the Anglican Communion', *Anglican Communion News Service* website, 13 May 2008 <http://www.anglicannews.org/news/2008/05/archbishop-of-canterburys-pentecost-letter-to-the-bishops-of-the-anglican-communion> accessed 30.8.14

—— 'Archbishop's Pastoral Letter to Bishops of the Anglican Communion', *Anglican Communion News Service* website, 26 August 2008 <http://www.anglicannews.org/news/2008/08/archbishops-pastoral-letter-to-bishops-of-the-anglican-communion> accessed 3.6.13

—— 'Communique from the African Anglican Bishops' Conference', *Anglican Communion News Service* website, 1 November 2004 <http://www.anglicannews.org/news/2004/11/communique-from-the-african-anglican-bishops-conference> accessed 3.5.13

—— 'Communiqué from the Primates' Meeting 2016', *Anglican Communion News Service* website, 15 January 2016 <http://www.anglicannews.org/features/2016/01/communique-from-the-primates-meeting-2016.aspx> accessed 28.3.16

—— 'Deeper Communion; Gracious Restraint: A Letter from Alexandria to the Churches of the Anglican Communion', *Anglican Communion* website <http://www.anglicancommunion.org/media/68372/Pastoral-Letter.pdf> accessed 26.3.15

—— 'Education/Studies', *Anglican Communion* website <http://www.anglicancommunion.org/mission/theology/educationstudies> accessed 15.7.14

—— 'French-speaking Anglicans set Theological Education, Translation as Priorities', *Anglican Communion News Service* website, 10 August 2005 <http://www.anglicannews.org/news/2005/08/french-speaking-anglicans-set-theological-education,-translation-as-priorities> accessed 16.8.07

—— 'House of Bishops adopts "Covenant Statement"', *Anglican Communion News Service* website, 16 March 2005 <http://www.anglicannews.org/news/2005/03/house-of-bishops-adopts-covenant-statement> accessed 15.6.13

—— 'Lambeth Conference Set for Canterbury 2008', *Anglican Communion News Service* website, 28 June 2005 <http://www.anglicannews.org/news/2005/06/lambeth-conference-set-for-canterbury-2008> accessed 15.6.13

—— 'Member Churches', *Anglican Communion* website <http://www.anglicancommunion.org/structures/member-churches> accessed 13.7.13

—— 'Report of the Meeting of Primates of the Anglican Communion', *Anglican Communion News Service* website, 17 April 2002 <http://www.anglicannews.org/news/2002/04/report-of-the-meeting-of-primates-of-the-anglican-communion> accessed 4.6.13

—— 'Resolutions Passed Today At ACC-13', *Anglican Communion News Service* website, 22 June 2005 <http://www.anglicannews.org/news/2005/06/resolutions-passed-today-at-acc-13> accessed 15.6.13

—— 'Statement by the Secretary General', *Anglican Communion News Service* website, 26 September 2007 <http://www.anglicannews.org/news/2007/09/statement-by-the-secretary-general.aspx> accessed 17.12.15

—— 'Statement from the Church of the Province of Uganda', *Anglican Communion News Service* website, 15 February 2008 <http://www.anglicannews.org/news/2008/02/statement-from-the-church-of-the-province-of-uganda> accessed 28.5.13

—— 'The Anglican Communion Covenant', *Anglican Communion* website <http://www.anglicancommunion.org/media/99905/The_Anglican_Covenant.pdf> accessed 14.4.13

—— 'The Primates' Meeting, February 2005 Communiqué', *Anglican Communion* website <http://www.anglicancommunion.org/media/68387/communique-_english.pdf> accessed 12.7.14

—— 'The Windsor Continuation Group', *Anglican Communion* website <http://www.anglicancommunion.org/media/100354/The-Windsor-Continuation-Group.pdf> accessed 1.8.15

Anglican European Provincial Consultation, 'Europe Partners in Mission Consultation: Madrid, 16-18 May 2003', *Anglican European Provincial Consultation* website <http://europeconsultation.anglican.org/may03pimreport.html> accessed 5.6.13

Anglican Relief and Development Fund, 'Values', The Anglican Relief and Development Fund website <http://ardf.org/values/> accessed 10.8.15

Angola London Mozambique Association, 'A Brief History of the Anglican Church in Angola', ALMA Link website <http://www.almalink.org/dioceses/bhistang.htm> accessed 7.7.13

Archbishops' Council, Just Pray website <http://www.justpray.uk/what/> accessed 27.1.16

Archdiocese of Indianapolis, 'Pope Speaks of Unity and the Council', The Criterion, vol. 1, no. 40 (7 July 1961), Archdiocese of Indianapolis website <http://www.archindy.org/criterion/

local/1961/07-07-preview.html> accessed 17.12.15

BBC, 'Funeral for British Victim of Paris Attacks', BBC website, 21 December 2015 <http://www.bbc. co.uk/news/uk-england-essex-35152849> accessed 8.1.16

Bible in the Life of the Church Project, 'What the Anglican Communion Has Said About the Bible 2: Themes and Principles', Anglican Communion website <http://www.anglicancommunion.org/ media/98270/22-Themes-Principles.pdf> accessed 28.8.15

Bible Reading Fellowship, Messy Church website <http://www.messychurch.org.uk/> accessed 6.4.14

Bowcott, Owen, 'Cross Ban Did Infringe BA Worker's Rights, Strasbourg Court Rules', The Guardian website, 15 January 2013 <http://www.theguardian.com/law/2013/jan/15/ba-rights-cross-european-court>, accessed 28.3.16

Bristol Post, 'Christ Church in Clifton Recreated in China' on Bristol Post website, 22 February 2015 <http://www.bristolpost.co.uk/Christ-Church-Clifton-recreated-China/story-26059370-detail/story. html> accessed 28.3.16

Broadbent, Pete, 'Simplicity Itself: The Future Shape of the Church of England...', Fulcrum website, 14 April 2015 <http://www.fulcrum-anglican.org.uk/articles/simplicity-itself-the-future-shape-of-the-church-of-england/> accessed 16.4.15

Canadian Great War Project, 'Canadian War Diaries: Medical Units', Canadian Great War Project website <http://www.canadiangreatwarproject.com/warDiaryLac/wdLacP09.asp> accessed 29.4.13

Christian Today, 'Archbishop Akinola Responds to Eames' Comments in Open Letter', Christian Today website, 19 October 2005 <http://www.christiantoday.com/article/4279> accessed 26.1.16

Church of England, The, 'Church Commissioners' Annual Report 2007', Church of England website <http://www.churchofengland.org/media/49938/2007report.pdf> accessed 8.2.16

—— 'Developing Discipleship', GS1977, Church of England website <http://www.churchofengland. org/media/2144200/gs%201977%20-%20developing%20discipleship.pdf> accessed 5.4.15

—— 'House of Bishops' Declaration on the Ministry of Bishops and Priests', Church of England website <http://www.churchofengland.org/about-us/structure/general-synod/about-general-synod/ house-of-bishops/declaration-on-the-ministry-of-bishops-and-priests> accessed 21.12.15

—— 'House of Bishops Pastoral Guidance on Same Sex Marriage', Church of England website, 15 February 2014 <https://www.churchofengland.org/media-centre/news/2014/02/house-of-bishops-pastoral-guidance-on-same-sex-marriage.aspx> accessed 28.3.16.

—— 'Liturgical Revision', The Church of England website <http://www.churchofengland.org/prayer-worship/worship/texts/introduction/litrevis.aspx> accessed 22.12.15

—— 'Main Volume: Authorization, Preface, and Declaration of Assent', Church of England website <http://www.churchofengland.org/prayer-worship/worship/texts/mvcontents/preface> accessed 8.2.16

—— 'Making New Disciples: The Growth of the Church of England', GS Misc 1054, Church of England website <http://www.churchofengland.org/media/1783339/gs%20misc%201054%20-%20 making%20new%20disciples.pdf> accessed 8.7.15

—— 'Of Holy Orders in the Church of England', Canon C1, The Church of England website <http:// www.churchofengland.org/about-us/structure/churchlawlegis/canons/section-c> accessed 21.12.15

—— 'Report of the Task Force on Resourcing the Future of the Church of England', GS Misc 1978, Church of England website <http://www.churchofengland.org/media/2139976/gs%201978%20-%20 resourcing%20the%20future%20task%20group%20report.pdf> accessed 8.7.15

—— 'Section C Ministers, their ordination, functions and charge', Church of England website <http://www.churchofengland.org/about-us/structure/churchlawlegis/canons/section-c.aspx> accessed 21.12.15

Church Society, 'Conflict in the Diocese of Recifé, Brazil', Church Society website <http://www. churchsociety.org/issues_new/communion/division/iss_communion_division_recife.asp> accessed 17.12.15

CNN, 'Princess Diana's Anti-Mine Legacy', CNN website, 10 September 1997 <http://edition.cnn.

com/WORLD/9709/10/diana.angola/> accessed 17.12.15

Corpus Christi College and the Stanford University Libraries, Parker Library website <https://parker.
stanford.edu> accessed 8.2.16

Cottrell, Stephen, 'A Message from Bishop Stephen' in parish vacancy document on Halstead Area
Team website <http://www.halsteadchurches.co.uk/uploads/Halstead%20Area%20Team%20Profile.
pdf> accessed 28.3.16

Darwall-Smith, Robin, 'Revd W. G. D. Sykes, MA, Fellow and Chaplain', obituary on University
College Oxford website, 19 January 2015 <http://www.univ.ox.ac.uk/Billsykes> accessed 28.1.15

Davies, Lizzy, 'Church of England Votes against Allowing Women Bishops', 21 November 2012, The
Guardian website <http://www.theguardian.com/world/2012/nov/20/church-of-england-no-women-
bishops> accessed 28.3.16.

Desmond Tutu Peace Foundation, The, The Desmond Tutu Peace Foundation website <http://www.
tutufoundation-usa.org/exhibitions.html> accessed 30.8.15

Doe, Michael, 'USPG and Theological Education', Rethinking Mission website (2009) <http://www.
rethinkingmission.org.uk/article_doe0609.html> accessed 3.6.13

Eastman, Peggy, 'Tears of God', Living Church website, 26 March 2013 <http://www.livingchurch.org/
tears-god> accessed 17.12.15

Episcopal Church, The, 'Affirm Commitment to the Anglican Communion', Resolution A159
of the 75th General Convention, The Archives of the Episcopal Church website <http://www.
episcopalarchives.org/cgi-bin/acts/acts_resolution-complete.pl?resolution=2006-A159> accessed
15.6.13

—— 'Bishops' "Mind of the House" Resolutions', Episcopal News Service website, 20 March 2007
<http://archive.episcopalchurch.org/79425_84230_ENG_HTM.htm> accessed 15.6.13

—— 'Consider Blessing Committed, Same-Gender Relationships', Resolution C051 (5) of the 75th
General Convention, The Archives of the Episcopal Church website <http://www.episcopalarchives.
org/cgi-bin/acts/acts_resolution-complete.pl?resolution=2003-C051> accessed 15.6.13

—— 'Exercise Restraint in Consecrating Candidates', Resolution B033 of the 75th General
Convention, The Archives of the Episcopal Church website <http://www.episcopalarchives.org/cgi-
bin/acts/acts_resolution-complete.pl?resolution=2006-B033> accessed 15.6.13

—— 'House of Bishops: Message to God's People', Episcopal News Service website, 21 March 2007
<http://archive.episcopalchurch.org/78695_84233_ENG_HTM.htm> accessed 15.6.13

—— 'Support Development of an Anglican Covenant', Resolution A166 of the 75th General
Convention, The Archives of the Episcopal Church website <http://www.episcopalarchives.org/cgi-
bin/acts/acts_resolution-complete.pl?resolution=2006-A166> accessed 15.6.13

—— 'The Report of the Joint Standing Committee to the Archbishop of Canterbury on the Response
of The Episcopal Church to the Questions of the Primates articulated at their meeting in Dar es
Salaam and related Pastoral Concerns', The Episcopal Church in Vermont website <http://www.
diovermont.org/archived-site/EpiscopalChurch/HoBNewOrleans/JSC%20Report%20on%20
New%20Orleans%20071003.pdf> accessed 30.8.14

Espir, Helen, 'Wemmergill Hall—Memories of School Days During the Second World War, 1940–44',
Lunedale Heritage project website (2007) <http://www.lunedaleheritage.org.uk/wemmergill_hall.
htm> accessed 4.5.13

Faith and Order Commission of the Church of England, 'Senior Church Leadership: A Resource
for Reflection', Church of England website, <http://www.churchofengland.org/media/2145175/
senior%20church%20leadership%20faoc.pdf> accessed 8.2.16

Feast, The, The Feast website, <http://www.thefeast.org.uk> accessed 3.6.13

Forebears, 'Binchester Genealogy & History', Forebears website <http://www.forebears.io/england/
durham/byers-green/binchester> accessed 4.3.13

Fresh Expressions, 'What is a Fresh Expression?', Fresh Expressions website <http://www.

freshexpressions.org.uk/about/whatis> accessed 13.7.13

Global South Anglican, 'Communiqué of the Global South Primates during their visit to China in September 2011', Global South Anglican website, 14 September 2011 <http://www.globalsouthanglican.org/index.php/blog/comments/communique_of_the_global_south_primates_during_their_visit_to_china_in_sept> accessed 30.6.13

—— 'Economic Empowerment: Consultation, Networking and Partnership within Global South—May 2006', *Global South Anglican* website, 7 June 2006 <http://www.globalsouthanglican.org/index.php/blog/comments/economic_empowerment_within_global_south> accessed 12.7.14

—— 'Global South Primates Kigali Communiqué, September 2006', *Global South Anglican* website, 23 September 2006 <http://www.globalsouthanglican.org/index.php/comments/kigali_communique/> accessed 15.6.13

—— 'Third Trumpet: Communique from 3rd South to South Encounter', *Global South Anglican* website, 14 November 2005 <http://www.globalsouthanglican.org/index.php/comments/third_trumpet_communique_from_3rd_south_to_south_encounter/> accessed 12.7.14

Government of Canada, 'Statement of Apology to Former Students of Indian Residential Schools', *Indigenous and Northern Affairs Canada* website, 11 June 2008 <http://www.aadnc-aandc.gc.ca/eng/1100100015644/1100100015649> accessed 7.11.14

Griswold, Frank T., 'Statement from the Most Revd Frank T. Griswold on the Windsor Report 2004', *Anglican Communion News Service* website, 18 October 2004 <http://www.anglicannews.org/news/2004/10/statement-from-the-most-revd-frank-t-griswold-on-the-windsor-report-2004> accessed 3.5.13

House of Commons Debates, 'Vesture of Ministers Measure' Hansard: 30 July 1964, vol. 699, cc1865-935, *Hansard* website <http://hansard.millbanksystems.com/commons/1964/jul/30/vestures-of-ministers-measure> accessed 8.2.16

House of Lords Debates, 'Pastoral Reorganisation Measure', Hansard: 11 July 1949, vol. 163, cc1047-58, *Hansard* website <http://hansard.millbanksystems.com/lords/1949/jul/11/pastoral-reorganisation-measure-1949> accessed 8.2.16

Inclusive Church, *Inclusive Church* website <http://inclusive-church.org.uk> accessed 21.3.16

Ingham, Michael, 'Bishop of New Westminster Windsor Report Statement', *Anglican Communion News Service* website, 26 October 2004 <http://www.anglicannews.org/news/2004/10/bishop-of-new-westminster-windsor-report-statement> accessed 3.5.13

Lambeth Palace, 'Presence and Engagement: The Churches' Task in a Multi Faith Society', *Presence and Engagement* website <http://www.presenceandengagement.org.uk/presence-and-engagement-report> accessed 7.7.13

Law and Religion UK, 'CofE Simplification Report—Key Recommendations', *Law and Religion UK* website, 15 January 2015 <http://www.lawandreligionuk.com/2015/01/15/cofe-simplification-report-key-recommendations> accessed 6.8.15

Meijer, Guus and David Birmingham, 'Angola from Past to Present', *Accord* online journal, iss. 15, 2004 <http://www.c-r.org/accord-article/angola-past-present> accessed 7.2.16

Ministry Council, 'Ridley Hall Report: November 2011', *Church of England* website, 2012, <http://www.churchofengland.org/clergy-office-holders/ministry/ministerial-education-and-development/quality-assurance-in-ministerial-education/inspection-reports> accessed 2.5.12

National Archives, 'Church of England (Worship and Doctrine) Measure 1974 (No. 3)', *National Archives* website <http://www.legislation.gov.uk/ukcm/1974/3/contents> accessed 21.3.16

—— 'Parsonage Measure 1938', *National Archives* website <http://www.legislation.gov.uk/ukcm/Geo6/1-2/3/contents> accessed 8.2.16

—— 'Parsonages (Amendment) Measure 1947', *National Archives* website <http://www.legislation.gov.uk/ukcm/Geo6/10-11/3/contents> accessed 8.2.16

Newman, Cardinal, 'Thoughts on the Ministerial Commission, Respectfully Addressed to the Clergy',

Newman Reader website <http://www.newmanreader.org/works/times/tract1.html> accessed 15.12.15

No Anglican Covenant Coalition, 'Ten Reasons Why the Proposed Anglican Covenant is a Bad Idea', *No Anglican Covenant* website <http://noanglicancovenant.org/resources.html> accessed 23.4.16

Out of Battle, 'Festubert 1915—5th Sussex in Action', entry for 17 July 2008 on *Out of Battle* blog <http://outofbattle.blogspot.co.uk/2008/07/festubert-1915-5th-sussex-in-action.html> accessed 24.2.14

Pew Research Centre, 'Regional Distribution of Christians', *Pew Research Centre* website, 19 December 2011 <http://www.pewforum.org/2011/12/19/global-christianity-regions/> accessed 2.9.14

—— 'Religion in China on the Eve of the 2008 Beijing Olympics', *Pew Research Centre* website, 2 May 2008 <http://www.pewforum.org/2008/05/01/religion-in-china-on-the-eve-of-the-2008-beijing-olympics/> accessed 2.9.14

Potts, Lauren, 'Remembering the York Minster Fire 30 Years On', *BBC News* website <http://www.bbc.co.uk/news/uk-england-york-north-yorkshire-28112373> accessed 28.8.15

Redeemed Christian Church of God, 'Church Finder', *RCCG* website <http://www.rccguk.church/places/churches/> accessed 23.6.13

Roberts, S., 'Summary Report of the Papers of Arthur Stafford Crawley (1878–1948) and Anstice Katharine Crawley (1881–1963) in the muniments of St George's Chapel Windsor', Historical Manuscripts Commission, GB-0260-M.126, *National Archives* website, 1996 <http://www.nationalarchives.gov.uk/nra/lists/GB-0260-M.126.htm> accessed 10.7.13

Rosenthal, James M., 'European Anglicans Set Common Goals at Madrid Consultation', *Anglican Communion News Service* website, 20 May 2003 <http://www.anglicannews.org/news/2003/05/european-anglicans-set-common-goals-at-madrid-consultation> accessed 5.6.13

Ryle, John Charles, 'The Teaching of the Ritualists not the Teaching of the Church of England', Church Association Tract 4, *Church Society* (archived) website <http://archive.churchsociety.org/publications/tracts/CAT004_RyleRitualism.pdf> accessed 22.2.13

Sengulane, Dinis and Jaime Goncalves, 'A Calling for Peace: Christian Leaders and the Quest for Reconciliation in Mozambique', *Accord* online journal, iss. 3, 1998 <http://www.c-r.org/accord-article/calling-peace-christian-leaders-and-quest-reconciliation-mozambique> accessed 7.2.16

Sheridan, Sharon, 'General Convention Approves Marriage Equality', *Episcopal News Service* website, 1 July 2015 <http://episcopaldigitalnetwork.com/ens/2015/07/01/general-convention-approves-marriage-equality/> accessed 28.3.16

Sison, Marites N., 'Primate Urges Synod Members to Embrace Ethic of Respect', *Anglican Journal* website, 20 June 2007 <http://www.anglicanjournal.com/articles/primate-urges-synod-members-to-embrace-ethic-of-respect-7318> accessed 7.11.14

Smock, David, 'The Alexandria Process', *United States Institute of Peace* website <http://www.usip.org/programs/projects/alexandria-process> accessed 21.10.15

Solange De Santis, 'Synod Narrowly Defeats Same Sex Blessings', *Anglican Journal* website, 24 June 2007 <http://www.anglicanjournal.com/articles/synod-narrowly-defeats-same-sex-blessings-7329> accessed 7.11.14

St Mary's Basingstoke, *St Mary's Basingstoke* website <http://www.stmarys-basingstoke.org.uk> accessed 16.4.14

Sterr, Jeff, 'Drumheller: From Coal to Cool', entry for 29 May 2013 on *Retroactive: Blogging Alberta's Historic Places* blog <http://www.albertahistoricplaces.wordpress.com/2013/05/29> accessed 8.2.16

University College Oxford, 'Memorial Service for The Reverend William Sykes', *University College Oxford* website <http://univ.ox.ac.uk/univ-news/memorial-service-reverend-william-sykes> accessed 1.7.15

Vatican, The 'Address of Cardinal Walter Kasper at the Lambeth Conference, July 30, 2008', *Vatican* website <http://www.vatican.va/roman_curia/pontifical_councils/chrstuni/angl-comm-docs/rc_pc_chrstuni_doc_20080730_kasper-lambeth_en.html> accessed 7.7.13

Vines, Alex, 'Sant'Egidio and the Mozambique Peace Process', *Accord* online journal, iss. 3, 1998

<http://www.c-r.org/accord-article/calling-peace-christian-leaders-and-quest-reconciliation-mozambique> accessed 7.2.16

Vinovium, 'Binchester: A Short History', Vinovium website <http://www.vinovium.org> accessed 4.3.13

Welby, Justin, 'Archbishop Justin's Presidential Address to General Synod', *Archbishop of Canterbury* website, 12 February 2014 <http://www.archbishopofcanterbury.org/articles.php/5251/> accessed 8.2.16

—— 'Archbishop of Canterbury calls for Primates' Gathering', Archbishop of Canterbury website, 16 2015 <http://www.archbishopofcanterbury.org/articles.php/5613/> accessed 8.2.16

—— 'Archbishops Recall Commitment to Pastoral Care and Friendship for All, Regardless of Sexual Orientation', *Archbishop of Canterbury* website, 29 January 2014 <http://www.archbishopofcanterbury.org/articles.php/5237/> accessed 8.2.16

—— 'Reconciliation', *Archbishop of Canterbury* website, <http://www.archbishopofcanterbury.org/pages/reconciliation-.html> accessed 27.1.16

—— 'Statement on behalf of the Archbishop of Canterbury', *Archbishop of Canterbury* website, 1 February 2017 <http://www.archbishopofcanterbury.org/articles.php/5833/statement-on-behalf-of-the-archbishop-of-canterbury> accessed 12.6.17

Williams, Rowan, 'A Society that does not Allow Crosses or Veils in Public is a Dangerous one', *The Times*, 27 October 2006, available online at <http://www.globalsouthanglican.org/index.php/blog/comments/a_society_that_does_not_allow_crosses_or_veils_in_public_is_a_dangerous_one> accessed 28.3.16.

—— 'Address at Opening Ceremony Sant'Egidio International Meeting of Prayer for Peace—Palais de Congress, Lyons', *Dr Rowan Williams: 104th Archbishop of Canterbury* website, 11 September 2005 <http://rowanwilliams.archbishopofcanterbury.org/articles.php/1289/> accessed 12.5.13

—— 'Archbishop and Pope: "Our Churches Share Witness and Service"', *Dr Rowan Williams: 104th Archbishop of Canterbury* website, 23 November 2006 <http://rowanwilliams.archbishopofcanterbury.org/articles.php/1459/> accessed 25.5.13

—— 'Archbishop of Canterbury's Presidential Address at ACC-13', *Anglican Communion News Service* website, 20 June 2005 <http://www.anglicannews.org/news/2005/06/archbishop-of-canterburys-presidential-address-at-acc-13> accessed 15.6.13

—— 'Archbishop—Sangla Hills Apology "a hopeful sign"', *Dr Rowan Williams: 104th Archbishop of Canterbury* website, 27 November 2005 <http://rowanwilliams.archbishopofcanterbury.org/articles.php/1287/> accessed 26.1.16

—— 'Archbishop's Presidential Address—General Synod November 2010', *Dr Rowan Williams: 104th Archbishop of Canterbury* website, 23 November 2010 <http://rowanwilliams.archbishopofcanterbury.org/articles.php/919/> accessed 26.3.15

—— 'Archbishop's Visit to Pakistan', *Dr Rowan Williams: 104th Archbishop of Canterbury* website, 24 November 2005 <http://rowanwilliams.archbishopofcanterbury.org/articles.php/1288/> accessed 19.5.13

—— 'China—Press Conference, British Ambassadors' Residence, Beijing', *Dr Rowan Williams: 104th Archbishop of Canterbury* website, 24 October 2006 <http://rowanwilliams.archbishopofcanterbury.org/articles.php/748/> accessed 11.9.08

—— 'China—Universities Have "Essential Role" in Public Life', *Dr Rowan Williams: 104th Archbishop of Canterbury* website, 13 October 2006 <http://rowanwilliams.archbishopofcanterbury.org/articles.php/1468/> accessed 11.10.15

—— 'First Invitations Sent for "Reflective and Learning-Based Lambeth Conference"', *Dr Rowan Williams: 104th Archbishop of Canterbury* website, 22 May 2007 <http://rowanwilliams.archbishopofcanterbury.org/articles.php/1418/first-invitations-sent-for-reflective-and-learning-based-lambeth-conference> accessed 30.8.14

—— 'Forum Debate: Is Europe at its End?—Sant'Egidio International Meeting of Prayer for

Peace', *Dr Rowan Williams: 104th Archbishop of Canterbury* website, 12 September 2005 <http://rowanwilliams.archbishopofcanterbury.org/articles.php/1180/> accessed 12.5.13

—— 'Notes from China—Day by Day Highlights', *Dr Rowan Williams: 104th Archbishop of Canterbury* website, 23 October 2006 <http://rowanwilliams.archbishopofcanterbury.org/articles.php/628> accessed 11.9.08

—— 'The Archbishop's Advent Letter to Primates, 2007', *Dr Rowan Williams: 104th Archbishop of Canterbury* website, 14 December 2007 <http://rowanwilliams.archbishopofcanterbury.org/articles.php/631/> accessed 30.8.14

—— 'The Challenge and Hope of Being an Anglican Today: A Reflection for the Bishops, Clergy and Faithful of the Anglican Communion', 27 June 2006 <http://rowanwilliams.archbishopofcanterbury.org/articles.php/1478/> accessed 15.6.13

World Christian Database, 'Pie Charts: Anglican Communion & The Episcopal Church', entry for 28 June 2008 on *God, Christ: Questions of Faith* blog site <http://www.one-episcopalian-on-faith.com/2008/06/pie-charts-angl.html> accessed 8.2.16, originally sourced from the World Christian Database (research version, May 2008)

Manuscripts, Reports and Other Unpublished Works

Anglican Theological College of Vancouver, 'Anglican Theological College Bulletin: 1922', Vancouver, Anglican Diocese of Vancouver Archives, 1922

—— 'Anglican Theological College Bulletin: 1923', Vancouver, Anglican Diocese of Vancouver Archives, 1923

—— 'Student Body Minute Book', Vancouver, Anglican Diocese of Vancouver Archives, 1923

Archdeaconry of France, minutes of the Annual Archdiaconal Synod in Chantilly 30–31 January 1998, author's collection, 1998

Ardingly College, 'The Ardingly Annals: Number 224', Haywards Heath, Charles Clarke, 1944

—— 'The Ardingly Annals: Number 254', Haywards Heath, Charles Clarke, 1954

—— 'The Ardingly Annals: Number 255', Haywards Heath, Charles Clarke, 1955

—— 'The Ardingly Annals: Number 256', Haywards Heath, Charles Clarke, 1955

—— 'The Ardingly Annals: Number 263', Haywards Heath, Charles Clarke, 1957

Barnett, James, report of the Strasbourg Chaplaincy Annual Archdeaconry Synod, author's collection, 1988

Beauvoir, William, 'William Beauvoir Papers', London, Lambeth Palace Library, 1715–20

British Embassy Church, 'The British Embassy Church', Paris, 1955

Brown, Donald, 'Weeley: Through the Ages', Weeley, Parochial Church Council, Weeley Parish Church, 1996

Carlisle Diocese, 'Growing Disciples: Vision and Strategy 2011–2020', Carlisle, Carlisle Diocese Church House, 2011

—— 'Growing Together: Three Churches Journeying as one for God's Kingdom in Cumbria', Carlisle, Carlisle Diocese Church House, 2013

CEC (Conference of European Churches), 'Charta Oecumenica', Strasbourg, 2001

Chelmsford Diocese, 'Transforming Presence: Strategic Priorities for the Diocese of Chelmsford', Chelmsford, Chelmsford Diocese Church House, 2011

Crawley Papers, 'World War One Correspondence', M126/F, Windsor: St George's House Archives, 1915–19

—— 'Italy Diary', M126/K/18, Windsor, St George's House Archives, 1918–19

—— 'Letters from Nancy', M126/B/549, Windsor, St George's House Archives, 1919

Diocese of Calgary Archives, 'H. L. Nobbs Archive Materials', Calgary: University of Calgary, 1926–28

—— 'H. L. Nobbs Archive Materials', Calgary: University of Calgary, 1992

Dominy, Peter John, 'Church and Change on the Jos Plateau, Nigeria', MLitt thesis, University of Aberdeen, 1983

Durham Church Register, 'Byers Green St Peter Parish', EP/13–132, Durham, County Records Office, 1901–85

Ferns, Stephen, 'Attendance at Bishops' Advisory Panels', London, Ministry Council, 2013

Fulham Papers, *Blomfield Papers*, vol. 65, 'Letters from Bishop Luscombe', London, Lambeth Palace Library, 1829

—— *Blomfield Papers*, vol. 38, 'Dieppe—Letter on Building a Church', London, Lambeth Palace Library, 1843

Government of Canada, 'Table 12: Population of Canada by provinces, counties or census divisions and subdivisions, 1871–1931' in Census of Canada, Ottawa, 1931, pp. 98–102, held by Statistics Canada

Holloway, David, 'Reform Discussion Paper No. 1', London, Reform, 1993

House of Bishops, 'Apostolicity and Succession', GS Misc 432, London, General Synod of the Church of England, 1994

—— 'Women in the Episcopate? An Anglican–Roman Catholic Dialogue', London, General Synod of the Church of England, 2008

Jennings, Anthony and Harry Thompson (eds), 'The Cherwell Guide to Oxford', Oxford, Oxford Student Press, 1981

Jesmond Parish Church, 'Jesmond Parish Church: A History of God's Work—150th Anniversary', Newcastle-upon-Tyne, Clayton Publications, 2011

Lambeth Conference, 'Lambeth Indaba: Capturing Conversations and Reflections from the Lambeth Conference 2008', Lambeth Conference, 2008

Leroy, Michael, 'Riots in Liverpool 8: Some Christian Responses', London, Evangelical Coalition for Urban Mission, 1983

Ministry Division, 'Relating Recruitment to Deployment', London, Ministry Division of the Church of England, 2009

Norman, Andrew, 'The White Man's God in the White Man's Grave', unpublished report, 1985

—— 'Anglican Mission en France', self-published report, 1994

—— 'Common Mission and the Case for Anglican Engagement in French Language Ministry in France', MPhil thesis, University of Birmingham, 2007

Ridley Hall, 'Ridley Hall College Handbook', Cambridge, Ridley Hall, 1992

—— and Westcott House, 'Bishops' Roundtable Report: What Kind of Clergy Do We Need?', Cambridge, Ridley Hall, 2012

Royal Sussex Archive, 'Diary: An Account of the Proceedings of the 5th Cinque Ports Battalion: 18 February 1915–31 March 1919', RSR/MSS/5/72, Chichester, County Records Office, 1915–19

—— extract from letter dated 14 May 1915 from Lt Col. Langham commanding 5th Royal Sussex Regiment, MS/5/79, Chichester, County Records Office, 1915

—— 'Order of Service for Temporary Laying of Colours', RSR/MSS/11/23, Chichester, County Records Office, 1915

Smith, David, 'The Communication of the Christian Faith in Africa', Emem Publications, 1983

SPG Archive (Society for the Propagation of the Gospel), 'SPG Reports', Oxford, Rhodes House Library, 1926–27

St Andrew's PCC, AGM minutes, Weeley, Weeley Parish Church, 1959

St Andrew's PCC, AGM minutes, Weeley, Weeley Parish Church, 1960

Wilmot, Laurence, 'The St John's College Story: A Documentary', Winnipeg, St John's College, 2002

Index

Page numbers in *italics* denote illustrations.

Anglican Church relations *(continued)*
  with other faiths, 202, 225–26, 234, 238,
    264, 282–83, 321. *See also* interfaith
    dialogue; multifaith contexts
  with Pentecostal churches, 111–12
  with the Methodist Church, 42, 135, 167
  with the Roman Catholic Church, 119–20,
    126, 157–58, 159, 162, 174, 176–77, 179–80,
    190, 205, 222–25, 244–47, 289–91, 302. *See
    also* ARCIC; IARCCUM; unity: between the
    Anglican and Roman Catholic Churches
Anglican Communion, 2, 3, 33, 200–202, 248,
  298, 300, 334–35, 338
  and division, 2, 118, 213–14, 219–21, 247–52,
    254–55, 266, 286–94, 300, 303, 309, 335–37.
    See also communion (Christian): impaired;
    disagreement: good
Anglican Consultative Council (ACC), 149, 151,
  201, 209, 221, 247–48, 252, 255, 261, 287
Anglican Covenant, 221, 222, 249, 250, 287–88,
  295, 306, 308, 309–10, 323, 335
  drafts of: 2007 Nassau draft, 250–52, 255,
    261; 2008 St Andrew's draft, 263–64;
    2009 Ridley–Cambridge draft, *286,* 287
Anglican Formularies, 143, 305–6, 316
Anglican Healing Home (Igbo-Ukwu), 112
Anglican Hymn Book, The, 71
Anglican International Conference on Spiritual
  Renewal (1978), 84–85, 115
'Anglican Mission en France', 160, 161, 186–87,
  188, 190
Anglican Relief and Development Fund, 300
Anglican–Roman Catholic International
  Commission. *See* ARCIC
Anglican three-legged stool, 247, 310, 326
Anglican Way, 4, 215, 264, 321, 323, 326. *See also*
  'Signposts' document
Anglican World, 240
Anglo-Catholicism, 38, 43, 86, 157, 177, 289, 302
Angola, 129–30
Angolan Civil War, 129–30
Anis, Mouneer, 258
Annan, Kofi, 322
Anstee, Margaret, 130, 133
Anthony of Sourozh, 95
anti-slavery, 105–6, 193, 208, 254, 302–3, 316, 323
Aotearoa, New Zealand and Polynesia, Province
  of, 150, 215, 288
apartheid, 260, 322

Apologia ecclesiae Anglicanae, 142–43, 306, 310, 314
Apology for the Church of England, 142–43, 306,
  310, 314
Apostles' Creed, 308, 325
Apostolic succession, 313, 332
Apostolic Tradition, The, 154
apostolicity, 306–8, 339
Arabic-language ministry, 207
Archbishop of Canterbury, 80, 199, 200, 201,
  202, 207, 221, 235, 242, 258, 259, 301, 322
  as Focus of Unity, 5, 215, 220, 335
  See also individual Archbishops of Canterbury
Archbishop of York. *See individual Archbishops
  of York*
Archbishop's Commission on Evangelism. *See*
  Commission on Evangelism
Archbishops' Council, 196, 200, 228, 295, 299
Archbishops' Doctrine Commission, 143
L'Arche, 224–25, *225*
ARCIC (Anglican–Roman Catholic International
  Commission), 158, 180, 244–47, *246,* 329
Ardingly College, 46–48, 64–68, *68, 74,* 75–79, 82
Ardingly College Junior School, 64–65, 75
Arnold, Thomas, 46, 47, 55
Articles of Religion. *See* Thirty-Nine Articles
Asaba, Diocese of, 107, 110
ASB *(Alternative Service Book)* 85, 167, 178–79,
  198, 207
Ashimolowo, Matthew, 284
Assisi, 224–25
attendance, declining, 303, 323, 324, 331–32
Auckland Castle, 41, *41*
Augustine, Saint, 53, 291
Australia, Province of, 251, 288
autonomy, provincial, 213, 220, 221, 249, 251,
  286, 287, 295, 301, 334
Ayer, A. J., 95

Bangladesh, Church of, 234, 332
baptism, 39, *39,* 261, 308, 327–28
  in the Holy Spirit, 84
'Bash' (Eric J. H. Nash), 78, 304
'Bash' camps, 78–79, 81, 90, 103, 190, 304, 331
Basingstoke, 125–26, 128–29, 276
Bassenthwaite, 54–56, *55,* 60, 273–74
Beauvoir, William, 161
Bebbington Quadrilateral, 80 (n.26)
Bede, the Venerable, 54
Bedminster, 34, 35

Cinque Ports Battalion, *9*, 9–11, *10*, 113
Clayton, Tubby, 19
clergy
    geographical deployment of, 58, 60
    pastimes, 60–62
    numbers, 31, 60, 72, 134, 151, 270, 273,
        274–75, 279, 294–95, 304
    roundtable on, 271, 281
    training. *See* ministerial education
    See also ordained ministry; priest(s)
Cleverly, Charlie, 176
Clifton, 193. *See also* Christ Church, Clifton
CMS. *See* Church Missionary Society
Cocksworth, Christopher, 267 (n. 2)
Coggan, Donald, 165, 201
Cole, Alan, 82
College of Canons, 291
Colley, Jim, 83, 97, 171–72
Colonial and Continental Church Society
    (CCCS), 163–64, 165, 166. *See also* ICS
Colonial Bishoprics' Fund, 232
colonial churches, 33
colonialism, 300–301
Commission on Evangelism, 57–58, 66. See also
    Towards the Conversion of England
Committee for Theological Education, 134
Committees of Enquiry, 20
Common Declaration, 158, 246
common good, the, 322–23. *See also* injustice
Common Worship, 189, 198, 211, 306, 321
Communion, Anglican. *See* Anglican
    Communion
Communion, Holy. *See* Holy Communion
communion (Christian), 334–35
    with autonomy and accountability, 286,
        287, 295
    autonomy in, 220, 221, 249, 251
    Churches in, 207, 226–27
    impaired, 280, 312, 336
    instruments of. *See* Instruments of
        Communion
    provinces out of, 262, 300
    with the See of Canterbury, 301, 335
communities, religious, 49, 52, 98, 150, 235, 297,
    330. *See also individual communities*
Community of St Andrew, 148
Community of St Anselm, 292
comprehensiveness (of the Anglican Church),
    3, 336

Conference of European Churches (CEC), 209,
    227, 228, 300
confession, 47, 307, 327
conflict. *See* Anglican Communion: and division;
    disagreement; war
Congregation for the Doctrine of the Faith
    (CDF), 245, 246
Congregation for the Evangelization of
    Peoples, 265
Congresses. *See* Lausanne Congress (2010);
    pan-Anglican Congresses
contextualisation, 298, 304–5, 320–21, 339
    in Africa, 108–112, 115, 130, 253–54
    in England, 124, 211, 268
    in Melanesia, 218
    See also ministry: foreign language
Convocation of Episcopal Churches in Europe,
    177, 207
Coote, Roderic, 72
Cope, Margaret, 50–51
Corpus Christi College, Cambridge, 140, *140*,
    141, *141*, 142
Cottrell, Stephen, 274–75 (nn. 22–23)
Council of European Bishops' Conferences
    (CCEE), 209
Councils, Ecumenical, 257–58, 307, 313–14, 325
Country Parson, The, 59
Covenant. *See* Anglican Covenant; Lausanne
    Covenant
Covenant Design Group, 250–51, 258, 261, 263,
    286, 287. *See also* Anglican Covenant
Cowper, William, 80
CPAS (Church Pastoral Aid Society), 190
Cranmer, Thomas, 86, 138–39, *139*, *140*, 178, 328.
    See also individual works by Cranmer
Crawley, Arthur Stafford, 16–20 *passim*, 21
Cray, Graham, 136, 267, 268, 269
creeds, 72, 306, 308, 325–26
Crockford's Clerical Directory, 127–28
Croft, Steven, 269
Cromwell, Oliver, 80, 307, 332
Cromwell, Thomas, 138
Croos, John Princely, 182
cross-border interventions, 221, 222, 239, 249,
    257–58, 261, 266, 308, 334
Crosse, Ernest, 20, 47, 48
Crown Appointments Commission, 201
Crowther, Samuel Ajayi, 106–7, 108–14 *passim*
Cultural Revolution, 239–40, *239*, 241

Da Qin pagoda, *240*, 240–41
Darfur conflict, 219
Darwin, Charles, 62, 81, 302, 309
daughter churches, 33, 144
Davidson, Randall, 12, 18, 20, 31, 32–33, 34, 55, 71, 202, 325
Davison, Andrew, 270
Dawn, Maggi, 147, 149, 152, 314
de Clermont, Jean-Arnold, 175
de Leyritz, Marc, 224
de Pemberton, Roger, 65–66
de Waal, Hugo, 135–36
deaconesses, 147–48, 169, 185, 308
deacons, 23, 147–48, 150, 166–67, *167*, 178, 330
Decade of Evangelism, 144
Declaration of Assent, 143, 168, 306
Deeper Life Ministries, 104, 283–84
Delhi, 97–98
    Cambridge Mission to, 97–98, 118, 232, 233
demographics. *See under* Anglican Church
Descartes, René, 94
Diana, Princess, 83, 120, 129, 183–84, *184*, 198, 327
Diaz, Ivan, 265
Dikko, Umaru, 102–3
disagreement, 335–36
    within churches, 27–28, 182–83, 184–85
    good, 293–94, 335–37
    See also Anglican Communion: and division
division. *See* disagreement; *and under* Anglican Communion
Dix, Gregory, 154, 308
Dobinson, Henry Hughes, 111
Doctrine Commission, 143
Doe, Michael, 209
Domingos, Alexander, 130
Doria Pamphilj family, 244
Dow, Andrew, 194
Dow, Graham, 159
drama and mission, 90, 100–101
Draper, Martin, 177, 183
Drumheller, 24–26, 32–33,
    candles controversy in, 27–28, 81
Dry Drayton, parish church of, *x*, 1
Duncan, Bob, 178, 204, 205, 286
Durham, Diocese of, 272, 280

Eames, Robin, 150, 214, 219, 220
Eames Commission, 150, 214, 219, 313–14
early church. *See* tradition

East African Revival, 229, 325
East India Company, 99
Eastwood, Mike, 279
Ecclesiastical Commissioners, 44, 60, 196
Ecclesiastical History of the English People, 54
'ecumenical bishops', 284
Ecumenical Councils, 257–58, 307, 313–14, 325
ecumenism, 3, 125, 135, 234–35, 237, 267, 283–84, 289–90, 301, 327, 332–33. *See also* Charta Oecumenica; *and under* Anglican Church relations
Edinburgh, Duke of, 67
Edinburgh Missionary Conference (1910), 333
education. *See* ministerial education; schools; theological colleges; theological education; *and individual institutions and programmes*
Education Act (1944), 71
Edward VI, King, 138–39
Edwardes College, Peshawar, 234
Edwards, David, 79
L'Eglise de la Madeleine, Paris, *170*, 176, 184
L'Eglise Réformée de Belleville, Paris, 176
L'Eglise Réformée du St Esprit, Paris, 175–76
Elizabeth I, Queen, 140–41, 307, 326
Elizabeth II, Queen, 16, 67, 116, 124, 172, 264
Elizabethan Settlement, 141, 143
Elsmore, Guy, 277
Embassy Church, Paris, 163–65, *164*, 223, *310*. *See also* St Michael's Paris
Emmanuel, Bristol, 276
L'Emmanuel, Communauté de, 224
End of an Era, The, 102
England, Church of, 18–21, 57–58, 72–73, 79–85, 138–52, 268–71, 287–91 and *passim*
Enlightenment, the, 94, 110, 302, 316
Episcopal Church (USA), 150, 152–53, 248–50, 254–55, 257–58, 286, 288, 293–94. *For other Episcopal Churches see names of countries or provinces*
Escomb Church, 54, *240*
Eucharist. *See* Holy Communion
Europe
    Anglican activity in, 159, 161–62, 207–8, 209–10, 228–29. *See also* French-language ministry
    Diocese in, 160, 161, 177, 226
    the place of religion in, 226–28
    See also House of Bishops' Europe Panel
European Constitution, 210
European Union (EU) 210, 227–29

Green, Stephen, 174 (n. 1)
Greenacre, Roger, 177
Greenbelt Arts Festival, 90
Grief Observed, A, 5, 338
Griswold, Frank, 219, 249
Group for Urban Ministry and Leadership, 124
Growing Together in Unity and Mission, 246
Guinness, Os, 94, 155–56
GUML, 124
Gunstone, John, 84, 157

Handford, Clive, 264 (n. 75)
Hare, Richard, 84, 88, 92
Harper, David, 155
Harper, Michael, 84
Harper, Stephen, 256
Harris, Barbara, 150
Harvest Festivals, 48, *56*, 71
Hastings, *9*, 9–10
Hastings, Adrian, 119
Hausa language minstry, 115
Hawker, Robert Stephen, 71
Hawkins, Clive, 129, 276
Hawkins, David, 284
healing, 85, 112, 198
Heasewood Farm, 31, 46
Heirs Together Consultation, 209
Hemingway, Ernest, 15
Henry VIII, King, 138, *138*, 139, 297, 321
Henson, Hensley, 42, 50, 81, 253, 302, 325, 336
Herbert, George, 59–60, *311*, 325, 329
Higginson, Richard, 174
Hind, John, 160, 166, *167*, 186, 188, 189–90
Hines, John, 155
Hislop, Ian, 77–78
Hobson, George, 189
Hocken, Glen, 78
holiness, 325, 339
Holloway, David, 128, 280–81
Holy Communion, 76–77, 154, 178, 179, 308, 339
     prominence of, 21, 43, 62, 180
     presence of Christ at, 141, 142, 328
Holy Sepulchre, Church of the, 206
Holy Spirit, 77, 84–85, 167, 229, 305, 317
Holy Trinity, Brompton, 194, 224, 277
Holy Trinity, Brussels, 227, 228
Holy Trinity, Hastings, 10, *10*
Holy Trinity, Nice, 187
Holy Trinity, Paisley, 40

Holy Trinity, Paris, 177
Holy Trinity, Sliema, 127
Holy Trinity Cathedral, Shanghai, *239*, 239–40
Homilies, Cranmer's, 316–17, 320, 327
homosexuality, 155, 214, 220, 221, 247, 252,
     266, 286, 293, 294, 304. *See also* bishops:
     homosexual; marriage, same-sex; same-sex
     blessings
Honest to God, 72, 136–37, 143, 156, 204, 302
Hong Kong, 83, 149–50, 151, 243, 288
Hook, Walter, 162, 163
Hooker, Richard, 179–80, *296*, 310, *311*, 311,
     315–17 *passim*, 326, 328, 329, 332, 336
Hoopell, Robert, 40
House of Bishops' Europe Panel, 228
Huddersfield, 92–93
Huddleston, Trevor, 77
Humphries, John, 205
Hurd Report, 202
Hurricane Katrina, 257, *257*
Hutchison, Andrew, 256
Hwang, Jane, 150
Hyatt, Suzanne, 150
hymn singing, 76, 80, 297, 313, 337
Hymns Ancient and Modern, 70, 76, 111, 304

IARCCUM (International Anglican Roman
     Catholic Commission for Unity and Mission),
     246, 247
IASCOME (Inter-Anglican Standing Commission
     on Mission and Evangelism), 251
Ibadan, 103
Ibo-language ministry, 111
Ibrahim, Malam, 115–16
ICS. *See* Intercontinental Church Society
Idahosa, Benson, 105, 125
Ijaz-ul-Haq, Muhammad, 233
impaired communion, 280, 312, 336
'incompleteness' (of the Anglican Church),
     311–12
inculturation. *See* contextualisation
Indaba groups, 259, 264
India, 96, 97–100, *98*. *See also* North India,
     Church of; South India, Church of
Indian residential schools (Canada), 23, 256, 322
indulgences, 179
Industrial Christian Fellowship, 21
Inge, Dean, 42
Ingham, Michael, 219

Partners in Mission consultations, 207–8, 209
Passchendaele, Battle of, 14–15, 19–20
Pastoral Reorganisation Measure, 63
Patterns for Worship, 198
Patterson, Archibald, 130, 304
Patteson, John Coleridge, 215–16
Paul vi, Pope, 158, 180, 290
Paul Report, 134
Pawley, Bernard, 244
Payne, Claude, 203
pccs (Parochial Church Councils), 150–51
pcpcu, 208, 225, 246, 247
peace-building. *See under* Anglican Church
Pentecost Mountain, 216, 217
Pentecostalism, 6, 104–5, 112, 283–85
Peshawar, 232, 234
Phillipson, Christopher, 70
philosophy and faith, 94–95
Piave, Battle on the, 15
pim consultations, 207–8, 209
Pinkham, Cyprian, 23, 24, *25*, 331
pioneer ministry, 269, 273. *See also* leadership,
    pioneering
Pittsburgh, Diocese of, 204–5
plants, church, 144, 268, 276–77, 280, 284
Plea for the Middle Classes, A, 47
Pole, Reginald, 139, 140
Polge, Nick, 102
Policy Sub-Committee (General Synod), 128
Pontifical Council for Promoting Christian
    Unity (pcpcu), 208, 225, 246, 247
Poperinghe, 12–13, *13*, 19
popular culture, as driver for change, 304
Portuguese Lusitanian Church, 207
Porvoo Communion of churches, 227, 332–33
practical considerations, as driver for change,
    315, 316
prayer, 291–92
Prayer Book
    by country: American (1928 and 1979), 154,
        306; Church of England. See *Book of
        Common Prayer, The*; New Zealand, 321;
        Nigerian (1996), 219; Tanzania (1995),
        253–54; Zanzibar (1919), 253
    by language: in Ibo (1871), 111; in Swahili
        (1919), 253; in Urdu (1901), 99
    See also *Common Worship*
'Prayer of Humble Access', 154
Presbyterian Church of Scotland, 34, 232

presbyters, 166, 178, 179–80, 328–29
presence and engagement (concept), 304
Presence and Engagement (report), 281–82
priest(s), 178–80, 185, 328–30
    slum, 38
    women, 147–52, 169, 290, 337
    See also clergy; Jesus Christ: as High Priest;
        ordained ministry; priesthood, of the
        Church
priesthood, of the Church, 179, 328–29, 330
Primate of All England, 202
Primates' Council (gafcon), 262
Primates' Meetings, 201, 251
    by year: (2002 Canterbury), 200–202, 268;
        (2003 Lambeth Palace), 209, 213–14;
        (2005 Dromantine), 220–22, 247, 293,
        301; (2007 Dar es Salaam), 249, 251,
        252–55, 257; (2009 Alexandria), 286, 287;
        (2011 Dublin), 293; (2016 Canterbury),
        293–94
Primates' Standing Committee, 220, 252
Primitive Methodist Church, Binchester, 42
Princess Diana, 83, 120, 129, 183–84, 184, 198, 327
processes, church, 286, 312, 313, 316, 317, 334–35.
    See also individual bodies, meetings and groups
prophecy, gift of, 89
proselytism, 159, 187, 188, 190, 191, 208, 228–29
Protestant Episcopal Theological Seminary of
    Virginia, 153–54. *See also* Virginia Theological
    Seminary
provinces, 103. *See also* autonomy, provincial *and
    individual provinces*
Provincial Episcopal Visitors, 152
Pullinger, Jackie, 83–84
Puritanism, 307, 310, 332
Pusey, Edward, 38

Quadrilateral. *See* Bebbington Quadrilateral;
    Lambeth Quadrilateral
Queen Anne's Bounty, 63, 196

Raiwind, Diocese of, 232
Ramsey, Michael, 3, 158, 180, 201, 223, 244, 290,
    310, 311, 328, 330
Ratzinger, Joseph, 245, 246. *See also* Benedict
    xvi, Pope
rccg (Redeemed Christian Church of God), 284
reason, 247, 310, 315–16, 326, 335
reception, open, 152, 169, 313–14

reconciliation, 131, 173, 206, 285
    in the Anglican Church, 220, 245, 249, 287, 291, 293–94
    See also National Unity and Reconciliation Commission (Rwanda); Truth and Reconciliation Commission
Rector's Wife, The, 63
Redeemed Christian Church of God (RCCG), 284
Reform, 128, 197, 280
Reformation, Protestant, 81, *137,* 138–43, 157, 178, 179, 306, 327, 337. *See also individual Reformers*
Reformed Church, 175
Rein, Katherina, 50
religions, non-Christian. *See* interfaith dialogue; multifaith contexts; Anglican Church relations: with other faiths
religious communities, 49, 52, 98, 150, 235, 297, 330. *See also individual communities*
renewal, 337, 339
    charismatic, 77–78, 84–85, 89, 90, 155, 198, 305, 313, 337
resource churches, 90
Resourcing Ministerial Education, 294–95
Resourcing the Future Task Group, 315
Reuilly, Deaconesses of, 185
Reuilly Conversations, 175, 185
revival, evangelical, 79–80, 337
Reynolds, Charles 'Charlie', 38, 39
Reynolds, Elizabeth 'Birdie', 38, 39, 52
Reynolds, Margaret. *See* Nobbs, Margaret
Riah, Bishop, 206
Ridden, Sister, 60, 272
Riding Lights, 90
Ridley, Nicholas, 28, 135, 139–40, *140,* 328
Ridley Hall, 1–2, 132–33, 135–37, *139,* 143–44, 147–49, 267–69, 271, 284–85, *286,* 288, *296, 311*
rites, last, 19, 183. *See also* unction, sacred
Robinson, Gene, 209, 211, 214, 219, 248, 261
Robinson, John, 72, 73, 136–37, 156, 302
Roger, Brother, 223
Rogers, Tricia, 273–74
Rookery Farm, 31
Roman Catholic Church, 6, 125, 131, 156–57. *See also* Vatican, the; *and under* Anglican Church relations
Rowlandson, Maurice, 175
Rowthorn, Jeffery, 177, 188, 189, 305
Royal Niger Company, 113, 118
Royal Sussex Regiment, 10, *10,* 12, 232

Ruanda, 229. *See also* Rwanda
Rugby School, 46, 47, 55
Runcie, Robert, 79, 87, *88,* 95, 120, 128, 240, 241, 245
Rutayisire, Antoine, 285, 325
Rwanda, 229, 251–52, 261, 285, 325
Ryle, John Charles, 81, 307

Sacks, Jonathan, 265
sacraments, 289, 308, 327–28, 339
sacred unction. *See* unction, sacred
Salisbury Cathedral, 101
same-sex blessings, 204, 219–20, 221, 248–49, 250, 254, 256, 257, 266, 286, 303
Sanders, E. P., 137
Sandom, Carrie, 289
Sangla Hill incident, 233
Sant'Egidio, 131, 225–26
Sarum rite, 179
Satterthwaite, John, 165
schism. *See* Anglican Communion: and division
schools
    Anglican, 46–47, 49–50, Chs. 3 & 4 *passim,* 216, *216,* 230, 234, 324
    Indian residential (Canada), 23, 256, 322
    missionary, 108, *108,* 114, 115, 216, 326
    See also individual schools; theological colleges
Schütz, Roger, 223
Scotland, 33–40 *passim,* 298. *See also* Scottish Episcopal Church
Scottish Episcopal Church, 33, 34, 162, 169, 288
Scottish Presbyterian Church, 232
Scripture
    accessibility of, 320
    authority of, 213, 280–81, 307–10, 316–17, 325–26, 339
    interpretation of, 213, 289, 303, 309–10, 317, 326
    See also Bible
Scripture Union (SU), 103–4, *111,* 112, 283
    camps. *See* 'Bash' camps
Scriven, Henry, 178, 188
Scruton, Roger, 155
Seabury, Samuel, 153
Second Vatican Council, 156–57, 158, 169, 244, 290, 302, 327, 333
See of Canterbury, 288, 291, 301, 335
sees, 100, 291
selection conferences, 128, 129

war
as a driver of change, 9, 16, 20–21, 28–29, 33, 57, 149, 151, 297, 299
and ministry, 12–13, 15, 16, *17*, 18–21, 35, 44, 47, 60, 327
and missionary activity, 103–4, 182, 241, 300–301
See also Anglican Church: and peacebuilding; *and individual wars;*
Washington, George, 152
Waters, Nick, 75
Watkins, Brigadier and Sybil, 49, 53
Watson, David, *88*, 90–91, 92, 136
Watson, Tim, 278–79
Way, Lewis, 187
WCC (World Council of Churches), 235, 237–38, 284, 285, 300
Weeley, 56, 59–60, 62–63, *64*, 72, 274
Welby, Justin, 79, 83, 84, 272, 279, 291–94, 337
enthronment of, 291–93, *292*
Wells, Anthony, 190
Wells Theological College, 133
Weninger, Michael, 210
Wesley, Charles, 80, 152
Wesley, John, 79–80, 152
Wesley House, 135
West Africa, 100–118, 302
Anglican Province of, 103
Evangelical Church of, 114
See also individual countries
West Indies, Province of the, 250
Westcott, B. F., 98, 232, 326
Westcott House, 135, 269, 271
Weston, Frank, 253
White Horse Tavern, *137*, 138–40, *138*
Whitfield, George, 79–80
Wilberforce, William, 99, 106, 303, 316, 323
Wilkinson, Guy, 281
Williams, Jane, 205, 231, 234
Williams, Rowan, 201, 205–65 *passim, 212, 223, 225, 236, 246, 253, 257,* 268–71, 287–89, 291, 322
Wilmot, Tony, *104*
Wilton, Gary, 228
Windsor Continuation Group, 264 (n. 75), 287
Windsor Process, 214, 221–22, 223, 235, 247, 258, 264, 293
Windsor Report, 214, 219–21, 235, 239, 247–58 *passim*, 266, 301, 305, 334–36
Winslow, Jack, 65–66, 77, 91, 120
Women and Holy Orders, 151

women's ministry
as bishops, 150, 197, 288–91, 303, 313, 315, 326
as 'Bishop's Messengers', 151
as churchwardens, 150–51
as clergy wives, 38–39, 55–56, 62, 63, 181
as lay readers, 151, 304
as ordained priests, 147–52, 169, 290, 337
on Parochial Church Councils, 150
See also deaconesses
Woodard, Nathaniel, 46–47, 313, 327
Woodard schools, 46–47, 65, 66, 73, 304. *See also individual schools*
'Woodbine Willie', 19, 20, 21
Woollcombe, Kenneth, 151
Word, A Service of the, 198
Word of God. *See* Bible; Scripture
World Council of Churches (WCC), 235, 237–38, 284, 285, 300
World War One, 9–22, *9, 10, 11, 13, 16, 17,* 35–36, 50, *69,* 151, 173, 297, 299, 303, 304, 324, 327
World War Two, 44–45, *45,* 46, 51, 149, 217
Worlock, Derek, 120, 278
worship
accessibility of, 180–81, 320–21, *320,* 339
changing styles of, 85, 111–12, 275–78, 304. *See also* candles controversy
charismatic, 79, 85, 305
Wright, N. T., 95
Wuhan University, 243, 322
Wycliffe College, Toronto, 255
Wycliffe Hall, Oxford, 91

Xi'an, 240, 242

Year of the Young for Christ Crusade, 112
YMCA (Young Men's Christian Association), 21
Yoder, John Howard, 156
Yoruba people, 103
Yorubaland, 106

Zanzibar, 253–54, *253,* 331
Zaria, 115–16

"A unique reflection on Anglican identity from someone who has ministered in a rich diversity of contexts and watched at close quarters the struggles of the last decade or so as to what Anglicanism is and might be. What is distilled is a vision that is realistic, theologically acute—and, above all, hopeful. This is a very significant book indeed, deserving the widest welcome."
  Rowan Williams, former Archbishop of Canterbury

"Andrew Norman offers an engaging and insightful analysis of the recent history and current situation of English and global Anglicanism from the perspective of a reflective insider. His book will be of great service not only to committed Anglicans but also to all who seek a rounded critical understanding of this major Christian tradition."
  John Wolffe, Professor of Religious History, The Open University

"This is a fascinating account of the Anglican Way. For anyone interested in the journey of today's Anglican Communion, with challenges confronting it and possibilities ahead, this perceptive book is a must."
  Mary Tanner, former European President of the World Council of Churches

"This is a timely encouragement to all Anglicans to appreciate afresh what we share in common and continue working at the gift of being a Communion. It moves between the local and the global, situating Anglican experience in its wider context, with challenges for the future carefully identified. I will be recommending this informative and thought-provoking resource to all who rejoice in being Anglican."
  Josiah Idowu-Fearon, Secretary General of the Anglican Communion

"With broad horizons and a visionary eye to the future, this book provides an accessible introduction to the essentials of the Anglican landscape, weaving the author's own story with the Church's wider story."
  Steve Benoy, Diocesan Director of Ordinands, Peterborough Diocese

"Discreetly observed and diligently documented, this patient memoir interweaves autobiography with shrewd perspectives from inside Lambeth Palace, the Church of England and the Anglican Communion."
  Graham Kings, Mission Theologian in the Anglican Communion